HONG KONG HANDBOOK

INCLUDING MACAU AND GUANGZHOU

HONG KONG HANDBOOK

INCLUDING MACAU AND GUANGZHOU
SECOND EDITION

KERRY MORAN

MOON
TRAVEL
HANDBOOKS

HONG KONG HANDBOOK
INCLUDING MACAU AND GUANGZHOU
SECOND EDITION

Published by
 Moon Publications, Inc.
 P.O. Box 3040
 Chico, California 95927-3040, USA

Printed by
 Colorcraft Ltd.

ISBN: 1-56691-108-7
ISSN: 1079-0675

Editor: Diane Wurzel
Map Editor: Gina Wilson Birtcil
Copy Editors: Diane Wurzel, Asha Johnson
Production & Design: David Hurst
Cartography: Chris Folks and Mike Morgenfeld
Index: Sondra Nation
Chinese characters: Maureen Ho Newlin

Front cover photo: White-breasted Kingfisher © Pete Oxford/ENP

Distributed in the United States and Canada by Publishers Group West

Printed in China

Although the author and publisher have made every effort to ensure that the information was correct at the time of going to press, the author and publisher do not assume and hereby disclaim any liability to any party for any loss or damage caused by errors, omissions, or any potential travel disruption due to labor or financial difficulty, whether such errors or omissions result from negligence, accident, or any other cause.

Please send all comments,
corrections, additions,
amendments, and critiques to:

HONG KONG HANDBOOK
MOON TRAVEL HANDBOOKS
P.O. BOX 3040
CHICO, CA 95927-3040, USA
e-mail: travel@moon.com
www.moon.com

Printing History
1st edition—August 1995
2nd edition—February 1998

For Cassandra and Colin

ACKNOWLEDGMENTS

Thanks are due to many people for their help with this edition: first to John Cremer for his still unflagging hospitality in Hong Kong; May Ng, Claire Lau and Pauline Ngan at HKTA for their resourcefulness in providing information; Lina Ding at GIS, Helka Ahokas, Leong Ka-Tai, Grant Morrison, Thomas and Jessica for a nightlife run-down; and Jen Schwerin for dining support.

Thanks also to readers who have written or e-mailed contributions: Mark Schaeffer, Jon Giorgini, Andreas Horvath, E. Delambertye, Jay Johnson, and Spod (Lisa Donovan).

CONTENTS

CHARTS AND SPECIAL TOPICS

ABBREVIATIONS

/F—floor

C—Celsius

CITS—China International Travel Service

CPA—Country Parks Authority

d—double

HK$—Hong Kong dollars

HKHA—Hong Kong Hotel Association

HKTA—Hong Kong Tourist Association

IYHA—International Youth Hostel
  Association

KCR—Kowloon-Canton Railway

km—kilometers

kph—kilometers per hour

LRT—Light Rail Transit

MTR—Mass Transit Railway

PLA—People's Liberation Army

PRC—People's Republic of China

ptc—Portuguese *pataca* (currency)

s—single

SAR—Special Administrative Region

CHARTS AND SPECIAL TOPICS

WE'D LIKE YOUR INPUT

No place changes faster than Hong Kong. Prices rise; buildings go down and new ones go up in the wink of an eye; and restaurants and bars start, flourish and die of terminal trendiness within a year. Even the land is regularly transformed, as reclamation alters the coastline—not to mention large-scale transformations like the new airport and the recent handover.

To help keep this book up to date I'd appreciate readers' comments and evaluations. Take some time to list the best and worst things about your trip to Hong Kong— specifics like hotels and restaurants, and also sights, experiences and general impressions. What surprised you most about Hong Kong? Was that highly rated restaurant a disappointment? Did you find a new hotel or guesthouse worth listing? Did a Tsimshatsui camera salesman actually provide polite and helpful service?

Please e-mail us at travel@moon.com

Or write to:

Hong Kong Handbook
Moon Publications
P.O. Box 3040
Chico CA 95927, U.S.A.

MAPS

MAP SYMBOLS

— — — INTERNATIONAL BORDER	MARSH	✻ MTR STATION ACCESS
—·—·— PROVINCE BORDER	WATER	○ LRT STATION ACCESS
——— MAIN ROAD		■—■—■ KCR
——— OTHER ROAD	▲ MOUNTAIN	– – – – – LRT
– – – UNPAVED ROAD	✱ AIRPORT	||||||||| MTR
—·—·— PATH, TRAIL	O CITY	·········· TRAMLINE
═══ BRIDGE	o TOWN, VILLAGE	▟ CATHEDRAL, CHURCH
⊰══⊱ TUNNEL	■ POINT OF INTEREST	⛩ TEMPLE, MONASTERY, PAGODA
— — FERRY	● HOTEL, ACCOMMODATION	▟ MOSQUE
⚓ SWIMMING		△ BOATING

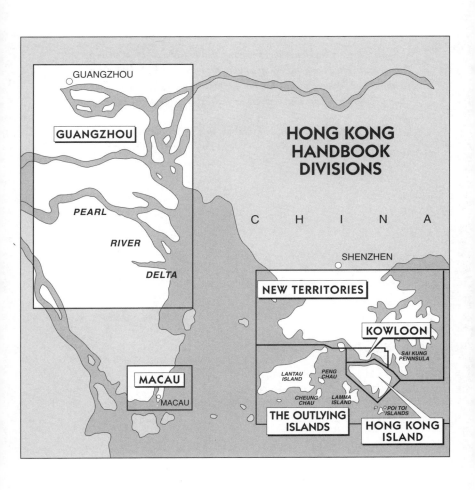

I began to wonder how it was that foreigners, that Englishmen, could do such things as they had done, for example, with the barren rock of Hong Kong within 70 or 80 years, while China in 4,000 years had no place like Hong Kong. Where did I get my revolutionary ideas? It was entirely in Hong Kong.

—*Dr. Sun Yat-sen, in a 1922 address to students at the University of Hong Kong*

BOB RACE

INTRODUCTION
SETTING THE SCENE

Hong Kong is one of the world's most sophisticated and exciting cities, a vibrant, futuristic port on the South China Sea. Prosperous, colorful, and busy, it's a city-state composed of superlatives, a cosmopolitan mixture of East and West. Writer Jan Morris describes Hong Kong perfectly: ". . . hard, rich, opportunist, hospitable, and like it or not exhilarating."

The British acquired Hong Kong Island from China in 1841 by near-accident, and for a long time regarded it with scorn. Gradually they expanded the tiny colony, adding a chunk of mainland peninsula and a collection of scattered islands. What was once a "barren Island with hardly a House upon It" today ranks among the world's 15 largest trading entities. British administration combined with Chinese entrepreneurial energy proved to be a magical blend. Modern Hong Kong is a financial, commercial, and manufacturing powerhouse, and a transportation and communication crossroad for all Asia.

It's also Asia's major tourist destination, drawing over ten million visitors a year. It offers an unrivaled setting on a magnificent deepwater harbor, superb food, and world-class shopping. Exotic enough to satisfy even the most sophisticated world traveler, Hong Kong is also well-organized, comfortable, and easy to get around—a unique blend of Western luxury and Eastern ambience.

Hong Kong's appeal lies in its sheer dynamism and pure energy. Its intense and vital Chinese essence makes other regions of China look like a pale replica of the real thing. So much of traditional China was obliterated in the Cultural Revolution, but in Hong Kong it coexists alongside the glitz and glitter. Beneath its glossy facade, Hong Kong is Chinese to the core.

At midnight on 30 June 1997, the British Crown Colony of Hong Kong became the Hong Kong Special Administrative Region of China (SAR). The uniquely peaceful transition, made under the terms of a Sino-British agreement,

THE HANDOVER: WHAT HAPPENS NEXT?

From the British point of view, Hong Kong has always been a "borrowed place, living on borrowed time." Time ran out in 1997, when Hong Kong reverted to Chinese rule. Now the question is what will happen to Hong Kong since it is no longer borrowed? The end of British rule does not mean the end of Hong Kong. In fact, it may finally come into its own.

At the stroke of midnight on 30 June 1997, the British Crown Colony of Hong Kong vanished and the Hong Kong Special Administrative Region of China (SAR) was born. Four thousand dignitaries gathered in the new Convention Centre (thrown up in typically record time for the event) to watch the Union Jack and the old Hong Kong flag being lowered for the last time. The five-star flag of China was raised, along with the Hong Kong SAR's new red-and-white flag. And that, apparently, was that.

The next day, Hong Kong got back to work with its typically high-octane energy. It seemed to matter not a bit that the Chinese flag had replaced the Union Jack. Journalists were puzzled at the apparent anti-climax to such a hugely important event, and felt peeved that they'd come all that way to report that on 1 July the sun rose and it was business as usual.

Life in the Hong Kong Special Administrative Region should not differ much from life in the British Crown Colony of Hong Kong. Social and economic systems, and, by implication, Hong Kong's lifestyle, are guaranteed to remain unchanged for 50 years— by which time optimists hope China will be capitalized. At the very least, the 50 years of limited autonomy will pass the problem on to the next generation.

Can Hong Kong really remain a self-governing, thoroughly capitalistic society under the sovereignty of Communist China? Or will China swallow it? The worst-case scenario envisions a post-1997 meltdown: political repression, emigration restrictions, People's Liberation Army soldiers patrolling the streets of Central—maybe even mobs pouring over the border to loot the city's riches. Optimists, and there are many of them, focus instead on the tremendous economic opportunity that will be created by Hong Kong's incorporation into China, the world's fastest-growing and largest market. Couple China's huge manpower and thirst for economic advancement with Hong Kong's entrepreneurial and management skills, and an economic juggernaut is born.

It may have been that the links between Hong Kong and South China made 1997 a nonevent. Hong Kong and China were already welded together by powerful economic forces—Hong Kong investment in South China, *and* massive Chinese

provided a spectacle of history in the making that was simultaneously fascinating and disturbing. No one really knows how one of the world's most notoriously capitalist city-states will fare under Chinese rule. The impact of the handover will take several years to become clear. In the meantime, Hong Kong is moving ahead with its characteristic frenetic energy and optimism.

One perspective is that Hong Kong is part of China, and always has been. The British borrowed it long enough to allow it to flourish in a framework of their providing. Now it's back to the China it has economically and culturally always belonged to. No one can yet say what China will do to Hong Kong, but the real question may well be: what will Hong Kong do to China?

Images and Impressions

The slopes of Victoria Peak yield a sweeping vista of Hong Kong Island, the peninsula of Kowloon, and the surrounding island-dotted sea. Victoria Harbour, Hong Kong's raison d'être, is a constantly busy place filled with boats of all types: fishers and trawlers and tugs, ferries and lighters and police boats.

The harbor is rimmed by a forest of skyscrapers crowding against one another, tall buildings outdone by still taller and more audacious ones. The city renews itself every few years as buildings are ripped down to make room for newer, bigger structures. They sprout with astonishing rapidity. Late into the night, you hear jackhammers relentlessly clawing down through bedrock, the percussive thump of pile drivers, the crash of rubble rattling down sheathed chutes. The pace of change is brutal, an expression of the pure energy to make, to earn, to create: that is Hong Kong.

Sightseeing here is not a matter of working through a list of monuments and exhibits. The real thrill is in weaving your way through the investment in Hong Kong. China had been Hong Kong's largest trade partner, biggest market, and leading commodity supplier, as well as its largest foreign investor. From this point of view, the border was an artificial construct. Removing it merely underscored what was already reality: that South China and Hong Kong were a single, inseparable, and highly successful economic unit—before the handover.

Hong Kong's economic importance is its sole strength when it comes to China. Chinese politicians, whoever they may be, can ignore bluster about human rights, but their political survival depends on Hong Kong's foreign exchange earnings. And making money is what Hong Kong does best. With no real control over its own political fate, it's busy cultivating the only power it knows. More than the goose that laid the golden egg, Hong Kong is the catalyst for China's recent emergence as an economic power. Its economic potential may protect it from major changes—but many fear that China will not be able to help tinkering with the fantastic money-making machine that is Hong Kong, and will somehow botch things up.

China will show its hand eventually. 1997 is not the crucial point for Hong Kong; it's 1998 and 1999 that really count. What kind of place will Hong Kong be in a few years? There are valid worries: that Chinese bureaucracy will raise taxes and plunder Hong Kong's foreign exchange funds; that party politics will intrude into Hong Kong's excellent civil service; that bribery will reappear, and the pervasive mainland practice of *guanxi* or connections will erode the rule of law and fair economic competition. Freedom of the press will definitely be reduced—voluntarily, if reporters know what's good for them. And it will become harder to hold political demonstrations, but then, political freedoms have always taken a back seat to economic ones in Hong Kong's book.

Consider another, still more intriguing possibility: that Hong Kong will instead transform China. It's possible that Hong Kong can prove to be a laboratory for political changes which will spread to China. The acceptance of this heroically capitalist society may work alchemical wonders on the Motherland, in ways politicans and pundits cannot yet clearly forsee.

A benevolent British dictatorship allowed Hong Kong to develop a unique character and way of life. Hong Kong is Chinese in character and spirit, but, along with Taiwan, it embodies a whole new way of being Chinese—a lot more successful than the totalitarian model espoused by Beijing. Is it a hothouse plant that will wilt without colonial protection? Or is it the face of a new China? Anyone familiar with Hong Kong's resilience and energy suspects the latter, but the future is far from certain.

vital, crowded streets, taking the fast-beating pulse of the city. People are everywhere, shopping, working, eating, walking, chatting, even—somehow—sleeping. The gregarious Cantonese appear immune to crowds and noise. Over one million people live jammed onto Hong Kong Island's 78 square km, while the Kowloon Peninsula has some of the most crowded neighborhoods on earth.

Hong Kong typifies the staggering energy level of south China. Like New York, it's a city in a hurry, with the same energy and hustle, the same loud, fast, pushing crowds (Hong Kong's are even louder and pushier), and the same infectious excitement. Unlike New York, there's no alienation or lurking violence: Hong Kong's urban culture is purposeful, focused, and extremely pragmatic.

Hong Kong is focused on the pursuit of money, embodying a strain of capitalism as pure as can be found on the planet. Money is its lifeblood, business and shopping its leitmotivs. Hong Kong's post war transformation is testimony to the power of capitalist enterprise, and to the strength, tenacity, and drive of its people. Its status as a city made largely of immigrants gives its sense of transience, resilience, and a stubborn certainty that the future can be improved through hard work.

At first glance Hong Kong may seem thoroughly Westernized, but that is a sophisticated illusion. At its core are traditional Chinese customs, beliefs, festivals, and religious rituals that have continued largely uninterrupted, unlike the rest of China, where traditions were ravaged by the vicious Cultural Revolution of the 1960s.

Hong Kong's side streets reveal glimpses of a traditional China long vanished from the other provinces. Old-style pharmacies display glass jars of mysterious dried roots, pickled snakes, and wizened antlers, essential ingredients in Chinese medicine. Bakeries dispense

SOUTHEAST ASIA

© MOON PUBLICATIONS, INC.

flaky pastries filled with bean paste, lotus seed, and duck egg. Food shops are festooned with long strings of red-and-white Cantonese sausages and shiny pressed ducks. Other stores sell lacquered chopsticks, carved ivory chops, and padded silk jackets.

Hong Kong is the rattle of mahjong tiles, the slow graceful movements of early morning tai chi, colorful "flower boards" advertising parties and weddings, noisy restaurants crammed day and night with groups enjoying some of the best food in the world. Old ladies in black *samfu* (loose-fitting collarless tops worn with loose,

straight trousers) burn incense in front of animistic shrines, and gaudy Taoist temples are crammed with supplicants and soothsayers. Even the smells are evocative: the big-city scent of auto exhaust dominates, but underneath is the ocean's salt tang, meat frying in a wok, the delicate fragrance of the purple *bauhinia* flower, sandalwood incense drifting from a doorway shrine.

Hong Kong is best embodied in the cheerful pandemonium of street life: stalls selling noodle soup and chicken feet and squid-on-a-stick, the gaudy neon signs, the surging, pushing

WHAT'S CHANGED, WHAT HASN'T

From the visitor's point of view, the Hong Kong Special Administrative Region is no more difficult, nor less fascinating, than the British Crown Colony of Hong Kong. Visa regulations have remained unchanged, and Hong Kong retains the use of its own currency linked to the US dollar. English is still an official language and English signs are maintained. And of course the stunning array of sights, including the spectacular skyline, haven't disappeared and aren't likely to no matter what. Hong Kong is too big and powerful and energetic a place to vanish overnight—and vanishing seems to be the last thing it has on its mind.

Post-handover changes focus on the political system. Instead of a governor appointed by London, the SAR is run by a chief executive appointed by Beijing. The old Legislative Council has been replaced by a Provisional Legislature, which shares more than half of the original Legco's members. Elections for the new 60-seat legislature, slated for March 1998, will include direct election of 20 seats—the same proportion as the controversial 1995 elections in which China accused the British of trying to sneak in democratic reforms.

According to the Basic Law, Hong Kong retains full autonomy except in matters of foreign affairs and defense. While People's Liberation Army Soliders have replaced British troops at 14 locations throughout the SAR, they keep a low profile. Domestic security is still maintained by the (formerly Royal) Hong Kong Police. Hong Kong will keep its separate membership in organizations like the World Trade Organization, and is negotiating for the right to send a "Hong Kong, China" Olympic team.

The legal and judicial system remains the same, based on common law, although the Chinese language has finally been introduced to the courtroom. China is retaining strict border controls to avoid a deluge of immigrants, or even visitors—Chinese still need a special permit to visit the Motherland's latest acquisition, much to their disappointment. According to the terms of a 1995 agreement, 55,000 mainland Chinese will be allowed to settle in Hong Kong each year—a number large enough to strain Hong Kong's overburdened housing resources, yet hardly significant in the big picture.

---

crowds. Jackhammers beat out the rapid pulse of the city as crowds of workers hurry across crosswalks, driven by the whirring tick-tick-tick of the green light. Time is always running out, and there are things to do, money to be made. Even the striped barbershop poles spin at double speed, as if to keep pace with the frantic activity.

Beyond Urban Hong Kong

Hong Kong has its peaceful side too. Most of its area consists of green hills, rugged coastline, and isolated islands. Visitors seldom realize that nearly 70% of the SAR is undeveloped, 40% of it preserved in an extensive series of country parks. Try to spend at least one day beyond the urban canyons, exploring a glossy New Town or a quiet fishing village on one of the Outlying Islands.

Don't expect to experience all that the SAR has to offer in two or three days. Most travelers devote that much time merely to shopping. A week is the minimum allotment to see Hong Kong, after which you can venture farther afield. A recommended first stop is the tiny Portuguese enclave of **Macau,** an hour's boat ride away on the opposite side of the Pearl River Delta. Macau's tangled old streets are a charming blend of old and new, Chinese and Mediterranean, and superb food, plentiful wine, and lower costs only add to its appeal.

Another option is a visit to the south China city of **Guangzhou** (formerly Canton), accessible from both Hong Kong and Macau. This big, busy metropolis ranks among China's most progressive cities. A visit here provides insights into the speed and frenzy with which the rest of China is striving to catch up to Hong Kong. Viewed together, Hong Kong, Macau, and Guangzhou neatly encapsulate Chinese life, both traditional and modern—always vital and fascinating.

THE LAND

The Hong Kong Special Administrative Region (SAR) consists of a peninsula, a tiny piece of the Chinese mainland, and 236 islands scattered about the South China Sea. Set at the eastern entrance to the wide, muddy Pearl River estuary, it lies 135 km southeast of the important city of Guangzhou, and some 2,000 km south of Beijing. In the past, it was unflatteringly described as "a pimple on the posterior of China."

At first glance Hong Kong appears an inhospitable place for a prosperous settlement, with a rugged coastline, infertile land, very little water, and virtually no natural resources. What it *does* have is the strategically located deepwater port of Victoria Harbour, ideal for an enormous transit shipping trade. This, plus the determination and energy of its people, has created a truly

great capitalist machine. Hong Kong has parlayed its position on the southernmost tip of China into a powerful trump card, successively transforming itself into an international trading port, a manufacturing base, and most recently a major financial center.

Hong Kong encompasses a tremendously varied terrain of green mountains, steep if not high, an intricate coastline indented with sheltered bays, and 236 mountainous islands. It's not that big to begin with, and an excellent transportation system makes it easy to get around. The interior is surprisingly rugged, and in many places the scrub-covered hills roll right up to the sea. Settlements and roads are concentrated on the few flat areas, mainly along the shoreline.

With flat land and open space at a premium, developers have found that filling in new land along the shoreline is cheaper than leveling hills. Constant reclamation means that Hong Kong's area is growing steadily —11 square km in the 1980s. The current total area is 1,091 square km.

Topography

Hong Kong's mainland and scattered islands were originally a single landmass. During the Ice Age the sea level was 100 meters lower than today, and the South China Sea lay far east of Hong Kong. The melting of the glaciers around 8000 B.C. caused the ocean to rise, submerging the mountainous region and transforming peaks into islands. The coastline is believed to have assumed its present form around 4000 B.C.

Hong Kong's topography remains exceptionally rugged. "We are a tiny territory whose terrain seems specially designed to impede development on land," bemoaned a government report. There is little flat land, most of it found in the northwest New Territories, in pockets of valleys and at the heads of sea inlets. Three-quarters of Hong Kong is hills, the tallest (Tai Mo Shan) rising 950 meters. Not coincidentally, three-quarters of Hong Kong is countryside: built-up urban areas occupy a mere 150 square km, less than 20% of the total.

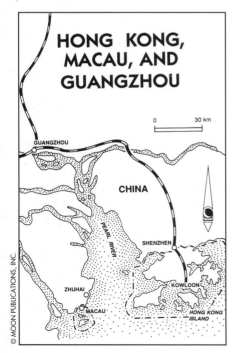

HONG KONG, MACAU, AND GUANGZHOU

0   30 km

GUANGZHOU

CHINA

SHENZHEN

PEARL RIVER

ZHUHAI

KOWLOON

MACAU

HONG KONG ISLAND

Hong Kong By Region

Hong Kong Island was the original British territory, acquired in 1841. The north shore provides the SAR's archetypal image: a skyline worthy of New York City, set around a strikingly beautiful harbor and backed by towering green hills. Its curving northern shore is densely packed with businesses and crowded apartment blocks; the southern shore, with its indented coastline, is more sparse. Some 22% of the area's population lives on this 80-square-km island.

A short ferry ride across the harbor is the **Kowloon Peninsula,** a major commmercial, shopping, and residential area that connects with Hong Kong Island by undersea tunnel and subway. The southern tip, Tsimshatsui, harbors the SAR's highest concentration of hotels and tourist-oriented shops. The area up to Boundary Road was taken by the British in 1861; beyond are the urban neighborhoods of **New Kowloon,** acquired some 30 years later as part of the New Territories but for all practical purposes an extension of Kowloon. Some 36% of Hong Kong's population lives here, in some of the most crowded neighborhoods on earth.

The **New Territories** are relatively huge—790 square km, 91% of Hong Kong's total area—but are largely ignored by tourists. The British acquired the land from China by a 99-year lease in 1898, and it was the impending lapse of this agreement that led to the return of the entire territory. Formerly Hong Kong's rural heartland, the New Territories still support farmers and fishermen, but the rice and vegetable fields are disappearing fast. Over 40% of the population lives here, most in the recently developed New Towns. Pockets of wilderness are laced by hiking trails and dotted with small traditional villages, many now abandoned as the population migrates to more developed areas.

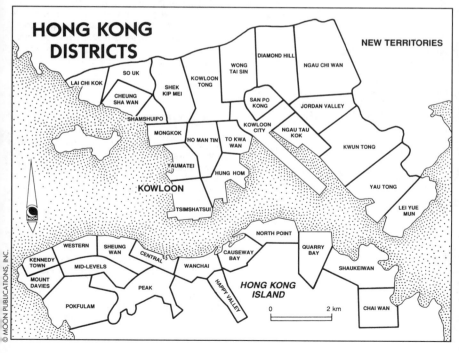

The 235 **Outlying Islands** were leased as part of the New Territories in 1898. They form another face of busy Hong Kong: isolated and tranquil outposts where cars are often banned and traditional life still lingers. Many are uninhabited, sea-washed rocks. The big four are Lantau, Lamma, Cheung Chau, and Peng Chau, but even these are sparsely populated. With an appealing mix of fishing villages, beaches, and good seafood, they are a favorite playground for residents as well as tourists.

CLIMATE

Hong Kong lies just south of the Tropic of Cancer, at the same latitude as Hawaii and Calcutta. Its subtropical climate is shaped by the great Asian landmass and the surrounding oceans. Weather comes in two modes: hot, humid, and rainy during the southwest monsoon (March to September), and cool and dry during the northeast monsoon (October to February, the best time to visit).

"Cool" is a relative term, as is "dry." Average relative humidity is 77%, soaring to 90% in the hot summer months. But many visitors who arrive in the winter months expecting a year-round hot and humid climate can be seen shivering in sleeveless dresses and shorts.

The single best time is November through early December. Weather is generally sunny and clear, with comfortable temperatures and relatively low humidity. Around Christmas and New Year's the skies may become gray for days on end, with chilly drizzle and mist blanketing the views. February is the coldest month, though still mild; temperatures seldom drop below 8° C and rare reports of frost on New Territories hilltops draw crowds of sightseers.

Spring is brief in Hong Kong, and temperatures rapidly heat up in March. This is probably the second-best season to visit, though clouds and rain are more frequent. May is very hot, and by June the monsoon is moving in.

Summer temperatures average 28-35° C; three-quarters of the annual rainfall falls in this season, alternating with hot sun. It is possible to visit Hong Kong and barely leave air-conditioned buildings, and the monsoon has its charms—vivid green vegetation, billowing cumuli, and the occasional excitement of a typhoon—but the incessant stickiness is tiresome. Hongkongers themselves seem unfazed, somehow managing to look cool and crisp in long-sleeved shirts and trousers.

AVERAGE MONTHLY TEMPERATURES AND PRECIPITATION

(temperatures expressed in degrees Centigrade, precipitation in millimeters)

	Maximum	Minimum	Precipitation
Jan.	19	14	23
Feb.	19	14	48
March	21	17	67
April	25	20	162
May	29	24	317
June	30	26	376
July	32	27	324
Aug.	31	26	392
Sept.	30	26	300
Oct.	28	23	145
Nov.	24	19	35
Dec.	21	15	27

THE NATURAL WORLD

Somehow you just don't associate Hong Kong with nature: it often appears to be an entirely man-made phenomenon. Surprisingly, 70% of Hong Kong is undeveloped land, much of it preserved in an extensive series of country parks.

Flora
Falling just within the Tropic of Cancer, Hong Kong supports a rich variety of plant life, combining temperate and tropical species.

The subtropical forest that once covered all of Indochina has nearly vanished in the face of human activity. Hong Kong Island was indeed a "barren rock" when the British arrived, picked nearly clean by centuries of firewood gathering. The colonists introduced new species, coaxing forth a profusion of greenery.

TYPHOONS

The Cantonese call them *dai feng,* "great wind." These tropical cyclones typical of the South China Sea whirl up between May and November; they're most common from mid-July through September. The mere edge of this tropical storm brings rain and wind; its spinning center can bring winds up to 267 kph—enough to sway tall skyscrapers.

Direct hits on Hong Kong are rare, but even peripheral winds can wreak tremendous damage. In the old days typhoons would sweep in without warning, sinking boats and killing thousands. The monster typhoon of 1906 killed perhaps 10,000 fishermen and their families, their boats reduced to matchstick kindling by the force of the great winds.

In those days people relied on folk methods to predict typhoons: for instance, dragonflies were believed to hatch in huge quantities on the eve of a storm. Nowadays weather satellites give plenty of warning. Regular warnings are broadcast on radio and TV, or call 2835-1473 for signal enquiries.

Typhoons are rated according to a scale of numbered signals. Signal No. 1 is a standby alert, meaning a typhoon has been sighted within 800 km of Hong Kong. Signal No. 3 means a storm is approaching, with winds expected up to 60 kph and gusts nearly double that. People start to get ready, as things can worsen rapidly within the next 12 hours. Schools are closed, boats go into typhoon shelters, storm shutters are raised, and supplies laid in. Try not to travel anywhere long-distance after this point,

as ferries and public transport may shut down on short notice.

The next level, Signal No. 8, is reached only once or twice a year, but this is when things start to get serious. Winds up to 117 kph and gusts up to 180 kph are anticipated, and offices and shops close to allow employees to get home before transport ceases entirely. Ferries stop running first, and taxis become scarce. (You can still take the MTR to cross the harbor.) Outgoing airline flights may be canceled and incoming ones rerouted.

It's exciting to brave the gusts, but falling branches and flying debris make being outdoors dangerous. Stock up on food and entertainment, as 12 hours trapped in a hotel room can get boring. Chinese residents pass the time by playing mahjong, while expats rent videos.

If you're lucky enough to have a harbor view, you can watch boats being blown clear across the harbor. Winds are strongest near the waterfront and up on the Peak, where air conditioners may be sucked out of mountings and windows shattered by the force of the gale. Inland, the buildings reduce the wind's force somewhat.

Higher signals are rare: Signal No. 9 means the wind force is expected to increase and the storm will brush very near Hong Kong; Signal No. 10 is used for a direct hit hurricane of 118 kph and up, with gusts of 220 kph and over. A direct hit comes only once every eight years or so.

There are 2,500 species of plants, trees, and ferns in the SAR, around half of them native, including the Chinese red pine, dwarf mountain pine, fig, laurel, oak, camphor, and chestnut. Flowering shrubs are particularly beautiful: camellias, magnolias, rhododendrons, and the cerise-flowered "King of the Hanging Bells Tree" *(Rhodoleia championi)* found only on the south side of Hong Kong Island. The *bauhinia (Bauhinia blakeana),* an evergreen with drooping branches and scented mauve flowers, blossoms in the winter months. It is the carefully neutral symbol of the Special Administrative Region's political identity, appearing on its flag and replacing the portrait of Queen Elizabeth II on the back of coins.

British settlers encouraged the widespread planting of pine trees to control erosion. Refor-

estation efforts diversified and expanded after WW II, and much of the formerly bare countryside is now forested, albeit sparsely. The thin red topsoil covering large swaths of the mountainous countryside supports only grasses and stunted shrubs. The valleys by contrast are intensively farmed, mostly producing vegetables today. Market prices have been too low to justify rice farming for at least 30 years, but the brilliant green of paddy still flashes forth from patches. Less than three percent of Hong Kong's land is devoted to crop production, one of the lowest ratios in the world.

Some of the oldest vegetation is found in the *feng shui* groves flanking New Territories villages. Here, plants like bamboo, ficus, and *Aquilaria sinensis,* the incense tree, were allowed to grow untouched for geomantic rea-

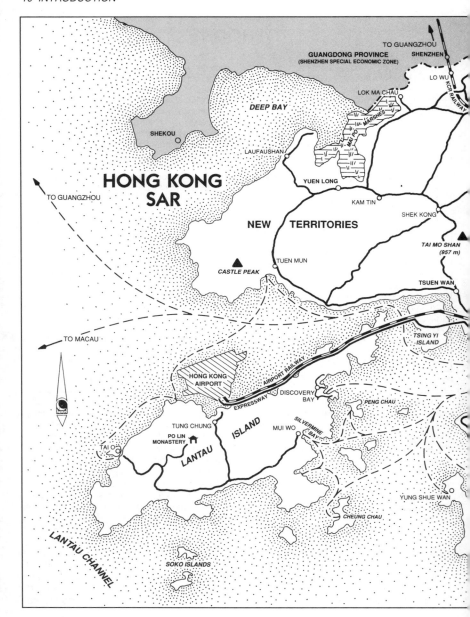

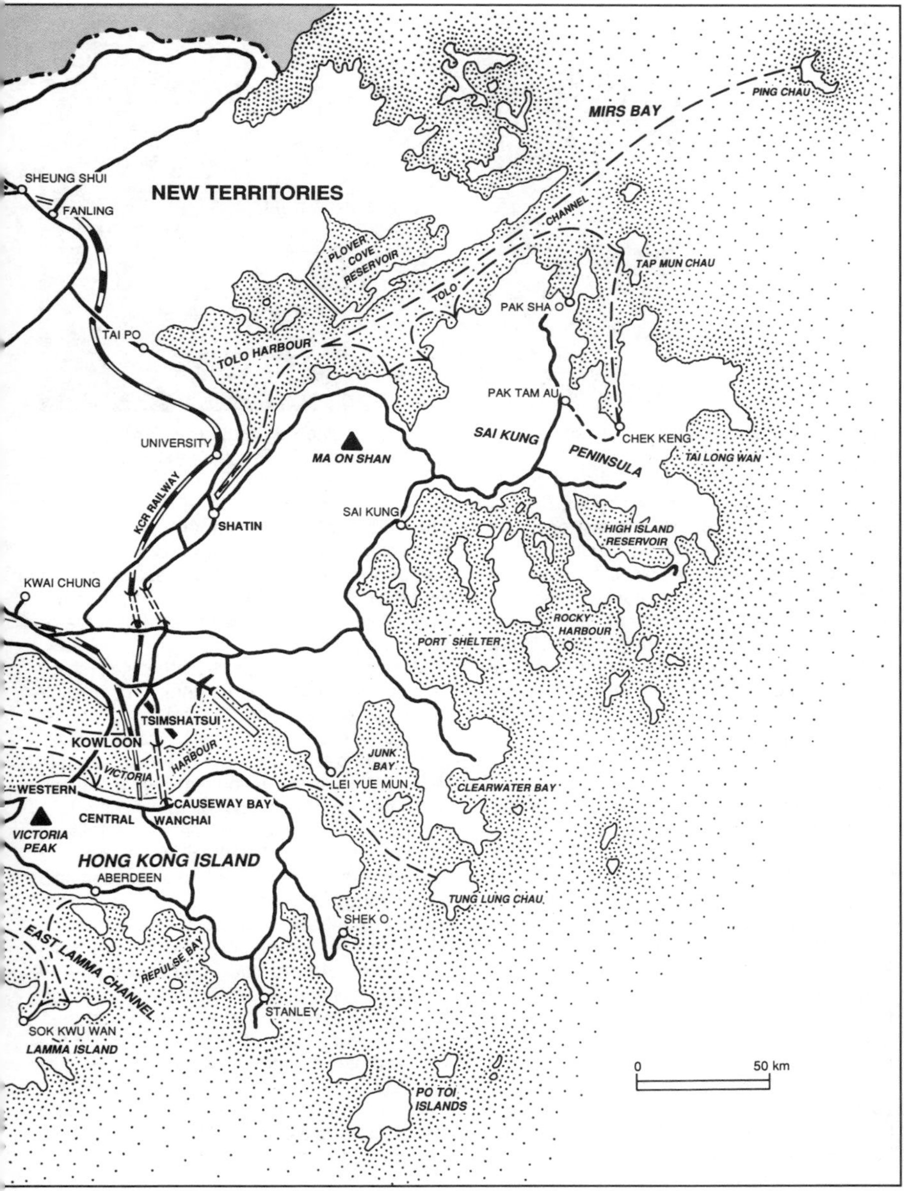

SHEUNG SHUI

FANLING

NEW TERRITORIES

MIRS BAY

PING CHAU

PLOVER COVE RESERVOIR

TAP MUN CHAU

TOLO CHANNEL

TAI PO

PAK SHA O

TOLO HARBOUR

PAK TAM AU

UNIVERSITY

MA ON SHAN

SAI KUNG

CHEK KENG

TAI LONG WAN

PENINSULA

KCR RAILWAY

SHATIN

SAI KUNG

HIGH ISLAND RESERVOIR

KWAI CHUNG

PORT SHELTER

ROCKY HARBOUR

TSIMSHATSUI

KOWLOON

VICTORIA

HARBOUR

JUNK BAY

LEI YUE MUN

CLEARWATER BAY

WESTERN

CENTRAL

WANCHAI

CAUSEWAY BAY

VICTORIA PEAK

HONG KONG ISLAND

ABERDEEN

TUNG LUNG CHAU

EAST LAMMA CHANNEL

SHEK O

REPULSE BAY

SOK KWU WAN

STANLEY

LAMMA ISLAND

0   50 km

PO TOI ISLANDS

© MOON PUBLICATIONS, INC.

Hong Kong Harbour

KERRY MORAN

sons: they were believed to shelter settlements from evil influences.

Mention should be made of the ubiquitous all-purpose bamboo, idealized by ancient Chinese culture for its flexibility and resiliency. The wood is used for scaffolding, baskets, chopsticks, brooms, hats, water pipes, furniture, musical instruments, and boat masts; the sheaths and fiber for paper; the leaves as rain hats and cloaks. Books were once written on split and flattened bamboo slips. New bamboo shoots are prized as the "queen of vegetables," and the pith, sold in minute quantities, is a highly valued delicacy.

Fauna

South China's original fauna, including beasts like crocodiles, tigers, and leopards, vanished long ago with the destruction of the primeval forests. Of Hong Kong's 38 remaining mammalian species, 27 are bats and rodents. Wild boar and rhesus monkey populations have been reestablished with reforestation: rarer are deer, fox, otter, and the pangolin or anteater. Most of these animals are nocturnal. Domestic cattle, pigs, chickens, and dogs are the creatures you're most likely to encounter on a New Territories hike.

There are 47 snake species, 18 of them poisonous. Over 200 types of butterflies appear in the spring and autumn months. Hong Kong is home to 352 bird species, an unusually large number for such a tiny place. Birdwatchers should visit the Mai Po Nature Reserve or the Yim Tso Ha Egretry.

The Underwater Environment

Much of Hong Kong's ecological diversity is hidden underwater. The SAR's western waters tend to be brackish and clouded by silt from the Pearl River Delta; the eastern side is clearer and more oceanic.

Mirs Bay on Hong Kong's northeastern shore has a unique marine ecosystem combining elements of temperate and tropical environments. Temperate marine environments generally harbor large populations of only a few species, while tropical seas support smaller populations of tremendous biological diversity. Mirs Bay blends both, making it the best scuba-diving site in Hong Kong. Currents, which keep the water exceptionally warm in winter, support kelp beds along the shoreline, and these attract oceanic sharks, rays, dolphins, and garfish.

Hoi Ha Wan, a small inlet off Mirs Bay, boasts 37 species of hard coral and a rich marine ecosystem. It was recently designated Hong Kong's first Marine Park, and study and educational centers are planned here. While the cove is protected from damage or incursion, its diversity is threatened by pollution from Tolo Harbour and the new towns at Tai Po and Shatin. Coral is a delicate organism, extremely vulnerable to sewage and sediment. Formations take years to develop, and can be seriously disturbed by a diver merely brushing against them.

Mirs Bay itself is increasingly menaced by pollution, especially silt spills from dredging operations that mine sand for construction use. The marine mud washed off the sand settles on the bottom, suffocating corals and other lifeforms. Fishermen have long complained that dredging reduces their stocks.

The marine environment around the Nine Pins, a favorite dive site 15 km south of Mirs Bay, has been devastated by nearby dredging. Mirs Bay is under threat from other regions of China as well, as the Shenzen Special Economic Zone expands eastward, accompanied by pollution.

Environmental Issues

Until 20 years ago, competitors dove into Victoria Harbour to swim a one-km race from Kowloon to Hong Kong Island. The prospect is now beyond unappetizing, considering the sewage, sludge, and bobbing waste that fill the harbor. Marine Department barges and commissioned sampans skim about 20 tons of floating garbage from the surface of the harbor every day. Meanwhile, 1.5 million cubic feet of untreated sewage and industrial wastes are spewed out daily into the surrounding ocean.

Pollution tends to accumulate in Hong Kong's narrow bays, and the resulting flood of nutrients has seriously damaged the once abundant and diverse marine life. A prime example is Tolo Harbour, devoid of marine life since 1975 due largely to human waste. Fish farming, in which commercial species are fattened in undersea wire cages, also upsets the balance of nutrients, killing off many species while encouraging a few. Other problems involve the waste dumping of sludge and building refuse (which often ends up onshore), overfishing, increased siltation from reclamation projects, and commercial sand-dredging operations which dump tons of mud and silt on the ocean bottom, suffocating coral and other life-forms.

The government is aware of the problems, but hesitates to impose potentially costly controls on businesses. Obstacles are mainly attitudinal, and include the capitalistic ethic of extract-

---

CHINESE WHITE DOLPHINS

They're not actually white—more like a pinkish gray—but the *Sousa chinensis* of the Pearl River Delta was designated the official mascot of the 1997 handover by China. Observers found the symbolism a bit worrisome, as only 80 to 100 of these endangered mammals are believed to be left. The waters north of Lantau Island have been designated a dolphin sanctuary, though the dolphins are not likely to be happy about the jets soon roaring overhead.

Hong Kong Dolphinwatch runs cruises out to visit the dolphins every Monday, Wednesday, and Friday. Trips leave from Queen's Pier and Tsimshatsui and include a buffet lunch aboard a luxury cruiser; cost is HK$400. The company has a 95% sighting record and offers a go-again guarantee. Ten percent of profits go to the Hong Kong branch of Friends of the Earth. Call 2983-1630 for information.

---

ing the maximum profit in the minimum time, and a general sense of apathy. Some recent signs of progress: the government is moving to clean up Tolo Harbour's coating of sewage sludge, and recently approved a HK$20 billion water treatment project.

Air pollution is considered the most serious problem. In heavy traffic areas, pollutants are 15-40% over government standards, and are expected to rise to 60% by 2001. Vehicles are the single worst source, and the amount of cars continues to increase despite a registration tax of 90-120% of the value of the vehicle. Hong Kong has an exceptionally low number of private vehicles per inhabitant, but the world's highest ratio of vehicles per kilometer of road, making traffic jams a regular occurrence. Compounding the problem, pollutants tend to be trapped at ground level by the surrounding mountains and ubiquitous high-rises.

A broader environmental issue is the voracious appetite of Chinese communities across South Asia for exotic plants and animals, either compounded into traditional medicines and aphrodisiacs, or simply consumed as status symbols. Local consumption aside, Hong Kong serves as a clearinghouse for the international trade in shark fins, and more illicitly, tiger bones and rhino horn. Botanical diversity is threatened as well, as fragile Himalayan medicinal herbs are uprooted by the ton for use in traditional medicines.

Environmental awareness remains low, as evidenced by the litter filling country parks on weekends and the forest fires, mostly resulting from carelessness, that ravage five percent of the SAR's area every year. Slowly public awareness is increasing, partly due to advertising campaigns.

HISTORY

The southeasternmost tip of China is an unlikely setting for one of the world's great cities. It seems almost ludicrous that the Asian equivalent of Manhattan has appeared in this typhoon-whipped region of rugged seacoast and relentless hills, a region where 80% of the land is too mountainous to farm and 70% of it is too hilly to inhabit.

A century ago it must have seemed absurd to imagine this would become Britain's "Gibraltar of the East," the farthest outpost of the British empire—but here it is today, a repository for the ultimate the West has to offer: Rolls Royces and chic boutiques, French cognac and cellular phones.

Hong Kong is a capitalist version of China, what China could have been, or perhaps could still be. Perched at the edge of the Asian continent, Hong Kong tilts toward the future. The sight of its skyscrapers rising along the harbor can still send shivers up the spine: the utter audacity and undiluted energy of this city-state is dizzying.

Hong Kong's historical parallels to Shanghai are often cited today: Shanghai, the cosmopolitan Chinese city that flourished through WW II, only to fall with the arrival of the Communist regime. Hong Kong has assumed Shanghai's mantle as a sophisticated and energetic entrepôt, and those who draw the metaphor hint darkly that it may suffer the same fate.

EARLY HISTORY

Lord Palmerston's sneering epithet—"a barren Island with hardly a House upon It"—has given the false impression that Hong Kong was uninhabited before the British arrived. In fact, human habitation here dates back to 4000 B.C., when Neolithic hunters and fishers roamed its coastline, leaving behind stylized carvings etched onto boulders. Later came the Yue people, seafarers whose day-to-day lives resemble those of the present-day Tanka and Hoklo.

Early inhabitants lived near the seashore, fishing, panning salt, and making lime. Archaeological excavations on Lantau, Lamma, and Cheung Chau have uncovered pottery fragments and the ruins of lime kilns. Later enterprises included pearl diving in Tolo Harbour and the export of the fragrant yellow wood of the incense tree, *Aquilaria sinensis.*

By the Tang dynasty (A.D. 618-907), the Pearl River was an important international trade corridor. Arab traders sailed up it to Guangzhou, where they acquired silks and porcelains for foreign export. Tuen Mun in the southern New Territories was another major trade port, and a Chinese garrison was established there to protect the area from pirates.

Sea trade expanded in the Song dynasty (A.D. 960-1279). In the latter half of this peri-

miniature clay house found in Han Tomb

THE GUIDEBOOK COMPANY

od, the first Cantonese settlers arrived in present-day Hong Kong, cultivating the fertile areas of the New Territories. The founding member of the Tang clan, a scholar from Jiangxi Province, retired at Kam Tin. The Tangs were followed by the Pang (also from Jiangxi), Hau, Liu, and Man, who together make up Hong Kong's "Five Great Clans."

Early settlers huddled together in walled villages, seeking protection against robbers, pirates, and unfriendly neighbors. Life was isolated and simple, based around agriculture and the family. An atypical bit of drama transpired in 1276, when the nine-year-old emperor of the Song Dynasty, fleeing the Mongol invaders, encamped at Silvermine Bay on Lantau and at what is presently Kowloon City. It is said that he was drowned in the arms of his prime minister in 1279 to avoid his capture by the Mongols.

The Qing Dynasty

The tranquil life of villagers was disrupted in 1662 by an imperial edict ordering the district's entire coastal population, some 16,000 people, to move inland. The intent was to cut off support for Ming rebels and Japanese pirates who roamed the China coast. Imperial soldiers enforcing the edict wreaked more havoc than the pirates ever had, destroying crops and razing villages. Uprooted from their land and way of life, people suffered greatly.

Following the Ming rebels' defeat in 1669, the order was rescinded through the intervention of two government officials, still revered in some New Territory temples for their efforts. As part of the resettlement effort, the government encouraged the immigration of Hakka people from northeast Guangdong Province.

By 1819 nearly 700 small, agriculturally based villages were located in what is present-day Hong Kong, inhabited mainly by Puntei (Cantonese) and Hakka. The staple crop was rice, supplemented by vegetables, fruit, pigs, and chickens. Other en-

BOB RACE

> *Hong Kong is a barren rock, producing nothing—not leading to any place—surrounded by no trading or populous communities.*
>
> —*Robert Martin,*
> *colonial treasurer, 1844*

terprises included lime and pottery kilns, fishing, and piracy, a tradition on the south China coast that continues today.

Hong Kong Island was entirely unnotable at that time. In 1840 it had a population of around 7,400, mainly Hakka people. As Lord Palmerston would sneer, it was indeed barren, denuded by centuries of firewood gathering. British sailors knew it only as a supply point for fresh water. The biggest settlement was Chek Chue (today's Stanley), but even it was nothing more than a fishing village.

THE BRITISH AND THE CHINESE

This quiet backwater was an unlikely setting for the meeting of two profoundly incompatible cultures. In retrospect it seems the clash was inevitable. Britain, the world's leading trading nation, possessed a powerful navy and the conviction that free trade and profit were its right. Insulated China considered itself the sovereign of the known world, and received trade missions as suppliants, accepting their gifts as tribute. Serene in its superiority, China allowed the "Outer Barbarians" to trade on the fringes of its empire, a minor loophole in a basically isolationist policy. The Chinese needed nothing from the West, but they believed Westerners could not live without tea and rhubarb, the latter popular as a spring purgative.

tomb figurine with horse

It is difficult to say which side was more ethnocentric and closed-minded. Neither made any effort to understand the other's motivations, neither of which were lofty to begin with. Chinese officials considered trade a degrading occupation and perceived foreign traders as money-grubbing, basically inferior beings—a sentiment wholeheartedly returned by foreign traders.

Development of Trade

China had allowed the Portuguese to establish a trading colony at Macau in 1557. Guangzhou was opened to European traders in 1685 on a limited basis, and in 1714, Britain's East India Company was granted permission to build a "factory" or warehouse there. Other Europeans and the Americans joined them, but the East India Company, the world's largest commercial organization, dominated the China trade until its monopoly was abolished in 1834.

Life in Guangzhou was not easy for foreign traders, who were restricted to their factories on the fringes of town. They could not enter the city, ride in sedan chairs, stay out after dark, travel in groups of over 10, bring their wives or families to Guangzhou, study Chinese, or even get drunk (though of course they did). Only the pariah Tanka people were allowed to work as their servants. Most irritating to traders, all business had to go through the Co-hong, a guild of Chinese merchants. Corruption and "the squeeze" flourished. All these constraints begat dreams of a base on the southeast China coast where traders could operate freely.

The Opium Trade

The most pressing problem was the tremendous trade imbalance favoring China. Europeans had an insatiable appetite for tea, not to mention silk and porcelain. The balance of trade in tea alone ran 6:1 in China's favor. "Our Celestial Empire possesses all things in prolific abundance" proclaimed the emperor: China had not "the slightest need" for imported manufactured goods, and accepted only silver.

Searching for a solution, traders discovered a demand for opium, which had been introduced to Guangzhou via Malaysia in the late 17th century, possibly by Chinese merchants. The East India Company, which held a monopoly on Indian opium, auctioned it to British merchants, who shipped it in swift clippers to the China coast and smuggled it in with the connivance of corrupt Chinese officials.

The trade expanded rapidly despite imperial decrees against it. By 1836 opium was the world's most valuable commodity. Among the leading opium traders were a pair of shrewd Scotsmen, James Matheson and William Jardine, whose company was to became the greatest of Hong Kong's hongs.

In retrospect, the opium trade was a nasty

Hong Kong Island's streets decorated for Queen Victoria's Jubilee in 1897

THE GUIDEBOOK COMPANY

business, but it suited the mercantile ethic of the time. Opium traders shrugged off scruples by maintaining that trade, and the missionaries that automatically followed, would benefit China—even if China had to be forced to open up. It also benefited the traders; a single trip could earn £53,000 in silver.

The Chinese government became increasingly concerned about opium, described as an extravagant habit that ruined minds and morals. The trade imbalance was now in China's disfavor, and roughly a tenth of its annual revenues went to pay for opium.

The First Opium War
In 1839 the emperor assigned the governor of Hunan Province, Lin Tse-Hsu, to Guangzhou with orders to end the opium trade. Lin was an exceptionally intelligent and incorruptible official who had successfully stopped the trade in Hunan. He immediately took action, demanding that Guangzhou's foreign traders turn over their stores of opium. The British Chief Superintendent of Trade (a position translated in Chinese as the "Barbarian Eye") was Captain Charles Elliot. Much to the dismay of merchants, he acceded, relinquishing 20,000 chests of opium valued at almost £3 million, which Lin promptly had destroyed.

Perturbed, the British withdrew to Macau and to ships anchored in Hong Kong's harbor. The squabble turned nastier after a Chinese man was killed in a brawl, and the British were prevented from getting food and water. Lin made further threats, and Elliot ordered the Navy to fire on three Chinese warships.

Goaded by the influential opium traders (MPs Jardine and Matheson foremost among them), Britain seized upon the issue to press for an expansion of trade. The British Foreign Secretary, Lord Palmerston, dispatched an expeditionary fleet of 4,000 from India, which arrived in Hong Kong in June 1840. Its mission was to obtain compensation and an apology from China for the destroyed opium, and to secure a British foothold on the China coast.

What ensued was the Anglo-Chinese War of 1839-42, popularly called the Opium War. As one historian has pointed out, it could just have easily been the Molasses War, had molasses been the main commodity. The real motive was

Britain's desire to regularize and broaden trade with China. Not everyone agreed it was a good thing. William Gladstone raged of the Opium War: ". . . a war more unjust in its origin, a war more calculated in its progress to cover this country with permanent disgrace, I do not know, and have not read of."

China was ill-equipped to deal with Britain's powerful warships. Following the death of 500 Chinese soldiers in an attack on forts at the mouth of the Pearl River, China agreed to the January 1841 Convention of Chuenpi, promising to provide compensation for the confiscated opium and to permit British merchants to return to Guangzhou.

Hong Kong Island
The treaty also ceded Hong Kong Island to the British. On 26 January, a naval survey crew landed at Possession Point to plant the British flag and drink to the health of Queen Victoria.

Both sides were unhappy with the treaty, which was never actually signed. The Chinese emperor found it impossible to accept, while the British were disgruntled with their apparently meager acquisition. Queen Victoria lamented "the unaccountably strange conduct of Chas. Elliot," who had "tried to obtain the lowest terms from the Chinese." The London *Times* grumbled: "A worse situation could not have been selected for trade, and that is the reason why the Chinese have so readily ceded it. It may be considered as a banishment from the more civilised parts of the empire by the Chinese authorities, who have insulted, tricked and cajoled us."

Elliot, by all accounts a decent and unaggressive man, was sent packing as counsel-general to the new Republic of Texas (his Chinese counterpart was booted off to Tibet). His replacement, Sir Henry Pottinger, was charged with obtaining a better deal for Britain—either a more suitable island, or permission to trade from Chinese ports.

Treaty of Nanjing
A new British expeditionary force sailed up the China coast, seizing port cities all the way up to Nanjing, whereupon the Chinese gave in. The 1842 Treaty of Nanjing forced China to pay $21 million in compensation; open the port cities of Shanghai, Xiamen, Fuzhou, Ningpo, and Guang-

zhou to British trade; and confirm the cessation of Hong Kong Island "in perpetuity," so that the British might have "some Port whereat they may careen and refit their Ships, when required, and keep Stores for that purpose."

More important, they had a base for commerce that lay outside of Chinese interference and corruption. Jardines shifted its godown and counting houses from Macau to the island even before ratification of the treaty, and other traders followed suit.

Western historians have paid the fact scant attention, but being forced to hand its land over to aliens was a profoundly humiliating experience for China, one that has neither been forgotten nor forgiven. In the aftermath of Britain's success, other European countries moved in to carve their own trade ports out of helpless China.

HONG KONG'S EARLY YEARS

Hong Kong Island was originally to be developed as a military position, but the British foreign secretary who gave that order in 1842 was far too late. Buildings had started going up immediately after the British landed in January 1841, and by October the population had swelled to 12,000, nearly all Chinese. At first everything, even the governor and the Anglican church, was housed in bamboo mat sheds, but soon the outlines of a proper settlement could be discerned: a cricket ground, a majestic cathedral, military barracks, a racecourse, police stations, and hospitals.

Elliot and his replacement, Pottinger, organized land sales. Central was reserved for the government, including a huge swath of grassy land sweeping down from Government House to the water. Western and Wanchai were Chinese neighborhoods, while prime oceanfront lots went to the Army and Navy—the beginning of a trend that has disrupted urban planning to the present day. Streets were named for British civil servants, though the disgraced Captain Elliot is nowhere commemorated. A constitution was drawn up in 1842, and Hong Kong became a British Crown Colony in 1843.

The early years were hard for the colonists, who struggled against malaria, typhoons, and piracy. The malaria epidemics of 1841-43 killed hundreds of soldiers, earning the colony a reputation as a "white man's grave." "You can go to Hong Kong for me," became a popular saying of contempt in England. One journalist of the period noted that Hong Kong was always associated with pestilence, war, or internal struggle.

The population grew to 20,000 by 1844 and was nearly double that nine years later. Most residents, whether Chinese or British, were temporary settlers hoping to make their fortune. An early colonial treasurer described Hong Kong's Chinese inhabitants as "the scum of Canton," but the British eventually came to admire their industriousness, respect for learning, and close family ties.

Turmoil in China proved to Hong Kong's benefit, as the Taiping Rebellion (1859-65) forced refugees across the border and the population topped 100,000. Among the refugees were wealthy businessmen who established the Nam Pak Hong, trading houses that supplied emigrant overseas Chinese with goods from the homeland.

Social Life

Of a population of 24,000 in 1845, only 600 were Europeans, and of these only 90 were women. The young men of the hongs led a collegiate life in compounds that combined office, godowns, and living quarters. A visiting Shanghai doctor described a typical dinner. It started with soup and sherry, went on to side dishes with champagne; and meat with champagne or beer; then game, pudding, jelly, and champagne; followed by cheese, salad, bread, and port; fruit and claret; and at long last, coffee and cigars.

When ships were in town, sailors outnumbered residents three to one. A missionary sniffed: "They drink like fishes, ride round the town in rickshaws, making night hideous with their shouts, eat overripe fruit from street stalls, are stricken with cholera, and die in a few hours."

The same man's description of Hong Kong's get-rich-quick mentality applies equally well to the present day: "The large salaries paid, the desire to make a fortune quickly, together with the uncertainty of health and life consequent on fast living, give a certain feverishness to the pulse of the community." Horse racing was popular, as was prostitution, then concentrated around Hollywood Road. A 19th-century madame ran a discreetly risqué newspaper advertisement: "HONEY at Mrs. Randall's—a small quantity of HONEY in small jars."

The opening of the Suez Canal in 1869 shortened the 100-day voyage from England and increased Hong Kong's importance. Clipper ships were replaced by faster and more comfortable steamships, and wives and children traveled out more frequently, changing the tenor of the community.

Opium War Redux

Relations between Europe and China remained strained. Lord Palmerston, now prime minister, noted "these half-civilised governments" such as China "require a Dressing every eight or ten years to keep them in order." The pretext for this "Dressing" was the Arrow Incident.

In August 1856, Chinese authorities in Guangzhou boarded a suspected pirate ship, the *Arrow,* arrested the crew, and tore down the Union Jack. Britain seized on the fact that the ship was registered in Hong Kong and had a British captain to press for further concessions on the part of China. Joining forces with France, Britain besieged the China coast again in the Second Anglo-Chinese War. The skirmishes ended with the 1858 Treaty of Tientsin, which leased Kowloon to the British and allowed them diplomatic representation in Beijing.

China reneged after signing the treaty, and hostilities resumed. British and French troops occupied Beijing in October 1860, forcing the signing of the Convention of Peking. This version dispensed with the lease and ceded outright the tip of the Kowloon Peninsula up to what is now Boundary Road, as well as Stonecutter's Island. This new acquisition greatly expanded Hong Kong's military defenses, provided room for growth, and allowed authorities to control the pirates and robbers based at Tsimshatsui.

The treaty also essentially legalized opium in China. The Chinese government was allowed to handle internal trade and excise a modest tax. Hong Kong's government did the same, first by licensing opium divans, later by auctioning off the monopoly on the preparation and sales of opium. From 1914 to 1941 the government took over the monopoly itself, earning a substantial portion of its revenues from it. The practice ended only with WW II and the Japanese occupation.

The New Territories Lease

In 1898, Britain took its last and biggest bite out of China, hoping to improve the colony's military defensibility against other European powers busy carving out concessions for themselves. The Second Convention of Peking turned over a chunk of land north of Kowloon, plus 233 surrounding islands—790 square km of land in all. These New Territories, as they came to be known, constitute 91% of Hong Kong's area.

The Chinese government objected to an outright grant, and the British foreign secretary, who had hoped for an open-ended lease to be terminated on mutual agreement, rather carelessly agreed to a 99-year term. That probably seemed as good as forever in 1898.

Economic Growth

Hong Kong developed quickly as a trading port: "a little England in the Eastern Seas, the creation of British energy, enterprise and industry," a Londoner described it in 1886. By 1895, it was the world's fourth-largest port. The population continued to grow, but the percentage of Westerners remained miniscule. The Chinese and European communities led separate lives, neither comprehending the other.

Hong Kong's elite was quite a snooty bunch. Social rank was indelibly fixed by one's race, nationality, position, and accent. The hierarchy took visible form on the Peak, where the rich retreated in the stifling summer months. On its upper reaches lived the British taipans and civil servants. Wealthy Chinese and other Europeans lived in the Mid-Levels; borderline acceptables like Portuguese, Jews, Armenians, and Parsis at the foot of the Peak, and the Chinese masses in crowded, unsanitary slums in Western and Wanchai districts.

Epidemics of bubonic plague frequently ravaged the Chinese community. In the 1894 outbreak, nearly 3,000 died and 100,000 fled to China, disturbed by British efforts at plague control, which included immediate burial of victims and the burning of infected homes. The plague returned yearly, and in the next 12 years over 13,000 would die.

Political turmoil and civil war in China periodically sent masses of refugees streaming into Hong Kong. The toppling of the Manchu dynasty in 1911 boosted the population to 500,000; by 1937, it was over one million. Despite its growth, Hong Kong had a reputation as a relatively dull colonial outpost: Shanghai was considered a far more cosmopolitan and exciting city.

JAPANESE OCCUPATION

Beginning in 1933, Japan marched across China, occupying Beijing and Shanghai in 1937 and taking Guangzhou the following year. Refugees poured into Hong Kong, swelling the population to 1.65 million by 1941.

Hong Kong hadn't a chance against a concerted attack, but Winston Churchill insisted the colony could not surrender outright. Defense plans were drawn up to hold Hong Kong Island, and a line of pillboxes was installed across the New Territories. British citizens were conscripted in 1939, and the following summer British women and children were evacuated to Australia.

The Japanese invaded Hong Kong the morning of 8 December 1941, as part of a simultaneous attack on the Philippines, Malaysia, and Pearl Harbor (which lay across the International Dateline). The tiny RAF (Royal Air Force) detachment at Kai Tak was destroyed within minutes, and Japanese soldiers quickly overran the New Territories, forcing troops to withdraw to Hong Kong Island. After several days of heavy bombardment and threats, Japanese forces landed there on 19 December.

British efforts to hold out against Japan were suicidal, and the British suffered heavy casualties, including two Canadian battalions that had been sent the preceding month to boost local morale. Hong Kong's governor, Sir Mark Young, signed the British surrender on Christmas Day. The island's defenders were shunted off to prison camps for three and a half years of forced labor on two bowls of rice a day. Some men were sent to work in Japan coal mines or factories; others labored on an extension of Kai Tak airport's runway. British civilians were interned at Stanley, where they suffered from disease and food shortages.

The Japanese occupiers alternately ignored and terrorized the Chinese population. Starvation was an ever-present threat, and to reduce the strain on scanty resources they urged the return of Chinese to the mainland. Many were dumped into unseaworthy boats and sent off to watery graves. By the time a British naval squadron arrived to a subdued welcome on 30 August 1945, Hong Kong's population had been reduced to 600,000.

THE POSTWAR YEARS

Reconstruction
The British expected to return to a shambles, and Hong Kong was in a sorry state, but government officials were astonished at the energy with which the inhabitants rebuilt their shattered economy. Following the Japanese surrender, exiles returned at rates approaching 100,000 per month.

The years 1948-49 saw an even greater influx, as the Communist drive into south China sent supporters of the Kuomintang fleeing to Taiwan and Hong Kong. Members of the upper class arrived with business acumen and suitcases of gold ingots. Most of the new immigrants, though, were peasants and laborers with nothing but a fierce desire to make good. Capital, knowledge, and labor proved the precise combination necessary to launch Hong Kong's industrial revolution.

Mao announced the creation of the People's Republic of China from Tiananmen Gate in Beijing on 1 October 1949. Hong Kong braced itself for the expected invasion—there was no reason to believe the Communists would respect the old regime's agreement with the British—but the People's Liberation Army troops stopped at the border.

Hong Kong sighed with relief and went on with the business of growth. Before the war, the colony had flourished as a trade entrepôt. After the war, and especially following the 1952 UN embargo on trade with China, it turned to making things itself: first textiles, followed by plastics, electronics, and watches. Businessmen seized the opportunities the embargo provided to make money, and Hong Kong became an important source of goods for China, as well as a "laundry" for the re-export of Chinese-made goods. In the '60s, the Vietnam War boosted Hong Kong's economy further with the military procurement trade and the influx of up to 3,000 soldiers a month on leave.

Political Turmoil

In the late '50s, China's disastrous "Great Leap Forward" brought famine even to fertile Guangdong Province. The Cultural Revolution, which followed, wreaked even greater havoc, throwing the country into turmoil for nearly a decade and spilling over into Hong Kong as well.

Political conflicts had flared up occasionally between Nationalist and Communist sympathizers. In 1956, 60 people died in clashes sparked by the removal of posters of Chiang Kai Shek from a housing estate (ironically, officials had merely been concerned the glue would damage the building).

A decade later, rioting flared up over a five-cent increase in the Star Ferry fare. Hong Kong's most uncomfortable moment came in 1967. A labor dispute at a plastic flower factory triggered political unrest, and the virulent rhetoric of the Cultural Revolution swept into Hong Kong. Crowds shouting slogans from *The Thoughts of Mao Tse-tung* beseiged the gates of Government House. Homemade bombs exploded throughout the summer, inspiring a ban on fireworks that endures today; anti-British graffiti was scrawled on walls, and political slogans were unfurled from the windows of the Bank of China. Along Queen's Road Central, loudspeakers blared out opposing messages from the Bank of China and the Government Information Office. Protestors took refuge in the giant emporiums of Chinese product stores, as a dusk-to-dawn curfew was imposed and residents huddled at home. The situation remained tense for nearly six months, but without clear support from China things slowly calmed down.

In the aftermath the Chinese border was virtually sealed, making crossing much more difficult for Hongkongers and impossible for tourists. An assortment of Sinologists, journalists, and scholars came to roost in Hong Kong, where they could monitor China and read between the lines of the official press. Hong Kong remained a center for exiled China watchers through the late '70s, when they moved into Beijing.

> *. . . in its time the Colony has been an entrance to China, an escape from China, a window into China and the one sure base from which the world can contemplate China in bad times and make its contracts with China in good.*
>
> *—Jan Morris*

An International City

Hong Kong hit its stride in the late '70s, blossoming into a great international city. Political conditions in China relaxed, trade improved, and the '80s proved to be a decade of prosperity. Buoyed by a succession of fiscal surpluses, the government began to improve working and living conditions. Compulsory free education to age 15 was provided by 1974, and money was channeled into cultural facilities, hospitals, and transport. A particular focus was the massive public housing program, with its eight New Towns slated to eventually house 3.5 million residents.

1997, AND BEYOND

Things were going so well, in fact, that some dared hope that the issue of 1997 and the expiry of the 99-year lease on the New Territories might not come up at all. China had deferred Portugal's offer to return Macau; perhaps, optimists argued, it would realize Hong Kong's benefits were too great to risk.

Fat chance.

The issue came up like clockwork, 15 years before the return date—just when businessmen were getting nervous. Fifteen years is the usual maximum term for mortgages, and nobody knew if China would honor existing leases and mortgages on property it would be taking over.

Prime Minister Margaret Thatcher visited Beijing in September 1982, launching two years of negotiations between the British and Chinese leaders. Details of proceedings were kept secret, but apparently the British were made to quickly realize that the return of Hong Kong was not a question: China would have it back.

The truth is that Hong Kong has no choice: full independence was never an option. China wished to regain face by regaining the colony, plus absorb the advantages of a multi-billion dollar economy. Britain had relatively little at stake. Hongkongers, of course, had plenty at stake—their way of life, their security, their freedom—but they were not consulted in the matter. No Hongkongers participated in the negotiation process, which resulted in the Sino-British Joint Declaration of 1984.

The Hong Kong SAR

The Sino-British Joint Declaration of 1984 outlined a timetable by which Hong Kong would revert to Chinese control at the stroke of midnight 30 June 1997. Under the terms of this agreement, elaborated on in later documents, Hong Kong was to become a Special Administrative Region or SAR, possessing a fairly high degree of internal autonomy, with its own currency and laws and its own elected government, to be headed by a China-nominated chief executive. Freedoms of speech, the press, travel, religion, and assembly were guaranteed, at least on paper, and China agreed that Hong Kong's current social economic system was to remain intact for at least 50 years, under the slogan "one country, two systems."

The entire joint declaration was carefully crafted to give China maximum flexibility while inspiring the maximun degree of confidence in the people of Hong Kong. China was fully aware that lacking these reassurances, up to one-third of the population was prepared to flee Hong Kong, just as their ancestors had fled the advent of Communist rule on the mainland.

Tiananmen Square

Hong Kong's moment of truth occurred in the spring of 1989. Democratic protests erupted in China in April following the death of Hu Yaobang, the former secretary-general of the Communist Party. Crowds gathered in Beijing's Tiananmen Square, China's symbolic center of power. For six weeks demonstrators occupied it, the original student protesters joined by all ages and classes of Chinese.

It was an extraordinary and moving display, watched with great hope by Hong Kong. Students brought up money to support the protest-

ers, and pro-democracy advocates organized giant demonstrations in Hong Kong. The situation in Beijing soon became unendurable for the Communist Party leaders who had become the target of unprecedented criticism. Martial law was declared and troops sent in, only to be overwhelmed by the protesters. Finally, tanks and troops were sent into Tiananmen the evening of 3 June, and under cover of darkness brutally cleared the square of demonstrators. Nobody knows how many were killed, but Amnesty International later estimated there to be some 1,700 victims.

The optimism which had preceded the slaughter only served to double Hong Kong's sense of horror and outrage. Suddenly liberals, pro-Communists, and even the normally apathetic majority were out on the streets. Monster rallies held 4 June and the following two Sundays attracted nearly a million people. Demonstrators wore black armbands to signify mourning, and buried the Cenotaph memorial with heaps of floral offerings to the dead.

The sorrow and anger also evoked pride and a previously lacking sense of identity. Suddenly it seemed everyone cared about Hong Kong's future—and virtually everyone was afraid. Crowds seeking foreign passports mobbed embassies, and newspapers were full of advertisements for immigration seminars. Tiananmen Square was Hong Kong's nightmare come true, proving that China's leadership could and would brutally crush even peaceful opposition.

Things quieted down in the years following Tiananmen Square, and Hong Kong got back to business. The lack of certainty about the not-so-distant future gradually became less of an issue as Hong Kong once again resolved to make the 1997 transition work—or at least to appear to for as long as possible, because determined optimism breeds more money.

Democratic Reforms

Hong Kong has no real tradition of direct elections or public participation in government, nor of public debate on issues. The Confucian view of people as sheep and the government as shepherd blended with colonial instincts to create what was until recently a very comfortable situation.

Still, Hong Kong has historically possessed

THE EMIGRATION RUSH

Rule by China was not necessarily a pleasant prospect for six million of the world's most ardent capitalists, even if they are themselves Chinese. Some Hongkongers—mainly those with the most to lose—were understandably disturbed at the recent transition. Perhaps half a million chose to express their opinion of Hong Kong's future in the most dramatic way possible: leaving. Panic set in after the Anglo-Chinese agreement on the return of Hong Kong was announced in 1984. Emigration rates rose from an average of 20,000 a year in the early '80s to 40,000 in 1987, then soared after the 1989 Tiananmen massacre, peaking at 66,000 in 1992. The pace cooled considerably by 1996, as those who had the means to leave also had the foresight to prepare well in advance.

Traditionally Chinese emigrants have been coolies, laborers, and merchants. Modern emigrants were skilled, often wealthy professionals, "yacht people" rather than "boat people." Even for those with the education, skills, and wealth to have the option, leaving was not an easy choice. It's a tough call: to move with insufficient capital to guarantee a good life, or to risk everything they've built in Hong Kong. For most the issue was economic rather than political.

The 1981 British Nationality Act denied 2.6 million Chinese their status as British subjects, rescinding their rights to reside in the United Kingdom. Most British still oppose giving it to them, although the British economy could certainly use an injection of Hong Kong-style enterpreneurialism. Criticized for its abandonment of Hong Kong, Britain in 1990 announced a program to grant citizenship to up to 50,000 key Hong Kong residents. With family members included, it was estimated this Nationality Selection Scheme would accommodate a total of 225,000 people. Response was less than overwhelming, though. Justified or not, Britain has a reputation as a cold, gloomy, and unfriendly place. Hongkongers prefer Australia, the U.S., and most definitely Canada, where around 20,000 end up annually. Many of them have settled around Vancouver, B.C., causing it to be dubbed "Hongcouver." Other less-qualified emigrants have obtained passports from more accessible countries like Tonga, Peru, and Argentina.

Middle-aged couples may send adult children abroad to establish a refuge. Some have a child in each of three different countries. Another common solution is for one spouse to go abroad to establish residence, while the other keeps working in Hong Kong. Those who stay behind are known as *tai hong yen*, "astronauts," alluding to their solo orbit. The long-term separation is more difficult than many couples anticipate, and split-ups are common. Another problem is the breaking up of tightly knit families, as middle-aged children leave their elderly parents behind.

The brain drain has peaked by now, and some 12% of emigrants have returned to live in Hong Kong, new passports in hand. They report that between unemployment, high taxes, and cold weather, life abroad is not so great. Many of these returning émigrés are fence-sitters who will probably leave at the slightest hint of trouble.

what it considers the most important freedom: the freedom to create wealth and to get ahead. Economic benefits are widely preferred to messy issues like elections. Expanding local democracy was proposed after WW II, only to be shelved following the 1949 rise to power of China's communist government. The idea was never seriously revived: China would have disapproved of increased political freedom; Britain was happy enough with its cozy colonial arrangement; and Hong Kong people were largely apathetic in the matter.

Gradual political reforms instituted in the 1980s allowed direct elections of minor posts like local district boards and half the seats on the Urban Council. Public interest and voter turnout remained low, until the Tiananmen Square massacre of 1989 provoked an acute awareness of Hong Kong's vulnerability. One result was the direct election of 18 members of the Legislative Council (see Government section) members in the 1991 elections—a first for the territory, though still largely symbolic. Of the balance of Legislative Council members, 10 were appointed and the remainder were chosen through a byzantine system of functional constituencies, involving a tiny fraction of voters and designed to favor corporations.

Whether to expand democracy further in the 1995 elections became a subject of bitter dispute between Britain and China. A controversial reform package presented by Governor Patten in October 1992 proposed changes which would let Hong Kong people elect, either directly or indirectly, all 60 legislators in 1995—for the first time ever, and only two years before Hong Kong's return to China. Although China bitterly denounced the reform package as a violation of the Basic Law, (Basic Law is the document that outlines the Hong Kong SAR government, released in 1988 by Beijing.) Patten eventually forged ahead with the proposals.

The dispute revolved more around the mechanics of elections than actual democracy. Even the Basic Law provides for a gradually increasing percentage of directly elected seats in the new SAR legislature, from 20 in 1997 to 30 by 2003. (In fact, the Basic Law allows for the eventual possibility of direct elections for all leg-

islative members and the chief executive—which would be far more political freedom than Britain ever gave Hong Kong.) The truth is that China didn't take kindly to what it regarded as underhanded tactics to change the terms of its earlier agreements with the British—and China held most of the cards. Relations thawed in mid-1994 as talks on economic issues got back on track, but China dismantled the Legislative Council the moment it took over, replacing it with a Provisional Legislature with the power to pass laws until regular elections could be held in 1998. Some local observers wondered if the two years of improved democracy had been worth the bad feelings generated. Others maintained the reforms didn't go far enough to ensure a strong local government—a case of too little, too late on Britain's part.

GOVERNMENT

n July 1, 1997, the British Crown Colony of Hong Kong became the Hong Kong Special Administrative Region of China. The Sino-British Joint Declaration of 1984 guarantees the HK SAR a "high degree of autonomy" in all except foreign affairs and defense. The Hong Kong SAR government is outlined in the Basic Law, a document released by Beijing in 1988. The keystone is *gangren zhigang* or "Hongkongers rule Hong Kong." As party secretary Jiang Zemin told a group of Hong Kong visitors: "The well water does not interfere with the river water."

Hong Kong remains a free port and a separate customs entity with independent financial and taxation systems. Legal and governmental systems are comprised of local people, ruled by a Hong Kong chief executive appointed by Beijing. The Basic Law serves as a sort of mini-constitution, as interpreted by the National People's Congress in Beijing.

Numerous minor details were taken care of in the transition. Queen Elizabeth's profile disappeared from Hong Kong coins, replaced by the carefully neutral *bauhinia* flower, the official symbol of the Hong Kong SAR. A flag was developed as well, a stylized white *bauhinia* flower on a red ground, bearing China's five red stars on its petals. Hong Kong's new coat of arms also fea-

tures the *bauhinia*. This heavy reliance on the flower is symbolically disturbing, for, as Jan Morris has pointed out, the *bauhinia* is a sterile hybrid.

Chief Executive
The post of colonial governor has been replaced by a chief executive appointed by Beijing. The first office holder, announced in 1996, was Tung Chee Hwa, a 59-year-old shipping tycoon of Shanghai origin. In his early months in the post, Tung proved to have moderate skills retaining both power for himself and space for Hong Kong. No sweeping changes were evident with the transition. Tung reappointed all of the previous government's civil service policy secretaries, though it appears that policy-making will increasingly be delegated to his own appointees.

Legislature and Elections
The Legislative Council, often called Legco, is invested with the modicum of democracy Hong Kong possesses. For a long time all of its members were either civil servants or appointees, but in 1985 around half its seats were transferred to indirect elections. In 1991, in response to demands provoked by the Tiananmen Square massacre, 18 of the 60 seats were directly elected, a first for Hong Kong.

Political parties are a recent phenomenon, one resisted for a long time for fear of polarizing the electorate into Communist and Kuomintang (Taiwan) camps. Even Hong Kong's liberals are fairly conservative by the standards of most places. The United Democratic Party (UDP) won 12 of the 18 seats in the 1991 elections: it's led by lawyer Martin Lee, an outspoken and steadfast advocate of democratic reforms. The UDP has since merged with Meeting Point, another liberal faction, to form the Democratic Party, which swept the 1995 polls. The Liberal Party, supported by conservative and business forces, is moderately pro-Beijing, while the recently founded Democratic Alliance for the Betterment of Hong Kong is even more so.

The 1995 Legco was originally supposed to sit its full four-year term, but China, irritated at the unilateral British decision to implement democratic reforms, took matters in its own hand, dissolving Legco July 1st and replacing it with a hand-picked Provisional Legislature. This body is to make laws and organize elections within 12 months of the handover.

As China is concerned that Hong Kong not become a base for subversive activities, the Provisional Legislature is likely to pass laws making it more difficult to hold demonstrations and start political organizations. The new government will also redefine treason, sedition, and subversion, and set punishments for these crimes. Just how severe new restrictions will be remains to be seen.

Judiciary
The judicial branch remains the least changed by the handover. Chinese has been introduced into court proceedings, but English common law will remain the basis of practice for the next 50 years. Traditional outfits remain as well—Chinese tourists reportedly adore the justices' horsehair wigs. A local Court of Final Appeals has replaced Britain's Privy Council as the ultimate arbiter, though China's National People's Congress has the power to overrule its decisions in "acts of state"—a vague clause which could be interpreted a number of ways.

Local Government
Local government encompasses 19 district boards, a Regional Council, and an Urban Council. Half of the seats on the latter are elected, half are appointed. Turnout for these elections remains low, perhaps because these bodies deal with uninspiring issues like sanitation and zoning.

The 1998 Elections
The Hong Kong SAR's first elections are to be held within 12 months of the handover, probably in March 1998. It's up to Tung's government and the Provisional Legislature to determine exactly who can run and who will vote, but according to Basic Law, 20 seats in the new legislature will be directly elected, just as in the controversial 1995 reforms. Thirty seats will be chosen by professional groups, and ten by the election committee. Liberal politicians are planning to participate, and if Tung and Beijing are at all smart they will encourage this, rather than cast them outside the fold and make automatic heroes of them.

ECONOMY

Hong Kong works. It works hard, and it works well—well enough to raise itself from squalor to prosperity in less than 50 years. The SAR's booming economy is the envy of many countries, its colonial masters included. It is a happy blend of a Confucian-inspired immigrant work ethic and a government that, up until 1997, at least, knew the difference between support and interference.

For the past two decades, Hong Kong's GDP (gross domestic product) has grown over seven percent annually, twice as fast as the world's economy. It's the eighth-largest trading entity in the world, and is the largest exporter of clothing, watches, toys, radios, clocks, plastics, and candles, among other things. The Kwai Chung container terminal is the world's largest and vies with Rotterdam and New York as the world's busiest, and Hong Kong's merchant fleet controls one-eighth of world shipping. Hong Kong is also Asia's financial center, the third most important in the world after New York and London.

Hong Kong's per capita GDP was over US$24,000 a year in 1996. (Across the border in China the figure is something like US$700.) Average annual income was only US $9,300, but disposable income is higher than these figures indicate, since taxes are low, most housing is subsidized, medical care and social services are virtually free, and excellent public transport makes a car unnecessary. Adjusted for purchasing power, the average Hong Kong worker's income ranks in the world's top 10, above Britain's, and slightly below that of France.

> *Hong Kong subscribes to Victorian economic principles: these are the only economic principles that have ever actually succeeded.*
> —*District public official, quoted by Jan Morris in "Anglo-China," Travels, 1976*

Even more amazing is how this standard of living was created. Hong Kong has no natural assets except its harbor, and its extraordinarily ambitious and diligent people. They feel there is opportunity, and they are determined to make the most of it. People work hard (44 hours is the usual workweek, but 70 hours is not uncommon), save fiercely, cut corners, and count costs for their families' long-term benefit. Partly it's a characteristic of an immigrant society, still hungry, not quite believing it's got it made. Partly it's faith that hard work and brains will bring rewards. Even street hawkers and fast-food cashiers display a fierce diligence and energy. Only a few will become fabulously wealthy, but the general standard of living has improved tremendously over the past few decades.

There are problems: cramped and unsafe sweatshops, huge disparities between rich and poor, heavy and unregulated environmental pollution, and an inadequate social welfare system. But the general prosperity that has resulted sounds like an economic fairy tale. The government budget boasts a chronic surplus. Private companies complete gigantic civil-engineering projects like the Cross-Harbour Tunnel or the MTR well ahead of schedule, providing superb service at low cost. Hong Kong's transport system and all its utilities except water are privately owned profitmakers. Even the government postal service makes money.

Government Role

Hong Kong's reputation as a laissez-faire play-ground is not entirely accurate. No government running the world's largest public housing authority could be accused of a hands-off policy. But in purely economic terms Hong Kong is as close to laissez-faire as things get. No less an expert than Milton Friedman cites Hong Kong as the place "to see how the free market really works." A 1996 survey of 103 countries ranked Hong Kong's economy as the world's freest.

Paternalistic and colonial though the past government may have been, it created an environment in which businesses flourish. Customs procedures are simple, shipping and communications excellent, regulations straightforward, and bureaucratic interference minimal. Taxes are deliberately low: 16.5% on corporate profits, a maximum of 15% on salaries, and no capital gains tax. Trade unions have limited power, strikes and labor unrest are rare, and there is no fixed minimum wage.

The legal and judiciary system has so far limited the network of favoritism and *guanxi* (connections) that plagues businesses operating in China. Elaborate gifts and lavish entertainment are part of doing business, and corruption certainly exists, though it's well below the Asian standard.

The environment encourages competition. Market pressures encourage flexible, resilient companies that can adapt to new situations faster than any government edict could ever hope to. Most businesses are small (the average manufacturing concern employs only 17 people) and thus can easily switch to whatever is profitable or popular at the moment. Hong Kong long ago outgrew its reputation as a colony of sweatshops churning out cheap imitation goods. Today it's professional, flexible, and utterly dedicated to the bottom line.

"Little Dragons"

Hong Kong shares its phenomenal economic growth with Southeast Asia's other three "Little Dragons": Singapore, South Korea, and Taiwan. The quartet has much in common: easy access to new technology and services, excellent communications, stable workforces, minimal regulations, low taxes, and centralized governments receptive to business needs. The stunning success of their export trade has created a new urbanized Asian middle class with a standard of living comparable to the middle class in Western countries.

ECONOMIC SECTORS

Hong Kong is extremely industrialized: farmland constitutes less than seven percent of total area (one of the lowest percentages in the world), and only two percent of the population fish or farm. With a dearth of natural resources, practically everything—raw materials, fuel, equipment—must be imported, even manufactured goods, as local factories produce mainly for the export market.

Hong Kong's economy is based on "value-added" production and services: raw materials and unfinished components flow in to be exported as finished goods. Today even more money is made from services like financing, insurance, warehousing and shipping, and tourism. Hong Kong is *the* Asian business center: located at the crossroads of the Pacific, it's more cosmopolitan than Tokyo, more business-oriented than Singapore, more English-speaking than just about anyplace.

Manufacturing
Hong Kong's economic trajectory was launched in 1949 with the convergence of two crucial

HONG KONG BY SUPERLATIVES

Some of the categories in which Hong Kong holds the title for world's biggest, busiest, or best:

- World's highest per capita horse race betting revenue (adult men spend nearly one of every seven dollars they earn on horse races)

- Highest per capita brandy consumption (0.57 liters)

- Highest per capita consumer of oranges (many of them used for temple offerings)

- World's tallest outdoor bronze statue (the Buddha at Po Lin Monastery)

- World's largest nightclub (Club Bboss)

- World's largest oceanarium and aquarium (Ocean Park)

- World's largest outdoor escalator system (Mid-Levels Hillside Escalator)

- 25 of the world's 50 busiest McDonald's

- World's largest Pizza Hut

- Most Rolls Royces per capita (around 1,600 total)

- Largest number of Mercedes-Benz cars outside Germany

- World's highest density of vehicles (271 per km of road)

- World's largest civil engineering project (Port and Airport Development Scheme)

- World's longest rail and road suspension bridge (Tsing Ma, 2.2 km)

- Tallest building outside the U.S. (Central Plaza, 79 stories)

- World's largest neon sign, with over 13 km of neon tubing (the San Jiu sign next to the Shun Tak Centre, Central)

- World's largest wall of glass (Hong Kong Convention and Exhibition Centre)

- World's highest percentage of land conserved in country parks (40%)

- World's most expensive retail rents (Causeway Bay, followed by Pedder Street in Central)

- Highest annual average of hours worked (among 48 major cities)

- World's largest annual fireworks display (the Urban Council's Chinese New Year show)

- Highest proportion of residents living in subsidized public housing (3.19 million in 290 estates) elements: over a million Guangdong peasants blessed with entrepreneurial talent and a drive to work, and several hundred Shanghai capitalists with the skills to harness this raw energy. The result transformed Hong Kong from a trade entrepôt to a manufacturing center in its own right.

Local industries began with textiles and clothing (still the largest industrial employer), expanding into plastics, electronics, watches and clocks, photographic equipment. Through the '80s, the annual growth of domestic exports was 11%, double the world average. Today, 83% of the value of total exports is reexports, to China, Japan and Taiwan.

In recent years, much of the manufacturing has shifted across the border to China, and Hong Kong has moved gracefully into services. The manufacturing workforce, over 800,000 in 1981, has slipped to less than 450,000 today, but unemployment remains virtually nonexistent, hovering below 3%. Newspapers print enormous "Help Wanted" sections, and hotels have permanent windows for hiring—not a Help Wanted sign set in a window, but an engraved metal plaque embedded in the wall, a good indicator of the permanence of the situation.

Financial Services
The service sector, primarily banking, business, and tourism, now constitutes nearly three-fourths of Hong Kong's economy. The SAR has a more diverse range of financial services than Tokyo, with more than 400 financial institutions, including 75 international banks, on Hong Kong Island alone. The local time zone complements London and New York, causing banks to choose it as the logical Asian center for round-the-clock operation.

Hong Kong is an exciting but risky place to make money, with a notoriously jittery stock market. There are four stock exchanges, but everyone watches the blue-chip Hang Seng Index, which soared to new records in the days following the handover.

Tourism
Hong Kong's tourism industry began with the influx of U.S. servicemen during the Korean and Vietnam wars. Since then it's grown into Asia's top destination, attracting 10.2 million visitors in 1995.

A complementary international mix of Asian and European travelers evens out the difference between high and low seasons. Nearly 40% of tourists are from China and Taiwan, the latter often stopping off in Hong Kong to buy gifts for relatives in other parts of China.

The average tourist spends a little over half of his or her money on shopping: without a doubt it remains Hong Kong's favorite sightseeing attraction. If shopping has recently lost its glamour for Western tourists, it still appeals to wealthy Asians who appreciate Hong Kong's huge range of luxury goods.

Shipping
This traditional moneymaker remains an important element in trade. Many ships are unloaded by lighter in the middle of the harbor, while the container terminal at Kwai Chung is the busiest in the world. Here consignments of goods are broken down or consolidated into shipments for China, northeast and southeast Asia. Container traffic grew nearly 30% in 1992 and even more in 1993, resulting in tremendous bottlenecks and a constant scramble for berthing space.

HONG KONG AND CHINA

Even before their political merger, the Hong Kong and China economies had been growing steadily closer since economic reforms began in the late '70s. Hong Kong investors were quick to seize the opportunity to invest in Chinese enterprises and establish joint ventures, first in the free market Special Economic Zones, more recently expanding into the Guangdong countryside.

Hong Kong is China's main trading port and true economic center, handling 40% of its trade and providing nearly two thirds of all foreign investment in China. It's also a convenient route for the unofficial US$5 billion Chinese trade with South Korea and Taiwan. Hong Kong provides the Communist government with a window on the capitalist world, and serves as its largest supplier of foreign investment and managerial expertise.

Things work both ways: China has long been the largest single foreign investor in Hong Kong.

THE PRINCELY HONG

"Hong" (which bears no relation to the name Hong Kong) is the local term for the old established British trading companies like Jardine Matheson, Butterfield and Swire (now the Swire Group), and Hutchison Whampoa. The hongs' origins lie in the trading houses established in Guangzhou in the 19th century. Combined, warehouses, offices, and quarters were called "factories." The buildings were set up in a row in a sort of international bazaar: Dutch, French, Austrians, Danes, Swedes, Spaniards, Americans, and of course the British, whose East India Company was the biggest of all.

The quintessential hong remains Jardine Matheson, which predates the territory itself and is still intimately associated with Hong Kong, though it's no longer locally based. William Jardine was a Scottish merchant who entered the Far East trade in Bombay, first as a "country trader" dealing in Indian cotton, spices, and indigo.

In 1827 Jardine shifted to Canton and Macau, where he soon became the leading merchant. Breaking the monopoly of the East India Tea Co., he shipped the first free consignment of tea to London. Eventually he teamed up with fellow Scotsman James Matheson to make a fortune in the opium trade. Strict Calvinists, they prided themselves on being honorable, in a fashion: their opium was unadulterated. Jardine is on record as describing his business as "the safest and most gentlemanlike speculation I am aware of."

Jardine earned a reputation as a shrewd, tough character: according to company legend, there was only one chair in his office—his own. The Chinese called him the "iron-headed old rat," following an incident in Guangzhou when he was struck on the head with a bamboo staff and didn't even flinch. He left Asia in 1839 a rich man, giving up his business to become a Member of Parliament, along with partner Matheson. The pair played a major role in lobbying for the First Opium War, and are thus considered among Hong Kong's founding fathers, though Jardine never actually visited Hong Kong.

Jardine Matheson was formally established in 1841; its opium godown at what is now Causeway Bay was Hong Kong's first permanent building. The company rapidly expanded, its business opportunities boosted by an exceptionally fast clipper fleet. It became one of the first companies to enter Japan in the 1850s, and participated in the building of several Chinese railroads.

The seemingly permanent British control of the hongs was brought to an end in the '80s, when billionaire Li Ka Shing became the chairman of Hutchison Whampoa. Swire, still controlled from London by family members, remains successfully involved in the shipping trade and much else, including Cathay Pacific Airlines. As for Jardine Matheson, the Mathesons had long ago quit the company, while the last Jardine was bought out in 1961 by the distantly related Keswick family when the company went public. Distrustful of Chinese intentions, it transferred its headquarters to the Bahamas in 1984, in a move compared by an indignant local commentator to "the Queen emigrating to Australia."

Jardines today is a multinational conglomorate active in over 50 countries. In Hong Kong it has a finger in every lucrative pie: its Hong Kong Land Company owns huge chunks of Central, while Gammon, its joint venture construction associate, is active in the building trade. Other interests are the Mandarin Oriental, merchant bank Jardine Fleming, the Dairy Farm and Maxim's chains, and Pizza Hut and 7-Eleven franchises. Jardines' past history is far from forgotten, as revealed in a survey mounted to test a revamped company logo. The design depicts a Scottish thistle: when questioned, most local Chinese revealed they thought it was an opium poppy.

One indication of what Jardines' future may hold was hinted at in August 1997, when Li Ka Shing revealed that he had purchased a three percent stake both in Jardines and in Hong Kong Land. Li made a previous attempt to buy Hong Kong Land in the '80s, which ended in a promise that he would make no further attempts to buy any of Jardines' businesses until 1995. Now that deal has expired, and Li appears to be mounting another bid, this time with the apparent backing of China. The betting in Hong Kong is that this time he will succeed.

Private investors and government agencies have bought into manufacturing firms, banks, hotels, office and apartment blocks, seeking higher profits than they could dream of on the mainland. Much investment is disguised or unreported, but investment from other regions of China accounts for a third of Hong Kong's economy.

Optimists argue that Hong Kong's best reassurance against a post-1997 economic meltdown is that China won't want to trash its own investments. Which poses the question: Did China really take over Hong Kong in 1997? Or had Hong Kong already taken over China?

The Guangdong Connection

Hong Kong has invested some $24 billion in China in recent years, bringing south China into its vibrant economy. Since the mid-'80s, increasing wages and rents in Hong Kong have driven manufacturing jobs into Guangdong Province. Manufacturers find the lowered production costs more than cover the extra transportation expenses, and the new six-lane highway linking Hong Kong and Guangzhou knits the region together even more closely.

The economic integration is already enormous: Hong Kong companies have set up over 10,000 factories in Guangdong, and employ some two to three million workers. As wages and expenses increase in the Special Economic Zones, manufacturers are burrowing deeper into the Guangdong countryside. It's all part of an emerging, and formidable, partnership, in which Hong Kong provides the foreign exchange, equipment, and expertise, and Guangdong the cheap land and labor.

Past 1997

"One country, two systems," is a political, not an economic, doctrine. China and Hong Kong are already blended together, and China would cut its own throat with any deliberate actions to ruin Hong Kong's economy. This much seems certain. What the future holds for Hong Kong's economy, though, is less clear.

The HK$64 billion question is: Will Hong Kong's orderly brand of capitalism be subverted by mainland corruption, or will the opposite process occur? Whatever happens, it will be big. China is already developing into the world's largest sales and labor market. Combining China's massive natural resources and pent-up marketing demand with Hong Kong's marketing skills may be a recipe for economic success on an unimaginable scale.

Again, there are two scenarios. The optimists foresee Hong Kong and China becoming even more interdependent, as mutual investment increases. Hong Kong's role will gradually shift from trade and investment to raising global funds for Chinese enterprises, as with "red chips," listed Hong Kong firms backed by mainland funding. In this scenario, the SAR will remain China's international financial center for a long time to come.

What could go wrong? China's economy might crash, igniting a financial crisis in Hong Kong. High costs could drive businesses to other Asian locations, like Singapore or Shanghai. More likely, as China develops, Hong Kong will slowly lose its comparative advantage—but that's a long way in the future.

The key for Hong Kong is political stability, the necessary prerequisite to making money. The 50-year transition period from 1997 is supposed to provide this, by guaranteeing the continuation of a free market economy under common law, a convertible Hong Kong dollar, unrestricted freedom to travel, and freedoms of speech, religion, and the press. What will actually happen is anyone's guess. It's widely feared that China will consider some freedoms more essential than others—economic freedom it will accept, but political freedom may be less palatable. Just how essential political freedoms are to Hong Kong's economic success is the crucial question.

Hongkongers remain optimistic by virtue of necessity. Many people are betting cautiously on the "economic miracle" scenario. They point out that China took over Hong Kong politically in 1997, but South China was already taken over by Hong Kong, commercially. While politicians bickered, businessmen were quietly cementing the financial links which may prove more powerful than any paper agreement.

As ultimate insurance, Hong Kong has its capacity for hard work and quick change. Hongkongers have turned past crises—the 1950s trade embargo with China, the 1980s rise in labor costs—to their advantage. They are prepared again to adapt to unexpected changes, and anyone who knows them is betting that they'll win. In the end, however, all the predictions and projections are nothing more than guesses. History here is still very much in the making.

THE PEOPLE

Hong Kong's six million people are 96% ethnic Chinese, about 70% of them Cantonese from Guangdong Province. The remainder come from southern coastal regions like Chaozhou, Fujian, and Shanghai, while a small fraction are tribal peoples like the Tanka, Hoklo, and Hakka.

Cantonese

Hong Kong is essentially a Cantonese city. The outside world does not often recognize the differences between Chinese regions, but the people of Guangdong Province are distinctly different from northern Chinese. A Hong Kong governor once described them as "the Irishmen of China"—independent-minded, charming, and talkative. Beijing regards Guangdong as wayward and possibly renegade territory, with good reason: South China has produced more than its share of revolutionaries, most notably Sun Yat-sen.

But the Cantonese are less concerned with politics than with economics. The urbane folk of Beijing and Shanghai disdain the Cantonese as uncouth, loud, and mercenary. "Mercantile"

A QUESTION OF IDENTITY

Identity is a painful subject for Hong Kong, beginning with its political definition. More than a city, it is still something less than a country. "Special Administrative Region" has a less than inspiring ring to it (some joke that SAR stands for "Small Area under Repression.") What does a Hongkonger specify on an immigration form? He can no longer even pretend to be British—few ever felt they were—yet he is not quite Chinese. Asked to describe themselves, 70% of Hongkongers use the term "Hong Konger" or "Hong Kong Chinese." Only 20% say "Chinese," a fact which might give Beijing pause.

Culturally, Hongkongers are Chinese to the core, yet most feel uncomfortable with mainland politics. They are Chinese evolved in a different direction, shaped by enterpreneurial forces and a refugee mentality. They share classical Chinese Confucian and family-oriented values, yet have been deeply influenced by the British colonial system.

The British provided the framework that has allowed Hongkongers' energies to flourish: security, civil liberties, and freedom from arbitrary revenge and political intrigue. But Hong Kong was made with Chinese effort, Chinese ingenuity, Chinese innovation.

Hong Kong at the time of the handover exemplified colonialism inverted. The natives were not being exploited; instead, they were running amok in financial fields and making a good show of it. Hong Kong is purely Chinese, but its essence is modernized and slightly Westernized. In this sense it's a perfect stepping stone between China and Western culture.

The 1997 handover has helped the formation of Hong Kong's unique identity in some ways. The process was encouraged by a deliberate government campaign to make people consider Hong Kong their home rather than a temporary stopping-point, but much of it is a natural result of the steady increase in Hong Kong-born residents, now 60% of the population. China's political upheavals, especially Tiananmen, have served to define differences more clearly.

It's not a question of secession or revolt: Hongkongers are essentially pragmatic, with little regard for political dogma, and will adapt to China as long as they can make money. But it's becoming clear that they are their own people—a fragile identity still being formed, and one which may never be officially acknowledged. To put it another way, Hong Kong (the British name) has become Xiang Gang (the Mandarin name), without ever acknowledging Heung Gong, the name by which the local Cantonese have always called it. No wonder there is an identity problem.

might be more apt: the Cantonese are capitalists at heart, and form the backbone of prosperous overseas Chinese communities around the world. They share the Chinese ethics of discipline, family loyalty, and hard work, and add their own special enthusiasm for earning money.

Hong Kong was settled by several mutually exclusive and suspicious ethnic groups long before the arrival of the British. The largest of these was the Puntei (the term means "local inhabitants"), descendents of Cantonese who arrived from the 11th century onwards to farm the best land. Many were emigrants from the Sze Yap of Guangdong Province, four villages about 40 km north of Hong Kong that spawned the bulk of overseas Chinese communities. Descendents of the Puntei "Five Clans" still predominate in the northwest New Territories.

Hakka

The Hakka (their name means "guest families") are the gypsies of China. Driven out of Shandong Province around 200 B.C., they assumed a life of wandering, moving south into Guangdong and Fujian around the 11th century. Arriving in Hong Kong in the late 17th century, they settled in the rugged eastern New Territories, where they still predominate. Many Hakkas are farmers, but they also monopolize the stone quarry and bean curd industries, while black-clad Hakka women can be seen working on construction sites. They are distinguished by a fondness for gold teeth and the bamboo hats

FILIPINAS IN HONG KONG

The largest foreign community in Hong Kong is neither British nor American, but Filipino. There were some 128,000 Filipinos at last count, more than 90% of them women hired on domestic service contracts. As old-style Chinese *amahs* have moved on to more lucrative work in factories, Filipina women have taken their place. Employers prefer them because they will work for less than Chinese, are literate in English, and will work on a fixed contract—often 14 or 16 hours a day, six days a week, for several years.

Many of the women are nurses, teachers, or midwives with university degrees. Their skills are desperately needed in the Philippines, but the local economy is chronically crippled, and Hong Kong is only a three-hour plane ride away. The standard contract salary of HK$3,200 a month plus room and board (a special low rate set for domestics) is triple that of a schoolteacher in Manila. Most of the women live frugally and send back most of their salaries in the form of remittances to support families in the Philippines. Some try to save up enough money to buy a shop, or a tractor, or a business. Many women go into debt just to get their position—employment agencies in the Philippines charge exorbitant fees—and spend the first year working to pay it off.

It's seldom a happy life in Hong Kong: the women must contend with loneliness, homesickness, the drudgery of menial work, and the strain of living in an unreceptive foreign culture. Workers frequently report beatings, sexual abuse, unfair dismissal, or the withholding of wages and passports. Some employers force their servants to work illegally in factories, restaurants, or relatives' homes, doing double or triple duty for the same pay.

The women have few alternatives. A foreign domestic servant needs permission from the Department of Immigration to change employers, and must leave the territory two weeks after her contract terminates. Many overstay their contract or stay illegally.

The number of Filipinos in the area has increased dramatically in recent years as word has spread of employment opportunities. Philippine clubs around Hong Kong now offer discos, videos, and remittance services in pesos. On Sunday, their day off, thousands of women go to Sunday Mass, then congregate around Statue Square in Central, where they meet friends, catch up on news, and share or sell special home-cooked food in an all-day outdoor reunion that carries on regardless of weather. The crowds are huge, to the dismay of the area's owner, the Hong Kong Land Co.

The big question, of course, is how has the handover affected the Filipinos. While China has promised to allow domestic helpers to remain, the local expectation is that workers from the mainland will replace them—whether gradually or quickly remains to be seen.

ON *GWEILO*

The word *gwei* means "monster, demon, evil being"; another meaning is "odd, strange, or queer." This unflattering term has been used to describe Westerners since the earliest days of Chinese-Western contact. Modern expats have cheerfully appropriated the term, taking the sting out of its use.

Some historians insist that no insult was originally intended, and that the term originated from the first glimpse of Macau's Portuguese, who looked remarkably like the stock Chinese idea of a devil. Commissioner Lin gave a chilling description of them in his diary:

"The bodies of the men are tightly encased from head to toe by short serge jackets and long close-fitting trousers, so that they look like actors playing the parts of foxes, rabbits and other animals. Their hair is very curly, but they keep it short, not leaving more than an inch or two of curl. They have heavy beards, much of which they shave, leaving one curly tuft. Indeed, they do really look like devils, so calling them 'devils' is no empty term of abuse."

The complete term is *fan gwei lo,* "savage devil fellow": if you're concerned with proper grammar, *gwei po* is a woman devil, *gwei nu* a girl devil. Not that the term is limited to Westerners: Indians are *yun do gwei,* Japanese are *yut poon gwei,* and a *waung meen gwei* is a yellow-faced *gweilo,* an overly Westernized Chinese.

(liangmao) fringed with black cloth, which Hakka women wear to protect against insects and sun.

"Boat People"

The underdogs in Hong Kong's indigenous social hierarchy are the region's original inhabitants, a group the English have dubbed "Boat People" and the Cantonese derogatorily call Tanka or "Egg Families." They themselves prefer the term Sui Seung Yan ("People on the Water"). Historians believe they may be descended from the aboriginal Yue people who inhabited the South China coast in prehistoric times.

Another theory postulates that the Tanka are descendents of refugees who long ago fled to south China. Historically they were forbidden to move ashore or to marry into landed families, and even today they experience discrimination.

The British developed a friendly relationship with the Tankas, as by imperial edict only this pariah caste was allowed to work as their servants. The Anglicization "Hong Kong" is based on the Tanka pronunciation of the name.

The Tanka are Cantonese speakers who stay apart from the Chaozhou-speaking Hoklo, a smaller seafaring tribe who originated from Fujian Province. Both groups were historically fishermen, supplementing their income with trading, pearl-diving, ferrying cargo and passengers, and a smattering of piracy and opium-smuggling.

As recently as 1981 there were 80,000 boat people in Hong Kong. Today around 15,000 or so remain seagoing fishermen, living on boats anchored most visibly at Aberdeen. The floating life is not as romantic as it sounds—the boats are cramped and dirty, the work hard and dangerous. As the fishing industry becomes more mechanized and competitive, boat people are choosing a less adventurous but more reliable future, coming ashore to work in factories and live in housing projects.

Expats

Hong Kong's expatriate community totalled 438,200 in 1996, making it one of the largest in Asia. The number of foreign citizens has doubled over the past decade, though nowadays many of these are former residents returning on expat terms. The 1997 transition may create problems for expats who can't obtain a visa through their work. The Basic Law states that non-Chinese can obtain the right of abode if they have entered Hong Kong legally, have stayed continuously for a period of at least seven years, and declare Hong Kong their place of permanent residence. What this means in practice remains to be seen.

The largest expat group, numbering over 128,000, are Filipinos, nearly all women who come to work on domestic service contracts. Indonesians are joining this category as well. Among Westerners, Americans and Canadians both outnumber the British population, which is a mere 25,000. Most Western expats are in Hong Kong to work and get ahead. Their increasing population partly reflects the poor job market in the West, and partly a growing interest in the Asia-Pacific market.

The Thai population is surprisingly large (around 25,000), many of them women working in the euphemistically named "entertainment industry." A Japanese community of around 22,000 keeps a low profile (local resentment remains regarding WW II) but has heavily invested in the local economy.

Indians form another prominent community, with some 22,000 residents. Some of their ancestors arrived with the British as soldiers in 1841. Indian traders predominated in the young colony, and even today Indians and Pakistanis control about an eighth of Hong Kong's foreign trade, partly due to the extensive overseas Indian network in the Middle East, Africa, and Latin America. The post-1997 citizenship issue is particularly difficult for them, as many have huge amounts invested in Hong Kong. China will not automatically accept anyone but racial Chinese, and the British have turned down the Indian community as well. India has offered them a home, but to families who have lived in Hong Kong for generations, it's a foreign country, complicated by the fact India doesn't allow its citizens to hold other passports.

Vietnamese Refugees
For nearly 20 years Hong Kong has dealt with Vietnamese refugees, popularly called "boat people." They first arrived in the mid-1970s, having drifted hundreds of miles aboard leaky boats, fending off pirate attacks along the way. Hong Kong absorbed the first influx, originally housing them in open camps and granting them the right to work, but the numbers grew too large —65,000 by 1979. In 1982 the boat people were moved to closed "centers" (a polite term for detention camps), while Hong Kong sought an international solution to the problem.

Few countries showed interest in accepting the refugees, but to its credit, Hong Kong never turned any away (until recently). Between 1975 and 1986, 110,000 Vietnamese came; a core of 50,000 stayed. The government estimates it's cost over US$350 million to keep, process, and deport them.

In 1988 the UN High Commission for Refugees instituted a screening program to sort out economic from political refugees. Only those who could demonstrate "a well-founded fear of persecution" in Vietnam were eligible for emigration. Less than five percent qualified, and even they had to wait long periods to be accepted by another foreign country.

The vast majority of Vietnamese were classified as economic refugees, with nowhere to go but back home, a depressing thought to those who had spent five or ten years in the grim camps. The forcible deportation program instituted in December 1989 by the Hong Kong government caused international protests. A video on positive conditions in the new Vietnam, plus the realization that they had no alternative, persuaded most Vietnamese to return. China had made it quite clear it wanted the problem solved before the handover, and by mid-1997 only 2,000 or so Vietnamese were left.

Illegal Immigrants
From 1949 through 1962, Hong Kong absorbed over one million Chinese refugees. Hong Kong's population has long been fed by immigrants from China, and indeed the society possesses a refugee mentality: short-term view, highly pragmatic, and fast-moving. Things are completed early; money is made immediately if not sooner; and people save, save, save for the future, so that their children can do even better.

Illegal immigrants are popularly known as "I.I.s" ("eye-eyes"). During the '60s and early '70s I.I.s were not exactly welcomed, but if they managed to "touch base" by reaching the urban area, they were eligible for an identity certificate granting residence in Hong Kong. It was almost a game, and for every one caught, two or three others made it home free. By the late '70s over 1,000 a day were slipping into Hong Kong, seriously straining its resources. The "touch-base" policy was revoked, and an identification card system instituted to determine legal residents from illegal ones.

Immigration legislation enacted the following year allowed the legal immigration of 150 people a day, who must prove the existence of a close relative in Hong Kong. The current list has around 600,000 names.

And still the I.I.s continue to come: in 1996 some 37,000 were deported, and an equal number slipped through. Attempts increased in the runup to the handover, with rumors flying that immigrants would be allowed to stay. With jobs plentiful, most find a niche quickly—often working on construction sites—but those who don't make it in this highly competitive society may turn to crime or drugs. Periodic sweeps are conducted to round them up and deport them. But periodic amnesties are also granted, and those who come hope they will be lucky enough to coincide with one.

Population

The natural population growth rate is around 1.5% annually, but the other regions of China provide a limitless supply of would-be immigrants: between 1978-80, 500,000 flooded into Hong Kong. The population—6.3 million in 1995—is projected to rise to 8.1 million by 2011, much of this growth fueled by illegal immigrants and an annual legal quota of 55,000 mainlanders allowed to settle in Hong Kong.

Compounding the problem, much of the SAR consists of uninhabited rugged mountains and barren islets. Residents huddle together in the relatively scarce flat areas and in the equally crowded New Towns. The waiting list for public housing is long and growing longer—seven years at last count.

The average population density rate in inhabited areas is 20,811 per square km, compared to 9,068 per square km for Manhattan. Kowloon neighborhoods regularly vie for the title of most crowded on earth: the latest winner was Shamshuipo, with 165,445 people per square km. Someone once calculated that if everyone came out from their high-rises simultaneously, there would be six square meters of space per person, a figure which has no doubt dwindled since then.

The Housing Crunch

Houses in Hong Kong are only for the very, very rich: even a small patch of lawn is a rare luxury. With flat land at a premium, life proceeds in vertical mode, in massive housing estates where a 500-square-foot flat may house a family of ten. No wonder people spend much of their free time away from home, shopping, in restaurants, or working long hours in the office.

Hong Kong is among the most expensive cities in the world for renters: a flat that rents for US$1500 a month in New York may cost US$4000 here. Recent speculation has driven up prices even further. Skyrocketing land values

and limited facilities caused the government to long ago opt for high-rise, high-density development. Today it runs the world's largest public housing program, housing nearly 50% of the population.

The tremendous post-WW II influx created an acute refugee problem. By the early '50s squatter shanties were spread along hillsides everywhere, east of Central all the way to Chai Wan and all over Kowloon. The government was reluctant to do anything to encourage immigrants to stay, until a disastrous fire at the squatter settlement of Shek Kip Mei left 55,000 homeless and prodded it into action. The area was quickly redeveloped into a housing estate, the first of over 150 to date.

WHAT'S IN THESE NAMES?

Hong Kong names are often inspired combinations of East meets West. Business names may be picked for their auspicious ring: the Sovereign Superb Shipping Co., the Prosperity Steamship Co., the Smart Rich Company. Then there's the cheerful Ho Ho Co. in Wanchai, which is just across the street from the Healthy Mess (a restaurant, no less).

Other company names reveal a sly sense of humor: the Tin Tin Motor Company, the Ping Pang Piano Factory, Hop On Bicycle Company, and Lee Kee Boots Enterprise. Sometimes the humor borders on perverse, as in Hang On Tailor or the Wo Clinic. How about One Way Electric Company? And who wants to work in Chao's Building?

The wit extends to given names as well. Taking a Western name is a rite of passage for young people, who typically add it before their Chinese name (as in Martin Lee Chu-Ming or Rita Fan Hsu Lai-Tai). Less staid Hongkongers have adopted sobriquets like Apple, Creamy, Cinderella, Jackal, or Quicktrip. Money is an understandably popular name. The fabled Milky Wei is joined by a chef named Mango Tsang, a truck driver named Hitler Wong, and Dr. Ziggy Kwok, DDS. The list continues through Thankie Yue and Angel Sin, reaching the outer edges of believability (and decorum) with Nausea Yip and Pubic Ha.

The Hong Kong Housing Authority was founded in 1954 to provide reasonable permanent housing for everyone in Hong Kong, a tall order indeed. HKHA builds and manages flats whose rents are determined by the tenant's ability to pay—usually five times below market value. It also sells flats, again considerably below market value. "Laissez-faire" is not in the government vocabulary with respect to housing. HKHA has also sponsored the development of the completely self-contained New Towns, where over 40% of Hongkongers now live.

The flood of Chinese immigrants has been temporarily staunched, but the demand for housing continues to increase as nuclear families break away from larger units and young married couples want their own quarters. The government has housed over 2.8 million people, but a waiting list remains, and there are still people living in pedestrian underpasses, stalls, and shops. In Mongkok, old men sleep in 6-by-3-by-3-foot cages, stacked in tiers and rented for HK$1000 a month. About 300,000 people remain in "tolerated squatter settlements," areas which have been improved with communal lavoratories and concrete paths.

Critics of the government program say if these are one-story slums, the housing projects are high-rise ghettos. Apartments in the earliest buildings were concrete cubicles with communal bathrooms and no kitchens—residents cooked in the hallways. Things have improved markedly since then, though quarters are still incredibly cramped by Western standards. A family of eight might live in four rooms.

Inside are color TVs and air-conditioning—Hongkongers are not poor, except in the sense of quiet and space. Resident expats sometimes wonder why they aren't invited to a colleague's apartment for dinner: it may well be because there is no room to entertain. Crowded conditions drive Hongkongers onto the street, accounting for the old people drowsing in parks, the packed restaurants, and the vivid public life —not to mention the "love hotels" renting rooms by the hour to married couples starved for a bit of privacy.

Aspects of modern city life resemble an urban jungle, with children getting their fresh air in caged playgrounds. Still, wealth is distributed far more equitably than the last century, when wide open spaces and quaint rambling colonial buildings contrasted with the crowded squalor of Chinese neighborhoods. Ugly as they may be, modern housing estates provide a minimally decent standard of living for everyone.

Urban Stresses

With a population density 30 times greater than that of urban London, life in Hong Kong involves a tremendous amount of stress. It has been named the noisiest city in the world; one survey ranked it among the world's most stressful cities—just after Beirut. The pressure is increased for young people: teenagers facing school exams, and even younger children under parental expectations to succeed. Suicides of children as young as eight years old are not uncommon, and are often attributed to school pressures.

Surprisingly, Chinese University researchers found a lower rate of depression in the general population than high stress levels would indicate. Researchers speculate it's due to strong family ties and the intensely social nature of the community. Despite the crowding, there is little alienation or vandalism. People seem to have no time to be depressed; they're busy, forward-looking, and either prosperous or expecting to become so soon. It's worth remembering that, stressed or not, Hongkongers have the second-highest life expectancy in the world (80 years).

CONDUCT AND CUSTOMS

Hong Kong's unique cultural makeup means that social interactions and behavior are a mix of East and West. Certain local characteristics are apparent to even the casual observer. People place great value on appearance, right down to the perfect shoes, watch, and handbag. Virtually everyone is neat and well-dressed, even in the steamiest summer months. The gregariousness and talkativeness of Hong Kongers is also readily apparent. People thoroughly enjoy company—they even hike in cheerfully noisy groups. Solitude is virtually unknown, and so, fortunately, is the need for it.

Visitors are often culturally shocked about Hong Kong's relentlessly enormous crowds. While the pushing and shoving that used to characterize public places has markedly improved in recent years, don't try crossing the Chinese border during the Mid-Autumn Festival. or you'll be trampled by determined little old ladies wielding enormous bags. (Little old ladies seem to push the most, in fact.) In such a situation, discard your finer sensibilities and push back, or you'll never get anywhere.

Public displays of anger are a serious loss of face. Avoid trying to prove someone wrong, especially in front of others. Always leave an out to save face—even a token concession is appreciated. Be patient and persistent rather than aggressive. And remember that the disconcerting Asian tendency to laugh in serious or embarrassing situations is simply an attempt to defuse tension.

Social Interactions

While Westerners emphasize one-on-one relationships, Chinese interactions focus on groups of relatives and friends. The elaborate Confucian system of social interaction covers all possible permutations within familial and business relationships, but there are no rules governing treatment of strangers—thus the chaos in public situations. Shoving in crowds is acceptable: after all, they're strangers.

Psychologists point out the difference stems in part from methods of child-rearing. Children in the West are taught to be independent and as-sertive. Conflicts are brought up and dealt with openly, and disagreements are looked at as something to be discussed and resolved by mutual compromise. The cult of the individual permeates Western society, from elaborate birthday parties complete with cake and presents to separate checks at restaurants.

Chinese society, on the other hand, emphasizes the importance of groups. Family solidarity dominates the individual to a much larger extent than in the West, and children generally obey their parents. Modern adults may try to persuade their parents, but will seldom disobey them outright.

The Western and particularly American emphasis on independence and individuality seems downright selfish to such a mentality. When I was teaching at a Chinese university in the early '80s, an apocryphal story making the rounds concerned an American family who shared a nice home-cooked meal. At the end the father whipped out his calculator and tallied up a bill for each member. Students repeated this anecdote in a tone of smug horror, and no one really believed my protestations that such things didn't occur. Another frequently cited shocker, this one undeniable, was the American custom of putting old people into nursing homes—in Chinese eyes, separating them from their families and the respect they had rightfully earned.

"Face" and Conflicts

"A man needs face like a tree needs its bark," goes an old saying. Face is not some bizarre Asian concept: everyone everywhere wants to look good and avoid social shame. But because Chinese society focuses on groups and group interactions, face becomes a matter of unspoken cooperative behavior.

Face has multiple aspects: on the individual level, a person gains face by displays of wealth or generosity. This constant quest for social status fuels Hong Kong's obsession with the best, be it cognac, gold watches, or shark's fin soup.

On a broader level the concept of face structures interactions in subtle but far-reaching ways. People try to avoid unduly damaging the prestige and self-respect of others as well as themselves. Confrontation and criticism are guaranteed face-destroyers. If criticism must be delivered, it is done subtly, in the form of advice.

If disagreement arises, it is never stated outright. The participants might discreetly figure out who is the dominant figure among them, and let him (it's invariably a man) win. Or a higher-ranking third party might be brought in to resolve the conflict.

It's interesting to consider the political implications of this point of view, which supports and stems from a hierarchical political tradition. True loyalty precludes publicly contradicting someone and causing him to lose face. Thus, students and employees dislike speaking up, because they either risk making a mistake and losing face themselves, or they threaten their superior with loss of face. The concept of a "loyal opposition" is an oxymoron in this system. Obedience is valued more than self-assertion, and individualism, rather than being a shining virtue, is perceived as simply being selfish and ill-bred.

FENG SHUI: THE WIND-WATER SCIENCE

Feng shui (pronounced "fung soy" in Cantonese) is the art and science of positioning manmade structures in harmony with the vital cosmic energy *(chi)* coursing through the earth. It is quintessentially Chinese in its concern for harmony and proportion, and for balancing man, nature, and spirit.

Traditional cosmology describes how invisible energy currents, or "dragon veins," run from the sky down into mountain peaks and then along the earth, blending heavenly and earthly energies. Natural topography—the form of hills, the direction of streams—is believed to modify the natural energies, creating auspicious and inauspicious sites.

Feng shui experts study this invisible geography, looking at the positioning of mountains, valleys, and streams. Using the *luo pan* compass, a magnetic disc set in a divining board, they scan the hillsides for hidden dragon veins, then follow these down to the valley floor. Sites where yin and yang meet in proper proportions—where "dragon ridges" intersect "tiger hills"—are favorable locations for villages, houses, and ancestral graves.

The ideal site faces south, with rising land to the east and softly undulating hills to the west. It is fronted by a stream and backed by mountains, is open to breezes in front, and is dry, with no white ants. Often these sites are used for graves: ancestors must be appeased with the best of everything. The omega-shaped form of old brick graves is considered ideal from a *feng shui* perspective.

Feng shui's ancient principles (the system dates back to the Sung dynasty) have been successfully transferred to modern urban environments. Hong Kong is the center of the international *feng shui* scene, exporting geomancers to Chinese communities around the world. Since poor placement of a building could bring bad luck to both businesses and workers, multimillion-dollar office buildings are vetted by geomancers who adjust their design.

"Why go against what everyone believes in?" said an American businessman who regularly consults *feng shui* experts. "Besides, it just might work." If the recommended adjustments seem too expensive, he added, property agents can recommend an understanding *feng shui* consultant who will keep costs in mind.

At the Regent Hotel, *feng shui* experts were called in even before the architects' plans were approved. The Regent's spectacular waterfront location was a particularly tricky matter, as dragons are said to sweep down from the hills each day at dawn to bathe in the ocean and would be peeved to find their route blocked by a building. Dragons, however, can pass through glass unimpeded—thus the hotel's spectacular 12-meter-high windows and the glass doors on its Salisbury Road entrance. *Feng shui* experts also advised on the placement of doors, windows, and elevators inside the hotel, right down to the positioning of room furniture.

The Hong Kong and Shanghai Bank building, the world's first billion-dollar office building, underwent a similar process. Its site is considered nearly ideal from a *feng shui* point of view, but the consulting geomancer placed the ground floor escalators at slightly oblique angles to counteract the negative influences of the building's diagonal bracing. The bank's trademark bronze lions were also repositioned so as not to face one another, and were set in place one Sunday at the auspicious hour of 4 a.m.

Banquet Etiquette

Eating is a highly social and symbolic event, epitomized in the formal banquet. The meal will be elaborate, but the host is expected to ritually deprecate its quality. Do not agree with him! Instead, vehmently compliment him on the superb food. Expensive fresh fish, fine cognac, or shark's fin soup are all signs of the host's respect for his guests, and earn him status.

In a similarly complex ritual, the host plies his guests with food and drink, and they decline two or three times before graciously accepting.

If you *really* don't want any more, state it in a very convincing yet polite manner. At banquets, save enough room to eat something of every dish. But don't completely finish the rice or noodles served at the end, as this implies the food was insufficient.

Toasts are raised to every possible subject. You needn't drain your glass each time; a symbolic sip is sufficient. If it's your turn to toast and you've run out of ideas, you can always raise a toast to the next dish.

Watch other guests for cues on behavior.

HONG KONG TOURIST ASSOCIATION

The lou pan, *or geomancer's compass, has eight points representing heaven, water, fire, thunder, wind, rain, hills, and earth. Each of these in turn is associated with eight animals: horse, goat, pheasant, dragon, fowl, swine, dog, and ox.*

The neighboring Bank of China tower, all sharp edges and acute angles, is an anathema from a *feng shui* standpoint. The malevolent "secret arrows" it shoots out onto the neighboring Government House have been deflected by a weeping willow tree planted at the order of a *feng shui* master.

Feng shui principles influence interior decorating as well, accounting for the abundance of mirrors inside Hong Kong offices. Small octagonal mirrors called *pat gwa* are strategically placed to scare away demons, who fear the sight of their own ugly faces. Aquariums are another solution to pending evil: the fishes' movement and the play of light on the water deflect bad influences. The fish absorb the bad luck, acting as a sort of filter—and if they die, they're replaceable.

A manager hoping to improve business may call in a *feng shui* consultant to rearrange the office fur-

niture; families experiencing difficulties do likewise. A local magazine runs a monthly *feng shui* column, detailing common problems. A typical column described the case of Mr. and Mrs. Wong, a "Western Earth" couple inhabiting an "Eastern Wood" flat, who were beset by a series of quarrels and illnesses. The geomancer called in to remedy the situation pinpointed a beam set into the surface of the ceiling, which "pressed" and "cut" the couple's bed. A west-facing sofa attracted the "star of illness," as did the bay window in their bedroom. The Wongs needed a northwest-facing flat but couldn't afford to move. On the advice of their geomancer, they switched bedrooms and moved the bed and sofa to face advantageous directions. Then they temporarily moved out of their flat, to return on a lucky hour of a lucky day, and presumably lived happily ever after.

Minor faux pas on the part of foreigners are expected and easily forgiven. Generally guests leave soon after the food is finished. If you dine out with someone, don't attempt to split the bill: either accept the meal graciously or pay the bill discreetly without any public pondering of the matter.

Meeting People
Business cards are important indicators of social status for professionals, indicating one's role in the hierarchy. They're printed in English on one side, Chinese on the other. You can get these made up within 24 hours from the little shops on Man Wa Lane in Central, or by instant machine. (To fit further into society, you can rent a cellular phone and pager and indulge in the local habit of animated lengthy conversations in public places.) Present a card with both hands as a gesture of respect.

People are generally addressed formally—Mr. Lee, Miss Wah. In the Chinese fashion, family names come first: Lee Chu-ming is Mr. Lee. Professionals often adopt a Western given name instead of or in addition to their Chinese name: thus Martin Lee Chu-ming, or simply Martin Lee.

LANGUAGE

Cantonese and English are the official languages, and things like road signs, government documents, and public notices appear translated into both (written Chinese became an official government language with the handover). There are perhaps one million passable English speakers in the SAR, and many more poor ones. English use is declining in recent years, as educated professionals emigrate abroad and pragmatic Hongkongers increasingly turn to studying Mandarin. The long-term prospects for English are dimming: starting in 1998, secondary schools which previously used English will switch to Chinese.

It's easy to get by in English in Central and Tsimshatsui, but outside the main tourist destinations, communication can become difficult. Usually a passerby can be enlisted to help: look for a student or a teenager, who is more likely to speak it than someone older. English-speaking policemen wear red badges on their uniforms. Many taxi drivers know the English names for the most popular destinations, but it helps to have someone write down your destination in Chinese, or show the driver on a street index or map. As a last resort, the driver may radio his main office and have you explain your destination—or he may pull into a police station for assistance.

CHINESE

Chinese is spoken by more people than any other language: some 907 million, compared to 456 million English speakers. "Chinese" is not a single language, but nine groups of dialects embracing countless subdialects, many of them mutually unintelligible. Were China not a unified country, these would be considered separate languages rather than dialects, because they differ as much as Spanish, Italian, and French. What they have in common is an ingeniously flexible system of non-phonetic writing.

The dominant version of Chinese, spoken by 70% of mainlanders, is the Beijing dialect, known in the West as Mandarin. The Chinese government promotes a standardized form of it, Putonghua, as the national language.

Most of the Chinese subdialects developed in the isolated coastal regions south of Shanghai, and retain archaic features which Mandarin shed long ago, including a more complex tonal system—nine in Cantonese, compared to four in Mandarin. While all dialects share the same written system, a Hong Kong businessman needs a translator in Beijing, and vice versa.

Dialects differ mainly in pronunciation, somewhat in vocabulary, very little in grammar. Chinese structure and syntax is straightforward, and sentences have a telegraphic simplicity. Words do not change according to number, gender, case, or person; verbs are not inflected, and the ideographic writing system spares the learner the difficulties of spelling. The main difficulty for Western students lies in mastering the tones. It helps to have an ear for music.

Tones originated as a means of differentiating an extremely limited repertoire of sounds. Linguists term spoken Mandarin "phonetically impoverished," with only 420 possible monosyllables. Depending on the tone, the word *bei* can mean "teacup," "sad," "north," "shellfish," or "quilt." Different tones avoid confusion only to a point: the rest must come from context. For example, *bei* spoken in a level tone can mean "cup," "inferior," "to carry on the back," "sad," "compassion," or "stone stele"—among other things. *Gwei* can mean "honorable" or "devil," depending on the tone, and *shi shi shi shi shi shi* inflected in just the right way means "ten lions are eating the carcass of a pig." Even native speakers get confused sometimes, but they quickly clarify matters by sketching out the character in question on their palm.

Written Chinese

Chinese script is said to have been invented by a minister of the legendary Yellow Emperor, who copied down the footprints of birds and animals. Originally characters were a sort of primitive picture, with the elements reduced to essentials and stylized down to a few lines. A few modern pictographic characters, like *shan* (山) for mountain and *yu* (雨) depicting drops of rain, remain in the modern language, but most have been stylized beyond recognition.

Ideographs or indirect symbols were developed a mere five or six thousand years ago, greatly expanding the written vocabulary. It's fascinating to dissect the composition of characters and examine the associated ideas. "Bright" is expressed by the characters for sun + moon, "good" by woman + child. The character for "man," read literally, combines strength + field, while "woman" is peace + home.

The greatest invention was the development of determinative phonetic characters, which now constitute 90% of Chinese characters. These combine a specifier indicating the meaning of the word with a phonetic element indicating the pronounciation. For instance, a character which contains the component *mu* nearly always has something to do with wood, as *mu* in its basic form means "tree." Chinese dictionaries operate on this principle, arranging characters first by the 214 radicals or root components which serve as sense indicators, then in order by number of strokes.

The system is cumbersome to learn, but its non-phonetic nature allows speakers of different dialects to share the same written language. Learning Chinese requires an enormous amount of memorization, and much schooling is devoted to rote drills and writing exercises. Chinese has a huge vocabulary: the largest dictionaries list 50,000 characters and 300,000 words and phrases, most of these literary. There are around 6,000 words in common use, and you'll need to know a minimum of 1,500 in order to read a newspaper.

Characters are written with a set order of strokes, drummed into students from an early age. A single character can have as many as 33 strokes, though in the PRC, modernizations of some 2,000 characters were introduced in the 1950s as part of a drive to increase literacy. The simplifications reduced the number of strokes, though purists complain the changes damaged the abstract beauty and logical structure of characters. Outside of the PRC, only Singapore has adopted these changes so far. Hong Kong has kept the older, more complicated forms so far, but changes will presumably occur in the next few years.

Before the invention of paper in the first century B.C., Chinese was originally written on dried slips of bamboo sewn together to form scrolls. Each slip was wide enough for a single line of characters—thus the vertical nature of traditional Chinese writing, which proceeds top right to bottom left. Modern (mainland) Chinese is read horizontally, from left to right.

CANTONESE IN HONG KONG

Cantonese, the main dialect of Guangdong Province, is Hong Kong's lingua franca, spoken in 89% of households and understood by nearly everyone. Other Chinese dialects, primarily Chiu Chau, Shanghaiese, and Hakka, are also spoken by seven percent of the population.

"Cantonese" is an Anglicism: its 65 million speakers worldwide call it Guangdonghua, "the language of Guangdong (province)." It's the most widespread of all Chinese dialects, spoken in Chinese communities around the world.

To northern Chinese, Cantonese sounds like Mandarin run through a mangle and delivered through a bullhorn: *feiji chang* (airport in Man-

| SUNG | GRASS | CURSIVE | PATTERN | ANCIENT | SEAL |

six styles of Chinese script

darin) becomes *fegei cheung; ching wen* is *cheung mun; san dian zhong* is *sam din jung.* Northerners also remark on the high decibel level of speech in Hong Kong and Guangzhou. If it's not loud, it's not Cantonese.

Cantonese is a living, vibrant dialect, full of humor and rich expressions. People play on the monosyllabic nature of the language with punning slang. "Dog" and "nine" are both *gou,* so the code for dog becomes "three-six" *(sam lok).*

Hong Kong Cantonese has absorbed many Anglicisms. "Chinglish" is spoken especially among the upper classes, and useful terms like "percent," "I.Q.," "jogging," and "par-tee" sprinkle Cantonese conversations. Other words are rendered into Cantonese characters, sometimes with tongue-twisting results: taxi is *dik si,* coffee *ga fai,* strawberry *si do be lei,* and, most laboriously, golf is *go yih fu kauh.* It's interesting to note that *mun* (from "money") is the local word for the Hong Kong dollar.

Traffic the other way has been limited. The most prominent Chinese word in English is ketchup (from *ke-tsiap,* fish sauce). Other loans are tycoon, kowtow, and typhoon. Hong Kong English is further enriched by quaint Anglo-Indian words like shroff (cashier) and nullah (small ravine or gully). Then there are purely local terms like *gweilo* (literally "foreign devil," referring to Westerners), taipan (a big businessman), hong (a big business firm), sampan, kaido, and junk (originally a Malay term). The Portuguese have contributed their share: joss or luck comes from the Portuguese Deos, as does *amah* (female servant). The word "mandarin" itself comes from the Sanskrit *mantri,* minister or counselor.

Learning Cantonese

Cantonese's nine tones are intimidating, but learners can take heart in the fact that only six are essential. While you certainly don't have to speak any Cantonese to get around Hong Kong, even a few words will enhance your experience immeasureably. *Joi gin* (goodbye) and *m'goi*

(please/thank you) are easy enough to pick up, as are basic numbers for prices.

For anything more, tones are crucial: you can't just read Chinese phrases out of the book. Get a friendly hotel clerk or waiter to help you pronounce the basics, and practice. Tonal languages are not too difficult for anyone with a sense of musical pitch, but Cantonese is not something you pick up overnight.

Western students need all these characters transliterated into Roman script. Old systems like Wade-Giles rely on superscripted numbers to indicate tones, and apostrophes to denote pronunciation quirks. The PRC's Pinyin system has reasonably straightforward pronunciation, and was responsible for many spelling changes in the Western press—Mao Tse-tung to Mao Zedong, Peking to Beijing, and so on.

Mandarin is a more pragmatic option than Cantonese, both internationally and, increasingly, for Hong Kong. But Hong Kong remains frustrating to Mandarin students because pronunciation differs so greatly, and while local people understand quite a bit, they aren't likely to recognize that *you're* speaking it until you've become fairly fluent.

Both the YMCA and the Chinese University of Hong Kong offer courses in Cantonese and Mandarin. The YWCA, 1 MacDonnell Rd., Mid-Levels, tel. 2522-3101, has afternoon classes in Basic Cantonese. The **Chinese Language Society of Hong Kong,** 18/F, Kam Chung Commercial Building, 10 Hennessy Rd., Wanchai, tel. 2529-1638, offers individual tuition starting at HK$300 per hour. The **Translanguage Centre,** 3/F, 6 Queen's Rd., Central, tel. 2868-3812, holds longer-term language courses. Private teachers advertise in the classifieds of periodicals like *HK Magazine,* or look in the *Yellow Pages* under "Language Instruction." For more details, consult the Glossary, which lists common words and Cantonese phrases you'll encounter in Hong Kong.

RELIGION

Popular Chinese religion remains alive and vital in Hong Kong, unlike the mainland, where the Communist government did a good job of either squelching rituals and beliefs or driving them underground. There's little difference between Hong Kong's present-day religion and that of 1000 years ago.

The thoroughly Chinese philosophies of Taoism and Confucianism permeate society, shaping ideals of how individuals and societies should act. Religion is a loose syncretism of the "Three Teachings" (San Jiao) of Taoism, Buddhism, and Confucianism. Most people consider themselves Taoist *and* Buddhist, but it's difficult to disentangle religion from custom, culture, and superstition.

Hong Kong's people practice a religion that is as profoundly practical as they are, one based on the here-and-now rather than philosophical speculation. Worshippers are concerned with improving their lives and luck rather than seeking spiritual guidance. Wealth, health, long life, many children, and social status—religion is a way to obtain these favors, by either persuading the gods and ancestors to grant them, or at the very least to prevent misfortune. Huge offerings of incense and food are made to back up supplications. Religious symbols and charms are important, as are rituals and fortune-telling. Much emphasis is placed on placating one's ancestors, who also have the power to influence human life.

One result is that there is no strict demarcation between faiths, for who knows what might be effective? Many people appear to operate on the theory that if they cover all the bases, *someone* will bless them. There are some 350 temples in Hong Kong, most of them Taoist, but even these may hold images of Buddhist deities, and vice versa. The grandest example of this

BOB RACE

popular faith is the Wong Tai Sin Temple in Kowloon, full of fortune-tellers and images and always crowded with supplicants.

TAOISM

Like all major religions, Taoism has both esoteric and exoteric levels. Its philosophy has deeply influenced traditional Chinese thought.

Taoism's main teachings are codified in a slim volume, the *Tao Te Ching* or *The Way and Its Power*. Of an almost maddening simplicity and profundity, it is said to express the teachings of Lao Tse, a philosopher of the 4th-3rd century B.C. It has become the world's most translated Chinese work.

Tao is described as the very essence of existence, not a personal being like God, but a *state* of being. The term roughly translates as "The Way," but more accurately it's a label for a limitless state that is beyond description—though not beyond experience. "He who speaks does not know; he who knows does not speak," advises the *Tao Te Ching*.

Many Taoist doctrines were adopted from even older philosophies, like the concept of yin and yang, which are described as polar forces. Yin (the character literally signifies "the shady side of a mountain") is receptive, feminine, cold; yang is "the sunny side of a mountain"— dynamic, masculine, hot. They are two sides of the same coin, one endlessly yielding to the other, and the constantly shifting interplay between them brings forth everything in existence. Taoism acknowledges that change is perpetual, and devotes much energy to analyzing its cyclic patterns.

Taoist philosophy allows one to accept the vicissitudes of life

Taoism's eight trigrams

with equanimity. The Tao is not something to be worshipped, but to be understood. Serenity and contemplation are emphasized in order to accommodate oneself to the universal process of flux. This is crystallized in the doctrine of *wu wei,* literally "no activity," implying a lack of interference or wasteful exertion—no calculation, greed, or anxiety. *Wu wei* is the art of leaving alone, of spontaneous action in accordance with present need. It is symbolized by flowing water, which is powerful, patient, and always moves with the terrain.

Mystical Taoism involves the "Inner Alchemy," practices which aim to transform one's subtle physical energies in order to attain immortality. This may be implied in a figurative rather than literal sense, but actual old age is heavily emphasized.

Popular Taoism, on the other hand, is a folk faith for the masses. It has absorbed the traditional superstitious dread of spirits as well as a large pantheon of folk deities. The Taoist hierarchy is topped by the "Three Pure Ones" ruling over heaven, earth, and man, but the most actively worshipped gods are patron saints, many of them deified humans. They are supplicated with offerings and prayers in the hope of improving one's present life.

BUDDHISM

Buddhism is not an indigenous Chinese religion but an import introduced from India in the first century A.D. It began 700 years before that, with an Indian princeling named Siddhartha Gautama who renounced his crown to seek the ultimate truth of existence through asceticism and meditation. Buddhism retains a reliance on meditation to discover the true nature of the mind, though the popular religion is more concerned with offerings and supplications.

Buddhism's profound philosophy postulates an ultimate state of being, which, like the Tao, transcends dualistic thought and categories. Sentient beings pass through an endless series of rebirths, according to the karma created by their past actions. These lives are viewed as a succession of suffering, which can end only with the realization of non-ego, the state of enlightenment or nirvana. As in Taoism there

are no real gods, though compassionate enlightened beings or bodhisattvas are believed to provide spiritual assistance, and are commonly worshipped as deities. Most popular are Amitabha and the female bodhisattva Kwun Yam, both of whom appear in Taoist temples as well.

Buddhist shrines tend to be less colorful than Taoist temples, and are often more remote. Major Buddhist temples are at Castle Peak, Shatin, and Po Lin Monastery on Lantau Island.

CONFUCIANISM

Confucianism is not a religion at all, but an ethical system concerned with the ordering of human relations. Kung Fu Tsu (it was the Jesuits who Latinized his name into Confucius) was a reformer and teacher of the fifth century B.C., who taught the virtues of loyalty, altruism, respect for one's superiors, and wisdom. The correct attitude leads to harmony with the eternal order of the cosmos, Confucius said, while an imbalance leads to strife and turmoil. The emphasis on obedience appealed to the Chinese sense of history and continuity, and of course the Emperor liked it as well.

Confucius had little impact in his lifetime, but after his death his followers recorded his teachings in the *Five Classics* (the most popular being *The Analects*), which became the basis of traditional Chinese education for nearly two millenia.

Confucianism is supremely Chinese in its concentration on family and social relations, and its emphasis on the supreme virtue, filial piety. There is no mention of deities—Confucius resolutely refused to talk of the existence or nonexistence of spiritual beings—and it is quite ironic that he himself has become deified. A special patron of scholars, he was decreed an "Ancestral Saint" in 1370.

ANCESTRAL WORSHIP

The real Chinese religion is ancestral. All formal religions emphasize respect for one's forebears and incorporate rites to honor and placate them; even many Christian converts maintain this practice. In part this stems from the Chinese esteem for blood ties, which are considered all-important: nothing matters as much as one's family. Part is a common-sense wish to avoid trouble and bring good fortune, for it's believed one's ancestors have the power to dispense both. Descendents and ancestors have a reciprocal arrangement—they do each other favors.

To understand this it's necessary to look at beliefs regarding an afterlife. Humans have a two-fold soul. The spiritual, male element goes to heaven, while the material, female portion remains on earth, and can benefit or harm the living. To avoid trouble, one's ancestors must be placated with offerings and a well-sited tomb: then they will bring blessings and good fortune. Rather than worship, it's a matter of respect.

Burial rituals are elaborate: the body is first interred in a coffin in a temporary grave, and is exhumed after about 10 years. The bones are cleaned by a specialist and placed in a ceramic urn, which is stored in a special shelter. Eventually the urn will be placed in a traditional omega-shaped tomb, sited according to the dictates of *feng shui*. Many ancestors get stuck indefinitely in the second stage, as it's expensive to find a good site—though a run of bad luck might prompt descendents to do something.

In ancient China, the dead were buried with possessions, even servants and concubines to provide for them in the afterworld. The typical Chinese family will keep their *tso sin* or "former holy founders" well-supplied with the possessions represented by paper offerings and well-fed with lavish feasts. The dead need things just as the living do, and burning is believed to transmit the essence of offerings in a symbolic fashion.

In temples you'll often see white-clad family members industriously folding and arranging the paper offerings commonly burned at the end of the mourning period. Look for "spirit money," rectangles printed with "gold" and "silver" lines to represent ingots, or $5 million notes drawn on "The Bank of Hell." (It's said the deceased need such funds to bribe judges in the underworld to avoid punishment. Some families provide paper "passports" with visas into the underworld.) In addition there are elaborately crafted possessions—paper limousines, boats, portable phones, or houses complete with furniture and tiny paper servants. The tra-

altar with portraits of ancestors, Poon Uk

dition may result from Buddhist influences, which replaced flesh sacrifices with more innocuous substitutes.

Ancestors are also taken care of in the annual grave-cleaning festivals, and in regular offerings made in front of ancestor tablets—wooden blocks inscribed with the name (and sometimes photograph) of the deceased, set up on an altar in the home or a temple. Prayers, incense, and food are regularly offered here, usually by the women of the family.

Other Religions

There are about 500,000 Christians in Hong Kong, the result of decades of active proselytizing by Western missionaries in China. They are evenly divided between Roman Catholic and Protestant denominations. Around half the SAR's 50,000 Muslims are Chinese. Hong Kong's 10,000 Hindus gather at the main temple on Wong Nai Chung Road, while the small local population of Jews meets at Ohel Leah Synagogue on Robinson Road in the Mid-Levels.

INSIDE TEMPLES

Hong Kong's colorful temples are intriguing, but at first glance it can be difficult to figure out what's going on. Festival days and the 1st and 15th days of the Chinese lunar months (the full and new moons) are the most interesting times to visit, as offerings increase dramatically.

Temples usually retain the gray brick and mortar and high pitched tile roofs of traditional Chinese architecture, even if they're recent restorations. Roof ridges are often adorned with glazed porcelain figures depicting figures from Taoist legend, like the Sun God and Moon Goddess bearing their orbs.

Inside, the main hall is often filled with eye-stinging smoke from the incense burned in offerings to ancestors and gods. Spirals of incense in all sizes may hang from the ceiling: the biggest of these will burn for two weeks. The red tags dangling from them hold the names of donors, and their wishes for good fortune, thanks for past favors, or pleas for future ones.

On the main altar stands the temple's ruling deity, his or her name and title often displayed on a richly embroidered silk altarcloth mounted above. Side shrines hold other deities, often of a different religion. The Buddhist goddess Kwun Yam, for example, is popular even in Taoist temples.

In front of the altar are offering tables for food, and cushions for supplicants to kneel upon as they pray. Worshippers may try to divine their future by casting the bamboo *chim* (fortune sticks) or *bui* (fortune blocks), which are laid out on side tables. A common sight is tiny children being taught to make offerings in the proper fashion, moving their joined hands up and down in a gesture of respect.

Side halls may hold more deities, ancestral tablets, or figures representing the Tai Sui, gods of the 60-year calendar cycle. Another common feature are the small "smoke rooms" where caretakers dispose of blazing offerings so that the main temple doesn't get too stuffy.

Offerings

As in most Asian religions, worship is an individual occasion. There are no intermediaries or particular set times; instead, people drop in throughout the day to light incense and candles and make brief offerings and requests. They are either supplicating for favors or against illness and misfortune.

The simplest offering is three sticks of lit incense held in folded hands: it's said this formula represents one for heaven, one for the underworld, and one for oneself. Incense are traditionally offered at dawn and dusk to household guardians, and you'll see sticks smouldering in niches set in doorways.

Next up on the list is tea and fruit. Anything red, gold, or orange is considered auspicious; thus the abundance of apples, persimmons, and oranges (Hong Kong is the world's largest consumer of oranges, and most seem to end up in temples).

Most elaborate are the massive food offerings made three times a year, for Lunar New Year, the Ching Ming festival, and the celebration of one's local or patron deity. These might include whole chickens or ducks, jars of golden cooking oil, or plates of pork or vegetables. The supreme offering is a whole roast pig (called "golden pig"), which is basted with a sugary glaze to attain the auspicious golden-red shade and is said to protect against sickness and misfortune.

spirit money is offered to the gods

THE BOOK OF EVERYTHING

The Chinese almanac, called the *Tung Sing,* is the oldest annually published book in the world. It was commissioned in 2256 B.C. by the Chinese emperor in order to calculate the arrival of seasons and the movement of celestial bodies. Mass-printed as early as the eighth century (the British Museum has a copy from A.D. 877), it was suppressed on the mainland from 1949, but has reappeared recently. Throughout, it's continued to flourish in Chinese homes around the world, where, hung from a red loop sewn into the binding, it is revered as a magical charm.

The book is popularly known by the nickname *Tung Sing,* "Good Fortune in Everything," but its proper title is *Tung Shu,* the "Book of Everything." This is scarcely an exaggeration: it covers all imaginable subjects that could impact the well-being of the reader.

Part of it is like a western almanac. The section on "24 Joints and Breadths of the Solar Year" describes fortnights by seasonal changes: the fortnight of Rain Water is followed by that of the Waking of Insects, the Spring Equinox, Pure Brightness, and the Grain Rain. Other chapters detail protective charms (to prevent sickness, purify water, and protect pregnant women) and explain dream interpretation and fortune-telling. Another section assigns numeric values to Chinese characters, so that messages can be sent by telegram and decoded at the other end with the aid of the same table.

Most important and extensive is the calendar, where the profitable days are marked in red and the inauspicious in black. The *Tung Sing* provides a complete guide to behavior, specifying the good-luck days (some lasting only a few hours) used for weddings, well-diggings, moving house, and property purchases. Some days are good for travel, others for cleaning gutters, sowing seeds, or launching boats. On "broken" days, everything is unlucky, and readers are advised to avoid even religious ceremonies and simply rest.

While the almanac's popularity is dwindling in modern cities, it remains important in rural areas. Hong Kong street vendors and joss paper shops stock various editions, recognizable by their bright red covers. At around HK$20 a copy it makes a good cheap souvenir, full of fascinating woodcuts.

Offerings are briefly deposited on tables in front of the altar for the spirits to imbibe their essence, then are carted away for consumption by the donor family. Hongkongers have so far not descended to the level of Chinese in Malaysia. There, a single roast pig might be rented out to 20 families over the course of a day, all of whom offer its essence to their ancestors.

Fortune-Telling

Fortune-telling is a major activity in temples, most commonly involving the *chim,* a set of numbered bamboo sticks in a cylindrical container. The supplicant lights incense sticks in offering, kneels before the altar to make a wish or pose a question, then gently shakes the container until one of the sticks falls onto the floor. Its number is then checked against a series of written fortunes.

Each temple has its own book of fortunes, written in archaic language and referring to old legends. Number 39, for instance, may read "Yuen Chi Ling goes back to the fishing ter-race," signifying highly unfavorable prospects. The cryptic revelations require the consultations of a resident soothsayer for interpretation, especially as the reading of the same fortune will differ for each person.

Another method is *man bui,* "asking the blocks," involving two pieces of wood that are convex on one side, flat on the other. A question is asked or a wish made, and the blocks are dropped onto the floor three times. To get one of each side up is considered a well-balanced affirmative reply, while two sides the same way is negative. The blocks are thrown three times in a row, and meaning is sought in the combination.

Usually it's women doing the asking. Often their concerns are economic, but family problems, illness, and children are also issues. They may also consult professional fortune-tellers who rely on the reading of faces or palms. The biggest collection of fortune-tellers is at Wong Tai Sin Temple in Kowloon; another group of streetside soothsayers sets up at the Temple Street Night Market.

IMPORTANT DEITIES

There are gods at every level, from household to neighborhood and on to the patron deities of trades and professions. At the top of the Taoist hierarchy are the "Three Pure Ones": the Jade Ruler or Pearly Emperor; Tao Chun, who controls yin and yang and the principles of nature; and Lao Tsu. Because they're considered beyond the fluctuations of time and the supplications of humans, these three are basically ignored. People devote their energies to worshipping more accessible deities, whose popularity depends on his or her reputation for efficacy.

Tin Hau

The compassionate Taoist goddess Tin Hau originated from the daughter of a 10th-century Fukian fisherman, a saintly girl who died at an early age. Several years later, fishermen began reporting her apparition had appeared to save them from death. Ships started to carry her image, and shrines to her were built along the South China coast. She was canonized as "Saintly and Diligent Saviour" in the 12th century, and promoted to "Queen of Heaven" (Tin Hau) in 1683.

Tin Hau is the protector of sailors and fisherman and a special patroness of mothers and children. The goddess is still credited with miracles and frequent cures of illnesses. Hong Kong has at least 40 Tin Hau temples, all of them originally built on the waterfront, but most now far inland due to reclamation.

Kwan Ti

Also known as Kwan Kung, this God of War is among the most powerful of all deities, and is another example of a human elevated to divine status. His origins are linked with Kwan Zhong, a great warrior of the late Han dynasty. The adventures of this Chinese Robin Hood are related in *The Romance of the Three Kingdoms,* a Ming dynasty classic retold in contemporary operas and comic strips.

Armed with a sword called Green Dragon, astride the horse Red Hare, Kwan Ti is the embodiment of integrity and courage. Like Tin Hau, he was posthumously promoted by Imperial edict, first to "Warrior Prince," then in 1594 to "Faithful and Loyal Great Deity, Supporter of Heaven, Protector of the Realm." He is the patron of many different trades and professions, including anyone who works with sharp objects—cooks, soldiers, police, gangsters, and actors.

Kwun Yam

The Buddhist Goddess of Mercy, this compassionate protectoress is the best-loved of all the deities. White-robed and serene, she is depicted bearing a vase of the elixer of healing, with which she sprinkles the sick. Her origins lie in the Indian Buddhist deity Avalokitesvara, who was introduced into China around the fifth century and was gradually transformed into a goddess.

Other Deities

Amitabha is another much-beloved Buddhist deity, a bodhisattva who presides over a Pure Land where the faithful are reborn in bliss merely by the act of repeating his name.

Wong Tai Sin is a local Taoist deity renowned for his effectiveness in bringing luck and healing the sick. His main temple is in Kowloon, near an MTR station of the same name, but his image is found in many other temples as well. Other gods include **Hung Shing,** a patron of seafarers; **Tam Kung,** a local fishermen's protector who controls weather; and **Pao Kung,** god of justice. **Pak Tai,** "Ruler of the North," is a fierce black-bearded god in charge of structuring and protecting society. **Tai Si Wong,** a sort of policeman from the afterworld, is represented by towering papier-mâché figures that preside over offering ceremonies at festivals.

The 60 **Tai Sui** deities, always displayed ensemble, represent the 60-year Chinese calendar cycle; people worship the one affiliated with the year of their birth. The Taoist **Eight Immortals** represent the eight stages of existence and are supplicated for good fortune and protection from evil. Their legend stems from the deification of historical sages and hermits.

Earth, City, and Household Gods

The local **To Tei** or Earth Gods stem from a 2000-year-old animistic tradition. "Territory god" would be a more accurate term, as they rule not the earth in general but a specific area.

The local Earth God is visualized as a sort of civil servant in the celestial administration; he is subordinate to and reports to **Shing Wong,** the City God. Dwelling in small shrines set in the side of doorways, he presides over shops, apartments, neighborhoods, villages, and fields, protecting the area and overseeing the behavior of its inhabitants. Worshippers offer him incense at dawn and dusk, appeal to him in sickness or distress, and inform him of births, deaths, or marriages occurring in his territory.

Households also have their own shrines to family ancestors, local guardians, the God of Wealth, and their own particular **Kitchen God**— the last represented only by a name written in gold characters on red paper, pasted up every New Year. Offerings of candles (red light bulbs are the modern substitute) and incense are made daily before the shrine.

Homes are protected from evil influences by posters of **door guardians,** a pair of deified generals from the Tang dynasty said to repel demons with their ferocious expressions. It's said they must be pasted up facing each other or disharmony will result.

Other posters appear most frequently at Lunar New Year. Five rectangles of gold-speckled red paper pasted over the lintel represent the "Five Happinesses": long life, wealth, health, love of virtue, and a natural death after a full lifespan. Couplets written on strips of paper flanking the entrance extend the wish for good fortune and happiness.

ACCOMMODATIONS

Eating and shopping may be bargain-priced in Hong Kong, but places to stay are not. Skyrocketing land prices put space at a premium. Budget travelers in particular are put in a bind: they pay more here than in many Asian countries, and get less.

HK$200 per night brings a tiny box of a room in a dilapidated Tsimshatsui tenement. Somewhere around HK$500 per night will rent a reasonably decent room; around HK$1000 a downright pleasant one. Above HK$2000 a night, luxury opens up. Hong Kong's top hotels are among the world's finest, with 18-carat gold bathroom fittings, breathtaking harbor views, and impeccable service. In the Marco Polo Suite at The Peninsula (HK$22,000 a night and designed like an English country manor house), the butler's pantry alone is bigger than the average room at Chungking Mansions across the street.

Fed by a consistently huge flow of business and tourist travel, Hong Kong hotels have one of the world's highest occupancy rates, an average of 82%, peaking at close to 95% in October-November and again around the lunar New Year. Try to book in advance, especially if you're hoping for one of the few reasonably priced places like the YMCAs (the immensely popular Salisbury YMCA recommends three months' advance notice). If you don't book in advance, though, don't worry: there's always something.

The Hong Kong Hotel Association booth at the airport can be helpful in conjuring up rooms for late-night arrivals, but they'll only book at member hotels, which means the cheapest rooms are HK$800.

Hong Kong's number of hotel rooms more than doubled between 1986 and 1991, and new hotel construction is rocketing ahead. Despite the intense competition, room rates only seem to ascend. Rates are highest in the main tourist season, October-December; March-June is another crunch. All add a 10% service charge and 5% tax onto the bill.

Off-season travelers will have better luck at getting a discount or negotiating an upgrade to a better room, especially in summer months, when many hotels offer discounted packages. It never hurts to inquire about "special rates," or to matter-of-factly request a hotel's business discount. The latter is most effective if you have a business card and are credibly dressed. A little chutzpah can net a 10-50% discount. Another way to economize is to book a hotel or an airfare/hotel package through a travel agent. This can cut your hotel bill in half—savings enough to persuade even freewheeling individual travelers to visit an agent.

Where To Stay

Urban transportation is so good that it really

doesn't matter where you stay. Most tourists choose glitzy Tsimshatsui, which has the highest concentration of hotels and nearly all the cheap guesthouses. But the relentlessly materialistic atmosphere and hordes of shoppers can be depressing. Yaumatei and Mongkok, north of Tsimshatsui, are cheaper, more Chinese, and altogether more interesting. The elegant highly commercial district of Tsimshatsui East features a string of pricey hotels.

Hong Kong Island offers a more local feel. The few hotels in Central draw mainly business travelers—nobody else can afford them. Wanchai and Causeway Bay are vital, interesting areas with plenty of life but without the hassles of Tsimshatsui. Trams make short hops along the island easy, while the MTR and several ferries allow for fast cross-harbor commutes.

Staying on an outlying island may be worth considering for long-term visitors. Lamma, Lantau, and Cheung Chau are all quiet, pleasant, and cheap, and connected to the city by an excellent ferry service. See The Outlying Islands chapter for details.

CAMPING AND HOSTELS

Camping

The HKTA (Hong Kong Tourist Association) leaflet "Campsites of Hong Kong Country Parks" outlines nearly four dozen camping facilities, most located on Lantau and the Sai Kung Peninsula. Official campsites have toilets, barbecue areas, and water sources; nominal charges are levied (up to HK$38 a night). You must bring your own food and equipment.

Camping at youth hostels is allowed everywhere except the Mt. Davis and Tai Mei Tuk facilities. You can use their washrooms, and some provide sheets and blankets. Fees again are low. Try to avoid weekends, when campsites are flooded with young backpackers.

Youth Hostels

Hong Kong's seven International Youth Hostel Federation hostels charge HK$25-50 a night for a bed in men's or women's dormitories. Most have cooking facilities, and bedding is available on request. Bring your own towels and food.

HONG KONG YOUTH HOSTELS

Ma Wui Hall, Mt. Davis Path, Hong Kong, tel. 2817-5715. HK$40, 112 beds.

Sze Lok Yuen, Tai Mo Shan, Tsuen Wan, tel. 2488-8188. HK$22, 92 beds.

Bradbury Lodge, Tai Mei Tuk, Tai Po, tel. 2662-5123. HK$32, 94 beds, some a/c rooms.

Bradbury Hall, Chek Keng, Sai Kung, tel. 2328-2458. HK$22, 100 beds.

Pak Sha O Hostel, Hoi Ha Road, Sai Kung, tel. 2328-2327. HK$22, 112 beds.

Jockey Club Mong Tung Wan Hostel, Lantau, tel. 2984-1389. HK$22, 88 beds.

S.G. Davis Hostel, Ngong Ping, Lantau, tel. 2985-5610. HK$22, 48 beds.

Ma Wui Hall is the only hostel in urban Hong Kong: it's on a hillside a long hike from town. The others are located in rural areas, generally empty during the week but crowded on weekends. Check-in times are roughly 7-10 a.m. and 4-11 p.m. You may have to be out of the building 10 a.m.-4 p.m. Lights-out is usually around 11 p.m.

IYHF membership is required for all guests. Get a card through the **Hong Kong Youth Hostels Association,** Room 225-226, Block 19, Shek Kip Mei Estate, Shamshuipo, Kowloon, tel. 2788-1638. Bring your passport, one photo, and HK$150 for the card. Hong Kong Student Travel in Star House, Tsimshatsui, can also issue a card. Or, easiest of all, pay an extra HK$25 per night for the first six nights of your stay until you achieve member status.

Ma Wui Hall, Mt. Davis Path, tel. 2817-5715, has 112 beds and is air-conditioned, with harbor views; rates are an exemplary HK$50 a night. It's a bit tricky to find. Take Citybus 5B from the stop in front of the Hongkong and Shanghai Bank headquarters to the Felix Villas terminus on Victoria Road. (Or take Bus 47 from Exchange Square to the same stop.) Walk back 100 meters and follow the hostel signs onto Mt. Davis Path—*not* Mt. Davis Road. Walk uphill 20-30 minutes to the hostel. This is not something to do with lots of luggage.

Most of the outlying IYHF hostels listed in the accompanying chart are closed one or two days a week, and normally closed between 10 a.m.-4 p.m. weekdays. Call either the hostel or the main office in Shamshuipo to check before showing up. Weekends can be crowded with local backpackers, but weekdays may be virtually deserted.

BUDGET (UNDER HK$300)

There's never been an abundance of cheap places to stay in Hong Kong, but the budget scene underwent a further crunch when tougher safety laws were enforced following the deaths of two tourists in hotel fires in 1991. Budget guesthouses were forced to remodel, and about a third closed down instead. Those that reopened have definitely improved, but prices have risen noticeably.

Budget travelers congregate in small, dingy guesthouses lodged in high-rise blocks in Tsimshatsui, where rooms start at HK$180 d without bath, HK$250 d with bath. The recent remodeling has produced some surprisingly bright, clean, and cheerful places, and has introduced windows into what were often dark shoe boxes. Still, the tendency is towards tiny: a "double" may be a single-sized room with a bunk bed crammed in behind the door.

Room prices and quality vary within each guesthouse, so make it a point to view the room before taking it. Offering several nights' stay should allow you to negotiate a lower price, but commit to only a single night at first in order to check out nighttime noise levels, cockroach emergence, and other possible flaws.

Chungking Mansions

The center of the budget universe is Chungking Mansions, 36-44 Nathan Road (see the special topic "Chungking Mansions: The Archetypal Experience"). Dozens of guesthouses crammed inside this prime location make it a budget mecca. Quality is a different matter. While decent rooms do exist—the recent upgrade has produced some surprisingly nice places—the overall atmosphere is stiflingly dingy, and getting to and from your room can be highly unpleasant. If you're set on staying in

DORMITORIES

For real budget travelers this is the only way to stay in Hong Kong. Even sharing the room with other backpackers, it's hard to find a bed for less than $HK100 a night. Address and phone details for these places are provided in "Accomodations" section.

Victoria Hostel, 3/F, 33 Hankow Rd., tel. 2376-0621, has dorm beds from HK$90-160 depending on the size of the dorm. Lockers for gear ensure some degree of security. Discounts are available if you're prepared to pay weekly, but there are no refunds.

The following Tsimshatsui guesthouses have dorm beds for HK$70-100: **Travellers' Hostel,** 16/F "A" Block, Chungking Mansions; **City Guesthouse,** 9/F Mirador Mansions; **Golden Crown Guesthouse,** Golden Crown Court; and **Lily Garden Guesthouse** and **Garden Hostel,** both 3/F Mirador Mansions.

STB Hostel in Mongkok is more expensive than most with HK$200 dorm beds; still, it's popular and often full.

Ma Wui Hall, described under "Youth Hostels," has the cheapest beds in Hong Kong at HK$50 a night. Access is less than convenient, however.

Cream of the crop are the HK$190 beds in the **Salisbury YMCA's** four-bed dorm rooms—viciously popular, but they can be reserved.

Tsimshatsui, consider one of the other mansion blocks listed here: guesthouses in these have slightly higher prices and a much nicer ambience.

Don't be fooled by the glossy chrome-and-glass facade of the World Trade Centre, part of Chungking Mansion's ground-floor shopping arcade. Penetrate inside and you'll find the building is organized in five lettered blocks, each with separate lifts for even- and odd-numbered floors. The elevators are tiny and old, and lines form rapidly for the busiest blocks. Guesthouses in each block are listed on signboards above each lift.

"A" Block: The most popular block for budget travelers, with long lines for the elevator and surprisingly clean stairwells which will hopefully not lapse into their previous state of horrendous filth.

16/F: Travellers' Hostel, tel. 2368-7710, is tremendously popular—undeservedly so, as it's noisy and crowded, and the long elevator ride up is an ordeal. A bed in the big dorm is HK$100; double rooms w/bath are HK$250 and up.

15/F: Ocean Guesthouse is a good example of the new Chungking Mansions: spotless, bright rooms with windows starting at HK$150 s, HK$220 d. Recommended.

14/F: Tokyo Guesthouse, tel. 2367-5407, has tiny, newly remodeled rooms for as little as HK$130 s, HK$200 d. **Hawaii Guesthouse** on the same floor, tel. 2366-6127, is redolent with family cooking, and has rooms for HK$130-250 s, HK$250-300 d with bath.

13/F: Rhine Guesthouse, tel. 2367-1991, managed by the ebullient Madame Cheung, is a very friendly clean place with a real find: a sunny double room for HK$350 with a view of the harbor (well, at least a piece of it). Normal rooms are HK$250-270 d, as low as HK$160 s.

12/F: Peking Guesthouse, tel. 2723-8320, is a friendly place with new rooms for HK$160-200 s, HK$240 and up d. **Super Guesthouse,** tel. 2368-3767, is newly remodeled, with quiet, clean, and fairly large rooms, some with windows, running around HK$200-300.

8/F: Tom's Guesthouse, tel. 2722-4956, has dim little windowless rooms for HK$160 s, HK$180 d. Tom's also exists on 16/F "B" and "C" Blocks.

7/F: Welcome Guesthouse, tel. 2721-7793, is run by the very friendly Jon Wah, who speaks good English. The cheapest rooms (nearly all have windows) are HK$160-220 s, HK$280-250 d; there's a triple for HK$300. Recommended. **London Guesthouse,** tel. 2366-5010, has basic, not-so-clean rooms for HK$150-160 s, HK$180-200 d.

"B" Block:
15/F: New Carlton Guesthouse, tel. 2721-0720, has rooms with bath for HK$220 s, HK$250 and up d.

13/F: New Washington Guesthouse, tel. 2368-2228, is uninspiring but cheap: HK$130 s, HK$150-180 d.

9/F: Happy Guesthouse, tel. 2368-1021, has its reception here: rooms are on the 10th floor and have fan and TV. Prices run from HK$160 d without bath to HK$250-300 for a triple with bath.

4/F: Harbour Guesthouse, tel. 2368-1428,

has nice a/c rooms for HK$250 and up.

3/F: Dragon Inn, tel. 2368-2007, is a reasonably pleasant place with rooms for HK$150-200 s, HK$200-250 d.

"C" Block:
16/F: Tom's Guesthouse, tel. 2367-9258, is a popular, fairly clean and quiet place, though the long elevator up remains an ordeal. Rooms are HK$200 s, HK$250-350 d.

Mirador Mansions
Just down the street from Chungking Mansions at 56-58 Nathan Rd., this block is smaller and more pleasant—the stairwells are airier, built around an open courtyard; there's no ground floor arcade to wrestle through, and the lift lines are short. Interspersed with several dozen guesthouses are tiny sweatshops where workers make clothing, jewelry, and Chinese medicine. Note there are separate lifts for even- and odd-numbered floors.

3/F: Garden Hostel, tel. 2921-8567, is extremely popular, and often full, especially the HK$100 dormitory. Rooms are HK$260-320.

3/F Lily Garden Guesthouse, tel. 2366-2575, is an easy stop. The manager runs four other guesthouses in Mirador Mansions (including City Guesthouse, 9/F) and should be able to come up with the right room at the right price. Private rooms run HK$250-300 d with bath; HK$200 without bath; dorm beds are available for around HK$70.

6/F: Man Lee Tak Guesthouse, tel. 2739-2717, is the place for basic windowless cheapies, as low as HK$260 d. Tolerable, though nothing to get excited about.

7/F: Great Wall Guesthouse, tel. 2311-6987, is a good choice: quiet, clean, friendly, with seven small but bright rooms with windows for HK$260 s, HK$300 d. Recommended.

9/F: City Guesthouse, tel. 2724-2612, charges HK$70 for dorm beds; rooms are HK$250 s, HK$300 and up d. **Mini-Garden Guesthouse,** tel. 2367-8261, under Indian management, is not as pleasant as the name or cheery signboard suggest, but rooms are exceptionally cheap, from HK$150 s, HK$180 d. There are some HK$70 dorm beds as well.

13/F: Kowloon Hotel, tel. 2311-2523, has good rooms for around HK$300 with bath, HK$250 without.

14/F: Man Hing Lung Guesthouse, tel. 2722-0678, is a good choice, with modern if small rooms with bath, TV, a/c and phone for HK$300 s, HK$380 d. On the same floor, the **Wai Lee Guesthouse,** tel. 367-2220, has tiny new rooms for HK$300 d.

16/F: First Class Guest House, tel. 2722-4935, is a decent place with rooms for HK$250 s, HK$320 d. The manager, who is actually quite pleasant, is fed up with backpackers performing a routine that certain guide books recommend of starting at the top floor and descending downward to compare prices, and flatly refuses to negotiate room rates.

Golden Crown Court

Access into this small, low-key block at 66 Nathan Rd. is less of a hassle than either Chungking or Mirador Mansions, though there's only a few guesthouses here.

5/F: Golden Crown Guest House, tel. 2369-1782, has dorm beds for HK$100 and small, none-too-clean rooms from HK$250 s, HK$300 d. Like the **Silver Crown** and **Copper Crown** next door, it's run by friendly Thai women. On the same floor is **New World Guesthouse,** tel. 2366-7882, an upmarket place with pristine little rooms complete with wallpaper. Sadly overpriced at HK$500 s, HK$700 d.

INEXPENSIVE HOTELS (HK$300-600)

Tsimshatsui

Lee Garden Guesthouse, 8/F, 34 Cameron Rd., tel. 2367-2284, is an excellent well-maintained guesthouse with small, clean, modern rooms with bath, a/c, and TV for HK$420 s, HK$450 d. The Lee Garden's sister guesthouse across the street, **Star Guesthouse,** 6/F, 21 Cameron Rd., tel. 2723-8951, is a smaller, even quieter place with a handful of rooms for HK$450 d, HK$400 s. Both are recommended.

Also check **Champagne Court,** 16 Kimberley Rd. (behind the Miramar Hotel). The arcade is filled with camera and tailor shops; two lifts lead up to a few guesthouses, including **Tourist's Home** (6/F, "G" Block, tel. 2311-2622), a friendly, clean place with minimal English and rooms for HK$380 s, HK$430 d.

Chungking Mansions, described in the Budget category above, has expensive places also. **Chungking House,** 4-5/F "A" Block, tel. 2366-5362, is pricey for the location. Fairly large though gloomy rooms have bath, TV, and a/c and cost HK$320 s, HK$400 and up d.**Marria Guesthouse,** 11/F "C" Block, tel. 2724-3788, has relatively large, bright rooms with a/c and refrigerator for HK$350-420 s or d. **New Chungking Mansion,** 7/F "C" Block, tel. 2368-0981, is a bit pricey but the rooms are well-maintained and possibly bargainable: HK$340 s, HK$380 and up d.

The **Lyton Building** at 42 Mody Rd. has the same confusing setup as Chungking Mansions, with four blocks (this time numbered) served by separate lifts, and a directory above each. Dive into the arcade and hunt about for the lifts. Few tourists straggle down this way.

Up Lift 2, 6/F, is **Lyton House Inn,** tel. 2367-3791, a dingy though clean place with enormous (for Hong Kong) doubles starting at HK$500. Singles are HK$300, and there's a room that sleeps four for HK$600.

Lift 4, 7/F: **Frank Mody House,** tel. 2724-4113, has average rooms for HK$350-450. On the sixth floor is a nameless establishment advertising "Rooms for Tourists," tel. 2366-0579. Run by a family which speaks minimal English, it's a bit noisy, and charges HK$300 s, HK$350 d.

Yaumatei

This is a far more interesting and altogether less exhausting neighborhood than Tsimshatsui, and the Yaumatei MTR provides easy access to just about anywhere. There are a few places in **Cumberland House,** 227 Nathan Rd., including **International House,** 5/F, tel. 2730-9276, where rooms are HK$480 s, HK$580 d. **City Guesthouse,** 6/F, tel. 2730-0212, charges HK$350 s, HK$400 d.

New Lucky Mansions, 300 Nathan Rd., at the corner of Nathan and Jordan roads is another good place to explore for guesthouses. **Great Wall Hotel and Sky House,** 14/F, tel. 2388-7675, is old but clean and decent, with rooms for HK$320-350 s, HK$380 d.

Mongkok

Again, a good neighborhood for those who prefer a less commercial atmosphere than Tsimshatsui. **STB Hostel,** 2/F Great Eastern

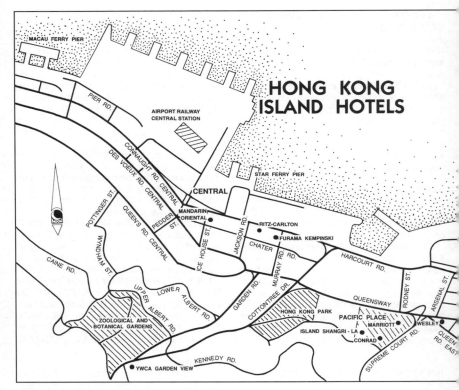

HONG KONG ISLAND HOTELS

Mansion, 255 Reclamation St., tel. 2710-9199, is a spotless place with small, a/c rooms, run by Hong Kong Student Travel Ltd. The out-of-the-way location is compensated for by an interesting neighborhood and good MTR access. Call first, as it's often full. Dorm beds are HK$200; rooms are HK$500 s or d, HK$600 triple.

Hung Hom
Holy Carpenter Guest House, 1 Dyer Ave., tel. 2362-0301. This tiny place has about one dozen rooms, which are clean but, again, tiny. Reserve one month in advance. HK$570 s or d, HK$680 triple.

Causeway Bay
Noble Hostel, Flat A3, 17/F Paterson Building,

37 Paterson St., tel. 2808-0117, reservations 2576-6148. This is a great alternative to Tsimshatsui, and people who stay here are generally pleased at their find. The hostel manages a total of 40 a/c rooms in three different locations in Causeway Bay. Prices start at HK$340 for a modern, bright room with no bath, to HK$440-460 for doubles with bath. Contact the head office at the address above for arrangements. Recommended.

Also check with Judy at **Yee Woo House Co.,** Flat A, 3/F Hyde Park Mansion, 53 Paterson St., tel. 2887-8025. She manages a number of rooms in different locations in Causeway Bay, including a few at the above address, where large doubles are around HK$350.

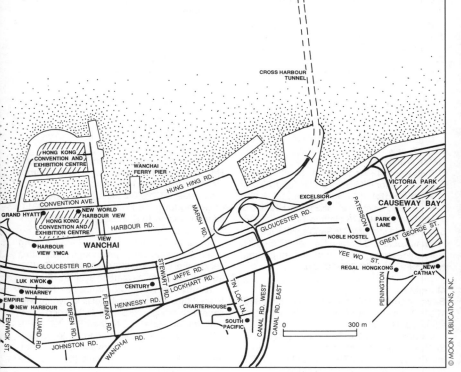

MODERATE HOTELS
(HK$600-1000)

Hotels listed below have rates and standards somewhere between those of guesthouses and regular hotels. HK$600-1000 will buy a clean, quiet but small room, with bath, a/c and a window view of something, if only a brick wall (don't laugh—budget rooms often have no windows at all). Not surprisingly the accommodations listed here are usually crowded; try to book in advance. Some of these hotels are run by religious organizations like Caritas or the Salvation Army. Even the Boy Scouts and the Methodist Church are property owners that benefit from running hotels.

Tsimshatsui

China-H.K. Hotel, 1 Parkes St., tel. 2730-8023, is a small, simple, new place, with rooms starting at HK$600. A related hotel with similar standards and prices is the **Baccarat,** 29 Chatham Rd., tel. 2311-8977.

The **Grand,** 14 Carnarvon Rd., tel. 2366-9311, is an old refurbished hotel with plain rooms. HK$720-1000 d.

An elderly, basic hotel in the heart of Tsimshatsui is the **International Hotel,** 33 Cameron Rd., tel. 2366-3381, at the high end of this price category: HK$900 s, HK$1120 d.

Yaumatei

Bangkok Royal Hotel, 12 Pilkem St., tel. 2735-9181. Basic small rooms that are cheap for a Hong Kong hotel, with a good Thai restaurant;

located near the Jordan MTR. HK$420-620 s, HK$520-700 d.

Booth Lodge, 7/F 11 Wing Sing Lane, tel. 2771-9266. Run by the Salvation Army, this lodge has a friendly, helpful staff, and small, clean if bleak rooms for HK$580-950 s or d.

Caritas Bianchi Lodge, 4 Cliff Rd., tel. 2388-1111. Operated by the Catholic charity organization Caritas and quite nice: all rooms are AC, with bath and TV. Continental breakfast included in the price: HK$650 s, HK$750 d, HK$920 triple.

Chung Hing Hotel, 23 Saigon St., tel. 2780-8222. A new hotel, nothing fancy. HK$750 s, HK$820-980 d.

Evergreen, 42 Woo Sung St., tel. 2385-8584. Basic rooms for HK$550 s and HK650-700 d.

King's Hotel, 473 Nathan Rd., tel. 2780-1281. A basic older hotel. HK$450 s, HK$570 d.

Nathan Hotel, 378 Nathan Rd., tel. 2388-5141. An old standby. HK$800 s, HK$980 d.

Shamrock, 223 Nathan Rd., tel. 2735-2271. *Very* old—circa '50s—but still operating. HK$750-970 s or d, HK$850-1070 d.

Mongkok

Beverly Hotel, 157 Waterloo Rd., tel. 2336-1381. A small newer hotel with decent rooms starting at HK$600.

Caritas Lodge, 134 Boundary St., tel. 2339-3777. A small (40-room), friendly place, close to the Prince Edward MTR. HK$490 s, HK$560 d, HK$790 triple, breakfast included.

YMCA International House, 23 Waterloo Rd., tel. 2771-9111. Recently expanded, this modern, pleasant place has small but adequate rooms for HK$800-1000 s or d.

YWCA Guest House, 5 Man Fuk Rd., tel. 2713-9211. Bet you can't wait to call your mom and tell her the address. Rooms are HK$350 s without bath, HK$470-720 s or d with bath.

Central/Mid-Levels

Garden View International House, 1 Macdonnell Rd., tel. 2877-3737. Run by the YWCA, it has a great location across from the Botanical Gardens above Central. Exceptionally cheap at HK$800-900 s or d; some rooms women only.

Causeway Bay

New Cathay, 17 Tung Lo Wan Rd., tel. 2577-

8211. An older, renovated hotel with modest rooms for HK$650 s, HK$900-1180 d, triple rooms for HK$1380.

EXPENSIVE HOTELS (HK$1000-1800)

Tsimshatsui

BP International House, 8 Austin Rd., tel. 2376-1111. The BP stands for Baden-Powell—it's run by the Boy Scouts. This new, big place adjoining Kowloon Park has rooms for HK$980-1700 s or d, and family rooms for HK$1050-1250.

Grand Stanford Harbour View, 70 Mody Rd., tel. 2721-5161. Most rooms have a harbor view, and there's an exceptionally wide range of room rates: HK$1260-2260 s, HK$1360-2380 d.

Guangdong, 18 Prat Ave., tel. 2739-3311. Catering mainly to Chinese groups. HK$1200-1600 s or d.

Imperial, 30 Nathan Rd., tel. 2366-2201. An older, renovated, pleasant enough hotel with a very central location. HK$950-1400 s, HK$1100-1500 d; family suites starting at HK$2100.

Kimberley Hotel, 28 Kimberley Rd., tel. 2723-3888. This newish hotel is a favorite with Japanese groups. HK$1300-1800 s or d.

Kowloon Hotel, 19 Nathan Rd., tel. 2369-8698. Very modern, oriented to business travelers with an information terminal in each room, and right behind The Peninsula (it shares the same management). HK$1320-2300 s or d.

New Astor, 11 Carnarvon Rd., tel. 2366-7261. An older hotel with small rooms for HK$1100-1600 s or d.

Park Hotel, 61 Chatham Rd. South, tel. 2366-1371. Built in 1961, this hotel has unusually big rooms and is popular with Australians. HK$1400-1600 s, HK$1500-1700 d, HK$1850-2050 triple.

Prudential, 222 Nathan Rd., tel. 2311-8222. Relatively big rooms, and an MTR station right below. Pool and gym too. HK$1200-1750 s or d.

Ramada Hotel Kowloon, 73 Chatham Rd. South, tel. 2311-1100. HK$1080-1780 s or d.

Salisbury YMCA, 41 Salisbury Rd., tel. 2369-2211. *The* ideal accommodation at the low end of this price category, with pleasant recently renovated rooms and a great location right beside The Peninsula. Rooms are HK$1030-1270 d (the higher price brings a harbor view), with a very

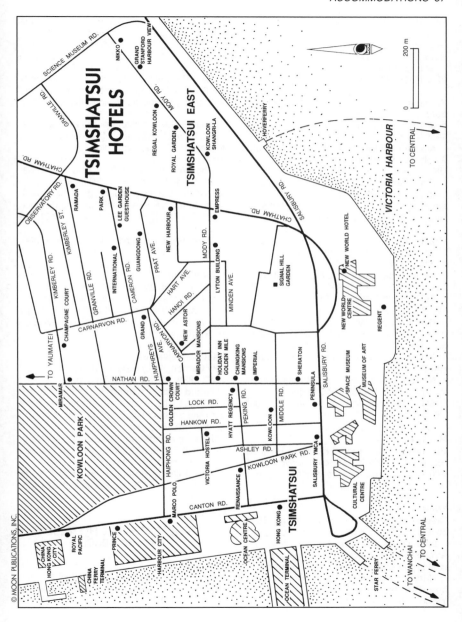

few single rooms for HK$880; family suites HK$1720. Extremely popular dorm beds are HK$190. Try to reserve one to two months in advance (reservations accepted for dorm beds also).

Stanford Hillview, 13 Observatory Rd., tel. 2722-7822. HK$1200-1700 s or d.

Yaumatei

Eaton, 380 Nathan Rd., tel. 2782-1818. A newer hotel with smallish modern rooms for HK$850-1450 s or d.

Majestic, 348 Nathan Rd., tel. 2781-1333. An old standby with surprisingly high standards. HK$1200-1600 s or d.

Pearl Seaview, 262 Shanghai St., tel. 2782-0892. Small rooms and no sea view, but an interesting location, and it's close to the MTR. HK$780-1180 s, HK$1180-1480 d.

Mongkok

Most of these cater to Asian business travelers and tour groups:

Concourse Hotel, 22 Lai Chi Kok Rd., tel. 2397-6683. HK$1050-1850 s or d.

Fortuna, 355 Nathan Rd., tel. 2385-1011. HK$800-1100 s or d.

Grand Tower Hotel, 627 Nathan Rd., tel. 2789-0011. A new hotel with large rooms, set in a shopping center way up on Nathan Road. A shuttle bus runs regularly to Tsimshatsui. HK$960-1500 s or d.

Newton Hotel Kowloon, 58 Boundary St., tel. 2787-2338. HK$890-1460 s or d.

Stanford Hotel, 118 Soy St., tel. 2781-1881. HK$1100 s, HK$1100-1600 d.

Mid-Levels

Bishop Lei International House, 4 Robinson Rd., tel. 2868-0828. Tucked up above Central, with inexpensive rooms considering the location: HK$980 s, HK$1380 d.

Wanchai

Charterhouse, 209 Wanchai Rd., tel. 2833-5566. HK$1200 s, HK$1550 and up d.

Empire Hotel, 33 Hennessy Rd., tel. 2866-9111. An oldish place favored by Chinese groups, with a rooftop pool and gym. HK$1300-1800 s or d.

Harbour View International House, 4 Harbour Rd., tel. 2802-0111. Operated by the YMCA and an exceptionally good value for the

prime location. HK$950-1400 s or d, with the higher end charged for harbor view rooms.

Luk Kwok, 72 Gloucester Rd., tel. 2866-2166. Suzie Wong's old bordello, reborn as a family-oriented hotel. HK$1500-1700 d.

New Harbour, 41 Hennessy Rd., tel. 2861-1166. A CITS affiliate, older but renovated, usually hosting groups from China. HK$980-1480 s or d.

South Pacific, 23 Morrison Hill Rd., tel. 2572-3838. New, elegant, and a little out of the way, though good transport is close by. HK$1300-1900 s or d.

The Wesley, 22 Hennessy Rd., tel. 2866-6688. Owned by the Methodist church and operated by a private company, this hotel is well-sited on the tramline, within walking distance of Pacific Place. HK$1000-1800 s, HK$1200-2200 d.

Wharney, 61 Lockhart Rd., tel. 2861-1000. HK$1450-1750.

Happy Valley

The Emperor Byron, 1A Wang Tak St., tel. 2893-3693. An odd though not bad location amid residential blocks just north of the Happy Valley tram loop. Decent rooms average HK$1580.

Past Causeway Bay

City Garden, 9 City Garden Rd., North Point, tel. 2887-2888. HK$1450-1950 s or d.

Grand Plaza, 2 Kornhill Rd., Quarry Bay, tel. 2886-0011. This hotel comes with its own sports club and is located right next to a big shopping center. HK$1060-1880 d.

Newton Hongkong, 218 Electric Rd., North Point, tel. 2807-2333. New, near the Fortress Hill MTR. HK$1250-2200 s or d.

South China Hotel, 67 Java Road, North Point, tel. 2503-1168. New, simple, HK$1300-1800 s or d.

VERY EXPENSIVE HOTELS (HK$1800-2800)

Tsimshatsui

Holiday Inn Golden Mile, 50 Nathan Rd., tel. 2369-3111. An extremely popular location. HK$1550 s, HK$1900-2510 d.

Two men engrossed in a game of Chinese chequers. A common sight which always attracts a crowd of bettors.

Hyatt Regency Hong Kong, 67 Nathan Rd., tel. 2311-1234. Built in 1969, and now outdone in luxury by the Grand Hyatt in Wanchai. HK$2150-2850 s or d, triples for HK$2500-3200.

Miramar, 130 Nathan Rd., tel. 2368-1111. An older hotel across from Kowloon Park, favored by tour groups . HK$1700-2800 s or d.

New World, 22 Salisbury Rd., tel. 2369-4111. Part of a giant shopping center next to the Regent; while it's on the waterfront, it lacks harbor views. HK$1750-2600 s, HK$1950-2600 d.

The Hongkong, Harbour City, 3 Canton Rd., tel. 2736-0088. This and its sister hotels (listed below) are set in the midst of a giant shopping mall, and are good value. HK$2200 and up s, HK$2300 and up d.

The Marco Polo, Harbour City, 3 Canton Rd., tel. 2736-0888. HK$1700-2100 s or d.

The Prince, Harbour City, 3 Canton Rd., tel. 2736-1888. HK$1850-2000 s or d.

Renaissance, 8 Peking Rd., tel. 2375-1133. Newish, good value for this category, with a rooftop health club and pool. HK$2050-2900 s or d.

Royal Pacific, 33 Canton Rd., tel. 2736-1188. In China Hong Kong City, connected by walkway to Kowloon Park. HK$1250-2750 s or d.

Sheraton, 20 Nathan Rd., tel. 2369-1111. Popular with business travelers; some rooms with harbor views. HK$2400-3480 s or d.

Tsimshatsui East
Kowloon Shangri-La, 64 Mody Rd., tel. 2721-2111. Elegant decor, favored by business trav-

elers. HK$2100-3800 s or d.

Nikko, 72 Mody Rd., tel. 2739-1111. Great skyline views from many rooms, but a little far from central Tsimshatsui. HK$1980-3180 s or d.

Regal Kowloon, 71 Mody Rd., tel. 2722-1818. HK$1500-2250 s, HK$2000-2700 d.

Royal Garden, 69 Mody Rd., tel. 2721-5215. Glass elevators soar above a stunning garden atrium, and there's a gorgeous rooftop swimming pool—a lot of ambience for the price. HK$1900-2500 s or d; recommended.

Hung Hom
The Harbour Plaza, 20 Tak Fung St., tel. 8121-3188. New hotel in a hitherto unpopular location; easy access to the Hung Hom ferry pier, however. There's a fitness center and a rooftop swimming pool. HK$1900-3000 s or d.

Wanchai
New World Harbour View, 1 Harbour Rd., tel. 2802-8888. Located on the other side of the Convention Centre from the Grand Hyatt, it's lost some of its harbor views to the convention center extension, though higher-up rooms retain them. HK$2030-3350 s, HK$2280-3600 d.

Causeway Bay
Excelsior, 281 Gloucester Rd., tel. 2894-8888. An older but still comfortable hotel that's popular with groups; some rooms have harbor views. HK$1600-2700.

HONG KONG'S BEST HOTELS

"Opulence" is the operative word here. The following three hotels are among the world's finest, combining Western luxuries with Asian service. Their selling point is the personal touch: the waiter who remembers your brand of beer; the concierge who discreetly produces the book you casually mentioned; the maid who duplicates the layout of your toiletries each morning after cleaning the bathroom.

Hotels that arguably qualify for this list include the Grand Hyatt, the Kowloon, and Island Shangri-Las. The following three, however, are firmly ensconced as the best hotels in Hong Kong:

The Peninsula, Salisbury Rd., Tsimshatsui, tel. 2366-6251. This gracious 1928 building near the Tsimshatsui Star Ferry exemplifies colonial elegance. A string quartet plays in the gilt-rococo lobby and there's a fleet of Rolls Royces to serve guests. Rooms are huge, and suites huger. Top restaurants are a trademark: Gaddi's, the Verandah Grill, Felix. A 17-story tower opened in 1993 added 90 more rooms to the total and reclaimed The Peninsula's harbor views. Rooms are HK$2600-3800; suites HK$4900-38,000.

Mandarin Oriental, 5 Connaught Rd., Central, tel. 2522-0011. Built in 1963 as competition for The Peninsula, the Mandarin regularly places among the world's best hotels. The nondescript exterior hides an elegant lobby of black marble and gilt; European and Asian styles are blended throughout. A superb health center includes a pool lined with Roman columns. Restaurants like the Mandarin Grill, the Man Wah, and Pierrot are some of the best in Hong Kong. Impeccable service is its hallmark: the Mandarin's staff-to-room ratio is 2:1. Superbly located across from the Central Star Ferry. Rooms start at HK$2400; suites are HK$5000-24,000.

The Regent, Salisbury Rd., Tsimshatsui, tel. 2721-1211. Opened in 1981, the Regent quickly made its mark on the local scene with its prime waterfront positioning. A sprawling building of red marble and acres of glass, it projects out over the harbor, and most rooms have harbor views, even from the sunken Italian marble bathtubs. Rolls Royces to spare, and again, great restaurants: Plume, and Lai Ching Heen. HK$2200-3500, suites for HK$3800-22,000.

Park Lane, 310 Gloucester Rd., tel. 2890-3355. Right across from Victoria Park. HK$1980-3080 s, HK$2280-3380 d.

Regal Hongkong, 88 Yee Woo St., tel. 2890-6633. New and glittery, right on the tramline in the middle of the shopping district, with rooms for HK$2300-2500.

LUXURY HOTELS (HK$2500+)

Central/Admiralty
Conrad, Pacific Place, 88 Queensway, tel. 2521-3838. New and ultra-modern, with spacious rooms overlooking the Peak or the harbor. HK$2550-3500 s or d.

Furama Kempinski, 1 Connaught Rd., tel. 2525-5111. A favorite with business travelers. Rooms are HK$1850-3000 s or d.

Ritz-Carlton, 3 Connaught Rd., tel. 2877-6666. Opened in 1993, this small, deluxe hotel is popular with Americans and Japanese. HK$2400-3800 s or d.

Island Shangri-La, Pacific Place, Supreme

Court Rd., tel. 2877-3838. A plush, new highrise hotel featuring luxurious big rooms with all the amenities, including great views, and some excellent restaurants. HK$2400-3400; recommended.

Marriott, Pacific Place, 88 Queensway, tel. 2810-8366. A similarly plush place located right in the shopping center. HK$2450-3400 s or d.

Wanchai
Grand Hyatt, 1 Harbour Rd., tel. 2588-1234. The last word in opulence, with a lobby decorated to resemble a 1930s cruise ship, several superb restaurants, and rooms outfitted with 18k-gold bathroom fixtures, most with harbor views. HK$2800-3600 s, HK$3050-3850 d.

RENTING

Give up the idea of living on Hong Kong Island unless you're independently wealthy or your company will pay for it. The latter is how most expats manage to live in the Mid-Levels, where a small two-bedroom flat with a view can run HK$30,000 a month. Something nice on the Peak might be HK$90,000 or more. A tiny studio in Western or Wanchai for HK$8000 is a rare commodity indeed.

Beyond the city, prices become more reasonable. Commuting is inevitable: you need only choose the method—living on an island and taking the romantic but slow ferry, or settling in the New Territories and relying on bus, MTR, or KCR. Shatin on the KCR line or Tsuen Wan on the MTR line are closest in and worth considering for that reason alone. Rents get cheaper the farther out you go, and it doesn't have to be that far: a flat in Taikooshing might be HK$10,000-12,000 monthly.

Expats who needn't bother with a daily commute often take advantage of the pleasant environment and cheaper rents of the outlying islands, particularly Cheung Chau and Lamma. A reasonably sized flat on Cheung Chau might go for HK$8500 a month, a third of the cost of a similar accommodation in the city. The excellent ferry system means you're less than an hour from downtown. So-called "holiday flats" are reasonable if rented for a period of several weeks.

Look in the *South China Morning Post* classifieds, where flats are listed by area (measured in square feet). Sharing an established flat with a roommate is an the easy way to settle in. Check the "Share Flats" section and the classifieds in *HK Magazine*. House-sitting opportunities are listed under "Short-Term Flats," but be prepared to pay.

Or call an agent, listed under "Estate Agents" in the Yellow Pages. Offices are dotted about town—just look for small clusters of people staring at the small cards displayed in the window.

FOOD AND RESTAURANTS

Chinese cooking, as Chinese will tell you, is the world's best cuisine. And the best of all the varied Chinese cooking styles is generally considered to be Cantonese. An old saying outlines a recipe for happiness:

Be born in Suzhou (said to have China's most beautiful women)
Live in Hangzhou (the loveliest city)
Eat in Guangzhou (the best food)
Die in Lizhou (the best coffins)

There is a universe of difference between the gluey slop of chop suey (a dish unknown in China —one suspects it was concocted especially for unappreciative barbarians) and the supremely fresh, impeccably prepared cuisine of Guangdong Province. Cantonese food is refined, vivid, and varied, with the fresh ingredients cooked in such a way as to intensify the special nature of each. Hong Kong is the repository of centuries of cooking talent, rivalled only by Taiwan.

Eating is *the* major social and recreational activity in Hong Kong, where brightly lit, noisy restaurants are packed day and night. It's no wonder the local greeting is *"Neh sek joh fan, meiya?"*—"Have you eaten yet?" The average Hong Kong family eats out once a day: restaurants are cheap and plentiful, and offer an escape from the cramped quarters of housing estate flats. They come in all different price ranges, from cheap open-air *dai pai dongs* to the luxurious gourmet shrines of top hotels.

The cheapest meals—rice and roast meat, or a bowl of noodles—can be had for as little as HK$15. At the other end of the spectrum, an elegant French dinner for two with drinks will easily run into four figures. In general, you won't get away for less than HK$60-70 a meal unless you resort to fast food.

Around HK$150 per person provides a much tastier range of options (that's not including alcohol, which can be pricey). More expensive restaurants can run HK$400-500 per person, an occasional splash may be worth some scrimping.

EATING CHINESE

Street Food

Dai pai dongs or open-air street stalls are cheap and fun places to eat. Small metal carts dispense grilled fish balls or squid-on-a-stick and various steamed and fried tidbits that vary seasonally—roast chestnuts and sweet pancakes, for example, and, less pleasant, chicken feet and reeking squares of fermented tofu *(chao doufu)*. Other vendors produce steaming bowls of fresh noodle soup in under a minute, dipping a mesh basket of noodles into boiling water and adding bits of fish, meat, tofu, or vegetables.

Things get more elaborate where *dai pai dongs* are clustered together, like the Temple Street Night Market or the huddled stalls on Graham Street in Central. There's seldom a menu at such places; just point and eat. You get great views of the street, and the street gets great views of you.

The cooked food markets crammed into local market blocks serve a variety of tasty, cheap dishes. Try the one at Aberdeen, or the 2/F of the Sheung Wan Market Complex in Western.

Restaurants

The classic Chinese restaurant is decorated in lucky hues of red and gold, with walls of mirrors improving the *feng shui* and tanks of live fish at the entrance displaying soon-to-be-eaten wares. Seating in the biggest places is arranged by hostesses clad in slinky *cheongsam*s (tight long dresses with a slits up the sides) and equipped with walkie-talkies.

The large round tables are meant for groups of 10 or 20. Often smaller parties end up sharing a table with strangers. The overall atmosphere is one of cheerful clamor: the air is filled with the sounds of clashing crockery, shouted conversations, and boisterous toasts, which only get louder as the evening goes on. One study concluded the typical Hong Kong restaurant is loud enough to drown out 40% of normal table conversation—and that peak decibel levels are high enough to damage hearing.

RESTAURANT PRICES

Restaurant ratings are as follows:

Inexpensive: under HK$150 per person

Moderate: HK$150-250

Expensive: HK$250 and up

Telephone numbers are listed if reservations are recommended.

Ordering

Chinese food is best eaten with a group, which maximizes the chance to sample different dishes. Place yourself in the hands of a Chinese friend, if possible. The general rule is one dish per diner, plus one extra. A classic meal for a group of six might be a cold appetizer, followed by pork, chicken, vegetables, seafood, soup, and noodles or rice. Try to balance flavors—salty, sweet, spicy, sour—and textures too: crunchy, chewy, crisp, creamy.

English menus in Chinese restaurants seldom list everything available; seasonal specialties in particular are usually described only in Chinese. You can always point to an appealing dish at a neighboring table—but confirm the price first, as some specialties are ridiculously expensive. Or ask your waiter for advice.

Dining Etiquette

Dishes are brought to the table as soon as they're cooked, while soup usually comes at the end of the meal. Everything is served communally—even the soup comes in a tureen to be ladled into individual bowls. At bigger tables, dishes are placed on a spinning tray in the center of the table to give everyone easy access to each.

Diners serve themselves with chopsticks. Food is briefly touched or paused atop individual bowls of rice, a nicety which breaks the continuity of everyone eating from the same dish. Inedible bits like bones and crabshells are spat out more or less delicately onto the tablecloth.

Porcelain spoons are provided for soup and pudding, but everything else is eaten with *fai tse* or chopsticks, an elegant method which is not as difficult to master as it first appears (practice with shelled peanuts). Think of them as a set of pincers: the top one moves, while the bottom one rests atop the thumb and third finger. It's easiest to hold them fairly far up. Except at a banquet or other formal occasion, it's perfectly acceptable to raise the rice bowl to one's lips and use the windmill technique. Chinese prefer chopsticks to metal tableware, which they say spoils the true taste of food. When not in use, chopsticks should rest across a plate or on a chopstick rest.

Tables are set with small dishes of dipping sauce which vary with the food being served:

OFFBEAT DINING

These suggestions for offbeat dining experiences are selected from the text, see the appropriate chapters for more details.

Felix: Perched atop The Peninsula, tel. 2366-6251, this dramatically decorated restaurant/bar had the whole town talking for months when it opened in 1995. (Check out the men's room to see what people were talking about.) Food is East/West cuisine, delicious and expensive.

Peak Cafe: Take the Peak Tram up to Victoria Gap and cross the road to this big old fieldstone building at 121 Peak Rd., tel. 2849-7868. Built in 1901 as a shelter for sedan-chair bearers, it was saved from demolition in 1989 and renovated into a casual but classy cafe. A small outdoor terrace offers views of Lamma and the South China Sea. The menu is suitably intriguing, mixing Californian, Italian, and Asian cuisines—sometimes all in the same dish, as in Grilled Scallop Brochette with Thai Salsa Vinaigrette. Inexpensive-moderate.

Cafe Deco Bar and Grill: A giant place seating nearly 500, featuring elegantly stylized decor and period appliances like a 1920s Parisian oyster bar. Food is elegant and eclectic—the menu encompasses Indian, Italian, and Asian cuisines—but go most of all for the views, the house jazz band, and the Italian coffee bar. It's in the Peak Galleria, 118 Peak Rd., tel. 2849-5111; moderate.

Revolving restaurants: La Ronda atop the Furama-Kempinski in Central, tel. 2525-5111, is the best, with harbor views and extensive international lunch and dinner buffets. Early evening is the most popular time for a seat, as the light changes. The **Revolving 66** atop the Hopewell Centre, 183 Queen's Rd. East, Wanchai, serves Continental cuisine, a daily lunch buffet, and high tea.

Nautical gimmicks: At **Bamboo Village Fishermen's Wharf,** 250 Jaffe Rd., Wanchai, the booths are modeled after Chinese junks, complete with rigging and set around a moat. The food is seafood, of course, including crab and shark's fin; moderate.

The Other Side: Hong Kong Island's laid-back south side offers some intriguing dining options, like the romantic **Stanley's French,** at 86 Stanley Main St., tel. 2813-8873. **The Verandah,** 109 Repulse Bay Rd., tel. 2812-2722, serves French food in a reconstruction of the stately old Repulse Bay Hotel. Besides lunch and dinner there's a weekend champagne breakfast 8-10:30 a.m., and tea 3-5:30 p.m. A favorite weekend outing is to hike down Dragon's Back Ridge to Shek O, ending at the big, busy **Thailand-China Seafood Restaurant.**

Floating Restaurants: "Floating cliches" is more like it—still, they're gorgeous at night when lit up like birthday cakes. Take the private boat service from Aberdeen Pier to either the **Jumbo** or **Tai Pak,** anchored side by side. Prices and quality are moderate at both: the Jumbo is more ornate on the outside; the Tai Pak on the inside. The Jumbo serves dim sum 7:30 a.m.-4 p.m., a cheap way to sneak a peek inside.

Dinner Cruise: A more mobile floating restaurant is the gaudy pink, triple-decker ferry *Pearl of the Orient,* which cruises Victoria Harbour offering live entertainment and a Western dinner buffet. Reserve through hotels or travel agents or call 2561-5033. A two-hour dinner cruise is around HK$400; there's also a Chinese dinner buffet available on the *Pearl of Hong Kong,* operated by the same company.

Pigeon Restaurants: On weekends city dwellers visit the pigeon restaurants of Shatin. The favorite is the 50-year-old **Lung Wah Hotel Restaurant,** 22 Ha Wo Che, Shatin, tel. 2691-1594, where over one million pigeons are served each year, prepared in an astonishing range of styles. Go on a weekday, and try roasted Shek Ki pigeon, pigeon satay, baked pigeon, or minced pigeon wrapped in lettuce. **Yucca de Lac Restaurant,** Ma Liu Shui, Shatin, tel. 2692-1835, is rightfully famous for its huge garden terrace overlooking Tolo Harbour. The extensive, reasonably priced Cantonese menu features pigeon as a specialty.

Seafood Restaurants: Take the ferry to Lamma for a seafood meal at **Sok Kwu Wan's** strip of brightly lit waterfront restaurants. Alternatively, **The Waterfront** at Yung Shue Wan serves food from Indian to pizza, salad, and burgers, all very good and reasonably priced. Farther afield, and cheaper, are the seafood restaurants on **Peng Chau** and **Po Toi.** Closer and more expensive is **Lei Yue Mun,** a tiny enclave on the eastern approaches to Victoria Harbour. Choose live fish, crabs, clams, and giant prawns from fishmongers, then carry your picks to one of the 20-odd restaurants lining the main street. Try **Hoi Tin Garden** or the **Lei Yue Restaurant. Sai Kung** is another good place to view and consume colorful live seafood at outdoor tables—choose from the string of restaurants lining the waterfront.

most common are soy sauce, hot mustard, and plum or chili sauce. Soy sauce goes only on dark foods (salt is added to light foods); it's uncouth to dump it onto rice. Small bottles of vinegar and sesame oil may be provided for seasoning noodles. Dessert is rare, fortune cookies nonexistent (they're an American invention).

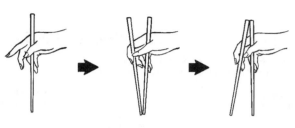

To get the bill, say *"mai dan"* or make the international scribble gesture. The 10% service charge levied in most restaurants should cover the tip, though it's common to leave the small change as well. If there's no service charge, tip 10%.

Banquets

Chinese culinary ingenuity comes into its own at banquets, which showcase dish after elaborate dish. Banquets consist of at least 12 dishes: four cold plates, four sautéed dishes, and four more substantial main courses, plus soup and rice or noodles at the end. Pace yourself so you can sample modest portions of each dish, and

CHEAP EATS

Saving up for a splurge at a great restaurant is a noble goal, and the cheaper eateries frequented in the process are not exactly an adversity. Some of the best food in Hong Kong is encountered in tiny local restaurants and street stalls. There are no English menus, so the recommended method is point-and-eat. Wonton soup, noodles, and roast meat with rice can be found in virtually every neighborhood. Try **Mak's Noodles** at 77 Wellington St., Central, for a particularly good example of tasty cheap food tucked away in an expensive neighborhood. Other cheapies include **Ser Wong Fun,** 30 Cochrane St., Central; and **Ocean Empire Food Shop,** 137 Johnston Rd., Wanchai.

Cheapest of all are the open-air *dai pai dong*s found in markets and on street corners, though the Urban Council's zest for over regulation is driving these to extinction. (The goal is eventually to move all hawkers into covered markets, which would be a real shame.) The shellfish restaurants in the Temple Street Night Market are a highly visible example, but there are many other little clusters tucked away in various neighborhoods.

Only slightly more expensive, and easier to cope with for non-Cantonese speakers, are places like the **Ah Yee Leng Tong** café chain, furnished in old-fashioned style and serving health-oriented soups and homestyle cooking. There are branches at 68 Canton Rd., Tsimshatsui; 505 Lockhart Rd., Causeway Bay; and 13 Fleming Rd., Wanchai. **Dai Pai**

Dong has a retro decor and serves snacks and light meals; there's one at 20 Russell St., Causeway Bay; another at 128 Queen's Rd. Central, Central.

Other tricks in the budget repertoire include searching out lunch specials. The fixed-price menus and buffets at otherwise expensive restaurants can be real bargains. Remember that some cuisines—notably Indian, but also Thai, Vietnamese, and vegetarian Chinese—are markedly cheaper than others (French, American).

Don't scorn judicious reliance on fast food. Especially in Central, most of the bill goes to pay for a table to sit at rather than the food one consumes. A takeout meal consumed in a park or promenade, scarce as they are, is more tranquil than a jam-packed restaurant. Try picnicking in Hong Kong Park, on the Tsimshatsui waterfront promenade, or in Signal Hill Garden.

Unfortunately many of the local fast food chains, like Café de Coral, are terrible. **Oliver's Super Sandwiches** is a decent exception, with several dozen outlets scattered around town. Japanese fast food is another option; look in the basements of Causeway Bay's department stores, or in Central, where little places do takeout sushi boxes. Many Chinese restaurants pack up takeout boxes for harried workers to eat at the office. The Cantonese restaurant **Yung Kee** at 32 Wellington St., Central, dispenses boxes of its famous roast goose and rice to lunchtime crowds.

remember the rice or noodles shouldn't be entirely finished, as this implies the food has been insufficient.

Toasts are a banquet essential. "Bottoms up" is *yum sing* in Cantonese or *gan bei* ("dry glass") in Mandarin. This need not be taken literally—Chinese *jiu* is far too strong to gulp—but do take a symbolic sip of something each time. Rather than guests ordering separate drinks, a single kind of alcohol—often cognac—is served to everyone. Glasses are topped up with each course at the host's insistence, and guests are expected to do the same for him. Drinking games (see "Nightlife" under "Entertainment") are a distinct possibility.

DRINKS

Tea

Chinese food is accompanied by tea, which comes in countless regional varieties but is always drunk in small cups, without the addition of sugar, milk, or lemon. The basic types are green (unfermented), red (fermented, and what the Western world calls "black"), and oolong (semi-fermented). Lighter green teas may be scented with chrysanthemum, rose, narcissus, or jasmine. Foreigners are generally served jasmine tea *(heung ping),* while Cantonese drink the stronger fermented *bo lei.* Strongest of all is Iron Goddess or Iron Buddha tea from Chiu Chow, a variety of oolong. For more on tea, see the special topic "The Intricacies of Tea."

Tea is generally served free with a meal, though a minimal charge may be levied for it and for appetizers like peanuts, pickled garlic, and preserved eggs. To get the teapot refilled, simply turn over the lid.

> *The people there gave us a certain Drinke called Chaa, wich is only water with a kind of herbe boyled in it. It must bee Drancke warme and is acompted wholesome.*
>
> —*Peter Mundy,*
> *Travels in Europe and Asia (1637)*

Tapping three fingers on the tabletop signals a silent thanks for one's cup being refilled—a pleasingly subtle gesture. For proper British tea with all the trimmings, visit one of the grand hotels.

Coffee

Good coffee was once almost impossible to find in Hong Kong, and the standard remains Nescafé, though hotel restaurants serve brewed coffee. However, a Seattle-imported fad for authentic brewed coffee has made life more tolerable for caffeine addicts. See the listings in the special topic "Breakfast, Lunch, and Dinner." Causeway Bay's Japanese department stores have little coffee shops serving expensive, impeccably brewed coffee—try Jamaican Blue Mountain for HK$38 a cup.

Other Drinks

All the major soft drinks are available. Milk comes in cartons and in Tetra Pak boxes, which needn't be refrigerated until opened. Sweetened soy milk is a popular alternative for the frequently lactose-intolerant Chinese. Fruit juices come in cartons, and fresh juice is sold from little street stalls.

Alcohol

The most popular beers are the locally brewed San Miguel and Carlsberg, and the Chinese-German Tsingtao. Imported brands are also available, the most popular being Heineken and Blue Girl, often found in the refrigerators of obscure New Territories shops. A single local microbrewery produce ales with names like Crooked Island and Dragon's Back—worth a try.

Wine is expensive, as atop the flat tax on alcoholic beverages a 30% tax is levied based on wine's value. Wine in general does not mix well with Chinese food. Avoid the overly sweet Chinese wines. (Dynasty white wine, produced in a joint venture with Rémy Martin, is a tolerable exception.) If you really want to drink wine, go to Macau.

Chinese call all alcohol *"jiu"* and translate it into English as "wine." So beware of the tendency to call all alcohol "wine," which usually refers to potent distilled liquor like *go leung* and the notorious millet-based *mao tai.* The rice-based *siu hing* (also known as *shaoxin*) is better, especially if served warm—but guard your intake of all these. Distilled up to 12 times, they are up to 70% pure alcohol, and deliver a lethal hangover.

THE INTRICACIES OF TEA

For the Chinese, as for much of Asia, tea is a symbol of hospitality and courtesy, and its consumption is surrounded by a web of social intricacies. It is said to have been discovered long ago by the emperor Shen Nung, the same ruler who identified the vast pharmacopoeia of Chinese medicine. Seated under a tree one day, he idly watched camellia leaves drift into a cauldron of boiling water. He sampled the brew, and the rest is history.

The Chinese were drinking tea as early as the 11th century B.C., as a medicinal remedy and a sort of soup taken at meals. By the Han dynasty, southern Chinese were boiling tea leaves together with flavorings like ginger, dates, green onion, or mint. The practice spread to northern China, and by the middle of the Tang dynasty tea had become a national obsession.

The eighth-century scholar Lu Tu outlined elaborate instructions for proper tea preparation in his *Tea Classic.* Add powdered, roasted tea leaves and a pinch of salt to boiling water. When the water generates bubbles "large as fish eyes" and sounds like "wind blowing through the pines," it has reached the first boil. Fresh-boiled water was considered essential in bringing out the full flavor of the tea, and the quality of water received as much attention as that of the leaves. Finest was icy water from a free-flowing mountain stream, followed by river water, with well-water a lowly third.

Lu Tu and his contemporaries considered tea consumption an aesthetic experience, one best enjoyed in open-air pavilions surrounded by rustling groves of bamboo. A Ming dynasty *Tea Treatise* discussed "Times for Drinking Tea": "When bored with poetry or when one's thoughts are confused . . . during late-night conversations or studying on a sunny day . . . when playing host to scholars, pretty girls . . . or visiting friends returned from afar."

There are hundreds of varieties of tea, and the subtle differences between them require a discerning tongue and a philosophical nature to fully savor. Top-quality blends can cost thousands of Hong Kong dollars per pound. The names of the different types border on poetry: "Ten-League Fragrance," "Jewelled Cloud," "Long-Life Eyebrows."

The best tea is said to grow on high mountain peaks, where fog and snow impart a delicate flavor. The leaves are picked, sorted, rolled to release the flavor-bearing sap, and dried. Green tea, which is oilier than most, undergoes only a single run-through of this process; other types of teas are repeatedly rolled and roasted or sun-dried.

The finest green tea is top-graded Lung Ching, "Dragon's Well," which is picked in early spring when the leaves are still tiny buds. It's prized for its ability to remain jade-green no matter how long it sits. Oo-

tea on display

long is a special kind of semi-fermented tea prepared through an elaborate curing process: it's brewed very strong, in tiny pots stuffed three-quarters full of leaves. Tei Guanyin or Tit Kwan Yin, literally "Iron Goddess of Mercy," is a popular blend from Fujian Province that can be sampled in Hong Kong's Chiu Chow restaurants. Other varieties are "Hairy Crab," "Water Fairy," and "Clear Fragrance."

Black tea (called "red" in Chinese after the color of the infusion) is popular among the masses, though connoisseurs scorn it as good only for export. Low-quality leaves are fermented, heated, then dried. It's the only type of tea strong enough to stand up to the English treatment of dumping in milk and sugar.

Pu-erh tea from Yunnan Province comes in all colors and has a distinctive flavor and reputed medicinal qualities. The names of its varieties reach rhapsodic levels: "Cloud-Burner," "Height-Hater," "Handful of Snow," "Drunken Concubine Yang." The robust pu-erh variety called *bo lei* is the most popular brew in Cantonese restaurants. Teas infused with dried flower petals are another popular innovation; foreigners are inevitably served jasmine tea; other blends feature chrysanthemum, rose, or narcissus.

The paraphernalia of tea preparation is equally complex. In the Song dynasty, green tea powder was mixed with boiling water and whipped into a froth with a bamboo whisk, much as the Japanese do today. Epicures held tea contests to see whose froth lasted the longest.

The practice of steeping tea leaves in boiling water became widespread during the Ming dynasty, when teapots with spouts, handles, and lids were developed. Their tiny size ensures freshness (tea becomes bitter if it sits too long). Porcelain pots were admired for their cleanliness, pewter-coated pots for their ability to preserve heat; but the reddish-purple clay pots of the Yixing region were said to retain the tea's color and flavor best of all. The finest teapots were miniature works of art, signed by their makers. Their graceful, smooth forms, tiny enough to nestle in the palm of the hand, were modelled after flowers, leaves, or vegetables.

Miniature tea sets are highly prized even today, and are sold in expensive specialist stores. The Museum of Teaware's shop stocks Yixing pots priced HK$120-7000. Recommended shops for browsing for both tea sets and tea varieties include Fook Ming Tong on Theatre Lane in Central (also in Harbour City), the Best Tea House at 3 Lock Rd. in Tsimshatsui, and Chan Chun Lan Tea Co. on Cochrane Street.

Perhaps in light of this, the Chinese are not big drinkers. The most popular booze is cognac, indiscriminately mixed with ice, soda, lemonade, or 7UP, and drunk steadily throughout a meal via ritual toasts. Hongkongers consume more cognac per capita than anyone else in the world—5.4 million bottles in 1990, nine percent of the world's total market.

Like shark's fin soup, the cognac bottle set on each table at a party signals the host's prosperity and respect for his guests. Cognac would not be popular if it were cheap. It has the additional virtue of being made from grapes, which are considered "heating" in Chinese thought; thus it's associated with strength, power, and potency. Whiskey and gin, made from "cooling" grain, are not so popular, though whiskey sales are on the rise.

CHINESE FOOD

The most essential ingredient in Chinese cooking is *fan,* or boiled rice, called "the foundation of all tastes." There's logic behind Asia's passion for rice: it supports more people per acre than any other food grain. Rice-growing requires minimal inputs but maximum labor, a requirement easy to meet in populous countries. Asia has thousands of different indigenous rice varieties, each with a subtly different fragrance and texture. In recent years many of these have vanished, replaced with a few highly productive strains.

In the cuisines of colder north China, rice may be replaced by steamed bread or noodles. This staple serves as the base for what Cantonese call *sung,* main dishes of vegetables, meat, fish, eggs, or tofu. Chinese cooking combines these basic ingredients to create a tremendous diversity of textures and flavors. The Cantonese will shop twice a day to guarantee absolute freshness, seeking fish which are still flopping, just-picked vegetables, and pork butchered that very morning.

Cantonese
The distinctive cooking of Guangdong Province is considered the most varied and interesting

DIM SUM

Dim sum is one of the most enjoyable forms of Cantonese cuisine, a kind of culinary merry-go-round in which carts of sweet and savory tidbits are paraded about the dining room for diners to select from. Dim sum can be either breakfast, lunch, or a snack, as most large Cantonese restaurants serve it between 7 a.m.-5 p.m. On Sunday and holidays, multi-generational families pack the big, round tables for hours of *yum cha* (literally "drinking tea")—the word used to describe the highly social process of consuming dim sum.

The Chinese characters for dim sum mean "to touch the heart," though the literal meaning applies only about as much as does "hot dog" in English. The term encompasses all varieties of dumplings, buns, croquettes, puffs, tarts, cakes, and puddings. Standard favorites include steamed buns stuffed with barbecued pork *(cha siu bau),* translucent shrimp dumplings *(har gau),* yellow-white pork dumplings *(siu mai),* fried meat dumplings *(jin fun gwor),* crispy small spring rolls *(chun kuen),* glutinous rice with meat bundled in lotus leaves *(nor mai gai),* and egg custard tarts *(dan tat).*

Portions, usually two or four small pieces, are kept warm in round bamboo steamer baskets stacked in metal carts. These are pushed by weary-looking women who announce their wares in loud voices, adding to the general hubbub. Flag the server over to get a closer view, and try whatever looks good. Prices are determined by the size of the plate and run around HK$20-30.

Dim sum in its purest form is incredibly simple to order and deal with, since everything is displayed. Unfortunately the modern trend involves ordering dim sum from menus (invariably in Chinese), and bringing the plates straight from the kitchen. The food may be fresher, but the experience is not the same. Try to find an old-fashioned place where the food is presented in carts—the bigger and noiser, the better. Dim sum is meant to be a cheerfully rowdy event.

Lunchtimes are extremely busy and tend to decimate supplies for the rest of the afternoon. Mid-morning is probably the best time to visit a dim sum restaurant. Avoid Sunday and holidays, when families descend in full force (and many places extend dim sum serving hours).

Highest ratings go to **Maxim's,** which has dim sum 7:30 a.m.-5 p.m. It's at 1 Yee Woo St., Causeway Bay, tel. 2894-9933. The elaborate **North Sea Fishing Village** in the basement of Auto Plaza, 65 Mody Rd., Tsimshatsui East, tel. 2723-6843, serves treats 11 a.m.-2:30 p.m. **Ocean City,** New World Centre, 18 Salisbury Rd., Tsimshatsui, tel. 2369-9688, ranks as the world's largest indoor Chinese restaurant, a gigantic place that fits in 6,000 diners at once. Dim sum is served 8 a.m.-5 p.m.

A good place to check it all out is **Dim Sum,** decorated in old-fashioned style, where traditional dishes depicted on a picture menu are served 11 a.m.-11 p.m. It's at 63 Sing Woo Rd., Happy Valley, tel. 2834-8893.

As dim sum is so cheap, you can use it as an excuse to visit somewhere unusually swanky, like **Lai Ching Heen** at the Regent, noon-2:30 p.m., or the elaborate **Shang Palace** at the Kowloon Shangri-La, where excellent dim sum is available from a menu

of all Chinese cuisines. Partly this is due to south China's subtropical climate, which produces a huge range of fruits and vegetables and all kinds of seafood.

Cantonese cooking uses steaming and quick stir-frying to enhance the qualities of food. The expert cook knows when a dish is done by the sizzling sound emanating from the wok. It's the lightest and least oily of all regional cooking styles, seasoned by a wide variety of sauces, rather than spices. Vegetables, seafood, pork, and chicken are the main ingredients.

Specialties include steamed prawns with chili sauce, steamed crab with vinegar, prawns or crab in black bean sauce (made from fermented, salted soya beans), whole steamed fish, barbecued roasted meats (often served as an appetizer), and roast pigeon dipped in soy sauce and seasoned salt. Dim sum is another Cantonese invention, experienced in its fullest glory in Hong Kong.

The typical Cantonese restaurant is a vast, crowded, noisy palace. A classic example is **Yung Kee,** 32 Wellington St., Central, tel. 2522-1624, which has been selling its famous roast goose with plum sauce since 1942. It has a huge menu with all the standards, plus seasonal dishes like tiny rice birds in autumn or snake soup in winter; moderate.

*stacked bamboo
steamers filled
with dim sum*

noon-3 p.m. The **Summer Palace** at the Island Shangri-La is similarly plush, with a limited but exquisite menu of nouvelle dim sum from 11:30 a.m.-3 p.m.

Dim sum hours for selected restaurants:

Capital, 2/F Chungking Mansions, 40 Nathan Rd., Tsimshatsui: 7 a.m.-5 p.m.

City Hall Chinese Restaurant, 2/F City Hall Low Block: 10 a.m.-3 p.m.

Diamond Restaurant, 267 Des Voeux Rd., Central: 6:30 a.m.-4 p.m.

East Ocean Seafood Restaurant, 3/F Harbor Center, 25 Harbor Rd., Wanchai: 11 a.m.-6 p.m.

Fontana, 6 Prat Ave., Tsimshatsui: 11 a.m.-3 p.m.

Golden Crown Shark's Fin Seafood, 2/F The Charterhouse, 209 Wanchai Rd., Wanchai: 11 a.m.-4:30 p.m.

Golden Leaf, Conrad Hotel, Pacific Place: noon-3 p.m.

Jade Garden, Swire House, 11 Chater Rd., Central: 2:30-6 p.m.

Jade Garden, 25 Carnarvon Rd., Tsimshatsui: 7:30 a.m.-5 p.m.

Super Star Seafood Restaurant, 1/F 83 Nathan Rd., Tsimshatshui: 11 a.m.-3 p.m.

Vegi Food Kitchen, 8 Cleveland St., Causeway Bay: 11 a.m.-5 p.m.

Yung Kee, 32 Wellington St., Central: 2-5 p.m.

Zen Chinese, Pacific Place: 11:30 a.m.-3 p.m. Expensive, nouvelle Cantonese.

City Hall Chinese Restaurant is popular for its harbor views, reasonably priced food and dim sum; it's on the 2/F City Hall Low Block, Central, tel. 2521-1303; moderate.

Enormous, perennially busy **Tsui Hang Village Restaurant** serves all the standard specialties. There's one at 2/F New World Tower, 16 Queen's Rd. Central, tel. 2524-2012, and another in the Miramar Shopping Mall in Tsimshatsui; moderate.

Yaik Sang is an old standby—nothing special about the setting, but the food is very, very good. It's at 2/F Lee Theatre Plaza, 99 Percival St., Causeway Bay, tel. 2882-3426; inexpensive-moderate.

Farm House dishes out superb home-style Cantonese cooking in a fashionable setting in the AIA Plaza, 18 Hysan Ave., Causeway Bay, tel. 2881-1881; moderate.

Tin Tin Seafood Harbor is a good place for excellent reasonably priced fresh seafood; it's at 4/F, 250 Gloucester Rd., Causeway Bay, tel. 2833-6683; moderate.

Orchard Court 37 Hankow Rd., Tsimshatsui, tel. 2317-5111, has a big menu that combines traditional and innovative dishes, with a special emphasis on seafood; inexpensive-moderate.

The "Garden" restaurants, part of the Maxim's chain, provide reliable, moderately priced food in an unintimidating setting and are good if unadventurous choices for an introduction to Chinese food. **Jade Garden** is the Cantonese version, with outlets in Swire House, 11 Chater Rd., Central, tel. 2526-3031, and at 25 Carnarvon Rd., Tsimshatsui, tel. 2369-8311. Its Beijing, Sichuan, Chiu Chow, and Shanghai counterparts are listed in the appropriate sections below.

Fook Lam Moon is very highly rated, partly through snob appeal: its specialties are pricey items like shark's fin soup and abalone; deep-fried crispy chicken is another, cheaper, specialty. It's located at 35 Johnston Rd., Wanchai, tel. 2866-0663; also 53 Kimberley Rd., Tsimshatsui; moderate-expensive.

The very best place for shark's fin is said to be **Sun Tung Lok**, 1 Sunning Rd., Causeway Bay, tel. 2882-2889, and 17 Canton Rd., Harbour City, Tsimshatsui, tel. 2730-0288; expensive.

Zen began as an upmarket place in London and now has branches all over the world serving nouvelle Cantonese. It's in Pacific Place Mall in Queensway, tel. 2845-4555; elegant and moderate-expensive.

The Cantonese restaurants in hotels can be authentic yet unchallenging places to sample dishes, though they're not cheap. Try **Loong Yuen** in the Holiday Inn Golden Mile or **Celestial Court** in the Sheraton, both moderate-expensive.

Cantonese food is delivered in its finest form at chic hotel restaurants: the elegant, intimate **Man Wah** atop the Mandarin, or nouvelle Chinese with a view at **Lai Ching Heen** in the Regent. At either, a superb dinner for two with drinks might run around HK$1500. Slightly more

---

CULINARY EXOTICA

"If its back points to heaven, you can eat it," maintains one Cantonese adage. Another asserts, "The Cantonese will eat anything with four legs but a table, anything that flies but an airplane, anything that swims but a submarine."

Chinese cuisine is generally practical and survival-based. Every available bit of food is utilized—chicken feet, duck web, fish lips, clotted chicken and pig blood (mixed into winter soups), and the brains and intestines of various animals.

Cantonese are extremely liberated in this respect, dining on creatures other Chinese shun, such as snake and dog. Both are winter dishes believed to "warm" the body and fight off disease. Snake shops in Western and Wanchai keep their writhing wares in wooden drawers or mesh cages. The meat is boiled in soup, or the bile duct may be squeezed into a glass of brandy or *jiu* and taken as a tonic. Out of respect for British sensibilities, the sale of dog meat has been banned in Hong Kong,

though it's available in the New Territories. It's openly sold in Macau, though, and in wintertime the roasted carcasses of man's best friend dangle prominently in Guangzhou markets.

Another Cantonese cult involves expensive delicacies like bird's nest, abalone, and shark's fin—luxury foods consumed for status rather than their admittedly bland flavor. By serving such exotica the host acknowledges the specialness of the occasion and impresses his guests. The custom is *de rigueur*

preserved snakes

HONG KONG TOURIST ASSOCIATION

affordable (especially at lunch) is the all-red **Shang Palace** at the Kowloon Shangri-La. The Grand Hyatt's romantic **One Harbour Road,** tel. 2558-1234, regularly tops surveys of Hong Kong's best restaurants, with its lovely airy decor and light, innovative Cantonese cooking. **The Golden Leaf** at the Conrad in Pacific Place, tel. 2521-3838, also takes a lighter hand with unusual ingredients. All are expensive.

Hakka

The Hakka are descendants of a wandering south Chinese tribe who settled in the New Territories in the 17th century. Theirs is a relatively minor cuisine, but certain popular dishes appear on Hong Kong menus. Hakka specialties like blood soup and fish lips use every bit of the animal. Tastier dishes include salt-baked chicken; duck stuffed with glutinous rice, lotus seeds and chopped meat; and tofu stuffed with minced fish. Try these and more at **New Home Hakka and Seafood Restaurant,** 19 Hanoi Rd., Tsimshatsui, tel. 2366-5876; moderate.

Chiu Chow

Another south China cuisine, based on the cooking of the seafaring people settled around the Shantou (Swatow) coastal area, Chiu Chow cooking is basically Cantonese in style and preparation, but oilier and more strongly flavored. Starters you probably won't desire are coagulated pig blood stir-fried with green onions, and chicken blood, sliced and served with an array of sauces.

---

for banquets and special events.

Bird's nest is the congealed saliva of cliff-dwelling sea swallows, collected from caves of islands in the South China Sea. The clear, tasteless substance is considered nutritious and good for the complexion. It's boiled in chicken stock as a soup, or soaked in rock sugar syrup and served as a dessert.

Shark's fin is similarly tasteless and is generally simmered in chicken broth to give it flavor. Dried fins of all sizes are displayed in restaurants and in the seafood shops of Western, the most expensive installed in locked glass cases. The Chinese taste for shark's fin is wreaking havoc with the world's shark population. Growing demand has pushed the price of fins and tails up to US$100 a pound in the case of the most prized species, the great white shark. Many fishermen now simply cut off the fins and dump the live but helpless animals back into the sea, where they drown, unable to move. Apart from the damage to sharks themselves, which are wonderfully complex creatures with highly developed sensory systems, the decimation of the food chain's top predator is seriously harming marine ecosystems.

A subsidiary aspect is the cult of the aphrodisiac. Business banquets in particular may feature expensive items such as rhino-horn powder or "bullwhip soup" made of bull penis (sometimes the organ of a deer or dog is substituted). Ginseng and bêche-de-mere are other items, and Hong Kong's obsession with cognac is explained in part by the fact that cognac is considered an aphrodisiac, while whiskey is a depressant. Much of this is motivated by the desire to preserve vigor and health, rather than lascivious reasons.

Bullwhip soup is nothing compared to the exotic dishes presented in the Man-Han banquet, a tradition originating from the imperial demand for ever-more refined and unusual fare (the name is an amalgam of "Manchu-Han"). Its standard form involves 365 dishes presented over the course of several days, accompanied by entertainment, gambling, and pretty young women.

While it's impossible to get such a decadent display on the mainland nowadays, Hong Kong still appreciates conspicuous consumption. Rare dishes are presented on gilt-edged or gold-plated dinner services, and consumed with ivory or silver chopsticks. Dishes may include double-boiled white crane with ginseng and fish maw, stewed elephant's trunk, snow frog fat and moose nose, and tongues of ricebirds. The more bizarre the better, it seems. Sliced bear paw is a popular dish (not only at Man-Han banquets), but it's the *left* paw of the bear that's preferred: it's supposed to be softer than the right, as bears are said to lick their left paw more frequently.

The meal is rounded out with the obligatory shark's fin and bird's nest concoctions. The bill might be US$25,000 for a 12-person banquet, and the recent implementation of the CITES treaty prohibiting trade in rare species has rather hampered grocery shopping. Still, chefs at major resturants are prepared, indeed proud, to put on such extravagant events, and several are held in Hong Kong each year.

Specialties include goose simmered in a "mother stock" of chicken, soy, wine, and spices; boiled crab with red rice vinegar; and steamed lobster with tangerine preserves. Chiu Chow chefs have also perfected the cooking of shark's fin and bird's nests, the latter sometimes served sweetened with coconut milk as a dessert. Chiu Chow restaurants serve a dark, strong, slightly bitter tea known as Iron Goddess or Iron Buddha Tea. A type of oolong, it is said to aid digestion, and will keep you up all night if you're not careful.

Golden Island Bird's Nest Chiu Chow offers different varieties of bird's nest soup. There's one at 25 Carnarvon Rd. in Tsimshatsui, and another in Causeway Bay Plaza; 489 Hennessy Rd.; moderate.

New Golden Red Chiu Chow, 13 Prat Ave., Tsimshatsui, tel. 2366-6822, serves a wonderful soyed goose; moderate. Or try **City Chiuchow,** 98 Granville Rd., Tsimshatsui East, tel. 2723-6226; moderate. **Carrianna Restaurant** is famed for sweet and sour fried noodles, sliced goose, and cold crab; moderate. There's one at 1/F 151 Gloucester Rd., Wanchai; another at 2/F 96 Granville Rd., Tsimshatsui.

Beijing

Northern China's cold climate has inspired an oiler and more substantial cuisine. Because wheat flourishes here, steamed breads, noodles, and dumplings supplement rice as a staple. Mutton and lamb are popular, as is cabbage, the sole winter vegetable. Influences from the imperial court are apparent in theatrical touches like *lie mien,* noodle dough stretched out to great lengths to entertain diners.

Specialties include steamed or fried meat dumplings, cold meat appetizer plates, fried onion cakes, and the multi-course banquet built around Peking duck. An air-dried duck is coated with a syrup-soy sauce mixture, then roasted. The first course consists of the crisp skin, which diners wrap into thin pancakes with spring onions or leeks and dip in plum sauce. Next comes the duck meat, and finally a broth made from the bones.

Beggar's chicken is often served in Beijing restaurants, though it actually originated in Hangzhou. The bird is stuffed with pork, black mushrooms, and pickled cabbage, wrapped in lotus leaves, and baked in a coating of wine-soaked clay, which diners then smash with a silver-plated hammer. One day's advance order is recommended.

Hong Kong's Beijing restaurants are a good choice for informal, friendly service. The menu at the noisy, friendly **American Peking** includes Peking duck, dumplings, onion cakes and tasty beggar's chicken. It's at 20 Lockhart Rd., Wanchai, tel. 2527-1000; inexpensive. **Yin King Lau,** 113 Lockhart Rd., Wanchai, serves Beijing and Sichuan food in variously sized portions, and is very reasonable and friendly; inexpensive. For delicious dumplings *(jiaotze),* fried or steamed, go to **Peking Shui Jiao Wong,** 118 Jaffe Rd. and 202 Johnston Rd., Wanchai; inexpensive

Kowloon-side, try **Peking Restaurant,** 227 Nathan Rd., another old-fashioned place with a superb menu; inexpensive. **Spring Deer** 42 Mody Rd., Tsimshatsui, tel. 2723-3673, is another old favorite, famous for its Peking duck; moderate.

Peking Garden offers a wide menu and nightly noodle-making displays. There's one in Alexandra House, 6 Ice House St., Central, tel. 2526-6456, another in Star House, Tsimshatsui, tel. 2735-8211; inexpensive.

Shanghai

Shanghai is China's main seaport, and its oily, sweet, strong-flavored cuisine reflects diverse influences. Considered "warming," it's a favorite in winter. Shanghai restaurants in Hong Kong tend to be cheerfully informal, with immense menus encompassing cuisines of other regions. Specialties include eels, "drunken chicken" cooked in rice wine, and red-fried meats cooked in soy sauce.

Most celebrated are the hairy crabs flown to Hong Kong every fall, advertised on giant signboards posted in front of restaurants. You'll see them displayed in street-side stalls, still alive and trussed with bamboo. Demand always exceeds supply, although the freshwater crabs can run HK$150 apiece in a restaurant (they're much cheaper in the market). They're steamed and eaten with the hands, and accompanied by warmed rice wine. The roe is the most prized part, and is said to be best in males.

Andy's Kitchen is a popular local place with simple, delicious home-cooked Shanghai food at

25 Tung Lo Wan Rd., Causeway Bay, tel. 2890-8137; inexpensive.

Sanno Lo Ching Hing is a busy Shanghai restaurant with all sorts of dishes; also dumplings, noodles, and wonton soup. Find it at 46 Wellington St., Central; inexpensive.

Great Shanghai is a wonderful place to explore Shanghai cuisine, or any other, for that matter. Friendly waiters will guide you through the giant menu. It's at 26 Prat Ave., Tsimshatsui, tel. 2366-8158; inexpensive.

Wu Kong is another old-fashioned, cheerfully crowded restaurant with Shanghai dishes plus Peking duck. Try the famous cold pigeon with wine sauce appetizer. The original is at 27 Nathan Rd., Tsimshatsui, tel. 2366-7244; there's another in Times Square, Causeway Bay, tel. 2506-1018; moderate.

Shanghai Shanghai, in the basement of the Ritz-Carlton Hotel, 3 Connaught Rd. Centra., tel. 2869-0328, is a fun and funky place with authentic mainland decor and good, straightforward food. Expensive.

Sichuan

China's spiciest cuisine relies on chili, fragrant peppercorns, fennel, star anise, coriander, and lots of garlic. Steamed breads absorb the intense flavors of specialties like *mapo doufu* ("pock-marked Grandma's bean curd"), garlicky eggplant, and crispy beef with kumquat. Sichuan smoked duck is seasoned with orange peel and cinnamon, marinated in rice wine, steamed for two hours, then smoked over a fire of camphor wood chips and tea leaves.

At many restaurants the food is several degrees below authentic fieriness, but it remains plenty hot for most diners. Most Sichuan restaurants serve dishes in two or three sizes, depending on the size of the party, so groups can easily sample a range of items.

In Causeway Bay, try the excellent **Szechuan Lau,** 466 Lockhart Rd., tel. 2891-9027, and the more touristy and also good **The Red Pepper** at 7 Lan Fong Rd., tel. 2577-3811. Both are moderate.

Crystal Palace is recommended for its sizzling dishes; try to reserve in advance. It's at 1/F 16 Cameron Rd., Tsimshatsui, tel. 2366-5784; moderate.

Fung Lam is among the older Sichuan restaurants in town: small, authentic and popular with locals, it's at 1/F 21 Prat Ave., Tsimshatsui, tel. 2367-8686; moderate.

Sichuan Garden is more expensive; the extensive menu here includes duck's tongues. There's one in The Landmark, Central, tel. 2521-4433, another at Pacific Place, tel. 2845-7537.

Hunan Garden, another elegant place, showcases the equally spicy food of neighboring Hunan Province—though to tell the truth, the dishes served here are not very spicy. It's at 3/F The Forum, Exchange Square, Central, tel. 2868-2880; moderate.

Vegetarian

Meat in small quantities is practically unavoidable in Chinese restaurants unless you stick to greens and rice—and even then, vegetables may be cooked in a meat-based stock. Try visiting a specialist vegetarian restaurant, or a Buddhist or Taoist temple—many of the big ones have canteens serving superb, inexpensive vegetarian dishes. Religious beliefs support vegetarianism, and many Chinese take periodic meatless days to purify both body and soul.

The vegetarian staple is tofu, dried or fresh. Imitations of roast duck, chicken, pork, and sausage fashioned from tofu are real enough to fool both eyes and tongue. Mushrooms and other fungi (cloud's ear, wood ear) also figure prominently, as do bamboo shoots, hailed as "the queen of vegetables" for their purity and delicacy. A standard dish is *lohan tsai,* "monk's vegetables," featuring tofu, mushrooms, and vegetables.

Most of the following restaurants serve vegetarian dim sum as well, and some do takeout. Marvel at the magic things chefs can do with tofu at one of a trio of excellent vegetarian restaurants: **Wishful Cottage,** 336 Lockhart Rd., Wanchai; **Vegi Food Kitchen,** 8 Cleveland St., Causeway Bay; or **Bodhi,** 384 Lockhart Rd., Wanchai; 56 Cameron Rd., Tsimshatsui; or 32 Lock Rd., Tsimshatsui. All are moderate.

Healthy Mess is a great name for this little place with a wide variety of tofu dishes. It's at 51 Hennessy Rd., Wanchai; inexpensive.

Fat Heung Lam serves veggie Cantonese food, simple and very cheap. Located at 94 Wellington St., Central, tel. 2543-0404; inexpensive.

Kung Tak Lam is a simple place serving delicious Shanghai-style vegetarian food. There are branches at 45 Carnarvon Rd., Tsimshatsui, and 31 Yee Wo St., Causeway Bay. Try the cold Shanhai style noodles with seven different sauces and toppings, or the vegetarian "fish" with pine nuts; inexpensive.

Vegi-Table is difficult to find, tucked away at 1 Tun Wo Lane, but worth seeking out for lunch: self-serve soup and rice, and different entrees every day; inexpensive.

Desserts
Sweet Dynasty at 88 Canton Rd., Tsimshatsui, specializes in Chinese sweets and serves congee, noodles, and dumplings as well; inexpensive.

ASIAN FOOD

When you tire of Chinese, eat your way around the rest of Asia. Japanese restaurants are usually expensive, but the Indian restaurants catering to Hong Kong's large Indian population are real bargains. Most are northern Indian, serving tandoori-cooked meats, chewy unleavened bread *(naan),* and richly spiced meat and vegetable dishes. Malaysian and Indonesian restaurants feature curries and milder dishes flavored with peanuts or coconut milk. Singaporean cooking is similar but incorporates influences from India and China. Then there's fiery, sophisticated Thai cuisine, and milder but equally varied Vietnamese food. The international smorgasbord is rounded out by food from Korea, the Philippines, Sri Lanka, even Nepal.

Indian
A very good bet for an inexpensive meal—every restaurant listed in this category is inexpensive. The real cheapies are the Indian and Pakistani "mess clubs" in Chungking Mansion, where you can get a huge and authentic set meal in a spartan setting for around HK$50. Pay just a few dollars more and the ambience improves. Many Indian restaurants have lunch buffets, so you can sample a range of flavors.

Inexpensive: Wyndham Street in Central is lined with curry clubs, like the excellent **Ashoka** at 57 Wyndham St., tel. 2525-5719. **Gunga Din's Club** is right next door at No. 59, and

HOTPOT AND BARBECUE

A dish served almost exclusively in the winter is hotpot or firepot (*ta pin lo* in Cantonese). Every region has its own variation, but basically diners sit around a communal pot of bubbling soup stock, dipping slices of meat, fish, and vegetables into the "moat" to cook, then into various sauces. The last item to go in is noodles, yielding a delicious bowl of soup as a finale. Hotpot is a fun and very social way to eat.

Most popular is Beijing-style with mutton, which can be sampled in winter months at **Cheung Chuk Lau (Pine and Bamboo),** 30 Leighton Rd., Causeway Bay, tel. 2577-4914, a tremendously popular place which serves dumplings and noodles, too. **Tin Tin Hotpot** is another option, with outlets at 74 Percival St., Causeway Bay, and 16 Cameron Rd., Tsimshatsui.

Mongolian barbecue involves filling a bowl from a buffet of raw veggies, meat, and sauces, and handing it over to the chef to be cooked on the spot. **Kublai's** is an inexpensive/moderate place to try this mix-your-own, all-you-can-eat setup. Locations are One Capitol Place, 18 Luard Rd., Wanchai; 1 Keswick St., Causeway Bay; and 55 Kimberley Rd., Tsimshatsui. The Wanchai restaurant has the advantage of a cyber-café on the premises.

Club Sri Lanka is at 17 Hollywood Road. A little farther down at 11 Lyndhurst Terrace is **Club Lanka II,** a vegetarian version with exceptionally cheap lunch and dinner buffets.

The Curry Pot, 68 Lockhart Rd., Wanchai, serves both northern and southern Indian specialties. **International Curry House,** 26 Tai Wong St. East, Wanchai, is another cheap place for dozens of kinds of very spicy curries.

Branto Snack Bar has "pure veg" South Indian food: idli (small fried cakes), dosa (flat lentil pancakes stuffed with delicious fillings), and special thalis (set meals of rice and various curries and accompaniments). It's at 1/F, 9 Lock Rd., Tsimshatsui. Or try **Woodlands,** at 61 Mody Rd., another all-vegetarian South Indian establishment.

Gaylord, 1/F, 23 Ashley Rd., Tsimshatsui, is slightly more upscale.

Finally, the **Sherpa Himalayan Coffee Shop** at 11 Staunton St., Mid-Levels (just off the escalator) is a pleasant place to hang out, with a full menu of delicious Nepali items that are not as shockingly spicy as Indian food.

Thai

Cheapest and most authentic are the dozen or so Thai restaurants along Kai Tak Road in Kowloon City, near the old airport. Look for **Golden Harvest, Thai Wah,** or **Heng Thai.**

Good Luck Thai, 13 Wing Wah Lane, Lan Kwai Fong, is a tiny place with tables set outside to watch the streetlife. Very inexpensive, especially for Central.

> *Food is heaven.*
> *—Chinese proverb*

Two simple, inexpensive places serving good food are **Thai Delicacy,** 44 Hennessy Rd., Wanchai, tel. 2527-2598; and **Thai Kitchen,** 2/F 68 Canton Road.

Thai Chili Club is wildly popular with expats: the management flies in bushels of chili peppers from Thailand twice a week. It's at 88 Lockhart Rd., Wanchai, tel. 2527-2872; inexpensive-moderate.

In Tsimshatsui, try **Her Thai** in China Hong Kong City, which has outdoor seating and great harbor views; inexpensive.

Golden Elephant has an innovative take on Thai food; a big menu and lunch and dinner buffets. There are branches in Harbour City in Tsimshatsui, tel. 2735-0733, Pacific Place in Admiralty, tel. 2522-8696, and Times Square in Causeway Bay, tel. 2506-1333. Moderate.

Wyndham Street Thai is a pricey upmarket place with delicious food at 38 Wyndham St., Central, tel. 2869-6216. Moderate-expensive.

Indonesian/Malaysian/Filipino

Tiny **Java Rijsttafel,** 38 Hankow Rd., Tsimshatsui, tel. 2367-1230, has cramped quarters (it's best to reserve a table) but a big menu, including a 16-dish rijsttafel for HK$140.

All of the following restaurants are inexpensive, starting with several restaurants behind the Sogo Department Store in Causeway Bay, including the **Restaurant Indonesia** at 514 Lockhart Road.

Cinta serves a range of Indonesian and Filipino food, and puts on an inexpensive lunch buffet. It's at 10 Fenwick St., Wanchai.

Authentically spicy food can be had at **Indonesian Restaurant,** 28 Leighton Rd., Causeway Bay, and **Bali,** 10 Nanking St., Tsimshatsui.

At **Banana Leaf Curry House,** spicy Indian and Malaysian dishes are indeed served on a banana leaf, and you can eat with your fingers. There's one at 440 Jaffe Rd., Causeway Bay, and another at 3/F Golden Crown Court, 68 Nathan Rd., Tsimshatsui.

Mabuhay, 11 Minden Ave., Tsimshatsui, is a very cheap place for Filipino stews and such.

Korean

The specialty is *bulgogi,* in which diners grill marinated meat and seafood at the table; it runs around HK$90-150 per person. All the restaurants listed in this category are inexpensive or the low end of moderate.

3-5 Korean Restaurant, 6 Ashley Rd., Tsimshatsui, is a tiny place with *bulgogi* and lots of side dishes.

Koreana serves creative Korean food in a pleasant cafe setting at 55 Paterson St., Causeway Bay, tel. 2577-5145.

Korea House, a noisy, popular place at 119 Connaught Rd., tel. 2544-0007, has a notably huge array of kimchee (pickled cabbage).

Arirang offers *bulgogi* and a good fixed-price lunch; it's at 2/F, The Gateway, Canton Road, Tsimshatsui, tel. 2956-3288, and in Times Square, Causeway Bay, tel. 2506-3298.

Japanese

While Japanese food has a reputation as expensive, there are an amazing number of cheap places to be found, starting with Japanese fast-food:

Genryoku Sushi Express is a fast-food sushi joint which does takeout sushi boxes at HK$8 a piece—great lunchtime fare. There are shops in Worldwide Plaza in Central, Jaffe Rd. in Causeway Bay, and Chatham Road South in Tsimshatsui.

Gomenbo is unremarkable, but the setting and service are great for the price—HK$50 for a set meal, HK$25 for noodles. There are several outlets, including 8 Wyndham St., Central.

Gomitori, very popular with visiting Japanese, serves virtually every part of the chicken, very cheap (HK$24-38). The menus on the wall are in Japanese and Chinese only, so ask the waiters for help. It's in the basement at 92 Granville Rd., Tsimshatsui East.

Tomokazu at 17 Percival St., Causeway Bay, has good food and exceptionally good-value lunch specials; inexpensive.

Yorohachi is a cut above, in both quality and price (which is moderate). It's at 5 Lan Kwai Fong, tel. 2524-1251. Down the street is **Tokio Joe** at 16 Lan Kwai Fong, tel. 2525-1889, serving grilled dishes and noodles, big bento boxes, and a sushi bar; moderate-expensive.

Benkay, tel. 2521-3344, features Kyoto-style cuisine, sushi, and teppanyaki in a calm setting in the basement of The Landmark, Central; expensive.

Some of the best Japanese restaurants are in hotels. Try **Unkai** in the Sheraton (moderate), or, if price is no object, expensive **Nadaman** in both the Island and Kowloon Shangri-La.

Vietnamese
Saigon Beach is a tiny hole-in-the-wall at 66 Lockhart Rd., Wanchai. Another fine choice is **Perfume River Vietnamese** at 89 Percival St., Causeway Bay, tel. 2576-2240, a popular place with an extensive menu. Both are inexpensive.

W's Paris 13th serves French-Vietnamese food in a spacious dining room with a view at Toyo Mall, 94 Granville Rd., Tsimshatsui East, tel. 2723-6369; inexpensive.

Moving upscale, there's the very popular mainstream **Golden Bull** in Harbour City, tel. 2730-4866, and New World Centre, Tsimshatsui, tel. 2369-4617, and in Times Square; moderate.

At the elegant **Indochine**, 30 D'Aguilar St., Lan Kwai Fong, tel. 2869-7399, the exquisite food blends Vietnamese and French influences. Expensive.

Pan-Asian
If your companions can't agree on what to eat, head to one of these restaurants for an international feast.

Tiger's, in the basement of Pacific Place, blends cuisines from Vietnam, Thailand, India, Burma in an ornate Eastern setting; moderate.

The Viceroy has added Thai, Vietnamese and Indonesian dishes to its previously Indian menu. Great lunch buffet. It's at 2/F Sun Hung Kai Centre, 30 Harbour Rd., Wanchai, tel. 2827-7777; moderate.

The **Peak Cafe,** tel. 2849-7868, serves a range of Asian and Western dishes—the Asian are best—in a pleasing colonial setting at Victoria Gap, right across from the upper Peak Tram station; moderate.

It's hard to choose between the Peak Café and **Café Deco** in the Peak Galleria, tel. 2849-5111. The latter is an Art Deco concoction with stunning views and decor, and a very good Asian-cum-international menu; high-moderate.

The eclectic menu at **Roy's at the China Max** combines cuisines from California to Japan—call it Pacific Rim fusion food. It's at 11/F Times Square, Causeway Bay, tel. 2506-2282, moderate.

Stanley's Oriental is worth the trip out to the island's south side. The restaurant blends Thai, Chinese, and Indian foods in a lovely setting at 90B Stanley Main St., tel. 2813-9988; moderate.

Spices, at 109 Repulse Bay Rd., tel. 2812-2711, serves all sorts of Asian dishes in a beautifully decorated setting; there's an outdoor terrace too. Moderate; the weekday lunch buffet is an especially good deal.

At **Felix**, 28/F The Peninsula, Salisbury Rd., tel. 2366-6251, the fantastic views are merely the icing on the cake. Even the notably good East-West fusion cuisine is second to the theatrical decor. It's expensive, but save up and go anyway—it's an event. Open for dinner only.

WESTERN FOOD

You can get anything from hamburgers to haute cuisine: enchiladas, jambalaya, Scottish smoked salmon, Swiss raclette—though you'll pay for the more exotic items. The best and most expensive Western restaurants are at the big hotels, where tabs are driven up by the high price of drinks, especially wine. The fixed-price lunches here are a notably good value, maybe one-third the price of an a la carte dinner.

French
Au Trou Normand, 6 Carnarvon Rd., Tsimshatsui, tel. 2366-8754, is a mercifully casual French restaurant. The HK$110 lunch buffet is an especially good deal. Moderate.

Cafe de Paris excels in salads; it's at 2/F California Tower, 30 D'Aguilar St., Lan Kwai Fong, tel. 2524-7521.

Papillon, tel. 2526-5965, is a tiny, unpretentious yet highly romantic place just off Lan Kwai Fong at 8 Wo On Lane, with excellent food and a good-value set lunch; expensive.

Gaddi's in The Peninsula has been ranked the best restaurant in town since 1953. Some say it's overrated, but the French cooking is exquisite, the wine cellar huge, and the fixed-price lunch surprisingly reasonable. Rivals are the Mediterranean cuisine of **Plume** in the Regent (with fantastic harbor views), the elegant nouvelle Française of **Margaux** at the Kowloon Shangri-La, **Restaurant Petrus** at the Island Shangri-La, and the **Pierrot** at the Mandarin. A dinner for two with wine at any of these can easily exceed HK$2500.

Italian

Two old standbys are **La Bella Donna** in the Shui On Centre, 8 Harbour Rd., Wanchai, tel. 2802-9907, and **La Taverna,** an Italian bistro with an extensive menu and two locations: 24 Ice House Street, Central, tel. 2522-8904, and 34 Ashley Rd., Tsimshatsui, tel. 369-1945. Both are moderate.

The chic café/bar **La Dolce Vita,** 9 Lan Kwai Fong, tel. 2810-9333, has exquisite light food, and a menu concluding with a dozen kinds of gelato; moderate. Down the street at 34 D'Aguilar St. is the more standard **Ristorante II Meracto,** with a great antipasto bar, pasta and pizza; moderate.

The Pizzeria in the Kowloon Hotel, 19 Nathan Rd., Tsimshatsui, tel. 2369-8698, is a moderately priced place for pizza and pasta, with notably good lunch specials.

Grappa's is a casual, popular restaurant in Pacific Place (the one in Ocean Centre is not nearly as good). Moderate-expensive. **Rigoletto** serves standard Northern Italian cuisine—good pizza, pastas, and grilled meats—at 14 Fenwick St., Wanchai, tel. 2527-7144; expensive.

There are plenty of very **expensive** places. Among the best is **Va Bene,** with a good bar, great ambience, and wonderful Venetian cuisine. It's at 58 D'Aguilar St., Lan Kwai Fong, tel. 2845-5577. Its sister, the just slightly cheaper trattoria-style **Tutto Bene,** is in Tsimshatsui at 7 Knutsford Terrace, just off Observatory Road, tel. 2316-2116. Then there's **Tutto Meglio,** serving rustic Tuscan cuisine based on olive oil and

tomatoes, at 33 D'Aguilar St., Lan Kwai Fong, tel. 2869-7833. **Grissini** in the Grand Hyatt Hotel in Wanchai, tel. 2588-1234, serves superb Milanese food in an elegant setting. **Nicholini's** is even more formal and equally highly rated; it's in the Conrad Hotel at Pacific Place, tel. 2521-3838.

German

Weinstube is an inexpensive winebar at 22 Ashley Rd., Tsimshatsui, serving simple meals, sausages, and such.

Delicatessen Corner in the basement of the Holiday Inn at 50 Nathan Road has a large meat-laden German menu (pork knuckle, sauerkraut, dumplings) food, and an excellent takeaway counter for breads, pastries, cold cuts and salads. Breakfast also; inexpensive-moderate.

Mozart Stub'n, 8 Glenealy, Central, tel. 2522-1763, is a lovely small place featuring lightly and wonderfully prepared Austrian cuisine and superb souffles, expensive.

Spanish

Local efforts at tapas bars tend to be disappointing, but **El Cid,** 14 Knutsford Terrace, Tsimshatsui, tel. 2312-1898, does a good job with 50 varieties of tapas and meals as well. There's another at Shop C, Cleveland St., Causeway Bay; moderate.

Rico's at 44 Robinson Rd. is another good choice, and inexpensive too; ride the Mid-Levels escalator up.

La Bodega, 31 Wyndham St., tel. 2877-5472, has a tapas and wine bar in the basement, Spanish-influenced food above; moderate.

American

American food is popular and becoming only more so, with a number of new restaurants opening in the past few years. **Dan Ryan's Chicago Bar and Grill** serves giant sandwiches, Hong Kong's best hamburgers, apple pie, and steak-oriented dinners. There's one in Ocean Terminal, Tsimshatsui, tel. 2735-6111, and another at Pacific Place, tel. 2845-4600; moderate.

L.A. Cafe has a West Coast slant to its generous servings, a popular bar, and widescreen TVs delivering sports events. It's in the Lippo Centre, Admiralty, tel. 2526-6863. **The Jump**

BREAKFAST, BRUNCH, LUNCH, AND TEA

Breakfast

The traditional Chinese breakfast is congee or *jook,* a bland porridge of soaked rice with the addition of salty bits of seafood or meat. Accompanied by deliciously greasy fried dough-sticks, it's served at *dai pai dongs* throughout the day.

If you can't face congee and have ruled out dim sum, you probably need a good injection of caffeine. **Pacific Coffee Company** in the Bank of America Tower in Admiralty is a genuine Seattle transplant, with powerful latte and cappuccino, baked goods, and an assortment of magazines and newspapers for browsing. Other outlets are in Quarry Bay, Pacific Place, and CitySuper in Times Square. **Uncle Russ** is a tiny stand-up gourmet coffee bar with baked goods to go. There's one at the corner of Canton and Peking roads in Tsimshatsui, and others in Times Square in Causeway Bay and at 30 D'Aguilar St. in Central. **Espresso Americano,** G/F Star House on Salisbury Road, is a supremely convenient location for a mostly take-away business.

For a cheap breakfast, HK$15-25, Oliver's Super Sandwiches, or the widespread **Delifrance** chain for French pastries and coffee plus the morning papers. More substantial breakfasts for around HK$45 are available at the **Mall Cafe** in the Salisbury YMCA, the **Can Do** restaurant chain, **Jim's Eurodiner** at 5 Stanley St., Central, or **Cable Car Coffee Shop** in Barnton Court, Harbour City, and in the Peninsula Centre in Tsimshatsui East. **Sherpa Himalayan Coffee Shop** at 11 Stuanton St., Mid-Levels, has *puri tarkari* and other subcontinental delicacies, as well as reasonably priced Western breakfasts.

If you've overslept, **Al's Diner** in Lan Kwai Fong serves breakfast daily from noon to 1 a.m. **Dan Ryan's** serves breakfast on weekends 9-11:30 a.m.

All the big hotels sponsor fancy breakfast buffets 7-10 a.m. for around HK$150. Spreads go beyond eggs and toast into luxuries like papaya, smoked salmon, and flakey croissants. Eat strategically, and it will take you well past lunch. The **Island Shangri-La** in Pacific Place and the **Royal Garden** in Tsimshatsui East are good choices.

Sunday Brunch

Late sleepers can try the HK$275 brunch buffet at the **Mandarin Grill,** served 11 a.m.-3 p.m.

The American Pie in Lan Kwai Fong puts out a well-laden brunch table starting at noon, with lots of delectable desserts and a wide selection of coffees.

Post 97, 9 Lan Kwai Fong, is open Sunday from 11 a.m. for a leisurely brunch.

Cyrano atop the Island Shangri-La in Pacific Place is a lovely place for brunch at HK$198, or try the HK$280 brunch in the **Lobster Bar.P>**

Grissini in the Grand Hyatt in Wanchai puts out an unusual spread for HK$295. Lavish antipasti and dessert tables; noon-2:30 p.m.

Bostonian in the Hong Kong Renaissance, 8 Peking Rd., Tsimshatsui, is a relaxed place for brunch, HK$198, served 11:30 a.m.-3 p.m.

The Verandah Restaurant at 109 Repulse Bay Rd., tel. 2812-2722, (reservations a must) preserves a bit of colonial lesiure with its HK$250 champagne brunch 11 a.m.-2:30 p.m.

Lunch Buffets

Many hotel restaurants put on daily lunch buffets for HK$150-200. At minimum these encompass Western, Japanese, and Chinese food. Prices and crowds increase on Sunday and public holidays. Check the "What's On" section of the *South China Morning Post* for current listings. Indian and Thai

features similarly casual American dining and a huge drink list; it's a very popular nightspot after 10 p.m. It's at 7/F Causeway Bay Plaza II, 463 Lockhart Rd., tel. 2832-7122. Both are moderate.

Planet Hollywood 3 Canton Rd., Tsimshatsui, is part of a chain owned by a consortium of American movie stars. It combines cosmopolitan fast food—burgers, fajitas, salads—with a film memorabilia theme. Dine within view of a cyborg from *Terminator 2,* or Bruce Lee's leather jacket, or the knife from *Psycho.* Just

down the street at 100 Canton Rd. is the **Hard Rock Cafe,** another chain, this one featuring rock 'n' roll memorabilia and expensive hamburgers. There's another in Swire House on Pedder St., Central. All of these are moderate.

Lan Kwai Fong has plenty of American places. **Al's Diner** at 37 D'Aguilar St. is outfitted with leatherette booths and a Wurlitzer playing bad rock 'n' roll; it serves hot dogs, sandwiches, burgers, banana splits, and all-day breakfasts; moderate.

restaurants are also good bets for inexpensive lunch buffets.

Most famous is the enormous international spread at **La Ronda,** the revolving restaurant atop the Hotel Furama-Kempinski, tel. 2525-5111. Lunch is HK$230 from noon-2:30 p.m.; there's a HK$280 dinner buffet 6:30-11 p.m.

At Pacific Place, coffee shops in both the **Marriot** and the **Island-Shangri-La** host notable upmarket buffets.

The Oasis, 8/F New World Harbour View Hotel, Wanchai, has an excellent weekday lunch buffet centered on healthy food, including a great salad bar.

Lunch buffet options in Tsimshatsui include the Sheraton's **Sidewalk Cafe** or the HK$118 Asian buffet at **Spice Market** in The Prince in Harbour City. The lunch buffet in the coffee shop of The Marco Polo is notably inexpensive, only HK$98 on weekdays.

For salad bars, try the **Lau Ling Bar** in the Furama-Kempinski, or **San Francisco Steak House** at 7 Ashley Rd., Tsimshatsui.

fresh fish at the market

Afternoon Tea

High tea is not a meal as much as an institution, a civilized way to revive after a long day. Sink into a plush armchair and enjoy the quiet. If you're not careful, the cakes and cucumber sandwiches and scones with clotted cream will ruin your dinner. Too bad. Standard hours for tea are 3-6 p.m.

The grandest setting for high tea is the gilt rococo lobby of **The Peninsula,** where a string quartet plays from an upper balcony. The fare is not quite as elegant as some other places, though. High tea is served 3-6 p.m. for HK$165.

Locals prefer tea in the Mandarin Oriental's **Clipper Lounge,** where rich *tai-tais* parade their Chanel suits and a Filipino combo plays popular music. Abundant tea fare is HK$70 for one, HK$120 for two.

The **Tiffin Lounge** at the Grand Hyatt puts on an extensive, elegant tea buffet for HK$125 from 3-6 p.m.

The extensive HK$128 buffet tea in the **Marriott Lobby Lounge** in Pacific Place will take you well into dinner.

The **Lobby Lounge** at the Island Shangri-La serves tea for HK$120 from 3-5:30 p.m.

The California Entertainment Building at 34 D'Aguilar St. is jammed with restaurants, starting with **California,** tel. 2521-1345. This popular nightspot includes a good if trendy restaurant serving excellent Cal-Mex food (great hamburgers) in a surreal setting of multiple TVs, blacklights, and hair-flipping blondes; moderate. **Tony Roma's** on the first floor dishes out enormous slabs of gloriously messy BBQ ribs in five flavors, tel. 2521-0292; moderate-expensive. **The American Pie** on the fourth floor has an outdoor balcony and all sorts of salads and sandwiches, but dessert is its raison d'etre. Try the banana cream or mango lime pies. There's another outlet in Times Square Galleria, Causeway Bay; inexpensive-moderate.

Trio's, just around the corner from LKF at 9 Wo On Lane, tel. 2877-9773, is a cozy New-England style place serving steak and lobster and cheaper items too; moderate-expensive.

Steaks

W's Entrecote in Times Square, tel. 2506-0133, specializes in steak: one kind only (you choose the size), served with fries, bread, and salad; moderate.

San Francisco Steak House features beef, seafood, and a good salad bar; it's at 7 Ashley Rd., Tsimshatsui; moderate.

The Steak House at the Regent, tel. 2721-2111, has perhaps the best salad bar in town, and the dessert buffet isn't bad either; expensive.

Mexican

Mexican food doesn't get much attention in Hong Kong: the best bet for nachos or a fajita may be West Coast restaurants like California or L.A. Café.

The Mexican Association serves reasonably good food, sangria by the pitcher, and margaritas. It's at 11/F Hankow Centre, 1C Middle Rd., Tsimshatsui, tel. 2367-4535; inexpensive-moderate.

Zona Rosa is a pricier way to enjoy southwest and Tex-Mex cuisine—call it Nouvelle Mexicane. It's at 2/F, 1 Lan Kwai Fong, tel. 2801-5885; moderate/expensive.

Aussie/British

Brett's Seafood Specialists, 86 Lockhart Rd., Wanchai, is a plain cafe serving a big, basic chunk of fish with chips or rice; inexpensive.

Harry Ramsden's is a branch of the famous Yorkshire fish 'n chips shop, bringing mushy peas and Yorkshire bitter to Hong Kong. There are two parts to the restaurant at 213 Queen's Rd. East, Wanchai; an inexpensive self-serve café and a more formal restaurant.

Notably good pub food is served at the Irish bar **Delaney's,** at 3 Prat Ave., Tsimshatsui, and 2/F One Capitol Place, 18 Luard Rd., Wanchai; inexpensive.

Classiest is **Bentley's,** a spinoff of the famous London club, in Prince's Building, Central, tel. 2868-0881; moderate-expensive.

Wildlife

The Cantonese are not the only people to eat everything that walks, swims, or flies, as proven by the following: **Mr. Rhino,** 3/F 1 D'Aguilar St., Central, has bizarre dishes like ostrich medallions, crocodile kebabs, and springbok. At **City Jungle,** 24 Percival St., Causeway Bay, the heavily Canadian menu is interspersed with kangaroo, emu, and venison dishes. Both are moderate.

Diners at **King of Snake,** 24 Percival St., Causeway Bay, can watch public executions of snakes on the restaurant's floor before consuming snake soup and less exotic dishes like roast meat and rice; inexpensive.

Miscellania

Bacchus, in the basement at 8 Hennessy Rd., Wanchai. Mediterranean cuisine, plate-smashing allowed on Tuesday; other nights are quieter. Expensive.

Desert Sky specialises in Mid-Eastern food, including roast baby goat, a previously unfulfilled niche in Hong Kong cuisine. It's at 36 Elgin St., Mid-Levels; take the escalator up; expensive.

How about an Austrian, Finnish, and Greek take-away restaurant—most likely the only one in the world. **O'Wien** at 5 Staunton St., Mid-Levels, fits the bill; inexpensive

Cafes and Light Food

La Cite, a Parisian café in the basement of Pacific Place, is a good place to hide out for a while and relax, with a selection of light dishes and a very reasonable fixed menu; inexpensive-moderate.

The Original Health Café is a vegetarian's delight, with good three-course set lunches and a vast selection of veggie juices. It's at 27/F Wing Shan Tower, 173 Des Voeux Rd. Central; inexpensive.

The Source of Health, 2 D'Aguilar St., Central, has extensive organic and vegetarian fare, good breads and baked items, sandwiches, and vegetarian items. Take-away counter too. Inexpensive, especially for Central.

The Big Apple has an extensive sandwich listing plus entrees, a salad bar, and a deli counter. It's in the Ruttonjee Centre on Duddell Street, Central; inexpensive.

Midnight Express is a tiny place serving kebabs, samosas, and curries to the LKF late-night crowd. It's at 3 Lan Kwai Fong and is open till 3 a.m., 6 a.m. on Fri.-Sat. nights; inexpensive.

Post 97, an ultra-chic café/bar, serves interesting light food, desserts, and all sorts of excellent coffee. Open 8:30 a.m.-2 a.m., 'round the clock on weekends, it's at 9 Lan Kwai Fong, Central, tel. 2810-9333; moderate.

Wyndham St. Deli at 36 Wyndham St. is a friendly café with a delicious array of specials, sandwiches and salads; moderate

Joyce Cafe in the Galleria at 9 Queen's Rd., Central, is a designer restaurant serving elegantly healthy meals and salads; open until 7:30 p.m. weekdays. There's another outlet at Exchange Square, with a take-away counter and a small deli. Moderate-expensive.

Big John, at 17 Lock Rd., Tsimshatsui, is a simple, small cafe with a surprisingly large range of sandwiches, salads, specials, and desserts; espresso and cappuccino too. Open only till 5:30 p.m.; very inexpensive.

Coffee Shops

Some days, what's needed is not adventure but an unintimidating, ordinary coffee shop with good air-conditioning. The following fit the bill:

Can Do serves "bloody good cheap Chinese food" and Western food too. Branches are at 37 Cameron Rd., Tsimshatsui, and 78 Johnston Rd. and 139 Hennessy Rd. in Wanchai; inexpensive.

The **Mall Cafeteria** at the Salisbury YMCA has a three-course set lunch for HK$50, though the food is nothing to get excited about. The YMCA's fourth-floor dining room is a little classier but still convenient and moderately priced. Both are inexpensive.

Singapore Restaurant is a funky, basic place with a soda fountain and a menu that covers Western, Malaysian, and Chinese food. It's at 23 Ashley Rd., Tsimshatsui; inexpensive.

Jim's Eurodiner is a bright, spotless cafe serving decent if dull fare. There's one at 5 Stanley St., Central and another in Cityplaza, Taikoo Shing; inexpensive.

Queen's Cafe is a local classic, founded and run by White Russian immigrants and recently relocated to Hysan Avenue in Causeway Bay. Its inexpensive set lunches and dinners draw crowds; try the borscht and/or the excellent raisin bread.

Jimmy's Kitchen is a 1920s transplant of the famous Shanghai restaurant for merchent seamen, with a menu vast enough to satisfy anyone (bangers and mash, corned beef and

cabbage?) It's at 29 Ashley Rd., Tsimshatsui, and 1 Wyndham St., Central; moderate-expensive.

Hotel coffee shops are always reassuringly tame retreats (see the buffet listings in the special topic "Breakfast, Brunch, Lunch, and Tea" for more on this). The **Grand Cafe** in Wanchai's Grand Hyatt gets top ratings for its elegant setting and innovative menu. In Tsimshatsui, the Regent Hotel's glassed-in **Harbourside** projects out over the water for fantastic views. The menu in the elegant lobby of **The Peninsula** is not nearly as pricey as you'd expect. All are moderate.

Fast Food

Fast food restaurants are tremendously crowded around lunchtime, but that's the price you pay for a cheap, quick meal and an air-conditioned seat.

Hong Kong's **McDonald's** are among the busiest in the worldwide chain. Adapting to local culture, McDonald's markets "McLai Sees" at Chinese New Year—gift certificates substituting for the traditional *lai see* packets of lucky money. There are branches at 37 Queen's Rd., Central; 302 Hennessy Rd., Wanchai; 46 Yee Woo St., Causeway Bay; and all over Tsimshatsui, including 2 Cameron Rd., 21 Granville Rd., 12 Peking Rd., and 3 Salisbury Road. Also on the list are **Wendy's, Burger King, Jack in the Box, Kentucky Fried Chicken, Pizza Hut,** and local chains like **Cafe de Coral** and **Fairwood,** neither of which can truly be recommended.

A few fast-food chains deserve special mention. **Oliver's Super Sandwiches** charges HK$20-32 for big sandwiches, and serves salads and baked potatoes too. You'll find outlets everywhere, including Exchange Square, Prince's Building, and Pacific Place in Central; Gloucester Road in Wanchai; and Ocean Centre and Granville Road in Tsimshatsui. **Delifrance** is another classy enterprise, selling French pastries, set breakfasts, sandwiches, and coffee. Shops are at Queensway Plaza, Admiralty; Worldwide House in Central; and at 20 Carnarvon Rd., Tsimshatsui.

Local versions of fast food begin with the open-air *dai pai dongs.* Independent hawkers used to sell delicious cheap food on the street in Central until the Urban Council decided they were unsanitary and in the way. Office workers must now cram into restaurants, or settle for polystyrene takeout boxes of rice-and-dish. This stuff is cheap and good enough, but avoid the gluey, awful Chinese fast-food at chains like Maxim's.

Big shopping centers often have fast-food courts, usually in the lower level and frequently featuring Chinese, Thai, and Malaysian food. Try the food courts at **Ocean Terminal** or **Silvercord Centre** in Tsimshatsui, or the 24-hour **IFJ Food Plaza** in the basement of Chungking Mansion. **Seibu Food Hall** in Pacific Place houses a number of upscale little establishments, like the **Gastro Primo Sandwich Bar.** Sogo in Causeway Bay has a Japanese fast food emporium in its basement, but best is the bright, pleasant Food Hall in **CitySuper,** Times Square, where diners slurp down giant bowls of ramen and other Japanese delights.

Takeout pizza can be obtained from **Numero Uno**—thick crust or thin, delivered by moped. Look in the phone book for the branch nearest you. **Marco Polo Pizza Gourmet,** 23 Lan Kwai Fong, Central, tel. 2868-1013, also delivers, and there's a Domino's Pizza chain too.

SHOPPING AND MARKETS

Local supermarket chains like **Park'N'Shop** and **Wellcome** provide the fixings for picnic fare or cheap meals. Bakeries sell fluffy bread, rolls, buns, and cream-filled cakes: easiest are the do-it-yourself operations with tongs and trays.

Delicatessen chains include the tony **Lucullus** and **Oliver's Delicatessen** (there's one in Ocean Centre, Tsimshatsui, another in Prince's Building, Central). **Seibu Food Hall** in the basement of Pacific Place is an upper-class super-

market with an elegant takeout section. **Daimaru Household Square** and **Sogo** in Causeway Bay both have big supermarkets with Japanese food and takeouts. The supermarket in **City-Super** in the basement of Times Square, Causeway Bay, is a truly incredible shopping experience, with edibles from arond the world.

In Tsimshatsui, **Delicatessen Corner** in the basement of the Holiday Inn Golden Mile has a deli counter with carryout pate, lunchmeat, pastries, and excellent bread.

Street Markets

Street markets are among Hong Kong's most interesting sights, and make shopping for fresh produce fun. Pick out what you want and have it weighed on the hand-held balance. Produce is sold by the catty, equivalent to 1.3 pounds or 600 grams. Price per catty is written on cards (usually in Chinese); it helps to have a sense of the going rate, but sellers are usually honest. You'll pay a lot more for fruit from stalls in Tsimshatsui.

Look for exotic seasonal fruits like the spikey durian, the subject of much hyperbole regarding its "fetid, exciting reek." Other seasonal fruits are litchi, which look like large hard-skinned strawberries but have translucent sweet fruit, papaya, mango, giant jackfruit, the hairy rambutan, purplish mangosteens, red-and-white longan, and yellow-green carambola or star fruit, with its crisp, juicy flesh. The pomelo, a giant citrus, is a winter favorite; it tastes somewhat like a grapefruit.

If you enjoy vegetable shopping, look for giant winter melon (which perversely appears only in summer), corrugated small bitter melon, hairy taro, neatly bundled soybean sprouts, two-foot-long green beans, tubular lotus root, and all kinds of mysterious greens.

SHOPPING

Consumerism is Hong Kong's most popular sport, and *the* major form of entertainment for tourists. The typical tourist spends over half of his or her budget on shopping, pumping HK$17 billion a year into the local economy.

Professional shoppers visit Hong Kong expressly for the world-class shopping, arriving with only a carry-on bag and leaving with suitcases full of bargains (they buy the luggage in Hong Kong, too). This approach works best if you're ordinarily a big spender and can gloat over the killing you've made on custom-made copies of designer clothes, furniture, and jewelry.

Less professional shoppers can benefit as well. Bargains are easiest to find in clothing, luggage, and optical goods. Shop for cameras and electronic goods at your own risk: there are too many ripoff artists in Tsimshatsui to make these items a good deal.

Consumerism presses many of Hong Kong's buttons—the urge for status, the urge to get ahead, the urge to be out in public amid a cheerful crowd. There is a tremendous variety of goods, among the widest selections in the world, crammed into small row shops, modern shopping malls, elegant hotel arcades, department stores, boutiques, emporiums, and open-air markets. The acquisitive urge fairly assaults you upon stepping off the airplane. Shopping in Hong Kong is intoxicating and addictive, a supreme example of capitalism run amok.

The phenomenon centers around the huge flow of goods moving in and out of Hong Kong. Cheap labor, linked to an outstanding financial, transport, and communication infrastructure, has attracted foreign manufacturers, especially in garments, plastics, and electronics. Overruns for the unpredictable world market are sold in the local marketplace at a fraction of their normal price.

In addition, Hong Kong is a duty-free port, and charges no VAT or import taxes. Most locally made goods cost 30% less than in the U.S. or Europe. Some items are even less here than in their country of origin, notably Japanese electronic gear and photo equipment (but then, Japan has never been known for its bargain prices).

Hong Kong's reputation as a bargain paradise is tarnishing, however. With prime retail rents 130% higher than Tokyo or New York, it now ranks as one of the most expensive cities in the world for merchants, and high shop overheads have inevitably driven up prices.

Still, international surveys consistently rank Hong Kong top among major cities for shopping bargains, with prices 30-50% below the average for clothing, watches, gold necklaces, and video cameras. And sales are still climbing, boosted by an influx of wealthy Asian shoppers: first the Japanese, then the Taiwanese, and most recently mainland Chinese.

STRATEGY AND WARNINGS

Bargaining

Shopping in the West is largely a matter of passive acquisition. Bargaining transforms it into an active skill. A good bargainer steps into the role like an actor, and never takes the game too seriously. Bargaining in Asian societies is business: it's also a battle of wits and a source of entertainment. Finding good deals in Hong Kong will to a large extent depend on your bargaining skills.

Prices are fixed in department stores, hotel shops, chains, and boutiques, and increasingly in other types of shops as well. If there's no price tag, as in street markets and smaller shops, expect to bargain. A very mild form of bargaining is to ask "What kind of discount can you give me on this?" or "What's your best price?".

A few basic rules apply. Establish a reasonable price range for a particular item by visiting three or four different shops *before* you buy. Fixed-price department stores can also provide indications, though prices tend to be 10-20% higher than in smaller shops.

Assume that prices are negotiable unless a sign states otherwise. Aim for a 20-40% discount off the asking price—less in arcade shops, more in traditional areas like outdoor markets.

Discounts on jewelry can run up to 60-70%, but don't bargain with tailors, lest they cut corners on the finished product. In street markets, bargaining needs to be faster and more ferocious.

Having done your research and targeted a likely place, stay light. Try to establish personal contact with the seller. Drop the names of mutual acquaintances if possible; present him with your business card; make small talk; be civil and charming. Attitude is all-important: a patient, personal approach shows that you know the rules of the game.

State precisely what you want, and show that you mean business (saying "I will pay cash" often helps.) Never, ever make the first offer, despite a probable invitation to do so. Ask the seller for his best price, and respond with a counteroffer based on your previous research. If you haven't done that research, try offering 40% below the first price, and work your way up from here slowly. Set a mental ceiling of what you'll pay for the item and stick to it. As you approach it, appear increasingly disappointed but firm. Take your time. Look at other items; don't give away your attattchment to a particular one. Play around with the calculator and make a final offer. If he won't budge, you can try to get him to throw in a few small extras to sweeten the deal.

When to give in depends on your assessment of the item's value to you personally. Often the HK$50 gap remaining between you is not worth the hassle of going to another shop and starting the process all over again.

Scams

Be alert to the point of suspicion, especially when shopping for expensive items. HKTA recommends shopping only at stores that belong to the HKTA Merchants Association (identified by a sticker with the HKTA red junk logo). Members are required to maintain ethical standards, provide value for money, and promptly rectify valid complaints. HKTA has no legal responsibility to enforce this, but will investigate complaints involving members. Shopping at HKTA members is good advice—except that there are several hundred HKTA member shops, and several tens of thousands of stores. Also note that HKTA members don't necessarily offer the lowest prices.

Aggressive Tsimshatsui merchants often try to bully customers into a sale. In one case a shopkeeper leapt over the counter and thrust a ballpoint pen up the nose of an indecisive customer—a story you will well believe after meeting some of these guys.

A common trick is to promise an apparently good deal, take the customer's credit card, then try to hook him or her into buying a more expensive item. The salesman may even refuse to return the card! In such a situation, walk out of the shop and immediately inform the police and HKTA; cancel the card if necessary. In another case, a customer was persuaded to sign several blank credit card slips for goods to be shipped to him. He returned home to find the HK$30,000 in promised goods—and debits to his account totalling HK$270,000.

If after purchasing an item you find, or suspect, you've been taken, go back to the shop and explain the problem. The shopkeeper's attitude should soon tell you if a problem was an honest mistake or a deliberate ripoff. Exchanges may be given if an item is defective, but refunds are rare. If problems remain, contact HKTA's Membership Department, tel. 2801-7278. If the shop is a member, they can lean on the merchant; if not, they or you can pass the complaint on to the government's Consumer Council, tel. 2304-1234, though don't expect anything to result.

Precautions

It's a jungle out there, especially in the tourist ghetto of Tsimshatsui—*especially* in the camera and electronics shops, though jewelry, antiques, and watches are also frequently misrepresented. The first rule: **shop around.** Compare prices at department stores, boutiques, arcades, small shops. If you're looking for a big-ticket item like a video camera, know what you'd pay at home. If the savings aren't spectacular, it may not be worth the trouble, not to mention your valuable vacation time.

A good baseline is to check the recommended local retail price for an item by calling a brand's sole agent (listed in the back of the free HKTA *Shopping Guide*). There are sole agents for all kinds of brand-name items: electronic goods, cosmetics, perfumes, crystal, stationery. They are good resources for questions about accessories, compatibility, and other details merchants may not know.

The second rule is to **carefully examine the item.** Reconditioned used cameras are often passed off as new: being sealed in plastic is no guarantee. False labels or tags are often attached to clothing, so shop for quality rather than names. The shopkeeper may try to make up for the bargain he's given you by overcharging for accessories (camera case, connecting wires) that should come with the purchase. Or he may take the item in the back room to wrap it for you, and substitute lower-quality stock. Never accept a "fresh" item from the back room without thoroughly examining it.

Having successfully navigated thus far, there is still the matter of guarantees. Local guarantees are worthless if you don't live in Hong Kong. You want a worldwide or international guarantee, which must carry the name and/or symbol of the local sole agent (again, see the HKTA *Shopping* brochure). Make sure the guarantee has a complete description of the product, including serial and model number, the date of purchase, and the name and address of the shop. Often only authorized agents can provide a one-year worldwide guarantee; other shops may sell items more cheaply. It's up to you to decide whether a bargain is worth the risk.

For any purchase, **get a detailed, legible receipt,** listing the brand name, model and serial numbers and price of the item, or in the case of jewelry or watches, a description of the precious metal content and stones.

All these precautions can make shopping for certain items an exhausting process, and you'll want to seriously think about whether the sum you save is worth the aggravation, risk, and time.

Payment

Credit cards are a good way to pay for major purchases. Companies give a decent exchange rate, and charging an item provides inexpensive insurance against fraud and damaged goods. Some cards automatically cover damage or loss in transit, and you can stop payment if an item does not arrive. Don't count on it to work if the item does arrive and it's not what you wanted, though. It's always best to carry major purchases out of the store yourself.

Shopkeepers must pay a four or five percent commission to the company, and often this is built into the price when purchasing with a cred-

street barbers

it card. Bargained prices are generally considered to be in cash, so clarify in advance how you'll pay. Keep the receipts, and at bill-paying time make sure the final amount has been calculated on the basis of HK$ rather than US$.

Generally there's no need to give a deposit unless something is being specially ordered for you, in which case 10% is the maximum. For custom-made items like suits or eyeglasses the deposit will be around 50%. Deposits are not refundable, and goods are not normally returnable or refundable.

Shipping

All these bargains can leave you with a surfeit of stuff to schlep around or schlep home. Most shops will pack and ship items for you, either by parcel post, air freight, or container ship. Their insurance may only cover loss in transit; for big purchases, get all-risk insurance to cover damage or loss. And don't leave the shop without detailed receipts for the purchase and shipping.

HONG KONG TOURIST ASSOCIATION

Mailing items is cheap, reliable, and surprisingly easy, thanks to the excellent postal system (see "Communications and Media" under "Information and Services."). Surface mail takes six to eight weeks to the U.S. or Europe, air mail one week. Contents can be registered and insured against loss or damage.

For big items, check the Yellow Pages for companies handling sea freight (look under "Freight Forwarding/Consolidation"). Air cargo companies have offices at Kai Tak Airport; shop around for competitive rates.

Airlines are unusually strict on luggage weight limits on flights leaving Hong Kong. If your bags are declared overweight on checking in, first try another counter. A different clerk may not charge you. Bribery, unfortunately, does not work. If you're determined to take something with you, consider checking it as unaccompanied baggage—much cheaper than excess baggage, though it may take longer to clear customs on arrival.

Shopping Hours and Holidays

Consumption is an all-day, everyday affair. Shops open around 10 a.m., while closing times vary by neighborhood: 6 or 7 p.m. in Central and Western, 7:30 p.m. in Tsimshatsui East, 9 or 10 p.m. in Tsimshatsui and Yaumatei, and 10-10:30 p.m. in Causeway Bay and Wanchai. Night markets stay open even later, to 11 p.m. or so.

The only time everything shuts down is two or three days at Chinese New Year. Shopping malls and shops in Central may close on Christmas and New Year's, but smaller shops stay open virtually year-round. Sunday, the usual day off work, is also the big shopping day.

Big department stores and many boutiques hold huge sales in late December and June. The December sales are a response to the upcoming Chinese New Year: an estimated 40% of all retail sales take place between Christmas and Chinese New Year.

Shopping Services

Professional companies, often run by expats, offer custom-designed shopping tours. These are especially helpful if you have limited time or specific needs; guides help with bargaining if necessary and make sure you pay reasonable prices. The hourly cost depends on services and

transport, but a top-of-the-line service will whisk you about in a Mercedes to New Territories workshops, hidden factory outlets, and private homes filled with antiques for sale. Fees run around US$200 for a three-hour custom tour. Look in the Yellow Pages under "Shopping Services."

WHERE TO SHOP

Often it seems like the city is one big wholesale market. The chunk of Tsimshatsui south of Kimberley Road, between Chatham Road South and Canton Road, is where tourists shop, but it long ago lost its bargains. Contrary to popular belief, Nathan Road is not a shopping paradise—and the cheap neckties you see everybody buying here aren't real silk.

Prices improve (though selection dwindles) in locally oriented neighborhoods like Yaumatei and Mongkok. Tsimshatsui East is new, expensive, and flashy, popular with trendy locals. Kaiser Estates in Hung Hom is packed with "factory outlets" selling jewelry and clothes, but sadly there are few bargains to be found here any more.

Hong Kong-side, it's Western for dried scallops, ginseng, bear paws, and deer antlers. Central has the highest rents and highest prices, and is full of sophisticated boutiques. Try Wanchai for tattoos, Happy Valley for shoes, and Causeway Bay for (small-sized) women's clothes, especially the boutiques between Yee Woo St. and Leighton Road. The gigantic shopping malls east of here, like Cityplaza and Kornhill, are good low-hassle shopping resources.

Shopping Malls

Even if you loathe malls you're bound to end up in a few, because there are so many, and because they're streamlined, air-conditioned ways to get from one place to another. Malls have become embedded in local culture: a visit to observe these pleasure domes of shiny chrome and polished marble is practically mandatory for anyone who seeks to experience the real Hong Kong. The biggest shopping centers are destinations in themselves, equipped with spacious atriums, entertainment complexes, and fast-food centers.

Notable are **The Landmark** in Central with its

soothing air of exclusivity, the gleaming new **Mall at Pacific Place** in Admiralty, and the giant **New World Shopping Centre** next to the Regent. The gigantic **Harbour City** complex next to the Tsimshatsui Star Ferry is good for a day's wallow in its 600 shops. Newest and temporarily most popular with locals is **Times Square** in Causeway Bay.

Farther out, there's **New Town Plaza** in Shatin, **Cityplaza** in Taikoo Shing (accessible by tram or MTR), or **Whampoa Garden** in Hung Hom. These aim squarely at the local market, with family-oriented entertainment like ice rinks, musical fountains, and cultural shows. Prices are reasonable and goods reliable, but few tourists venture out here.

Department Stores

Again, blessedly air-conditioned and stuffed with stuff. British stores have imported British prices along with the merchandise. Most prestigious is locally owned **Lane Crawford,** at 70 Queen's Rd., Central, and in Harbour City and Pacific Place. Mere mortals wait for its famous twice-yearly sales, which are held in July and after Christmas. **Dodwell** is more utilitarian, with shops in Harbour City and Melbourne Plaza, Central. Dependable old **Marks & Spencer** is known for clothing: find it in Pacific Place, Times Square, The Landmark, and Harbour City.

Prices are more reasonable at local chains like **Wing On,** 26 Des Voeux Rd., Central, and 62 Mody Rd., Tsimshatsui East. **Dragon Seed** 39 Queen's Rd. Central, and **Sincere** 173 Des Vouex Rd., Central, are other local department stores.

The Japanese department stores in Causeway Bay are popular with late-night shoppers (they stay open till 10 p.m.). Bargains are generally found at the basement levels. The most Japanese is **Daimaru,** a sprawling complex with two branches: Fashion Square on Paterson St. (clothing) and Household Square on Kingston St. (furniture, housewares, and a good supermarket in the basement).

Mitsukoshi, 500 Hennessy Rd., is the swankiest, filled with high-priced designer boutiques; there's another at 28 Canton Rd., Tsimshatsui. The biggest store in all Hong Kong is **Jumbo Sogo,** 555 Hennessy Rd.; it's cheaper and more family-oriented. **Matsuzakaya,** 20

Paterson St. is also mid-market; there's a second branch at Queensway Plaza in Admiralty. **Seibu** in Pacific Place targets the yuppie market with ultrasmart furnishings and clothing. **City-Super** in Times Square is similarly slick.

On the Kowloon side, **Isetan** in the Sheraton Hotel focuses on clothing; across the street in New World Centre is **Tokyu.** Out in the New Territories, **Yaohan** dominates the local family trade. There's a gigantic Yaohan in New Town Plaza at Shatin.

Chinese Products Stores

Forget about China's Friendship Stores. The Chinese product stores in Hong Kong offer a far bigger array of goods at reasonable fixed prices, along with typically unresponsive staff. These emporiums are great places to browse and buy souvenirs, though prices are not as low as they used to be. The Tsimshatsui branches are the most spectacular; those in other neighborhoods are more oriented to the local market and tend to have better prices.

Goods range from practical—down jackets, medicinal products, clothing, silk dressing gowns —to HK$60,000 cloisonne camels and ornamental "trees" with jade leaves. There's lots of embroidered tableware, porcelain, cork carvings, painted scrolls, and cashmere.

Chinese Arts & Crafts is the most upscale, with eight outlets. The biggest is in the Silvercord Building in Tsimshatsui; there are others in Star House in Tsimshatsui; at 233 Nathan Rd., Yaumatei; and in Pacific Place and Prince's Building, Central. **China Products Co.,** at 488 Hennessy Rd., Causeway Bay, is just the place for a pair of antlers or a snake soaking in a jar of medicinal liquor. There's also **Chung Kiu Chinese Products Emporium,** 17 Hankow Rd., Tsimshatsui, and 528 Nathan Rd., Mongkok. **Yue Hwa Chinese Products** has a good blend of local and touristic merchandise: there are shops at 54, 143, and 301 Nathan Rd. and 24 Paterson St., Causeway Bay.

WHAT TO BUY

The best deals are on items made with cheap labor, often sold under international labels. Look for ready-made and tailor-made clothing, luggage, porcelain, optical goods, and jade. Shop carefully for jewelry and watches; very carefully for cameras, electronic goods, and computers; extremely carefully for antiques. Foreign-made goods are generally not a bargain except to Japanese, who pay lots more at home. Look to save at least 30% on home prices, and if not, don't buy.

Ready-Made Clothing

Check the labels in your wardrobe to see how many say "Made in Hong Kong" (or China, or Macau). Hong Kong is among the world's largest clothing exporters, with annual exports worth over US$7 billion. Nearly half the industrial workforce is employed in the garment industry, and Kowloon is bursting with tiny rooms full of women turning out piecework. The surplus, overruns, and seconds from this giant industry are sold in some 40,000 local retail outlets, ranging from boutiques to factory outlets or clearinghouses specializing in cheap sales. Prices can be 70% below retail cost in the U.S.

Cheap clothing on the local market generally falls into three categories: excess stock, overruns (items produced in excess of the quantity specified in delivery contracts, and sold for next to nothing in local shops), and seconds (rejected because of some flaw, anything from a near-invisible speck to a sleeve sewn in backwards). You never know if something is an overrun or a second, so inspect bargain garments with an eagle eye, especially as there are no refunds or returns.

Locally popular chains like **Giordano, Episode,** and **U2** sell casual first-run unisex sportswear at very reasonable prices. A few factory outlets specialize in menswear; try **Leighton Stock Sales** (868 Cheung Sha Wan Rd., Lai Chi Kok). The trendiest place for women's clothing at the moment (small sizes only, please) is Beverley Centre in Tsimshatsui, with dozens of tiny boutiques.

Garments bearing designer labels like Hermes, Cardin, and St. Laurent are locally made and sold in fixed-price designer boutiques that are somewhat below U.S. prices. Hong Kong is also the world's largest exporter of fur garments (mostly ranch-bred mink and fox), with prices as low as half the U.S. standard.

Chinese products stores sell some unique items: slithery satin cheongsams (tight long dresses with a slit up the side), satin brocade pajamas and robes, and padded or quilted jackets. In addition there are silk blouses, cashmere sweaters, lingerie, down jackets, silk long underwear—all of lovely fabrics, but often not very stylish.

A unique local venue is Shanghai Tang in the Pedder Building in Central. Run by local mega-entrepreneur David Tang, it sells traditional Chinese fashions—slinky cheongsams and mandarin jackets—in modern colors and gorgeous fabrics, not to mention Deng Xiao Ping watches. Not cheap, but beautiful.

Shoes are not such great bargains: quality varies, and sizes above 6 for women and 10 for men are hard to find. Main areas are the ladies' shoes stores lining Leighton Road (near the Happy Valley racetrack) and the hip Beverley Centre in Tsimshatsui. You'll also find shoe bargains in boutiques in Central, along Li Yuen St. East and Li Yuen St. West, which run between Des Voeux Rd. and Queen's Road. The labels say "Made in Italy," but they're not. For sports shoes visit Stanley. You can also have shoes custom-made.

Custom Tailoring

This business was pioneered by Indian tailors in postwar Hong Kong catering to U.S. servicemen—thus the quick turnaround time. Tailor-made men's clothing is one of the luxuries of Hong Kong, but having a suit made requires some planning. The 24-hour suit is a myth if it ever did exist (though a local tailor once whipped up a suit in one hour, strictly for the record books). Allow a minimum of three or four days and two fittings for a tailored suit. Six days and three fittings is better.

Prices are not negotiable, and a nonrefundable deposit, generally 50%, is required upon placing an order. If you run out of time at the end the finished garment can be shipped to your home. The tailor will keep your measurements on record so you can mail-order more suits or shirts.

A top-class suit runs around HK$4500, though adequate garments are half that. Shirts are made too, for around HK$300-500 each. Most men's tailors also do women's wear, though they're best at copying things or rendering classic tailored garments.

Steer clear of the unreasonably cheap package deals advertised in tourist publications ("one suit—one blazer—two shirts—two ties only HK$1800!"). The best and most expensive tailors are found in shops in and near the major hotels, like **H. Baromon** in Swire House or **Ah Man Hing Cheong** in the Mandarin. For shirts, try **Ascot Chang** in Prince's Bldg. and the Regent Arcade, or **David's Shirts,** 33 Kimberley Rd., Tsimshatsui, and the Mandarin.

Cheaper but still good is **Eddie Siu Fat Tai,** 2/F, 2 Hanoi Rd., Tsimshatsui. Burlington House, 94 Nathan Rd., has some good tailors like **W.W. Chan & Sons,** which also makes women's clothes, and **Sam's Tailor,** which has made clothes for everyone from Margaret Thatcher to David Bowie.

Fabric

Chinese emporiums sell crepe de chine, brocade, and printed and raw silk in every imaginable color (try Chinese Arts & Crafts and Yue Hwa). They're not cheap, but the selection is huge. Main cloth neighborhoods are around Jardine's Bazaar in Causeway Bay and the Lanes in Central. A reduced contingent of vendors from Wing On Lane (the old "Cloth Alley") has been relocated in the renovated Western Market, where they still sell everything from dress silk to upholstery material. **Mountain Folkcraft** at 12 Wo On Lane (off Lan Kwai Fong) has unusual indigo paste-dyed cloth from southwest Chinese hilltribes.

Jewelry

There are more listings under jewelry shops than any other category in HKTA's membership pamphlet, and it's the most popular item for tourists, as there are no taxes or duties on gems. Hong Kong is a major international jewelry exporter and diamond trading center. But scams abound, and buyers need to be knowledgeable and aware. Watch out for imitation stones made of colored glass or synthetic resins, or semiprecious stones passed off as precious ones. Sometimes two or three slices of a cheaper stone like beryl will be stuck together with green adhesive to create an "emerald."

Shop around, don't believe everything you're told, and bargain hard everywhere. If you care to wade into these murky waters, HKTA's *Shopping Guide to Jewelry* provides an introduction to precious and semiprecious stones. The Diamond Importers Association, tel. 2523-5497, provides shopping advice and a listing of members. The very finest jewelry shops are in the hotel arcades and The Landmark.

See the special topic "Know Your Jade" for advice on jade, the local favorite. Hong Kong has among the world's biggest and best selections, as seen in the Jade Market at Yaumatei. It's a good place for cheap trinkets and souvenirs, but don't invest heavily unless you know what you're doing. Chinese products emporiums are reliable if expensive places to buy jade.

Pearls, from Japan and the South Pacific, are priced according to size and luster. Shape

embroidery on silk

and color depend on personal preference, but look for evenly matched strands. Inexpensive pearls are sold at the Jade Market; again, for quality, shop at reputable jewelers like International Pearl Centre, 49 Peking Rd., Tsimshatsui.

Local gold stores mount dazzling displays of enormous necklaces, charms, and figurines, watched over by shotgun-toting guards. Gold is sold by the tael (1.3 ounces or 38 grams) at international prices. The real deal is the workmanship, much cheaper than in the West. Hong Kong jewelers can replicate a piece, mount unset stones, or copy a design from a photo. In case you're wondering, the glittering pure gold figurines of ships and deities displayed in shop windows are usually given as wedding gifts.

Watches

There's a huge selection, as befits the world's largest watch manufacturer, from Van Cleef & Arpels through Citizen and Seiko, down to the famous though illicit "Carter" and "Rollex" imitations sold by street vendors in lanes and markets. Be suspicious of huge discounts, which might indicate a scam like an inferior or used mechanism inserted into an expensive case. If you want a name brand, contact the sole dealer for that brand. Get a receipt and the manufacturer's international warranty, and check that the movement's serial number matches the guarantee's. If you just want a decent watch, **City Chain** is a good mid-priced chain with shops all over town.

Optical Goods

A good yet unpublicized bargain: regular lenses run around HK$160-200; bifocals HK$450; soft-lens contacts HK$650. All kinds of European frames are available (along with designer sunglasses). Shops give computerized eye exams (often unreliable) and can fill a prescription in a day or two. You can also have your current glasses copied or your prescription filled. Two reliable chains are **The Optical Shop** and **Optical 88.**

Cameras

Virtually everyone expects to get a bargain on cameras in Hong Kong, but you have to know your stuff. There is a bewildering selection of brands and models, both up-to-the-minute and out-of-date. If you don't know which is which,

you can get stuck. Don't rely on shopkeepers to educate you—they have their own agenda. Contact sole agents for information on recommended prices and models, then shop around. Buy a camera with an international guarantee—it may be more expensive, but it's worth it. See "Scams," above for more advice, as camera shops are hotbeds of abuse.

Most importantly, try to check prices at home before leaving so you have a base for comparison. Discount mail-order houses in New York usually sell goods 10-20% cheaper than the best Hong Kong prices, and you don't have to bargain. Check ads in the Sunday edition of the *New York Times.*

There are dozens of camera shops along Lock Road and lower Nathan Road in Tsimshatsui, though merchants here have some of the worst attitudes around. Hassles are less likely along Hennessy Road and Percival Street in Causeway Bay. Local professionals recommend **Mark's Photo Supplies,** 20 Des Vouex Rd., Central; entrance on Theatre Lane, or **Photo-scientific** at 6 Stanley St., Central—not cheap, but reliable.

Video Cameras and Sound Equipment

Electronic shops beckon with huge stocks of the latest models, including products that have not yet reached the U.S. Prices are not necessarily a bargain, however, and you must shop carefully. Big department stores like Sogo are good places to preview the selection, though prices aren't the best.

Video cameras may be available for half of U.S. prices. Be aware of the 110-220 volt difference between Hong Kong and the U.S.; also the different types of broadcast standards (PAL, NTSC, SECAM) for video cameras, VCRs, and TVs. Pick up a copy of HKTA's *Shopping Guide to Consumer Electronics,* which explains these and lists the most popular models of camcorders, disc players, and VCRs, plus sole agents. Electronics shops are found along with the camera shops on Nathan Road in Tsimshatsui and Hennessy Road in Wanchai.

Computers and Software

Again, it pays to know what you're shopping for: an uneducated consumer is probably going to get taken. Mail-order houses in the U.S. may

STREET MARKETS

There's a market for everyone and everything in Hong Kong: men, women, and thieves; jade, fruits, and vegetables. Some are semi-permanent establishments set up under tarps and tents; others materialize wherever vendors appear with their pushcarts.

Markets are among the cheapest places to shop for clothing, though the selection is limited and there's no fitting allowed (some vendors offer tape measures in compensation). They're especially good for minor items—tights, socks, underwear, sweaters, luggage, and handbags—and kid's clothes. The bigger street markets branch out into cheap jewelry, clocks, toys, and watches. There are no guarantees, refunds, or returns, so check everything carefully and bargain hard. Watch your wallet, as pickpockets are rife.

Probably the most famous markets are two narrow alleys running between Queen's Road and Des Voeux Road in Central: **Li Yuen Street East** and **Li Yuen Street West**. Vendors sell all manner of women's and children's clothing, stockings, gloves, handbags, makeup, and accessories (lots of brand-name fakes). They're open 10 a.m.-7 p.m., and are used to tourists, so it may be difficult to bargain.

Smaller lanes in Central and Western specialize in various oddities. **Fat Hing Street** sells traditional Chinese baby clothes, **Pottinger Street** haberdashery and sewing notions, **Man Wah Lane** carved Chinese chops. The cloth merchants who once inhabited Wing On Street have been moved into the second floor of Western Market, more spacious but not as much fun. Farther west, the vendors on Upper Lascar Row or "Cat Street" deal in all manners of bric-a-brac, everything from old abacuses to hubcaps.

Over in Causeway Bay, **Jardine's Crescent** has rows of stalls selling women's and children's clothing and accessories. After the shops close around 10 p.m., the late-night vendors emerge to sell fake designer goods and gadgets. Further down the tramline, there's a basic clothing market on **Marble Road** in North Point.

On the south side of the island, the famous **Stanley Market** is touristy but features tons of clothes and souvenirs, at rising but still-decent prices. Take Bus 6 or 260 from Central, and try to avoid Sunday or holidays.

In Kowloon, the famous **Temple Street Night Market** in Yaumatei should be visited just for the experience. It's good for clothing (especially menswear), T-shirts, socks, tapes, luggage, watches, clocks and other gadgets, and there's the added bonus of opera singers, fortune-tellers, and open-air food stalls. It's in full swing 8-11 p.m.

The lively **Ladies' Market** on Tung Choi Street (near the Mongkok MTR) is similar but less touristy and more for locals, with a heavier emphasis on women's clothing. Visit in afternoon or evening.

Yaumatei's **Jade Market** at the end of Reclamation Street is a huge bazaar specializing in jade jewelry and carvings and pearls (open 10 a.m.-4 p.m.). The **Bowring Street Market** west of the Jordan MTR is a good example of a typical local market. The big daytime **Kowloon City Market** on Lion Rock Road is a little out of the way, but a favorite with locals.

---

be as cheap or cheaper than Hong Kong, and more reliable. If you want a name-brand computer, contact the sole agent for a list of authorized dealers, and make sure to get the international guarantee. Make sure your computer will run on the voltage back home. And don't forget to get the manual.

Pirated software is illegal but plentiful—HK$25 for US$500 packages—and some dealers shower you with freebies with a computer purchase. Also popular are cassettes crammed with up to 100 video games for a fraction of the original price. Of course there are no instructions or warranties with these. Some are good copies, some are not; all are illegal, and generate occasional police raids on shops selling them. Some merchants readily admit they're selling copies, while others will deny it, but it's easy to tell, as prices are much, much lower than the originals. Pirated CD-ROMs are another hot item, at prices up to 70% off the U.S. standard.

Larger established outlets are fairly reliable, but try to get a personal recommendation for smaller ones. The reputable place to shop is **Star Computer City,** several dozen shops clustered on the second floor of Star House near the Tsimshatsui Star Ferry.

The *disreputable* place is **Golden Shopping Arcade** on the corner of Kweilin and Fuk Wah streets in north Kowloon. (Take the MTR to Shamshuipo.) The arcade is just across the street, with over 100 shops selling computers (mostly clones), accessories, and pirated software. It's an exciting place if you know your stuff, but it's no place for amateurs, as used computers and fake brands are very real dangers.

Furniture and Carpets

Hand-knotted Chinese carpets of silk and wool are sold at Chinese product emporiums. **Tai Ping Carpet Factory** is famous for its wool carpets (its main showroom is in Hutchison House, Central, and there's a salesroom at the factory at Tai Po). Wyndham Street in Central is lined with shops selling old and new carpets from Turkey, India, Afghanistan, Pakistan, and Tibet.

Traditional Chinese wooden furniture is a good buy, though shipping costs may eat up whatever savings are achieved. Long-grained, fragrant rosewood is popular; there's also teak, camphorwood, and blackwood, often inlaid with mother-of-pearl or set with marble. You can also find imports from Korea and Japan, both antiques and reproductions. Queen's Road East, Hollywood Road, and Canton Road in Tsimshatsui are the main furniture areas. **Tequila Koala,** 1/F Prince's Building, Central, has furniture, pottery, and housewares from many different countries. **Banyan Tree** emphasizes larger items like Asian antiques, reproductions, and furniture (Prince's Building, Central and Ocean Galleries, Tsimshatsui).

Antiques

Hong Kong is a crossroads for rare and valuable goods from across Asia, and is the world's greatest source of Chinese art, much of it illegally obtained. As prices rise and supplies shrink, the market is expanding into Korea, Japan, Thailand, and Burma. Dealers fear the supply of Chinese artifacts will dry up post-1997, given China's laws forbidding the export of art more than 200 years old. As a precaution, collectors shipped tons of their best pieces to safety in Singapore and the US.

You'll pay high prices for genuine Chinese antiques—and for fake ones too, if you're not careful. New Territories factories churn out a suspiciously continuous supply of "100-year-old wood carvings," snuff bottles, and "Ming dynasty" vases. There is no policing on the part of the government, and the authenticity papers issued by a shop don't necessarily mean a thing.

This leaves you with three choices: know your stuff; shop at reputable and expensive stores; or hire a local expert to shop with you (look under "Oriental Art Consultants" in the *Buyer's Guides*). Shops have lots more in back rooms, so if you're searching for something in particular, ask.

Wyndham Street, which turns into Hollywood Road, is lined with antique and curio shops selling a mishmash of the rare and bizarre: gorgeous embroidered silk robes from the Dowager Empress's court, Neolithic pottery, giant porcelain vases, temple drums, calligraphy brushes, Mao buttons, Japanese *netsuke,* Edwardian china cabinets. Local specialties include tiny, intricately painted snuff bottles of porcelain, crystal, or bamboo, and *huang huali,* an orange wood with a twisting grain used for scholars' brush boxes and brush pots.

Hollywood Road culminates in "Cat Street," Upper Lascar Row, just below the Man Mo Temple, a narrow passage lined with more expensive stores, fronted by street vendors selling everything from manual typewriters to jade bracelets. There's another conglomoration of antique stores on the third floor of Harbour City in Tsimshatsui.

Reputable, top-priced shops include **Charlotte Horstmann & Gerald Godfrey,** Harbour City, Tsimshatsui, **C.P. Ching,** Pacific Place and 21 Hollywood Rd., Central, **Luen Chai,** 22 Upper Lascar Row, **Honeychurch Antiques,** 29 Hollywood Rd., **Chak's Gallery,** 67 Hollywood Rd., and **Ian Mclean Antiques,** 73 Wyndham Street. **Asian Collectors Gallery,** 19 Wyndham St., Central, specializes in old prints and paintings and Asian maps. Antique showrooms in the China products stores may be good for Chinese ware, but the "Tibetan" statues sold here are Nepali, new, and tremendously overpriced.

Antiques also turn up at auctions: local auction houses Lammert Brothers and Victoria Auctioneers advertise sales in the *South China Morning Post* classifieds, and Sotheby's and Christie's hold auctions in late fall and early spring at downtown hotels. The International

Asian Antiques Fair is held in Hong Kong each May.

Porcelain

Competitively priced bone china is sold in luxury outlets. For Chinese porcelain ranging from giant urns to tiny snuff bottles, shop the China products stores or Hollywood Road. Or visit factory outlets: **Ah Chow,** 7/F Block B, Hong Kong Industrial Centre, 489 Castle Peak Rd., Lai Chi Kok; the giant **Wah Tung China Company,** 12-17/F Grand Marine Industrial Bldg., 3 Yue Fung St., Tin Wan Hill Rd., Aberdeen; or **Overjoy Porcelain,** 1/F 10 Chun Pin St., Kwai Chung.

Chinese Arts and Crafts

Chinese emporiums display objects ranging from ornate to downright vulgar: cloisonné, silk paintings, embroideries, papercuts, carvings, porcelain. **Chinese Arts and Crafts** in Star House, Tsimshatsui, has an especially huge selection. Finely detailed embroideries and drawnwork are found in Chinese products stores, in small shops around D'Aguilar St. and Lan Kwai Fong in Central, and in Stanley.

For contemporary Chinese paintings visit **Hanart TZ,** 5/F Bank of China building, Central or **Plum Blossoms** at 17/F, Coda Plaza, 51 Garden Rd., Central. Colorful folk paintings from mainland China are HK$500 and up at **The Paintbox** in Western Market.

Ivory Carvings

The international ban on ivory trading has hit the local industry hard. Stringent regulations introduced in 1990 make it necessary for buyers to obtain both a Hong Kong export license and an import license from their home country. Hopefully this will help save the dwindling population of African elephants. Carvers are now turning to bone, or dentin from hippos, walruses, boars, and whales to render their famously intricate scenes and jewelry.

Asian Crafts

Amazing Grace Elephant Co., Harbour City, carries all sorts of reasonably priced Asian handicrafts; a great place for unique small gifts. **Mountain Folkcraft,** 12 Wo On Lane, Central (off D'Aguilar Street), has a fascinating collection of Chinese and Thai hill handicrafts: indigo-dyed fabric, porcelain, wood carvings, embroideries, Chinese folk paintings, wooden dumpling molds, puppets, toys, tribal costumes, jewelry.

Souvenirs

Tsimshatsui shops overflow with silk scarves and pajamas, kung-fu outfits, T-shirts, and "happy coats." Most of these are available at slightly lower prices at Stanley Market. HKTA sells items like T-shirts, posters, and coffee mugs at its main information centers, as well as a "Wonders of Hong Kong" CD-ROM.

Small tins of tea make nice presents. HKTA sells a gift box of six Chinese teas complete with brewing instructions, or shop at **Fook Ming Tong Tea Shop** in the rear of the Pedder Building, Central, or **The Best Tea House,** 3 Lock Rd., Tsimshatsui. For tiny, whimsically shaped purple clay teapots from Yixing (expensive) try the shop at the Museum of Teaware in Hong Kong Park.

Local designer Alan Chan does a range of elegantly presented traditional motifs printed on trays, coasters, containers, and T-shirts, available in The Loft on Wellington Street; Seibu in Pacific Place; and the Tai Yip Art Book Centre in the Art Museum in Tsimshatsui.

A chop carved with three initials or Chinese characters runs around HK$100-350 depending on material (ivory, bone, soapstone, marble). Stalls along Man Wa Lane in Central can carve a design in a few hours.

"Olde Hong Kong" memorabilia—cigarette posters, toys, funky souvenirs—is sold at **Six Bugs Curio Shop** in Western Market. For kitschy Cultural Revolution paraphernalia and posters, try **Lowprice Secondhand Store,** at the junction of Hollywood Road and the escalator, or **Sun Chau Book Co.** at 32 Stanley St., Central.

More unusual items are found in traditional shops in neighborhoods like Yaumatei or Wanchai: junk gods, a geomancer's compass *(luo pan),* small eight-sided *ba gua* mirrors to hang outside windows and deflect evil influences, chunks of fragrant sandalwood and huge incense sticks, paper funerary objects and spirit money, ink sticks and brushes, and colorful, cheap Chinese almanacs.

ENTERTAINMENT

CULTURAL EVENTS

Hong Kong's old reputation as a soulless, money-grubbing enclave is now obsolete. New venues like the Hong Kong Cultural Centre in Tsimshatsui and the Hong Kong Arts Centre and Academy for Performing Arts in Wanchai have done much to improve its image, as have several lively arts festivals. And local culture is thriving, as demonstrated by vigorous Canto-pop and film industries and the perennially popular Chinese opera.

> *The city appears at the foot of its radiant mountains: it blazes like a great flower of light with stamens and petals of floodlit stone.*
> *—James Kirkup, Streets of Asia, 1980*

Arts Festivals
Much of the credit for Hong Kong's newfound cultural reputation goes to the organizers of its annual cultural festivals. HKTA can provide more information on timing and venues; tickets are available through Urbtix.

Each February/March the **Hong Kong Arts Festival** presents three weeks of classical music, opera, ballet, and theatre from around the world, including Asian specialties like Vietnamese water puppets and Tibetan dance. It's complemented by the three-week alternative **Hong Kong Fringe Festival,** sponsored by the local Fringe Club in January/February. Call 2521-7251 for details and tickets.

The **Festival of Asian Arts** held every other October/November presents drama, opera, dances, and music, while the **Hong Kong International Film Festival** plays every March/April. The annual **Art Asia** exhibition and sale, held in the Hong Kong Convention Centre each November, displays contemporary paintings and Chinese and Western antiques.

Music
The Hong Kong Philharmonic Orchestra, tel. 2721-2320, performs September through June. The Hong Kong Chinese Orchestra, tel. 2853-2600, performs traditional and modern Chinese and western music with Chinese instruments. Both generally appear in the Hong Kong Cultural Centre and City Hall.

Lunchtime recitals of classical music are held at St. John's Cathedral on Garden Rd., and free vocal and instrumental performances are often presented in the foyer of the Hong Kong Cultural Centre. For up-to-the-minute listings, check *Hong Kong This Week* or *HK Magazine*. Amateur musicians gather Sunday afternoons in Kowloon Park.

Hong Kong is the world center of overseas Chinese pop culture. The local "Canto-pop" scene sprouted up in the '80s after decades of domination by Mandarin songs. Cantonese songs used to be considered second-class: now local megastars sell out the 12,500-seat Hong Kong Coliseum for weeks on end (a 25-day series of concerts Jackie Cheung gave in fall '93 sold out in *four days*). Songs are generally middle-of-the-road romantic ballads, usually Cantonese covers of Japanese, English, or Taiwanese songs, though a few homegrown political protest anthems came out after Tiananmen. While the music is not to everyone's taste, attend a concert if you get a chance—it's a genuine cultural experience.

Theater and Dance
Drama groups include the Hong Kong Repertory Theater and the Hong Kong Drama Club. Zuni Icosahedron puts on innovative theatre-dance performances. Dance companies include the City Contemporary Dance Company, the Hong Kong Ballet Company, tel. 2573-7398, and the Hong Kong Dance Company, tel. 2853-2460, featuring modern Chinese dance. Shows are generally held at the Hong Kong Academy for Performing Arts.

Cultural Performances
Festivals offer the most authentic, lively displays: opera performances, lion dances, processions,

HONG KONG MUSEUMS

This listing covers Hong Kong museums both major and minor, with addresses, hours, and admission fees (generally HK$10, HK$5 for children and adults over 60). More specific descriptions are in the text. Hours on public holidays are the same as Sunday. A special HK$50 monthly pass allows unlimited admission to the Hong Kong Museum of Art, Museum of History, Space Museum, and Science Museum. It's available at participating museums and HKTA offices.

Hong Kong Museum of Art, 10 Salisbury Rd., Tsimshatsui. A well-presented display of traditional and contemporary Chinese art: paintings, ceramics, jade, textiles, stone. Open daily except Thursday 10 a.m.-6 p.m. (Sunday 1-6 p.m.); admission HK$10/HK$5.

Hong Kong Space Museum, 10 Salisbury Rd., Tsimshatsui. Exhibits on space science and astronomy, along with a large planetarium with an Omnimax projection system. Open weekdays except Tuesday 1-9 p.m., weekends and holidays 10 a.m.-9 p.m.; admission HK$10/HK$5 (HK$30/HK$15 for planetarium shows).

Hong Kong Museum of History, Kowloon Park, Haiphong Rd., Tsimshatsui. Well-arranged exhibits emphasizing Hong Kong's rich pre-colonial history. Open daily except Friday 10 a.m.-6 p.m. (Sunday 1-6 p.m.); admission HK$10/HK$5.

Hong Kong Science Museum, 2 Science Museum Rd., Tsimshatsui East. Fascinating collection of hands-on exhibits, including a 22-meter-high Energy Machine. Open Tues.-Fri. 1-9 p.m., weekends and holidays 10 a.m.-9 p.m.; admission HK$25/HK$15.

Flagstaff House Museum of Teaware, Hong Kong Park, Central. Well-documented collection of teaware displayed in the former colonial residence of the British commander-in-chief. Open daily except Wednesday 10 a.m.-5 p.m.; free.

Tsui Museum of Art, 11/F Bank of China Building, 2A Des Voeux Rd., Central. Beautiful private collection of antiquities. Open weekdays 10 a.m.-6 p.m., Saturday 10 a.m.-2 p.m.; admission HK$30/HK$15.

University Museum and Art Gallery, University of Hong Kong, 94 Bonham Rd., Mid-Levels. A mildly interesting collection of bronzes and ceramics. Open Mon.-Sat. 9:30 a.m.-6 p.m.; free.

Police Museum, 27 Coombe Rd., Wanchai Gap. Showcases history of the local police force, with special exhibits on the Triads and narcotics. Open Wed.-Sun. 9 a.m.-5 p.m., Tuesday 2-5 p.m.; free.

Hong Kong Racing Museum, Happy Valley Race Course. Galleries and a cinema tell the story of horse racing's phenomenal success in Hong Kong. Open Tues.-Sat. 11 a.m.-7 p.m., Sunday 1-5 p.m.; free.

Hong Kong Museum of Medical Sciences, 2 Caine Lane, Mid-Levels. Exhibits comparing traditional Chinese and Western approaches to medicine are housed in the Old Pathological Institute. Open Tues.-Sat. 10 a.m.-5 p.m., Sunday 1-5 p.m.; admission HK$10/HK$5.

Law Uk Folk Museum, 14 Kut Shing St., Chai Wan. A 200-year-old Hakka residence exhibiting period items. Open Tues.-Sat. 10 a.m.-1 p.m. and 2-6 p.m., Sunday 1-6 p.m.; free.

Lei Cheng Uk Museum, 41 Tonkin St., Shamshuipo. A Han Dynasty tomb preserved under glass, with a few pottery and bronzes displayed. Mon.-Wed. and Fri.-Sat. 10 a.m.-1 p.m. and 2-6 p.m., Sunday 1-6 p.m.; free.

Chinese University Art Museum, Institute of Chinese Studies, Shatin. Fine collection of traditional art, including seals, rubbings, ceramics and jade. Daily 10 a.m.-4:30 p.m., Sunday and holidays 12:30 p.m.-4:30 p.m.; free.

Railway Museum, On Fu Rd., Tai Po Market. Six old coaches for kids to clamber through, and a small historical display. Daily except Tuesday 9 a.m.-4 p.m.; free.

Sam Tung Uk Museum, Kwu Uk Lane, Tsuen Wan. Restored walled village displaying furniture and handicrafts. Daily except Tuesday and holidays 9 a.m.-4 p.m.; free.

Sheung Yiu Folk Museum, Pak Tam Chung, Sai Kung Country Park. A restored Hakka village with exhibits on traditional life. Daily except Tuesday and holidays 9 a.m.-4 p.m.; free.

puppet display at
Sung dynasty
village

HONG KONG TOURIST ASSOCIATION

puppet shows. More stagey are the cultural shows put on daily at Sung Dynasty Village and Middle Kingdom at Ocean Park.

HKTA sponsors free Chinese cultural shows weekly at various locations, including the New World Centre in Tsimshatsui and Cityplaza at Taikoo Shing (contact HKTA for dates and times). Performances include acrobats, puppets, music, and martial arts displays.

Art Galleries

Current art exhibitions are listed in "What's On" in the *South China Morning Post* and in *HK Magazine.* Major venues include the **exhibition galleries** in the Cultural Centre and **Pao Galleries** in the Hong Kong Arts Centre in Wanchai.

Private galleries offer an ever-changing selection of classical and modern art. Likely venues are **Oriental Arts Centre,** 1/F 19 Connaught Rd., Central; **Plum Blossoms,** 17/F Coda Plaza, 51 Garden Rd., Central; **Hanart TZ** in the old Bank of China; **Alisan Fine Arts** and **Altfield Gallery** in Prince's Building, 10 Chater Rd., Central; and the **Dragon's Back Gallery** and the **Fringe Gallery** in the Fringe Club, 2 Lower Albert Rd., Central.

Information and Tickets

For up-to-the-minute information, check the daily "What's On" listings in the *South China Morning Post,* the Saturday edition of the *Hong Kong Standard,* or the weekly *TV and Entertainment Times. HK Magazine,* a free weekly distributed in popular restaurants and bars, lists more offbeat performances, including live music. *BC* is another glossy modern publication focusing on the club scene and live music.

Pick up an Urbtix monthly flyer at City Hall for a listing of events and ticket prices. Two HKTA publications, the glossy *Hong Kong This Week* and the basic *Hong Kong Diary,* list exhibitions and performances, including Cantonese opera and Chinese cultural shows. *Hong Kong Now!* is another glossy flyer listing weekly events for visitors. Both the Hong Kong Arts Centre and the Hong Kong Academy of Performing Arts publish monthly brochures of events and exhibitions.

Tickets for most events are distributed through the computerized Urbtix system. Order tickets by phone and collect them at one of 18 outlets, including the Arts Centre in Wanchai, City Hall in Central, and the Cultural Centre in Tsimshatsui. For general info and ticket reservations, call 2734-9009.

MOVIES

Somebody should make a film with the Chinese word for "movie" *deen ying,* "electric shadows" as the title. Hong Kong's film industry is the third-largest in the world, cranking out an average of 10 films a month and exporting them to

CHINESE OPERA

With its shrill falsettos and clashing percussion, Chinese opera can grate on unaccustomed ears, but Hong Kong adores it. Regardless of the melodic qualities, the elaborate costuming and makeup are always fascinating.

Modern Chinese opera belongs to a tradition dating back to the 13th century. Most plots developed during the Yuan and Ming dynasties, based on well-loved folk epics of self-sacrifice, courage, filial piety, and tragic love. Vigorous action—mime, dance, acrobatics, swordfighting—carries the plot, and the clashing of gongs and drums heightens the drama at significant twists. Audiences know the themes by heart, but to an untutored observer the plot can be difficult to discern. It helps to have the story outlined in advance.

Actors rely on ornate costumes and symbolic gestures rather than props or stage sets. Performers dress in platform shoes, elaborate headdresses, and embroidered and sequinned robes. Their role is signaled by details like the color of robes, the pattern of makeup, even the type of beard (there are 18 distinct styles).

The heavy makeup, derived from painted masks used in older forms of opera, has its own language. A black face signifies an honest but uncouth character, while a white-faced one is treacherous and cunning. Villains have a white patch on the nose; devils are green-faced; gods yellow.

Gestures are relied upon to tell the story and move the plot along; they are accentuated by "water sleeves" of white silk attached to actors' robes. Particular motions indicate weeping, walking in the dark, dismounting from a horse and crossing a threshold. Theatrical conventions provide more cues: death is symbolized by a red cloth thrown over the face; two men with black flags are evil spirits seeking a victim.

Actors spend years perfecting the stylized falsetto demanded in opera. They specialize in particular roles: clown, bandit, wife, concubine, father, young hero. Traditionally, men played women's roles—the best of these "actresses" were said to be even more alluring than the real thing—but nowadays women participate on stage.

Hong Kong supports several dozen professional companies and regularly hosts visiting mainland troupes. Opera is traditionally associated with festivals, when communities sponsor public performances as offerings to the gods. Performances may be held in mat sheds, where audiences casually chat, eat, talk, and move in and out. Hong Kong's opera theaters developed in the '20s and '30s and are still vital centers. Modern fans smuggle in concealed recorders to make bootleg tapes of performances, and trade tapes of the best events.

An evening at the opera is a highly recommended cultural event. Ask HKTA or your hotel desk for ticket booking advice. Major venues are the Ko Shan Theater, the Paladium Opera House in Lai Chi Kok, and the Sunbeam Theater at 423 King's Rd. in North Point, tel. 2563-2959. URBTIX sells tickets for performances in New Town venues like town hall auditoriums or civic centers. Prices for these range HK$60-150. For impromptu street opera, visit the upper end of the Temple Street Night Market in Yaumatei, where women backed by traditional orchestras sing snatches of opera favorites—fascinating even without the costuming frills.

Taiwan, Singapore, Malaysia, and Chinese communities in the West.

Local films are relatively cheap, and focus on slapstick comedies, costume dramas (lots of sword fighting), or martial arts, often combining all these elements in the same package. The epitome was Bruce Lee, who though born in San Francisco became a local hero, starring in classics like *Fists of Fury* that appealed to both Chinese and Western tastes. Even if you don't follow Cantonese, local films are endearingly energetic, and the audience's enthusiastic response is gratifying.

Theaters

Check the papers for what's playing, you can expect a mix of English-language releases and locally made movies. There are 30-odd cinemas, many of them in Causeway Bay. Theater addresses are not provided in ads, so call for directions. Tickets are around HK$55; you pick your seat from a chart or video monitor at the box office. Most theaters allow advance telephone bookings.

Some local theaters which frequently show English-language releases: **Astor Classics,** 380 Nathan Rd., Tsimshatsui, tel. 2781-1833; **Co-**

lumbia Classics, Great Eagle Centre, Wanchai, tel. 2827-8291; **Majestic,** 348 Nathan Rd., Tsimshatsui, tel. 2782-0272; **New York Cinema,** 463 Lockhart Rd., Causeway Bay, tel. 2838-7380; **Silvercord Cinema,** 30 Canton Rd., Tsimshatsui; **UA Queensway,** Pacific Place, Admiralty, tel. 2869-0322; **UA Times Square,** Times Square, Causeway Bay, tel. 2506-2822.

Classic and art films are shown at the small **Lim Por Yen Theatre** in the Hong Kong Arts Centre in North Wanchai, tel. 2582-0292. **Cine-Art House** in Sun Hung Kei Centre, Harbour Rd., Wanchai, tel. 2827-4820, shows foreign films. **Alliance Française** and the **Goethe Institute** sponsor occasional showings of foreign films. The **Omnimax Theater** in the Hong Kong Space Museum shows grand naturalistic epics on Antarctica and such on its huge curved screen. Occasionally special film series are put on at the Arts Centre or City Hall, with tickets available through Urbtix outlets.

NIGHTLIFE

Hong Kong prides itself as Asia's most exciting city after dark, offering an enormous range of nightlife options. Young locals favor the trendy restaurants, bars, and discos of Lan Kwai Fong in Central. Hotels offer elegant rooftop bars with sparkling harbor views, or rowdy karaoke lounges full of Chinese businessmen. More glittery are the high-priced nightclubs for businessmen on expense accounts, where pretty cheongsamed "hostesses" charge by the hour for conversation and dances. Wanchai's pubs and discos, traditionally favored by hard-drinking expats and sailors, increasingly draw a younger, trendier crowd; it's the place for *serious* partying.

For up-to-the-minute listings, check *HK Magazine,* a free weekly distributed at trendy restaurants and bars, the glossy *BC,* which specializes in the club scene, or the *South China Morning Post.* Hong Kong nightlife is fairly fashion-conscious, and the trendiest clubs employ fashion police who reject those they deem underdressed. Drinking is not as popular as simply dancing, and the local discos are good fun.

Bars and Pubs

These run the gamut from scruffy to stuffy, encompassing rowdy sailor dives, plush hotel bars, and British pubs complete with steak and kidney pie. Beer is the cheapest drink; a pint averages HK$45 in a pub, HK$10-15 more in a bar. Cocktails run around HK$50 and up. Take advantage of happy hours, which run from 4 or 5 p.m. to around 8 p.m. and generally offer two-for-one drinks. Bar hours are roughly 11 a.m.-2 a.m., with plenty going on till 4 or 5 a.m. on weekends, and some in Wanchai operating around-the-clock.

Discos and Nightclubs

Hong Kong's relentlessly competitive scene—and skyrocketing rents—means that nightlife venues are constantly changing. Few succeed for more than a year or so, unless they really hit the local pulse.

A few discos cater mainly to tourists, but most are frequented by local young people—both expats and Chinese—who come mainly for the dancing. Cover averages around HK$100-150 on weekends, and often includes two drinks. (Some places don't charge covers on weekdays.) Discos are a late-night affair: nothing opens until 9:30 p.m. or closes before 2 a.m., 4-6 a.m. on weekends.

Live bands are increasing but still uncommon, though club nights with imported D.J.s spinning discs are popular. Most discos play Western music or Canto-pop. The larger discos are multifaceted "entertainment centers" with private karaoke rooms, video walls, and elaborate laser shows.

Karaoke Clubs

Japan's karaoke craze hit Hong Kong in the mid-'80s and isn't over yet. Karaoke literally means "empty orchestra." Clients sing along into a microphone to a taped instrumental track and visuals, usually on laser disc. Businessmen visit clubs at night to drink and sing (badly), and there is a growing trade in home karaoke units for the family market. Favorites include "Green Green Grass of Home" and "My Way." Poor renditions of these have led to "karaoke bashings" in which club patrons assault a particularly horrific singer.

Karaoke lounges range from downmarket to sophisticated, but they're generally expensive private affairs, often found in Causeway Bay and Wanchai. Some have practice booths and TV screens in the restrooms to allow clients to keep up with the action. Many discos have private karaoke rooms for rent, running about HK$700 for a small room for six people. Lounges have entertaining names like the Drunken Lounge and Kara O'Ke.

Drinking Games

"Finger games" are deceptively simple but highly entertaining ways of passing an evening, favored by middle-aged Chinese businessmen. There are many varieties: a popular Cantonese version is called *yu-ha-hai* ("fish-crab-shrimp"); another, popular on the mainland, is "scissors-paper-stone."

They involve two players, and usually a lot of drinking and noise. Each tosses out a hand displaying anywhere from one to five fingers, simultaneously shouting his guess at the combined total of fingers displayed. The winner is whoever guesses the right number; the loser must drink. These games can go on for hours, getting progressively noisier and more confused as drinks are downed.

Hostess Bars

It began with Vietnam-era servicemen: now Japanese businessmen are the lifeblood of Hong Kong's hostess bars. There are two distinct genres: the glittery, expensive Japanese nightclubs of Tsimshatsui East and Wanchai, where bevies of hostesses are available for conversation and dancing; and the less-elegant places (some can fairly be described as dives) of Tsimshatsui and Wanchai.

The system is set up to fleece the unwary, who may end up paying US$100 for one beer and a few words of poor English from a female companion. Hostesses try to extract money from customers quickly. Customers should determine the price of drinks in advance, and pay as they go rather than run a tab, which can easily grow to HK$1000 if you're not looking. Customers can also buy a girl out for the evening for a hefty charge; anything further will also cost. Though brothels and streetwalking are banned, straightforward prostitution is not illegal in Hong Kong.

NIGHTLIFE BY AREA

Tsimshatsui

While this is not necessarily the best neighborhood to sample Hong Kong nightlife, a lively scene has developed here. The cheapest places for a night out are inexpensive pubs, like the pleasantly seedy **Kangaroo Pub,** 35 Haiphong Rd., or the quieter German **Biergarten,** 8 Hanoi Rd., and **Schnurrbart,** 9 Prat Avenue. A particularly good Aussie pub is **Ned Kelly's Last Stand,** 11 Ashley Rd., where a good house jazz band plays nightly from 9 p.m. **Delaney's,** 3 Prat Avenue, is a slick Irish pub with Guinness on tap and a resident Irish band.

Mad Dogs at 32 Nathan Rd. is the Kowloon-side version of the Central original, a lively place popular with tourists and resident Brits, with regular live music. Locals steer away from Tsimshatsui with a few exceptions, like the little upstairs bar at the **Mariner's Club** on 11 Middle Rd., and **Someplace Else** in the basement of the Sheraton—the closest Hong Kong gets to a singles bar.

Knutsford Terrace is a quiet little alley lined with new trendy bars, for better or worse billed as "the new Lan Kwai Fong." (See "Lan Kwai Fong" section below.) It's a bit tricky to find as there's no vehicle access: either access it off Observatory Road or head up Carnarvon Road past the intersection with Kimberley Road and climb the steps.

Bahama Mama's, 4 Knutsford Terrace, is a friendly beach-themed place with loud partying and lively music on Friday and Saturday nights. The English pub **Chaser's,** 2-3 Knutsford Terrace, has an older expat clientele.

Tsimshatsui's premiere pickup joint is **Rick's Café,** in the basement at 4 Hart Ave., a Casablanca-themed bar packed with a gyrating mix of locals, expats, and tourists. The American cultural behemoth **Hard Rock Café** at 100 Canton Rd. has either a live band or a D.J. spinning tunes from 10 p.m. nightly.

More expensive discos include the campy **Catwalk** in the New World Hotel, 22 Salisbury Rd., a favorite with the young, wealthy and fashionable, with an in-house salsa band, a giant video wall, and a karaoke lounge. The cover here is HK$200 on weekends; HK$120 (men only) weeknights. **Bar City** in the basement of the New World Centre encompasses country and western, Latin, and disco.

PERFORMANCE VENUES

Hong Kong Cultural Center: The building has been maligned as a "ski slope," a "public toilet," and a "crushed cigarette carton," but inside are exhibition areas, a 2,100-seat concert hall and two theaters. Stop in the foyer for the free performances (recitals, mime, folk dancing). 10 Salisbury Rd., Tsimshatsui, tel. 2734-2010.

City Hall Low Block: A good place to preview posters and flyers of upcoming events: facilities include a 1,500-seat concert hall and theater. 7 Edinburgh Place, Central, tel. 2921-2840.

Hong Kong Academy for Performing Arts: Training and performances in drama and music. 1 Gloucester Rd., Wanchai, tel. 2584-8514.

Hong Kong Arts Centre: Music, art, and drama performances, art exhibits, and a cinema screening foreign films. 2 Harbour Rd., Wanchai, tel. 2877-1000.

Hong Kong Stadium: A new 40,000-seater sponsored by the Jockey Club, site of rock concerts and the annual Rugby Sevens match. Eastern Hospital Rd., Causeway Bay, tel. 2895-7895.

Hong Kong Coliseum: A 12,500-seat venue for pop concerts and sporting events. 9 Cheong Wan Rd., Hung Hom, tel. 2355-7233.

Queen Elizabeth Stadium: Anything from Thai boxing championships to ballroom dance competitions, plus comedy and music shows. 18 Oi Kwan Rd., Wanchai, tel. 2591-1347.

Ko Shan Theater: An open-air venue for rap concerts, or more commonly, Chinese opera. Ko Shan Road, Hung Hom, tel. 2330-4742.

The Fringe Club: Alternative performances and exhibitions. 2 Lower Albert Rd., Central, tel. 2521-7251.

The hostess club scene in Tsimshatsui is pretty depressing. **Bottoms Up,** 14 Hankow Rd., is a tame topless bar with waitresess who look as if they've been there since the place opened in 1971. **Red Lips** at the intersection of Lock and Peking roads is a similarly grotesque institution. At **Adam's Apple** in the basement at 81 Nathan Rd., half-naked "hostesses make scintillating conversation while you drink." **Caesar Karaoke Nightclub** in the Hotel Miramar at 118 Nathan Rd. has drink prices and prices for hostess time conveniently itemized on table cards.

Savor the spectacular harbor views from a plush cocktail lounge like the **Sky Lounge** on the 18th floor of the Sheraton, or another **Sky Lounge** at Hotel Nikko. **Club Shanghai** at the Regent is a glamorous Art Deco lounge overlooking the harbor, with an excellent resident band playing from 9 p.m.; cover is HK$120; HK$150 weekends. Finally, the bar at **Felix** atop The Peninsula deserves a visit for the spectacularly theatrical decor, not to mention the views, which take in the harbor on one side and Kowloon on the other.

Tsimshatsui East
Nightlife here is characterized by gigantic, glittery Japanese-style nightclubs—expensive, but worth a visit just to marvel. The epitome is **Club BBoss** in Mandarin Plaza, tel. 2369-2883, a monster nightclub with a dance lounge as big as two football fields. Drinks are delivered by a full-sized electric replica of an old Rolls Royce, and 1000 cheongsam-clad hostesses slither about earning money, while digital clocks in seating areas monitor the time they spend with customers. Other, similar places are **China City Night Club** at 4/F Peninsula Centre, 67 Mody Rd., tel. 2723-3278, and **Club de Hong Kong,** 3/F Tsimshatsui Centre, 66 Mody Rd.

The other neighborhood marvel is the enormous multi-themed **Club Lost City** in Chinachem Golden Plaza, 77 Mody Rd. (just across from Club BBoss). It boasts 100,000 square feet of seriously overdecorated space, including two dance floors and a dozen different theme bars, and must be seen to be believed.

Lan Kwai Fong (LKF)
Local yuppies and Chuppies party in Lan Kwai

Fong, a small L-shaped street off D'Aguilar Street packed with trendy bars, chic restaurants, and discos. The scene is typified by numbers of self-consciously gorgeous young people, a roughly even mix of Chinese and Westerners. A night at "The Fong" doesn't come cheap, but it's an authentically swanky Hong Kong locale. On weekend evenings the action spills out onto the streets in open-air revelry.

Nineteen 97, 9-11 Lan Kwai Fong, is a triumvarate consisting of **Post 97,** a casual cafe/bar with a tasty menu, **La Dolce Vita,** an ultra-chic Italian café/bar frequented by beautiful people; and the small, cool disco **Club 97,** which is members-only on weekends. The tiny, unpretentious **F-Stop** right next door draws a young crowd on weekends for its very loud live music.

More streetside dining and drinks are available at trendy **Oscar's** at 2 LKF, if you can find a seat. Most people stand in front, creating a street party that's become a regular event. Ultrachic **California,** 24 Lan Kwai Fong, makes its statement with good Cal-Mex food, lots of beers, blacklight, and TV screens. There's a disco here Thurs.-Sat. nights starting at 11 p.m.

One floor above California is the **Jazz Club and Bar,** tel. 2845-8477, one of the best places in town for live music. International acts perform monthly—Herbie Hancock and Wynton Marsalis have played unannounced—but normally the bill is a mix of local bands and CDs. Music starts around 11 p.m.; the cover is $150.

Bit Point, 31 D'Aguilar St., is a neighborhood German bar, as is **Schnurrbart** next door, which features several dozen varieties of schnapps. The very popular **Mad Dogs** at 1 D'Aguilar St. is a yuppified British pub with live music some nights. Across D'Aguilar Street is little Wing Wah Lane, with the happily unpreten-

---

LIVE MUSIC

Hong Kong's selection of live music is spotty. Jazz is the best bet. Performances start around 10 p.m., and there's no cover unless listed:

Ned Kelly's Last Stand: A lively Dixieland jazz band, the "Kowloon Honkers," holds forth nightly from 9 p.m. 11 Ashley Rd., Tsimshatsui, tel. 2376-0562.

Mad Dogs: Popular pub with a lone singer-guitarist and weekend discos. 32 Nathan Rd., Tsimshatsui, tel. 2301-2222, and 1 D'Aguilar St., Central , tel. 2810-1000.

Delaney's: Delaney's house Whiskey Jug Band plays Irish folk from 8 p.m., switching between the two locations. 3 Prat Ave., Tsimshatsui, tel. 2301-3980, and 2/F 18 Luard Rd., Wanchai, tel. 2804-2880.

The Jazz Club and Bar: Quality jazz, blues, sometimes rock and folk; some of the best music in Hong Kong. Cover HK$150. 2/F 34 D'Aguilar St., Lan Kwai Fong, tel. 2845-8477.

F-Stop: Loud live rock music on weekends in this tiny place. 14 Lan Kwai Fong, tel. 2868-9607.

Fringe Club: Jazz, classical, and folk performances in the Dragon's Back Gallery Wednes-

day and Friday; cover for major acts around HK$200. 2 Lower Albert Rd., Central, tel. 2521-7251.

Visage One: Impromptu local jazz performances in an establishment that by day is a hair salon, Saturday from around 9 p.m. Mainslit Bldg., 42 Stanley St., Central (entrance on Pottinger Street).

Rickshaw Club: Live blues and jazz in this piano bar. 22 Robinson Rd., Midlevels (entrance on Mosque Street), tel. 2525-3977.

J.J.'s: A good house band plays most nights. Cover HK$120 Sun.-Thurs., HK$170 Fri.-Sat. In the Grand Hyatt Hotel, Wanchai, tel. 2588-1234, ext. 7323.

The Wanch: Live folk and rock performances most nights, and a low cover. 54 Jaffe Rd., Wanchai, tel. 2861-1621.

bb's Bar and Brasserie: Occasional jazz, soul, blues, and rock performances. 114 Lockhart Rd., Wanchai, tel. 2529-7702.

TOTT'S Asian Bar and Grill: Blues, rock, and pop most nights except Sunday. Excelsior Hotel, Causeway Bay, tel. 2837-6947.

tious **Club 64** and **Le Jardin,** with its small outdoor terrace.

There's more good nightlife in the immediate vicinity of LKF. **Propaganda,** 1/F 30 Wyndham St., draws a gay crowd onto its roomy dancefloor. **Zip,** 2 Glenealy, is a popular place with outdoor seating, while the tiny neighborhood pub **The Globe,** 39 Hollywood Rd., has a variety of good beer on tap. **Petticoat Lane,** 2 Tun Wo Lane, is a charming, intimate little place with baroque decor that's actually quiet enough to talk in. **Uncle Eric's Vintage Wine Bar,** 19 On Lan St., fills up fast, as happy hour, with $19 drinks, *starts* at 8 pm.

The **Fringe Club,** 2 Lower Albert Rd., Central, tel. 2521-7251, is an alternative arts center with a spacious bar doubling as exhibition room. It's a favorite hangout for students and artists; you can get instant one-night membership for HK$70, and drinks are cheap. Live entertainment ranges from jazz and South American bands to folk and pop.

More Central Nightlife
There's life in Central beyond Lan Kwai Fong, but it tends to wear business suits, like the clientele of **The Jockey,** an upscale pub in Swire House. **Brown's Wine Bar** in Exchange Square Two is filled with bankers and brokers loosening up after work. **Hard Rock Café** perpetrates American cultural imperialism from the basement of Swire House at 11 Chater Road, with DJs and dancing from 10 p.m.

For harbor views, stalk the hotels: the chic, expensive **Harlequin Bar** atop the Mandarin Oriental, **La Ronda** in the Furama, or **Cyrano** on the 56th floor of the Island Shangri-La at Pacific Place. The Mandarin also has the **Captain's Bar,** with live music, and the quiet, exclusive **Chinnery Bar.** Ultimate views, and Hong Kong's best dry martini, are obtainable from the swanky bar at **Café Deco** in the Peak Galleria, 118 Peak Road. **Cossacks,** in the basement of the Ritz-Carlton, lacks views but offers 30-plus varieties of vodka, classy Russian decor, and occasional dancing.

The walls of **The Godown,** in the basement of the Furama Hotel at 1 Connaught Rd., are adorned with photos of long-forgotten celebrities and a collection of ties left by drunken visitors. There's live jazz on Wednesday nights and disco

on other nights. **The Bull and Bear** in Hutchison House on Harcourt Road is an authentically rundown British pub, with lots of beer varieties and excellent sausages and chips.

Stylish crowds dance up a storm at the spacious, glassy **JP Encounter** in the Bank of America Tower at 12 Harcourt Road. **L.A. Cafe** in the Lippo Centre is a popular American bar/restaurant with occasional club nights. Across the street in Pacific Place, the bar at **Dan Ryan's Chicago Bar & Grill** is circled by an overhead toy train, and crowded on Friday nights.

Wanchai
Some partiers still expect to find bawdy nightlife in Wanchai, as immortalized in the '50s film *The World of Suzie Wong.* Lockhart Road still provides a mix of British-style pubs, hostess clubs, massage parlors, and rowdy disco bars, but the Wanchai area has recently undergone a nightlife revolution. New, upscale bars and nightclubs are drawing a younger, wealthier—though still wild—crowd. This is the area to head for at 2 a.m., as you're sure to find fellow souls partying till past dawn.

bb's bar and brasserie, 114 Lockhart Rd., typifies the new upscale Wanchai, a chic place filled with suits sampling local microbrews like Dragon's Back Ale and Crooked Island. The Irish pub **Delaney's,** 2/F One Capitol Place, 18 Luard Rd., is another new and popular place with an Irish house band.

Less refined, and less expensive, is the **Beer Castle,** 15 Luard Rd., a cheerfully grungy pub drawing a mixed crowd of Chinese and Westerners. The nearby **Big Apple** pub/disco is *the* place on Saturday after 2 a.m.; a twilight zone of travelers, amahs, businessmen, hookers, and Mick Jagger when he's in town. It's in the basement at 20 Luard Road.

Across the street at **Joe Bananas,** 23 Luard Rd., the dance floor is packed on weekends. This combination bar-disco-restaurant has an American diner motif and a meat-market reputation. It draws a big expat crowd, though you'll have to meet the stringent dress code (no T-shirts, shorts or sandals for men). If it's all too crass for you, try **Dali's,** 76 Jaffe Rd., which experiments with more alternative music like acid jazz and hip-hop.

The **Flying Pig,** 2/F 81 Lockhart Rd., is a beer bar with a clubby dance floor. One floor below is **Ridgways,** on weekends a dance bar full of either "crazy, friendly," or obnoxious, drunken people, depending on your perspective.

The rowdy pub **Carnegie's,** 53 Lockhart Rd., is notorious for its wild nights and topless male waiters on Ladies' Nights (Wednesday); there's often live music. **The Wanch,** properly known as the Wanchai Folk Club, is a quieter spot at 54 Jaffe Rd., featuring local bands on weekends and a resident guitarist during the week, along with a bar that's a mockup of the green-and-white Star Ferry.

J.J.'s in the Grand Hyatt is a huge entertainment complex with a great R&B house band, a disco, restaurant, bar, and game room. Sensible decor separates loud and quiet sections; highly rated for fun, and dancing, though you should show up fairly well-dressed. The Grand Hyatt also has an ultra-expensive Art Deco **Champagne Bar,** and jazz in the Tiffin Lounge to midnight. At the opposite end of the Convention Centre in the New World Harbour View Hotel is **Westworld,** a rather futuristic entertainment center with a big dance floor drawing well-heeled young locals.

Old China Hand at 104 Lockhart Rd. is a genuinely dumpy pub, expat-owned and-frequented. Other pubs on Lockhart Road include the **Horse & Groom** at No. 161 and **Horse & Carriage** at No. 117. Cheap pub food is available at all these.

Wanchai's disco bars are a favorite with Filipina *amahs,* who on Sunday, maid's day off, crowd into places like the seedy **Makati Inn** at 100 Lockhart Rd., and **Neptune's** at 62 Lockhart Road. The latter is popular with post-rave clubbers from 5 a.m. until way past sunrise on weekends. These places are more fun and less expensive than hostess bars like the **Suzie Wong Club** on Fenwick Street and the nearby **An An Club** and **Club Gold Star.** Luard Road has several topless hostess clubs, like the **Superstar** and **Popeye.**

More upper-class nightclubs aim at Asian businessmen and are not as glitzy as their Tsimshatsui East counterparts. They include the enormous **New Tonnochy Nightclub** on Tonnochy Road and **Club Celebrity** at 175 Lockhart Road. The **Supernova Lounge** atop the China Harbour View Hotel, 189 Gloucester Rd., has good harbor views and incorporates a very popular karaoke club.

To wrap up the evening with a massage (strictly nonsexual), visit the **New Paradise Health Club** at 414 Lockhart Road. Here you can get Shanghai-style massage, in which the masseuse or masseur hangs from poles on the ceiling and walks on your back; there's also a sauna, steambath, jacuzzi, and regular massage, all quite respectable. It's open noon-8:30 a.m. the following morning; fees run around HK$250-350, and there are separate facilities for men and women.

Another offbeat idea, this one with permanent consequences, is to get a tattoo at the famous **Ricky's** on Lockhart Road.

Causeway Bay

Causeway Bay's lively night scene centers around shopping and dining, but more bars and clubs are popping up lately to round out the scene. A jazz band plays Sunday afternoons at the **Dickens Bar** in the Excelsior Hotel, a pleasant, reasonably priced English pub. Ride the elevators up to the very top to **Tott's Asian Bar and Grill,** a lively "total entertainment" place encompassing a sushi counter, a cognac bar, and an exceptionally spacious restaurant/bar with window seats and live music.

The Jump, 7/F Causeway Bay Plaza II, 463 Lockhart Rd., is one of Hong Kong's most popular night spots, a fiercely trendy restaurant/bar with a small dance floor and imported performing bartenders—vodka and ice cream drinks, anyone? Similarly decadent is **Roy's at New China Max** (11/F Times Square); a jungle-themed extravaganza whose decor must be seen to be believed; it also includes an excellent restaurant. Both these places charge HK$100 cover after 10 p.m. on Friday and Saturday nights. **Oscar's,** 3/F World Trade Centre, 280 Jaffe Rd., is less packed than its trendy Lan Kwai Fong counterpart but remains a chic bar/restaurant to see and be seen in.

Quieter places include the laid-back, artsy café-bar **Brecht's,** 123 Leighton Rd., and **Brewery Tap Pub** in Vogue Alley, 66 Paterson St., where a young professional crowd packs the roomier-than-usual pub for happy hour. The nearby **Bordeaux Cellar & Bar** at 58 Paterson

St. stocks more than 300 different wines to sample from the glass or by takeaway bottle. **Juliette's Wine Bar,** 6 Hoi Ping Rd., is a cozy, quiet place with an international wine list starting at $300-400 a bottle.

Other Ideas

You don't have to drink or spend a lot of money to enjoy evenings in Hong Kong. The Chinese thing to do is, of course, eat: see the special topic "Offbeat Dining" in the Food section for suggestions on jazzed-up dining.

Ride the Hong Kong Island tram to catch the neon lights and busy crowds of Wanchai and Causeway Bay. Trams run till midnight and are far less crowded than in the daytime. To make a party of it, hire your own tram from the Hong Kong Tramways Co., tel. 2311-3509,—HK$700 an hour, bar and snacks for an extra fee.

In a similarly extravagant vein, charter a junk for an evening cruise. Boats pick up passengers at Queen's Pier in Central and glide over to a Lamma seafood restaurant, passing great nighttime views of the city en route. Weekday evenings are about half the cost of weekends, maybe HK$1800 for a cruise to Lamma—not bad for a boat that can hold up to 30 passengers. Look under "Boats: Charter and Rental" in

HONG KONG SIGHTS: A BAKER'S DOZEN

You may be temporarily overwhelmed by Hong Kong's shopping, restaurants, and hotels, but there *are* sights out there. Some of the best are found in the process of getting around. The Peak Tram, the Star Ferry, the clanking old trams running along the north shore of Hong Kong Island and the ferries to the Outlying Islands are all worthy sights in themselves.

Tailor your activities to your taste and inclination. History buffs, power shoppers, gastronomes, hikers, nightclub habitues—Hong Kong can satisfy them all. Some visitors never manage to escape the air-conditioned shopping malls and are happy about it; others will want to seek out the quieter corners of the territory. It is possible to walk for hours over mostly unspoiled countryside, or lounge on secluded beaches (though this last takes a bit of doing).

A list of Hong Kong "must-sees" and sightseeing suggestions, from the general to the more specific:

1. Ride the **Star Ferry**—or take a harbor tour.

2. The best sightseeing of all is from the top deck of the **Hong Kong Island tram** (preferably the front seat). The best stretch is between Western and Causeway Bay—interesting day or night.

3. Ride the **Peak Tram,** then stroll around Lugard and Harlech roads or walk up to Victoria Gardens. Finish with dinner at the Peak Café or the Peak Galleria.

4. Join the crowds at **Happy Valley's racetrack** on a Wednesday evening or Sunday afternoon for a quintessential Hong Kong experience.

5. Wander through **Western** and savor the old-time atmosphere of rows of shops selling traditional medicine and dried seafood. Stop at the Man Mo Temple, and walk back to Central along Hollywood Road.

6. Stroll through the **Temple Street Night Market,** and don't miss the opera singers and fortune-tellers at the far end.

7. Take **afternoon tea** at The Peninsula or the Mandarin—both are institutions.

8. The biggest, liveliest Chinese temple of all is **Wong Tai Sin** in Kowloon. Visit on Sunday or the 1st or 15th of the Chinese month to watch crowds of worshippers laden with offerings of incense, fruit, even roast pigs.

9. Enjoy the noisy clatter of a **dim sum restaurant.**

10. Visit **Aberdeen** and take a sampan through the harbor.

11. Explore the mysteries of a **Chinese street market.** Wanchai's Cross Street market or the Reclamation Street market in Yaumatei are both good choices.

12. Take the **ferry to Lantau** and visit Po Lin Monastery and the fishing village of Tai O.

13. Cruise out to either **Cheung Chau** or **Lamma Island** for a leisurely walk and a supremely fresh seafood meal.

the Yellow Pages, or try Launch and Lunch Catering, tel. 2780-3577, Viking's Charters, tel. 2814-9899, or Image Water Tours, tel. 2736-5755. Call around, as some companies are notably cheaper than others.

The Peak Tram runs till midnight as well, and the harbor views are even more dazzling at night. The walk around the Peak via Harlech and Lugard roads takes about an hour; the path is level and well-lit. Hong Kong's other famous nighttime view is from Tsimshatsui's waterfront promenade, packed on weekends with young couples.

You can get a lot of mileage out of simply wandering about absorbing the atmosphere: the neon of Tsimshatsui, the crowded street of Causeway Bay, vendors selling from barrows in Wanchai till late.

Kowloon-side, the Temple Street Night Market is a must, with its clothing stalls, fortune-tellers, and opera singers in full swing 8-11 p.m.

Water World at Ocean Park is open till 9 or 10 p.m. on summer evenings—call 2555-6055. Horse racing in Happy Valley is the favorite event on Wednesday evening from September through May (see the special topic "Days at the Races").

FESTIVALS AND HOLIDAYS

There is no better way to penetrate Hong Kong's Chinese heart than to visit a festival. Along with Taiwan, Hong Kong preserves the last remnants of colorful celebrations suppressed on the Chinese mainland. Some are essentially religious and involve placating gods and ancestors with offerings and entertainment. Others commemorate historical events or folk legends. Often the origins of a festival are largely forgotten, but the excuse for feasting, family reunions, and gifts remains.

For visitors, festivals are a wonderful entry point into local culture, and a magnificent photo opportunity. The Dragon Boat Festival, Cheung Chau's Bun Festival, and the Mid-Autumn celebration are among the most photogenic.

Tracking festivals down can be a bit tricky. The traditional Chinese calendar consists of 12 months of 29 or 30 days each. Every few years an extra month is inserted to keep it roughly in accord with the solar calendar. Festivals are determined according to the lunar calendar, so their dates on the solar calendar vary from year to year. HKTA issues a detailed annual list of festivals and dates: consult it for minor celebrations not listed in the accompanying chart. With major festivals the public holiday often comes the day after, allowing time for recuperation.

Major holidays involving family reunions—Lunar New Year, Ching Ming, the Mid-Autumn festival—are a good time to avoid traveling, especially across the Chinese border, which is packed with trampling hordes heading both ways. On any festival day, be prepared for jam-packed public transport to any place worth getting to. Sharpen your elbows and dive into the crowd; it's advisable to get an early start.

Events

Festival celebrations may be found in modern housing estates or in traditional villages. Look for the mat sheds, temporary structures of bamboo roofed with tin. Generally one serves as a temple for the papier-mâché effigies of the gods; another is the communal kitchen; and a third is a theater where performances of Cantonese opera are staged, sometimes round the clock, as entertainment for gods, ghosts, and people alike. The best performances take place in the evening.

Huge colorful "flower boards" *(fa pau)* broadcast auspicious messages, and vendors sell incense, offerings, and souvenirs. Taoist priests perform ceremonies and purification rituals, while worshippers offer whole roast suckling pigs, fruit, rice, food, incense, and red candles to the gods. Firecrackers, a traditional ingredient of Chinese festivals used to drive away demons, have been banned in Hong Kong since 1967; you'll have to visit Macau for such ear-splitting revelry.

Some festivals involve processions of *fa pau wui,* clubs organized to honor the god, marching behind big "flower boards" of bamboo and colored paper. The parade is led by men costumed as dancing lions or unicorns, followed by groups carrying offerings of food, red candles, incense, and millions of dollars of spirit money to be burned.

Village Festivals

Ta Chiu are ancient Taoist village festivals of peace and renewal. While they are extremely interesting, you're not likely to find one except by chance, as dates are selected by divination. They involve groups of up to two dozen villages, and are held on cycles of 3, 5, 7, 10, 30, 60, or 100 years, generally in the 11th or 12th lunar months (December-January). The most famous example is the Cheung Chau Bun Festival, which, atypically, is held yearly.

Ta Chiu are major events, drawing even emigrants back to their ancestral homes in order to introduce children to old customs. Modern celebrations still closely resemble descriptions of temple fairs in Guangdong in the 1860s. Taoist priests perform esoteric rituals to invoke the power of the "Three Pure Ones," while villagers worship patron deities. There are the usual opera performances, mat sheds and flower boards, and gods and ghosts are feted with offerings and entertainment. The final night involves the ritual burning of a gigantic list of villagers' names, sending them heavenwards in the smoke. Offerings for hungry ghosts are burned as well, and the evening finishes with a communal feast.

ANNUAL FESTIVALS

Lunar New Year

The biggest festival of the year, this is a time for family reunions, gifts, and feasting. It's a private, family-oriented holiday rather than a public event. Businesses shut down for at least three days (and often for up to two weeks), and transport to and from other regions of China is tremendously crowded.

The New Year signifies renewal, a fresh chance, and is a time to pay debts and settle quarrels. The preceding month is devoted to preparation: houses are thoroughly cleaned and stalls do a brisk business in special treats like candied fruit, melon seeds, sugared lotus seeds, and sweets concocted of glutinous rice. Gift shopping is a major event. Workers receive a gratuity of an extra month's pay to help them meet expenses.

Among the few public events are the huge flower fairs held in the final week of the old year.

The biggest is in Victoria Park in Causeway Bay, but others are held at Shatin, Tai Po, and Yuen Long in the New Territories, and Fa Hui Park and Cheung Sha Wan in Kowloon. Blossoms include white jonquils, pussy willows, chrysanthemums, gladioli, and dahlias. Small peach trees are a favorite, and florists devote much effort to forcing the blooms at the precise moment. Peach wood protects against demons, while the fruit is a symbol of longevity. Similarly, potted kumquat trees symbolize long life and prosperity: the characters for kumquat sound the same as those for "gold" and "lucky," and the small golden fruit symbolizes wealth.

The day before the New Year, new posters of door guardians are pasted up to protect against demons, and red "lucky papers" bearing auspicious messages go up on door frames and lintels. That evening people throng the streets, visiting temples and the flower fairs. There's no countdown to midnight, just happy crowds milling about.

No cooking or work is to be done the first two days of the new year, so as not to cut or damage the new luck. The twin Chinese obsessions with food and punning fuse: dried oysters *(ho si)* are eaten as the name is a homonym for "good sales"; fish *(yue)* is another favorite dish, as another character for *yue* means "profit."

The days are used to visit relatives and friends. Children and unmarried youths receive *lai see,* gifts of fresh new banknotes wrapped in red paper packets. The season's greeting is *kung hei fat choi,* "best wishes and prosperity." Central's skyscrapers are lit up as for Christmas with gigantic designs of the year's designated animal, and the Urban Council sponsors a giant fireworks display over the harbor, best viewed from a boat tour.

Temples are crowded on the second and third days, as devotees worship and consult their fortunes for the year. The Wong Tai Sin temple in Kowloon and the Che Kung temple in Shatin are particularly popular. Celebrations officially end with Yuen Siu, the "Lantern Festival," 15 days into the new year, when lanterns are displayed in homes and shops and carried on the streets.

Ching Ming

Literally "Bright and Clear," this festival is a time

MAJOR FESTIVAL DATES

	1998	1999	2000
Chinese New Year	28 Jan.	16 Feb.	5 Feb.
Ching Ming	5 April	5 April	4 April
Birthday of Tin Hau	19 April	8 May	27 April
Cheung Chau Bun Festival	(Dates chosen by divination)		
Birthday of Lord Buddha/ Birthday of Tam Kung	3 May	22 May	11 May
Dragon Boat Festival	30 May	18 June	6 June
Maidens' Festival	28 Aug.	17 Aug.	6 Aug.
Hungry Ghosts' Festival	5 Sept.	25 Aug.	14 Aug.
Mid-Autumn Festival	5 Oct.	24 Sept.	12 Sept.
Chung Yeung	28 Oct.	17 Oct.	6 Oct.

for families to reunite and tend the graves of the dead. Weeds are cleared away, grave inscriptions repainted, and offerings of incense, candles, tea, food, paper clothing, and spirit money are made, followed by happy family picnics in the cemetery. Visit Aberdeen or Chai Wan cemeteries on Hong Kong Island, or the big cemetery at Wo Hop Shek near Fanling. In the New Territories, male members of the five great clans visit the graves of their ancestors for more formal rituals.

Tin Hau Festival

Though not a public holiday, this is a major and colorful occasion. The goddess Tin Hau is particularly beloved by fishermen: the daughter of a 10th-century Fujian fisherman, she was later deified as Queen of Heaven. There are over 40 Tin Hau temples in Hong Kong, and 24 of them host major celebrations around this holiday, featuring offerings, opera performances, and lion dances. Due to a shortage of professional opera companies, celebrations are staggered throughout the weeks surrounding the festival date. Check with HKTA for dates and locations of events.

Joss House Bay in the New Territories is the best place to visit on the actual festival day. The harbor is crammed with boats decorated with colorful silk banners, bringing their shrines to be blessed in the old temple. The goddess herself is said to visit here on this day, and as many as 20,000 people come to the shrine seeking her presence.

Cheung Chau Bun Festival

See the corresponding special topic in the "Cheung Chau" section in the Outlying Islands chapter.

Birthday of Lord Buddha

The birthday of Shakyamuni, the enlightened Buddha, is celebrated on the eighth day of the fourth moon. Worshippers crowd into important Buddhist shrines like the Temple of 10,000 Buddhas at Shatin and Castle Peak and Po Lin Monastery on Lantau.

Tam Kung Festival

Coincidentally, the Buddha's birthday is also the birthday of the Taoist deity Tam Kung, a fishermen's patron deity said to possess the power to quell storms, extinguish fires, and cure the sick. A spectacular party is held at the Tam Kung Temple on Ah Kung Ngam Road in Shaukeiwan. Decorated junks crowd the harbor, and there are opera performances, offerings, and ceremonies.

Dragon Boat Festival

This colorful festival is a particular local favorite. It's said to replicate the events surrounding the death of Wat Yuan, a fourth-century scholar, statesman, and poet who supposedly threw himself into a river to protest the corruption of government officials. Local fishermen raced to the site to try to save him, beating drums to scare away fish and scattering rice dumplings to feed his spirit. While Wat Yuan is a historical figure, there is no evidence he killed himself in such a manner. Most likely the festival is linked with the tribal water festivals of Southeast Asia held during the hot season.

visiting ancestral graves during Ching Ming

HONG KONG TOURIST ASSOCIATION

The main attraction is the long painted boats fitted with detachable carved dragon heads and tails, sponsored by associations or neighborhoods. The biggest are up to 30 meters long and seat 50 oarsmen, who row to the time set by a drum-beating coxswain. The boats are designed to travel backwards or forwards—it's easier for the crew to reverse itself than turn the long, unwieldy boat.

Watch rowers train the preceding month at Stanley, Shaukeiwan, Aberdeen, Chai Wan, or Sai Kung in the New Territories. Races are held at these places, as well as Tai Po, Lamma, and Cheung Chau islands. The biggest event takes place in Victoria Harbour, and is best viewed from the Tsimshatsui promenade (HKTA sells tickets for tourist seating). The following weekend is the International Dragon Boat competition, introduced in 1976, an equally enjoyable event in which overseas teams compete with local champions.

Maidens' Festival

Also known as Seven Sisters' Festival, the seventh day of the seventh moon commemorates the story of the Weaving Girl and her lover, the Cowherd. The jealous Queen of Heaven caused them to be separated by the chasm of the Milky Way, except for this Double Seventh day of the year, when crows fly up to the heavens and bridge the gap with their joined wings so that the couple can be reunited. It's a day for single girls to make offerings to the seven heavenly

sisters. Small-scale offerings take place in local neighborhoods, but the main event is at Lover's Rock, off Bowen Road overlooking Happy Valley, where girls and their mothers flock to pray for good husbands and a happy marriage.

Hungry Ghosts' Festival

This is one of the best occasions to observe a typical large community celebration. Ghosts are said to roam the earth during the seventh lunar month. The unsatisfied spirits of those buried without proper funeral rites, neglected by relatives, or with no descendents to care for them are said to be particularly resentful, and need to be placated so as to not harm the living.

Elaborate ceremonies, offerings, and operas are put on to keep the ghosts happy. A peculiar feature are the towering bamboo and paper images of Tai Si Wong, the King of Hell, who supervises the burning of paper offerings—clothing, cars, horses, furniture, spirit money—and ultimately is himself burnt as well.

Major celebrations are clustered around the full moon and are held virtually everywhere; just look for the mat sheds. The entire month is filled with smaller ceremonies, as families make offerings on the street or crowd into Taoist temples.

Mid-Autumn Festival

This is also called the Lantern or Moon Festival, as the moon is said to be at its biggest and brightest this month. It's the Chinese version of a harvest celebration, a time for family reunions and contentment. Everyone feasts on *yue bing,* "moon cakes," stuffed with red bean or lotus seed paste and salted duck eggs. With such dense, heavy-duty fillings, they're meant to be tasted rather than devoured. Their roundness is said to symbolize completion and happiness.

Stalls sell cakes and fat-bellied silk and paper lanterns, in both traditional form (rabbits, goldfish, flowers) and modern versions (rockets, airplanes, cars). In the evening, families gather for moonrise picnics and children run about with lanterns and candles, giddy with the magic of fire. Victoria Park hosts a full-scale carnival, with open-air opera concerts and cultural shows and a night market. The Peak is another popular place to watch the moon rise, as are the beaches at Stanley and Repulse Bay.

Chung Yeung

Similar to Ching Ming, this is also a time for making offerings and cleaning family graves, concluding with a picnic. Ancient custom dictates it's also a day for journeying to hilltops and high places, and public transport is crowded.

Other Holidays

China's acquisition of Hong Kong has put an end to traditional observances of the Queen's birthday in June and Liberation Day (marking Hong Kong's liberation from Japanese rule in WW II) on the last Monday in August. The new holidays are China's National Day (1 October) and Sino-Japanese War Victory Day (18 August).

The handover is not likely to dampen local zest for Christmas and New Year's. Crowds pour into the streets to purchase the season's latest gadgets (foam lizards suspended from a wire, flashing Santa caps), admire the Christmas lights in Central and Tsimshatsui East, and shop in stores blasting obnoxiously loud carols. Massive crowds can shut down traffic on Christmas Eve and night and New Year's Eve and night in Tsimshatsui, but people are amazingly well-behaved.

SPORTS AND RECREATION

It may seem that Hong Kong's favorite sport is getting ahead, but there's more to recreation than the pedestrian races across Nathan Road's crosswalks. The diverse terrain supports a wide variety of activities, from scuba diving in ocean waters to hiking in 21 country parks. Hong Kong is also a good place to shop for sporting equipment, with competitive prices on mountain bikes, scuba gear, and ski wear.

Residents plunge into sports with the same energy they apply to business. That means there's a good support system of sporting clubs and organizations. It also means that facilities are crowded, especially after office hours. Try to avoid doing anything recreational on weekends, which are crowded everywhere.

Events

A "Sports Diary" in the Urban Council's monthly magazine *City News* lists current events. The most popular annual event among expats is the **Rugby Sevens** held over Easter weekend to a sold-out stadium. The **Hong Kong International Marathon** is held each January in Shatin (contact the Hong Kong Amateur Athletic Association, tel. 2504-8215). There's also a **Coast of China Marathon** in March, tel. 2573-5292. The **Hong Kong Golf Open** is held at the course in Fanling in November. Other events include **Windsurfing Championships** and the **Trailwalker** charity fundraiser, both in October.

Facilities

The privately operated **Hong Kong Sports Institute** in Shatin has squash, badminton, and tennis courts, an Olympic pool, an outdoor track and running trail, and more. Nonmembers are admitted in off-peak hours (i.e., weekdays); call 2681-6888 for details.

The **Hong Kong Sportsworld Association** has tennis courts, a roller rink, and an Olympic indoor pool; membership is not necessary for use. It's at Telford Gardens in Kowloon Bay, tel. 2757-2211. The **South China Athletic Association** in Causeway Bay also sells day passes to visitors, tel. 2577-6932, and has indoor facilities for bowling, tennis, squash, and yoga, among others.

HIKING AND COUNTRY PARKS

It comes as a great surprise for most visitors to learn that roughly 70% of Hong Kong's area is undeveloped land, too rugged for even the most voracious developers. Much of it is preserved in an extensive system of country parks, set aside in the 1970s as green space, recreational playgrounds, and water catchment areas for reservoirs.

Hong Kong has 21 country parks, two special areas, and 17 reservoirs: over 41,000 hectares in all, encompassing white-sand beaches, rocky seashore, and a handful of lush forests. Most of it is rolling, scrub-covered hills, vaguely reminiscent of the Scottish highlands, but offering sweeping vistas of the South China Sea.

HKTA doesn't promote it as an attraction, but a day spent exploring a country park or hiking a trail can be a welcome respite from urban Hong Kong. In typical local fashion, even the wilderness is well-organized. Each park has an information center with detailed map boards outlining hiking routes. Most are easily reached by public transport. Trails are signposted, well-maintained, and often paved.

The park system is luring a new generation of Hongkongers further afield. Each year over 10 million visitors use the parks for group hikes, barbecues, and picnics. Still, if you avoid weekends and manage to dodge school field trips, you'll gain a big dose of peace and quiet.

Some hiking tips:

• Get a good map. The *Countryside Series* from the Government Publications Center in the GPO at Connaught Place is the most detailed.

• Bring more water than you think you'll need, as well as water purification tablets or iodine to treat water collected en route.

• Use good sun protection, and don't overestimate your abilities in the hot season.

• If you're camping, cook only in designated trailside barbecue pits (hill fires are a serious problem), and bring mosquito repellent for the evenings.

• Leave word of your whereabouts and expected return time. Hong Kong may seem tame, but hikers have gotten lost and died on its trails.

Many hikes are described in the text: Sai Kung's 80 km of trails; Hong Kong Island's accessible country parks, like Pokfulam and Aberdeen; the panoramic Dragon's Back down into Shek O; the high slopes of Tai Mo Shan. *Selected Walks in Hong Kong,* by Ronald Forrest and George Hobbins, describes over 75 possible routes, while *Hong Kong Pathfinder* by Martin Williams documents 21 day hikes. Consult the Booklist for other recommended guidebooks.

The MacLehose Trail

The centerpiece of the system is the 100-km MacLehose Trail (accent on the "Mac," and named after a former governor). It stretches the entire length of the New Territories, from the Sai Kung Peninsula to the new town of Tuen Mun, linking seven country parks and providing a varied sampler of peaks, city panoramas, wildlife, waterfalls, traditional fishing and farming villages, and remnants of WW II fortifications. The eastern portion is the most scenic; the westernmost section fairly boring. Still, a walk along any section reveals the older, rural Hong Kong that abides beneath the urban roar.

The trail is divided into ten stages, most connected to public transportation, so you can do a stretch or two and return to your hotel the same night. Hikers doing the entire trail usually take five days—a total of 34 hours walking at a comfortable pace. In the annual Trailwalker charity fundraiser, four-person teams have 48 hours to hike the entire trail. The record is 13 hours, 18 minutes, set by Nepali Gurkha soldiers.

There are 31 designated campsites along the route, two IYHA hostels, and an occasional store or small restaurant. Leaflets issued by the Country

---

The Urban Council operates Indoor Games Halls with facilities like basketball, tennis, volleyball, and squash courts. Courts must be booked in person. Convenient locations include 11/F Sheung Wan Complex, 345 Queen's Rd., Central, tel. 2853-2575; 27 Harbour Rd., Wanchai, tel. 2827-9684; and Kowloon Park, Hai-

phong Rd., Tsimshatsui, tel. 2724-3344.

Gyms and Health Clubs

Local gyms charge around HK$150 a day for use of their facilities. **The Gym,** 18/F Melbourne Plaza, 33 Queen's Rd., Central, tel. 2877-8337, has aerobics classes, steam and weight rooms,

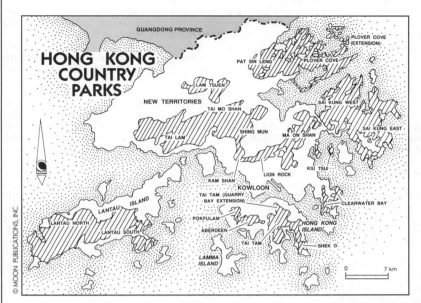

Parks Authority detail the MacLehose Trail's stages and outline public transport to each. The CPA also puts out a 1:25,000 map of the trail, available at its office (12/F Government Offices Bldg., 393 Canton Rd., Tsimshatsui) or at the Government Publications Center in Central.

The trail's finest sections include Stage One, a three-hour stroll from Pak Tam Chung around High Island Reservoir to a beach campsite at Long Ke, and Stage Two, five hours hiking past spectacular coastal scenery and the fine white-sand beaches of Sai Wan and Ham Tin, ending at the Bradbury Youth Hostel at Chek Keng. The trail's middle portions encompass a tough up-and-down trek over rugged ridges, crossing a saddle just below the 702-meter volcanic massif of Ma On Shan.

Stage 5 (three hours) is a breathtaking ridge walk offering views of Victoria Harbour and the Kowloon/Hong Kong Island skyline. To reach the trailhead, take a Sai Kung minibus from the Choi Hung MTR station to Fei Ngo Shan, then walk up to Tate's Cairn.

For hiking on Hong Kong Island, see the special topic of that name. See the chapter on Lantau for a description of the circular 70-km **Lantau Trail,** which leads hikers past secluded gardens and traditional monasteries.The CPA booth at the Lantau ferry pier distributes leaflets with a simple map.

and a sauna. **Beth's Workout** offers exercise and aerobics classes (you pay by the class); it's at 5/F 14 Wellington St., Duke of Wellington House, Central, tel. 2522-5793.

Hotels often allow outsiders to use their facilities for similar fees. Try the health center at the **Marriot** in Pacific Place, tel. 2810-8366, or the Sports Deck at the **Excelsior Hotel** in Causeway Bay, tel. 2894-8888.

Sports and Recreation Tour
Every Tuesday and Friday HKTA's "Sports and Recreation Tour" allows a daylong visit to the Clearwater Bay Golf and Country Club, with its

18-hole golf course, tennis and squash courts, swimming pool, and saunas. The tour costs HK$330, including lunch and transport; equipment rental and facilities are extra—from HK$30 for use of the pool to HK$850 for the golf course. Call HKTA at 2801-7390 for more details.

SPORTS DIRECTORY

Bowling
Bowl at **South China Bowling Centre,** 88 Caroline Hill Rd., Causeway Bay, or **TopBowl** at Whampoa Garden in Hung Hom.

Cycling
The most popular bicycling paths are around Tolo Harbour in the New Territories. Start at Tai Wai (on the KCR Line), and ride through Tai Po and on to Tai Mei Tuk and Bride's Pool on Plover Cove Reservoir (see The New Territories section for details). Rental cycles are available in front of the Tai Wai KCR as well as at Tai Po and Tai Mei Tuk. Shek O, Silvermine Bay on Lantau, and Cheung Chau are other popular bicycling sites. Bike trails are crowded on Sunday; rentals cost HK$10-35 per hour, HK$40-60 per day.

   Mountain biking is restricted to roads in country parks, greatly reducing potential terrain. Getting out of town with a cycle is another problem—fighting Kowloon traffic is less than inspiring. Ferries take bikes on board as long as you buy an extra ticket, making outlying islands like Lamma and Lantau good destinations.

   Out in the New Territories, the coastline route from Laufashan toward Tuen Mun, skirting the base of Castle Peak, is a current favorite. On Lamma, try crossing from Yung Shue Wan toward Sok Kwu Wan, cutting south over the ridge toward Sham Wan, then looping back through Tung O and Mo Tat Wan to Sok Kwu Wan. Lantau bikers can take the road from Mui Wo to Po Lin Monastery, and end at a Tai O seafood restaurant.

   The staff at **Flying Ball Bicycle Co.,** 201 Tung Choi St., Mongkok, tel. 2381-3661, is a good source of information on local routes and cycle tours into China. The **Universal Bike Co.,** 13 Wood Rd., Wanchai, tel. 2834-0163, sells bicycles.

Fishing
Shore and bottom fishing are done from boats out of Aberdeen, Cheung Chau, Sai Kung, and Hebe Haven. The season for freshwater fishing in reservoirs is September-March. A license is required: call the **Water Supplies Department** at 2829-4500 for information.

Golf
With greens fees topping HK$1000, golf is an expensive proposition, unless you can find a member to sign you in. Clubs generally admit non-members only on weekdays. The **Hong Kong Golf Club,** tel. 2670-0647, has three 18-hole courses in Fanling; the greens fee is HK$1400. It also operates a course in **Deep Water Bay,** tel. 2812-7070, where visitor's fees are HK$450. The scenic **Discovery Bay Golf Club** on Lantau, tel. 2987-7273, has a course designed by Robert Trent Jones; the greens fee is HK$900 on weekdays, nearly double on weekends. **Clearwater Bay Golf and Country Club** on the Sai Kung Peninsula, tel. 2719-1595, charges HK$1100, HK$850 for participants in HKTA's "Sports and Recreation Tour." The Jockey Club's new course on the island of **Kiu Tsai Chau** near Sai Kung has visitor fees of HK$1000.

Horse Racing
The Hong Kong Jockey Club operates two tracks: the original at Happy Valley on Hong Kong Island and an ultramodern one in Shatin. Racing season is September through May; races are held Wednesday evening and Saturday afternoon (and occasionally on Sunday). See the special topic "Days at the Races" for details on what is undoubtedly Hong Kong's favorite sport.

Horseback Riding
Horses can be rented at the **Tai Yuen Riding School** on Castle Peak Road, tel. 2471-8492, or the **Hong Kong Riding Union** in Kowloon Tong, tel. 2488-6886. The **Hong Kong International Riding Club,** San Tin., tel. 2482-1483, charges HK$150 for half-hour weekday sessions, HK$180 on weekends.

Martial Arts
Briefly, there are two schools of kung fu: *ngoi*

TAI CHI

You see them especially in the early morning hours in Victoria Park: elderly people moving in a silent slow-motion ballet, in the graceful movements English speakers have dubbed "shadow boxing." Actually it's tai chi chuan, an ancient system of exercise based on Taoist principles of balance and tranquillity.

Tai chi originated in the Song dynasty as a system of self-defense, useful for priests who were prevented by vow from carrying weapons and were thus easy targets for robbers. It's said to have been developed by a Taoist priest who observed a bird attacking a snake curled up to fend off the attack. The bird eventually tired, and the snake killed it instantly with a single poised strike.

Tai chi involves a flowing cycle of movement through poses with poetic names like "Catching the Peacock's Tail," "Needle at the Bottom of the Sea," and "White Crane Spreads Its Wings." The center of gravity is kept low, the weight constantly shifted from one foot to another. The idea is to move as slowly as possible, without strain or exertion, in a continuous motion, thus cultivating not outer strength but awareness of the inner energy or *chi*. Judo, kendo, and tae kwon do have all evolved from similar principles.

There are several different styles of tai chi, all involving the coordination of mind, body, and breath but differing in the sequence of postures and movements. A single cycle can take 20-60 minutes, the slower the better. It's best done outside, as open air favors the circulation of *chi*, and in the early morning, when the *chi* is highest and most malleable.

Tai chi's unstrenuous nature and its emphasis on flexibility make it ideal for elderly people. Practitioners say it improves balance and muscle control, stimulates circulation and promotes relaxation. More esoterically, it's supposed to cultivate *chi* and balance yin and yang, thus improving overall health and preventing imbalances that can lead to disease.

kung is the more dramatic and violent, popularized by hundreds of films. *Chi kung* teaches a student to turn the attacker's weaknesses against him, and is based on internal strength and balance. Hong Kong movie theaters specialize in kung fu epics, but the martial art you'll see practiced most often is the gentler variety, specifically tai chi.

For information on martial arts schools and classes, contact the **Hong Kong Chinese Martial Arts Association,** Sport House, So Kon Po, tel. 2504-8164. The **Hong Kong Tai Chi Association** at 60 Argyle St., Mongkok, tel. 2395-4884, may have information on tai chi courses. The **South China Athletic Association** in Causeway Bay, tel. 2577-6932, organizes classes in tai chi, judo, and yoga, as does the YMCA.

Paragliding
The **Hong Kong Paragliding Association,** tel. 2803-2779, runs a four-day training course in Tai Po for HK$1500, and holds meets on Dragon's Back at Shek O and Sunset Peak on Lantau Island.

Rock Climbing
Three sites offer a range of good, if short, climbs: the southwest wall of **Lion Rock,** just north of Kowloon in Lion Rock Country Park; **Kowloon Peak,** which has remarkable views of the Choi Hung housing estate and Kai Tak Airport; and **Tung Lung Island,** which is accessible by ferry (weekend mornings only) from Sai Wan Ho. The tip of the Shek O headland is good for bouldering. In addition there are nearly a dozen artificial climbing walls, the biggest at the University of Hong Kong's sports center. Contact the Urban Council for more details.

Running
Running on the Peak is an unrivaled experience. The 3.5-km loop around Lugard and Harlech roads is paved, cool, nearly traffic-free, and offers superb views. Hong Kong typhoons and socialites exercise along shady, scenic four-km-long **Bowen Road,** in the Mid-Levels above Wanchai and Happy Valley. There's also a jogging track in Victoria Park in Causeway Bay. Tsimshatsui runners must settle for the waterfront promenade or Kowloon Park.

Skating
For the roller variety, try **Rollerworld** in Cityplaza (Taikoo Shing) or **Sportsworld Association** in Telford Gardens, Kowloon Bay. Though

the ice is a bit soft, ice skaters can try **Cityplaza Ice Palace** in Taikoo Shing, 7 a.m.-10 p.m., or **Whampoa Super Ice** in Whampoa Garden, Hung Hom. Rentals and fees for either variety run around HK$40 for weekdays, HK$50 on weekends.

Squash

Try the **Hong Kong Squash Centre,** 23 Cotton Tree Dr., Central, tel. 2869-0611; **Victoria Park** in Causeway Bay, tel. 2890-5824; or check the listings under "Facilities," above.

Swimming

The dozen or so public pools run by the Urban Council are not too badly crowded on weekdays, but avoid weekends and during school holidays. Kowloon Park has multiple indoor and outdoor pools. Victoria Park has several outdoor pools; there's a 50-meter-long pool in Aberdeen, 2 Shum Wan Rd., and a heated indoor pool at Morrison Hill, 7 Oi Kwan Rd., Wanchai. Hours are roughly 7 a.m.-9 p.m. (some close for lunch), while admission runs around HK$17, HK$8 for children. Also check under "Facilities," above. Finally, **Water World** at Ocean Park features a wave pool and giant water slides. For a rundown of Hong Kong's beaches, see the special topic "Beaches."

Tennis

You're best off relying on your hotel, as the few courts are in great demand, especially after office hours. Otherwise, contact the Hong Kong Tennis Association in Victoria Park, tel. 2890-1132, for information, or try the public tennis courts: at **Victoria Park** in Causeway Bay, tel. 2570-6186; **King's Park** in Yaumatei, tel. 2577-6932; or the **Tennis Centre** on Wong Nai Chung Gap Rd., Happy Valley, tel. 2574-9122. Also see "Facilities," above.

WATER SPORTS

Windsurfing

Conditions are less than superb, but with the world's two biggest sailboard manufacturers locally based, windsurfing is popular—especially since Cheung Chau resident Lee Lai-san won Hong Kong's first-ever gold medal in the 1996 Olympics. Six centers scattered throughout the SAR offer tuition (HK$400-500 for a one-day beginners' course) and rentals (HK$50-80 per hour). Most popular are **Stanley Windsurfing Centre** on Stanley Main Beach, tel. 2813-9937, and **Cheung Chau Windsurfing Centre** on Tung Wan Beach, tel. 2981-8316. **Shek O Windsurfing Centre,** tel. 2368-9169, and **Tai Po Boardsailing Centre,** tel. 2366-9911, are also good.

In addition, three **Watersports Centres** run by the Regional Council offer inexpensive windsurfing classes and rentals as well as dinghy sailing and canoeing; they are located at **Tai Mei Tuk,** tel. 2665-3591, in Plover Cove, **Wong Shek,** tel. 2328-2311, and **Chong Hing,** tel. 2792-6810, at the High Island Reservoir.

Scuba Diving

This is best along the east coast of the New Territories, where water visibility can sometimes exceed 15 meters (usually it's less than six meters). Pollution has reduced the tremendous diversity of tropical and temperate marine life, but some sites still have up to 30 different types of coral.

There are some decent shore-diving sites, like Lung Ha Wan in Clearwater Bay, but the best dive spots are found by chartering a boat out of Sai Kung or Central to explore the eastern coastline. Table Island, Trio Island, and Basalt Island are all recommended. North of these, the beaches of Long Ke Wan and Tai Long Wan are fine destinations, which can also be reached by hiking.

Mirs Bay is another good choice. Jones' Cove or Hoi Ha Wan, a small inlet off of Mirs Bay, has been declared Hong Kong's first marine park because of its diverse undersea life.

Contact the **Hong Kong Underwater Centre,** tel. 2512-9388, for information on the SAR's 13 dive clubs, which often organize trips. The **International (Elite) Divers Training Centre,** tel. 2381-2789, and **Dive Venture,** tel. 2856-1700, both offer diving trips, instruction, and equipment rentals, though you have to bring your own suit, mask, and fins.

Water Skiing

Skis and boats can be rented for about HK$450 an hour from the **Deep Water Bay Speedboat Co.,** tel. 2812-0391.

Surfing
Body boards are for hire at Big Wave Bay, up the road from Shek O on Hong Kong Island.

Boat Rentals
Old fishing junks are converted into pleasure junks with a few simple modifications, like adding benches and tables—the latter with holes cut in them to hold beer cans, a very important feature. A weekday trip out to Sai Kung or Lamma might run around HK$2500.

Consult the Yellow Pages under "Boats: Charter and Rental." Or try **Charterboats,** G/F Aberdeen Marina Tower, tel. 2555-7349; **Viking's Charters,** tel. 2814-9899; **Rent-a-Junk,** Mongkok, tel. 2780-0387; or **Tsui Wah Ferry Service,** tel. 2527-2513.

In a different vein, pedal boats and rowboats are rented on Wong Nai Chung Reservoir for HK$40-60 an hour.

GETTING THERE

Hong Kong is a worthwhile destination in itself, but its excellent airline connections make it an ideal base for a longer trip through China, East Asia, and/or Southeast Asia. It's strategically located at the intersection of major air routes, three hours by plane from Beijing and Singapore, two hours from Bangkok and Manila. And when you've finished exploring Burma or Nepal or Cambodia, Hong Kong, with its modern amenities, is a great place to re-emerge, refuel, and continue on from refreshed.

BY AIR

Airline Tickets
Tickets purchased through airlines can be first class, business class, economy class, or even cheaper. APEX or Advance Purchase Excursion fares average 25% below economy prices. Generally these allow no stopovers, have minimum and maximum stays, fixed departure and return dates, and require three weeks' advance purchase. Excursion fares are more flexible, and still well below full fare. Fares depend on stopovers and vary by season (peak is summer) and possibly even day of the week.

Cheap Fare Ideas
Really cheap tickets (25-40% below economy fares) are sold by flight consolidators, who buy blocks of seats at charter prices, then unload them individually through discount travel agents. Roundtrip West Coast-Hong Kong can be as little as US$600, depending on the season. Check the Sunday travel sections of major newspapers, and try to buy such tickets well in advance for maximum savings.

Courier firms are another option, as Hong Kong gets a lot of business travel. Sometimes couriers are limited to carry-on baggage for personal use (hardly a problem, as you can buy a full wardrobe and several suitcases in Hong Kong with the money saved on airfare). Other times they need only deliver a document. Fare is significantly discounted, as little as US$350 roundtrip, and even less for flights booked within a few days of departure. Stays may be restricted to two to four weeks. Try TNT Skypack, UTL Travel, or Crossroads in San Francisco or Los Angeles, or Now Voyager, Discount, or Courier in New York.

Student discounts of 20% or more are sometimes available to anyone under age 26, so ask. STA Travel in New York (tel. 800-777-0112) arranges discount travel for students under 25. Children ages 2-12 pay 50 to 67% of adult fare, depending on the airline. Under-twos who are not occupying a seat pay 10%.

Hotel-airfare packages can be an exceptionally good deal in pricey Hong Kong, reducing room rates by 50% or more. Check with travel agents. Finally, including Hong Kong on a Round-the-World ticket packs in a maximum number of stops for a minimum fare; see "Routing Ideas," below.

From the U.S. and Canada
Roundtrip economy fare to Hong Kong is US$900-1200 from the West Coast (depending on season), US$1200-1450 from New York—but with a minimum of planning and research, you can find even cheaper fares. Call airlines for baseline information, then shop

around among discount and student travel agencies. One such possibility is Council Travel, with offices in many major American cities (New York tel. 212-882-2700). Air Brokers International in San Francisco (tel. 800-883-3272) is a good flight consolidator.

Cheap Asian fares are advertised in the Sunday travel sections of the *San Francisco Chronicle, Los Angeles Times,* and *New York Times.* You should be able to pick up a roundtrip ticket from the West Coast for around US$800; less than that in the off-season.

Direct U.S.-Hong Kong carriers include Northwest, Singapore, and United, all flying from the West Coast. (East Coast departures are bound to include at least one stopover, and average over 20 hours.) Cheaper fares are available on stopover flights on Asian airlines like China Airlines (via Taiwan) and Asiana Airlines and Korean Air (via Seoul). Hong Kong's own carrier, Cathay Pacific Airways, is one of the 20 largest airlines in the world and regularly ranks among the top five for service.

Flights from Canada are increasing as the Hong Kong population of cities like Vancouver grows. Canadian Airlines flies daily to Hong Kong direct from Vancouver, Toronto and Montreal. Cathay Pacific, Air Canada, Asiana Airlines, and China Airlines also fly out of Vancouver.

If Hong Kong is not your only Asian destination, consider adding an inexpensive stopover–less than US$100—onto your ticket to another city, like Bangkok (Thai International) or Singapore (Singapore Airlines).

DEALING WITH JET LAG

Jet lag is your body's normal physical reaction to being violently wrenched across multiple time zones. The miracle of modern travel disrupts the subtle circadian rhythms that regulate physical cycles involving hormones, sleep, and body temperature. The resulting fatigue and disorientation can ruin the early days of a trip.

Apart from being a waste of precious vacation time, jet lag causes people to function at lowered efficiency. Severe fatigue, impaired sleeping and eating rhythms and poor vision are some of the symptoms. A rough rule of thumb prescribes 24 hours recovery for every two hours of time difference, which means a traveler from the West Coast of the United States would need four days to feel up to snuff in Hong Kong.

Fortunately, much of this can be influenced by behavior. Pre-departure, avoid last-minute running about and try to get enough sleep. Beginning a few days before you leave, gradually shift your sleep patterns. If you're flying east, go to bed early and get up early. Westward-bound travelers should stay up late and get up late.

The efficacy of the "feast and fast" jet-lag diet has been substantiated by studies on animals, though few people are disciplined enough to follow it diligently. Starting four days before departure, "feast" on a high-protein, high-carbohydrate diet—dairy products, beans, meat, rice, potatoes, bread, desserts—which is supposed to induce sleep. The following day, adhere to a low-calorie "fast" diet (soup, fruit, toast, rice), which is supposed to deplete the body's carbohydrate store. Continue like this for the next two days, avoiding caffeine (coffee, tea, cola) throughout.

Once aboard the plane, move immediately into the sleeping and eating schedule of your destination. It helps to set your watch to Hong Kong time upon boarding. Some specialists recommend taking a low dosage of a mild sleeping pill to aid in-flight rest; consult your doctor.

Compounding jet lag is the "long-haul syndrome," the punishing routine that all airline passengers are subjected to. Cabins are pressurized to simulate an altitude of 1500-2000 meters, a lot higher than where most of us live. Among other things this causes mild edema or swelling, so wear loose clothing and shoes.

The stale, pressurized air tends to dehydrate passengers, as does the typically dry airline food. Drinking caffeinated or alcoholic beverages will dry you up still further. Load up on water and juice, relax with a wet washcloth over your nose and mouth, and periodically get up to exercise and keep the blood moving.

After landing, move immediately into the local schedule. Most long-haul flights land at Hong Kong late at night, so go straight to bed. No doubt you'll be up at dawn: wander down to a nearby park and watch the practitioners of tai chi, a favorite early morning sport.

From Europe
In Europe, the best deals are from London bucket shops or in Amsterdam. In London, try Trailfinders, tel. 0171-938-3666 or Council Travel, tel. 0171-437-7767. European airlines flying direct to Hong Kong include Air France, British Airways, Virgin, Lufthansa, and Swissair; Cathay Pacific has an extensive European network, including London, Paris, Manchester, Amsterdam, Frankfurt, Rome, and Zurich. Cheaper fares (which

HONG KONG'S NEW AIRPORT

The old Kai Tak Airport in the heart of urban Kowloon, with its single runway jutting into Kowloon Bay, was not only spectacular, it was stretched to full capacity years before the ultra-modern new airport opened. Built on a platform of reclaimed land off the north coast of Lantau Island, the new airport allows Hong Kong to retain its title as Asia's busiest air traffic point, and the fourth busiest airport in the world. Now there can be 24-hour takeoffs and landings, as there are fewer neighbors to complain, and two runways rather than the overworked singleton of Kai Tak. The dual runway airport is designed to handle up to 35 million passengers a year upon its opening in April 1998, and will eventually be able to process more than twice that number.

The saga of the airport's construction is one of history's more impressive feats of civil engineering. The tiny island of Chek Lap Kok (former pop. 194) was levelled and the fill pushed into the sea to create over 1200 hectares of new land—the world's largest reclamation project, at one point involving four-fifths of the international dredger fleet. The Airport Core Programme encompasses ten interlinked projects, including an elaborate system of expressways, bridges (including the world's longest suspension bridge at Tsing Ma), a high-speed rail line, and an undersea tunnel—the HK$7.5 billion Western Harbour Crossing. Container port facilities, dockyards, typhoon shelters, public housing, and a new China Ferry Pier are also part of the package. Crucial to the program is the ongoing Central-Wanchai Reclamation Project (see the special topic "The Expansion of Hong Kong"), which has created new land for the Airport Railway Station.

This Airport Core Programme is the centerpiece of a wildly ambitious effort to transform Hong Kong through massive land reclamation, a project that ranks as the world's biggest ongoing civil engineering scheme and among the most expensive public works projects ever—almost half again as much as the English Channel "Chunnel." The current estimated minimum cost of the entire package is HK$154 billion, with inflation taken into account.

Disputes regarding the new airport's cost and environmental impact dogged it since the first study was done in 1979. The idea was temporarily shelved when the international economy slowed in the early '80s, then revived as the need became apparent. In 1989 China signed a Memorandum of Understanding with Britain on the airport, confirming the project, but substantial foot-dragging followed—enough to ensure the airport would not be completed in time for the 1997 handover. It's slated to open in April 1998. The Airport Authority Home Page, which begins with an animated runway landing on the new site, displays photographs of current stages of development: it's at http://www.hkairport.com.

Transportation Center
The Transportation Center at the east end of the passenger terminal provides access to the Airport Express Railway, taxis, buses, and cars. The high-speed railway is the easiest option, linking the passenger terminal with stations at West Kowloon and Central on Hong Kong Island. With trains operating at 135 km per hour, travel time from the airport is only 18 minutes to Kowloon, 23 minutes to Central. Fares are HK$40 to Kowloon, HK$50 to Central. Trains depart every eight minutes, from 6 a.m. to 1 a.m. the following day. Trains have been designed with ample seating and space for baggage: as an additional plus, travelers needn't change floors within the terminal.

The airport is also served by special lowfloor Airbuses with luggage compartments and luggage handling assistance. Airbus fares range from $17 to $45 (exact change required), with concessions for passengers over 65. The A11 runs to Causeway Bay (Moreton Terrace); the A21 to the Kowloon KCR Station, and the A22 to the Lam Tin MTR station, while the E220 operates all day and night from the Star Ferry Pier. Check at the Airbus customer service center for more information on routes, or call 2745-4466.

entail more inconvenient routing) are available from Middle Eastern and Eastern European airlines like Gulf Air and Air China.

From Australia and New Zealand
Australia's Qantas flies to Hong Kong from Sydney, Brisbane, Melbourne, and Perth; Ansett flies from Sydney and Cathay Pacific from Sydney and Melbourne. Cheaper fares are available on Asian airlines like Philippine Airlines and Garuda Airlines. Air New Zealand and Cathay Pacific fly direct from Auckland. Cheap Australian flight specialists include STA Travel (toll-free 1800-637-444), Asian Travel Centre in Melbourne (tel. 03/9654-8277), and Sydney Flight Centre (tel. 02-9241-2422).

Routing Ideas
You may well be visiting Hong Kong as part of a longer trip. The rest of China naturally fits into the itinerary, as do Manila, Bangkok, and Singapore. Tokyo is a popular stopover on flights from the United States. Investigate mileage tickets, which allow multiple stops en route between two points, and the Circle-Pacific fares on United, Northwest, and Canadian.

Another way to get to Hong Kong cheaply is to include it on a Round-the-World fare. These

---

AIRLINE OFFICES

These move frequently, so if the number given no longer applies, check under "Airline Companies" in the *Yellow Pages,* and always double-check the address on the phone.

Air Canada: Wheelock House, 20 Pedder St., Central; tel. 2522-1001

Air India: Room 1002, Gloucester Tower, The Landmark, 11 Pedder St., Central; tel. 2522-1176

American Airlines: Room 1738 Swire House, 25 Chater Rd., Central; tel. 2826-9269

Air New Zealand: Fairmont House, Cotton Tree Drive, Admiralty; tel. 2524-9041

British Airways: 30/F Alexandra House, 7 Des Voeux Rd., Central; tel. 2868-0303

Cathay Pacific Airways: G/F Swire House, 25 Chater Rd., Central; tel. 2747-1888

China Airlines: G/F St. George's Building, 2 Ice House St., Central; tel. 2868-2299

Dragonair: Wheelock House, 20 Pedder St., Central; tel. 2868-6777

Delta Air Lines: Room 2915, Two Pacific Place, Queensway; tel. 2537-9795

Garuda Indonesia: 2/F Sing Pao Centre, 8 Queen's Rd., Central; tel. 2840-0000

Japan Air Lines: 20/F Gloucester Tower, The Landmark, 11 Pedder St., Central; tel. 2523-0081

KLM: Room 3201 World Trade Centre, Causeway Bay; tel. 2808-2118

Korean Air: 11/F Tower 2, South Seas Centre, 75 Mody Rd., Tsimshatsui East; tel. 2733-7111

Lufthansa: Edinburgh Tower, 15 Queen's Rd., Central; tel. 2846-6388

Malaysia Airlines: Room 1306 Prince's Bldg., Chater Rd., Central; tel. 2521-8181

Northwest Airlines: 29/F Alexandra House, 7 Des Voeux Rd., Central; tel. 2810-4288

PanAm: Room 1205 Alexandra House, 7 Des Voeux Rd., Central; tel. 2523-1111

Philippine Airlines: East Ocean Centre, 98 Granville Rd., Tsimshatsui East; tel. 2369-4521

Qantas: Room 1443, Swire House, Chater Rd., Central; tel. 842-1438

Royal Nepal Airlines: Room 704, Lippo Sun Plaza, 28 Canton Rd., Tsimshatsui; tel. 2375-9151

Singapore Airlines: 17/F United Centre, Queensway, Admiralty; tel. 2520-2233

Thai International: United Centre, Queensway, Admiralty; tel. 2529-5681

United Airlines: 29/F Gloucester Tower, The Landmark, 11 Pedder St., Central; tel. 2810-4888

tickets combine two or more airlines and allow for unlimited stopovers, as long as you don't backtrack. RTW fares out of the U.S. average around US$2000; tickets are valid for one year.

Getting Away

As the airfare hub of South Asia, Hong Kong is a good place to arrange flights and buy discounted air tickets. Check the *Post Services Guide* for ads on air ticket prices, then call around and do some comparison shopping, as prices can vary HK$500-600 between agencies. Be wary of exceptionally cheap fares. Try to avoid giving a deposit on air tickets: at unscrupulous companies, fares sometimes mysteriously rise after the customer has been hooked.

The lowest one-way airfares from Hong Kong in 1997 were as follows:

Auckland HK$4220
Bali HK$2000
Bangkok HK$1150
Beijing HK$1700
Canada HK$3220
Darwin HK$3300
Europe HK$3050
Hanoi HK$1060
Jakarta HK$1820
Kathmandu HK$2050
Manila HK$970
Phnom Penh HK$1900
Rangoon HK$1850
Saigon HK$1000
Seoul HK$1700
Shanghai HK$1780
Singapore HK$1520
Sydney HK$3500
Taipei HK$1050
Tokyo HK$1920
U.S. West Coast HK$2720
U.S. East Coast HK$3700

Also check the *Post Services Guide* for cheap tickets with courier companies, both one-way and roundtrip. These may allow only hand baggage, and usually require a deposit. Try Jupiter Air, tel. 2761-1303, TNT Skypak, tel. 2305-1413, or Linehaul Express, tel. 2735-2163, or look in the Yellow Pages under "Courier Service."

The new Hong Kong airport is served by express train from Central and Kowloon, as well as a fleet of lowfloor double-deck Airbuses. (See the special topic "Hong Kong's New Airport" for information on transport.) Advance check-in is available for luggage at the Central Airport Railway Station.

Security inspectors at the airport are thorough, as well as strict about overweight baggage (anything over a few kilos) and oversized carry-ons. Remember, maximum size is 22.5 cm by 35 cm by 55 cm; you can pick up a cheap bag at the Temple Street Night Market, among other places. Departure tax is currently HK$50 for adults (lowered from the outrageous rate of HK$120, but who knows how long this will last.) No departure tax is charged for children 12 and under.

BY TRAIN

Crossing Europe and Asia by train to Hong Kong is a long, slow, adventurous way to get there. This route takes a minimum of two weeks travel, commencing in London and heading across Eastern Europe into Russia. The Trans-Siberian Express runs from Moscow across Mongolia and into Beijing. From here it's two or three days more down to Hong Kong.

The Trans-Siberian is not any cheaper than flying. You do it for the adventure, not for the comfort, nor the fine cuisine. It's a gruelling trip unless you plan a lot of stopovers. For more details, consult a specialist guide like the *Trans-Siberian Handbook* by Bryn Thomas.

Most travelers entering Hong Kong from other areas of China arrive by train. There are two choices for the 182-km trip from Guangzhou: either take a local train to Shenzhen, then walk across the border to Lo Wu and hop on the local Kowloon-Canton Railway (KCR); or take one of four daily direct trains to the Hung Hom KCR Station. Departure times for the latter are currently 8:15 a.m. and 10:10 a.m. and 4:50 p.m. and 6:15 p.m.; the trip is under three hours.

Arriving In Hong Kong

The Hung Hom KCR Station is only about one km east of Nathan Road, though the walk is not much fun laden with luggage. To get into town, catch a taxi out front, or ride Bus 1K, 5C, 8 or 8A to the Tsimshatsui Star Ferry. Or, walk 10 minutes southeast down to the Hung Hom Ferry

Pier, from where ferries run across the harbor to Wanchai, Central, and North Point.

Getting Away

See the Guangzhou chapter for more details on train travel into China. If you're thinking about riding the Trans-Siberian back to Europe, consult a travel specialist like MoonSky Star Ltd., 4/F 'E' Block, Chungking Mansions, tel. 2723-1376.

BY BUS

The new Guangzhou-Shenzhen highway makes this method much easier than before. CTS buses from Guangzhou stop at Sheung Shui, Shatin, and the Kowloon Tong MTR Station, ending at the Hung Hom KCR Station.

BY BOAT

Not so long ago, most of Hong Kong's visitors floated into port aboard tea and opium clippers, later on P&O's trusty steamers. Now only the wealthiest enjoy the thrill of entering Hong Kong by water. Cruise ships anchor in Tsimshatsui, right beside the mammoth Harbour City shopping complex.

The only affordable choice is the ferry from Guangzhou, which leaves Zhoutouzui Wharf nightly at 9 p.m., arriving in Hong Kong at 5 a.m. the next morning. Tickets are available at the wharf, the CTS office, or the White Swan Hotel. Classes range from a reclining seat for HK$150 (not recommended) to a second-class dorm (quite tolerable) for HK$250, up to a deluxe cabin for HK$300. Remember to factor in the savings of a night's hotel room.

Jetcat is the other option: the trip takes a little over three hours and there's one departure a day from Guangzhou at 1 p.m. Tickets are HK$250. All arriving boats dock at the China Ferry Pier on Canton Road in Tsimshatsui, a 10-minute walk north of the Star Ferry Pier.

Getting Away

Consult the Guangzhou and Macau chapters for details on hovercraft and ferry departures from Hong Kong. Hovercraft depart several times a day to Shekou, while jetcats run to Panyu, Zhongshan and Shenzhen. It's also possible to take a steamer to Shanghai, a 60-hour trip with four departures a month, or boats to Shantou, Xiamen, Wuzhou, Zhuhai, or Hainan Island. Perhaps most intriguing is the weekly steamer to Shanghai, which takes 60 hours and costs HK$800-1350. Ask CTS for details, or pick up a copy of their leaflet *Sea Transportation to China.*

GETTING AROUND

Getting around Hong Kong is marvelously easy. The SAR is serviced by a wide range of cheap, efficient public transportation. Some of these, like the Star Ferry, Hong Kong Island's trams, and the Peak Tram, are attractions in themselves. Public transport is almost frighteningly well-run, and it's worth noting that all are privately owned and profit-making enterprises.

Hong Kong's compactness is an added advantage: it takes only a few minutes to zip between Hong Kong Island and Kowloon, and even seemingly distant New Territories towns like Sheung Shui are only a half-hour train ride from Kowloon. Victoria Harbour serves as a basic landmark, as well as a gorgeous backdrop for a fleet of ferries and hovercrafts.

Some practical advice: carry a pocketful of coins, as buses, ferries, the tram, and the MTR demand exact change and it's inconvenient to visit cashier windows or change machines too frequently. Rush hour is a problem everywhere. Try to avoid traveling 7:30-9:30 a.m. and especially 5-6:30 p.m. The same goes for sunny Sundays and holidays, when transport to the Outlying Islands, the New Territories, and the beaches is packed.

Late-night carousers should note that the MTR and regular bus service shut down by 1 a.m., and the Star Ferry stops at 11:30 p.m. To cross the harbor late at night, take a taxi, a *walla-walla* from Queen's Pier in Central, or catch Cross-Harbour Bus 121, which runs 12:45-5 a.m.

FERRIES

Star Ferry

Every visit to Hong Kong ought to begin with the six-minute Star Ferry crossing between Tsimshatsui and Central, and should include a liberal sprinkling of this glorious commuter voyage throughout. Views on a clear day are superb, but the romance is there even in the mist.

The Star Ferry service dates to 1898; the green-and-white ferries have been refurbished many times since then, but they retain their old-time elegance, their quirky names *(Northern Star, Twinkling Star, Celestial Star, Meridian Star)* and their sailor-suited crew.

The fleet of 12 double-deck ferries makes over 400 crossings daily. The vessels are double-ended, which means they can be steered from wheelhouses at either end. Ferries are divided into first and second class, a vestige of colonial days when Europeans rode on the top deck and "coolies" on the bottom. The glassed-in top deck costs HK$2 and is worthwhile on cold days, but second class (HK$1.70) has more interesting passengers. There are separate entrances, none too clearly marked, in the ferry concourses. Drop the fare in the turnstyle and head down the ramp. If you don't have exact change, first class has a cashier's window. Ferries run every few minutes 6:30 a.m.-11:30 p.m.

Other Ferry Routes

Most visitors think the cross-harbor service begins and ends with the Tsimshatsui Star Ferry. Actually there are about 16 cross-harbor ferry services, greatly increasing your flexibility if you keep them in mind. The exact location of piers may change with the ever-changing harbor waterfront.

Star Ferries run between Central and Hung Hom 7 a.m.-7:20 p.m. daily, and Wanchai-Tsimshatsui 7:30 a.m.-10:50 p.m.; the Wanchai Ferry Pier is near the Convention Centre. The Hong Kong and Yaumatei Ferry Co. operates passenger services between Wanchai-Hung Hom, Wanchai-Yaumatei (Jordan Road), North Point-Hung Hom, and North Point-Kowloon City. Fares are HK$4.40.

Faster, bumpier hoverferries run between Central (Queen's Pier) and Tsimshatsui East (behind the Kowloon Shangri-La) every 20 minutes 8 a.m.-8 p.m.

Kaidos, Walla-Wallas, And Sampans

Kaidos are small local ferries, anything from a sampan with a tarpaulin roof to a sturdier junk. About 120 *kaidos* ply set routes between outlying islands, hauling kids to school, farmers to markets, villagers to shopping, and, on weekends, carrying city dwellers out to the islands.

There are scheduled services between places like Lamma and Aberdeen; informal local services between remoter places operate on demand. Fares are usually under HK$20.

Chugging little *walla-wallas* patrol Victoria Harbour, ferrying sailors to and from ships and providing cross-harbor service after the Star Ferry closes at 11:30 p.m. Catch one from Queen's Pier, east of the Star Ferry terminal in Central. They charge around HK$10 per head, or you can rent the whole boat.

Sampan means "three planks," and that's practically all the simplest boats are. Sampans bobbing about in Aberdeen Harbour and the Yaumatei and Causeway Bay typhoon shelters can be rented for around HK$50 for a half-hour tour.

For information on ferries to Lantau, Lamma and Cheung Chau, see the special topic "Outlying Islands Ferries."

TAXIS, CARS, AND BUSES

Taxis
More expensive than other means of transport, taxis are still reasonably priced compared to most big cities, and wonderful if you're hot, harried, or in a hurry, as they're air-conditioned and blessedly private. They're generally easy to find except from 4-6 p.m., on rainy days, or very late at night. Remember, a double yellow line edging the pavement indicates a restricted zone where taxis can't stop.

If you can't find one on the street, join the orderly queues at the bus or ferry terminals, or look on Pedder Street in front of the Central MTR station. Look for the red "For Hire" flag on the meter, or the illuminated "Taxi" sign on the roof at night. A rag wadded over the meter means the driver is off-duty, but might be persuaded to go somewhere for an extra charge.

Hong Kong Island and Kowloon taxis are red with silver roofs. Fare is HK$14 for the first two km, HK$1.20 for each additional 200 meters. Rides around town are seldom longer than two or three km, but fares start to rise if you use the Cross-Harbour Tunnel, as you're expected to pay the HK$10 toll plus an extra HK$10 for the driver's return. Other rates are clearly outlined on the inside back door, like baggage (HK$5 per

STREET NAMES

Among the more prominent remnants of Hong Kong's colonial past are its street names. Central's cityscape is studded with the names of former governors (Bonham, Kennedy, Bowring, MacDonnell, Pottinger, Des Voeux), commanders-in-chief (D'Aguilar), harbormasters (Pedder), speculators (Duddell)—even a few old landmarks (Ice House Street immortalizes a warehouse for imported American lake ice). A few other nationalities edge their way in: Mody Road in Tsimshatsui is named for the Indian philanthrophist Sir Hormusjee Mody; Chater Square and Catchick Street for the Armenian Sir Paul Catchick Chater.

Chinese street names have traditionally existed alongside the official versions, often totally unrelated to them and instead describing local landmarks. Stretches of Connaught Road were called "The Goldfish Bowl" and "The Salt Fish Market." A Kennedy Town neighborhood was "The Rubbish Dump." Gap Road was, more poetically, "The Severed Dragon." Most names were relentlessly practical: "Earth Street," "Iron Street," the "Water Tank," "Bamboo Pier."

While it's hard to imagine a Chinese city with such overwhelmingly Anglophile street names, it's also difficult to imagine a Hong Kong without them. China, and the new government, have announced that street names will remain unchanged, as part of local culture. Queensway is not likely to become Jiefang Lu, or "Liberation Road"—at least not soon.

piece) and waiting time (HK$1.20 per minute). For a tip, just round up to the next dollar.

Most drivers speak enough English to understand major destinations, but it's wise to get more obscure ones written in Chinese. Some drivers carry an HKTA-sponsored "Communications Card" listing major destinations. In a pinch, he'll radio headquarters and have you describe your destination.

In a recent survey, locals voted taxi drivers the rudest of all Hongkongers, topping even Immigration Department officials. The 24-hour police hotline for taxi complaints (including lost items and overcharging) is 2527-7177. Take down the license number if you think you've been ripped off.

The New Territories have their own fleet of green-and-white taxis: for service call 2476-4247 (New Territories Taxi Merchants Association) or 2657-2267 (Association of New Territories Radio Taxicabs). Flagfall is HK$11, while fares are HK$1 per 0.2 km. These are restricted to serving the New Territories, whereas the red cabs of urban Hong Kong serve all. Lantau Island also has taxis, blue with a silver roof.

Rental Cars

With so much efficient and cheap public transport available, renting a car is unnecessary. Parking in Central is horrendous anyway, part of a deliberate effort to discourage use of private cars, and driving on the left side of the road is confusing for those not used to it. If you really need the flexibility of a car, it may be better (and cheaper) to hire a taxi for the day.

Rental cars, generally Japanese models, come with or without chauffeur. A Honda Accord rents for around HK$700 a day, plus a HK$9500 credit-card deposit against damage. A driver is HK$200 per hour. You'll need a valid driver's license or international driving permit to drive yourself. While the legal driving age is 18, companies often won't rent to anyone under 25. Look under "Motorcar Renting and Leasing" in the *Yellow Pages,* or try **Avis**, 85 Leighton Rd., Causeway Bay, tel. 2890-6988; or **Trinity,** 653 King's Rd., North Point, tel. 2563-6117. If the occasion demands, hotels hire out chauffered limousines, or call **Ring-a-Benz** at 2845-3376.

Buses

British-built double-decker buses run everywhere; they're particularly handy for visiting the south side of Hong Kong Island and many destinations in the New Territories. Seats on the top deck give the best view. Air-conditioned buses are worth the extra fare in hot weather.

The Kowloon Motor Bus Co. is the biggest passenger carrier in the SAR, making nearly one million journeys a year. Its red-and-cream buses run from the Tsimshatsui Star Ferry (also Hung Hom and the Jordan Road Ferry Pier) all over Kowloon and the New Territories.

Hong Kong Island is served by the China Motor Bus Co. (most of its blue-and-white buses start from the terminal beneath Exchange Square) and by the brightly colored vehicles of Citybus Ltd.

Buses operate 6 a.m. to midnight. Fares range from HK$1 to HK$35 for the longest hauls; most short trips are under HK$6. Drop the exact fare in the coinbox as you enter (the amount is posted on a card above). Press the black rubber bell strip on the ceiling to signal for the next stop. If you're not certain about a bus's destination, ask passengers—signs threaten "It is an Offense in Law for a Passenger to Talk to a Driver Whilst the Vehicle is in Motion."

Minibuses

Bus service is supplemented by privately owned minibuses, popular with locals but seldom used by tourists. The destinations on the front are hard to decipher, routes are arcane, and drivers speak little English.

Minibuses are air-conditioned 14-seat vans, yellow with a red stripe. They ply the regular bus routes but are faster and slightly more expensive, especially good for runs down Hennessy Road, Queen's Road Central, and Nathan Road. Flag them down like a taxi, and holler when you want to get off; they'll stop anywhere except regular bus stops and restricted zones. Fares are posted near the driver, and run HK$3-10 but vary according to demand. Pay as you exit; change is sometimes given. The main minibus terminal on Hong Kong Island is at Exchange Square in Central, just beside the China Motor Bus Terminal.

Green minibuses, called maxicabs, are a different beast: yellow with a green stripe, they run to popular areas which lack full bus service. Several start from alongside City Hall in Central. Fares range from HK$3-10; pay exact fare as you board. Useful routes include the Tsimshatsui Star Ferry to Tsimshatsui East, City Hall to Bowen Road and Ocean Park, and City Hall to the Peak.

THE MTR

The Mass Transit Railway, Hong Kong's marvelously efficient, clean, and fast subway, transformed public transport when it opened in 1980. The US$3.4 billion system has none of the grunge or gloom of many urban counterparts. Stations are sparkling clean and graffiti-less and everything is air-conditioned. Trains run every few minutes from 6 a.m. to 12:30 a.m.

The MTR has its limitations—no smoking, no eating, and no large bags allowed; there are no toilets in the stations, and trains can be horrendously crowded in rush hour (weekdays 8-9 a.m. it becomes the world's busiest railway). It lacks the soul of the Star Ferry or the tram, but remains the fastest and most efficient way to get about, especially for a cross-harbor journey. Fares (HK$4-12.50) are higher than buses or ferries but become more economical on long hauls.

The system is fairly easy to decipher as there are only a few lines. Check the name of the station at the end of your line, and follow the signs down to the right train. The **Island Line** runs along the north shore of Hong Kong Island, from Sheung Wan in the west to Chai Wan in the east. The **Tsuen Wan Line** starts from Central, burrowing beneath the harbor through Kowloon and into the western New Territories—handy for quick harbor crossings or getting up or down

Nathan Road. The **Kwun Tong Line** makes a semicircle from Yaumatei through east Kowloon to Quarry Bay on Hong Kong Island; you'll probably only use it to visit Wong Tai Sin Temple.

A fourth **Lantau Line** is scheduled to open along with the new airport, providing domestic service from north Lantau and joining the Tsuen Wan Line into Central. It should take some of the pressure off the ultra-crowded Nathan Road corridor.

The electronic ticketing system is also clearly diagrammed. Check the fare on a ticket-dispensing machine and feed in the appropriate amount of coins (change is dispensed by machines or bank counters nearby). The plastic ticket that emerges resembles a credit card, with a magnetic coding strip on the back. Feed it into the slot on the entry gate, and retrieve it on the other side of the turnstile. You'll have to feed it into the exit gate at the end of your journey. This time it will not reemerge unless the

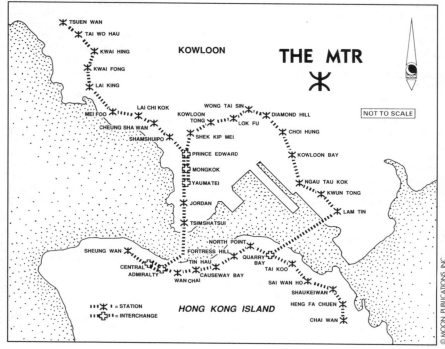

value exceeds the cost of the ride. MTR tickets are only valid for 90 minutes from purchase, so don't overbuy.

Stored-value tickets available from machines or the cashier's window save a lot of fumbling with change. They come in HK$70, HK$100, and HK$200 denominations, and can be used on the KCR as well as the MTR. The special HK$25 Tourist Ticket sold at HKTA offices and MTR stations is no bargain, as it gives only HK$20 worth of rides (the extra HK$5 allows you to keep the ticket as a souvenir).

The local tendency to shove seems to be quelled underground, though heavy pressing is quite common. Passengers usually wait meekly in queues for other passsengers to exit, then move forward, still in line, to board. Since the doors stay open for only 30 seconds, this is quite an achievement.

The trickiest part is navigating your way back to the surface: big stations like Central and Admiralty sprawl for blocks underground. Follow the direction cards and consult the mapboard placed near the exit, and you'll surface fairly near your intended destination.

THE KCR

When the Kowloon-Canton Railway opened in 1911, it represented the final link in the epic trans-Asian journey from Europe to the tip of south China. The classic old railway station near the Kowloon Star Ferry was demolished in the early '70s to make room for the Cultural Centre, and the new station at Hung Hom is not nearly as imposing.

The KCR now serves mainly as a commuter line through the central New Territories. It's an excellent way to sightsee beyond urban Hong Kong, even if you don't get off at any of the nine stops along the way. The high-speed electric cars take a bit over a half-hour to travel the 34 km from Hung Hom to Lo Wu. Without a Chinese visa, the farthest you're allowed to go is Sheung Shui (HK$8).

Remember that stored-value MTR tickets can be used on the KCR as well. Trains run every few minutes 6 a.m.-midnight. If you're coming from Central or Wanchai, you could take a ferry straight to Hung Hom and walk ten minutes to the station; otherwise, it's easy to catch the KCR from the interchange with the Kowloon Tong MTR station.

The KCR tracks are also used for express trains to Lo Wu and Guangzhou. For details on this service, see "Getting There" in the chapter on Guangzhou.

Light Rail Transit
The newest of Hong Kong's transport links, the LRT is an above-ground electric train linking Tuen Mun and Yuen Long in the western New Territories. It consists of six lines, the most convenient (No. 610) starting at the Tuen Mun Ferry Pier. The system is nowhere near as difficult to use as the complicated map implies. Tickets cost HK$4-6 and are sold from vending machines on station platforms: find your destination and drop in enough coins for the appropriate zone. The LRT operates on the honor system—there are no turnstiles, just sporadic spot checks. Trains run 5:30-12:30 a.m. For information call 2468-7788.

OTHER TRANSPORT

Rickshaws
The rickshaw was introduced in the 1870s from Japan, where a Baptist missionary had invented it as a humane (wheeled) substitute for the sedan chair which was carried by sweating bear-

---

PUBLIC TRANSPORT INQUIRY HOTLINES

Hongkong Tramways Ltd. 2548-7102
Peak Tram Co. 2522-0922
MTR 2811-8888
KCR 2602-7799
LRT 2468-7788
China Motor Bus Co. 2565-8556
Kowloon Motor Bus Co. 2745-4466
Citybus Ltd. 2873-0818
Star Ferry Co. 2366-2576
HKY Ferry Co. 2310-4091

Or call HKTA at 2801-7177 for fares and timetables.

ers. The term comes from the Japanese *jinrik-isha,* literally "man + power + vehicle." For several decades they were the preferred means of transport in Hong Kong, replacing sedan chairs for the upper classes. The advent of motor vehicles wiped them out, though rickshaws enjoyed a brief resurgence after WW II when vehicles and gasoline were scarce.

The government fully intends to let this anachronistic form of transport fade away: the last rickshaw license was issued in 1975. The handful of old rickshaw men hanging out in front of the Hong Kong Island Star Ferry make their living posing for photographs; their numbers decline yearly.

Helicopter

As several best-selling books of aerial photographs demonstrate, the city by helicopter is breathtaking. **Heliservices,** tel. 2523-6407, operates flightseeing tours with five-seat Squirrel helicopters. Fifteen-minute tours of Hong Kong Island and Victoria Harbour run HK$2235, while a half-hour over Lantau is HK$4470. There's a half-hour minimum on tours, though they can be taken in 15-minute blocks.

Walking

Hong Kong is eminently walkable, and combined with judicious doses of public transport, it's how to get the most out of the city. For serious walking—hiking in the New Territories or on the Hong Kong Trail—see the special topic "Hiking and Country Parks."

There are some peculiar aspects to pedestrian travel in Central. If you don't walk quickly enough to keep up with the scurrying lunchtime crowds, you risk being bowled over. And it's not wise to circumvent the maze of pedestrian walkways stretching east of the Star Ferry or around Admiralty, as walking below is very unpleasant.

The "Hillside Escalator Link" is a series of elevated moving walkways and escalators designed to carry commuters down from the Mid-Levels to Central in the morning and back up again in the evening. The 800-meter-long system runs between Central Market and Conduit Road. It carries about 20,000 passengers a day, running downhill 6-10 a.m., then uphill until 10:30 or 11 p.m.

While it cost over HK$200 million to build, it's not doing as much to solve traffic problems as hoped. One problem is that it's quite slow—the 20-minute descent from Conduit Road takes several minutes more than traveling by taxi or bus. Still, the Urban Council is considering building similar systems in a half-dozen other locations.

ORGANIZED TOURS

Tours By Bus

A set circuit of the New Territories is not a bad idea if time is limited, and the sunset harbor cruises are definitely worthwhile. The standard offerings, best left to those with *very* limited time, include half-day tours of Hong Kong Island or the New Territories, evening trips to Victoria Peak and Aberdeen, and daytrips to Shenzhen, Guangzhou, and Macau. Don't go out of your way to book tours with meals, which tend to be Chinese tourist food of the sweet 'n' sour pork with fried rice variety.

Tours can be arranged through hotels or travel agents, or directly through companies. One of the biggest is **Gray Line Tours,** 5/F 72 Nathan Rd., tel. 2723-5262, with a full menu of boat, tram, and bus tours of Hong Kong, and excursions to China and Macau as well. Another is **Splendid Tours,** tel. 2316-2151.

Boat and Tram Tours

As the ads for evening cocktail cruises imply ("Unlimited Free Drinks!"), some of these trips are merely excuses to slosh around the harbor. Simple harbor cruises are the best deal; you can get a better, cheaper meal in town. The biggest company, **Watertours,** offers over a dozen different excursions, from a two-hour morning harbor cruise for HK$200 to a sunset dinner cruise to Aberdeen for HK$680. Perhaps most interesting is the HK$260 cocktail cruise from 6:30-8 p.m. Call 2739-3302 for reservations, or book at the floating pier in front of Ocean Terminal in Tsimshatsui.

MP Tours runs hour-long cruises on old green-and-white Star Ferries, and open-top antique tram tours, both day and night. Prices for either are HK$180 for adults, HK$140 for kids. Call 2188-6241, or stop at the booths located at both Star Ferry piers.

TRAVEL AGENTS

The travel agents listed below sell cheap air tickets and may also provide Chinese visas, and train, bus, or boat tickets into China.

Hong Kong Student Travel: Friendly and helpful service for cheap flights, China visas, boat and train tickets, and rail passes for Europe and Japan. There's an office at 10/F Star House, Tsimshatsui, tel. 2730-3269; also in Room 305 Entertainment Bldg., 30 Queen's Rd., Central, tel. 2810-7272; and 11/F Circle Plaza, 499 Hennessy Rd., Causeway Bay, tel. 2833-9909.

Phoenix Services Agency: Recommended by veteran travelers; it's located at 6/F Milton Mansion, 96 Nathan Rd., Tsimshatsui, tel. 2722-7378.

Shoestring Travel: Cheap and reliable, on a par with Time Travel across the street. It's at 4/F Alpha House, 27 Nathan Rd., Tsimshatsui, tel. 2723-2306; e-mail shoetvl@hkstar.com.

Time Travel: Popular with budget travelers, but not necessarily cheaper than other companies, and inconveniently located when you consider Chungking Mansion's elevators. On the 16/F "A" Block, Chungking Mansions, 36 Nathan Rd., Tsimshatsui, tel. 2366-6222; e-mail timetrvl@hkstar.com.

MoonSky Star Ltd.: Specialists in the Trans-Siberian Express, located on the 4/F "E" Block, Chungking Mansions, Tsimshatsui, tel. 2723-1376.

Travel Expert: 301 United Chinese Bank Bldg., 31 Des Vouex Rd., Central, tel. 2845-3232; and Room 303, Trans-HK Commerical Bldg., 1 Lock Rd., Tsimshatsui, tel. 3267-0963.

HKTA Tours

These are well organized, relatively inexpensive, and not too hokey. There's even a bit of social conscience exhibited in the "Family Insight Tour" (HK$260), which visits a family in a public housing estate and a nursery or community center for the elderly, along with Wong Tai Sin Temple.

"The Land Between" (HK$365) takes in the New Territories: New Towns, a Buddhist monastery, the Luen Wo market, the bird sanctuary at Luk Keng, and a fishing village. The "Heritage Tour" (HK$310) visits historical sites like the restored 18th-century walled village of Sam Tung Uk, the scholar's home of Tai Fu Tai and the ancestral hall of Man Shek Tong in Sheung Shui. The "Come Horseracing Tour" (HK$530) provides access to the Visitor's Box at the Happy Valley racetrack, plus lunch or dinner. (Visitors must be 18 or over and have been in Hong Kong less than 21 days.) The "Sports and Recreation Tour" (HK$400) provides access to the Clearwater Bay Golf and Country Club in Sai Kung for a day of golf, tennis, and swimming. Lunch is included, but you'll pay extra for use of the facilities.

All tours are discounted for those over 60 and under 16, and can be booked at HKTA information centers or through hotels or travel agents. For information, contact HKTA's Information and Tours Department at 2807-6390 (2807-6177 Sunday and holidays).

INFORMATION AND SERVICES

VISAS

Visa regulations have remained relaxed after the handover, though British and residents of Commonwealth countries will find their length of stay reduced. Most visitors from Western countries need only a valid passport to enter Hong Kong. British get a six-month visa-free stay; residents of France, Canada and Australia can stay up to three months; while Americans, Germans, and Japanese get a 30-day visa-free visit. Scruffy or impecunious-looking travelers may be asked to show an onward ticket and evidence of enough funds to cover their stay.

If you have any questions, consult a Chinese embassy or consulate before arrival. To obtain a longer stay, it's usually easy enough to visit Macau or Guangzhou for a weekend and return for another round. Or, contact the Immigration Department, located in Wanchai Tower 2, 7 Gloucester Rd., Wanchai (general inquiries, tel. 2824-6111).

Customs

The duty-free allowance is one liter of wine or spirits, 60 milliliters perfume, 250 milliliters toilet water, 200 cigarettes or 50 cigars or 250 grams tobacco, and "reasonable quantities" of other goods. Duties are levied on petroleum products and alcohol (liquor and perfume); everything else is duty-free. Prohibited items include fireworks, firearms, drugs, and drug paraphernalia. Backpackers arriving from suspicious countries like India or Thailand undergo the most scrutiny; to customs officials, backpackers and drugs are synonymous.

Identification

Hong Kong residents are required to carry proof of identity at all times and are issued I.D. cards for this purpose. Visitors are "advised," but not required, to do this; a photo I.D. such as a driver's license is sufficient if you don't want to carry your passport. Visitors who plan to remain in Hong Kong more than 180 days are supposed to apply for an identification card within 30 days of arrival. Contact the Immigration Department, tel. 2824-6111, for information.

Driving

Visitors with a valid overseas driving license can drive for 12 months on it, provided they have motor vehicle insurance. You must carry your license and another form of identification with photograph.

Working and Staying On

New visa regulations for Brits have ended the heyday of the FILTH—"Failed in London, Try Hong Kong"—who found employment in the territory. Now they, like everyone else, must obtain a work visa from the Hong Kong Immigration Department *before* arriving in Hong Kong. Contact the Hong Kong Immigration Department at 7 Gloucester Rd., Wanchai, tel. 2824-6111, for details.

Professional jobs in business and finance are available, but most are assigned from abroad. If you have the right qualifications (fluency in Chinese is a big plus), scan the massive "Help Wanted" sections of local papers. If you manage to land a job as a tourist, you'll have to leave Hong Kong to apply for a work visa.

Travelers do work on the sly, of course, but the options are limited and the pay generally low. The standard options are teaching English, either freelance or through a school, and waiting tables or bartending at pubs. More exotic jobs are modeling (Caucasians are in demand for commercials and advertisements) or working as a film extra. Women, especially young blonde ones, may be approached to work as "hostesses" or "escorts," a profession best avoided. The bulletin board at the Travellers' Hostel in Chungking Mansions advertises other dubious occupations, such as distributing pornographic films.

Travelers are sometimes recruited as "mules" to carry luxury items like mink coats and gold watches into Asian countries. Payment is often only the free airfare. Smuggling gold or drugs into certain countries risks imprisonment in extremely unpleasant conditions or even the death penalty for drugs. Don't carry luggage for someone unless you're positive about what's inside.

A more innocuous scam is working as a business impersonator. Hong Kong companies sometimes hire presentable *gweilos* to pose as their customers or employees at trade fairs or opening banquets. The job is not too strenuous—it involves passing out a few fake busi-

FOREIGN CONSULATES

Australia: 23/F Harbour Centre, 25 Harbour Rd., Wanchai; tel. 2827-8881

Britain: 1 Supreme Court Rd., Admiralty; tel. 2901-3000

Canada: 14/F One Exchange Square, Central; tel. 2810-4321

Denmark: 24/F Great Eagle Centre, 23 Harbour Rd., Wanchai; tel. 2827-8101

France: 26/F Tower II, Admiralty Centre, Admiralty; tel. 2529-4351

Germany: 21/F United Centre, 95 Queensway, Admiralty; tel. 2529-8855

India: 16/F United Centre, 95 Queensway, Admiralty; tel. 2528-4028

Indonesia: 6 Keswick St., Causeway Bay; tel. 2890-4421

Israel: Room 702, Tower II, Admiralty Centre, Admiralty; tel. 2529-6091

Italy: Room 805, Hutchison House, 10 Harcourt Rd., Admiralty; tel. 2522-0033

Japan: One Exchange Square, Central; tel. 2522-1184

Korea: 5-6/F Far East Finance Centre, 16 Harcourt Rd., Admiralty; tel. 2529-4141

Malaysia: 24/F Malaysian Bldg., 50 Gloucester Rd., Wanchai; tel. 2527-9350

Myanmar: Room 2421, Sun Hung Kai Centre, 30 Harbour Rd., Wanchai; tel. 2827-7929

Netherlands: Room 301, China Bldg., 29 Queen's Rd., Central; tel. 2522-5127

New Zealand: Room 3414, Jardine House, 1 Connaught Place, Central; tel. 2525-5044

Norway: Great Eagle Centre, 23 Harbour Rd., Wanchai; tel. 2587-9953

Pakistan: 38/F China Resources Bldg., 26 Harbour Rd., Wanchai; tel. 2827-0681

Philippines: United Centre, Admiralty; tel. 2866-8738

Portugal: Harbour Centre, 25 Harbour Rd., Wanchai; tel. 2802-2587

Singapore: 9/F Admiralty Centre, Admiralty; tel. 2527-2212

Spain: 8/F Printing House, 18 Ice House St., Central; tel. 2525-3041

Sri Lanka: 2243 Dominion Centre, 43 Queen's Rd. East, Wanchai; tel. 2866-2321

Sweden: 8/F Hong Kong Club Bldg., 3 Chater Rd., Central; tel. 2521-1212

Switzerland: 37/F Gloucester Tower, 11 Pedder St., Central; tel. 2522-7147

Thailand: 8/F Fairmont House, 8 Cotton Tree Dr., Central; tel. 2521-6481

United States: 26 Garden Rd., Central; tel. 2523-9011

Vietnam: 20/F Kam Chung Bldg., 19 Hennessy Rd., Wanchai; tel. 2527-0221

(There is no Taiwanese consulate in Hong Kong. Visas for Taiwan are handled by Chung Hwa Travel, 4/F Lippo Tower, Lippo Centre, 89 Queensway, Admiralty; tel. 2525-8315).

ness cards and making social chitchat, and perhaps sitting through a multi-course banquet. Typical renumeration might be HK$50 per hour, or HK$1200 plus expenses for an overnight China trip. Check local employment agencies for openings.

Foreign Consulates

Hong Kong is not a country, so there are no embassies or ambassadors posted here. Consulates do the everyday work of replacing lost passports, issuing visas for onward travel, providing information, and dispensing legal advice. Some will take urgent messages for their citizens, hold mail, or provide emergency cash.

Business hours are generally 9 a.m.-noon and 2-4 p.m., but it's advisable to telephone in advance, especially regarding the issuing of visas. For countries not listed here, look under "Consulates" in the Yellow Pages Buying Guide.

MAPS AND TOURIST INFORMATION

HKTA

The Hong Kong Tourist Association is a paragon of a tourism office, efficiently dealing with an annual load of over 10 million visitors. HKTA offices dispense free or reasonably priced brochures and leaflets on all conceivable aspects of local life. Its helpful staff will provide directions, advise on shopping and transportation, or help you rent a junk or get tickets to the Chinese opera.

Stop by one of its offices early in your stay to pick up a free map booklet and look through the many HKTA publications. These include a *Traveller's Guide,* a general *Sightseeing Guide,* and brochures on *Dining and Entertainment, Shopping,* and *Hotels,*which provide general information and list HKTA members. The monthly *Official Hong Kong Guide* (HK$15) contains maps, restaurant reviews, ads, and a rundown of current events; the latter are also covered in the glossy newsletter *Hong Kong This Week!* and the plainer but more detailed *Hong Kong Diary.* HKTA also issues "Factsheets" on various tourist destinations. There's much more available than what's displayed, so if you have a particular interest, ask.

HKTA has also produced a CD-ROM, *The Wonders of Hong Kong,* with music, videos, and photos depicting local Hong Kong's attractions.

Maps

HKTA's advertisement-studded free map booklet, *The Official Hong Kong Map,* is a handy flipthrough reference to major tourist areas.

Universal Publications issues detailed larger sheet maps of Kowloon and Hong Kong Island (HK$15). *The Hong Kong Arrival Survival Map* by Barbara Anderson and Leopoldine Mikula is a brightly colored hand-drawn assemblage of sights, shopping, and restaurants in popular neighborhoods—fun for wandering.

The most comprehensive resource is the Universal Press paperback *Hong Kong Guidebook,* a handy compilation of detailed neighborhood maps, transport timetables, and bilingual indexes of streets and buildings. It's available in bookstores for around HK$60; or look for the government-published *Hong Kong Guide: Streets and Places.*

Serious hikers will want selected sheets from the *Countryside Series,* produced by the Buildings and Land Departments. These 1:20,000 topographic sheets cover the entire SAR and run around HK$30 per sheet. The over-all maps make nice souvenirs. They're available at the Government Publications Centre at 66 Queensway, next to Pacific Place.

Bookstores

No single store outshines the rest. You must hunt for items of local interest, and books are shockingly expensive—HK$160 for a paperback that retails for US$8.

The utilitarian **Government Publications Centre,** G/F Low Block Government Office, 66 Queensway, Admiralty, stocks a mind-boggling array of government documents. *Bats of Hong Kong,* anyone? Or perhaps a "Manpower Survey Report in the Catering Industry"? There are also topographic maps and a small selection of photographic books and guidebooks at unbeatably low prices.

Hong Kong Book Centre, 25 Des Voeux Rd., Central, is one of the best overall bookstores, with particularly good sections in fiction and local interest.

HKTA OFFICES

The Hong Kong Tourist Association's foreign offices provide general information and glossy brochures. For more detailed information, contact HKTA's Head Office: 11/F, Citicorp Center, 18 Whitfield Rd., North Point, Hong Kong (tel. 852-2807-6543, fax 852-2806-0303). To access HKTA's 24-hour infofax menu from overseas, dial 852-177-1128. The HKTA Website "Wonder Net" (http://www.hkta.org) provides all sorts of up-to-date information.

ABROAD

USA: 590 Fifth Ave., New York, NY 10036-4706, tel. (212) 869-5008
Suite 200, 610 Enterprise Dr., Oak Brook, IL 60521, tel. (630) 575-2828
Suite 1220, 10940 Wilshire Blvd., Los Angeles, CA 90024, tel. (310) 208-4582

Canada: Hong Kong Trade Center, 9 Temperance St., Toronto, Ontario M5H 1Y6, tel. (416) 366-2389

UK: 125 Pall Mall, London SW1Y 5EA, tel. (0171) 930-4775

Germany: Humboldt Strasse 94, D-60318 Frankfurt/Main, tel. (069) 95-91-29-0

France: Escalier C, 8eme etage, 53 rue Francois 1er, 75008 Paris, tel. (01) 4720-3954

Australia: 55 Harrington St., The Rocks, Sydney, NSW 2000, tel. (02) 9251-2855

Japan: 4/F Toho Twin Tower Bldg., 1-5-2 Yurakucho, Chiyoda-ku, Tokyo 100, tel. (03) 3503-0731

Singapore: 9 Temasek Blvd., #34-03 Suntec Tower Two, Singapore 038989, tel. (65) 532-3668

Taiwan: 9th Fl, 18 Chang An East Rd., Sec. 1, Taipei, tel. (02) 581-6061

IN HONG KONG

Airport Buffer Hall daily 8 a.m.-10:30 p.m.

Tsimshatsui Star Ferry Concourse: Mon.-Fri. 8 a.m.-6 p.m., weekends and holidays 9 a.m.-5 p.m.

Basement, Jardine House: 1 Connaught Place, Central; Mon.-Fri. 9 a.m.-6 p.m., Saturday 9 a.m.-1 p.m.

HKTA operates a multilingual information hotline at 2807-6177; Mon.-Fri. 8 a.m.-6 p.m., weekends 9 a.m.-5 p.m.

Swindon Book Co. has perhaps the broadest selection. The main shop at 13 Lock Rd., Tsimshatsui is a paradise for browsers; the Harbour City outlet specializes in paperbacks, and there's a smaller shop in the Tsimshatsui Star Ferry concourse.

The **South China Morning Post Family Book Shop** has a good selection of Hong Kong topics and paperback fiction. Outlets are at the Central Star Ferry concourse and Harbour City in Tsimshatsui; the main store is in Cityplaza at Taikoo Shing.

Bookazine has lots of magazines and fiction. Shops are in Alexandra House, Prince's Building and the basement of Jardine House, Central; in Shui On Centre and Hopewell Centre in Wanchai; and in Tsimshatsui Centre, Tsimshatsui East.

Kelly & Walsh, Level 3, Pacific Place, is a colonial oldtimer relocated with its oak shelves and incandescent lights intact. It's especially good for art and travel.

Tai Yip Art Book Centre in the Hong Kong Museum of Art, 10 Salisbury Rd., stocks over 8,000 titles in the visual arts, emphasizing Chinese topics, as well as posters, T-shirts, and art supplies.

Libraries

For research, casual reading, periodicals, or just some air-conditioned peace and quiet:

City Hall Library, City Hall High Block, Central, has children's, lending, and reference libraries and a periodical room. Open Mon.-Thurs. 10 a.m.-7 p.m., Friday 10 a.m.-9 p.m., Saturday 10 a.m.-5 p.m., Sunday 10 a.m.-1 p.m.

British Council, 3 Supreme Court Rd., Admiralty, tel. 2913-5125, is open Monday, Tuesday, Thursday, Friday 9:30 a.m.-8:30 p.m.; Wednesday noon-8:30 p.m., Saturday 9:30 a.m.-6:30 p.m. There's a HK$160 membership fee for the lending library.

Goethe Institute, 14/F Hong Kong Arts Centre, Harbour Rd., Wanchai, tel. 2802-0088, has German and English books and periodicals.

Alliance Française, 2/F 123 Hennessy Rd., Wanchai, tel. 2527-7825, has French books and films.

Both the **University of Hong Kong** and the **Chinese University** have large collections. Contact the registrar for information on access.

Miscellanea

The **Royal Asiatic Society** focuses on history and culture, with lectures, field trips, a lending library, and publications. For further information write to GPO Box 3864, or call 2551-0300.

The **Government Information Services Department** acts as an information source and clearinghouse for specific requests; it's in Beaconsfield House, 4 Queen's Rd., Central, tel. 2842-8777.

The **Community Advice Bureau** run by St. John's Cathedral answers practical questions for tourists and new arrivals. Call 2815-5444, Mon.-Fri. 9:30 a.m.-4 p.m.

COMMUNICATIONS AND MEDIA

Like everything else in Hong Kong, postal and communications services are reliable and prompt.

Postal System

The post office prides itself on next-day service within Hong Kong. Its efficiency is demonstrated by the story of a Central business firm that mailed a query in the morning and received a reply, by post, that same afternoon. Airmail to the U.S., Australia, and Europe takes four or five days; sea mail parcels to the U.S. or U.K. take 6-10 weeks.

The General Post Office is at 2 Connaught Place, Central (beside the Star Ferry). Poste restante letters go here unless the envelope specifies another post office. Bring your passport for identification and go to the window on the first floor. Letters are held for two months.

The Kowloon Central Post Office is at 405 Nathan Rd., between the Jordan and Yaumatei MTR stations. The post office at 10 Middle Rd., Tsimshatsui, is more convenient. Post office hours are Mon.-Fri. 8 a.m.-6 p.m., Saturday 8 a.m.-2 p.m. In off-hours, use the stamp vending machines and mailboxes. A 30- gram letter costs HK$1.30 for local mail, HK$4.60 to Macau, Taiwan or Japan, HK$5.40 for all other destinations. Aerogrammes are available for a flat rate of HK$2.30. For information, call 2921-2222.

Packages must be wrapped in plain paper; padded envelopes, boxes, and string are available; bring your own tape and paper. A five-kilogram parcel to the U.S. costs around HK$211 via surface mail, HK$419 airmail. Insurance is extra: HK$2.50 for each HK$500 of insured value. For information on commercial shipping, see "Shopping."

Local Phone Calls

Local calls are free from private phones, and shops and restaurants generally won't charge for use of their phones. Hotel charges for room calls—even local calls—are quite high, however.

Local calls from public pay phones calls are HK$1. There are no local area codes. The hardest part is finding an unoccupied pay phone: look in and around MTR stations, ferry terminals, or hotel lobbies. Privately owned pay phones are usually bright yellow, installed in small shops and restaurants, with a coin slot on top. The standard telephone greeting, a snarled *"wei,"* can be off-putting in its abruptness, but it's the Chinese version of "hello."

Hong Kong has a massive multivolume telephone directory, encompassing a Yellow Pages Buying Guide, a Commercial and Industrial Guide, a business directory, and a residential directory. So few people bother to use the residential guide that the telephone company has stopped distribution. Given the rapidity with which telephone numbers change, it's easiest to call **directory assistance** (1081 for English speakers). The Classified Business directory can also be accessed at http://www.yp.com.hk/.

Long-Distance Calls
International direct-dial (IDD) calls are much cheaper than operator-assisted or hotel phones. Dial 001, then the country code, followed by the area code and number. The country code for the U.S. and Canada is 1. (Hong Kong is 852, Macau 853.) The standard IDD rate for the U.S. is HK$1.23 per six seconds. Dial 013 to inquire about codes and charges for other countries. Rates are 20 percent less on Sunday and from midnight to 7 a.m. weekdays, and 1 p.m. midnight Saturday.

There are three types of IDD phones: coin, card, and credit card. Phone cards are sold in various denominations of HK$50-100-250 at HKTA offices, Hong Kong Telecom service centers (see below), or at any 7-11 store. Or, calls can be charged to major credit cards (Visa, AmEx, MasterCard) from about 100 creditcard phones found in major tourist locations. Dial 013 for details on the latter two methods. Collect calls can be arranged by dialing the operator at 10010.

You can also make collect and card calls using the Home Direct service to reach an operator in your country. For the U.S., dial 800-1111 for AT&T; 800-1121 for MCI; 800-1877 for Sprint. The code for Australia is 800-1611; Canada 800-1100; U.K. 800-1144.

Long-distance and collect calls can be made from Hongkong Telecom Service Centres. Twenty-four-hour offices are at 102A One Exchange Square, Central and 10 Middle Rd., Tsimshatsui. There are others at the airport, at 3 Hennessy Rd. in Wanchai, and at 96 Granville Rd. in Tsimshatsui.

Fax, Telex, and Cables
The larger hotels have business centers offering secretarial, translation, telex, and fax services. Otherwise, visit one of the Hong Telecom offices listed above, or the 24-hour Cable and Wireless service, 37/F Exchange Square Tower II, Central. For international fax directory inquiries, dial 10014.

Internet
For those who travel with a laptop and want to

USEFUL PHONE NUMBERS

Directory Enquiries (English) 1081

International services inquiry 10013

Operator-assisted and collect calls 10010

Calls charged to overseas calling card 10011

Operator-assisted calls to China 012

International Customer Services (overseas directory enquiries and information on international calling, time zones, charges, and IDD codes) 10013

Time 18501

Weather 187-8066

Emergencies (police, fire, ambulance) 999

Tourist information hotline 2801-7177

---

keep up with their e-mail, Hong Kong has a number of Internet service providers, including: Compuserve (info@compuserve.com, tel. 2833-1500), Netvigator (info@netvigator.com, tel. 2183-3888), and HK SuperNet (info@hk.super.net, tel. 2358-1383).

Cyber-cafes are a growing phenomenon. **Café Internet,** at Soft and Hard: the Computer Department Store,118 Java Rd., North Point, is among the biggest places; for the price of a drink you get access to one of their ten computers. **Kublai's Restaurant,** 3/F One Capitol Place, 18 Luard Rd., Wanchai, has a cyber café across the hall from the main restaurant. It's free as long as you're eating there; you get a maximum of 20 minutes' use on one of six computers. Two branches of **Pacific Coffee** have a single computer each, and plan to add more: they're at 979 King's Rd., Quarry Bay, and Pacific Place 2, Shop 404, Admiralty.

Newspapers
With over 70 newspapers and 620 periodicals produced locally, Hong Kong is a media center for much of Asia. There's a huge selection of Chinese newspapers—over 50 dailies (New York has four), though an honest observer must admit that most are racing forms. Press freedom is an issue to watch in post-handover Hong Kong: observers noted an increased tendency towards self-censorship on the part of local re-

porters and editors even before July 1st 1997.

The two main English dailies are the *South China Morning Post,* which balances international and local coverage, and the slightly less polished *Hong Kong Standard.* The classified and entertainment sections in both are worth perusing, while the reporting will keep you informed on the latest twists and turns in local politics. Entertaining features in the SCMP include the "Courts" page, reporting murderers' alibis and dramatic bank heists. Letters to the editor provide another slice of Hong Kong life. Here are open dialogues on ferry crew uniforms, the size of the leopard cages in the zoo, the length of taxi queues at the airport, and the weight of schoolchildren's bookbags (too heavy, is the general consensus).

Other locally published papers are the Asian editions of the *International Herald Tribune* (a composite of the *New York Times* and the *Washington Post), The Asian Wall Street Journal,* and *USA Today.* European papers, including *Le Monde* and the *Times,* are available in specialist bookstores.

Magazines

The locally published *Far Eastern Economic Review* and *Asiaweek* survey the Asian business and political scene. Hong Kong is also the base for the Asia editions of *Time* and *Newsweek.* Internationl magazines are available but painfully expensive: HK$95 for a US$3 copy of *Vogue.* The best places for foreign magazines is **Tower Records** in Times Square, Causeway Bay; or **What's News?** on the first floor of Admiralty Centre, Harcourt Road.

The South China Morning Post puts out *Hong Kong Visitor,* a glossy monthly with restaurant reviews, shopping tips, maps, and general information. *The Peak* aims squarely at the local rich. *HK Magazine* is a funky free weekly surveying the entertainment and restaurant scenes (interesting classifieds), and available in bookstores and trendy restaurants and bars.

Radio

Three radio stations broadcast on 15 channels, half of them in English. Daily programming is printed in newspapers.

The government-run **Radio Television Hong Kong (RTHK)** operates Radio 3 at 567 AM

(news, talk), **Radio 4** at 97.6-98.9 FM (Western and Chinese classical music), and **Radio 6** at 675 AM (24-hour BBC World Service relay, but it can be hard to pick up).

Commercial radio's **Quote AM** at 864 AM plays pop, while **Hit Radio** on FM 99.7-102 plays Canto-pop; **104 FM Select** soft pop; and **Metro News** at 1044 AM broadcasts 24-hour news and finance.

Television

There are two television companies, Asia Television (ATV) and Television Broadcasts (TVB), each operating one Chinese and one English-language station. English stations are TVB "Pearl" (Channel 3) and ATV "World" (Channel 4). Programming is mostly imports from the U.S., England, and Australia, with a few local shows. Satellite TV in hotels includes MTV, BBC, and the Asian Star Plus network. Programming is listed in newspapers and in *TV & Entertainment Weekly.*

The Cantonese stations, TVB "Jade" (Channel 1) and ATV "Home" (Channel 2), are worth a scan if only to survey homegrown programming—mostly insipid clownish stuff featuring clean-scrubbed young people mugging for the camera. Ads are slicker and altogether more entertaining, providing insights of Hong Kong's self-image: young, cheerful, and peppy.

SERVICES DIRECTORY

Babysitting

Major hotels provide babysitting services, or call Rent-a-Mum Ltd., tel. 2523-4868.

Business Hours

Office hours are Mon.-Fri. 9 a.m.-5 p.m., Saturday 9 a.m.-1 p.m. Smaller businesses may close 1-2 p.m. for lunch. Banks close around 4:30 p.m. weekdays, 12:30 p.m. on Saturday. Shops are usually open seven days a week, 10 a.m. to 9 or 10 p.m., 6 p.m. in Central and Western.

Government offices and many shops close on public holidays, though it's usually possible to shop, except for the Chinese New Year in January-February, when nearly everything shuts down. See the special topic "Major Festivals Dates" for a list of public holidays.

HONG KONG TOURIST ASSOCIATION

The Chinese traditional form of a baby carriage.

Business Information
Contact the Hong Kong Trade Development Council, 36-39/F Convention Plaza, 1 Harbour Rd., Wanchai, tel. 2584-4333.

Counseling
Several places in Hong Kong offer free assistance to those with personal problems, including **St. John's Cathedral Counseling Services,** tel. 2525-7208; the **Samaritans** 24-hour hotline, tel. 2389-2221; and the **Suicide Prevention Hotline,** tel. 2896-0000.

Dry Cleaning
Most convenient are the shops inside many MTR stations, including Tsimshatsui, Admiralty, and Central.

Electricity
Electricity is 220 volts AC. You'll need a step-down transformer for 110 volt appliances, though hotels often have 110 volt sockets for electric shavers.

Another problem is created by the varying wall outlets: most accept three round prongs or two round and a rectangular. Adaptors are available in electric shops, or ask at your hotel.

Emergencies
Dial 999 and ask for police, fire, or ambulance.

Laundry
Hotels provide same-day laundry service but it's usually expensive. Every neighborhood, even Central, has local laundries that charge by the pound: just walk in and weigh it on the spot. A typical charge is HK$35 for up to six pounds, ironing extra.

Lost and Found
The MTR Lost Property Office is in Admiralty station, while the KCR Lost Property Office is in Shatin, tel. 2606-9392. Taxi drivers may turn lost property over to police, tel. 2860-2000. Newspapers recently reported the story of an honest driver who turned in a briefcase with US$300,000 (he got a huge tip).

Luggage Storage
The left-luggage room in the airport Buffer Hall charges HK$25 per piece for the first 24 hours, HK$40 for the second, HK$80 for the third and beyond. Luggage is transferred to the Departure Hall for pickup. Storing bags at your guesthouse or hotel is another possibility.

Measurements
Hong Kong converted in the '80s from imperial to metric measurements. Local Chinese weights are still used for some items: a tael (*leung* in Cantonese) is 38 grams or 1.33 oz; it's used to measure gold and silver. Produce and meat is sold by the catty *(gun),* equal to 0.6 kilograms.

Photos and Film Developing

Coin-operated instant photo machines are found in major MTR stations and at the Star Ferry. The Fotomax chain offers one-hour print processing, three hours for slides. Charges are HK$1.80 for a 3 x 5 print (more at the Salisbury Road shop), film processing is HK$18.

For specialist work, prints from slides, or color copies, try **Robert Lam Color** at 67 Wyndham St., Central; or 120 Canton Rd., Tsimshatsui; or **Color6 Lab**, 18A Stanley St., Central. The many camera shops around Stanley Street are reliable places for repairs and advice.

Police

Dial 999 in an emergency and ask for police, fire, or ambulance. The 24-hour crime hotline is 2527-7177 (it's also used for complaints about taxis). General inquiry is 2866-6166.

Time

Hong Kong Standard Time remains constant year-round, eight hours ahead of Greenwich Mean Time and 13 hours ahead of Eastern Standard Time (12 hours in summer). Noon in Hong Kong is 4 a.m. in London, 11 p.m. the previous evening in New York, 10 p.m. in Chicago, 8 p.m. in San Francisco. For the correct time in Hong Kong, dial 18501.

Toilets

Best bet is any hotel, department store, shopping mall, or fast-food restaurant. Note there are no toilets in the MTR. In upper-crust places like the Mandarin and The Peninsula, white-clad attendants leap to their feet to turn on the taps and hand you starched towels. Best Restroom award goes to the men's room at Felix atop The Peninsula, where glass(!) urinals are strategically placed on plate-glass walls overlooking Tsimshatsui.

MONEY

The local currency is the Hong Kong dollar, written HK$ or often just $. Since 1983 it's been pegged against the U.S. dollar, at a rate which usually fluctuates only a few cents from HK$7.80.

Rather unusually, private banks retain the responsibility of issuing Hong Kong's money, though the government bears the expenses. Most bills bear the image of the Hongkong and Shanghai Banking Corporation headquarters, but the Standard Chartered Bank and the Bank of China also participate. Bills are colored according to denomination: HK$10 is green, HK$20 orange, HK$50 blue, HK$100 red, HK$500 brown, and HK$1000 gold.

The government issues 10-cent, 20-cent, 50-cent, and $1, $2, $5 and $10 coins, the smaller denominations in bronze, the larger in silver (the thick $10 coin is a nickel/bronze mix). Coins issued since 1993 bear the *bauhinia* flower rather than the profile of Queen Elizabeth II.

Changing Money

Traveler's checks are the safest way to carry large sums; in fact, cash gets a slightly lower rate. Generally speaking, you'll get the best rate at banks, the worst at the airport and hotels. Bank rates for exchange run only a few cents below the official rate, but many slap charges of up to HK$50 on exchanges of traveler's checks, penalizing those who prefer to change small amounts frequently. Banking hours are Mon.-Fri. 9 a.m.-3 or 4:30 p.m. (some are open as late as 6 p.m.) and Saturday 9 a.m.-noon.

American Express offices offer a good rate and charge no commission on traveler's checks issued by any company. The main office is at 16 Queen's Rd., Central; there's another at 25 Kimberley Rd., Tsimshatsui.

Be very wary of the licensed money changers clustered in Tsimshatsui—rates are generally miserable. Some advertise decent rates, but charge commissions as high as 10%. Others, like the popular **Chequepoint** chain, offer as little as HK$7.07 per U.S. dollar—which is the equivalent of a 10% commission.

A favorite scam is to advertise "No Commission," which refers only to *selling* HK dollars and *buying* foreign currency. They will charge a commission on buying HK dollars. If you're unsure, ask for the total amount to be calculated before handing the money over. For large transactions, you can and should ask for a rate higher than the one posted.

An exception to the above is the conveniently located little window of the Hang Tai Finance Co. on Mody Road (just off Nathan Road). It gives HK$7.65, no commission—a better rate than most banks. Money changers in Chungking Mansions also tend to give decent rates.

Hotels are convenient and open at all hours, but the bigger ones offer their guests exceptionally poor rates. The airport is another poor place, offering only HK$7.32 per US$1.

One solution is to pay your hotel and restaurant bills with credit cards: you'll get the official bank exchange rate with no commissions and no hassles. Shopping with credit cards is a bit more difficult, as merchants often try to pass the card company's 5% charge onto the purchaser. Many shops do accept traveler's checks at the going rate, however.

Transferring Money

Credit card holders can get cash advances from banks. You may be able to use your credit card (Visa, MasterCard, American Express) or even your bank card at automatic teller machines— check with the credit card company or bank before departure. The exchange rate for ATM transactions is good, though transaction fees for withdrawals may be higher than you're used to.

Otherwise, find an international bank that's a correspondent with your home bank and ask it to arrange a telex transfer of funds, a process which shouldn't take more than one or two working days.

Expenses

Hong Kong is more expensive than many Asian countries, especially in terms of accommodations. Nightlife and restaurants run up the bill, as does impulse shopping, but much is free or nearly so: the great, cheap public transport, the colorful street life, the superb street food.

At the very cheapest, figure US$20-25 per day, and that means sleeping in dormitories and eating in noodle stalls. A more reasonable figure is US$100-150 per day, which will bring a decent room, a wider variety of meals and a few extras. There's no limit to top-end expenses, of course.

Tipping

The 10% service charge levied in many restaurants, bars, and hotels should cover tips, but waiters tend to conspicuously lurk about after your change is returned, hoping for more. The small change left over from the bill is sufficient for smaller places, up to 5% if you're feeling generous. If no service charge is included, leave 10%—but if service is bad, don't tip at all.

Taxi drivers needn't be tipped for short trips, beyond rounding up to the nearest dollar; give five to 10% for longer ones. Airport porters get HK$5 per bag; hotel porters a bit more; hairdressers and barbers 10% of the bill. Restroom attendants at plush hotels get HK$1-2, notwithstanding the HK$5 pieces laid out as bait.

HEALTH

Vaccinations

No vaccinations are needed to enter Hong Kong, unless you've visited an area infected with cholera or typhoid within 14 days of your arrival. Travelers to China or other less healthy places may want to obtain vaccinations in Hong Kong; cheapest are the government-run Port Health Vaccination Centres, which will also answer questions about travel. Offices are located at 2/F Centre Point Building, 181 Gloucester Rd., Wanchai, tel. 2961-8840, and 9/F Government Offices Building, 393 Canton Rd., Tsimshatsui, tel. 2368-3361.

Cholera vaccines are available here for HK$60; China travelers should also consider hepatitis, polio, and tetanus. Typhoid vaccines are no longer provided. Malaria prophylaxis, recommended for travel in certain areas of China, can be obtained from Hong Kong pharmacies.

Common Complaints

Hong Kong hasn't the sanitation problems of many Asian countries. Tap water is treated and safe, although locals still don't seem to believe it. Many people prefer to drink boiled water poured straight from the thermos, and are obsessive about rinsing chopsticks, teacups, and bowls at restaurants—leftover habits still applicable on the mainland but unnecessary in Hong Kong.

Food is pretty much worry-free too, even on the street. Cantonese food is supremely fresh,

EDIBLE CURES

Food is medicine in Hong Kong, where medicinal restaraunts serve dishes like steamed tortoise soup with apricot kernels, and gleaming brass urns dispense glasses of 24-herb tea, said to preserve the complexion and aid digestion. Eating as a science is detailed in ancient Chinese texts that outline the medicinal properties of food.

All foods affect the body in some way, depending on their predominate character of yin or yang. Some are remedial, others are damaging; some cooling, others warming. Illness is said to develop from an imbalance in yin and yang. "Hot" and "cold" foods (and to a lesser degree "damp" and "dry") must be balanced in the diet, or sickness will result. Disorders indicating an excess of one quality are treated by consuming the opposite type of food.

Warming foods—those which are oily, spicy, or fried, and most meats—stimulate vital energy or *chi,* but an excess can cause inflammation and infection. Cooling foods, including most vegetables and fruits, dried beans, shellfish, and bitter or salty foods, help to cleanse the body, but in excess they will weaken the system. The distinctions between categories can be exquisitely subtle: unpeeled ginger and white sugar are cooling, while peeled ginger and brown sugar are warming. Rice, as the mainstay of the Chinese diet, is neutral.

Few ordinary people could explain this system in detail, but everyone instinctively knows how to match foods to the system and weather, as well as their own body condition. Cooks understand that ginger, which is warming, goes naturally with tofu, which is cooling; that some vegetables should be stir-fried and others made into soup; that garlic is the perfect partner for greens.

Then there are the five basic tastes, each associated with an organ: sweet for the spleen, hot for the lungs, bitter for the heart, salty for the kidneys, sour for the liver. Each taste supports an organ, but overconsumption will damage it—which leads to all sorts of rules. Spinach, which is cold and slippery in character, must not be eaten with eel. Heart disease sufferers should avoid salty foods and eat more beans and dog meat. Snake and dog meat are good for rheumatism and winter ailments; shark's fin and bird's nest for the complexion; ginseg for digestion (as well as being a restorative, and, by implication, an aphrodisiac). Seasonal foods play an important role in this system, providing qualities suited to the changing weather, like winter-melon soup, consumed in summer to clear away excess heat. There's more to eating Chinese food than meets the eye.

and problems are limited to an occasional case of food poisoning from hotel buffets, and shellfish, which can carry Hepatitis A. Oysters in particular are undesirable, though safe if thoroughly cooked. Coming into too-close contact with polluted water (swimming at a dirty beach) can lead to gastroenteritis or skin infections.

More common are skin rashes caused by the heat and humidity. Even the early colonists complained of "Hong Kong boils." Prickly heat manifests as painful tiny red dots, the sign of inflamed sweat ducts caused by excess sweating. Treatment involves wearing loose cotton clothing, bathing frequently with soap, dusting with talcum powder and lounging about in air-conditioned rooms or shopping centers. Fungal infections like jock itch and athlete's foot are easily treated with antifungal powder or ointment.

Especially in the summer months, travelers should adapt schedules to local conditions. Structure days around air-conditioning and try to do outdoor exploring at night. Drink extra water and fluids, bathe frequently, wear loose-fitting cotton garments, and slow down.

AIDS

AIDS exists in Hong Kong as it does worldwide, though not yet in the proportions of Asian countries like Thailand. Thirteen cases were reported between 1985-92, and many more remain undiagnosed. As a public health brochure states: "The golden rule is refrain from promiscuity and never have sex with strangers." (Not to mention using condoms.) An AIDS Helpline provides information and referrals, tel. 2898-4422.

Treatment

Pharmacies are found all over town: Watson's and Manning's are the biggest chains. Pharmacists will prescribe for minor complaints. For more complicated cases, look in the *Yellow Pages* under "Physicians." Most doctors have trained overseas in English-speaking countries, and charges for basic consultations and medicines are reasonable (room visits by hotel doctors are expensive, though). A cheaper alternative, though it may involve several hours' wait, is to visit one of the 50-plus government clinics, listed under "Medical and Health Department" in the government listings at the beginning of the phone directory.

Government hospitals provide reasonably good services. Fees are higher for foreign visitors than for residents, but are still reasonable, at least compared to the United States. However, the potential need for hospital treatment is a good reason to arrange temporary health insurance *before* you begin your trip. Make sure it covers medical evacuation if you need to be transferred home for treatment.

Government hospitals include **Queen Elizabeth Hospital,** Wylie Rd., Yaumatei, tel. 2958-8888; **Queen Mary Hospital,** Pokfulam Rd., Pokfulam, tel. 2855-3111; and **Princess Margaret Hospital,** Lai King Hill Rd., Lai Chi Kok, tel. 2990-1111.

Private hospitals are more expensive but have better facilities and top-quality care: **Hong Kong Adventist Hospital,** 40 Stubbs Rd., Wanchai, tel. 2574-6211; **Baptist Hospital,** 222 Waterloo Rd., Kowloon Tong, tel. 2339-8888; and **Canossa Hospital,** 1 Old Peak Rd., Mid-Levels, tel. 2522-2181.

Queen Mary Hospital and Queen Elizabeth Hospital have 24-hour casualty wards. For emergency ambulance service, dial 999. The St. John's Ambulance Brigade operates a free ambulance service: call 2530-8000 for information.

SPECIAL INTERESTS

Women Travelers

Hong Kong, like most Chinese-influenced places, is an exceptionally safe and pleasant place for solo women travelers. Sexual harrassment of any type—even obvious sidelong leering—is rare. You're far more likely to be judged on the relative expense of your outfit than your physical attributes. It's still best to dress reasonably modestly, though shorts and short skirts are acceptable here, unlike many other Asian destinations. See the "Safety" section below for general advice.

Handicapped

Travelers with disabilities will find Hong Kong a relatively easy place to get around. Its ultramodern design makes wheelchairs fairly navigable, especially on the KCR and various ferries. Some MTR stations have wheelchair access as well. Contact HKTA before departure for more advice, and ask for a free copy of its *Guide for Physically Handicapped Visitors to Hong Kong.* If you need more detail, the Transport Department, tel. 2829-5258, 41/F Immigration Tower, Gloucester Rd., Wanchai issues a *Guide to Public Transport Services in Hong Kong for Disabled Persons.*

Gays and Lesbians

Homosexuality was only legalised in 1990, and Hong Kong's gay community keeps a fairly low profile. There's a gay/lesbian advisory service, **Horizons,** tel. 2815-9267. Gay nightlife can be found in a few Central bars and clubs. **Club 97,** 9 Lan Kwai Fong, has gay happy hour Friday

HONG KONG WITH KIDS

Hong Kong is eminently do-able with children of all ages: it's safe, clean, well-organized, and fascinating. Kids ages eight and above will probably get the most out of it. If you're traveling with small children, a toddler harness can be reassuring in busy crowds. Strollers are popular, though by the end of a long shopping day they're frequently used more for packages than for a child.

When traveling anywhere with children, pacing is important. So is patience. The first big challenge is the long-distance flight: Request bulkhead seats for the extra legroom (bassinets can be provided for infants), and bring a backpack full of interesting peaceful diversions. Stash a few small surprises and snacks in *your* bag to pull out at critical moments.

Sightseeing with kids requires frequent rest and snack stops, and a supply of toys and activities to get them through boring things you happen to be interested in. Try to intersperse such occasions with strategically timed fun concessions. Advance preparation helps a lot: discuss expected behavior before the morning spent shopping, or the dinner with friends.

Here are a few Hong Kong attractions children will find particularly appealing:

Public transport fascinates everyone, regardless of the destination. Ride the Star Ferry, ferries to the outlying islands, the top deck of the Hong Kong Island tram, the top deck of any bus.

The **Peak Tram,** with its breathtakingly steep ascent, is wonderfully scary, and the walks around the Peak are marvelous. The spacious grounds of the old **Governor's Lodge** in particular are great to run about in.

Centrally located **Hong Kong Park** offers a giant walk-in aviary, lagoons, and a padded playground. **Kowloon Park** has lots of attractions too, including turtles in the fishpond, a maze of clipped hedges, and preening flamingos.

On a rainy or hot day visit the **Space Museum,** with its Omnimax Theater and Planetarium, and the **Science Museum,** featuring hundreds of hands-on

exhibits. Or stop in to see one of the action-packed local **movies,** with enough slapstick and excitement to enthrall any child.

Hong Kong's **temples** are colorful and intriguing: among the best are the Man Mo Temple in Western, the Tin Hau Temple in Yaumatei, and Wong Tai Sin in Kowloon.

Ocean Park is a world-class attraction, and right next door is **Water World,** featuring giant waterslides. **Sung Dynasty Village** is a surprisingly classy historical theme park with regular performances by acrobats, monkeys, and dancers.

If meltdown threatens, take a ferry ride out to one of the **Outlying Islands** for a more low-key day.

Many country parks have designated **Family Walks:** easy, specially marked short trails, often with facilities, barbecue pits and playgrounds.

Beaches are always popular, and stalls at the bigger ones sell irresistible giant inflatable toys in the form of lobsters, sharks, and alligators.

If shopping is your thing, give your child an allotment and let him or her shop too. HK$100 will buy a decent supply of gaudy souvenirs or gifts for friends.

Older children can keep a journal of their trip, illustrated with photos, drawings, and scenic postcards.

The family suites at the Salisbury YMCA are highly recommended, and babysitters are available too (but book months in advance). BP International House at 8 Austin Rd., near Kowloon Park, also has family rooms for HK$1050-1250. For food, **Dan Ryan**'s supplies reassuringly American fries and burgers, and there are plenty of familiar fast-food outlets around town. **Aberdeen**'s floating restaurants are fun for the boat ride and the kitschy ambiance. There's an enormous **Toys 'R' Us** in the basement of Ocean Terminal. The toy sections and restaurants in the Japanese department stores of Causeway Bay are another good distraction. Finally, **Bookazine** in the basement of Jardine House has a good selection of locally oriented kids' books.

nights 6-10 p.m., but you'll have to find a member to get you in. **Petticoat Lane,** 2 Tun Wo Lane, is a hard-to-find little place with an increasingly straight clientele. There's always hot dancing at **Propaganda,** 32 Wyndham St., which has been termed a "gay meat market." **Zip,** 2 Glenealy, is another possibility.

SAFETY

Crime in Hong Kong is minimal, as evidenced by its graffiti-free MTR stations and gangs of scrubbed and wholesome-looking youths. Police are worried about problems ensuing from the increasingly porous Hong Kong/China border, including firearms smuggling and increases in corruption and illegal immigrants. And mainland gangs pull off spectacular bank and gold-store heists. The level of violent crime remains reassuringly low, however, and travelers have little to fear.

Theft

The biggest threat to travelers is pickpockets, many of them among Hong Kong's 40,000 drug addicts. Thieves often work in groups to discreetly slit a pocket or purse, remove valuables, and melt into the crowd. Japanese tourists, known for carrying big wads of cash, are a favorite target, while fast-food restaurants are a favorite venue.

To avoid problems, carry your valuables in a money belt or pouch. At the very least, carry purses slung diagonally across the body rather than over one shoulder, and place wallets in front pockets in dense crowds. Don't put anything valuable in a backpack or daypack, as these are ridiculously easy targets. Be especially careful in crowded places like the Temple Street Night Market or Nathan Road, and on public transport.

Don't leave valuables lying conspicuously about your hotel room, either; store them in the hotel safe if possible. As always when traveling, it's a good idea to keep a photocopy of your passport's front page in a separate safe place to expedite a replacement.

Police

If your passport or valuables are stolen, you'll need a police report for your embassy or insurance company. Contact the main police station for advice on how to obtain this. Hong Kong Island police headquarters is on Arsenal St. in Wanchai, tel. 2860-2000. Kowloon headquarters is at 190 Argyle St., Mongkok, tel. 2761-2228.

The police crime hotline is 2527-7177; general enquiries are at 2866-6166. In an emergency dial 999 and ask for police, fire, or ambulance.

Personal Safety

Personal safety is also a matter of common sense. You probably shouldn't wander about scruffy neighborhoods alone late at night, but areas frequented by tourists are safe. Women travelers will be relieved to find Hong Kong has none of the overt sexual harassment that characterizes many Asian countries. Most women travelers find that Western expats and travelers are more bothersome than locals. A lone woman is pretty much ignored, though you might attract a few stares if you're walking about late at night. Try to maintain a businesslike attitude and look as if you know exactly where you're headed.

A dramatic but extremely remote danger is getting in the way of the crossfire in the spectacular jewelry store heists periodically pulled off by mainland robbers. Look both ways when you pass a gold store. Another favorite technique is "ram raids," in which thieves use vehicles to smash shop windows displaying luxury goods. Fortunately for pedestrians, these generally take place at night.

CHINESE ALMANAC

WHAT TO TAKE

"An empty suitcase" is the first item that comes to mind, but with luggage so reasonably priced in Hong Kong, even that might be too much. Packing too many clothes for a trip to the world's largest garment exporter is definitely bringing coals to Newcastle, unless you hate to shop. Take an adequate wardrobe in case you don't find what you want, but don't overdo it.

Now, what to carry your streamlined wardrobe *in*. A backpack might be ideal for a multi-country Asian trip, but it's not a good idea if Hong Kong is your only destination. For one thing, it marks you as a low-rent traveler in the eyes of scornful concierges; for another, it's not all that convenient. With transport good and porters and bellhops plentiful, you needn't carry your bags long distances. Likewise, a daypack is useful for hiking, but it's not the best thing for city use—unwieldy in an MTR crush, vulnerable to pickpockets, and again somewhat scruffy.

Hong Kong is much more fashion-conscious than most places on the backpackers' circuit. Asian travelers may want to upgrade their wardrobe a notch—something which is easily done on the spot. Business travelers need to look properly businesslike. Jacket and tie are required for men in some of the smarter restaurants. Modesty and bare skin, within reason, is not an issue for women; short skirts and sleeveless dresses are almost universally worn in the summertime.

Clothing should be comfortable and breathable, extremely so in the summer months (May-September). But bring something to protect against the powerful air-conditioning in restaurants, hotels, and shopping malls. Spring and fall require a light jacket as backup for evenings. Winter (December through early March) requires long sleeves and long pants, a sweater or two, and a medium-weight jacket or overcoat. A surprising number of travelers arrive shivering in shorts and sundresses in these months.

Comfortable shoes are a must. Budget travelers might pack a pair of plastic sandals for communal showers, though thongs are frowned upon in public and will prevent you from entering the lobby of The Peninsula.

Other items to consider bringing (though all are locally available) are a small umbrella (essential in summer, but handy year-round), sunglasses, sunscreen, a Swiss Army knife for picnicking, and possibly clothespins and line for in-room clothes drying, though laundry service is inexpensive enough. Pack your glasses or contact prescription if you plan on buying new ones in Hong Kong.

Toiletries are widely available (British brands predominate). Likewise with film, cameras, and lenses, though buying photographic equipment in Hong Kong can be a hassle. Bring your own camera as long as you're happy with it; film is available everywhere at reasonable prices (developing is easy to arrange too). Finally, a photocopy of the front page of your passport tucked away in a safe place makes replacement much easier should you lose it.

BOB RACE

HONG KONG ISLAND

An Overview

A cluster of craggy green hills rising up from the blue South China Sea, Hong Kong Island provides a spectacular setting for one of the world's most intensely urban environments. Most of the island's interior consists of steep wooded hills, permanently protected from development by country parks. The bulk of the island's 1.3 million residents cluster along a narrow strip on the north shore.

Level building sites are at a premium on an island that's basically a mountain. Land reclamation has been an important aspect of life here since the first settlers arrived in the 1840s. It's easy to forget that a century ago much of downtown Hong Kong was underwater.

Central is Hong Kong's business and financial district, a thicket of soaring skyscrapers embracing the spectrum of modern architecture, from dramatic to mundane. It's backed by the **Mid-Levels**, a pricey residential district spread across the lower slopes of Victoria Peak. **The Peak**, as it's fondly known, is a major landmark in itself, and its upper reaches yield magnificent views of urban Hong Kong.

East of Central is **Admiralty**, another cluster of high-tech glass office towers, then **Wanchai**, where shiny new waterfront buildings front an intensely interesting older district. Lively **Causeway Bay** is where Hong Kong residents go for shopping and nightlife. Densely packed residential neighborhoods stretch on through **North Point, Quarry Bay, Taikoo Shing,** and the former old fishing village of **Shaukeiwan.**

Heading in the other direction from Central, **Sheung Wan** or **Western** is Hong Kong's Chinatown, a traditional old trading quarter specializing in delicacies like sharks' fin and medicinal herbs. It merges into **Kennedy Town,** an old shipping site and working-class settlement.

The island's south side is quieter and less crowded, though hardly spacious. Sights here include the busy town of **Aberdeen,** the world-class amusement center of **Ocean Park,** the crowded beach at **Repulse Bay,** touristy **Stanley,** the sleepy village of **Shek O,** and some fine if crowded beaches.

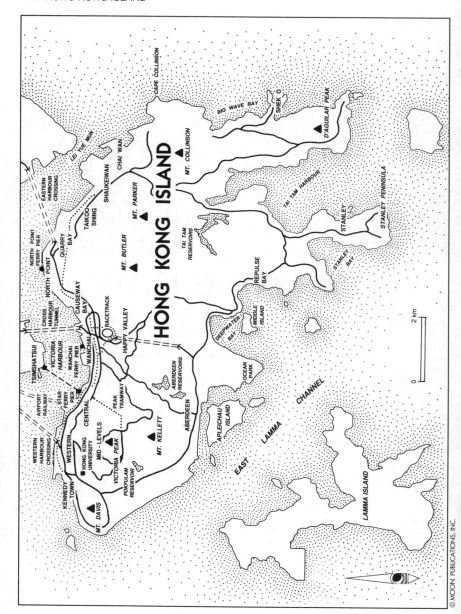

© MOON PUBLICATIONS, INC.

CENTRAL 中環

The scrap of Hong Kong Island's northwest coast below Victoria Peak is the symbolic center of the SAR and a business and financial axis for much of Asia. Early colonists dubbed it Queenstown; the first governor re-christened it Victoria in 1843. Once a city, now a district, it remains the administrative "capital" of Hong Kong.

Hong Kong's racing pulse beats faster here than anywhere else. Central is a seething cauldron of activity, set against a backdrop of moving planes and boats and cars, filled with hurrying crowds of people. The scene is both invigorating and exhausting. In terms of urban planning it's a hodgepodge, but even so it remains a marvel—one of the world's most exciting urban centers.

The relentless verticality of the place rivals Manhattan. Its elegant old colonial buildings were long ago knocked down to make room for densely packed office towers, their glass-curtain walls reflecting one another. Central is a virtual museum of modern buildings, both dreary conformist ones and light, elegant glass spires. Some of the most notable are Exchange Square, the Bank of China, and the Hong Kong and Shanghai Bank Building.

Central is constantly remaking itself: buildings are raised up and torn down within the space of a few years. The relentless pace of change is only accelerating in the last breakneck years before 1997, driven by the rattle of jackhammers, piledrivers, and pneumatic drills. Rents for prime office space here now vie with Tokyo as the world's most expensive.

Central displays Hong Kong's most cosmopolitan face. It's full of big banking and finance offices, expensive hotels and boutiques, and well-dressed crowds on the move. The rapid tick-tick-tick of green lights at pedestrian crossings sets the pace: a brisk walk that only dignity prevents from breaking into a run. There's no loitering in these crowds, no leisurely strolling here; even window-shoppers are jostled. Time is at a premium, and people pass one another like cars on an expressway, singlemindedly bent on getting ahead.

The highway metaphor extends to the sidewalks: much of Central is crisscrossed by elevated walkways raised over busy thoroughfares. Take them when they appear, even if the stairs seem inconvenient, or risk getting lost in the dark tangle of busy roads below.

ALONG THE WATERFRONT

Star Ferry Pier 天星碼頭

The very first thing to do on a Hong Kong visit is to ride the Star Ferry across the harbor. The seven-minute trip between Tsimshatsui and Central is one of the world's classic boat journeys, a superb way to first see Central's stunning facade. On a sunny day, with the water sparkling and the breeze blowing in your face, it's unforgettable; and no matter how often you do it, the crossing retains a mild thrill of excitement. The thrumming engines and shrill whistles, the slam of the gangway and slap of the waves, embodies Hong Kong. The ferry, which started in 1898, is pleasingly low-tech in every detail, from the sailor-suited crew to the piers painted and shaped to resemble the tubby green-and-white boats.

A few ancient rickshaw drivers lurk on the ferry concourse, elderly men in straw hats who pass their days waiting for tourists to pay them for a photo or a ride around the block. Their bright red rickshaws are the last of a fleet that once conveyed the important of Hong Kong. Human-powered transport may seem degrading by modern standards, but the rickshaw was originally a humanitarian device invented by a 19th-century American missionary wishing to spare Japanese coolies the difficulties of sedan chairs.

Stop and get your bearings before taking the pedestrian underpass beneath Connaught Road into the thick of Central. To your right is the large **General Post Office** (郵政總局). The **Jardine House** (怡和大廈) across the street was the first of Hong Kong's monster skyscrapers, twice as high as other buildings when it was raised in 1973, but now looking dated compared to its sleeker neighbors. Its distinctive porthole windows have lent it the sly nickname "House of 1000 Orifices." Stop in at the Hong Kong Tourist Association office in the basement if you haven't yet picked up a supply of brochures and maps.

Airport Railway Central Station

West of the Star Ferry Pier is a chunk of newly reclaimed land, site of the new **Airport Railway Central Station** scheduled for completion in early 1998. Construction on the accompanying developments, which include retail space, an office tower, and two new hotels, is likely to be ongoing for some time. Behind here is a string of ferry piers for the outlying islands of Lamma, Lantau, and Cheung Chau.

Exchange Square 交易廣場

Pushed inland by the new reclamation project are the three elegant pink granite and glass towers of Exchange Square, a business and financial center housing multitudes of important-looking young men in suits. The **Hong Kong Stock Exchange** operates here and can be observed from the glassed-in visitor's gallery overlooking the cavernous trading hall. Call 2522-1122 for arrangements; visiting hours are 10 a.m.-12:30 p.m. and 2:30-3:30 p.m.

Exchange Square is an "intelligent building" boasting such niceties as English-speaking elevators, computer-controlled microclimates, and an internal communications system which among other things provides tenants with an off-track betting service connected to their personal bank accounts. The main **Central Bus Terminal,** the place for buses to the Peak and the island's south side, is well concealed beneath the building.

A pedestrian walkway runs from Exchange Square all the way to the distinctive scarlet-and-black **Shun Tak Centre,** housing the Macau

THE EXPANSION OF HONG KONG

How many places on earth can say they are growing in size? Hong Kong grew 11 square km between 1981-91, but then, it's been growing for a long time. Land reclamation has been a part of local history since the first efforts to fill in Central's shoreline in 1842. A glance at any map reveals history embedded in the street contours: old shoreline streets like Queen's Road curve gracefully around the former coastline, while neighborhoods built on reclaimed land (like Yaumatei and Mongkok) followed a regimented grid pattern.

By WW II, nearly all of Hong Kong's north shore and much of Kowloon's coast had been expanded. City Hall and a new Star Ferry Terminal were added to Central in the mid-1950s, while an entire district—Tsimshatsui East—sprang full-fledged from the ocean in the 1970s. The process was not limited to the city proper: much of the New Towns have been built on reclaimed land. By 1980, one million Hong-kongers lived on manmade land that a generation or two ago did not even exist.

This power to limitlessly remake itself seems peculiarly appropriate to energetic, ever-changing Hong Kong. The process will culminate in the 1990s with grand plans to transform the urban cityscape over the course of the next decade. While elements of the program are linked to the new airport off the coast of Lantau, the entire project is independent of it—and of the squabbles it has inspired between China and Britain.

To fulfill plans for a 25-minute express service between the airport and Central, a massive system of roads, tunnels, and bridges will be developed to link the outer islands with metropolitan Hong Kong. New land is needed to provide space for the new transport hubs, as well as offices, hotels, and apartment buildings.

Reclamation work is expanding Hong Kong Island's northern shoreline in a swath stretching from the Macau Ferry Terminal all the way down to Causeway Bay. Central's shoreline from Rumsey Street to Pedder Street will be pushed an additional 150-350 meters into the harbor. A new station for the Airport Railway will be built on reclaimed land on the current site of the Outlying Districts ferry pier. The Star Ferry Pier and piers for the Outlying Islands ferries will be relocated in roughly their present location, but farther out into the harbor.

Reclamation will continue past the former military headquarters of the HMS *Tamar,* already being redeveloped as an office block, and into Wanchai, where an exhibition park will be built in front of the Arts Academy. Even the Causeway Bay typhoon shelter will be filled in.

Ferry Terminal. A boisterous night market nicknamed "Poor Man's Nightclub" used to operate in a parking lot nearby, but extensive reclamation work has wiped it out, and more buildings are due to sprout here soon.

Around Edinburgh Place 愛丁堡廣場

East of the Star Ferry Pier, the cemented promenade of Edinburgh Place offers splendid views of ships crisscrossing the harbor and airplanes gliding in for a spectacular landing at Kai Tak. Hong Kong's lack of planning becomes woefully obvious here. With one of the most magnificent urban locations available, Edinburgh Place is a bare cement plaza set with a few scrawny palms and benches. Two small battered cannons sunk into the cement, a remnant of colonial days, are unmarked by even a plaque. Pleasure boats and smaller vessels dock here at **Queen's Pier** to pick up passengers (hire a *walla-walla* here for cross-harbor transport after the Star Ferry shuts down).

Behind the square is the architecturally uninspired **City Hall** (大會堂), a relic of the early '60s. Low Block houses various performance venues and several good restaurants; flyers in the lobby advertise upcoming cultural events. High Block holds Hong Kong's main public library and a marriage registry, the latter filling the building's small garden courtyard with a steady procession of wedding parties posing for photos. The brides may wear slithery red cheongsams at their receptions, but the dresses here are Western with a vengeance: huge hoop-skirted gowns of white satin encrusted with rhinestones. Alongside City Hall is a secondary terminal for buses and minibuses, including the free shuttle bus to the Lower Peak Tram Terminus.

The new land (a total of 108 hectares will be added in Central and Wanchai alone) will be used for hotels, government buildings, and transport links to the new airport. A new MTR line and a tram loop will integrate the area into existing transport. High-rise development is to be more strictly controlled than the present generation of buildings, and the new land will include plenty of landscaped open space, including a broad two-km-long waterfront promenade linking a series of parks. Statue Square will be expanded into a palm tree-filled plaza, lined by government buildings and allowing an open vista from the Hong Kong and Shanghai Bank all the way down to the waterfront.

Things are happening across the harbor too: the West Kowloon Reclamation Area currently taking form will add a 330-hectare wedge of land between Yaumatei and Lai Chi Kok, significantly reducing the size of the harbor. A new underwater tunnel, the HK$7.5 billion Western Harbor Crossing, will run from Western (Sai Ying Pun) to the West Kowloon reclamation area, integrating the new area with the island and the airport transportation network. The old Kai Tak airport will be developed into an urban center housing over 250,000, served by an extension of the MTR.

Project expenses are predictably enormous, but revenues from the sales of the newly created land

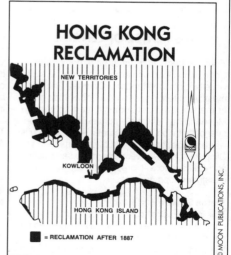

HONG KONG RECLAMATION

NEW TERRITORIES

KOWLOON

HONG KONG ISLAND

■ = RECLAMATION AFTER 1887

© MOON PUBLICATIONS, INC.

are anticipated to far exceed the cost of development. Completion is slated for 2000-2001, and if Hong Kong follows its usual track record, it will be finished on or ahead of schedule.

USEFUL BUS ROUTES FOR HONG KONG ISLAND

Look for the round bus stop signs (blue-and-white on Hong Kong Island). "M" after a route number means the bus connects with an MTR station.

BUS NO.	ROUTE
1	Central (Rumsey Street)-Happy Valley
6, 6A, 260	Exchange Square-Repulse Bay-Stanley
9	Shaukeiwan-Shek O
11	Central Ferry Pier-Causeway Bay-Tiger Balm Gardens-Jardine's Lookout
15	Exchange Square-The Peak
61	Exchange Square-Repulse Bay
70	Exchange Square-Aberdeen
70M	Admiralty MTR-Aberdeen

Green Minibuses

1	Edinburgh Place (City Hall)-Upper Peak Tram
6	Edinburgh Place (City Hall)-Ocean Park (Mon.-Sat.)
9	Edinburgh Place (City Hall)-Bowen Road

THE CENTER OF CENTRAL

Take the pedestrian underpass beneath busy Connaught Road and emerge beside the squat white block of the **Mandarin Oriental.** The unimpressive exterior does a good job of hiding one of the world's most sophisticated hotels: the Mandarin has always emphasized refinement over ostentation. The discreetly elegant lobby is worth a stop, or indulge in afternoon tea in the Clipper Lounge—silver trays of tiny sandwiches and cakes, and well-dressed *tai-tais* laden with designer shopping bags.

Statue Square 皇后像廣場

This nondescript collection of fountains and benches was once part of a much larger central plaza extending all the way down to the harbor, but the elegant whitewashed colonial buildings with their columned verandahs have all been pulled down. The figures of British monarchs that gave the park the name "Royal Square" were shipped off to Japan in WW II. While they were later retrieved, times had changed and they were not reinstated (except for Queen Victoria, who now reigns over Victoria Park). The only remaining statue is a regal bronze of Sir Thomas Jackson, a former manager of the Hong Kong Bank.

The square comes alive on Sunday, when huge crowds of Filipina women spill onto the surrounding streets to enjoy their day off, picnicking and visiting with friends. With a population of 128,000, Filipinos are the largest non-Chinese community in Hong Kong (see the special topic "Filipinas in Hong Kong").

Adjoining the square is equally uninspiring **Chater Gardens,** with its **Cenotaph** honoring Hong Kong's war dead. Hung with funeral wreaths, the Cenotaph was a rallying point for demonstrators in the aftermath of the Tiananmen massacre. Nearby looms the imposing neoclassical dome of the **Legislative Council Chambers,** housed in the former Supreme Court Building (look for the blindfolded statue of Justice on the pediment). Designed in 1912 by the architect who created the facade of Buckingham Palace and the Victoria and Albert Museum, the granite building is especially impressive lit up at night.

Three Banks

Across the tram tracks and Queen's Road is a trio of skyscraping temples to the real source of power in Hong Kong: its banks. On the right is a slender pink granite skyscraper topped with the double 'SC' logo of the **Standard and Chartered Bank.** The building is skinny for a reason—the architect had only a small plot of land to work with—but it rises a few significant meters higher than its neighbor.

Hong Kong and Shanghai Bank Building
香港上海匯豐銀行

Next door, the silver-gray tower of glass and metal designed by British architect Norman Foster is generally conceded to be one of the most exciting, or at least "interesting," modern buildings in the world. Its design is based on the prin-

Hong Kong and Shanghai Bank building, with the Standard Chartered Bank on the right.

This latest version was accounted the single most expensive building in the world when it opened in 1985: the total cost has been estimated at US$1.1 billion. Much of the bill was run up by doodads like the 30-ton sunscoop on the south facade, which lights the atrium through a system of reflective mirrors channeled through lasers. The helicopter pad atop the building inspired cynical comments regarding the bank's ability to transfer its reserves quickly, should the need arise.

Among the few nonfuturistic touches are the two noble bronze lions guarding the entrance, so different from the curly-maned imperial Chinese lions flanking many other important Hong Kong doorways. Dubbed Stephen and Stitt after two former chief managers, the lions were retrieved from the old bank office. Pockmarked with shrapnel from WW II, they serve as mascots for all Hong Kong. Their positioning was determined by *feng shui*, as was the oblique angle of the escalators rising up into the belly of the building. Ride up them to get a different perspective on the architecture.

Tsui Museum of Art 徐氏藝術館

Next door is the old stone **Bank of China** building, former headquarters of the mainland institution, now relocated in an ultramodern tower. The Tsui Museum of Art on the 11th floor is a privately owned 3,000-piece collection of paintings, carvings, furniture, bronzes, and ceramics that spans the Neolithic era to the Qing dynasty. Beautifully presented exhibits include Han dynasty tomb guardians, examples of different porcelain glazes, and replicas of old scholars' studies. The museum is open Mon.-Fri. 10 a.m.-6 p.m., Saturday 10 a.m.-2 p.m.; admission is HK$30.

Bank of China 中國銀行

Across Garden Road, the Bank of China headquarters rivals the Hong Kong and Shanghai Bank building with its dramatic design, a cluster of diminishing blue-glass pyramids twisting upwards into the sky. The building's form evokes the flexible, slender bamboo shoot. It manages to be at once modern and classically Chinese, an effect increased by the high-vaulted entrance hall. The 72-story structure ranked as the tallest building outside the U.S. when it was opened in

ciples of bridge technology, with floors suspended from huge steel trusses slung between two core towers. Conventionalities like support columns and concrete covering were avoided by using a special cladding of super-quality aluminium. The see-through walls thus reveal all the inner workings of elevators, escalators, and offices. Kids love it. Some critics find the exposed girders and trusses too steely and modern, but there's no denying the originality of the design.

The Hong Kong and Shanghai Bank has raised three different buildings on this prestigious site at 1 Queen's Rd., each immortalized on the back side of its banknotes. The 1865 original stood on the waterfront and had davits installed on its side to raise and lower the dinghies used to row out to ships anchored in the harbor. The building's 1930s replacement, commissioned as "the best bank in the world," was demolished in 1981 to make way for Foster's temple to technology.

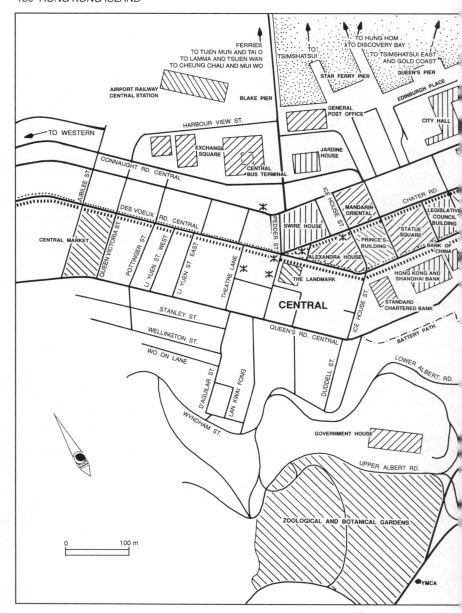

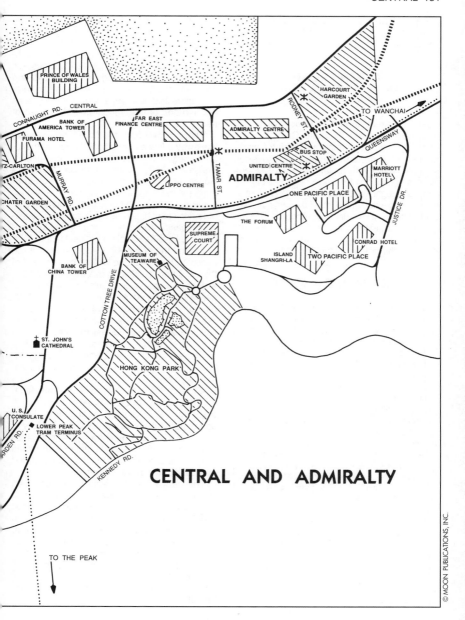

CENTRAL AND ADMIRALTY

1989. Its sharp angles are said to bode ill from a geomantic point of view, but then, American architect I.M. Pei had never heard of *feng shui*.

QUEEN'S ROAD AND DES VOEUX ROAD
皇后大道 德輔道

These two streets form the backbone of the district—central Central, if you like. Queen's Road, originally a shoreline track lined with the warehouses of European traders, has receded steadily inland with reclamation. Des Voeux Road was added in 1860 on a new layer of land, and Connaught Road was built in 1887; a further extension created in the mid-'50s forms the present waterfront—or did until recently. The ongoing Central-Wanchai Reclamation Project (see the special topic " The Expansion of Hong Kong") is the grandest of all.

THE LUK YU TEAHOUSE

This venerable Hong Kong institution at 24 Stanley St., Central, has been in operation more than 70 years, so it's not surprising that 'tradition' is the password here. Some clients are fourth-generation; others have a table booked daily. Perhaps that explains the lackadaisical attitude towards newcomers like tourists. A visit here requires either a Chinese companion or a reservation, and a lot of confidence.

It's worth the trouble, as the Luk Yu is the most authentic teahouse left in Hong Kong. The food is not particularly notable, but the original ambience of the shop on Wing Wo Street has been carefully re-created in the Stanley Street setting, with blackwood chairs and marble-topped tables and brass spittoons beneath lazily twirling ceiling fans (purely for atmosphere, as air-conditioning was installed long ago). The recipes for the famous dim sum are pre-WW II, and the menu changes four times a year. There's also an extensive a la carte menu offering all the standard Cantonese dishes. Go for dim sum either 7-11 a.m. or after 2 p.m., when it's easier to get a seat, and the waiters' attention. For reservations, call 2523-5464.

Downtown Central is a labyrinth of interconnected office buildings, arcades, and glitzy malls. Shopping is an obvious form of recreation if your credit cards can bear the stress of high-class boutiques, but it's fascinating to observe the bits of real life tucked away in nooks and crannies: the shoeshiners and shoemakers, keycutters and newspaper vendors eking out a living in one of the highest-priced patches of real estate on earth.

Veering west from the Mandarin, one can idle away a few air-conditioned hours in the interconnected shopping and office complex of Prince's Building, Swire House, and Alexandra House. Across Des Voeux Road is **The Landmark** (置地廣場), a plush collection of boutiques surrounding a huge atrium, with a fountain calibrated to spout higher as surrounding noise levels increase. Browse here for a HK$7000 handbag or a HK$80,000 diamond necklace.

Around the corner on Pedder Street, a red oval plaque set into the wall at the very end of the Landmark building marks the original 1841 waterfront. Passengers would land here at Pedder's Wharf and stroll up the tree-lined avenue, past the arcaded homes of prosperous merchants, to Queen's Road. Across the street, the handsomely restored **Pedder Building** (畢打街) (circa 1923) holds several floors of upscale factory outlets and the trendy Shanghai Tang boutique, featuring Chinese-style garments in cashmere and silk.

A few traces of the past remain in this high-priced area, with **Duddell Street,** with its granite steps and old-fashioned street lamps. Neighboring **Ice House Street** preserves history in its name. Nineteenth-century American ships laden with timber used Canadian lake ice as ballast; the product was unloaded and stored in special godowns on this street.

The narrow side streets running between Des Voeux Road and Queen's Road are worth exploration. "The Lanes," (**Li Yuen St. East** 利源東街 and **Li Yuen St. West** 利源西街) are crammed with street stalls selling cheap women's and kid's clothing, costume jewelry, umbrellas, handbags, and hair accessories. Vendors here are used to tourists, and prices may be higher than those of other street markets, but the selection and ease of access are unbeatable.

Farther down, the block-long, four-story **Central Market (**中央街市**)** on Queen Victoria Street is a typically bustling Chinese market with all sorts of live and freshly dissected creatures on sale (visit the veggies on the third floor if you're squeamish). The present simple building was built in 1939 on the site of an older market. It opens at 6 a.m. and is best visited early in the morning. While Hong Kong has more attractive and better-ventilated markets, Central's is easily accessible and exceptionally large. A walkway connects its second floor with the Hillside Escalator Link to the Mid-Levels (see "The Mid-Levels," below).

SOUTH OF QUEEN'S ROAD

Lane Crawford, Hong Kong's oldest and most prestigious department store, reigns supreme on Queen's Road Central. Behind it at 26 Stanley St. is the venerable **Luk Yu Teahouse,** a bastion of *yum cha* relocated in 1975 from its original location in Western. And a block behind *it,* at 32 Wellington St., the **Yung Kee Restaurant** dishes out classic Cantonese dishes (roast goose the specialty).

Wellington Street itself is good for a wander, leading past intriguing little side streets amid the usual pandemonium of jackhammers, delivery trucks, and office workers in search of a fast lunch. **Pottinger Street,** named for Hong Kong's licentious first governor, is in its upper reaches a "ladder street" of stone steps specializing in buttons, ribbons, and notions.

Lan Kwai Fong 蘭桂坊
Back near the Yung Kee, walk south a block down D'Aguilar Street to Wo On Lane, which has an excellent Asian handicrafts shop (**Mountain Folkcraft**) and an old **Earth God shrine** at the far end. Continue on another block to Lan Kwai Fong, an L-shaped cobblestone lane packed with a cosmopolitan mix of restaurants, discos, bistros and bars. (See "Entertainment" in the Hong Kong Basics chapter for a rundown of the area's nightlife.) In contrast to the tourist bars of Kowloon, "The Fong" draws locals, both expat yuppies and their Chinese counterparts (nicknamed "chuppies"). The scene is lively, expensive, and ruthlessly young and well-dressed.

Penetrating beyond LKF, you'll emerge at the top of the hill on Wyndham Street, lined with antique and carpet shops and inexpensive Indian restaurants. It's well worth a wander all the way down to the Man Mo Temple described in the "Western" section (the street becomes Hollywood Road about halfway down). En route you'll pass Hong Kong's largest remaining cluster of Victorian buildings: the gray and red-brick **Magistracy** (circa 1914), the old cream-and-blue **Victoria Prison,** where wardens' uniforms drying in the yard add a homey touch, and the enormous 1919 **Central Police Station.**

St. John's Cathedral 聖約翰大教堂
Behind the Hilton on Garden Road is the oldest Anglican church in the Far East, consecrated in 1849. Its Gothic angles, rendered in cream stucco, create a tropical Victorian ambience that's set off nicely by the quiet grounds dotted with old banyan trees. Inside, ceiling fans turn lazily above rows of carved teak pews, and light streams through the stained-glass windows. The north one depicts Jesus calming the waves, surrounded by local figures including a Hakka fisherwoman and British merchant seamen. It's dedicated to those who have lost their lives at sea, a common enough event in Hong Kong history.

Japanese soldiers, who used the cathedral as a social club during the occupation, tore out the old memorial plaques, but St. Michael's Chapel on the right holds books listing the original dedications. The cathedral hosts lunchtime musical recitals—anything from a string quartet to a brass band—Wednesdays around 1 p.m.

Government House 督憲府
The official residence of Hong Kong's governor was built in 1855. Its grounds originally included what later became the Botanical Gardens, and swept all the way down to the harbor. The architecture has been tampered with over the years, most notably by the Japanese governor who resided here during the occupation and oversaw certain design changes, turning up the roof corners and adding the Orientalesque central tower. The result is an appropriately grand mixture of East and West.

When the British governor was in residence, the site was off-limits except for one spring Sunday a year, when the public was admitted to admire the garden's azaleas and rhododendrons. Peer through the imposing wrought iron gates on Upper Albert Road at the sweeping drive and imposing facade. The best view is from the steps of the Botanical Gardens across the road, where Government House appears backed by the trio of skyscraping banks. It's an audacious display of power and privilege, tempered by the reflection that all things pass, and Hong Kong's last governor sailed off on the royal yacht *Britannia* in 1997.

IN SEARCH OF COLONIAL COLOUR

History doesn't last long in Hong Kong, where skyrocketing land prices have long prompted developers to rip down stately old buildings and replace them with sleek multi-storied towers. The relentless pace of change is driven by the territory's economic growth. There's little cash value in sentimentality, barring a few exceptions. Such a fuss was raised after the old Repulse Bay Hotel was knocked down to make way for apartment blocks that the developers eventually put up a replica of its facade. Elegant old Murray House in Central was dismantled in 1982 to make way for the Bank of China Tower. Its numbered stones rest in a shed at Tai Tam Reservoir, waiting to be resurrected at a less crowded site (possibly Stanley).

The few colonial relics that remain impart a much-needed sense of depth to Hong Kong's glossy facade. Most are concentrated in Central, among the earliest areas of British settlement. Herewith a listing of some of the lingering fragments of Hong Kong's colonial past:

- Duddell Street, with its stone steps and Victorian gas lamps (now electrified, but still romantic).

- The 1913 Dairy Farm Building on Lower Albert Road, now housing the Foreign Correspondents' Club and the artsy Fringe Club.

- Central Police Station and Victoria Prison on Wyndham Street, both still in use.

- The neo-Gothic Victorian bulk of St. John's Cathedral across from the Lower Peak Tram Terminus.

- Beaconsfield House, the stately old red-brick building behind the cathedral, once housed the French Mission and is now occupied by the Government Information Services Department. A small plaque describes its convoluted history.

- The Cathedral of the Immaculate Conception at the intersection of Caine and Upper Albert roads

was designed in the 1880s by an Italian architect. The interior features a trio of altars from Italy and stained-glass windows imported from France.

- The narrow "ladder streets," paved with granite slabs to ease the way for sedan-chair bearers. Too steep for vehicles, they continue to serve as pedestrian passageways.

- The Peak Cafe, housed in an elegantly restored 1901 fieldstone building.

- The tiny whitewashed Wanchai Post Office, opened in 1915.

Kowloon-side, there's even less to be seen. The grande dame of local hotels, the Peninsula, has a new tower stuck atop its balanced form, and all that remains of the dignified old Kowloon-Canton Railway Station is a lonely clock tower. Six granite columns salvaged from the old station now stand stranded in an Urban Council Park in Tsimshatsui East. A small park between the Science Museum and Chatham Road enshrines a 1921 KCR coach resting on a fragment of original track (the rest was torn up when the railway station relocated to Hung Hom in 1975). Across Chatham Road are St. Mary's Canossian College in cream stucco, and the red-tiled steeples of the 1905 Rosary Church.

The blue-and-cream Marine Police Headquarters sits primly atop a hill near the Star Ferry. Another anachronism is the towering mast preserved in the Signal Hill Garden across from the Regent: a hollow copper ball was once dropped from it daily at 1 p.m. to signal the time to ships anchored in the harbor. Down Nathan Road are St. Andrew's Church, built in 1905, and behind that the elegant Royal Observatory on a wooded hill. Nearby, the 1902 Kowloon British School now houses, appropriately, the Antiquities and Monuments Office.

Zoological and Botanical Gardens 動植物公園
This little oasis provides the birdsong, greenery, and space so lacking in Central. The main entrance is on Upper Albert Road, about 10 minutes' walk uphill from the Bank of China Tower. Visit early in the morning (6-8 a.m.) to watch the slow-motion ballet of tai chi practitioners.

The gardens were established in 1864 by the governor; Cantonese still call it *Ping Tau Fa Yuen,* "Head Soldier's Flower Garden." The 16 hectares embrace lush stands of camellias, hydrangeas, poinsettias, tree ferns, palms, bamboo, and orchids. There's also an aviary with 1,000 birds of 280 species, including flamingos, scarlet ibises, birds of paradise, and an excellent collection of peacock pheasants. Take the underpass beneath Albany Road to visit the smallish but good zoo, with jaguars, leopards, kangaroos, and the world's largest captive assembly of red-cheeked crested gibbons.

Hong Kong Park 香港公園
Opened in 1991 on the site of the old Victoria Barracks, this park is typically Hong Kong in that every bit of its 10 intensely landscaped hectares is used for *something:* a conservatory displaying plants of arid and tropical climates (the two divisions separated by an airlock), a padded playground, a spectacular walk-in aviary with 150 species of Asian birds, pools, fountains, and stunning views of Central's mirror-and-glass skyscrapers. Children frolic, old men read newspapers, and white-gowned brides pose for photos in the gardens after visiting the nearby Marriage Registry. A restaurant with indoor and outdoor seating serves snacks, sandwiches, and cappuccino. Access the park from Cotton Tree Drive or Supreme Court Road (behind Pacific Place).

Flagstaff House
Hong Kong Park also holds the **Museum of Teaware** (茶具文化館), situated in the stately former residence of the British commander-in-chief. Built in 1844, Flagstaff House is the oldest remaining colonial building in Hong Kong. Its cool, high-ceilinged rooms provide an elegant setting for a 500-item collection of teaware. Teapot aesthetics prove surprisingly compelling, and the collection is well-documented with narrative displays. The museum is open 10 a.m.-5 p.m. daily except Wednesday; admission is free.

ADMIRALTY 金鐘

The easternmost edge of Central, Admiralty offers more of the same: financial offices, shopping centers and glitzy boutiques, and a few remarkable buildings, like the **Lippo Centre,** its twin hexagonal towers blending sun and shadow in their multifaceted glass walls. The gold-mirrored glass encasing the glinting **Far East Finance Centre** has led to the nickname "the Hakka's (or Amah's) Tooth." Walkways connect these buildings with Queensway Plaza, Admiralty Centre, and Hutchison House—more offices and shops than you could reasonably hope to cover in a lifetime. From a terminal beneath United Centre, buses head to the Peak, Happy Valley, and Ocean Park.

The first foreign port on my journey was Hong Kong. It has a glorious bay, the movement of ships on the ocean is beyond anything I have seen in picture, excellent roads, trolleys, a railway to the mountains, museums, botanical gardens; wherever you turn you will note evidences of the most tender solicitude on the part of the English for men in their service; there is even a sailors' club. I drove around in a rickshaw, i.e., was borne by humans, bought all sorts of rubbish from the Chinese and got indignant listening to my Russian travelling companions abusing the English for exploiting the natives. Thought I to myself, yes, the English exploit the Chinese, the Sepoys and the Hindus, but they do give them roads, plumbing and Christianity; you exploit them too, but what do you give them?
—Anton Chekov,
1890 letter to a friend

HMS *Tamar*

Admiralty got its name from the British military headquarters which marked its shoreline until recently, part of a complex of naval dockyards that once stretched all the way into Wanchai. The compound was known as the HMS *Tamar,* after an old supply ship anchored here that served as naval headquarters for nearly 50 years until the Japanese blew it up in 1941. After the war, the military relocated in ordinary buildings here, but, upholding tradition, the entire compound was officially classed as a Royal Navy Ship (affectionately dubbed "the Stone Frigate"). In 1993 military headquarters moved to a new complex on Stonecutter's Island, despite protests from the Chinese, who would have preferred a military foothold in Central. The compound is now being developed as an office complex.

Pacific Place 太古廣場

The Mall at Pacific Place sets the tone for the new Admiralty: a spacious, shiny shopping center with an upscale veneer. Anchored by Seibu and Lane Crawford department stores, it boasts three luxury hotels (the Marriot, the Island Shangri-La, and the Conrad), a multiplex cinema screening international releases, and plenty of good if expensive restaurants. For a cheap meal, skip the fast-food court full of noisy teenagers and descend to Seibu's basement Food Hall, where counters sell everything from croissants to sushi (try the Gastro Primo sandwich bar or the giant bowls of Japanese noodles), and a grocery store stocks dozens of varieties of Japanese sake and French wine vinegar.

Also visit the world's most expensive tree: a 120-year-old banyan adjoining the Conrad's coffee shop, which cost an estimated HK$24 million to keep alive. A specially designed cylinder was sunk in the earth to contain the sprawling roots and allow three floors of shops and a two-level car park to be built beneath it. Preservation takes some strange twists in Hong Kong.

THE PEAK

Victoria Peak, "The Peak" in local terminology, is one of Hong Kong's undisputed must-sees. Its upper reaches reveal a stunning urban vista: the shimmering towers of Central backed by the magnificent busy harbor, Kowloon's packed peninsula across the way. At night the scene is a glowing neon paean to rampant capitalism. Make the trip up both day and night if possible, but if the days are cloudy (and the Peak is often swathed in mist), be assured that the views are most spectacular at night.

History

The Peak was developed in the venerable tradition of the British hill station, as an escape from the appalling dampness and heat of the summer monsoon—"envelopes stuck together and cigars like bits of sponge," fumed an early resident. Atop the Peak, "one can spend the summer in Hong Kong with a reasonable probability of being alive at the end of it," wrote another early resident. The colony's surgeon general recommended the Peak's salubrious air as early as 1867, and after the governor established a summer residence near its summit, civil

servants and taipans flocked to build their homes on the upper reaches.

The European Reservation Ordinance of 1887 restricted settlement on the Peak to Europeans—though this was not stated directly. Instead, building regulations required the governor to approve the construction of any Chinese-style residences in the area, which he of course did not. Colonial homes sprang up instead, imposing mansions with names like Brockhurst, the Bluff, Tor Crest, and Abergeldie.

The British were not averse to walking—morning constitutionals were de rigueur—but the Asian concept of face required the use of a sedan chair for ascending the Peak. The rope-supported seat, roofed with oilcloth and outfitted with a footrest, was set up rather like a swing on curving bamboo poles carried on the shoulders of bearers, who worked in relays for the three-hour ascent. "It is a distressing task for four coolies to carry one man up this incline," noted a colonist. Everything else—coal, food, supplies—was carried up too. In 1888 the Peak Tram was installed to link businesses with residences, easing the lots of both coolies and colonists.

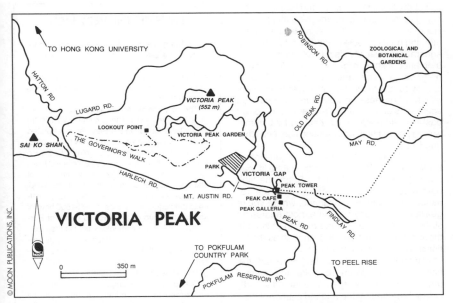

The lower reaches became more tolerable after the introduction of electric fans in 1908, but the upper class had by then settled comfortably into the Peak's rarified atmosphere. They probably enjoyed the way social status was so clearly delineated by altitude, with the governor's summer mansion nearest the summit and the colonists arrayed in descending rank about him.

Victoria Peak is only the most famous of the rugged mountains dominating the mid-section of Hong Kong Island: others are Mounts Gough, Kellett, Johnston, Parker, Davis, Cameron—good, solid, unromantic names, all belonging to former generals or governors. The Peak itself was previously known as Tai Ping Shan or "Great Peace Mountain," to mark the 1810 surrender of a local pirate band. Contemporary Chinese names are Shan Teng ("The Peak"), or Che Kei Shan ("Torn Banner Hill").

Victoria Gap

Contrary to what most tourists believe, the Peak Tram does not ascend to the Peak's 552-meter summit. The Upper Peak Tram Terminal is set in Victoria Gap (440 meters), which is about one-half km southeast of the main summit.

The upper tram terminus has gone through several incarnations; the most recent, described as resembling a "flying wok," opened in 1996. Packed with restaurants and souvenir shops, it's eventually supposed to include a movie theater and exhibits on Hong Kong's past, present, and future, as well as a Ripley's Believe It Or Not! Museum. The Peak Galleria, a high-class establishment across the road, offers more shops and restaurants and an amusing performing fountain spurting forth syncopated jets of water.

This area includes two not-to-be missed dining experiences: the quaint **Peak Café** across from the tram terminus, and the swanky, spectacular **Café Deco** in the Peak Galleria (see the special topic "Offbeat Dining"). A less quintessential but cheaper restaurant is Marche Movenpick on the 6th and 7th floors of the Peak Tower, a quick self-serve eatery with pizzas, salad, and Asian dishes.

Around the Peak

A mapboard across from the tram exit outlines possible walks. The classic is the hour-long circuit of the Peak via Harlech and Lugard roads, highly recommended for anyone suffering from Hong Kong urban-itis, or seeking a superb early morning running route. "Road" is a bit of an exaggeration: basically it's a level, paved 3.5-km path lined with lush groves of rhododendron, bamboo, jasmine, and giant palms. Circling clockwise, the views become ever more magnificent, first passing above the uninhabited southern slopes of the island stretching down past Pokfulam Reservoir, backed by Lamma, with its power plant, and dumbbell-shaped Cheung Chau.

From the recreation area at the junction of Harlech and Lugard roads, several trails lead out over the slopes of Sai Ko Shan, the high bare mountain rising up due west. It's a 15-minute scramble to the summit, where you're guaranteed privacy and an almost deafening silence—no sounds but the rustling of trees in the wind and the blast of distant ships' horns floating up from the Lamma Channel.

Continuing around onto Lugard Road, the path curves past millionaires' villas and an enormous Indian rubber tree. The island's north side is heralded by the muffled clamor of boat engines, jackhammmers, and traffic noises rising from far below. Suddenly the path rises above the forest, and Victoria Harbour unfolds below in a breathtaking wide-angled vista guaranteed to inspire awe no matter how often you've seen it.

If you haven't the time or inclination for this one-hour circuit, head directly down Lugard Road to get great views, fast. The best viewpoint is about 15 minutes' walk from the tram terminus.

Mountain Lodge

From the tram terminus, walk up steep Mt. Austin Road, passing a playground and rows of expensive condos with views. It's about 20 minutes to a little sky-blue and white gatehouse, all that's left of the governor's turn-of-the-century summer residence, Mountain Lodge. While it was noticably cooler atop the Peak, conditions were still less than idyllic: with the summit constantly wrapped in clouds, water streamed down walls to puddle on the floor. Modern air-conditioners and dehumidifiers have taken care of that, but the governors lost patience long be-

LIVES OF THE VERY RICH

Hong Kong is a place for the very rich, and for those who aspire to be so. Not for nothing are its television stations named Gold, Diamond, Pearl, and Jade. An American sociologist once noted punningly that Hong Kong's real religion is "money-theism."

The very rich are shameless about their condition: they revel in it. The epitome is Villa D'Oro on Victoria Road, which features gold-plated taps, gold coins embedded in the toilet seats, a gold dinner service, and a gold Rolls Royce Phantom. There are at least 899 other Rolls Royces in the territory: Hong Kong has more of them per capita than anywhere else in the world.

Extravagant expenditures are directly related to the acquisition of face. A HK$1500 bowl of shark's fin soup or a HK$6000 bottle of Bordeaux would be meaningless unless their purchase were observed, and admired. Hosts procure the best, the most exotic, the most expensive food and drink for their guests—VSOP cognac and fish worth their weight in silver.

Conspicuous consumption is an ideal firmly embedded in local culture. A quick glance through any uppercrust magazine reveals advertisements for Ferrari, Peugeot, and Alfa Romeo, while TV advertisements peddle Martell cognac, Cartier jewelry, and Lalique crystal. Few Hongkongers concern themselves directly with such acquisitions—the rich are a tiny fragment of the population—but the ostentatious display of wealth serves as an inspiration.

The key is opportunity. People believe they have a chance to get rich, whether it be through hard work or a lucky night at the racetrack. Hong Kong offers the chance to work hard, save, save, save, and get ahead. It will be quite interesting to see how the rest of China manages to tolerate this.

Westerners often deride the local obsession as avarice: "They're only interested in money" is a common lament. What really drives Hong Kong, however, is more ambition than greed, based on a collective memory of a generation's very recent poverty. Hong Kong has given its residents the chance for a new life, and they want it in a hurry. Luxury goods are simply the visible measure of success, the fruit of hard labor.

fore and transferred their retreat to Fanling in the New Territories. Mountain Lodge was eventually taken over by the occupying Japanese and was finally demolished in 1946.

The grounds have been converted into a landscaped park with magical little wooded corners

---

HALF THE FUN OF IT: THE PEAK TRAM

The Peak Tram is the steepest funicular railway in the world, with a gradient of 1 in 2 in certain stretches. Opened in 1888 by a pair of enterprising Englishmen, it reduced the three-hour sedan chair ride up the Peak to eight minutes. It remains the fastest and most exciting way to make the ascent.

The tram operates on the endless wire-rope system: two cars are pulled by 1,500-meter-long steel cables wound on separate drums at the top. As one ascends, the other descends; look for the brief run of double track in the middle where the two cars pass, just beyond May Road. Electric motors were substituted for the original steam boilers in 1926, and the old green mahogany cars were replaced in 1989 with sleek crimson ones, but the haulage gear is the original, well-maintained item. Reassuringly, there have been no accidents in over a century of operation.

Though it's a major tourist attraction, the Peak Tram is essentially practical. In the early morning it's filled with schoolchildren and briefcase-wielding businessmen making the downward commute to Central; traffic reverses in the evening rush hour. The tram stops along the way to discharge passengers at Kennedy, MacDonnell, May, and Barker roads. If you want to get off at any of these, press the signal button and exit from the front door.

The Lower Peak Tram Terminus is on Garden Road in Central, behind the Bank of China, and about 10 minutes' walk from the Star Ferry. A free double-decker shuttle bus runs from the Star Ferry every 20 minutes 9 a.m.-7 p.m. The tram operates every 10-15 minutes between 7 a.m. and midnight; be prepared for long lines on weekends and holidays. Tickets cost HK$14 one-way, HK$21 roundtrip.

Acrophobics dreading the alarmingly steep ascent can take a taxi or bus up the Peak, a longer but equally scenic ride. Bus 15 runs from the Exchange Square bus terminus; Minibus 1 from Edinburgh Place. Or walk up, an aerobic effort best made via 3.6-km Old Peak Road.

---

to fascinate dogs and kids. A little farther up the road is **Victoria Peak Garden,** a favorite viewpoint overlooking the island's backside. Visit it at sunset, when the boats slip silently through the East Lamma Channel and the lights flicker on in Aberdeen below. The Peak's summit—actually there are three summits, all marked by telecommunications towers—lies near here.

More Peak Walks
Victoria Peak's once-bare slopes are now thickly forested, thanks to the dogged British colonists who planted hundreds of trees to slow erosion and provide shade. The Peak's marvelous leafy walkways are enhanced by stunning views and well-appointed mansions, and it's always a few degrees cooler than town. Serious hikers should get a topographic map like *Countryside Series No. 1: Hong Kong Island* (available at the Government Printing Office in Admiralty). Here are a few ideas to get started:

The **Hong Kong Trail** starts from the Peak Tram station: the first 14-km stretch to Watford Road, heading around High West to Pokfulam and Aberdeen reservoirs, makes a good day walk. Or you could walk all the way to Shek O (50 km) in one *very* long day.

Pokfulam Reservoir Road starts south of the upper tram terminus and leads two km into **Pokfulam Country Park,** a popular picnic site. Returning, buses on Pokfulam Road run to Aberdeen or Central.

Twisting, turning **Old Peak Road** leads down to the Botanical Gardens in Central, a 3.6-km walk.

Circle the backside of the Peak via **Harlech Road,** then veer off onto **Hatton Road** to drop steeply down to Hong Kong University and, eventually, Kennedy Town.

The hour-long walk down the backside of the Peak to Aberdeen is also good: take Peak Road to shady **Peel Rise** and descend past a stunningly located giant cemetery into town.

For an aerobic workout, get off the Peak Tram at May Road and take shady, well-maintained **Chatham Path** up to Barker Road, a good, stiff 20-minute climb. From here, Hospital Path heads up to Severn Road, which leads to the Upper Tram Terminus.

Diehards can walk in about six hours from the Peak to **Stanley,** but bring a map as the route is complicated. From the Upper Tram Terminus head east along Finley Road to Barker Road, Peak Road, Coombe Road, then from Black's Link across Wong Nai Chung Gap and Stanley Gap, through Tai Tam Country Park, then Tai Tam Road into Stanley.

THE MID-LEVELS
半山區

This semi-swank residential district sandwiched between Western and the upper reaches of the Peak holds innumerable high-rise apartment buildings housing upwardly mobile young Chinese and expats. Views correspond to status, and a basic two-bedroom flat with a harbor view might rent for HK$25,000 a month.

The main attraction here for tourists is the HK$205 million **Hillside Escalator Link,** a series of 20 escalators and three "travelators" running from Connaught Road up to Conduit Road. The world's longest outdoor system at 800 meters, it's being observed with interest by other Asian cities thinking of replicating it. Hong-

---

HIKING ON HONG KONG ISLAND

While the island's shoreline hosts some of the most intense modernization in the world, much of the interior is uninhabited. You'll get a glimpse of the green interior if you hike even a portion of the 50-km **Hong Kong Trail** which runs from Victoria Peak to Big Wave Bay. It's actually a collection of linked trails, signposted and maintained, and broken only occasionally by an unavoidable road. Hikers can do bits and pieces—the trail traverses some of the most scenic areas of the island—or walk the whole thing in two long days.

The first 14 km takes about five hours and makes a good day walk. The route starts at the upper terminus of the Peak Tram and circles the backside of the Peak, veering off to head due west onto Sai Ko Shan (High West Peak) and gradually dropping down to Pokfulam Reservoir. It's hard to believe you're just one hill away from the urban blitz of Central. The multiple signposts can be confusing, but follow the ones with the Hong Kong Trail emblem of two hikers toward Peel Rise and spectacular views of Aberdeen. Eventually you'll emerge onto Watford Road, where buses run back to Central.

The trail heads on from here to Wanchai Gap and Tai Tam Reservoir, concluding at Big Wave Bay. A detour down Dragon's Back to Shek O and its Thai restaurant is highly recommended. The CPA issues a black-and-white *Hong Kong Trail Map,* or consult *Countryside Series Sheet No. 1, Hong Kong Island.*

---

kongers are less enamored of the system, which has had little effect on reducing rush-hour traffic jams in the Mid-Levels since its opening in 1993. Reportedly, however, it's a great pick-up site for young professionals. The ride takes 20 minutes end-to-end and is calibrated to demand, running downhill 6-10 a.m., then uphill till 10 p.m. Hop off it midway to explore the trendy small restaurants and bars lining **Staunton Street,** a recent phenomenon

WESTERN

If Central is the international financial center of Hong Kong, Western is the business district—but the businesses here are smaller, local concerns. Western is the place to glimpse a traditional China that has vanished from the mainland. Its side streets harbor fan makers and street barbers; dried ginseng and live snakes; warehouses of pungent herbal medicines and brightly lit shops displaying birds' nests and sharks' fins in locked glass cases.

Planting the British flag here at Possession Point in 1841, the British chose Western as their first area of settlement, but fled after it proved malarial, shifting first to Happy Valley, then to Central. Chinese settlers soon poured into the neighborhoods around Tai Ping Shan. Many of

CHINESE MEDICINE

Many shops in Sheung Wan trade in strange-smelling ingredients that sound like a recipe for witches' brew: deer antlers and dried sea horse; caterpillar fungus wine; crushed seed pearls ingested to improve the complexion or to soothe irritable babies. They are all part of a tradition dating back perhaps 4,000 years, when the legendary emperor Shen Nung is said to have tasted all herbs and discerned their uses, developing the basis for Chinese medicine and pharmacology.

Texts like *The Yellow Emperor's Classic of Internal Medicine,* written in 2600 B.C., elucidate an intricate system of health care. Disease is believed to result from an internal imbalance—too wet, too dry, too hot, too cold—which may be caused by a number of different influences. Treatment involves rebalancing the elemental forces through elaborate herbal preparations, or sometimes simply what one eats and drinks.

Prescription relies on subtle diagnosis of the pulse. More than 30 different kinds of pulses are outlined, including "slippery," "thready," "empty," "irregular," and "leisurely." The doctor may also check the patient's tongue. Once a diagnosis is arrived at—"wet heat" or the like—a specific remedy is prescribed to redress the imbalance.

If you come down with a cold or flu in Hong Kong, you might take the opportunity to visit an herbal doctor or chemist. Chronic conditions like asthma, eczema, and migraines are also responsive, especially as Western medicine often has little success with these. After listening to a description of your symptoms he will check your pulse in both wrists, and prescribe a treatment. The potion might include 20 or 30 different ingredients: roots, bark, twigs, dried leaves, seeds, or flowers; perhaps even insect parts (dried cicada shells are popular). The infusion is steeped in water for up to an hour, then drunk. Typically only a single dose is needed.

China's vast pharmacopia embraces some bizarre ingredients. Tiger bones, slowly roasted over a fire for seven to ten days at just the right temperature, are said to be good for rheumatism; deer's antler for fever. Sun-dried hornet bodies are mixed with herbs to cure the flu; dried sea horse is prescribed for nervous disorders; and snake gall mixed with wine cures arthritis. A cure for insomnia involves fossilized bones and teeth, ground up and mixed with date stones. It's feared that the bones of Peking Man, a forerunner of *Homo sapiens* unearthed in 1927 which disappeared during WW II, might have suffered this fate.

Bonham Strand West is also the center of trade in ginseng, a highly valued forked root attributed with magical properties. Like ginger, it is said to tone and invigorate the system and build up *chi* or vital energy; its reputation as an aphrodisiac stems from this.

Ginseng comes in some 30 varieties. Red ginseng from North Korea is said to enhance virility; white ginseng, often from America (Wausa, Wisconsin, is a major ginseng producer; so is Wyoming), is a relatively inexpensive variety often mixed with hot water and drunk as a general pick-me-up or a cure for hangovers. Most prized is wild ginseng from the mountains of northeast China, which must be extracted with wooden tools, as metal can damage its potency. It's said to have the power to prolong life for three days no matter how sick the patient might be, and is incredibly expensive—up to HK$60,000 per plant.

Western's residents were originally from around Swatow; some still speak the Chaozhou dialect.

Better than anywhere else, Western preserves the spirit of Hong Kong's old Chinese bazaar, but it's undergoing rapid transformation as rising property values push developers deeper into its old quarters. The old arcaded shophouses with overhanging balconies are being torn down and replaced by bland highrises. Visit Western now, before it changes even more. The tram provides excellent access: hop on whenever things get dull and get off a few blocks later to explore.

The neighborhoods between Central Market and Kennedy Town are all loosely termed "Western." More particularly the name refers to **Sheung Wan,** the area west of Central Market, densely packed with intriguing shops. Wanderers will want to visit **Hollywood Road,** with its antique and art shops, and the quaint old temples of **Tai Ping Shan** to the south. Farther west is **Sai Ying Pun,** with its Centre Street market and traditional stores. The neighborhood around the **University of Hong Kong** is largely residential but holds a few points of interest. Western terminates in **Kennedy Town,** an old seafaring district that's the end of the tramline.

SHEUNG WAN

This is Hong Kong's Chinatown, and wandering its busy streets you'll find just about everything. Long stretches of its east-west avenues are being rebuilt and modernized, but the old side streets running up from the water are still worth exploring. Here the air is thick with the old-time aroma of dried fish and pungent medicinal herbs.

Along Des Voeux Road
Taking the boxy block of the Central Market as your starting point, walk west down Des Voeux Road Central. The main road is noisy and crowded with traffic, but look for the colorful side streets running between here and Queen's Road Central. The shops and stalls of **Wing Kut Street** specialize in wholesale costume jewelry and accessories—vaster quantities of beads, bangles, and metallic trim than you ever would have believed. **Wing Wo Street** is being redeveloped, but a few shops still sell fluffy boas,

peacock feathers, and those chicken-feather dusters chauffeurs use to buff their cars.

Next is **Wing Sing Street,** a narrow lane specializing in all types of eggs: chicken, duck, quail, pigeon, goose. Buyers "candle" the eggs, holding them up to lightbulbs and peering at them through paper tubes to check for freshness. The "100-year-old" duck eggs here are soaked for one month in a mixture of tea leaves, lime, alum and salt, then plastered with mud and rice husks. In this state they can last six months without refrigeration, though the whites become a gelatinous amber and the yolks a slimy greenish black. Sliced eggs are served with pickled ginger as appetizers in Cantonese restaurants.

Around Man Wah Lane 文華里
Engraved seals or "chops" of all varieties are carved in the stalls lining this narrow street. Chops have been used since the 13th century B.C. to sign paintings, authenticate documents, and signify ownership. Tiny stalls display chops of ivory, bronze, soapstone, marble, wood, porcelain, and plastic, and small pots of vermilion paste, made of powdered cinnabar and oil.

Craftspeople will help you select Chinese characters to transliterate your name, perhaps adding a dragon or lion to the design. High or low relief is a matter of taste, though some say women should have low relief *(yin wen),* men high *(yang wen).* It takes an hour or two to carve a chop, during which you can further explore Western. Some stalls also print business cards in Chinese: look for tiny carved blocks, each bearing a single character, filed into cubbyholes.

Wing Lok Street, which bisects Man Wah Lane, was the old center of the rice trade. It's now being redeveloped. Back at 262 Des Voeux Road across from the Shueng Wan MTR station is the popular **Yat Chau Health Food Restaurant,** where customers have a quick medical consultation at the front desk before heading upstairs for on-the-spot refueling. A block north across Connaught Road, the scarlet and black towers of **Shun Tak Centre** house the Macau Ferry Terminal.

Western Market 西港城
This handsome red-brick Edwardian building at 323 Des Voeux Rd. Central dates to 1906; the

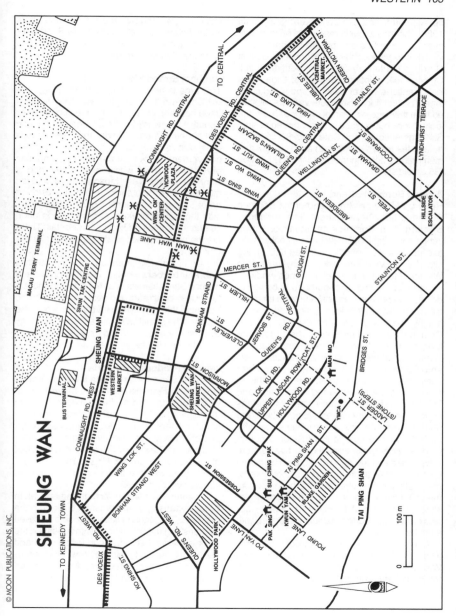

© MOON PUBLICATIONS, INC.

SHEUNG WAN

TO KENNEDY TOWN
TO CENTRAL

MACAU FERRY TERMINAL
SHUN TAK CENTRE
BUS TERMINAL

CONNAUGHT RD. WEST
CONNAUGHT RD. CENTRAL
DES VOEUX RD. CENTRAL

SHEUNG WAN

VICWOOD PLAZA
WING ON CENTER
MAN WAH LANE

WESTERN MARKET

BONHAM STRAND
HILLIER ST.
CLEVERLEY ST.

MERCER ST.

GOUGH ST.

QUEEN'S RD. CENTRAL

WELLINGTON ST.
ABERDEEN ST.
GRAHAM ST.
COCHRANE ST.
PEEL ST.
STANLEY ST.

CENTRAL MARKET
QUEEN VICTORIA ST.
JUBILEE ST.
HING LUNG ST.
WING KUT ST.
WING WO ST.
WING SING ST.
GILMAN'S BAZAAR

QUEEN'S RD. CENTRAL

LYNDHURST TERRACE
HILLSIDE ESCALATOR
STAUNTON ST.

JERVOIS ST.
QUEEN'S ST.
MORRISON ST.
SHEUNG WAN MARKET
LOK KU RD.
UPPER LASCAR ROW (CAT ST.)
HOLLYWOOD RD.

MAN MO
YMCA
LADDER ST. (STONE STEPS)
BRIDGES ST.

DES VOEUX RD. WEST
WING LOK ST.
BONHAM STRAND WEST
QUEENS RD. WEST
KO SHING ST.
POSSESSION ST.
HOLLYWOOD PARK
PO YAN LANE

PAK SING
SUI CHING PAK
KWUN YAM
PAK YAN LANE

TAI PING SHAN ST.
BLAKE GARDEN
POUND LANE

TAI PING SHAN

100 m
0

noisy poultry and fish stalls kept going until 1989. The meticulously renovated building has been reopened as an upscale shopping center, billed as the local version of London's Covent Gardens market. Pricey small boutiques sell Chinese folk paintings, images of Olde Hong Kong, antique wicker baskets and wood carvings. The first floor holds cloth vendors relocated from their age-old market on Wing On Street, looking a bit out of place in this sanitized setting. Six Bugs Antiques and Café provides cappucino and tea (and sandwiches) amid Hong Kong memorabilia, accompanied by a vintage jukebox ($5 an old song).

Around Bonham Strand

Head up Morrison Street and cross Bonham Strand, a busy bazaar street. The enormous **Sheung Wan Complex** here houses a civic center and a big food market with a cooked food section on the second floor. It was built on the site of an old Victorian market nearly identical to Western Market, with which it formed a pair.

The surrounding neighborhood is being redeveloped, but there are still a few old pharmacies displaying mysterious desiccated objects, and signboards advertising "Ship's Chandlers, Compradores and Hardware." The streets running between Bonham Strand and Queen's Road Central are particularly fascinating. **Jervois Street** (蘇杭街) is a center for the winter snake trade. Banded kraits, cobras, pythons, and rat snakes are imported from China and Thailand and brewed into a rather tasteless soup flavored with chicken stock, believed to protect against the cold. Hongkongers consume 50,000 cobras a year in this fashion. Another practice involves extracting the gall bladder from a live snake and mixing it with liquor. This potion is considered an aphrodisiac and a good cure for rheumatism (the snake survives this ordeal, as the gall bladder grows back). Look for the old-style snake shop at 13 Hillier St., where reptiles drowse in wooden drawers perforated with airholes.

Also stroll down **Cleverley Street** (急庇利街), which has a "Ginseng USA" emporium selling Wisconsin ginseng, a bird shop stocked with fresh crickets, and stalls selling woks, eight-sided *pa gwa* mirrors, and red wooden altars for the home. You'll exit on Queen's Road Central, just across from Ladder Street, which leads up to the Man Mo Temple.

Bonham Strand West 文咸西街

This area is home to the Nam Pak Hong, the old "South-North Trading Houses" specializing in trade between overseas Chinese communities ("south") homesick for the oil, beans, rice, and fruit of China ("north"). Today the trade focuses on wholesale medicinal goods, with ginseng a lucrative item. Walk past the busy warehouses of **Ko Sing Street,** which veers off the end of Bonham Strand West. Muscular bare-chested men unload burlap sacks and crates of dried herbs in a scene marked by much shouting. Inside the shops, workers sort and grade dried sea horses, antelope horn, and deer tail. There are more warehouses on Wing Lok Street a few blocks over.

Also in this neighborhood, look for old-style **open-air barbers** working with four chairs and no roof. Street barbers offer haircuts and shaves; they'll also clean ears and perform a ritual called "washing the eye," which involves scraping the inside of the eyelid with a small razor. You may even see a streetside lady barber, creaming and plucking the faces of female customers.

"Marine Products" Emporia

Bonham Strand West feeds into Des Voeux Road West. From here to Centre Street it's lined with shops devoted to dried seafood of every description: slugs, starfish, shrimp, abalone, squid, oysters, and scallops; all pricey examples of the local obsession with expensive, high-status food. The sharks' fins enshrined in locked glass cases can run over HK$500 per catty, depending on whether they're graded superior, superlative, or deluxe.

In winter the displays include red-and-white Chinese sausages and pressed duck from the mainland. The requisite flattened look is achieved by smashing the breastbone with a cleaver; the duck is then salted and hung in the wind and sun to dry. Around Chinese New Year, shoppers flock here to buy delicacies like dried melon seeds, lotus seeds, and tangerine peel.

ALONG HOLLYWOOD ROAD
荷利活道

South of Queen's Road, Hollywood Road winds back into Central, its entire length lined with antique shops.

Cat Street 摩羅上街
Ladder Street is typical of Hong Kong's steep lanes paved with stone slabs for the convenience of sedan-chair bearers. Climb up it to **Upper Lascar Row,** which once housed foreign seamen known as lascars. The nickname "Cat Street" came from the accompanying brothels.

This area has long been renowned for its bric-a-brac and antiques, dating from the post-1949 flood of Chinese immigrants, many of whom pawned valuable heirlooms. The dark little stalls cluttered with antiques, stolen items, and outright junk were spruced up in the 1970s into proper shops. With them went much of the local character and any chance of finding something cheap. Cat Street's shops are now reputable and high-priced, as exemplified by **Cat Street Galleries,** a four-story complex of expensive antique, art, and craft shops. In front of the stores, street vendors still display flea-market wares: cracked porcelain, old typewriters, broken steam irons, and crates of old abacuses, discarded in favor of the calculator.

Man Mo Temple 文武廟
At the corner of Hollywood Road and Ladder Street is Hong Kong Island's richest and best-known shrine, built in 1847. It's not much different from other big temples except that Man Mo's central location draws lots of tourists. You needn't feel obtrusive, at least, as worshippers seem accustomed to the groups marching through.

Giant incense coils hang in the hall, over a meter long and big enough to smoulder for weeks. The smoke alerts deities to the prayers written on dangling strips of red paper. A gilt-wood spirit screen blocks the entrance of evil spirits, which are believed to travel only in straight lines.

The temple is dedicated to a pair of historical figures transformed over centuries of veneration into deities—a common occurrence in

streetside keycutter

HONG KONG TOURIST ASSOCIATION

China. Man or Man Cheong was born Cheung Ah Tse in A.D. 287. As the god of literature, he controls the destinies of mandarins and civil servants. Mo (also called Kwan Kung or Kwan Ti), the god of martial arts and war, was born around A.D. 160. He protects people from war and serves as the tutelary deity of Hong Kong police. He is favored as well by the underworld, pawnbrokers, and curio dealers.

The two stand side-by-side on the main altar: Mo on the left in green robes and a pearl headdress, brandishing a sword; Man in red embroidered robes, wielding a calligrapher's brush. They are flanked by smaller shrines to black-faced Pao Kung, the god of justice, and richly robed Shing Wong, the "City God."

The temple's interior is exceptionally rich, with polished brass and pewter ritual vessels and a pair of shining meter-high brass deer symbolizing longevity and wealth. In a glass case on the side are the elaborately carved teak sedan chairs once used to carry the deities' images in processions. In front of the altar stand brass statues of the Eight Immortals, representing the different conditions of life: male, female, lord, peasant, age, youth, poverty, and wealth. A smaller room to the right holds images of Buddhist deities like Kwan Yum, plus the powerful Wong Tai Sin, Kwan Ti (the god Mo again), and others.

Worshippers pop in all day long for a quick intercession with the gods. The temple is a good place to see the *chim* in use. These numbered bamboo sticks are used to predict the answers to important questions: Will my business be successful? Will I pass the exam? Will my child be a boy? The narrow canister is shaken until a stick falls out; its number is used to obtain a prediction. You can always shake out another if you don't like the first result.

Hollywood Road

Hollywood Road all the way back into Central is one solid stretch of antique and furniture shops. The range of goods spans local Chinoiserie and British antiques, plus exotica like Tibetan carpets, Japanese fabrics, and Korean wedding chests. The days of bargains are past, bins of "100-year-old temple carvings" notwithstanding. But treat the shops as museums, and you can admire embroidered silk mandarin robes, elaborately carved rosewood chairs, and valuable old ancestral scrolls.

Cheaper stalls sell old postcards and mildly pornographic magazines, red-and-silver Mao buttons, wooden dumpling molds, fat porcelain Buddhas, and moldering old books. It's an in-

BAMBOO BOXES

Cast your gaze just about anywhere in downtown Hong Kong and you'll see a local peculiarity: buildings under construction encased in an airy cage of bamboo and swathed in green nylon mesh (the latter is to catch falling debris). Hong Kong is among the last of the Asian cities to use bamboo rather than steel scaffolding.

Scaffolders practice a craft that is thousands of years old, drawing on a practically instinctive knowledge of the marvelous strength and flexibility of bamboo. Lashing together individual lengths of bamboo with nylon ties, they create meter-square grids that serve as a framework for the workers who follow. Their work blends grace, flexibility, and acrobatics, requiring a head for heights and exceptionally calm nerves.

Gripping the poles with their legs, they select a length of nylon from the cluster stuck in their belts, twist it about and test the joint for firmness. There are no nets, and few workers use safety harnesses, complaining they limit their mobility. In such circumstances, the yellow hard hats seem to perch on their heads with an air of jaunty insouciance. "Fall of person" is the number-two cause of occupational fatalities in Hong Kong.

It takes workers 20 days to raise the scaffolding for an average building, and a single day to pull it down. Once the grid is erected, the buildings sprout upwards as rapidly as bamboo shoots, rising at the rate of one floor a week. Behind the scaffolders follow the "wet trades," masons and glaziers and plasterers and painters, all working within the bamboo cage. Scaffolders earn one of the highest salaries in the construction industry, as their craft involves the most skill—and danger.

There are around 300 scaffolding erectors in Hong Kong. With its emphasis on grace and precision, the trade attracts most of the few women in the construction industry. Some scaffolders are trained at industrial centers, but most learn the secrets of the trade from acknowledged masters, in an informal three-year apprenticeship which is often obtained through family connections.

Beginning students assemble models of traditional buildings from twigs and twine. They learn to *feel* the bamboo, acquiring an innate appreciation of its qualities. They learn to trust it, relying on instinct to judge how far it will go, and when it will give. A few Hong Kong buildings have been constructed using steel scaffolding, but local workers say they prefer bamboo, which, unlike metal, gives warning before it gives way.

Bamboo scaffolding is five times cheaper and four times faster to raise than steel, not to mention much lighter. Its resiliency allows it to withstand typhoons. Best of all, bamboo doesn't have to be manufactured: it grows, and it grows quickly. Hong Kong uses over three million pieces of bamboo each year, most of it from south China.

triguing half-hour walk back into Central, especially if you veer off to explore the small side streets running down to Queen's Road; like Peel Street with its stalls and religious offering stores, or Graham Street with its food market. Hollywood Road becomes Wyndham Road at the juncture with the old Central Police Station: head downhill at any point after this into Central.

TAI PING SHAN 太平山

Barely five minutes' walk west of Man Mo Temple, three local shrines seldom visited by tourists embrace a wide slice of the Chinese pantheon. The Tai Ping Shan neighborhood was among the earliest postcolonial Chinese settlements in Hong Kong. The story goes that after the notorious pirate Cheung Po Tsai surrendered and was granted amnesty by the Chinese government in 1810, he settled here with his followers, building a small temple on the site of the present Man Mo Temple. The name Tai Ping Shan ("Great Peace Mountain," referring to Victoria Peak) supposedly stems from the resulting truce.

By the late 19th century Tai Ping Shan was a squalid slum crowded with ramshackle dwellings, each housing dozens of people. Not surprisingly it proved fertile ground for epidemics of bubonic plague which swept through the community regularly from 1894 on, taking over 13,000 lives. British efforts to quell its course by razing buildings and imposing quick mass burials caused a general panic, as these clashed with the Chinese custom of waiting for an auspicious date for burial.

From Queen's Road West walk up Hollywood Road, passing **Possession Street.** Somewhere in this vicinity a British squadron hoisted the Union Jack for the first time in 1841, but the shoreline has advanced far to the north since those days.

Up another block on the left, **Hollywood Park** preserves a fragment of open space ringed by new high-rises. Shops across the street sell old round-ended coffins, a specialty of this neighborhood. Known as "four-and-a-half boards" for the amount of wood they require, they were traditionally purchased in advance and kept under the bed until needed.

Head up unsigned Po Yan Lane across from the park and take the first left onto Tai Ping Shan Street. Halfway down the block on the right side, the **Pak Sing Temple** (百勝廟) stands above the street. You can't miss the incense coils hanging under the green-roofed verandah, nor the old women selling offerings at the foot of the steps. The temple is full of people folding paper offerings and lighting red candles and incense.

The first temple established here in 1851 served as a hospice for the dying (it was considered bad luck to have a death occur in the house, and the dying were often abandoned on a hillside). Today it's a public ancestral hall—unusual, as most ancestral halls are dedicated to members of a particular clan. The present building houses over 3,000 small wooden ancestral tablets, many displaying photos of the deceased. Tablets may be placed here if there is no room in a home, or people may dedicate them for friends. Relatives come on festivals to offer incense and oil lamps, and groups of monks and nuns perform rituals for the dead in an outer room.

A block farther up the street on the opposite side is the **Sui Ching Pak Temple** (水月宮), dedicated to the "Pacifying General" who is said to be especially effective in curing illness. The temple was established during the 1894 plague epidemic, and was recently rebuilt. There are images of other deities, notably Kwan Yum and the 60 Tai Sui, each dedicated to a particular year in the Chinese calendar cycle. Worshippers come here before embarking on a journey or a new enterprise to make offerings to the deity presiding over the year of their birth. Outside is a popular Earth God shrine.

Across the street at No. 34 is a small new shrine to **Kwun Yam** (望夏觀), dedicated to the Buddhist goddess of mercy who helps women with domestic disputes, fertility, and sick children. The image is said to have been carved by the founder's wife from a mysterious block of wood found floating in the sea emitting golden rays.

To return to the Man Mo Temple and Hollywood Road, continue up the street past the old brick YMCA, built in 1918 for Chinese Christians. Turn left just past it and head down the steps of the aptly named Ladder Street.

Or, take a footpath to the right to Caine Lane, which runs off Caine Road, to visit the newly

TRIADS

The Chinese equivalent of the Mafia, Triad gangs are active in virtually every country with a large population of Chinese immigrants. They belong to a shadowy tradition originally linked to politics, now motivated by money and power.

The original Triad was founded after the 17th century overthrow of the Ming dynasty by the Manchus (their motto: "Restore the Ming, Overthrow the Qing"). The name comes from the primal triad of Heaven, Earth, and Man. Members were Robin Hoods, redistributing wealth from the rich to the poor and earning a romantic aura that remains to this day. Originally a symbol of nationalism—Sun Yat-sen was a Triad member—the groups have degenerated into a criminal underground.

The Triads arrived in Hong Kong very early on: the first anti-Triad laws were passed in 1845. Modern Triad groups are neighborhood-based and territorial. There are some 50 gangs, but only 17 are active, and only a handful of these are well-organized. These, however, are formidable. The 14K gang, a loose federation of ten groups founded in 1949 by the Kuomintang secret police, is active in the West, partly through its involvement in the heroin trade. The largest is Sun Yee On, composed mainly of Chiu Chow-speaking members and also involved in drugs. Dai Hoon or Big Circle is made up of mainland Chinese and specializes in dramatic robberies of gold stores.

The triads have their fingers in many pies: offbeat things like Green Minibus routes, lion dances, and wholesale markets, and more conventional corruptions like loan-sharking, gambling, and prostitution. Protection rackets are a highly lucrative enterprise. The entertainment industry is the main target for what's jokingly referred to as the TAT, Triad Added Tax. It's estimated more than three-quarters of Hong Kong's cinemas, restaurants, bars, and clubs pay protection money to triads, averaging around US$1100 a month. Film sets are a favorite target; so are construction sites. The new airport at Chek Lap Kok has been plagued by triad extortion.

Police are finding it difficult to deal with such increasingly sophisticated and internationally mobile adversaries. Fighting the Triads, a police superintendent complained, is "like trying to pick up lumps of mercury." The lack of a central organization makes them slippery and fluid, while a fiercely enforced code of secrecy make them difficult to penetrate. Triad members are bound by loyalty on pain of death, and death in such a case can be painful (one such murder was carried out with barbecue forks).

The Triads' enormous though vaguely diffused membership is another difficulty: there are said to be some 120,000 members in Hong Kong, of whom 15,000-20,000 are active. They are arranged in a strict hierarchy of bizarrely titled positions coded by symbolic numbers. The supreme leader is called the "Dragon Head," Number 489. "Red Poles" organize gang warfare and punishment, "White Paper Fans" are administrators, and "Straw Sandals" collect protection money. The average member is a "49 Boy."

---

established **Hong Kong Museum of Medical Sciences,** housed in the Old Pathological Institute, a colonial landmark. Exhibits here chart the development of medicine in Hong Kong and compare traditional chinese and Western approaches to medicine. Hours are Tues.-Sat. 10 a.m.-5 p.m., Sunday and holidays 1-5 p.m.; admission is HK$10; HK$5 children and seniors.

AROUND HONG KONG UNIVERSITY
香港大學

HKU opened in 1887 as the College of Medicine: its best-known student was Sun Yat-sen. The main building, completed in 1912, is a grand construction of granite colonnades flanking multiple courtyards. Bus 3 from Central (Rumsey Street) stops in front of the university's main gate at 94 Bonham Road.

University Museum and Art Gallery
This mildly interesting collection of bronzes and ceramics is housed in the red-brick building to the left of the university gate. It will occupy a half-hour or so, but if you've limited museum time, the Hong Kong Museum of Art in Tsimshatsui's Cultural Centre is far more comprehensive.

That said, the ground floor displays bronze mirrors, ritual implements, Shan dynasty oracle bones, and a huge collection (the world's largest) of bronze Nestorian crosses from the Chinese-Mongolian border region. Made around the 13th century by a small group of east Asian

Christians, these combine Western symbolism with Eastern geometric designs. Some are decorated with swastikas (an ancient symbol); others are in the form of birds, circles, or stars. Upstairs are ceramics in colored glazes typical of regional kilns, including several hard, cold ceramic pillows. The museum is open Mon.-Sat. 9:30 a.m.-6 p.m.; admission is free.

Lu Pan Temple 魯班廟

Cut through the university parking lot onto Pokfulam Road, a 10-minute walk past speeding vehicles. Just past No. 94 (Ricci Hall), descend the blue-tiled stairs on the right, grandly titled "Precious Dragon Terrace." The temple is on the third terrace down ("Green Lotus Terrace"), but its green roof tiles are visible long before. Veer off onto the upper terrace for a close-up view of the fine Shiwan pottery roof figures, including the Moon Goddess Heng-O bearing her orb and the elderly Sun God. Inside, the high-ceilinged shrine is quiet and dark, with its main deity encircled by a finely carved gilt altarpiece.

This is Hong Kong's only temple to Lu Pan, patron of builders and carpenters. He is a deification of a famously skilled Shantung carpenter of the 6th century B.C. An accomplished Taoist alchemist, he supposedly repaired the Pillars of Heaven and built a heavenly palace and a wooden kite upon which he flew. An old custom, still observed, requires a feast be laid out for him at the beginning of building construction. His temple, however, is largely ignored except for his annual festival each June, when builders gather at noon for a communal feast and offerings.

Leaving the temple, continue down the steps onto Belcher's Street, and turn left to explore Kennedy Town.

KENNEDY TOWN 堅尼地道

This busy working-class neighborhood is generally ignored by tourists but is interesting by virtue of authenticity. Its streets are filled with men unloading trucks, assembling boxes, and carving up pig carcasses. Women with small children in tow weave in and out among the shops gathering the day's groceries, and busy laundries process mountains of clothes.

Kennedy Town is built on land reclaimed in the 1870s under the governance of Sir Arthur Kennedy, who designed its most distinctive feature, the **Kennedy Town Praya,** a Portuguese-style waterfront promenade that now serves as a road. **Belcher's Street** is the area's other main artery. Belcher was the Royal Navy captain in charge of surveying Hong Kong's coastline: of the several dozen sites he named after himself, this is the only one the name stuck to.

Head down it to the **wholesale vegetable market,** which is in full swing by dawn and quiet by noon. Produce here is imported daily from mainland China. Double back, following the tramline down **Catchick Street,** where shops sell steel cables and huge coils of rope, reflecting the area's close ties to the adjacent harbor. On the left, the bustling **North Street Market** is worth a detour, with plenty of surprised-looking fish on ice, mouths opened in a last gasp. For a quick meal, stop at the open-air stalls in the market.

Farther down along the waterfront, boats offload goods from China, plucked by lighter from larger boats moored in the harbor. This stretch of harbor will soon be filled in with reclamation. The road and tramline run along the shoreline, but it's an uninspiring walk past the filthy water. Hop on the tram whenever you feel like it and ride up to Sheung Wan for more backstreet exploring, or into Central.

Mt. Davis 摩星嶺道

Rising, though hardly towering, up behind Kennedy Town is 269-meter Mt. Davis. Its summit was levelled around 1910 and a fort was installed to protect the harbor's western approaches. The defenses didn't last long in the face of the 1941 Japanese attack. The overgrown ruins of the fort remain, along with the remains of some old gun emplacements.The northern slopes are a good place to watch ships gliding through the harbor, and **Ma Wui Hall,** an HYIA youth hostel that's indisputably the cheapest place to stay in Hong Kong, is not far below the summit.

WANCHAI 灣仔

Wanchai comes as a relief after the sophisticated metropolitan veneer of Central. One of the five original neighborhoods set aside for Chinese inhabitants in the 1850s, it retains its distinct character in the face of recent "development." Real people still live here—and lots of them.

Tourists often associate Wanchai with the nightlife district centered around Lockhart Road, but Wanchai as a whole is a lot more than Hong Kong's Times Square—it's among its most vibrant, interesting neighborhoods, day and night.

The area is divided quite distinctly by the tramline, which once ran along the waterfront of a "Little Bay"—"Wan Chai"—that was long ago filled in. North of the tram is the New Wanchai, sparkling high-rises fronting the harbor. South of it is a maze of narrow market streets that make for some of the best wandering in Hong Kong.

WANCHAI NORTH

Skyrocketing land prices in Central are increasingly pushing businesses into neighboring Wanchai. Harbour Road, a strip of waterfront land reclaimed from the ocean in the late '70s, is now plastered with skyscrapers, offices, and hotels. The ongoing Central-Wanchai reclamation project is extending this neighborhood with another strip of waterfront buildings, which eventually will be linked by a waterfront walkway.

Arts Complexes
Walk down Fenwick Street to visit the **Hong Kong Academy for Performing Arts** (香港演藝學院), a training center for local dancers, musicians, and actors and a major venue for drama and dance productions. The impressive complex was built and is maintained by the Hong Kong Jockey Club.

Across Fenwick Street at 2 Harbour Rd., the less-spiffy **Hong Kong Arts Centre** (香港藝術中心) also hosts cultural events. There's a small cafe on the fourth floor with harbor views, and in the basement, the **Lim Por Yen Film Theatre** screens modern films. The **Pao Sui Loong Gallery** on the fourth and fifth floors displays contemporary works by international and local artists. It was donated by billionaire Y.K. Pao in memory of his father, but is disappointingly small and dingy considering the money that must have been poured into it.

Convention Centre 香港會議展覽中心
Cross Gloucester Road to reach the **Convention and Exhibition Centre,** recently expanded and the site of the 1997 handover ceremony.The opulent complex includes two giant exhibition halls and various banquet, theater, and meeting facilities, many with harbor views. Many of the events are open to the public: a typical day's schedule might include a Mercedes show or a cosmetics fair. The Design Gallery here retails locally designed new products like Felix the Cat watches, miniature violins, and HK$25,000 globes with the continents inlaid in semiprecious stones.

Grand Hyatt 君悅酒店
Two luxury hotels, the New World Harbour View and the ostentatious Grand Hyatt, anchor the convention center. Peek in at the art deco opulence of the latter's lobby, designed to resemble a 1930s cruise ship. The door handles here say it all: great slabs of black marble carved in the form of Greek columns and bound in brass, they require two hands to grasp; but the point is to impress, not to open a door. The Hyatt has an elegant coffee shop and some of Hong Kong's best restaurants, including Grissini and One Harbour Road.

The entire complex is connected with adjoining shopping centers, allowing, in best Hong Kong fashion, for hours of consumerism without ever setting foot on the ground. If you want to escape, there's a nice little park beside the Grand Hyatt that's good for an impromptu picnic. The waterfront promenade in front of the convention center runs all the way to the **Wanchai Ferry Pier** (灣仔渡海碼頭), from where Star Ferries chug over to Tsimshatsui and Hung Hom.

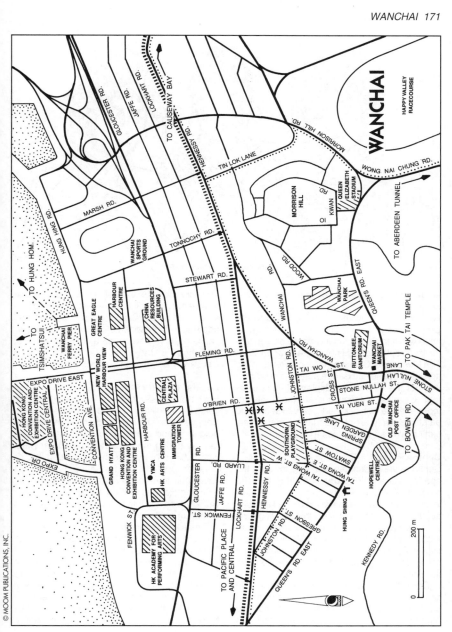

© MOOM PUBLICATIONS, INC.

WANCHAI

HAPPY VALLEY RACECOURSE

Chinese opera performers

Museum of Chinese Historical Relics
文物展覽館

Walkways lead across Fleming Road to the China Resources Building, with its giant Chinese Arts and Crafts and a Chinese garden featuring a replica of Beijing's Nine Dragon Wall. The Museum of Chinese Historical Relics in the adjoining Causeway Centre may sound promising, but the objects on display all have price tags. It's actually a mainland-affiliated outlet for top-of-the-line items like jade, carved seals, and paintings. Only an occasional archaeological exhibit allows it to call itself a "museum."

Central Plaza 中環廣場

Continue via pedestrian walkway towards the soaring spire of 78-story Central Plaza, the tallest building in Hong Kong (for a while, at least). Its fabulous views are maximized by its triangular shape. The architects thoughtfully blunted the edges so as not to point a sharp corner (bad *feng shui*) at its neighbors. At night, its distinctive illuminated spire is a local landmark, the colors changing every fifteen minutes to mark the time.

Central Plaza ranks as the tallest reinforced concrete building in the world: plasticizers had to be added to the concrete so that it could be pumped up to 374 meters without solidifying.

The gold and silver exterior is matched by an extravagant art deco interior of black marble pillars and potted palms. Sign in at the lobby desk and ride up the high-speed elevators to the observation gallery. Views wrap all the way around, and those of the Peak, Happy Valley, and Causeway Bay rival the harbor side.

Lockhart Road 駱克道

Hong Kong's red-light district has shifted over the years from Hollywood Road to Kennedy Town, Happy Valley, and most recently Wanchai. The neighborhood around Lockhart Road had its heyday during the Korean and Vietnam wars, when U.S. military personnel crowded into its bars for rowdy R and R. So ingrained is this image that, to Americans of a certain generation, all Hong Kong is embodied by *The World of Suzie Wong,* the tale of a Wanchai hooker with a heart of gold.

Times keep changing, and the nightlife scene (though not the prostitution) has diversified into Tsimshatsui and Lan Kwai Fong. When foreign fleets are in town, Lockhart Road regains some of its old character, but most evenings you're as likely to see clean-cut young couples, or even entire families, entering its establishments as sailors. Another sign of the times: the old Luk Kwok Hotel on Gloucester Road, the inspiration for Suzie's fictional Nam Kwok bordello, has been replaced by a solidly respectable hotel of the same name, and the surrounding tenements have given way to new skyscrapers. Property values are rising too rapidly to let the area remain undeveloped.

Wanchai's nightlife centers around Jaffe and Lockhart roads, particularly the stretch between Luard and Fleming roads. Here are pubs, bars, saunas, discos, tattoo parlors, seafood palaces, and tiny hole-in-the-wall restaurants. The **New Tonnochy Nightclub,** a Japanese emporium, sprawls the length of an entire block. See "Nightlife" in the general Introduction for more on this aspect of Wanchai.

Past the intersection with Fleming Road, the **Lockhart Road Market** has the usual collection of cooked-food stalls, though these are made redundant by the many good cheap restaurants in the area. Past here, the streets regain some of their old character: three- and four-story tenement buildings fronted with iron-barred balconies festooned with drying laundry and potted plants.

SOUTH OF HENNESSY ROAD

The tram trundles along Hennessy Road, Wanchai's main thoroughfare, diverting for a brief dip south onto Johnston Road. Ride it through here at night, enjoying the neon lights that tint the streets lavender and lime. The main road and side streets of this neighborhood hold dozens of small clothing outlets (incredibly cheap women's clothes for those willing to root through mountains of junk), plus camera, stereo, and shoe shops. The selection is oriented to the local market, and generally speaking things are lower-key and cheaper than in Tsimshatsui.

The small lanes running south off Johnston Road down to Queen's Road are among the most intriguing in Hong Kong, with shops selling man-sized sticks of incense, live snakes, and

MAHJONG

For sheer energy and velocity few games can rival mahjong. Chinese call the game *ma cheuk:* it was an American, Joseph Babcock, who copyrighted and marketed this ancient game as "Mah-Jongg," engendering a fad in the 1920s. In the Sung dynasty it was played with 40 pictures drawn on paper squares. Tiles of bamboo, ivory, or bone eventually replaced these, and the shuffling of these creates the glorious clatter that is the background music of Hong Kong life.

Everyone plays mahjong: at the beach, during lunch breaks, before dinner parties, at weddings. Rich *tai-tais* pass their afternoons playing in the dim sum restaurants of Central, Wanchai, and Causeway Bay. Men play faster and if possible more loudly, often for money. There are mahjong parlors in every Chinese neighborhood. The doors are kept closed for discretion's sake, but you can't miss the clatter of plastic tiles being shuffled and slammed on the table with each shouted call. Mahjong is one of the noisest games on earth.

It's played with 136 tiles, which are arranged by number and suite (winds, dragons, bamboo, and circles). Players try to make sets and sequences as in poker, but there are many variations and levels of complexity. Part of the game's appeal is that it allows for conversation while playing.

While mahjong can be played with cards, it's considered no fun—the noise of the tiles intensifies the emotions and feeling of a good time. The game's appeal revolves around the notion of *yit nau,* literally "hot and noisy," a phrase used to describe the atmosphere of happy excitement considered essential to a good time.

Mahjong resembles a wildly accelerated bridge. Like bridge, it's a social event as much as a game, and its excitement is positively addicting. Things get really serious on weekends, when mahjong sessions run around the clock with teams playing in relays. This is relaxation, Hong Kong-style, where the level of pandemonium fuels the fun. If you want to feel Cantonese, learn to play mahjong—or go to the races.

Mahjong is banned in other regions of China, at least in public, but the ubiquitous sound of the tiles being shuffled (or "washed," as the phrase goes in Chinese) is often heard on Guangzhou side streets. Evidently it's hard to keep a good game down.

coconuts in all forms. The small bird market on **Tai Wong Street West** sells beautifully crafted little bamboo cages, some carved with dragons or roofed like pagodas, tiny porcelain water bowls, and fresh crickets imported from China. **Tai Yuen Street** starts off with aquariums and fish. Halfway down is a snake vendor who dispatches his wares with brutal efficiency, cracking them on the pavement like whips.

Stretching along Cross Street and Wanchai Road is a magnificent **outdoor market** featuring vegetables, meat, gasping fish, and a dozen varieties of fresh-made noodles. Open shopfronts frame old-time scenes of butchers clomping about in thick wooden clogs and old women in black velvet caps methodically picking through heaps of bean sprouts. Food stalls alternate with welding shops and picture-frame businesses—thankfully for local color, zoning regulations have not yet been perfected. Many more vendors have been installed in the giant indoor **Wanchai Market** (灣仔街市) on Queen's Road East, a fine example of a Hong Kong wet market.

Pak Tai Temple 北帝廟

Across from the Wanchai Market is Stone Nullah Lane, *nullah* being the Anglo-Indian term for gully. Walk down it several blocks to a small Urban Council garden, and beside it a big, well-preserved Pak Tai Temple shaded by two enormous old banyan trees.

Pak Tai, also known as the "Supreme Emperor of the Dark Heaven," was the commander of the heavenly legions appointed to fight the Demon King. He is commemorated with a huge black-faced copper image cast in 1604 in Guangzhou. The main shrine houses many more deities, including a complete set of the Tai Sui or 60-Year Gods and a second Pak Tai image sprouting a beard of black horsehair. On the left is an ancestral hall; on the right, festooned with stacks of colored paper and lengths of flexible split bamboo, a room where paper offerings burned for the dead are made. Examples dangling from the ceiling include airplanes, limousines, and meter-high "mansions" made of paper patterned with a brick-and-mortar print.

Along Queen's Road East

As its curving shape indicates, this was the original waterfront road. Once it was famous for its rosewood and blackwood furniture makers, and shops still specialize in upholstery, curtains, carpets, and rattan. Despite the busy traffic, there's a neighborhood feel to it.

The little whitewashed **Wanchai Post Office** (灣仔郵政局) across from the market at 221 Queen's Rd. East was built in 1913, making it a veritable antique in Hong Kong terms. While the post office has relocated down the street to more modern quarters, the old building has been proclaimed a protected monument. It now houses an Environment Resource Centre.

A little farther down is the circular **Hopewell Centre,** the tallest building in Hong Kong until the Bank of China (and more recently Central Plaza) snatched away the title. The glass-walled elevator crawling up the exterior of the building ascends to a revolving restaurant; ride it for views alone.

The small **Hung Shing Kung Temple** (孔聖堂) at No. 129 dates to the 1860s. Inside the smoke-filled small interior, *chim* sticks rattle as women seek to divine their fortunes. The temple is dedicated to Hung Hei, a virtuous government official of the Tang dynasty who excelled in forecasting weather and thus became a patron of seafarers. Once it stood, appropriately, on the waterfront.

WANCHAI GAP 灣仔峽道

This neighborhood perched on the middle slopes of Mt. Cameron and Mt. Gough resembles the Mid-Levels with its high-class high-rises and spectacular views. It also provides some good walks.

Bowen Road 寶雲道

Bowen Road was originally an aqueduct carrying water from Tai Tam Reservoir to a point above Central: look for the old stonework still visible along the roadside. Much of it is closed to traffic and makes a shady, quiet stroll, popular with dog- and bird-walkers on weekends. On weekdays it's virtually deserted except for a few hard-core runners and tai chi practitioners. It's about four km in length, an hour and a half roundtrip, though one-way is easier.

Take Bus 15 or Minibus 7 from Central; get off at the Seventh-Day Adventist Hospital at 41

Stubbs Rd. and descend a flight of steps to Bowen Road. The path weaves along a forested slope, the steepest sections plastered with cement perforated with drainage holes for monsoon runoff. The route contours above the Happy Valley racecourse and high-rise apartment blocks, passing a few squatters' huts teetering on tiny ledges above a breathtaking dropoff.

Lover's Stone 姻緣石

The smell of incense proclaims the presence of several small Earth God shrines. These remnants of an ancient animistic religious tradition culminate in the strange garden of **Yan Yuen Sek** or "Lover's Stone." This massive nine-meter-high rock set in a rocky hillside grotto is visited by women praying for ideal husbands and offspring, or simply for good luck. Sandboxes of smouldering joss sticks stand beside rocks plastered with colorful paper offerings and groves of small paper windmills, the latter symbolizing a change in fortune. The most elaborate offering, the reward for answered prayers (often the birth of a child) is an entire roast pig.

A perennial crowd of fortune-tellers and incense sellers gathers here to counsel the lovelorn and sell talismans, while cheery old beggars request *cumsha* (the local term for a handout or tip). All in all it's quite a sight, especially on the busy and auspicious 6th, 16th, and 26th days of the lunar month and during the Maiden's Festival in mid-August.

A few minutes farther down Bowen Road is a small park set at a crossroads. From here, Wanchai Gap Road drops steeply down into Wanchai. If you follow this route, cross Kennedy Road to visit the Pak Tai Temple described above, then continue down to Wanchai Market. Or stay up on Bowen Road, which leads to Magazine Gap Road behind the Botanical Gardens. If you turn north onto Wanchai Gap Road, you'll eventually reach the Police Museum.

Police Museum 警隊博物館

Housed in the old Wanchai Gap Police Station at 27 Coombe Rd., the Police Museum documents the history of the formerly "Royal" Hong Kong Police Force with trivia both obscure and fascinating. Exhibits include the stuffed head of a tiger shot by a constable in Shueng Shui in 1915, a Narcotics Gallery displaying all sorts of drug paraphernalia, a Triad Societies Gallery with weapons and illegal devices, and, most moving, a fragile wicker coracle launched by Vietnamese refugees and intercepted by the Marine Police. The museum is open Wed.-Sun. 9 a.m.-5 p.m., Tuesday 2-5 p.m.; admission is free. Take Peak-bound Bus 15 from Central and get off at the intersection of Peak and Stubbs roads. Coombe Road is just off the latter.

Wong Nai Chung Gap 黃泥涌峽道

Wong Nai Chung Gap rests on the divide between Hong Kong Island's north and south sides. Buses to Stanley and Repulse Bay run past here (take Bus 6, 61, 64, or 262 from Central and get off at the Shell station at the Wanchai Gap roundabout).

A few minutes' walk from here is **Wong Nai Chung Gap Reservoir Park,** where you can rent a pedal or row boat or feed the fish. This area is also the launching point for many good walks across the undeveloped heart of Hong Kong Island. Consult Countryside Series Sheet No. 1 *(Hong Kong Island)* for details.

Here are some ideas: **Sir Cecil's Walk,** named after a former governor, runs north from here; **Lady Clementi's Ride,** named for his wife, goes south from Middle Gap to Wanchai Gap. Both are nearly level paths traversing the higher slopes, good choices for a jog or walk. **Black's Link,** a paved track connecting Wong Nai Chung, Middle and Wanchai Gaps, forms part of the fourth stage of the Hong Kong Trail and provides sweeping views of the south side of the island. It takes about an hour to walk the first section; or you can continue on down to Aberdeen in another hour or two. **Deep Water Bay Road** leads down seven km to the beach on the island's south side, passing elegant mansions en route. Many more long and short walks are to be had by heading east into **Tai Tam Country Park.**

HAPPY VALLEY 跑馬地

This euphoniously named area south of Wanchai and Causeway Bay was once slated to become Hong Kong's central business and residential district. Colonists relocating from malarial Western resettled here, but malaria struck again. Grandiose plans were scuttled, and the settlers retreated to drier ground in Central, abandoning their newly built villas and several barracks of long-suffering soldiers, who died of fever in droves.

Several years later Hong Kong's governor ordered the swamps drained and a racetrack built (see the accompanying special topic "Days at the Races"). Since the inaugural races were held in December 1864, Happy Valley has been synonymous with Hong Kong's enduring passion for horse-racing. At the turn of the century Happy Valley was known as the colony's playground, a place for football, cricket, tennis, bowls, golf, hockey, and even American baseball. It was also a center of prostitution. On hot evenings the women, many of them Viennese, would lounge about with their feet up on the verandah railing, affording riders on the top deck of the tram an interesting view.

Today the neighborhood is a sort of vestigial appendage dangling down from the juncture of Wanchai and Causeway Bay. You're not likely to explore more than the Happy Valley tramline reveals. It loops around the racetrack down Leighton Road, a neighborhood famous for shoe stores and designer interior decorating. The return route is via Tin Lok Lane, "Lane of Heavenly Happiness," which got its name from a government-licensed factory where coolies once stirred pans of steaming opium over charcoal fires.

Five Cemeteries

At the intersection of Queen's Road East and Stubbs Road, just past the turn-of-the-century Sikh Temple, an enormous tract of prime real estate is taken up by five cemeteries demonstrating the colony's diversity: Hindu, Parsi, Catholic, Protestant, and Muslim. Happy Valley's hillside was chosen for its auspicious *feng shui,* facing east and backed by hills. Apart from St. Michael's Catholic Cemetery, full of brooding marble angels, the most interesting is the old **Protestant Colonial Cemetery (**香港（紅毛）墳場**),** opened in 1845. Here are interred missionaries, soldiers, and civil servants. Epitaphs tell the tale of malaria, cholera, dysentery, and death in childbirth; the names are Russian, German, American, British, French. Famous residents include Lord Napier, the first British Chief Superintendent of Trade with China, and Bing Crosby's great-granduncle, who was an American sailor. There's an entrance near the tram stop on Wong Nai Chung Road (before the Aberdeen Tunnel) and another up on Stubbs Road. The cemetery is open 8 a.m. to dusk.

Happy Valley Racecourse

Few things are more quintessentially Hong Kong than a race night at Happy Valley's flat green oval. The track seats 40,000; average attendance is 35,000. Racing brings together rich and poor, albeit in different enclosures. Admission for the packed grandstand is only HK$10. From here you can barely see the horses until they hit the homestretch, but an enormous video screen remedies this problem. The elite sit up in the Jockey Club boxes with a splendid view of the whole scene. Everyone, grandstand or box, cheers frantically as the horses round the final turn and head into the homestretch.

Racing season is Sept.-June; meets are held on Wednesday evening and Saturday afternoon. Entrance is restricted to those 18 and over. Plush facilities at the Hong Kong Jockey Club can be arranged for short-term visitors who have been in the SAR for less than three weeks. Show your passport at the Badge Office at the main entrance to the Members' Enclosure, and you'll get tourist badges for HK$50, granting access to restaurants, bars, and top-level box seats. The HKTA's "Come Horseracing Tour" (HK$530) includes transport, dinner, and seating in the Visitors' Box. Bring your passport for the booking, which should be at least a day in advance.

Hong Kong Racing Museum

Opened in 1996, the museum's eight galleries

DAYS AT THE RACES

A Londoner cannot conceive of the excitement caused in this little distant island by the race week. It is the single holiday of the merchants. They spend weighty sums in importing horses from all parts and training them for the context. When we first see the racecourse in "Happy Valley" we are half tempted to declare that it is the most picturesque spot in the world. The grandstand, the booths and the stables, and all properties of the turf, by no means forgetting the luncheons and champagne, are all in first-rate order.

—China correspondent
George Wingrove Cooke, *The Times*, 1857

The Happy Valley racetrack has been the epicenter of local excitement since Hong Kong's earliest days. Colonists set up a rude track in a clearing in Pokfulam on the island's west side in 1845. Shortly thereafter the governor ordered a real racecourse built in conveniently flat Happy Valley. Inaugural meets were held in December 1846.

Describing a typical race day, a missionary wrote: "The excitement is intense; the city of Victoria is deserted, all the chairs and rickshaws are running in one direction . . . "It's said the weekly meeting of the legislative council was originally set for Wednesday (it still is), as members were sure to be in town for the races. The Happy Valley track became, and remains, one of the few social meeting grounds for Europeans and Chinese: "the Chinese are as much excited as the English and bet with much ardour," another observer noted.

The local passion is not for horseflesh, but for gambling—just take a look at any betting form, listing mounts with names like "Moneyland" and "Good Dividend." Horse-racing and the popular Mark Six Lottery (also run by the Hong Kong Jockey Club) are the only forms of legal betting in Hong Kong, though there's plenty of gambling going on in those ubiquitous mahjong games.

Gambling satisfies the Chinese fascination with numbers and omens, and offers the chance, however remote, of winning big. Complicated combinations prevail: most popular is the quinella (first and second in either order). The double trio involves picking the first, second, and third (in any order) in two races, but the potential yield is enormous: HK$32 million on a HK$10 bet.

Racing fever pervades Hong Kong. Betting papers (there are at least 20 racing dailies) are sold on every corner and pondered in buses and subways, and countless off-track betting centers are packed with people making "business investments," as the average Hongkonger views his bets. Local fascination with haute technology is turned to good use: Hong Kong boasts the world's most sophisticated computerized betting system, capable of processing 1,500 bets per second. An elaborate network of off-course shops, automatic machines, and miniature handheld Customer Input Terminals process five million bets each race day. The 1995-96 season's bets totalled HK$80.7 billion—that's over HK$13,000 per person. A single race might have HK$70 million put on it, and the record for an evening is HK$1 billion.

Eighty percent of the takings go to the winning bettors. The government excises a hefty tax on the remainder, collecting eight percent of its total revenues from here. The balance is funneled through the public-spirited Jockey Club into schools, hospitals, sporting facilities, parks, playgrounds, and community programs. Club funding has built Ocean Park, the Hong Kong University of Science and Technology in Sai Kung, Wanchai's Academy of Performing Arts, and the new 40,000-seat stadium at So Kon Po. Racing revenues return over HK$1 billion to the community each year, a tax in a palatable form. Most Hongkongers earn too little to be liable for income tax, but *everyone* bets.

and cinema tell the story of horse racing in Hong Kong, from the 1840s to today's record gambling turnovers. Features include interviews with jockeys and trainers and tips on the fine points of horseflesh. It's located in the racecourse's Main Building Stand on Wong Nai Chung Road, and is open Tues-Sat. 11 a.m.-7 p.m., Sunday and holidays 1-5 p.m.; admission is free.

CAUSEWAY BAY 銅鑼灣

Causeway Bay is *the* neighborhood for shopping, dining, and nightlife, intensely busy and open later than anywhere else in town. On a Saturday night, ride the tram down to the giant Sogo department store for a near-party experience. Hordes of neatly dressed young people pack the sidewalks, the milling crowds generating a feeling of excitement.

Causeway Bay is a good choice for shopping: prices are more reasonable and ripoffs rarer than in Tsimshatsui, despite a booming real estate market which has propelled shop rents to stratospheric levels. But you don't have to be in consumer mode to enjoy it: in fact, the utter overdose of things to buy can be intimidating. Just come to look, like everyone else does. The tram ride alone is worth it, and there are lots of movie theaters and restaurants.

History
Causeway Bay enters history books as a jumble of massive boulders called East Point. Its future was ensured when Jardine Matheson shifted its headquarters here from Macau in 1841. The hong's impressive business establishment was the first structure of note on the island. Soon opium junks were bobbing in the harbor, godowns were stacked with crates, and counting houses were adding up profits. Jardine's actions essentially founded Hong Kong even before the ratification of a formal treaty.

Other hongs soon established their headquarters and godowns here, and Causeway Bay's street names reflect this heritage: Jardine's Crescent, Jardine's Bazaar, Yee Wo Street (the Shanghai name for Jardine), Percival Street (named after a partner in Jardine), Keswick Street (another partner), and Russell Street (an early hong). Today, Daimaru stands on the site of Jardine's old godowns, and the "Princely Hong" has shifted its local office to the round-windowed Jardine House across from the Central Star Ferry. The company's main headquarters relocated in the Bahamas in 1985, causing a flurry of concern in Hong Kong.

Causeway Bay was indeed once a bay: Hennessy Road used to run along the shoreline until reclamation filled it in. Sprawling Victoria Park, the city's largest, was built on the new land, but the neighborhood remained an unremarkable mix of tenements and warehouses until the Cross-Harbour Tunnel opened here in 1973, allowing commuters to drive from the New Territories to their Hong Kong Island offices. Causeway Bay's newly reclaimed land sprouted with new hotels, restaurants, department stores, and clubs.

Today the area can be divided into distinct sections: toward the harbor are huge department stores and elegant shops, with cheaper establishments tucked away on side streets. South of Yee Wo Street are the older Chinese-style markets, tons of reasonable restaurants, and acres of small boutiques and shops. But big new developments like Times Square are slowly overtaking the interesting potpourri of small establishments. It may be only a matter of time before Causeway Bay is one giant shopping mall.

NORTH OF THE TRAMLINE

Japanese Department Stores
You probably don't want to spend HK$1850 for a linen suit or HK$540 for a teakettle, but Causeway Bay's Japanese department stores are worth a look. Ride the escalators up past floor after floor of goods just to experience the immensity of Daimaru, Sogo, Mitsukoshi, or Matsuzakaya. Sogo, which after a recent expansion regained its title as Hong Kong's biggest department store, seems to be most popular for the sport, as the escalators are conveniently placed one after the other.

The Hong Kong consumer, it seems, is doing the same as you—looking rather than buying. Stock includes but is not limited to Japanese goods; prices are not cheap, but there are some interesting items, like the Japanese porcelain in the housewares departments. Check out the basement of Mitsukoshi, where curious consumers crowd around demonstrations of reclining chairs, hot curlers, and electric massagers.

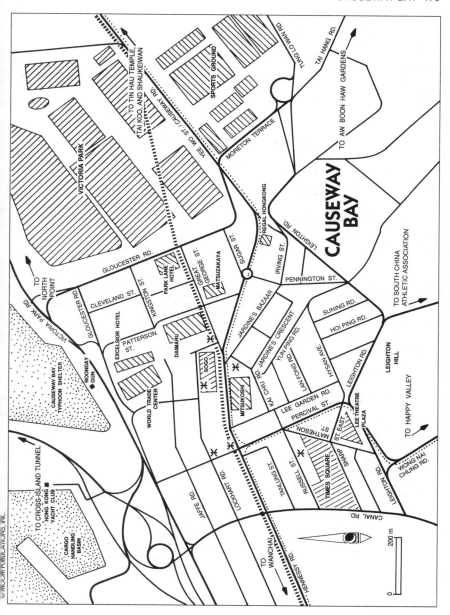

Sogo upholds the Japanese custom of superb if pricey coffee bars. Other points of culinary interest are Daimaru's Household Square for French bread and Japanese delicacies, the Japanese cafeteria in the basement of Sogo, and the Fook Ming Tong teashop in the basement of Mitsukoshi, with dozens of varieties of Chinese tea. The streets behind Sogo are sprinkled with restaurants of all varieties, including several cheap Indonesian places on Lockhart Road.

Noonday Gun 午炮

It's hard to figure out why this small brass-bound gun across from the Excelsior Hotel draws such attention. Perhaps it serves as an icon to notoriously unintrospective Hong Kong, a relic of colonial times when Jardine kept a manned bat-

---

HONG KONG ISLAND'S TRAMS

With their polished wooden benches and clacking wheels, Hong Kong Island's old double-decker trams are an endearing form of transportation—"leisurely clanking old aunts of vehicles," writer Nigel Cameron describes them. Like San Francisco's cable cars, they provide a touch of tradition amid harried city life. Trundling past the sleek skyscrapers of Central, they seem to be rolling anachronisms, turn-of-the-century remnants marooned in a sea of rush-hour traffic.

All anachronisms should be so useful. The 164 tram cars travel over eight million miles a year, carrying 130 million passengers up and down the north shore of the island, from Kennedy Town in the west to Shaukeiwan in the east. While they're a practical rather than touristic device, the trams provide the best sightseeing around. Grab a window seat and ride the entire length for a bird's-eye view of Hong Kong.

The first tram, inaugurated in 1904, ran through a considerably more pastoral landscape. The tram tracks originally ran along the waterfront; today, with the exception of Kennedy Town, they're a half km inland, the result of ceaseless reclamation. In 1914, Hong Kong Tramways was advertising "Bathing by Moonlight from the Beach at North Point," with special cars running from the post office and music from the band of HMS *Siberia*. The days of moonlit swimming in Victoria Harbour are long gone, as is North Point Beach, built over years ago.

Miraculously the tram has survived throughout, undergoing changes like the addition of upper decks and the abolition of separate "European" and "Native" cars. Today's trams may look antique, but they were built in the 1960s according to traditional design. The time-tested simplicity of the system endures: passengers enter through the double doors in the rear and drop the fare into the box upon exiting—it's HK$1 regardless of distance. Routes are simple,

too. Trams run either east or west (except for those marked Happy Valley, which detour from the main line), though not all go to the Kennedy Town or Shaukeiwan terminuses. They operate 6 a.m.-1 a.m., but avoid rush hour, when the 48-seater cars hold triple that number of passengers and it's a long, slow thrash through the crowd to the fare box.

At other times, the slow-moving trams offer a front-row seat for the street theater of Hong Kong life. When your feet get tired, hop aboard a tram, climb onto the top deck (the front seat is best if you can get it) and enjoy the ever-changing scenes sliding by: workers lounging over a mahjong game during an afternoon lull, shoppers haggling with a street merchant, an old man carrying a covered birdcage to a neighborhood tea shop. It's an ideal perch for photographers. Try to ride the North Point tram, which runs right through a street market, its stalls piled high with lotus root, sweet corn, and hundred-year-old eggs.

The trams themselves are bright splashes of color, the painted advertisments on their sides emblazoning the cityscape with mobile images of Swatch watches and giant bottles of soy sauce. The passengers too are worth a look: well-scrubbed schoolchildren with loaded bookbags, redoubtable old women in baggy black *samfu* and jade bracelets, conversing in duets of escalating volume.

Hong Kong is the only city in the world other than Blackpool, England, with functioning double-decker trams. The system's future looks bright: in fact, trams are Hong Kong's most-used form of public transport. Tram extensions are planned east into Aldrich Bay and west to Tsing Yi Island, with a loop to be added through the newly reclaimed areas of Central and Wanchai. One black cloud, however: the old-fashioned cars are slated to be replaced with modern steel ones.

Hong Kong Island tram

KERRY MORAN

tery here to protect its headquarters from pirate attack.

The gun is fired daily in a ritual of mysterious origins. One story maintains it was once fired to salute Jardine's taipan as he arrived by ship at East Point. A senior naval officer, peeved at this breach of etiquette, ordered the company to stop this practice, and to use up its supply of ammunition by firing a noontime signal, which it has done faithfully ever since.

In 1960, following complaints by local residents about the daily racket, the company traded its gun with the Marine Police for a smaller three-pounder. Every New Year's Eve, tuxedoed Jardine executives gather to shoot it off, and it was fired at midnight on 30 June, 1997, when Hong Kong reverted to China.

Unless you happen to be in the neighborhood at noon, you'll probably feel silly going out of your way to stare at a small gun mounted on a pedestal in a locked compound. Marooned across the speeding traffic of Gloucester Road, it's reached via a cleverly concealed pedestrian tunnel. Look for the door in the wall between the Wilson Car Park and the Excelsior Hotel, set back a bit from Gloucester Road.

Typhoon Shelter 避風塘

The last remnant of the original bay, Causeway Bay's typhoon shelter houses a dwindling population of several hundred people living on fishing junks and sampans. Stroll down here in the

evening and you'll be accosted by women touting sampan rides. Once in the harbor, kitchen sampans pull up; pick what you like to be prepared on the spot, and dine by lanternlight, your meal accompanied by drinks from bar sampans and musical entertainment from "sing-song boats." Everything must be bargained for separately, and none of it comes cheap. The popularity of this gimmick is waning as the sampan population shrinks and the traffic on Gloucester Road grows.

Victoria Park 維多利亞公園

A big chunk of the land reclaimed from Causeway Bay in the early '60s was developed into Victoria Park, the city's largest swath of green. The park's daily schedule begins at 6 a.m. with slow-moving practitioners of tai chi and old men strolling with bird cages. There's an Olympic swimming pool, 14 tennis courts, and a roller-skating rink, plus joggers, footballers, and kite fliers. The park blossoms twice yearly, with a flower market at Chinese New Year, and with bright paper lanterns during the Mid-Autumn Festival in September.

SOUTH OF THE TRAMLINE

Across Yee Wo Street, behind Mitsukoshi, the tone changes: the neighborhoods become more compact, more crowded if possible, more Chinese. This area was until recently an exciting mix of small restaurants, herbal pharmacies, boutiques, tea shops and pawnshops, but its character is rapidly changing, as old shops are razed to make way for glass-curtained office buildings.

Times Square 時代廣場

This new development on Russell Street (on the site of the old Causeway Bay tram station) is a prime example of the trend: it's Hong Kong's newest, trendiest shopping center, with a four-plex cinema and a posh interior outfitted with curving escalators. "Food Unlimited" is the ensemble name of the assortment of restaurants packing the 10th through 13th floors (these are reached via a separate entrance or from the ninth floor). **CitySuper** in the basement has a huge selection of imported foods and an excellent food court.

Jardine's Bazaar

This area gets its name from the old Chinese neighborhood once located behind Jardine's headquarters. The small street is lined with a dozen Chinese restaurants serving tofu, dim sum, noodles—a good place for a cheap meal. One block behind is **Jardine's Crescent,** an intensely crowded narrow bazaar resembling the famous Temple Street market in Kowloon, but catering to Chinese tastes and sizes rather than tourists'. Open day and night, it's packed with stalls selling clothes and accessories. Side alleys running off from it hold more small Chinese restaurants; in the evenings the tables spill out onto the sidewalk and everyone eats in jolly conviviality. The market culminates in a daytime food and flower market.

Tin Hau Temple 天后廟

Ride the tram past Victoria Park to visit this temple, one of the oldest in Hong Kong. The exact date of construction is unknown, but the bell inside is dated 1747, and an inscription says the temple was restored in 1868. It's obviously been rebuilt since then, but it's beautifully maintained and spotless. The goddess hides behind her pearl headdress, visited by supplicants who use the *chim* sticks and *bui* (fortune blocks) lying on side tables. Before reclamation the temple stood on the waterfront, visited by fishermen and seafarers who floated right up to the entrance. It's located on Tin Hau Temple Road just past its junction with Causeway Road. The Tin Hau MTR station across the street provides a convenient means of return to Central or Kowloon.

Aw Boon Haw Gardens 胡文虎花園

This kitschy array of peeling sculptures stands in the Tai Hang neighborhood behind Causeway Bay. It is the creation of Burmese-born Chinese businessman Aw Boon Haw, who made his fortune marketing Tiger Balm, a dubious concoction of menthol, herbs, and petroleum jelly said to cure everything from snakebite to headaches. Aw Boon Haw also developed a chain of Singapore newspapers and founded the *Hong Kong Standard.*

With the profits he built this collection of artificial caves and grottoes adorned with statues of legendary Buddhist and Taoist characters. (A larger version he raised in Singapore was recently demolished.) Words fail to describe the full gaudy horror, but "surreal," "bizarre," and "nightmarish" come to mind, and it's been described as "the Flintstones on acid." Contradicting this exercise in bad taste, Aw Boon Haw also built himself a lovely mansion on the same plot.

The gardens are open daily 9:30 a.m.-4 p.m.; admission is justifiably free. Bus 11 from Central runs through Wanchai and Causeway Bay; get off at 15 Tai Hang Road. On foot it's a 20-minute walk from Causeway Bay. Passing by, glance up at the squatter huts clinging to the hillside above. Once a common sight, these are now among the last on the island.

BEYOND CAUSEWAY BAY

Few travelers venture beyond Causeway Bay, perhaps because the HKTA-distributed tourist maps end there. While there's little of note beyond the usual bustling markets and residential streets, it's a thoroughly interesting tram ride down King's Road to the Shaukeiwan terminus, from where you can catch the MTR back to Central or Tsimshatsui.

North Point 北角
This crowded neighborhood was known as "Little Shanghai" in the 1930s for the quantities of Shanghaiese settled here. Today it's a typically jammed mass of tenements and office blocks. The shoreline is skirted by the Island Eastern Corridor, an ungainly highway on stilts raised up over the ocean.

Most fun is to take the North Point tram, which runs right through the busy street market on Chung Yeung Street, presenting fantastic photo ops of pressed ducks, live frogs, polished fruit, and vendors in rubber boots. The market spills over onto Marble Road, where the specialty is cheap clothing, from pajamas and brassieres to sweaters. A few blocks north is the **North Point Ferry Pier,** where ferries run to Hung Hom, Kowloon City, and Kwun Tong. Bus 10 runs from here through Central and all the way to Kennedy Town.

Back on King's Road, the tramline continues past shops selling embroidered red silk wedding dresses, the Sunbeam Theater (a popular venue for Chinese opera performances), and **Quarry Bay**'s new housing blocks.

Taikoo Shing 太古城
This area gets its name from Tai Koo, "Great and Ancient," the local name selected by Swire's when it set up business in Shanghai. Taikoo is Hong Kong's oldest industrial area, a shipbuilding neighborhood since the founding of the Whampoa Dock in 1863 and the famous Taikoo Dockyard in 1908.

The old dockyards have been redeveloped as Taikoo Shing, a huge private housing estate of identical towers it's easy to get lost amidst. The focal point is **Cityplaza (** 太古城中 **)**, an enormous gleaming shopping center oriented to local families, with casual fashion outlets and plenty of cameras and electronic goods. The low-key atmosphere comes as a relief after Tsimshatsui's hustlers. There are no fewer than 35 restaurants and fast-food establishments, including **Harbour Restaurant,** where seating is on the deck of a facsimile of a luxury cruise ship. Then there are ice- and roller-skating rinks, a cinema, a bowling alley, and a kid's entertainment center. Walkways lead across the street to **Kornhill Plaza** for more shopping, and to giant **Jusco,** a reasonably priced Japanese department store.

Shaukeiwan 筲箕灣
The tramline ends at this former small fishing village. At the time of the British arrival it was the second-largest settlement on the island, with a population of 1200. Shaukeiwan was once the anchorage for a fishing fleet second only to Aberdeen's in size, but the old Aldrich Bay Typhoon Shelter, once crammed with boats, is being filled in. The neighborhood is typically bustling and mildly interesting, though it's a very, very local sight.

Minor points of interest include the **Tin Hau Temple** opposite the wholesale fish market, and the **Tam Kung Temple** on A Kung Ngam Road. This deity is said to heal the sick (this particular image is credited with averting a cholera outbreak in the 1960s) and control the weather. To seafarers he is second in importance only to Tin Hau, and his "birthday" festival (usually May) is big and colorful. The 1905 temple holds images of various other gods, including a wooden Kwun Yam from China, holding a water pot and willow sprig as emblems of her mercy.

Across the harbor from here is Lei Yue Mun on the Kowloon mainland, renowned for its fresh seafood stalls and restaurants (see "Food and Restaurants" in the Hong Kong Basics chapter). A ferry runs to it from the Sai Wan Ho pier, just west of Shaukeiwan.

Chai Wan 柴灣
Minibuses and the MTR continue on to Chai Wan, a nondescript clump of housing estates

bordered by a cluster of cemeteries on the hillside south of town. The **Sai Wan War Cemetery** holds the graves of many of Hong Kong's WW II defenders. Tai Tam Road links Chai Wan with Shek O on the island's southeast tip.

Law Uk Folk Museum (羅屋民族館) at 14 Kut Shing St. (near the Chai Wan MTR) is one of two traditional Chinese houses remaining on Hong Kong Island. Built by a Hakka family about 200 years ago, it's been converted to a folk museum displaying traditional furniture and mildly fascinating items like a straw raincoat. It's open 10 a.m.-1 p.m. and 2-6 p.m. Tues.-Sat., 1-6 p.m. Sunday and holidays; admission is free.

THE SOUTH SIDE

In contrast to the heavily developed northern shore, Hong Kong Island's southern side remains more closely in touch with its rural roots, with few high-rises except for Aberdeen and Repulse Bay. This is partly due to the rugged coastline, rocky and set with inlets—which makes for some spectacular scenery. The island's south side has 14 official swimming beaches, and on summer weekends it seems every single resident of the north side descends upon them.

The island's southern shore was historically the more important one, the site of many small settlements, of which Stanley was the largest. Ships replenished their water supplies at a waterfall west of Aberdeen, possibly the "fragrant stream" (one of several translations of *heung keung*) that gave Hong Kong its name.

Present-day sights provide an interesting counterpoint to the relentlessly urban north shore: Aberdeen's crowded harbor, Stanley's market, the beaches of Deep Water Bay and Shek O, and Ocean Park's world-class oceanarium and amusement park. Access to all is easy: it's less than 40 minutes to any by bus or taxi from Central.

ABERDEEN 香港仔

No longer the quaint Chinese fishing village described in early guidebooks, Aberdeen's bustling residential streets now typify Hong Kong. Its busy harbor packed with bobbing sampans used to be a major tourist attraction, but the population of "boat people" has been drastically reduced, as many have resettled in the high-rises sprung up on the newly reclaimed shoreline.

The only other reasonably sized town on Hong Kong Island, Aberdeen—still called Heung Kong Tsai, "Little Hong Kong," in Chinese—gave Hong Kong its name, but lost its own in the process. The settlement began as a pirate's hangout and developed into a Hakka- and Hoklo-inhabited fishing village that served as collection point for the valuable scented wood of the incense tree, exported to China. British sailors may have mistakenly extrapolated the name of this "fragrant harbor" to cover the entire island. The British eventually named the town after the Earl of Aberdeen, Secretary of State for British colonies in the 1840s.

Aberdeen Praya 香港仔海傍

Twenty years ago, Aberdeen Harbor was packed solid with fishing boats, a floating community of perhaps 25,000, many of them Hoklo people from the coastal region of Swatow in Guangdong Province. Between the reclamation that has shrunk the harbor and government efforts to resettle floating families on dry land, only a handful of diehards remain today. The harbor's dwindling population reflects overall trends: Hong Kong's 1971 marine population of 80,000 was less than a quarter of that figure in 1991.

The harbor and the walkway skirting it (Aberdeen Praya) are still lively enough. The waterfront opposite the bus park has been developed into a park of sorts, with a viewtower, fountains, and a snack kiosk. The wholesale fish market at the east end is busiest in early morning and closes by noon.

The main problem here is fending off the charmingly persistent old sampan ladies hoping to take you on a harbor tour in their motorized wooden boats. Give into one, by all means, but negotiate the price down to about HK$50 a head. Watertours has a "legal sampan" dock here, the only apparent difference being that the asking price is HK$10 more.

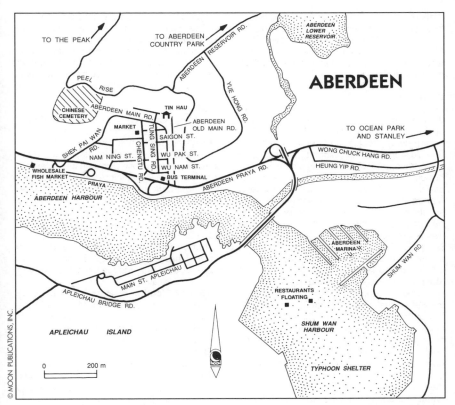

The set tour is a half-hour through the "lanes" of anchored boats, past vignettes of floating life: men mending nets and hanging fish up to dry in the fierce sun, grocery boats drifting between households, and women washing dishes on deck, amid potted plants, chained dogs, and toddlers wandering perilously close to the edge. (Boat mothers used to tie dried bottle gourds to their children's backs as life preservers.)

The sampan lady will also take you past the enormous **floating restaurants** farther out in Shum Wan Harbor (or catch the private restaurant shuttle boat in front of Aberdeen Centre). The restaurants are linked together by walkways: their ornate gilded and painted facades are particularly glorious lit up at night, but the utilitarian kitchens on the back side are interesting too, with gigantic pots bubbling away and delivery boats unloading fresh food. Underwater cages set around the edges of the restaurants guarantee supremely fresh seafood. A bit of trivia: the floating restaurant fire that forms the climactic scene of James Clavell's novel *Taipan* is based on fact—the newly built Jumbo went up in flames in 1971.

Apleichau Island

Across the harbor is Apleichau ("Duck's Tongue") Island, its ranks of high-rises alarmingly sterile in the daytime but dazzling lit up at night. The island's shoreline is being reclaimed, and Apleichau's old shipbuilding yards have been moved to the mainland side (look for them just beyond the bridge on your sampan tour).

Walk out onto the Aberdeen-Apleichau Bridge for excellent overviews of the harbor and the luxury yachts of the Aberdeen Marina and Boat Club. There's an old temple to Tin Hau on the island and another to the fishermen's weather-god Hung Shing.

Downtown Aberdeen
Aberdeen's bustling downtown, lying north of the bus terminal, is only a few blocks square and easily explored. Here are the usual shops selling gold, noodles, and herbal medicines, and old women worshipping at the local Earth God shrine, a roasted suckling pig on a trolley beside as an offering. The old street market has been packed off into the multistory **Aberdeen Market** at the corner of Nam Ning and Chengtu streets. Inside is clothing, produce, and all manners of poultry stuffed in bamboo cages, either freshly dissected or in the process of becoming so. The big cooked-food market on the third floor is crammed, cheerful, and cheap.

The **Tin Hau Temple (**天后廟**)** at the corner of Main and Reservoir roads indicates the location of the shoreline at the time of its construction in 1851 (virtually all of downtown Aberdeen is built on reclaimed land). Inside the small, smoke-blackened shrine, incense coils dangle from the ceiling. Offerings of roast chicken, fruit, and cooking oil are stacked on tables, and attendants whisk away smouldering bundles of incense almost as soon as they're lit, dousing them in a side room. The temple is a favorite haunt of the tough, tiny *samfu*-clad old ladies who are seen, bent and shuffling but indomitable, on Aberdeen's streets.

Chinese Cemetery
Head up Aberdeen Reservoir Road behind the temple and turn left onto Peel Rise, a steep though shady climb, to explore the enormous cemetery backing Aberdeen. To placate potentially troublesome ancestors, the dead are awarded the most auspicious sites—in this case a steep hillside facing the ocean (though their views have since been blocked by towering high-rises). The cemetery's hillside terraces are packed with neat gravestones engraved in red script, many inset with photos of the deceased. The multiple tiers echo the apartment blocks below: even the afterlife is crowded in Hong Kong.

If you'd like to get even farther away from it all, continue up Aberdeen Reservoir Road one km into **Aberdeen Country Park (**香港仔郊野公園**).** Here is a visitor information center with a natural history display, and marked trails winding past two reservoirs. It's a good picnic site, guaranteed private on weekdays.

Food
Downtown Aberdeen has plenty of local noodle shops and dim sum restaurants, as well as a few big fancy restaurants with burbling fish tanks at the entrance. Collect provisions at the supermarket in town for a picnic on the waterfront or at Aberdeen Reservoir. A snack kiosk at the waterfront park dispenses sandwiches, beer, and sodas. Or catch the *kaido* service to Mo Tat Wan on Lamma Island for a seafood feast at Sok Kwu Wan (see "Sok Kwu Wan" under "Lamma" in the Outlying Islands chapter).

Jumbo Floating Restaurant, Shum Wan Harbour, has touristy food but the setting is unbeatable, especially the rooftop patio. Dim sum is served 7:30 a.m.-4 p.m.

Tai Pak Floating Restaurant, Shum Wan Harbour, is smaller than but identical to the Jumbo and is connected to it by a floating walkway. Shuttles run out to the floating restaurants from a pier in front of Aberdeen Centre.

Blue Ocean, 9/F Marina Tower Complex, Shum Wan Rd., serves dim sum all day long.

Brazil Brazil, 8/F Marina Tower Complex, Shum Wan Rd., has samba-oriented food to the tune of jazz, Latin, country, and blues.

Getting There
Take Bus 7 or 70 from Central, Bus 70M from outside the Admiralty MTR, or Bus 73 from Stanley or Repulse Bay. Or hike down from the Peak in about an hour, taking Peak Road over to shady Peel Rise, which passes Aberdeen's giant cemetery on the way into town.

OCEAN PARK 海洋公園

This oceanarium/amusement park on a headland just east of Aberdeen bills itself as Southeast Asia's biggest entertainment complex. Ocean Park draws two million visitors a year, including 10 percent of all tourists. The Disney-like extravagance makes it difficult to remember that the park was originally funded by the Hong Kong Jockey Club. It's now a not-for-profit corporation engaging in marine research and an important dolphin breeding program.

The park is in two sections, linked by a spectacular 1.4-km cableway. Start at the **Lowland Gardens,** which features a greenhouse, a cocoon-shaped butterfly house, a Goldfish Pagoda full of bug-eyed Chinese fish, and a "Dino Island" film simulator ride. **Kid's World** offers rides, games, and shows at a "Dolphin University."

All this is just a warm-up for the **Headland,** reached by a 10-minute cable car ride over the hill. **Atoll Reef** is the world's largest deep-sea aquarium, with over 30,000 sea creatures, including sharks, rays, eels, and turtles. At **Wave Cove,** meter-high waves pour across a gigantic tank fashioned like a rocky coastline, providing a "natural" habitat for seals, penguins, pelicans, and cormorants, which can be viewed through an underwater gallery. Trained dolphins and a killer whale perform at the 3,500-seat **Ocean Theater,** and a **Shark Aquarium** features an underwater viewing tunnel. As if this weren't enough, your ticket buys unlimited rides on things like the Space Wheel, Crazy Galleon, and Octopus. The **Dragon Roller Coaster,** perched on the edge of a cliff and deemed too scary for younger children, shoots three loops— one in reverse—attaining a maximum speed of 77 kph.

The entrance fee also covers admission to the **Middle Kingdom** theme park, reached by a long, long escalator. Five thousand years of Chinese civilization are compressed into a few acres, with each of the 13 dynasties represented by a replica of a particular temple, pagoda, or palace. Craftspeople demonstrate skills like papermaking and silk-weaving, performers put on shows of acrobatics, juggling, dancing, and magic, and shops sell all kinds of souvenirs.

While Ocean Park is entertaining for just about everyone, it's a must if you're traveling with kids. For the most efficient visit, check theater show times upon arrival and plan your schedule around them. Allot an entire day, and avoid Sunday and holidays, when the lines for rides are unbearable. Hours are 10 a.m.-6 p.m. every day of the year. Admission is HK$150, HK$75

for kids under 11, and covers all rides, shows, and displays. Call 2552-0291 for English information.

Water World 水上樂園
This separate water-oriented amusement park adjoins Ocean Park's Lowland section. It features a wave pool sided by a "beach" and all sorts of rainbow-colored water slides, including a 60-meter long **Superslide,** which take all of six seconds from top to bottom. It's a great place for kids to let off steam. Parents who can't stand the excitement can retreat to the sundeck. Water World is open April-October, 10 a.m.-5 p.m. daily (closing time is 10 p.m. June-August). Admission is HK$70, HK$45 for children under 11. Call 2555-6055 for details.

Getting There
The Citybus to Ocean Park leaves the Admiralty MTR station every half-hour 8:40 a.m.-3:40 p.m.; a booth here sells all-inclusive tickets, currently HK$160. Minibus 6 runs from the Central Star Ferry to Ocean Park on weekdays 8 a.m.-6 p.m.

Otherwise, take Bus 6A, 64, 70, 260, or 262 from the Central Bus Terminus and get off just past the Aberdeen Tunnel at Ocean Park Road. It's a ten-minute walk to the entrance. Coming from Aberdeen, catch Bus 48, 70, or 73; from Repulse Bay or Stanley, Bus 73.

DEEP WATER BAY 深水灣

This is Sham Shui Wan or "Deep Water Bay," as opposed to "Shallow Water Bay" (Tsin Shui Wan, better known as Repulse Bay) just beside it, though really there's no difference. Deep Water Bay is one of Hong Kong Island's best beaches, at least on weekdays, when it's relatively uncrowded—though still not exactly clean. It's easy to reach by taxi from Central. The half-km of sandy beach is flanked by oceanfront promenades running to the Hong Kong Country Club to the west and around the headland to Repulse Bay, 1.5 km east. This latter route passes **Middle Island,** which is separated from the adjacent headland by a narrow channel. At low tide you can practically walk to it.

HONG KONG BEACHES

NEW TERRITORIES

TOLO HARBOUR

SHATIN

TSUEN WAN

TUEN MUN

APPROACH

LIDO

GEMINI

CAFETERIA

SILVERMINE BAY

PUI O

CHEUNG SHA WAN

LANTAU ISLAND

TAI LONG WAN

PAK SHA CHAU

SAI KUNG

TRIO

KIU TSUI

SILVERSTRAND

CLEARWATER BAY

BIG WAVE BAY

SHEK O

SHEK O

STANLEY MAIN

STANLEY

ST. STEPHEN'S

REPULSE BAY

MIDDLE BAY

DEEPWATER BAY

SOUTH BAY

CHUNG HUM BAY

KOWLOON

VICTORIA HARBOUR

VICTORIA

CENTRAL

HONG KONG ISLAND

ABERDEEN

HUNG SHING YE

LO SO SHING

LAMMA ISLAND

TUNG WAN

CHEUNG CHAU

SOUTH CHINA SEA

5 km

0

© MOOM PUBLICATIONS, INC.

BEACHES

It's doubtful if anyone comes to Hong Kong just to swim, but the territory's 43 gazetted beaches do provide welcome relief from the steamy city. The average Hongkonger visits the beach three times a year. Odds are at least one of those occasions is a July Sunday at Repulse Bay.

The main beach season is June to September, though swimming is possible from March through December. Late September until Christmas are virtually crowd-free, and the water doesn't get chilly until mid-November at the earliest. Surface water temperatures range from a minimum of 15° C in January through February up to 23-30° C in summer—about the temperature of chicken soup.

Water pollution is a well-publicized concern. It's concentrated in Victoria Harbour and around the industrialized western side of the Kowloon Peninsula, which also gets a lot of silt from the Pearl River estuary. The ocean is cleaner on the south side of Hong Kong Island and the eastern New Territories, and is best on Lantau Island. Water quality bottomed out in the late '80s and is slowly improving with tighter regulation and sewage system expansion. Avoid swimming after rainstorms, as runoff can contaminate the water; crowded weekends also muck it up. Pollution warnings are posted at affected beaches. In certain areas the bacteria count can be high enough to cause upset stomachs and ear infections. You most definitely don't want to open your mouth underwater.

Crowds are another irritant. Public beaches are a favorite destination for weekend overnights, complete with elaborate barbecues of squid and fish balls, Canto-pop boom boxes, and litter. Other perils include undertows and periodic invasions of stinging men-of-war. Most exciting are the periodic shark scares. Two swimmer deaths in June 1993 engendered a flurry of protective measures: shark nets were installed to protect threatened beaches, helicopters scanned the sea every hour, and speedboats followed dragon boat racers to pick up rowers fallen into the harbor. The actual level of danger from shark attacks is quite low.

The Urban Council maintains 43 gazetted beaches, most equipped with kiosks, showers, changing rooms, and lifeguards. HKTA puts out a beach leaflet listing facilities and public transport.

Beaches on Hong Kong Island are especially crowded: **Deep Water Bay, Shek O, Repulse Bay,** and **Stanley Beach** all have long lines for buses on weekends, though the first two are good bets on weekdays. **Big Wave Bay** is remote and fairly uncrowded: take the MTR or tram to Shaukeiwan, then Bus 9 to Shek O; get off at the intersection before town and walk 10 minutes north. Bus 14 from Shaukeiwan goes to **Turtle Cove** on Tai Tam Bay.

Outlying islands are another possibility. On Lantau, **Silvermine Bay Beach** is tremendously popular but often polluted. The island's south shore has some exceptional beaches, backed by Lantau and Sunset Peak. **Cheung Sha** is among the best in Hong Kong, with relatively clean water and over three km of white sand, big enough to absorb the crowds (who tend to cluster around the lifeguard stands at any rate). **Pui O** and **Tong Fuk** beaches are smaller and more developed. On Lamma, the best beach is probably **Hung Shing Ye,** a 20-minute walk from Yung Shue Wan. Cheung Chau's main beach, **Tung Wan,** is crowded and none too clean; it's better to walk down to the more isolated beaches on the southern end.

Beaches in the western New Territories, like the strip between Tsuen Wan and Tuen Mun, suffer from poor water quality, a combination of pollution and silt from the Pearl River estuary. The eastern New Territories (Sai Kung) has some exceptionally fine swimming, starting with popular **Silverstrand** and **Clearwater Bay Beaches #1 and #2** (Bus 91 from the Choi Hung MTR). *Kaido*s from Sai Kung Town promenade go to the island beaches of **Hap Mun Wan, Kiu Tsui,** and **Pak Sha Chau. Trio Beach,** a few kilometers south of Sai Kung Town, is also worth considering: get off Bus 92 at Pak Wai village and catch a *kaido* to the beach.

Best of all are the remote beaches on the easternmost side of Sai Kung Peninsula, accessible only by private boat or with several hours' hiking. Try **Sai Wan, Ham Tin,** or the ultimate, **Tai Long Wan,** a horseshoe bay with four wide beaches and crystal-clear water.

Getting There

Take Bus 64, 260, or 262 from Central, or Bus 73, which runs between Aberdeen and Stanley. Or take Bus 6 or 262 up to Wong Nai Chung Gap and walk seven km down Deep Water Bay Road to the beach, passing millionaires' mansions en route.

REPULSE BAY 淺水灣

Repulse Bay has long been Hong Kong's favorite swimming hole: Cooke's 1924 guide touted it as the "Riviera of the Far East." Much of its charm came from the elegant old **Repulse Bay Hotel,** with its afternoon teas and beachfront verandah. Built in 1920, the hotel endured even WW II, when British troops rolled grenades down its carpeted corridors at the Japanese invaders. But when its owners, the Kadoorie family, approved its demolition in the early 1980s, even public outcry could not save it. It was replaced by a bizarre rainbow-colored apartment block built with a rectangular hole smack in the middle—allowing the resident dragon to pass through freely, locals insist. A replica of the hotel's whitewashed facade has been reconstructed and now holds restaurants and a designer shopping arcade, but it's a sad mockery of former elegance.

Repulse Bay Beach (淺水灣匯 **)** remains the longest beach on Hong Kong Island, and also the most crowded, drawing up to 25,000 visitors on summer weekends. The crowds have inspired the predictable nickname "Repulsive Bay." Actually it was named for the HMS *Repulse,* a British ship engaged in anti-pirate warfare. Avoid weekends by all means: if it's still too crowded, try walking south to the beaches at **Middle Bay** or **South Bay.**

The baroque Chinese lifeguard station at the far end is flanked by huge statues of Kwun Yam and Tin Hau, installed as promotional devices by a local company. The kitschy images have achieved special fame with Japanese tourists, and tour buses disgorge groups to be photographed in front of them. More kitsch: each crossing of the "Bridge of Longevity" here is said to increase one's life by three days.

Food

Fast-food restaurants and food stalls line the beach, and there's a supermarket nearby. Other choices are expensive and situated in the Repulse Bay Shopping Arcade. **The Verandah,** tel. 2812-2722, is a classy re-creation of the colonial splendor of the old Repulse Bay Hotel, serving lunch, dinner, tea 3:30-5:30 p.m., and a recommended Sunday champagne breakfast 8-10:30 a.m. **Kagiya,** tel. 2812-2120, has an elegant, very expensive restaurant with French-Japanese cuisine. **Spices,** tel. 2812-2711, has an upmarket Asian smorgasbord spanning India, China, Indonesia, and Japan.

a summer Sunday at Repulse Bay Beach

HONG KONG TOURIST ASSOCIATION

Getting There

Take Bus 6, 61, or 260 from Central, or Bus 73 from Aberdeen or Stanley.

STANLEY 赤柱

When the British arrived in the 1840s, this peninsular settlement was the largest of Hong Kong's 16 villages. Its 2,000 inhabitants, mainly Hakka, called it Chek Chue, "Pirate's Stronghold." The name has stuck, though nowadays, residents remark, it refers to the vendors at Stanley's famed market. The British renamed the town for Lord Stanley, Secretary of State for British colonies in 1845.

Modern Stanley is a low-key, attractive little town, popular with expats, as the string of pubs along its main street demonstrates. Tourists flock to famed Stanley Market; there are also beaches, good restaurants, and a few pleasant walks.

Stanley Market 赤柱街市

Buses discharge passengers on the northern edge of town. The mapboard outside the stop is superfluous: just follow the crowds downhill to Stanley Market, an institutionalized tourist at-

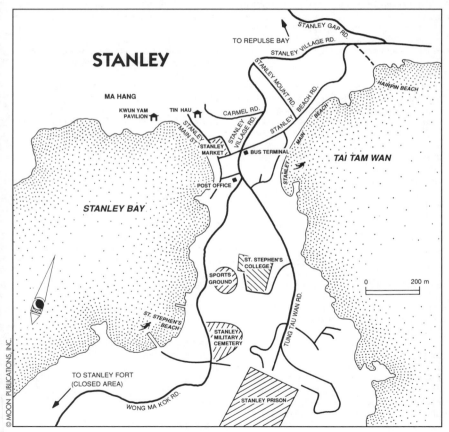

traction. The fabled bargains of yesteryear are gone, and prices are only slightly lower than the cheaper shops of Tsimshatsui, but there's still an amazing selection of casual and kid's clothes, silks, T-shirts, swimsuits, sports shoes, table linens, porcelain, and souvenirs. The stalls and shops go on and on, in a mind- and eye-boggling experience.

Stanley Main Street 士丹利街
When shopping pales, stroll past the busy restaurants and pubs lining Stanley Main Street. The grubby scrap of beach opposite has been overtaken by a reclamation project which will add 6,000 square meters of new land onto Stanley Bay. Current plans are to use this site for a reconstruction of **Murray House,** a graceful colonial building dismantled in 1982 to make room for Central's Bank of China building.

North of Town
Continue past some flower stalls, and in a few minutes you'll reach Stanley's **Tin Hau Temple,** believed to be the oldest on Hong Kong Island. It was founded in 1767 by the followers of Cheung Po Tsai, the pirate who controlled the area. The old drum and bell inside were used by pirate lookouts to send warnings. The temple itself isn't nearly as old—the present structure dates from 1938—but the dim interior with its smoke-stained walls has an air of great antiquity. The image of Tin Hau is surrounded by an array of other gods, some of them probably dating back to the temple's founding. Look for the beautiful old model junks on the left-hand side.

Five minutes' walk up the hill and slightly to the left is a modern **pavilion** to Kwun Yam, with a six-meter-tall statue of the goddess and nice views of Stanley Bay. To reach it you must wander through the redeveloped former shantytown of **Ma Hang (** 馬坑 **),** a village with some 400 years of history.

Beaches
Stanley Main Beach (赤柱正灣 **)** on Tai Tam Wan is a few minutes east of the bus terminal down Stanley Beach Road. It's crowded on weekends with couples, children, and dogs. The **Stanley Windsurfing Centre** here rents boards, but it's fun just to sit and watch the brightly col-

ored sails skimming over the water—or keeling over, as the case may be. From the frantic thrashing of beginners, it appears windsurfing is not an easy sport.

Much better swimming is to be had at **St. Stephen's Beach (** 聖士提反灣 **),** 10 minutes' walk in the opposite direction down Wong Ma Kok Road. Signed stone steps on the right lead down to the beach. Opposite the beach is **Stanley Military Cemetery (** 赤柱軍人墳場 **),** where lie many of the defenders in Hong Kong's ill-fated stand against the Japanese. A few colonial graves date from the early 1840s, when disease took a heavy toll among children. It's a poignant sight, but lofty thoughts are soon dispelled by the sight of Hong Kong girls preening for their boyfriends' cameras amid the headstones. (Evidently this problem is a longstanding one: a sign at the entrance warns sternly that "Games may not be played and food may not be eaten" in the cemetery.)

Just past is **Stanley Prison,** used as a civilian internment camp by the Japanese in WW II. The tip of the peninsula, off-limits to the public, is taken up by old **Stanley Fort,** a former British military installation now inhabited by the PLA.

Food
The *dai pai dong*s across from Stanley Market are cheap, good, and accustomed to tourists, with English menus on the tables. Look for **Relax Restaurant,** which has Chinese food and Western snacks too. There's a Wellcome Supermarket for picnic fare (best consumed at St. Stephen's Beach); or pick up a takeaway sushi box from **Fukishima Japanese Restaurant** on Stanley Main Street. Lively pubs along this road serve drinks and bar food, and the scene continues well into the night.

Stanley's French at 86 Stanley Main St., tel. 2813-8873, is romantically situated in an elegantly decorated old house filled with sunshine and flowers. It's not cheap, but the set lunches are a relative bargain and the whole experience is well worthwhile. Reservations recommended; expensive.

Down the street at 90B is **Stanley's Oriental,** tel. 2813-9988, run by the same owners, with an imaginative mix of Asian and Cajun cuisines; moderate.

Stanley's Beaches at 92B Stanley Main St.

has a create-your-own pasta menu, videos, and an evening D.J.; prices are moderate.

Lucy's, 64 Stanley Main St., behind the Park 'n Shop, is a small café with a simple, delicious Continental menu; moderate.

Less visible, and therefore less crowded, are the restaurants up the hill from the market. **At Village,** 40 Stanley Main Street, is a low-key cafe with some sidewalk tables serving moderately priced Asian and Western food (sandwiches, burgers, pasta). **Lorenzo Ristorante Italiano,** 64 Stanley Main St. (beside the supermarket), serves moderately priced Italian food; so does **Pepperoni's,** 18B Stanley Main St., where the menu includes excellent pizza; and **Firenze,** 126 Stanley Main Street.

To escape the crowds, catch a *kaido* from St. Stephen's Beach to Po Toi Island (Sunday mornings only) and enjoy excellent cheap seafood.

Getting There

Buses 6 and 260 depart from Central, while Bus 73 connects Stanley and Aberdeen. Returning is no problem—buses sail in every five minutes on Sunday. Taxis are a possibility, but can get expensive as the meter ticks away in the weekend traffic jams likely from Repulse Bay on. If air-conditioning is essential, take Minibus 40 back to Causeway Bay or Minibus 16M to Chai Wan, and catch the MTR.

SHEK O 石澳

The closest thing to a village on the entire island, Shek O is a cluster of tightly packed houses with hardly a high-rise in sight, so far. Set on a rocky headland on the easternmost tip of Hong Kong Island, it's isolated enough to really be away from it all, yet it's only an hour by public transport from Central. The local community remains surprisingly traditional, while the surrounding neighborhoods hold the elegant homes of Chinese taipans. On Sunday, day-trippers flock to Shek O to enjoy the good beach, popular restaurants, and superb hiking.

The road from Shaukeiwan heads down the lush, rugged D'Aguilar Peninsula, passing Tai Tam Reservoir and the swanky Shek O Country Club, the island's most exclusive. The bus stops at a roundabout on the edge of town. Stroll down the main road a few minutes to a big parking lot, flanked by small restaurants and stalls renting sturdy bicycles for use on the untrafficked roads. **Shek O Beach** lies behind, a long stretch of white sand that's crowded on weekends but not nearly as badly as, say, Repulse Bay. The rule seems to be Bring Your Own Kid—it's full of families with (well-behaved) children. Stalls here sell anything you might conceivably need: swimsuits, sun hats, straw beach mats and giant inflatable sharks, and bowls of cheap noodles.

There's another beach, **Rocky Bay,** on the opposite side of town, but water quality is so poor here it's closed to swimmers. Keep it in mind if you simply want great views and an uncrowded stretch of sand. The very best beach is **Big Wave Bay,** a half-hour's walk north (see below).

Shek O has few proper sights but some good leisurely walks. Explore the narrow streets of the old town and visit the small, brightly decorated Tin Hau Temple in the middle. Stroll through the village and slightly uphill to the road called **The Headland (** 石澳山仔 **),** an exclusive neighborhood of wealthy homes, each fronted by the ultimate Hong Kong status symbol—a patch of lawn. Farther back on the lower slopes of Dragon's Back ridge are the walled estates of the truly rich.

Down past The Headland, a paved path leads across a small footbridge onto the little islet of **Tai Tau Chau**—not even an island at low tide. A small sewage discharge plant recently built here has ruined the views of those expensive homes in Rocky Bay. Continue past it to find a secluded picnic spot on the island's rocky slopes. A little viewing pavilion offers incredible views north to Joss House Bay, south to the Stanley Peninsula, and straight down to pleasure craft floating lazily in the sparkling waters of the South China Sea. Scan the horizon for Waglan Island with its lighthouse, and one of the Po Toi Islands beside it.

Walks

A more adventurous hike leads down the peninsula south of town to **Cape D'Aguilar** (鶴咀道). Take either the narrow, winding paved road from Windy Gap, or the footpath cutting across the summit of 325-meter-high D'Aguilar Peak. It's around five or six km roundtrip.

To make a full day of it and work up an appetite for that Thai meal, you might hike into Shek O. The spectacular panoramic ridgewalk along **Lung Chek** (龍脊), "Dragon's Back Ridge" forms the eighth stage of the Hong Kong Trail. Take a taxi or Bus 9 from Shaukeiwan or Chai Wan and get off near the crematorium on Shek O Road, looking for the Shek O Country Park sign on the left. A mapboard nearby displays routes through the park. Climb up the steps behind the sign and keep going uphill. The trail heads along a windswept bare ridgeline for around two hours before dropping down into Shek O.

Food

A good meal is one of the main excuses for a visit to Shek O. **China-Thailand Seafood Restaurant,** just down the road from the bus stop, is run by the owners of the famous Heng Thai restaurant near the airport and offers authentic Thai food in a much nicer setting. Order up a slew of spicy dishes from the vast illustrated menu. Service is fast, prices reasonable, and beer cold and cheap. Across the street, **Welcome Garden Restaurant** serves good Sichuan food in an open-air setting. A few minutes' walk down the winding main lane at 452 Shek O Village Rd. is the tiny, offbeat cafe **Black**

Sheep, with an eclectic international menu starting at HK$70 and a nice selection of teas—just the place to hole up on a rainy afternoon.

Getting There

Take the MTR to Shaukeiwan and catch Bus 9 from the terminal outside. Departures are every 15-35 minutes; air-conditioned minibuses across the street leave more frequently. Sit on the right-hand side for spectacular views of the rugged peninsula and Tai Tam Harbor. A taxi from Central is faster (about 40 minutes), but drivers are often reluctant to go out to Shek O without the guarantee of a return fare.

Returning, there are plenty of taxis available on weekends (about $70-80 into Central), or frequent minibuses and buses. For a leisurely variation, ride the tram back from the Shaukeiwan terminus into Central.

BIG WAVE BAY 大浪灣

North of Shek O, this is one of the island's best and least-crowded beaches. The lack of public transport to it is a virtue in this respect. It's about a 30-minute walk from Shek O. If you're coming from Shaukeiwan or Chai Wan, get off the bus at the well-marked intersection about one km before Shek O and walk 10 minutes down the peaceful road towards the beach. Look for the exceptionally clear Bronze Age **rock carvings** on the headland a little north of the beach.

BOB RACE

KOWLOON 九龍

The 12-square-km chunk of the Kowloon Peninsula from the waterfront up to Boundary Street is the other half of the Hong Kong equation. Indeed it's *the* Hong Kong for most visitors, especially the tourist district of **Tsimshatsui** at the very tip, a hodgepodge of hotels, shops, and restaurants spilling over into even flashier **Tsimshatsui East.** It's easy to get sucked into this vortex and never escape, but you should definitely press north, into the more traditional neighborhoods of **Yaumatei** and **Mongkok.**

Boundary Street in Mongkok marks the division between Kowloon and the New Territories, but the neighborhoods immediately north are for all practical purposes an extension of Kowloon, served by the MTR. Here are some of the most crowded areas on earth, where the average resident has nine square feet of living space to himself—a bitter contrast with the stately mansions of the Peak.

Kowloon is a corruption of the Cantonese *gau lung,* "nine dragons," referring to the long range of rugged mountains backing the peninsula, and the *feng shui* tenet that dragons inhabit mountain peaks. Supposedly, when the young Sung emperor passed through here in 1277, the boy saw the peaks and commented, "eight dragons."

"Nine," corrected an obsequious counselor— "The emperor is also a dragon." Dragon or not, the boy emperor was driven into the sea by the approaching Mongols, and Kowloon's gently rolling hills have been bulldozed flat to make room for its densely packed buildings.

Kowloon's silhouette is presently unimpressive, a dull sprawl of boxy buildings with none of the splendid skyscrapers that adorn Hong Kong Island. When Kai Tak Airport, which falls right in the center of Kowloon, was active, buildings were restricted to a maximum height of 200 feet. This restriction will be lifted following the opening of the new international airport off the coast of Lantau. Kai Tak's prime real estate will be redeveloped, and Kowloon's existing buildings will shoot upwards, increasing their owners' profits.

History

Kowloon's modern history began at the tiny village of Tsimshatsui on 19 January 1861, when a Chinese mandarin handed over a packet of soil to a British officer, symbolizing the cessation of the Kowloon Peninsula under the terms of the Convention of Peking.

Britain's new acquisition embraced marshes, rice fields, and the scattered small villages of about 5,000 inhabitants, mostly Hakka farmers who paid little attention to the transfer of power. The far shore was rimmed by a fine beach—the "sandy point" that gives Tsimshatsui its name.

Kowloon in its early days harbored a reputation as an uncivilized place, the abode of outlaws, Portuguese, soldiers, and prostitutes. The opening of the Kowloon Railway Station in 1916 and the Peninsula Hotel across the road in 1929 marked the area's transition into respectability. It developed into a clutter of three- and four-story tenements, ground-floor shops topped by small workshops, factories, cheap guesthouses, and offices. The influx of foreign servicemen and tourists that began in the mid-'50s sparked Tsimshatsui's development, while the neighborhoods to the north retain more of their old character.

USEFUL BUS ROUTES FOR KOWLOON

Look for the round bus stop signs (red in Kowloon). "M" after a route number means the bus connects with an MTR station.

BUS NO.	ROUTE
1	Star Ferry-Shanghai St. (Yaumatei)-Chuk Yuen
1A	Star Ferry-Shanghai St. (Yaumatei)-Sau Mau Ping
1K, 2K	Hung Hom-Star Ferry-Mongkok (circular)
6A	Star Ferry-Lai Chi Kok Amusement Park
8	Star Ferry-Hung Hom-Jordan Rd. Ferry
8A	Canton Rd.-Hung Hom (Whampoa Garden)

Green Minibuses

1	Star Ferry-Tsimshatsui East
6	Hankow Rd.-Hung Hom (Whampoa Garden)

Cross-Harbor Routes (12:45-5 a.m.)

121	Macau Ferry terminal-Tsimshatsui East-Choi Hung
122	North Point-Tsimshatsui East-Lai Chi Kok

TSIMSHATSUI 尖沙咀

The first challenge is to pronounce it (say "Chim Sa Choy"). The second is to navigate this seething vortex of energy yet not get sucked into it. Tsimshatsui is Hong Kong distilled to a high-octane potency, a frenetic, fast-paced district focused on materialism and its pleasures.

Tsimshatsui is brash and hard, all scam and hustle and glitter, with an incredible vitality that propels it through the night. There are restaurants for every pocketbook and cuisine, hotels from the magnificent Peninsula and Regent to the fabled squalor of Chungking Mansions, and more shops than you could ever imagine. (See "Shopping" in the Introduction for details on Tsimshatsui's main activity.) Depending on your temperament and budget, it's either a nightmare or paradise.

STAR FERRY AND CANTON ROAD

Begin at the Star Ferry Pier (尖沙咀碼頭), set at the southwesternmost tip of the Kowloon Peninsula. Ferries run from here over to Central and Wanchai. There's an HKTA office set between the two piers, and over to the left is the floating dock for **Watertours,** the biggest harbor tour operator. Out in front is an outdoor terminal for Kowloon-side buses, and **Star House** with its big China Arts and Crafts outlet.

Harbour City 海港城

To your left as you disembark is a gigantic shopping center ranked among the largest in Asia. **Ocean Terminal,** built on a pier projecting out into the harbor, caters to cruise ships which dock here and discharge passengers straight into shopping. A basement food court dishes up all kinds of cheap Asian food.

Be careful: the unwary who stumble through this complex may not emerge for blocks. It continues through **Ocean Centre** and **Harbour City,** shops, shops, and more shops (over 500 in all), plus various hotels and a movie theater, all linked by moving walkways and pedestrian crossovers. Stores focus on clothing, shoes, jewelry, watches. Regardless of your opinion of shopping, it's a great place to spend a few air-conditioned hours. After it ends there's the **China Ferry Terminal (**中港城碼頭 **)**, where boats to Guangzhou (and a few to Macau) dock. It's contained in yet another shopping center, the big gold **China Hong Kong City.** The other side of Canton Road is lined with more shopping, including that contained in **Silvercord Centre.**

HONG KONG CULTURAL CENTER
香港文化中心

Back on the waterfront, the red-brick **Clock Tower** (circa 1921) represents the last trace of the old Kowloon-Canton Railway Station. Once you could travel all the way to London from here, passing through Guangzhou, Beijing, Ulan Bator, Moscow, and Paris before pulling into Victoria Station. The railroad was relocated at Hung Hom in 1975 and the classic old station demolished a

few years later to make room for the giant pink-brick Hong Kong Cultural Centre.

This HK$600 million complex has proven controversial since its opening in 1989. The vast sweeping walls have been uncharitably compared to a public toilet, a ski slope, and a crushed cigarette box. Certainly it's hard to understand why any architect would choose to place a virtually windowless edifice on a piece of magnificent harborfront property.

Close up, though, the buildings present some compelling angles, and the harborside plaza, set with palms, pillars, and reflecting pools, is a pleasant place to linger. The elevated waterfront walkway in front is appropriated by young lovers in the evening, when it becomes Hong Kong's premiere makout joint.

There's no reason to complain about the first-class facilities inside, either: a 2,100-seat concert hall, two theaters, a popular Chinese restaurant and a decent cafe, plus an arts library, museum, and planetarium in adjacent buildings. Half-hour tours of the center start at 12:30 p.m. daily; buy tickets at the Enquiries Counter in the main lobby.

Hong Kong Museum of Art 香港藝術館
Hong Kong's collection of traditional and contemporary Chinese art is finally displayed in a setting befitting its world-class status. Liberated from its cramped quarters in Central's City Hall, the new museum is a delight to browse through.

two boats from the Star Ferry's green-and-white fleet

KERRY MORAN

The serene scroll paintings of bamboo groves and streamside hermit dwellings on the second floor are calming antidotes to modern Hong Kong. The **Chinese Antiquities** section on the third floor is especially worthwhile. Here are well-presented displays of over 3,000 objects in ceramics, bronze, jade, textiles, and stone. The history of porcelain is outlined with richly glazed examples from the famous Shiwan kilns in Foshan. There are rhino horn cups (valued for their supposed ability to detect poison) and displays on minor arts like lacquer, cloisonne, metal

casting, and bamboo carving. An adjacent **Historical Pictures** section depicts the history of Hong Kong from colonial times through period paintings and sketches.

On your way out, visit the ground-floor Tai Yip Art Book Centre, which sells art and photo books on China and Hong Kong, posters, postcards, and some nice souvenirs. The museum is open Mon.-Wed. and Fri.-Sat. 10 a.m.-6 p.m., Sunday 1-6 p.m.; admission is HK$10, HK$5 for children and seniors.

Space Museum 香港太空館

Next door is the Space Museum, housed in an egglike building that looks best illuminated at night. The egg's interior supports the curved screen of the **Space Theater,** which alternates shows with Omnimax movies on natural wonders like Antarctica or volcanos. Shows start at 2:30 p.m., earlier on weekends, and cost HK$30. After an intensive day of shopping, a chance to sit in the dark may be welcome. The museum's **Exhibition Halls** have displays on astronomy, space history, and solar science and are open Monday and Wed.-Fri. 1-9 p.m., weekends and holidays 10 a.m.-9 p.m.; admission is HK$10.

SALISBURY ROAD

Across the road from the Cultural Centre is the **Salisbury YMCA,** built in 1924 and still clinging tenaciously to its prime plot of harborfront land. Location alone makes it among the best-value local lodgings. It's also among the busiest, with bookings running three months in advance.

The Peninsula 半島酒店

The grande dame of Hong Kong hotels, the Pen has reigned supreme in Hong Kong society since its opening in 1929. It was here that the British governor surrendered to the Japanese in

VICTORIA HARBOUR

Deep and well-sheltered, Victoria Harbour is the territory's finest, and virtually its only, natural asset—its centerpiece and raison d'etre. The harbor's 150-year history of intensive merchant shipping began with the export of opium. In those days it was filled with P&O steamers, the teak ships of the China "country trade," and elegant seagoing junks. Today the harbor hosts an international fleet of ships flying flags from Argentina to Vanuatu. Many are from China and Taiwan. Hong Kong itself has the world's third-largest merchant fleet, behind only Japan and Greece.

Victoria Harbour remains a tremendously busy place. In 1990 some 20,000 oceangoing ships arrived here, many of them container ships laden to the brim with brightly colored crates. The biggest ships can be the length of three football fields. They head for the Kwai Chung Terminal, which competes with Rotterdam and New York for the title of the world's busiest, and, with its recent expansion, is definitely the world's largest.

Smaller container ships and break-bulk carriers moor in mid-harbor. They are unloaded by lighters, which ferry cargo to handling areas at Causeway Bay, Western, Shaukeiwan, and Yaumatei. There are oil tankers and timber carriers and freighters, and cruise ships that berth at Ocean Terminal so that passengers can disembark directly into shopping.

Nearly 100,000 smaller ships engage in what used to be called the "country trade" along the south China coast and Pearl River Delta. Traditional boats, called "junks" after a Malay term, were two-masted

vessels with a sharp bow and high stern galley. They came in dozens of different regional styles, tailored to the peculiarities of different waters and the demands of work. Best of all, though now virtually extinct, were the oceangoing junks with their great bat-winged sails. The stock Hong Kong shot of junk backed by skyscrapers is no longer authentic: the only remaining junk is rented out for parties and film shoots.

Then there's the purely local traffic: the chugging old Star Ferries and vehicular ferries, the sleek hydrofoils and jetfoils bound for Macau, the hovercrafts whizzing out to Tuen Mun and Tsuen Wan. Holidays add dragon boats and pleasure craft to the mix, and every day, police vessels scurry about maintaining order.

Watching the boats come and go is one of the simple pleasures of Hong Kong. Best views are from the Tsimshatsui waterfront promenade or Edinburgh Place. Ferries to the outlying islands provide another perspective as they glide through the harbor en route to Lantau, Lamma, or Cheung Chau, while special tour boats concentrate solely on Victoria Harbour's charms.

The modern harbor has shrunk significantly from its original size. A long series of reclamation projects have encroached upon it, culminating with the ongoing effort to extend Hong Kong Island's northern shoreline another 330 meters. Local wits suggest that the logical end of the process would be a complete harbor reclamation, which would eliminate the hassles of ferry transport, provide plenty of new building space, and erase the guilt of water pollution.

WW II (it was promptly renamed the Toa Hotel). The hotel reopened under its own name in 1946. Despite periodic rumors of demolition, the dignified stone edifice remains one of Hong Kong's oldest landmarks. It's not been left unchanged, however: a 30-story tower newly plopped atop its midsection has added several dozen more rooms and a high-priced office block.

Step in to admire the hotel's ornate lobby, with gilt moldings on the ceilings, pillars, and cornices and a string quartet playing for afternoon tea (served 3-6:30 p.m.). Discreet engraved signs advise "appropriate dress": no plastic thongs allowed, and no sports shoes or jeans in the lobby after 7 p.m., please. The attached shopping arcade features names like Van Cleef & Arpels, Hermes, Cartier, Gucci, and Tiffany.

New World Centre and Signal Hill

Farther down Salisbury Road is New World Centre, an office/shopping complex with a Japanese department store, hotel, nightclub, restaurants, and a supermarket. The clock over the south entrance springs to life on the hour, as mechanical figures emerge from recessed doors in the granite facade for a three-minute show.

Across the road, **Signal Hill Garden** (迅號山公園) is almost invisible, wedged atop a rocky bluff well above street level. (Access is from Middle Road, past the Mariner's Club.) The steepish climb makes for few visitors. It's a nice quiet place for a picnic, with woods, a small pavilion, partial harbor views, and some old cannons, now aimed squarely at New World Centre. From the tall mast atop the hill, a hollow copper ball was once dropped daily to signal the time to ships anchored in the harbor.

The Regent 麗晶酒店

The red-marble Regent Hotel rivals the Peninsula and the Mandarin in elegance. It was built in the late '70s on a wedge of reclaimed land. The spectacular glassed-in lobby was a concession to the *feng shui* dragons said to sweep down from Kowloon's hills to bathe in the harbor here each morning. Stop in the glass-walled coffeeshop jutting out over the water, or have a drink in the bar. The **waterfront promenade** behind the Regent offers fabulous waterfront views and runs all the way to Hung Hom.

NATHAN ROAD 彌敦道

HKTA has dubbed it Hong Kong's "Golden Mile." Other, more cynical observers call it a "notorious tourist honey trap." Nathan Road is one unbroken line of shops, boutiques, and hotels ranging from the gloomy to the glittery.

When Governor Matthew Nathan ordered its development shortly after the turn of the century, the road was a banyan-lined lane leading to nowhere, so wide and straight and empty it was known as Nathan's Folly. Today it offers every imaginable object for sale: clothing, footwear, jewelry, watches, cameras, and electronic goods, interspersed with an enormous variety of restaurants, bars and pubs, hotels, and nightclubs. It's a shopping extravaganza, complete with pushy shopkeepers and street vendors sidling up to profer fake Rolexes. Acres of camera and electronics shops aim squarely at the tourist market: few locals would put up with the service, which is some of the rudest on earth.

Between the uncivilized shopkeepers, frequent ripoffs, and not-very-low prices, Nathan Road is not the place to shop, but to view the crowds you'd think it was. Some shoppers exhibit the glazed look of people overwhelmed by choices and driven by consumerism. One could almost wish for a warning to flash out occasionally over its neon signs: THIS IS NOT ALL THERE IS TO HONG KONG—although the neon signs here don't flash, lest aircraft mistake the road for the runway of the nearby airport.

Explore the web of side streets branching off from Nathan Road: mazes of shops and arcades from the tatty to the elite. The area to the west, including Lock and Hankow roads, is particularly tourist-oriented, with lots of camera, electronics, and silk stores.

The side roads to the east—Kimberley, Cameron, and especially Granville—are frequented by locals and are full of fashion outlets and overrun shops selling cheapish clothing, mostly women's. The Canto-pop is unbearably loud, the clothes are heaped in untidy piles, and you can't try anything on, but there are many bargains to be found.

CHUNGKING MANSIONS:
THE ARCHETYPAL EXPERIENCE

Chungking Mansions rank high on the list of archetypal experiences for the Asian budget traveler. Crouched on a chunk of prime real estate at 36-44 Nathan Rd., the building epitomizes the word seedy. Inside is a maze of shops, flats, guesthouses, sweatshops, curry restaurants, and travel agencies, plus nearly 100 guesthouses, providing the biggest cluster of cheap accommodations in Hong Kong. Stop in and take a look, if only for the unforgettable experience of crowding into one of its dirty, rickety, ancient elevators and praying it will take you safely up and down.

Built in 1962, Chungking Mansions enjoyed a brief stint as the tallest building in Tsimshatsui. Quickly, though, it degenerated into a center for gambling, drugs, and prostitution, the latter accelerated by the arrival of American servicemen on leave. In the '70s the Indians moved in, followed by an assortment of Asian and African workers. Then came the budget travelers, desperate for a cheap bed in expensive Hong Kong.

Today Chungking Mansions is a sort of international arcade of the poor, a refuge for illegal workers from India, Pakistan, Nepal, the Philippines, Nigeria, and Thailand, who live here for as little as HK$30 a day. "Sleaze City" blared the headline of a local magazine article, which described Chungking Mansions as "one of Hong Kong's most squalid public buildings, a home for whores, fly-by-night businessmen and illegal immigrants." It was not exaggerating.

Different nationalities congregate in different blocks. "A" Block is the cleanest and closest to the main entrance: here are plenty of Chinese-run guesthouses for Western travelers, averaging HK$250-300 for a tiny room with a bath and maybe a TV; HK$100 for a dorm bed.

"B" Block has a few guesthouses and more cheap restaurants. "C" Block is favored by Nepalis. A good number of the "guesthouses" here are brothels, where rooms are rented for no longer than 20 minutes. "D" Block is full of cheap, crowded guesthouses catering mainly to Asians, while "E" Block houses the Nigerian community.

The basement, originally intended to serve as a car park, is stuffed with shops, most owned by Indians. Plenty of curry restaurants ("mess clubs") serve excellent cheap food: the only drawback to late-night dining is that dining rooms become staff dormitories after 10 p.m.

Chungking Mansions' very setup is designed to evade responsibility. The building is divided into five 17-story blocks, carved up into 600 separately owned units. With ownership fragmented into individual lots, accountability is a major stumbling block to attempted cleanups. In addition, the Chungking Mansion Inc. Chinese owners don't get on with many of the Indian renters, and blame them (and the prevalent subcontinental habit of spitting) for keeping the property values down.

Veteran Asian travelers who simultaneously loved and hated the mansion's vivid imitation of Tenement Hell will be stunned to learn Chungking's guesthouses have recently cleaned up their act. Pressured by a 1993 government crackdown on fire-safety regulations, many places were closed for months for repairs. Some vanished for good: those that reopened are markedly improved, with clean, newly painted rooms, new furniture, clean sheets, and big, bright windows. Prices have risen as well, but it's worth it to be able to walk down stairwells free (for the moment, at least) of rats, cockroaches, and ancient piles of garbage.

Jamia Masjid Mosque 清真寺

This marble-domed building flanked by four minarets was built in 1984 to replace an 1896 mosque constructed for use by British Indian troops. It's the largest of three mosques in the SAR. Hong Kong has 50,000 Muslims, around half of them Chinese (Arab traders brought Islam to China centuries ago). Casual visitors are not allowed inside, but you can call 2724-0095 to arrange a tour.

Kowloon Park 九龍公園

Breathe a sigh of relief in this retreat, which is big (14 hectares) but easy to miss, raised up above the west side of Nathan Road. The park has been developed (some would say overdeveloped) by the Hong Kong Jockey Club. It's crammed with different sections, resulting in a dis-unified feel: various gardens, an indoor Olympic pool, an outdoor Sculpture Walk full of earnest art students sketching away, a maze fashioned of clipped hedges, and an aviary where flamingos preen gracefully against a backdrop of high-rise towers. Amateur music performances are sometimes held here on Sunday afternoons. The park is open 6:30 a.m.-11:30 p.m. daily; admission is free.

Hong Kong Museum of History 香港博物館

Housed in a former British Army barracks inside Kowloon Park, this well-put-together museum counteracts the Western bias of most historical accounts, which imply that Hong Kong's history began with the British. The emphasis here is

Tang dynasty tomb guardian

on local cultures, ethnic groups, and traditions. Exhibits lead visitors through Hong Kong's beginnings as a Neolithic settlement, through its development as an Asian trade entrepôt, and into modern times. Displays include a restored junk, a re-creation of an old market street, and a traditional Chinese apothecary, complete with odoriferous herbs, moved intact from Central in 1980. Old photos and a slick slide show round out the scene. The museum is open Mon.-Thurs. and Saturday 10 a.m.-6 p.m., Sunday and holidays 1-6 p.m.; admission is HK$10, HK$5 for kids and seniors.

TSIMSHATSUI EAST AND HUNG HOM 尖東, 紅磡

This district's parade of glittery hotels, shopping centers, and giant nightclubs sprang more or less fully formed from the sea in the early '80s. Everything east of Chatham Road is built on newly reclaimed land and is bright, shiny, and flashy. Hongkongers seem to prefer it to Tsimshatsui, which is more of a tourist hangout. A hoverferry runs between here and Central from the small dock behind the Shangri-La Hotel.

Even if you're not into Tsimshatsui East's expensive consumption or big Japanese-style nightclubs, don't miss the **Tsimshatsui East Promenade** running from behind the Regent Hotel all the way into Hung Hom. It's a favorite stroll with locals, especially during the holiday season (Christmas to Chinese New Year), when buildings on both sides of the harbor are lit up with elaborate displays. Year-round it's full of joggers and fishermen reeling in dubious-looking objects from the polluted harbor, and on Saturday nights the more secluded corners become a lover's lane.

Hong Kong Science Museum 香港科學館

This is Hong Kong's newest museum, orient-

ed to children but fascinating for adults as well. If you're coming from Tsimshatsui, the tail end of Granville Road leads right up to the striking broad plaza fronting the museum.

The pink-and-gray building holds some 500 exhibits, more than half of them hands-on demonstrations of how things work. View the 22-meter-high "Energy Machine," challenge a computer, or play in the video laboratory. There's a robot cyclist, a room full of distorting mirrors, even a display showing the amount of food a person consumes in a year. An excellent shop sells educational toys, posters, models, and experimental kits.

The Science Museum is open Tues.-Fri. 1-9 p.m., weekends and holidays 10 a.m.-9 p.m. Admission is HK$25, HK$15 for children and seniors.

HUNG HOM

Pedestrian walkways lead off from the Tsimshatsui East Promenade into Hung Hom, though the route loses its charm once it leaves the waterfront. Major landmarks include the 12,500-

seat **Hong Kong Coliseum,** a pillarless inverted pyramid hosting sporting matches and concerts, and the **Kowloon-Canton Railway Station** (九廣鐵路), the architecturally uninspired replacement for the old waterfront station torn down in 1978. This is the place for KCR trains to the New Territories or regular trains to Guangzhou. From there you can continue farther into China, or even reach London eventually via the Trans-Siberian Express.

Hung Hom's minor attractions lie north and east of the station. **Whampoa Gardens** (黃埔花園) is a housing and shopping complex at the corner of Hung Hom Road and Tak Fung Street, a 10-minute walk east of the Hung Hom Ferry Pier. Across the street is **The Whampoa,** a 100-meter-long concrete ship-shaped shopping mall that looks eerily authentic, especially when it's lit up at night. Inside are shops, restaurants, a movie theater, and a kids' entertainment arcade.

Ten minutes' walk north on Man Yue Street is **Kaiser Estates** (凱旋工商中心), three big blocks crammed with factory outlets. In the '80s the complex attained near-legendary proportions among power shoppers who bragged of the fantastic bargains they found on its grotty premises. Today most of the outlets have been jazzed up into boutiques for the tourist buses which disgorge in front, and the bargains, while still available, are not what they used to be.

Getting There

On a hot day, Hung Hom can be a bit of a hike even from Tsimshatsui East. Bus 2K runs from the Star Ferry to the KCR Railway Station (take the 1K for the return). Minibus 1 runs from the Star Ferry to Granville Square in Tsimshatsui East; Minibus 6 between Tsimshatsui (Hankow Road) and Whampoa Garden. The nicest way to get there is via the Star Ferries which run between the Hung Hom Ferry Pier and Central, Wanchai, and North Point.

YAUMATEI AND MONGKOK 油麻地 , 旺角

North of Jordan Road, Tsimshatsui's glitter fades into earthier neighborhoods of crowded tenements, busy local shops, street-side restaurants, and small shrines. The clatter of mahjong tiles floats out from upstairs rooms, and drying laundry hangs from the bamboo poles projecting from every open window. Even the street names suddenly change from English to Chinese. This area is not yet gentrified, and it's fascinating to wander the streets and observe the fundamentals of everyday life in a Chinese city.

The grid pattern of the streets indicate they were built largely on reclaimed land. The name *yau ma tei,* "sesame plant place," refers to early farming in the area. After the British acquired Kowloon, Yaumatei developed as a boatbuilding and repair center, and remnants of this trade linger along the streets that branch the old typhoon shelter, particularly Man Cheong Street.

Built after a huge 1915 typhoon devastated Kowloon's boat people population, the shelter once housed thousands of boats, including some famous floating one-woman brothels. The West Kowloon Reclamation Project is busy filling in the area, creating 330 hectares of new land which will be used for residential and commercial development, including a new Airport Railway station, and add some much-needed breathing and recreational space to this crowded area. The new typhoon shelter incorporated into here includes anchorage for the lighters that unload cargo vessels.

YAUMATEI TOUR

The local shopping district between Jordan Road and Kansu Street is well worth exploring, packed with shops selling richly embroidered wedding outfits, big wooden chopping blocks, and eight-sided *feng shui* mirrors. Other stores supply ritual paraphernalia for household shrines—red wooden altars, images of deities, brass incense burners, and permanent "candles" with red electric bulbs. The HKTA booklet *Yaumatei Walking Tour* describes the area in detail. Take the MTR to either the Jordan or Yaumatei stops and investigate the blocks west of Nathan Road.

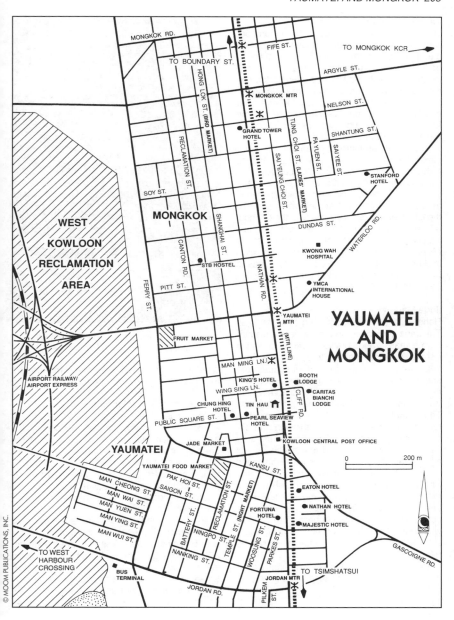

Tin Hau Temple 天后廟

Its main shrine is dedicated to the patron goddess of seafarers, but this temple embraces an exceptionally comprehensive collection of deities. Like most of Hong Kong's now-landlocked temples to Tin Hau, it originally stood on the waterfront in the days before reclamation extended the shoreline. It's located at the far end of Yaumatei's public square, in the daytime full of old men reading newspapers, playing Chinese chess, or furtively tippling.

The middle and largest building in the complex is Tin Hau's, with the usual giant incense coils smouldering above the entrance. Deities inside include the 60 Tai Sui gods, one for each year of the Chinese cycle, with No. 60 appearing at the top left and No. 1 at the bottom right. To the left are temples to Shing Wong, the city god, and To Tei, the earth god; to the right a *she tan,* reserved for fortune-tellers who interpret the *chim.* Look for the open-air collection of porcelain images resting beneath a giant banyan tree in front of the temple: women pray here for the health of their children.

Jade Market 玉器市場

Hong Kong is the world's leading center for jade. The trade centers around the streets surrounding Yaumatei's Jade Market, a permanent affair installed under the Kansu Street overpass. Over 400 vendors here sell jade in all shapes and shades: bracelets, beads, loose stones, statues, amulets, and protective and decorative devices. A few stalls sell pearls, mainly from Japan. The market is frequented by locals as much as tourists, and it's fun to prowl through and observe the customers—old women having their hands vigorously massaged so they can slide on a jade bracelet, or sorting intently though heaps of stones in search of an overlooked treasure. Some vendors still bargain in the old silent fashion, indicating price by pressing a certain number of fingers on a client's forearm—a technique developed to foil eavesdroppers. Formerly this was conducted with hands slipped inside wide-sleeved garments; today it takes place behind folded-up newspapers.

Prices range from HK$7 to no limit. Major purchases demand bargaining and a good eye, but it's fun to simply walk through and maybe pick up some inexpensive trinkets. The market

entrance to main shrine, Tin Hau Temple, Yaumatei

operates daily 10 a.m.-3:30 or 4 p.m., though many vendors begin packing up after lunch.

Reclamation Street Market 新填地街

Across Kansu Street, the indoor Yaumatei Food Market is redolent with odors of meat and fish by early afternoon. More entertaining is the bustling open-air market on Reclamation Street, with gilded coconuts, eight kinds of tofu, and flattened ducks. Prime shopping hours are 9-11 a.m. and again around 4-5 p.m. The traditional Cantonese housewife shops twice a day to ensure maximum freshness.

More jade shops are scattered about this neighborhood if you want to continue your pursuit. Two blocks east is Temple Street, dormant in the daytime but coming alive after dusk with its famous night market. Also explore **Saigon Street,** with its pawn shops and mahjong players; **Woosung Street,** the abode of Chinese herbalists and a snake-seller, and **Shanghai**

Street, the area's old main street and business center. Cross Jordan Road to find the busy local clothing market on **Bowring Street,** which runs right into the Jordan MTR station.

Temple Street Night Market 廟街

This is one of Hong Kong's absolute must-sees, a giant bazaar combined with a Chinese cultural show. Temple Street is just another Kowloon road in the daytime, but vendors start setting up around dusk and by nightfall the stalls are so crowded there's hardly room to move.

Visit from 6 p.m. on; by 9 p.m., it's in full swing.

The impromptu bazaar has its origins as an evening fair for working-class men, conducted by lantern- light until the 1970s. Now tourists and locals alike mill past row after row of T-shirts, jackets, belts, silks, socks, fake designer goods, watches, tapes, gadgets, and tables of shrilling alarm clocks. The small shops behind the stalls offer more bargains, and in quiet corners mild pornography and naked-lady cigarette lighters are proffered.

The *dai pai dong*s set up at strategic inter-

KNOW YOUR JADE

Jade is as valuable as gold or diamonds to the Chinese, who value its smooth texture as much as its lustrous appearance. Tradition attributes all sorts of magical qualities to the stone. It's said to absorb impurities, slow the effects of aging, and protect against evil influences. Beyond that, the wearer is believed to absorb its excellence, becoming more humane, intelligent, and brave.

To the Chinese, jade symbolizes the perfection of all virtues. "It is soft, smooth and shining like kindness," wrote Confucius in the *Li Ki.* "It is hard, fine and strong, like intelligence; its edges seem sharp, but do not cut, like justice; it hangs down to the ground like humility; when struck, it gives a clear, ringing sound, like music; the stains in it which are not hidden and add to its beauty are like truthfulness; its brightness is like heaven, while its firm substance, born of mountains and the water, is like earth."

Circular jade discs pierced by a hole *(pi)* were often placed with bodies in ancient Chinese tombs; they served as symbols of heaven and its celestial power. In the Han dynasty, the dead were encased in suits of jade squares linked with golden thread. Later, jade was worked into pendants worn on a girdle. Today women wear it as bangles, men in the form of amulets or rings.

An exceptionally hard stone, jade is extremely difficult to carve. Craftsmen use iron or steel tools and an abrasive paste to fashion jewelry, banquet ware, incense burners, and all sorts of vessels. Jade statues rely on traditional symbolism: dragons represent power, deer wealth, tigers good luck.

In Chinese jade is called *yu,* a term used for all semiprecious stones. The word "jade" comes from the Portuguese *mijada,* "kidneys," because Chinese reported to early explorers that the stone warded off kidney disease.

Loosely speaking, jade describes perhaps 170 different varieties of stones and colors. There are two main categories. Nephrite, sometimes called "old" jade, comes from Siberia, New Zealand, and Canada. Extremely hard, it's often used for carvings and beads. Colors range from off-white (called "muttonfat") to dark green. The yellowish or greyish brown shade is called "tomb" or "buried" jade and is caused by long burial in the yellow earth of China. Jadeite ("new" jade) is a rarer and more valuable stone. It comes mainly from Burma, and appears in all hues: white, apple-green, brown, red, orange, yellow, and lavender.

Jade appears in over 100 shades of green— spring, emerald, "moss-in-snow." Cantonese favor green jade, while northern Chinese prefer white. The most valued hue is emerald (often called "Chinese jade") or a bright apple-green. You'll save money if you pick another color. While the price of jade can equal that of diamonds among the Chinese, it's not nearly as valuable on the world market.

Serious jade-buying requires study and experience: jade is found all over Hong Kong, but quality stones are expensive and fairly rare. Plenty of other types of stone can be passed off as jade, including bowenite, quartz, feldspar, serpentine, and jasper. Sometimes these are dyed to improve the color, or stained brown with tea and sold as an antique. Watch out for thin slices of real jade glued onto another type of stone. Another clue: lick a fingertip and touch it to the stone. Real jade is cold, plastic is warm.

WARDROBE BARGAINS

Once upon a time Hong Kong's factory outlets were actually located inside factories, and shopping in them was a real adventure. Word of the bargains spread, and now it seems every second boutique calls itself a factory outlet, though its prices belie the term. Many authentic outlets have evolved into boutiques; others remain satisfyingly grungy and cheap. Some call themselves "fashion clearing-houses." Who cares, as long as the price is right?

The virtue of these places is that they sell export clothes at nearly wholesale prices. Items can be excess stock or overruns in mint condition, or quality-control rejects with flaws ranging from a tiny slub to a broken zipper. You never know which category an item falls into, so examine everything carefully, especially as returns are seldom allowed.

Usually there are no dressing rooms, though tape measures are provided for approximate fitting. Sizes are generally Western (i.e., large); though local labels mixed in may confuse the issue—a Hong Kong "small" dress bears no relation to a U.S. "small."

Fashions are subject to annual trends. One year denim shirts are everywhere; the next it's tie-dyed polyester. There is always a good range of casual clothes, with labels from The Gap, The Limited, Calvin Klein, and Banana Republic—though labels are not always applied to genuine garments. Some

items bear retail price tags, inspiring great satisfaction when you get a US$44 pair of trousers for HK$40 (again, though, the tags may be misapplied). Stock turns over rapidly, and the best shops are worth repeat visits every few days.

Most accessible are the joyfully crowded shops along Granville Road in Tsimshatsui, where shoppers rummage to the beat of blaring Canto-pop. Even cheaper shops are scattered about Wanchai and Causeway Bay—just wander about and look for the open storefronts revealing messy heaps of clothing. The shops along **Fa Yuen Street** are great for kid's clothes; so are a few stalls at Stanley Market.

For more upscale clothing, including silk, leather, and cashmere, check out the shops in the Pedder Building (12 Pedder St., Central); Star House (3 Salisbury Rd., Tsimshatsui); and the Sands Building (17 Hankow Rd., Tsimshatsui). Factory outlets in Lai Chi Kok are especially good for men's clothes, porcelain, and leather.

If you're at all serious, pick up a copy of the pocket-sized *The Complete Guide to Hong Kong Factory Bargains*, which has annually updated maps, addresses in Chinese, telephone numbers and hours for dozens of shops. Some outlets advertise in the classified section of the *South China Morning Post*.

sections provide a welcome break from the hustle. Dine on cheap shellfish and beer and watch the crowds surge past. There are bargains to be found, especially on men's clothes, but it's fun just to stroll through and observe the crowds.

When the stalls thin out, the street theater starts. Along Pak Hoi Street fortune-tellers ply their trade by lantern light, ready to read palms or faces and reveal past lives and future prospects. In tune with the times, one advertises "Advice for nice home and good career after emigration."

Fortune-tellers follow 500-year-old Chinese texts, which hold that facial features reveal more than the palm. Lines on the hand can change with circumstance, but the face does not. The science of physiognomy recognizes 48 different types of eye patterns, eight basic facial shapes, and a multitude of archetypal eyebrows and earlobes. If you're interested in exploring

further, look for a fortune-teller with a long line of customers, indicating he's a respected reader.

In makeshift stalls across from the Wilson Car Park, amateur Cantonese opera singers hold forth, without the elaborate makeup and costumes of full-scale productions, but still accompanying the words with stylized hand gestures. They are backed by orchestras of elderly men on traditional instruments—moon-shaped banjos *(yue chin)*, percussion instruments, xylophones, and dragon-headed fiddles.

Past here is a public square filled with old men drinking and playing chess. The street stalls continue, now specializing in housewares and toys and gadgets rather than clothes, with Nepali vendors selling silver jewelry and gilt statues.

Be aware that Temple Street is a favorite with pickpockets who ply their trade in the dense crowd. To get there, take the MTR to Jordan and walk west three blocks.

MONGKOK 旺角

Like Yaumatei, Mongkok is nitty-gritty real Hong Kong, and it's far enough from Tsimshatsui to be really off the tourist track. It once held the record for world's most densely populated urban area—a fact you will fully appreciate after slithering through the Mongkok MTR station during rush hour.

Bird Market 雀鳥市場
Narrow Hong Lok Street is packed with everything a bird or its owner might desire: specially toasted seeds packed in vials, fresh crickets imported from China, delicate porcelain water bowls, and bamboo cages, ornately carved and laquered like miniature palaces. There are birds too, stacked in high-rise cages mirroring Mongkok's apartment blocks: finches, tiny sparrows, mynahs, big white cockatoos, colorful parrots, and various nondescript Chinese songbirds, valued for their song rather than appearance. Birds are considered an elegant and refined pet, as well as a practical one in close quarters. Owners—invariably elderly men—dote on their charges, taking them for morning strolls in parks and serving up live grasshoppers and special honey drinks.

The market runs from around 9 a.m. to past dusk; try to visit in the morning. Take the MTR to Mongkok and exit onto Nelson Street; Hong Lok Street is two blocks west. You'll hear the twittering before you see the birds.

Ladies' Market 女人街
If you liked the shopping at Temple Street, you'll want to visit the Tung Choi Street Ladies' Market (Nui Yan Kai in Cantonese) for more of the same. The focus is ladies' wear—lacy underwear dangling from stalls seems to be a specialty—but there are also kid's and men's clothes and all sorts of accessories. The market starts in the early afternoon and continues till around 11 p.m., getting bigger and better as the day goes on. Take the Nelson Street exit of the Mongkok MTR station and walk two blocks east to Tung Choi Street.

Flower Market
Further north, Flower Market Road near the Prince Edward MTR is filled with hundreds of small stalls selling flowers, a colorful sight in the urban gloom.

NEW KOWLOON

Kowloon proper ends at Boundary Street, which runs in a ruler-straight line east-west. Until the 1898 acquisition of the New Territories, the border with China here was demarcated by a bamboo fence. In a technical sense, everything north of it belongs to the New Territories, but practically speaking the neighborhoods immediately north are an extension of Kowloon's seething urban masses. The attractions are minor, but the few temples and museums scattered about are worth visiting if only to glimpse how most of Hong Kong lives.

Shamshuipo 深水涉
This neighborhood holds the current Hong Kong record for highest population density: 255,000 per square km. As you might imagine, there's not much to see besides extremely crowded housing blocks, and a big, wriggly food market around Kweilin and Ki Lung streets, near the Shamshuipo MTR station.

The main attraction here, very minor though nicely presented, is **Lei Cheng Uk Han Tomb** (李鄭屋古墓), Hong Kong's oldest historic monument. The unearthing of this Han dynasty tomb in 1955 during construction of the surrounding housing estate drew huge crowds. It's believed to have been built around A.D. 220 for a Chinese officer from a local garrison.

Grave robbers long ago removed any valuables, but various pottery and bronze objects meant for use in the afterlife have been un-

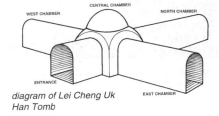

diagram of Lei Cheng Uk Han Tomb

earthed and are displayed inside the museum, along with lengthy explanations. Behind the building is the brick tomb itself, set in a hillside and preserved in a glass-walled, temperature-controlled cement vault. It's all about as interesting as it sounds, and is open Mon.-Wed. and Friday 10 a.m.-1 p.m. and 2-6 p.m.; Sunday and holidays 1-6 p.m. From the Cheung Sha Wan MTR station, follow the signs two blocks up to 41 Tonkin Street and the Lei Cheng Uk Resettlement Estate. Bus 2 runs from the Star Ferry terminal past Tonkin Street.

Shamshuipo is also home to the infamous **Golden Arcade Shopping Centre** (黃金商場), a three-story building crammed with over 100 shops selling cut-rate computer clones and bootleg software and CD-ROMS at ridiculously cheap prices. Take the MTR to Shamshuipo and exit onto the corner of Kweilin and Fuk Wah streets.

offerings arrayed on table, Wong Tai Sin Temple, Kowloon

KERRY MORAN

Lai Chi Kok 荔枝角

This neighborhood is reached by Bus 6A from the Star Ferry or a 10-minute walk from the Mei Foo MTR station. Tour groups crowd into **Sung Dynasty Village** (宋城), a small but well-done Olde China theme park re-creating the milieu of the Sung dynasty (A.D. 960-1279). A tree-lined stream is lined with elegantly carved pavilions and shops. Villagers in period costumes demonstrate crafts and put on periodic performances—acrobatics, noodle-making, martial arts, a Chinese wedding. There's a "House of the Rich Man" (air-conditioned, even) furnished with antiques, and a pricey restaurant serving genuine Sung dynasty dishes, accompanied by a "genuine Sung dynasty floor show." Downstairs, the **Waxworks Museum** features famous figures from 13 dynasties.

The complex is open 10 a.m.-8:30 p.m. weekdays, when admission is HK$120, HK$65 for children. Weekend hours are noon-5:30 p.m. Call 2741-5111 for details and performance schedules.

Right next door is **Lai Chi Kok Amusement Park** (荔園遊樂場), a purely local attraction with rides, ice-skating, and roller rinks, and evening performances of Chinese opera. Admission is free from Sung Dynasty Village; otherwise it's HK$15, HK$10 for kids. Open weekdays noon-9:30 p.m., Saturday 11-10:30 p.m., Sunday and holidays 10 a.m.-9:30 p.m.

Around the Old Airport

North-central Kowloon is dominated by housing estates and has little of interest. **Kowloon Tong** (九龍塘) was the site of the first New Town, built in 1957. The MTR station here serves as interchange with the KCR line. A temple at the nearby Sau Mau Ping housing estate is famous for a spectacular medium, who falls into trance to embody the mischievous Monkey God immortalized in the Chinese classic *The Journey to the West.* Kowloon Tong is also the site of **Festival Walk,** a new shopping and entertainment mall billed as "the Pacific Place of Kowloon," with top restaurants and a ten-screen cinema.

Next over is **Kowloon City** (九龍城), with a big day market on Lion Rock Road. Ferries run between North Point on Hong Kong Island and the **Kowloon City Ferry Pier** (九龍城碼頭). Very nearby, incongruous for such a built-up

THE WALLED CITY

Hong Kong's most notorious pocket of vice and squalor went out with a bang in 1993, with the demolition of Kowloon's old Walled City. In its long history it had progressed from quaintly scenic Chinese outpost to horrific slum, and on to complete obliteration.

The enclave began in pre-British days as a Chinese military outpost. After the British took over Hong Kong Island a granite-walled fortress was constructed, complete with watchtowers and cannon emplacements. An inexplicable slip in the New Territories lease of 1898 left the area under Chinese jurisdiction, and while British troops evicted Chinese officials the following year, the situation remained ambiguous. The Walled City was left as an autonomous anomaly, an unregulated plot of Chinese soil in the British-run New Territories.

Its old stone towers and narrow streets served as a quaint tourist attraction for many years. Most of the older buildings were demolished in the 1930s; the granite walls were pulled down under the Japanese occupation and the stones used for the new airport runway at Kai Tak.

For a while it seemed the Walled City would fade away of its own accord, but the thousands of Chinese refugees who jammed into it after the war gave it a new life. The area became a no man's land, a haven for all kinds of criminals and Triad members, "a cesspool of iniquity, with heroin divans, brothels and everything unsavoury," lamented Governor Alexander Grantham.

The Walled City had no zoning, no restrictions, and no laws. It grew into a crowded, dark warren of overlapping buildings, so closely packed that the old roads became tunnels, too narrow for vehicles. Inside were sweatshops, factories, and small industries, producing among other things 80% of the fish balls consumed in the territory. Tiny apartments housing far too many people were built without windows—there was nothing to look at, and the buildings were so close together no sunlight penetrated into the place. In short, the Walled City (it kept the name even after the walls were gone) was a supreme slum, an apocryphal urban horror story.

That's what it looked like to outsiders, at least. Inside, life was surprisingly orderly given the lack of external control. Plenty of normal people, including illegal immigrants, led ordinary lives in this unregulated setting. A genuine community existed here, entirely separate from Hong Kong. This aspect is illuminated in the book *City of Darkness* (the title is the literal translation of *Hak Nam,* the Cantonese name for the city).

Things might have continued indefinitely had Britain and China not reached an agreement in 1987 to rid themselves of this eyesore. By late 1992 some 33,000 residents had been compensated and resettled. The old buildings went up in a gigantic blast of dynamite in 1993, and a park was developed on the sight. With a layout based on the design of a classical Southern Chinese garden, it preserves architectural remnants like a Qing Dynasty almshouse and the city's old South Gate.

area, the single runway of **Kai Tak Airport** projects into the harbor. When it's replaced by the new airport at Lantau in 1998, the airport will be converted to housing and badly needed "solution spaces" to relieve the pressure of Kowloon's urban crowding.

Wong Tai Sin Temple 黃大仙

By far the best and busiest temple in Hong Kong, the Taoist shrine of Wong Tai Sin stands in the midst of a crowded housing estate of the same name, barely one km north of Kai Tak. The "Great God Wong" is the most powerful member of Hong Kong's pantheon, said to be especially good at curing illnesses and bestowing luck at the races. Recommendations from satisfied worshippers have made him a sort of village god for all Hong Kong, and three million visitors a year flock to his temple. Sunday and holidays are the most active times, when the yard is full of eye-stinging smoke from paper offerings and incense.

The cult originated with a portrait of the deity brought from Guangdong in 1915 and installed in a Wanchai temple. The image was moved to Kowloon in 1921, and the present large and lively temple complex was built in 1973.

From the signed MTR exit, walk down a lane lined with stalls selling colorful offerings—enormous round apples and oranges, joss sticks, and spirit money. Explore the long corridors of the "fortune-telling and oblation arcade," where several dozen face- and palm-readers practice their ancient arts. A few of them speak English and will for a hefty fee deliver a brief overview of what the future holds for you. Their reports invariably focus on money: health, family, and romance are purely secondary concerns.

The main temple is usually off-limits to the public, but the front doors are left open so the faithful can view the portrait of Wong Tai Sin, a shepherd boy who joined the ranks of the Taoist Immortals. The square facing it is crowded with devotees carefully arranging offerings and shaking out bamboo fortune sticks. Elderly women in black *samfu* kneel beside blue-jeaned young women and businessmen: Wong Tai Sin appeals to all. The *chim* can also be used to obtain a prescription from the Chinese medical clinic in the compound. Near it is a row of taps dispensing curative holy water (which, miraculously, flows from city lines).

Other shrines on the grounds include a "Three Saints Hall" dedicated to Kwun Yam, Kwan Ti, and Lui Tung Bun, a memorial hall with ancestor tablets, and shrines to Confucius and the Buddha. Behind the main temple is a painstakingly landscaped "Good Wish Garden" (entrance HK$2) with the odd-shaped rocks, waterfall, and zig-zag bridge typical of a Chinese landscape, and a replica of Beijing's Nine Dragon Wall.

Lei Yue Mun 鯉魚門

This former old fishing village and smugglers' lair guards the eastern entrance to Victoria Harbour and is set at the narrowest point between Kowloon and Hong Kong Island. The name means "Carp-Fish Gate." Lei Yue Mun is the closest and biggest of Hong Kong's fresh seafood specialty dining sites. The constant parade of tour buses means prices are high, though not unreasonable if you keep an eye out on what you're buying. It's a pleasant place to come out to admire the city lights and have a good meal.

The interesting part of town boils down to a single long street lined with restaurants and shops selling fresh seafood. This is participatory dining. Chose what you want (be sure to check the price first), have it weighed, and take it over to a promising restaurant to be cooked. **Hoi Tin Garden Restaurant** has an outdoor terrace overlooking the panorama of ships and neon signs.

Until fairly recently Lei Yue Mun was accessible only by boat, and a sampan through the harbor remains the most entertaining means of arrival. Take Bus 14C from the Kwun Tong MTR to its terminus at the Sam Ka Tsuen typhoon shelter. From here, sampans run to Lei Yue Mun. Or, catch the ferry from Sai Wan Ho on Hong Kong Island over to Sam Ka Tsuen.

THE NEW TERRITORIES

It's called the "The Land Between"—literally between urban Hong Kong and the rest of China, but also suspended between urban and rural, modernity and antiquity. The New Territories serve as an escape valve from the seething turmoil of the city. The British leased this 740-square-km chunk of mainland from China in 1898 for 99 years. The lease's impending expiration date was the direct impetus for the return of all Hong Kong, for the green hills and reservoirs of the New Territories supply Hong Kong's fresh water, and the city could not survive without it.

Technically speaking, the term "New Territories" includes everything north of Boundary Street in Kowloon up to the Chinese border. This chapter takes as the dividing line the Lion Rock Hills, which form a natural division between urban Kowloon and the more widely scattered New Towns.

History
Between the 10th and 15th centuries this area was colonized by Cantonese peasants, many of them members of the "Five Great Clans": Tang,

Hau, Pang, Liu, and Man. Collectively these settlers were known as Punti (from *pun tei,* "local inhabitants"). They were followed in the 17th and 18th centuries by the Hakka, a wandering clan who settled on the less fertile remaining land in the northeast. By the time the British took over in 1898, the New Territories had a population of around 8,000, mostly farmers and fishermen huddled together in isolated rural communities. Life continued in traditional patterns with remarkably little interference all the way through WW II.

Great postwar changes were in store, though. Remote villages were abandoned or left to a few elderly residents, as younger residents moved to the city to take advantage of the new economic development. Fields were taken over by Chinese immigrant tenant farmers, who switched the predominant crop from rice to more lucrative vegetables. Starting in the 1970s, impressive cities emerged from the former paddy fields: the New Towns of Tsuen Wan, Tuen Mun, Yuen Long, Fanling, Sheung Shui, Tai Po, and Shatin, many of these developed on reclaimed oceanfront land.

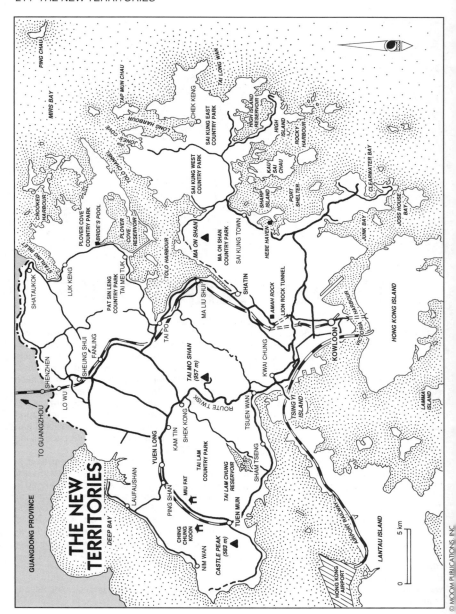

An Overview

Much of the rural New Territories is preserved in country parks, the result of a far-sighted decision made in the 1970s to provide recreational areas and guarantee water catchment areas for reservoirs. Many of the area's 14 country parks are connected by the 100-km MacLehose Trail, which traverses the region from west to east. Increasingly city dwellers are turning to the New Territories for recreation. Barbecuing has become a national sport, and on Sundays country park trails are full of happy, noisy groups of hikers. While Hong Kong's natural beauty is not likely to overwhelm visitors, there are some attractive destinations: the rugged coast of the **Sai Kung Peninsula,** isolated **Plover Cove,** the high, bare slopes of 957-meter **Tai Mo Shan,** and the Mai Po marshes near the northwest border.

The New Territories' original rural character remains in remote pockets, in duck farms and soft-eyed water buffalo and vegetable fields watered by hand. But the old rice fields have vanished entirely, replaced by more lucrative market crops like vegetables and flowers, and the huddled old villages with their ancestral halls are now overshadowed by towering high-rises.

The tone is now set by the New Territories' dynamic New Towns, miraculous cities of gigantic scale which in the past two decades have transformed the region. Eight New Towns have been built on old rural market centers, and newer developments are springing up at places like Junk Bay and Tin Shui Wai. As late as 1975, 90% of Hong Kong's population lived on Hong Kong Island and Kowloon; the New Territories had only around a half-million people. Currently its population is 2.5 million, with another million expected by 2000.

All this has been accomplished in barely 20 years, backed by huge investments and a massive government effort to relocate people from crowded urban tenements and squatter huts to high-rise towers. Living quarters are crowded,

USEFUL NEW TERRITORIES BUS ROUTES	
BUS NO.	**ROUTE**
34B	Tsuen Wan Ferry-Sham Tseng
51	Tsuen Wan Ferry-Kam Tin
53	Tsuen Wan Ferry-Yuen Long (East)
56K	Fanling-Luk Keng
59M	Tuen Mun Pier-Tsuen Wan MTR
59X	Tuen Mun Pier-Mongkok KCR
60M	Tuen Mun Town Center-Tsuen Wan MTR
60X	Tuen Mun Center-Jordan Road Ferry
64K	Yuen Long-Tai Po Market KCR
68	Yuen Long (East)-Jordan Road/Canton Road
68M	Yuen Long-Tsuen Wan MTR
68X	Yuen Long (East)-Jordan Road Ferry
75K	Tai Po KCR-Tai Mei Tuk (Plover Cove)
76K	Yuen Long-Kam Tin-Sheung Shui KCR
78K	Fanling-Shau Tau Kok-Sheung Shui KCR
91	Choi Hung MTR-Clearwater Bay
92	Choi Hung MTR-Sai Kung Town
94	Sai Kung-Pak Tam Chung-Wong Shek Pier
95R	Pak Tam Chung-Wong Shek Pier
234X	Tsuen Wan (West)-Tsimshatsui (Hankow Road)
299	Shatin-Sai Kung

and families make do with unbelievably limited space by Western standards, but most find the New Towns a better environment, offering more space, air, light, and recreational opportunities.

The New Towns' design, originally inspired by Britain's experimental New Towns, has taken time to evolve into the Chinese setting. While early developments were simply vertical concrete boxes, newer examples are marked improvements, with shopping, restaurants, and recreation areas integrated into the design to serve the entire community.

Hong Kong's urban planners are girding themselves for another gargantuan effort. Reunification with China means that 55,000 new Chinese residents will be entering Hong Kong each year, placing further strain on a system where the waiting lists for public housing are already seven years long.

Getting Around

Along with housing, an alphabet soup of transportation systems with acronyms like KCR, MRT, and LRT have been developed to serve the relocated population. The excellent transport makes it possible to explore the New Territories by day and return to your hotel in time for dinner. There's the Kowloon-Canton Railway, the Light Rail Transit system linking Tsuen Muen and Yuen Long in the west, the MTR line to Tsuen Wan, and plenty of buses, minibuses, and ferries, plus a fleet of green-and-white taxi cabs. See "Getting Around" in the Introduction for details.

HKTA's "Land Between Tour" is a popular way to cram a lot of sightseeing into one day: the current itinerary includes Cheuk Lam Sim Yuen Buddhist Monastery, Tai Mo Shan, the Luen Wo Market at Fanling, the Luk Keng bird sanctuary, Plover Cove Reservoir, Sam Mun Tsai fishing village, and Tai Po.

Ideally, though, you'll treat the region in the same way urban Hongkongers do: as a scenic escape from the pressures of urban life. Certainly a day here is essential if you want to see how most people live, and put your finger a little closer to Hong Kong's pulse. Read the descriptions and choose a trip that suits your fancy. Some suggestions:

- Take the KCR out to Shatin and the Temple of Ten Thousand Buddhas, with its mummified abbot enshrined on an altar; then continue up to Tai Po or Sheung Shui for a look at a typically bustling market and cheerful downtown.
- Hike in Plover Cove or Sai Kung country park.
- Enjoy a seafood lunch at Sai Kung Town, then bus to Wong Shek Pier to catch the ferry to the peaceful island of Tap Mun Chau, returning via the Tolo Harbour Ferry.
- Visit Tuen Mun's monasteries and explore the Ping Shan Heritage Trail.
- Hike out to Tai Long Wan in Sai Kung, undoubtedly Hong Kong's best beach.

The maps in this book should suffice for most sightseeing purposes, but serious explorers will want more detailed maps. For urban areas, consult the map books recommended in the Booklist, or Universal Publications' excellent *New Town Street Map,* which details all the major New Towns. Hikers should pick up appropriate topo sheets from the Countryside Series' 1:20,000 Survey Division maps; for short day hikes, you'll find the map boards at country park visitor centers to be sufficient.

ALONG THE KCR

The electric Kowloon-Canton Railway heading north to the border offers some of the New Territories' prettiest scenery and glimpses of rural life. The railway was completed by the British in 1911, joining the tracks to Canton. Service was suspended in the tumultous years between 1949-79. The Hong Kong portion of the system was electrified in 1983, and now provides mainly commuter service for residents of the central New Territories.

A ride down the KCR is a good choice if you've only a day to devote to the New Territories. The system is easy to use: it accepts stored-value MTR tickets and can be joined from the Kowloon Tong MTR station or the KCR terminus at Hung Hom (see "Getting Around" in the Introduction for more details).

You can get off at various New Towns, or just sit and watch the scenery flash by on the 50-minute ride out to Sheung Shui. The countryside becomes increasingly prettier and greener, the vegetable plots and fish farms interspersed with palm trees and an occasional old house, with the year of its construction emblazoned above the entrance. Stop at one of the old market towns (Tai Po Market and Sheung Shui are the best) to investigate a modern market. Traditionally held on certain days of the month, these drew not just shoppers but fortune-tellers, letter writers, and unofficial matchmakers. They still cater to the Cantonese obsession for fresh meat, fish, and produce, and the cheerful downtowns surrounding them are worth exploring.

TAI WAI 大圍

From Kowloon, the KCR ploughs through massive Lion Rock via an underground tunnel to emerge in the lush Shatin Valley. This area was once famous for its superb rice, sent all the way to the imperial table in Beijing. The first stop is the suburb of Tai Wai. Get off here and walk 20 minutes into Shatin to catch the modest attractions along the way—a couple of modern but intriguing temples and one of Hong Kong's better walled villages.

Amah Rock 望夫石

Emerging from the Lion Rock Tunnel you'll see a strange rock formation silhouetted against the eastern skyline: Mong Fu Shek ("Watching-for-Spouse Rock"), or Amah Rock to the English colonists, to whom all Chinese women were *amah*s or servants. Long ago, the story goes, a woman carrying her baby on her back climbed up here to watch for the return of her sailor husband. He never came, and the gods in pity finally turned her to stone.

The glimpse from the train is probably as close as you need to get, though during the Maidens' Festival in early August women flock here to make offerings for fertility and wealth (the rock is unabashedly phallic in form). A trail leads up from the end of Hung Miu Kuk Road, south of the KCR station. It's only one km to Amah Rock, and from here you can continue through **Lion Rock Country Park,** which, while hardly pristine (it's strung with huge powerlines), offers stunning views of the city to the south.

Tai Wai KCR

The enormous **bicycle rental lot** outside the station is a novelty that draws weekend crowds; on weekdays it's virtually deserted. Cycle paths lead from here along the river and Tolo Harbour up to Tai Po and Plover Cove—a pleasant way to explore. Rental fees are around HK$40 a day, HK$10 an hour. Next to the bike lot is **Happy Dragon Recreation Park,** with Ferris wheels, bumper cars, and water slides. Again, it's busy on weekends but eerily forsaken during the week.

Che Kung Temple 車公廟

Exiting from the station, pass the amusement park entrance, turn left on Che Kung Miu Road and cross it via an underpass. It's five minutes' walk to the well-maintained, large Taoist Che Kung Temple, dedicated to a deified general believed to have saved the area from the plague. During his festival on the third day of the Lunar New Year, the temple is packed with worshippers.

door gods, the New Territories

HONG KONG TOURIST ASSOCIATION

Continue up Che Kung Miu Road toward Shatin, passing a pretty **Buddhist temple complex** set in a small garden. Its brightly dyed orchid offerings and gilt statues (including a four-faced Buddha) indicate Thai influence, but the ancestor hall with urns set in labelled niches is distinctly Chinese.

Tsang Tai Uk 曾大屋

A few minutes farther, turn right onto Sha Kok Street, keeping an eye out for the gray stone walls of Tsang Tai Uk behind the recreation ground. It's a startlingly ancient oddity in the midst of new development: even more surprising, this authentic single-clan residence is still a viable community and not the sterile Urban Council display you might expect.

Tsang Tai Uk ("Tsang's Big House") was built by a wealthy quarry owner around 1850 in the style typical of the Hakka single-clan walled villages of Guangdong Province. It's a single immense fortress home, composed of two rectangles split by a public courtyard in the center. Impressive square watchtowers on each corner are topped with metal tridents to ward off evil spirits. The TV aerials sprouting from the rooftops and the air-conditioners wedged into small windows bring the picture up to date. Courtyards are cluttered with kids' bikes and laundry drying on bamboo racks, and the smell of cooking lingers in the air. Enter through the middle doorway to view the high-ceilinged ancestral hall, where Tsang ancestors stare down from faded photographs.

Back at the main road, cross via the underpass and walk north towards the orange-brown brick towers of Shatin's New Town Plaza.

SHATIN 沙田

Named for the "sandy fields" that once produced exceptionally tasty rice, Shatin is the among the largest, oldest, and nicest of Hong Kong's New Towns. Spotless, airy, and green, Shatin could almost be called pretty. Development started here in 1973, when the Lion Rock Tunnel and Tate's Cairn Tunnel were drilled through the Lion Rock Hills, linking Shatin to Kowloon. The old harbor was filled in, the Shing Mun River straightened into a sluggish canal, and 36-story housing blocks raised on old rice fields. Currently Shatin's population is half a million, projected to grow by half again by the end of decade.

For Hongkongers, Shatin is synonymous with the ultramodern **Shatin Racecourse,** opened in 1978 to soak up the overflow from the Happy Valley track. Weekend races are held in season (September to May), when special trains run to the KCR's Racecourse station. Non-gamblers might find the landscaped **Penfold Park** in the center of the racetrack more appealing; it's open daily except Monday and racedays.

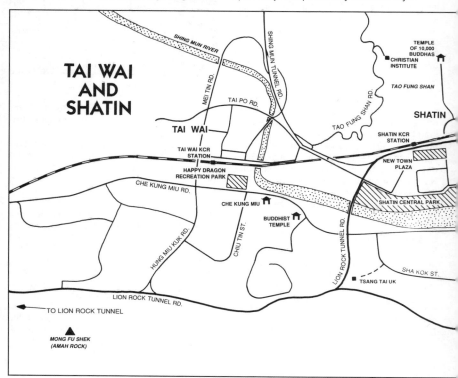

New Town Plaza 新城市廣場

The Shatin KCR station lies just across from the enormous New Town Plaza shopping center—Hong Kong's biggest and busiest—packed with dozens of restaurants, shops, department stores, and a six-screen UA Cinema. Prices are surprisingly reasonable, even in the Japanese department stores like Seiyu and Yaohan, and the complex is connected by walkway with other shopping centers for hours of air-conditioned distraction. If the indoor diversions pale, the nicely landscaped riverside park in front offers a glimpse of the real world.

Temple of Ten Thousand Buddhas 萬佛寺

This not-so-old but fascinating temple lies on a hillside one km northwest of the Shatin KCR station. Walk there in 20 minutes, following the signs around the bus lot and up the hill. Aim for the pink pagoda, and don't mistake your goal for the green-tiled white complex at the foot of the hill: that's the **Po Fook Ancestral Worship Hall,** a classy internment garden for urns and ancestral tablets. It's open to the public, and comes complete with tortoise ponds and an electric mini-tram gliding up the steep slope to its copycat nine-story white pagoda.

Past the ramshackle huts of Pai Tau village, the path heads steeply up a shady bamboo-covered hillside, some 400 steps in all. Superb *feng shui* was the reason behind the selection of this hard-to-reach site.

The temple is set in two levels: the lower one holds the main Temple of Ten Thousand Buddhas, 10,000 being the colloquial Chinese expression for "a lot." Actually there are some 12,800 gilt clay statues stacked up on the shelves covering the temple walls, each with a different posture and expression, all donated by devout worshippers since the temple's found-

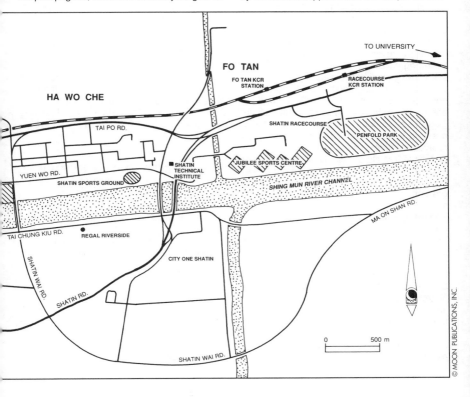

ing in the 1950s. Properly speaking these are not Buddhas but bodhisattvas, enlightened beings who have deferred their entry into Nirvana in order to help the suffering. The main temple is a favorite haunt of fortune-tellers, who set up consultation booths along the sides.

The forecourt is lined with funhouse-style statues of the 18 arhats plus a giant Kwun Yam and a pair of Buddhas atop an enormous elephant and a fantastical dog. You can climb up the distinctive nine-story pink pagoda for tremendous views of fast-growing Shatin below. There's also a small canteen serving the usual tasty temple vegetarian fare, heavy on the tofu and mushrooms.

The most bizarre sight lies on the upper level. Here are four more structures, including buildings dedicated to the Jade Emperor and Kwun Yam. The last shrine houses a giant standing Amita Buddha, and atop the altar in front of it, a gold-plated monk in a lotus position sealed inside a glass case. This is the body of the temple's founder and abbot Yuet Kai, a former philosophy professer from Kunming who arrived in Hong Kong after WW II to build the complex. Following his death in 1965 at the age of 87, his followers buried him seated inside a box: retrieved after eight months as per his instructions, they found no signs of decay, and his body is said to have emitted a phosphorescent glow. It was embalmed, lacquered, and gilded, dressed in robes and draped with chiffon scarves, then set on the altar as testimony to the beneficial "results of self-cultivation and strict discipline" (a quote from temple literature). His eyebrows and wispy beard are supposedly still growing.

Tao Fung Shan 道風山

From the lower terrace of the Temple of Ten Thousand Buddhas you can glimpse the white cross of the Christian center on the next hill over, Tao Fung Shan. This Chinese Mission to Buddhists was established in the 1930s to lure Buddhists onto the Christian path: the traditional architecture was designed to make its converts, many of them Buddhist monks, feel comfortable. To view the ornate architecture and visit the excellent porcelain painting workshop here, return to the KCR station and take the path branching left up to Tao Fung Shan Road,

which leads to the complex—about 20 minutes' walk from the station.

Practicalities

Shatin is a good place to eat. New Town Plaza is loaded with fine Chinese restaurants as well as the **Banthai** Thai restaurant. The stylish **Food Court** on the third floor of Seiyu Department Store serves everything from pizza to sushi. Shatin's most famous specialty, roast pigeon, is best sampled at the old Lung Wah Hotel Restaurant, 22 Ha Wo Che, tel. 2691-1594. One million pigeons are served here each year, prepared in an astonishing range of styles. Go on a weekday for dinner, and try roasted Shek Ki pigeon, pigeon satay, baked pigeon, or minced pigeon wrapped in lettuce. Or, for a pleasant al fresco lunch, take a taxi to Yucca de Lac Restaurant in Ma Liu Shui (described below). The **Oasis Restaurant** in the Regal Riverside Hotel puts on lunch, tea-time, and dinner buffets. The palatial **Treasure Floating Restaurant** serves dim sum and Cantonese food; it's on the Shing Mun River at 55 Tai Chung Kiu Rd., tel. 2637-7000.

Shatin also has the nicest New Territories accommodations: the **Regal Riverside** on Tai Chung Kiu Road across the river from the KCR station, tel. 2649-7878, has rooms for HK$1750-2100; the simpler **Royal Park,** 8 Pak Hok Ting St., tel. 2601-2111, has rooms for HK$1380-1980.

UNIVERSITY AND MA LIU SHUI
中文大學，馬料水

This minor stop serves the Chinese University of Hong Kong, its beautifully landscaped campus perched on a hillside above Tolo Harbour. The Institute of Chinese Studies here has a fine **art gallery** with an enormous 13,000-item collection including paintings and calligraphy by Guangdong artists, pottery, rubbings, carved jade flowers, and 2,000-year-old bronze seals. Unfortunately only a fraction can be displayed at any one time, so call 2695-2218 to find out what's being shown. The gallery is open Mon.-Sat. 10 a.m.-4:30 p.m., Sunday 12:30-4:30 p.m.

From the KCR station it's a steep climb uphill to the campus. Catch a free purple-and-white shuttle bus from behind the station, and get off at the top of the hill in front of Sir Run Run Shaw Hall. The gallery is over across the mall on the left (check the map board).

The area's other attraction is the **Yucca de Lac Restaurant,** tel. 2691-1630, on old Tai Po Road above the Tolo Highway. It has a spacious garden terrace overlooking Tolo Harbour and a huge, reasonably priced Cantonese menu —fried pigeon the specialty here.

Ten minutes' walk from the KCR station is the Ma Liu Shui Ferry Pier, the takeoff point for boats to Tap Mun Chau and Ping Chau (see "Other Islands" in the Outlying Islands chapter). Exiting the KCR station, cross the flyover to the waterfront and follow the bike path north to the pier.

Tai Po Kau Nature Reserve 大埔滘自然保護區
This 60-year-old nature reserve, an old forestry plantation grown wild, boasts the best trees around. Five signposted walks from one to ten km long lead past over 100 species of trees, including camphor, sweet gum, giant bean, acacia, and the fragrant joss stick tree *(Aquilania sinensis),* that may have given Hong Kong the name "Fragrant Harbor." The reserve is halfway between Ma Liu Shui and Tai Po. Take Bus 70 from the Jordan Road Ferry Pier and look for the signposted footpath entrance off Tai Po Road. Returning, you can catch the same bus into Tai Po or Sheung Shui.

TAI PO MARKET 大埔墟

Two km north of University, set at the western inlet of Tolo Harbour, Tai Po was an important market center as early as the 10th century. Ancient documents describe the local pearl-diving industry, a difficult and dangerous enterprise which involved tying stones onto the diver's body to make him sink more quickly. A tug on the rope signalled the need to pull him up— often too late.

Tai Po remained a sleepy local town into the late '70s, but its population has increased tenfold since then, to over 200,000. The north part of town is dominated by Hong Kong's first planned industrial park, built on reclaimed seashore. While this is less than compelling, enough remains in the south part of town to warrant a visit—in particular, the small and scrupulously maintained Hong Kong Railway Museum and one of the more colorful markets and downtowns.

The New Market
Exiting from the KCR station, turn right down the sidewalk paralleling the railway tracks. Turn right beneath the underpass, then left onto Heung Sze Wui Street, which runs into the big covered market, busiest in the morning but a worthwhile stop at any time of day. This is the latest incarnation of the "New Market," a mere century or so old, founded by members of the Man clan as a rival to the original 17th-century "Old Market" of the Tangs on the north bank of the river. Here is food in all possible forms— mountains of chicken feet, neat rows of unidentifiable internal organs, squirming fish and squiggly shellfish. The peaceable vegetarian stalls at the end, with their tranquil white squares of tofu, come as a positive relief.

Railway Museum 鐵路博物館
Behind the market is the Railway Museum, housed in the original 1913 Tai Po Market Railway Station. The tiny building is prettily decorated to resemble a Chinese temple, perhaps a gimmick to lure crowds to the nearby market. It was converted to a museum after the new, electrified KCR came on line in 1983. Inside is memorabilia from the inception of the KCR, including photos, old tickets, and posters. The old booking office has been restored, and down the banyan-shaded tracks are six old coaches dating from 1911-45, open for kids to climb through and fiddle with the levers. (A steam locomotive would round out the exhibition nicely, but the KCR has sold off all its old engines to China and the Philippines.) The museum is open daily except Tuesday 9 a.m.-4 p.m.; admission is free.

Downtown
Wander out onto nearby **Fu Shing Street,** the main old market area, where open shop fronts display cheap clothes, Hakka bamboo hats, clay hotpots, palm-leaf fans, and spirit money. Halfway down the street is the **Man Mo Temple,** a small but important shrine dedicated to the deities associated with war and literature. Look

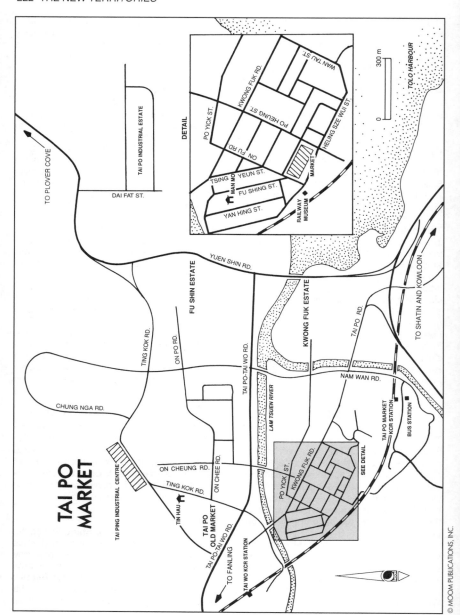

TAI PO MARKET

DETAIL

TOLO HARBOUR

300 m

0

TAI PO INDUSTRIAL ESTATE

DAI FAT ST.

TO PLOVER COVE

PO YICK ST.
KWONG FUK RD.
PO HEUNG ST.
WAN TAU ST.
ON FU RD.
HEUNG SZE WUI ST.
MARKET
RAILWAY MUSEUM
TSING MO
MAN MO
YEUN ST.
FU SHING ST.
YAN HING ST.

YUEN SHIN RD.

FU SHIN ESTATE

KWONG FUK ESTATE

TING KOK RD.
ON PO RD.
TAI PO-TAI WO RD.
LAM TSUEN RIVER
TAI PO RD.
TO SHATIN AND KOWLOON

CHUNG NGA RD.

NAM WAN RD.

TAI PING INDUSTRIAL CENTRE

PO YICK ST.
KWONG FUK RD.
SEE DETAIL
TAI PO MARKET KCR STATION
BUS STATION

ON CHEUNG RD.
ON CHEE RD.
TING KOK RD.

TIN HAU

TAI PO OLD MARKET

TAI PO-TAI WO RD.
TO FANLING
TAI WO KCR STATION

for rows of paper slips imprinted with fortunes for the *chim* arrayed by number and hanging on a board. The temple serves as a sanctuary for geriatric gamblers who play *pai kau* and mahjong in the palm-shaded courtyard, occasionally shuffling up to the altar to make an offering.

Tai Po's other attractions are minor. Across the river and up Ting Kok Road is the **Temple of the Sing Kung Cho Tang Charitable Association,** with an elaborate shrine dedicated to Kwong Sing Tai Sin, the teacher of the Yellow Emperor. A block farther (the location of the old shoreline, now far inland) is a 280-year-old **Tin Hau Temple.** The **Tai Ping Carpet Factory** up across Ting Tai Road offers guided afternoon tours through its workshops, by appointment only, tel. 2656-5161. There's a showroom, too.

To round out the day, you may like to rent a bike for the ride to Plover Cove (below): rental shops are clustered on Tung Cheung Street across from the Hong Kong Jockey Club at 158 Kwong Fuk Road. The **Ting Kok Road Cycle Track** (accessible from the Kwong Fuk Bridge) runs 6 km, past the industrial estate and along Plover Cove to Tai Mei Tuk. Or backtrack to the Chinese University, riding along Tolo Highway on the edge of Tolo Harbour.

If you're looking for a meal in Tai Po, there are plenty of cheap *dai pai dong*s around the market and moderately priced Chinese restaurants in town. The **Cosmopolitan Curry House,** 80 Kwong Fuk Rd., is packed evenings and weekends with crowds come to sample specialties like mango prawn curry and crab masala (for reservations, call 2650-7056).

PLOVER COVE 船灣淡水湖

The remote northeastern reaches of the New Territories have much to offer day-hikers: peace and quiet, mountains and woods, small secluded Hakka villages, and bare ridges yielding views of Tolo Channel to the south and Double Haven and Crooked Harbour to the north. The eastern fringes in particular are as isolated as one could wish, yet are still only 20 km from metropolitan Hong Kong. The rugged terrain is inhabited by Hakka people, who originated in Shandong Province and roamed for centuries before settling in the unpopulated highlands of the eastern New Territories several hundred years ago.

Plover Cove Reservoir (the name comes not from the bird but from an early British survey ship) was the world's first saltwater displacement project. The story goes that a British civil servant swimming in the harbor had a sudden brainstorm: dam up the mouth of the cove, drain it and fill it with fresh water to supply chronically thirsty Hong Kong. The dam has become a major water sports center, and the reservoir the centerpiece of **Plover Cove Country Park.** Combined with adjoining **Pat Sin Leng Country Park,** it's a relatively enormous area, crisscrossed with trails—a good place to get away from it all.

To Tai Mei Tuk 大美篤
Ride the bicycle path out of Tai Po, or catch Bus 75K from outside the Tai Po Market KCR station for the half-hour ride along Tolo Harbour. The bus ends at the tiny outpost of Tai Mei Tuk at the edge of Plover Cove Reservoir. There are bike and rowboat rentals here and a few *dai pai dong*s, as well as **Plover Cove Country Park Visitor Centre,** with displays on local flora and fauna and useful advice on hiking routes. It's open 9:30-11:30 a.m. and 1:30-4:30 p.m. daily except Tuesday. A few minutes south of the bus stop, out on the little peninsula toward the dam, is the **Bradbury Lodge Youth Hostel,** tel. 2662-5123, one of the better IYHA hostels, with air-conditioned rooms.

Bride's Pool and Other Walks
From Tai Mei Tuk, Bride's Pool Road curves north along the reservoir then runs up to Starling Inlet, cutting between Plover Cove and Pat Sin Leng Country Parks. Bus 75R runs down it on Sunday and holidays October to April and is predictably crowded; otherwise you'll have to walk, bike, or take the five-km signed nature trail from Tai Mei Tuk to **Bride's Pool** (新娘潭).

It's about an hour's walk to this pretty though often crowded series of waterfalls, the largest 15 meters high. Visit shortly after a rain to see the falls at their most impressive. The name comes from a local legend of a bride carried to her husband's village in a sedan chair; the bearers slipped on the slick trail, and she tumbled into the water and drowned. Neighboring Mirror Pool, a more impressive waterfall, is supposed to be where she combs her hair.

From Bride's Pool you can continue on to explore the northern half of the peninsula, dotted with small, nearly deserted villages. Consult a good map or the Visitor Centre at Tai Mei Tuk for ideas. The old Hakka village of **Wu Kau Tang** is only a few kilometers east of Bride's Pool.

About two hours' walk north is the remote settlement of **Lai Chi Wo,** its huddled houses overlooking the scattered islands of Crooked Harbour (Kat O Hoi). Or head west into **Pat Sin Leng Country Park.** The long ridge walk from

Bride's Pool across the summit of Wong Leng (639 meters) offers glorious views of Tolo Harbour before dropping down to the Sha Lo Tung roadhead north of Tai Po. Easiest is to continue up Bride's Pool Road another hour to **Luk Keng,** on the coast of shallow, mangrove-fringed Starling Inlet. From here you can catch a minibus to Fanling, on the KCR line.

Luk Keng Egretry 鹿頸

This small grove near the duck-farming community of Luk Keng is home to Hong Kong's population of 800 or so graceful, crane-like white egrets. Three species of egret nest here in win-

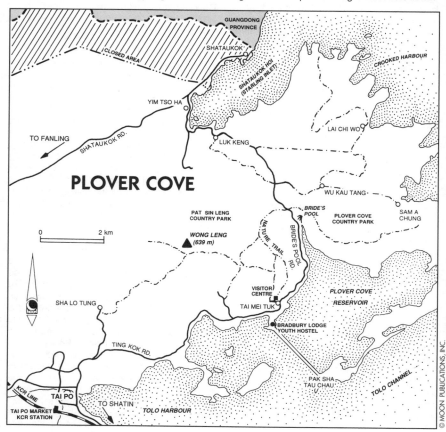

FARMING VILLAGES AND ANCESTRAL HALLS

Old farming and fishing villages remained the centers of New Territories life until rising land values and the postwar building boom transformed everything into vertical mode. People lived in small communities housing members of a single clan: sometimes members of smaller clans would group together for protection.

"Protection" is an important motif in traditional village architecture, as shown in the huddled layout of the narrow streets lined with thick-walled houses. Many rural villages were once walled and surrounded by a moat, with only a single door to control entry. On maps, the term *wai* (meaning "an enclosure") indicates an old walled village, *tsuen* an unwalled one. However, many *wai* have dismantled their walls. Villages were further protected by watchmen, and by local armories stocked with rifles, rusty spears, and a few old cannons.

All this was meant to defend against bandits, pirates, and feuding members of other clans. The actual level of threat was low, but suspicion is an ingrained feature of New Territories rural life, and even today outsiders are not warmly welcomed.

Villagers were equally wary of dangerous unseen forces and took appropriate precautions, building virtually windowless houses to prevent the entry of evil spirits, or placing strategic mirrors to deflect their path. *Feng shui* was an important element in this war with the supernatural, and geomancers were consulted in order to take advantage of the invisible forces permeating the landscape. The best site for a village was surrounded by hills, facing an open expanse of fields or water, with trees and bamboo planted in back to screen evil influences.

Within the village, buildings were laid out in symmetric fashion, with the most important ceremonial buildings in the center. Village life centered around the local ancestral hall *(tsz tong)*, the site of festivals, celebrations, ceremonies, and community meetings. A single village might have several halls, dedicated to different branches of a lineage. The greatest were built by the descendents of the "Five Clans," especially the powerful Tangs of the western New Territories.

Ancestral halls have been described as "the rural Chinese equivalent of cathedrals." They typically involve a central hall flanked by chambers and interspersed with internal courtyards open to the sky. External walls are often fine gray brick, cemented with white mortar. Elaborately carved wooden brackets support an overhanging tile roof adorned with porcelain figures, while engraved stone columns, frescoes, and highly decorated entrance gates all announce the ceremonial importance of the building.

The rear hall generally holds rows of wooden tablets inscribed with the names of the deceased. It's believed that one aspect of the deceased's spirit enters this wooden tablet; another goes to the netherworld, and a third remains with the body, which is buried at an auspicious site. Traditionally the bones would be disinterred after 10 years, arranged in a ceramic urn, then reburied near the village so that their power would benefit future generations of descendants.

A few villages boasted study halls where local boys were tutored for the imperial civil service exams. Considered the epitome of scholastic achievement, these rigorous examinations were used to select government officials. Success in them guaranteed material wealth and social prestige—not just for the individual but for his family, village, and clan as well. With the 1905 abolition of the examinations, studying moved into government-sponsored schools. Many of the halls were left to crumble; some were turned into ancestral halls. A very few have been restored, like the Kun Ting Study Hall at Ping Shan, among the most finely decorated of all traditional buildings in the New Territories.

*work and leisure in a
rural New Territories field*

HONG KONG TOURIST ASSOCIATION

ter. From April through July they breed at the nearby Yim Tso Ha Egretry off Shataukok Road. Bring binoculars or a zoom lens for easier viewing. Walk from Bride's Pool, or take minibus 56K from the Fanling KCR to Luk Keng, a half-hour ride.

FANLING 粉嶺

Though it's an ancient market center with centuries of history, Fanling is rather dull and depressing compared to other New Towns. For most purposes it's become a suburban extension of livelier Sheung Shui; there are some worthwhile attractions in the area, however.

Luen Wo Market 聯和墟
HKTA persists in promoting this relatively recent (1948) covered market, though there are far livelier ones in Sheung Shui and Tai Po. If you're stopping at Fanling anyway you might give it a look: it's best (and cleanest) in the early morning. Catch bus 52K, 70K, or 78K from outside the Fanling KCR for the brief ride, or walk straight up Shataukok Road less than one km and turn left on Luen Hing Street when the low covered stalls become visible.

Fung Ying Seen Koon Temple 蓬迎仙館
It's easier to recommend this elaborately decorated temple, which lies just across the high-

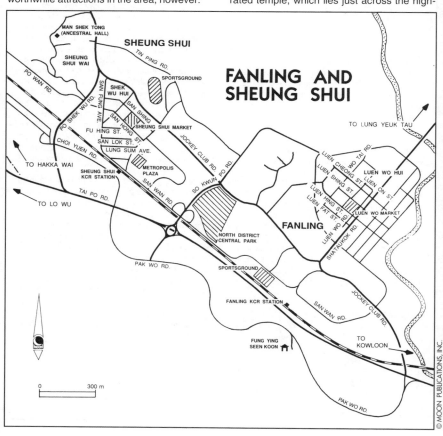

way from the KCR station. The lushly land-scaped complex was built in 1929 as the head-quarters of a Taoist sect. Typical of the Taoist emphasis on healing, there's a free herbal medi-cal clinic on the lower level; a canteen serves tasty, cheap vegetarian food (English menu available).

The main temple enshrines a blue-and-gold image of Lao Tze and other deities. Earnest *chim*-throwers kneel in front hoping to divine the future. In temples on the upper levels, paper of-ferings may be arrayed for ceremonies honoring the recently deceased, as family members clad in white (the color of mourning), fold gold paper "ingots" for burning, and shaven-headed nuns in yellow robes chant rituals for the dead.

Lung Yeuk Tau 龍躍頭

From Fanling, Shataukok Road runs northeast to the Chinese border and Luk Keng, cutting through peaceful fields tilled by Hakka and Can-tonese farmers. A little outside of Fanling is Lung Yeuk Tau ("Dragon Leap Head") district—11 villages, five of them walled, all dominated by the Tang clan.

Take minibus 54K (Lung Yeuk Tau) from the Fanling KCR and get off at the **Tsz Tong Tsuen** turning point, only a kilometer or so out of Fan-ling. This old unwalled village features a Tang ancestral hall (Chung Ling Tang Kung Tsz) that is around 650 years old and has undergone re-peated renovations. Among the largest in the New Territories, it serves all 11 villages of the district. Nearby is **Lo Wai walled village,** re-portedly the oldest of these Sung dynasty set-tlements—not hard to believe when you see its decrepit narrow streets.

Take the footpath across from the Tang an-cestral hall north, past Ma Wat Tsuen, Wing Ling Tsuen, and the formerly walled village of Wing Ning Wai. Cross Shataukok Road into **San Uk Tsuen;** down its main road is **Shin Shut Shue Shat** (try saying *that* fast), a Tang family study hall for imperial exams, now used as an ances-tral hall. A few minutes' walk north of here is **San Wai** (New Walled Village—"new" meaning a mere 250 years old), worth visiting for its ex-ceptionally fine old entrance gate. Back on Shataukok Road, it's easy to catch a minibus back into Fanling.

SHEUNG SHUI 上水

The last stop on the KCR for most travelers (you need a Chinese visa to travel on to Lo Wu), Sheung Shui is among the more attractive New Towns. An old Hakka settlement, it's far enough out to have escaped total mass development, and remains somewhat traditional, with a lively market area rivalling Tai Po's. Sheung Shui is the homeland of the Hau and Liu clans, who arrived in the 12th and 14th centuries, respec-tively, and left the usual traditional architecture.

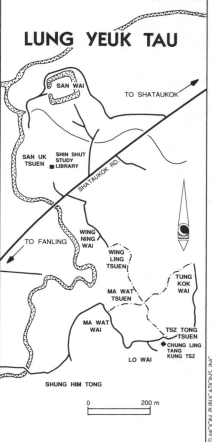

LUNG YEUK TAU

SAN WAI

TO SHATAUKOK

SAN UK TSUEN

SHIN SHUT STUDY
■ LIBRARY

SHATAUKOK RD.

TO FANLING

WING NING WAI

WING LING TSUEN

TUNG KOK WAI

MA WAT TSUEN

MA WAT WAI

TSZ TONG TSUEN

◆ CHUNG LING TANG KUNG TSZ

LO WAI

SHUNG HIM TONG

0   200 m

© MOON PUBLICATIONS, INC.

Shek Wu Hui Market 石湖墟

From the KCR station walk five minutes north, passing Metropolitan Centre and veering left into bustling "downtown" Sheung Shui. The market, bounded by San Shing Avenue and San Hong Street, consists of a series of covered stalls full of intense activity. Here are cheap clothes, salted fish, fish heads, tiny plucked birds, and a chaotic array of live and dead goods. It runs all day long; the *dai pai dong*s along the fringes are good places to eat and observe the street scene, and there are more small places scattered throughout downtown.

If you like old buildings and atmosphere, check out **Sheung Shui Wai,** an old formerly walled village on the west side of town, behind Po Shek Wu Road. This dank, dark maze of narrow alleys lined by old and new houses is entirely different in character from the towering blocks that hide it from the main road. Toward the back is **Man Shek Tong,** a Liu ancestral hall built in 1751 and superbly restored to its original condition.

Harder to reach but worthwhile for walled-village buffs is **Hakka Wai,** a well-maintained traditional settlement a little southwest of town. It was built around 1905 by a Hakka family named Wong, and the double row of neat interconnected little houses with an ancestral hall, surrounded by high walls, is one of the finest examples in the New Territories. Head south down Po Shek Wu Road and turn right on Tai Po Road; take the second lane on the right (to Tsung Pak Long), and Hakka Wai is just before the village.

LOK MA CHAU AND SAN TIN
落馬洲，新田

Only locals or travelers with a Chinese visa can proceed on to Lo Wu, the entry point into China. You can, however, take Bus 76K from the Sheung Shui KCR to **Lok Ma Chau** ("Dismount Hill"), the traditional lookout point into once-forbidden China. Get off at the intersection of Lok Ma Chau Road and Castle Peak Road, about a 15-minute ride (or take a taxi from Yuen Long or Fanling). The lookout point is about a half-hour walk up Lok Ma Chau Road; you may be able to flag down a minibus.

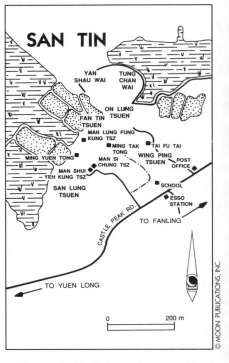

The grandly titled "observation terrace" here offers views of rice fields, farmhouses, and the sluggish Shum Chun River, which marks the actual border. Between here and China is a closed area—even the actual village of Lok Ma Chau is off-limits to tourists—but a steady stream of tourist buses keeps locals busy hiring out binoculars, selling souvenirs, and posing for photos.

With access into China so easy these days (you can get a visa in the morning and hop on an express train to Guangzhou that afternoon), Lok Ma Chau has become an anachronism. There's little reason to go except to say you've done it, in which case it's more impressive to say you've actually spent a day *in* China—even in Shenzhen or Zhuhai. If you do opt for Lok Ma Chau, the 76K can take you into Yuen Long on return, passing Kam Tin along the way.

San Tin 新田

West of Lok Ma Chau and near the Chinese border, the San Tin area remains the stronghold of the Man clan, whose members arrived in the late 14th century. With hard work they prospered off the inferior marshy land, raising a number of ancestral halls and other traditional buildings.

Take a taxi to Wing Ping Tsuen, or hop on Bus 76K, which runs between Sheung Shui and Yuen Long. Keep an eye peeled for signs for Wing Ping Tsuen and San Tin, and get off at the Esso station on Castle Peak Road. Cross the road and head behind the modern buildings to reach the old settlements *(tsuen)* of Fan Tin Tsuen, On Lung Tsuen, and Wing Ping Tsuen.

You'll have to hunt through the lanes to find **Man Lung Fung Ancestral Hall (**文公麟峰祠**)**, among the oldest (three centuries-plus), best-preserved, and largest of all traditional New Territories buildings. Its three halls are still used for ancestor worship, village meetings, festivals, and ceremonies. There are at least four other Man ancestral halls in the neighborhood, one of them raised in 1972 on the site of an old one.

The other important site is **Tai Fu Tai (**大夫第**)**, an elegant example of a scholar's home set in a big compound planted with lychee and longan trees. A prominent Man family member built it in 1865, calling in the finest craftsmen and sparing no expense in establishing his status. The Qing emperor awarded him the title "important person" or *taifu.* (The second "tai" in the title means "residence"; the whole is carved on a board over the entrance.) Squatters who took over the house after WW II were evicted in the 1980s, when the house underwent complete restoration with a HK$2.5 million grant from the Hong Kong Jockey Club—yet another example of gambling dollars at work.

Tai Fu Tai is open 9 a.m.-1 p.m. and 2-5 p.m. daily except Tuesday. The building's exquisite interior detail includes restored murals on the second floor (said to contain clues to buried treasure), rooftop decorations of Shiwan pottery, and plaster moldings and woodcarvings featuring auspicious Chinese themes like bamboo, chrysanthemum, orchids, deer, carp, and bats. Underneath the carved eaves are historical tableaux of fine pottery figures. Western influence shows in the painted glass panes and baroque plaster window moldings.

BOB RACE

Tai Fu Tai, San Tin

THE WESTERN NEW TERRITORIES

This region, the largest in terms of area, lacks the open space and sweeping rugged coast of the Eastern New Territories, or the cheerful bustling charm of the KCR New Towns. It's grittier, more industrialized, and becoming more developed by the day—but it's also among Hong Kong's most historically important areas, settled from the 10th century on. There is much of interest in the remaining pockets of traditional culture, particularly in the old temples and ancestral halls scattered amid the high-rises.

Points of Access

Hoverferries from Central to Tsuen Wan and Tuen Mun and the MTR line to Tsuen Wan make for easy access. The Light Rail Transit (LRT), an aboveground electric train, runs between Tuen Mun-Yuen Long. The KCR line is connected to Yuen Long by Bus 76K (Sheung Shui) and 64K (Tai Po Market). Plenty of buses run between towns, while minibuses operate between minor destinations. **Castle Peak Road** is the area's major highway, looping between Tsuen Wan, Tuen Mun, Yuen Long, and Sheung Shui. The other important road is Route Twisk, which cuts across the heart of the New Territories, running north from Tsuen Wan into Shek Kong via Tai Mo Shan.

TSUEN WAN 荃灣

The biggest of all the New Towns, Tsuen Wan (say "Choon Wan") is slated for an eventual population of one million. Its impressive ranks of white skyscrapers are visible from the Peak on a sunny day, looking like some miraculous Oz-like city. Close up, you'll see the uniform high-rise blocks have been painted different colors to help residents distinguish between them. Things are more interesting at street level, with old ladies in velvet caps playing chess in public gardens, and any number of small temples, mostly Buddhist, in the hills north of town.

From Central you can take the MTR straight here—it's the last stop on the Tsuen Wan Line, a 30-minute trip. The hoverferry is more inter-

esting, providing unique views of the rapidly changing shoreline. It runs every 20 minutes 7 a.m.-7 p.m. from Government Services Pier (west of the Central Star Ferry). It's a 20-minute trip past the newly risen West Kowloon Reclamation Area and the new military base on Stonecutter's Island—started by the British and handed over to the Chinese in 1997. Entering Rambler Channel, you see the busy container terminals of **Kwai Chung,** where brightly colored containers are stacked up like building blocks. The already gigantic volume continues to grow at a tremendous rate as shipping expands. Across Rambler Channel from Tsuen Wan is **Tsing Yi Island,** an overdeveloped and severely polluted wedge of land bearing the pathetic misnomer "Green Island." Recently it's been the site of extensive reclamation works that have made it a part of the airport railway transportation scheme.

Downtown Tsuen Wan

From Tsuen Wan Ferry Pier it's a 10-minute walk into the bustling modern downtown, centered around a giant public market complex. There's a fair amount of interest in poking around shops here, and the **Town Square** mall off Castle Peak Road has the usual decent New Territories prices. There are plenty of good local restaurants, too, like **Bo Lin Vegetarian Kitchen** at 115 Chung On Street. The **Food Plaza** on the second floor of Town Square dishes up designer waffles, Japanese noodles, and papaya shakes.

Sam Tung Uk Museum 三棟屋博屋館

Tucked beneath the high-rise towers of a housing complex, the crisp whitewashed buildings and black tile roofs of Sam Tung Uk are a distinct anachronism. A traditional single-family walled compound transformed into a mini-museum, it lies just a few minutes' walk east of the MTR station down Sai Lau Kok Road.

Sam Tung Uk was founded in 1786 by a group of Hakka immigrants from Fujian. The name means "three-beamed dwelling," referring to the three original main halls aligned in

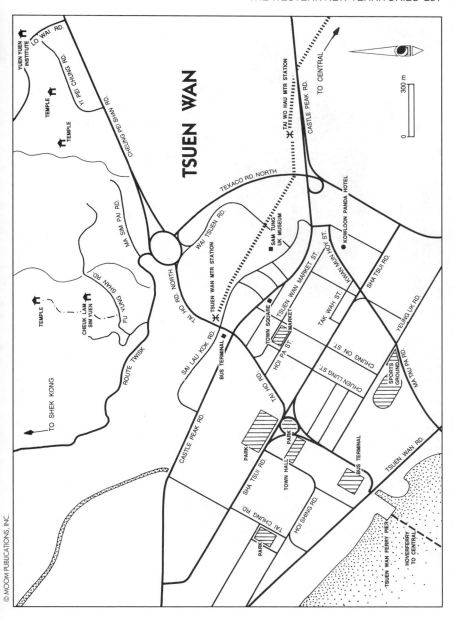

TSUEN WAN

HONG KONG TOURIST ASSOCIATION

A vendor in Tuen Mun market weighs out spring onions for a customer.

neat rows. The complex grew as the family did, but retained its original tight symmetry: four free-standing houses belonging to the original sons, walled in by rows of houses along the sides and back. Three interconnected halls running down the middle of the complex served as meeting places: the rear one, the old ancestral hall, has been repainted in bright red and green but looks a bit forlorn without its portraits or tablets. The double row of five pieces of speckled paper pasted up above the altar symbolizes the "Five Happinesses."

Sam Tung Uk's residents made their living farming the surrounding fields: these were gradually sold off, but photos on display show how the house existed in a rural environment through the 1970s. The last family members moved out in the early 1980s, and an extensive and painstaking restoration process began, detailed in the orientation hall. Authentic gray brick and roof tiles were imported from China, along with artifacts and furniture collected from Hakka villages in the Guangdong countryside. While it's

a bit *too* perfectly restored—verging on sterility—the tight maze of narrow corridors and small rooms is an interesting relic of a now-vanished way of life. It's open daily except Tuesday 9 a.m.-4 p.m.; admission is free.

Temples
Up in the hills behind town are a half-dozen or so monasteries and temples. The best choice is probably the **Yuen Yuen Institute** (圓玄學院), which has shrines to Hong Kong's three main religions: Taoism, Buddhism, and Confucianism. The canteen serves a good cheap vegetarian lunch. Take Minibus 81 from Shiu Wo Street (two blocks south of the MTR station) to the terminus on Lo Wai Road; the complex is just across from the bus stop. The other choice is **Cheuk Lam Sim Yuen** (竹林禪院), "Bamboo Forest Monastery," originally constructed of bamboo mat sheds in 1927 but by now developed into a more elaborate complex, with large statues of the three Precious Buddhas. Take Minibus 85 from Shiu Wo Street to the terminus on Fu Yung Shan Road.

Airport Core Programme Exhibition Centre
All the details of the world's largest civil engineering program—the construction of Hong Kong's new airport and its related transportation projects—are displayed at this center, which also provides stunning views of the graceful Tsing Ma suspension bridge. It's at 401 Castle Peak Rd., Ting Kau, and is open Tues.-Fri. 10 a.m.-5 p.m., 10 a.m.-6:30 p.m. Sat.-Sun.; admission is free. Take maxicab 96M (Tsing Lung Tau) from the Tsuen Wan MTR station, and look for the center's signboard, about 15 minutes down the road.

Practicalities
Tsuen Wan has one high-class hotel, the **Kowloon Panda**, 3 Tsuen Wan St., tel. 2409-1111, with over 1,000 rooms for HK$990-1650.

Buses and minibuses start from several places: the big bus station at the ferry pier is the place to catch the 34B to Sham Tseng or the 51 to Tai Mo Shan and Kam Tin (Bus 51 can also be caught on the flyover above the MTR station). Buses 59M (to Tuen Mun Ferry), 60M (Tuen Mun Centre), and 68M (through Tuen

Mun to Yuen Long) start from the central bus terminal across from the MTR station. Minibuses leave from Shui Wo Street, two blocks south of the MTR station.

Shing Mun Country Park 城門郊野公園

This country park up in the hills northeast of Tsuen Wan encompasses the catchment area around Shing Mun (Jubilee) Reservoir. Take Minibus 82 from Shui Wo Street to the **Country Park Visitor Centre,** open 9:30 a.m.-4:30 p.m. daily except Tuesday. Exhibits here focus on the local landscape and history—the WW II defenses are particularly fascinating. The two-km **Pineapple Dam Nature Trail** makes a very easy short walk, while the trail around the reservoir takes around two hours.

Not far from the reservoir trail is the **Shing Mun Redoubt,** a 12-acre underground complex of interconnected pillboxes and bunkers tunnelled beneath Smuggler's Ridge. The British built it in the late 1930s as a key part of the longer "Gindrinkers Line," a string of defensive structures meant to protect Kowloon from attack. The undermanned Shing Mun section was taken by the Japanese in a few hours' fighting in December 1941, leaving Kowloon open to invasion. The network of crumbling, overgrown tunnels remains, some still marked with the original London street names.

Kam Shan Country Park 金山郊野公園

East of Tsuen Wan, this area is known as "Monkey Hills," after the marauding bands of macaque monkeys descended from a handful released some 70 years ago. Watch out for them, as they may snatch food, or worse, your camera. The south end of the park includes the small Kowloon Reservoirs.

Take Bus 81 from the Jordan MTR station or Bus 72 from the Shamshuipo MTR (Kowloon Reservoirs), and get off on Tai Po Road, near the Sir Robert Black College of Education. The park entrance, and a mapboard, is near the next bus stop.

ROUTE TWISK AND TAI MO SHAN 荃錦公園，大帽山

"Twisk" comes from the acronym "Tsuen Wan Into Shek Kong." This rural highway cuts across the middle of the New Territories, across the slopes of Tai Mo Shan ("Big Hat Mountain," due to its shape). The hike up the side road to its 957-meter summit, the highest point in Hong Kong, is a favorite with locals. They are probably more inspired by the challenge than the scenery, which is merely high, bare ridges, steeper than most Hong Kong slopes. On the hillsides can be found traces of abandoned tea terraces.

Catch Bus 51 (Kam Tin) from Tsuen Wan, either at the ferry pier or on the flyover (overpass) above the MTR station. It's a spectacular, swaying ride on the top deck, as the road climbs into virtually alpine territory. To explore, get off at the top of the pass (about 15 minutes out of town) at the sign for **Tai Mo Shan Country Park.** You'll find picnic facilities here, and a small visitor center with map boards detailing local hikes.

Walk up quiet Tai Mo Shan Peak Road, passing the **Sze Lok Yuen Youth Hostel** in about 45 minutes. Advance booking is essential if you want to stay here; call 2488-8188. It's another hour up to the top—or near enough, as the actual summit has been taken over by government communications transmitters and is fenced off. (A steeper route without switchbacks heads straight up.) From the top there are splendid views of Tsuen Wan and the harbor to the south and the New Territories well into China to the north.

Back on the bus, Route Twisk descends to reveal views of the green countryside around **Shek Kong** (pronounced "Sek Kong"), a former British Army base now inhabited by PLA troops. Through the 1980s, Shek Kong was the site of a crowded detention camp for Vietnamese "boat people." The road passes the burned-out wreckage of the fire set in a dispute that killed 24 Vietnamese refugees in 1992, a sad chapter in a bitter saga now winding to a close as the refugees return to Vietnam.

The scenery degenerates further as the road continues: Shek Kong is a haven for new and used car lots, and the roadside is littered with mountains of rusting chassis. Bus 51 ends at Kam Tin, while the road continues into Yuen Long.

KAM TIN 錦田

A few kilometers east of Yuen Long down the Kam Tin Road to Shek Kong, this area is among the oldest settled regions in the New Territories. Tang clan immigrants claimed its fertile fields as early as the 10th century. The Tangs' wealth has inspired persistent legends of buried treasure left behind during the imperially decreed eviction of the 1660s. Supposedly nobody remembered the location of the treasure upon return—unlikely, as the eviction only lasted seven years, but it makes a good story.

The flowery name Kam Tin ("Embroidered Fields") was bestowed by a 16th-century magistrate who had been inspired by a generous donation from villagers. By the late 17th century over a half-dozen villages had been built in the area, huddled behind fortified walls raised to protect against bandits and rival clans. Today they constitute some of Hong Kong's last remaining examples of walled villages and are heavily touted as such. While the history is undeniably significant, don't expect quaint settlements amid green fields. Modernity, and a rather grim urban modernity at that, permeates all. Kat Hing Wai in particular is an overrated tourist trap, but if you're in the neighborhood you might want to stop by.

Kat Hing Wai 吉慶圍
Get off at the Bus 51 terminus on Kam Tin Road and look for the Park 'N Shop—Kat Hing Wai village lies just past it. The first glimpse is promising: the fine stone walls are topped with four corner towers, and the small moat and single entrance reinforces the air of antiquity. Deposit HK$1 in the donation box outside (the old ladies lurking in the entrance hall will make sure you do), and pause to admire the fine iron chain-link gate. It was seized by British troops in a skirmish during the New Territories takeover, and ended up on the Irish estate of former governor Sir Henry Blake before being returned several decades later.

Kat Hing Wai's narrow streets retain the typical geometric layout of an old village, but many of the houses are modern. The central lane, lined with souvenir stalls, runs into a rather barren village temple and ancestral hall. Residents, all members of the Tang clan, are mostly elderly and skilled at posing for photos for money.

Shui Tau and Shui Mei 水頭，水尾
Skip the old villages of Tai Hong Wai and Wing Lung Wai across the street, which lack even the fine outer wall of Kat Hing Wai. The best bets are the settlements of Shui Tau and Shui Mei, set amid fields. Continue down the road from Kat Hing Wai, heading toward Yuen Long, and turn right at the Mung Yeung Public School. In a few minutes you'll cross a bridge and begin to see old buildings interspersed with new tiled Mediterranean-style villas. The walls of Shui Tau are mostly gone now, but clusters of tight-packed old houses remain, along with temples to **Tin Hau** and **Hung Shing.**

Across the stream is **Chou Wong Yi Kwong Shue Yuen,** built in the 17th century as an ancestral hall to honor Chou and Wong, the viceroy and governor of Guangdong Province, who interceded with the emperor to reverse the disastrous coastal evacuation order of 1662. Later it became a clan study hall. Continue down the road another few minutes, and after the road curves left you'll come to Shui Mei village, with its recently restored triple ancestral hall and more densely packed old houses.

To continue into Yuen Long, catch a westbound Bus 54, 64K, 76K, or 77K (the destination card is likely to read "Un Long"). Eastbound buses 76K and 77K run to Sheung Shui; the eastbound 64K to the Tai Po KCR, while Bus 51 goes to the Tsuen Wan Ferry.

Tsuen Wan To Tuen Mun
There are two coastal routes, both yielding views: the old 1919 Castle Peak Road and the new Tuen Mun Road, slightly inland. If you just want to get to Tuen Mun, take the 60M or the 68M from the Tsuen Wan MTR. To explore the coast in more depth, take Bus 34B (Sham Tseng) from the Tsuen Wan ferry, or the 96M minibus from the Tsuen Wan MTR. Both these run down Castle Peak Road with its **beaches:** Approach Beach, then Lido (probably the best),

followed by Hoi Mei, Gemini, Angler's, and Dragon beaches. This isn't the best place for swimming, though, due to pollution. These are working waters: big ships and freighters glide past the coast, and the outskirts of Tuen Mun are stacked with offloaded containers.

Castle Peak Road passes through the coastal town of **Sham Tseng** (深井), another of Hong Kong's specialty dining niches, this one famous for roast goose (try the **Yue Kee Restaurant** at 9 Main St. or the **Jade** at 63 Sham Tseng Village, and remember, the goose's left leg is considered tastier and firmer). Bus 34B ends here, while the minibus continues to Tsing Lung Tau, just after Dragon Beach.

Most of the area inland between Tsuen Wan and Tuen Mun is taken up by giant **Tai Lam Country Park,** site of Tai Lam Chung Reservoir and many kilometers of footpaths. The scenery is not spectacular—the MacLehose Trail through here is definitely dull—but the valleys offer some passable day-hikes.

TUEN MUN 屯門

Tuen Mun means "garrisoned entrance": the old deepwater channel at the mouth of the Pearl River was a wealthy trading port guarded from pirates by an imperial fortress as early as A.D. 750. The Portuguese tried to establish a trade station here, building forts in the area, but were expelled by the Chinese in 1521 following a bout of pillaging and shifted to Macau.

All that remains of old Castle Peak Bay today is the murky waterway running through the middle of town. The harbor long ago silted up, and the remainder was reclaimed and covered in apartment buildings. It's good to keep Tuen Mun's rich history in mind, because the modern reality of a big New Town is pretty uninspiring, apart from a few temples in the area.

Tuen Mun Town Plaza, just off the Town Centre station of the LRT, has a musical fountain in the central lobby and tons of shops, including the giant Japanese department store Yaohan. There's a decent food court in the basement, along with a Japanese supermarket.

Castle Peak 青山
With its strangely shaped boulders and sacred

springs, Castle Peak was traditionally reckoned one of the eight wonders of Guangdong Province. An imperial decree of A.D. 969 declared it a sacred mountain, and it has been celebrated in verse by generations of Chinese poets. Over the centuries it has known many other names: "Holy Mountain," "Green Mountain" (Tsing Shan, still the local name), even "Goat Ditch Hill."

Castle Peak is crisscrossed with trails, but be careful not to wander onto the uninhabited back side, which is a government firing range. The map warns: "A danger of unexploded shells exists . . . Do not enter range areas during firing practice." There are better places to hike in Hong Kong.

Castle Peak Monastery 青山寺
The only remaining fragment of the area's past is the Buddhist monastery set on a slope above town. It was supposedly founded in the fifth century by Bei Du, a legendary monk, liar, and thief who is said to have stolen a golden Buddha image from a house he spent the night in. Pursued by his former hosts, he was nearly trapped at the river, until he managed to cross the water in his begging bowl—thus his name, which means "Cup Ferry."

The monastery has been rebuilt many times, passing hands from Buddhists to Taoists and back again. To get there, take the LRT to Technical Institute Station and walk uphill between the Technical Institute and St. Peter's Church. To avoid the steep half-hour climb, take a taxi all the way up to the temple entrance.

Inside you'll find the usual elaborate shrines tended by Buddhist monks, and a vegetarian restaurant. Behind the main temple is a cave housing a granite image of Bei Du, said to date from the tenth century. A nearby stone inscription, which reads "Kao Shan Dai Yat" ("High Mountain, First in Merit"), is said to be a replica of the original, now lost, inscribed on Castle Peak's summit by a Tang dynasty scholar. Enshrined in a cage under an old tree is a fossilized vertebrae said to be a 10,000-year-old dragon's bone.

Ching Chung Koon Temple 青松觀廟
This "Temple of Green Pines" (the pine tree symbolizes long life) is Hong Kong's most famous practicing Taoist shrine, its modern, spa-

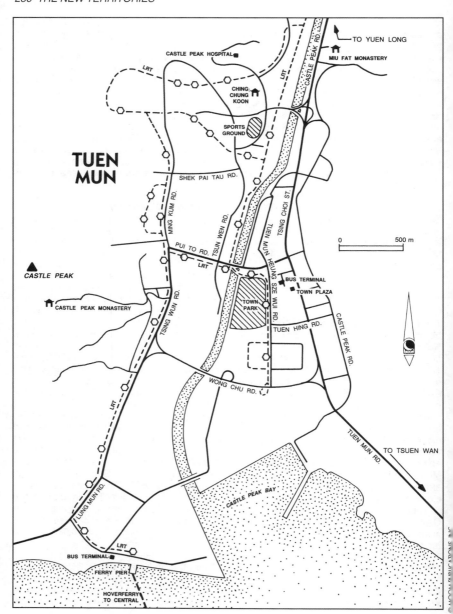

TO YUEN LONG

MIU FAT MONASTERY

CASTLE PEAK HOSPITAL

CHING CHUNG KOON

SPORTS GROUND

TUEN MUN

SHEK PAI TAU RD.

MING KUM RD.

TSUN WEN RD.

TSING CHOI ST.

TUEN MUN HEUNG SZE WUI RD.

CASTLE PEAK

PUI TO RD.

LRT

CASTLE PEAK MONASTERY

TSING WUN RD.

BUS TERMINAL

TOWN PLAZA

TOWN PARK

TUEN HING RD.

CASTLE PEAK RD.

WONG CHU RD.

TO TSUEN WAN

TUEN MUN RD.

LRT

LUNG MUN RD.

CASTLE PEAK BAY

0   500 m

MOON

BUS TERMINAL

FERRY PIER

HOVERFERRY TO CENTRAL

cious grounds crowded with worshippers on weekends and festivals. Though the complex was built in 1949, the **main temple** is superbly decorated with carved wood, wall frescoes, and antique artifacts. On the altar are images of sect founder Wong Chung Yeung on the left (bearing a fly whisk), Wong's teacher Lui Tung Bun in the center, and Wong's disciple Qiu Chang Chun (wielding a feather) on the right.

The most important of the trio is Lui Tung Bun, one of Taoism's legendary Eight Immortals. The main altar displays his implements: a magic sword to slay demons, a fly whisk to swish away bad luck, and a gourd of herbs to heal the sick. There's also a 1,000-year old jade seal and two beautiful goddesses carved of white stone. A map board here helps make sense of the wealth of artifacts.

Next to the temple is the booking hall for the temple's famous vegetarian lunches (minimum two people). Past it are two ancestral halls containing thousands of wooden tablets: families sponsor commemorative services here, with monks chanting and burning paper offerings. The compound also contains an herbal medicine clinic and a home for the aged—appropriate in view of Taoism's preoccupation with longevity. At the rear is a formal Chinese garden of odd-shaped rocks set in a pond, and a zig-zag bridge leading out to a small pavilion.

The temple lies north of town, behind Castle Peak Hospital. Take the LRT to Affluence station, cross the tracks and head right through the housing estate to the main road. You'll see the elaborate temple roofs to the right of the small sports ground across the street. Or take a different LRT line (slightly trickier) to Ching Chung Koon station, right across from the temple.

Miu Fat Monastery 妙法寺

This unusually ornate Buddhist temple lies a few kilometers north of town on Castle Peak Road. The 68M bus stops near a Mobil station across the street, or take the LRT to Lam Tei station. You can't miss this imposing, brightly painted temple right on the main road. Gold-leaf dragons set with mirrored

MAI PO MARSHES NATURE RESERVE

Tucked away in the northwest corner of the New Territories along the Chinese border, this 740-acre (300-hectare) reserve on the shore of Deep Bay provides a safe haven for tens of thousands of migratory birds commuting between Australia and their summer breeding grounds in northern China and Siberia. At peak times the reserve may shelter over 55,000 birds of more than 250 species; birdwatchers can easily spot 80-100 species in a single day. All this, amazingly, exists a 45-minute drive from Tsimshatsui.

"Deep Bay" is a misnomer: the average depth here is only nine meters, and at low tide wide expanses of mudflats are laid bare, drawing thousands of birds to feed. Thick green mangrove forests line the eastern shore of the bay. Similar groves once covered the south China coast, but most have been destroyed in the course of development. With them has vanished a unique ecosystem of salt-tolerant plants and animals. Behind the mangroves are marshes pocketed with large tidal ponds where farmers raise prawns and fish. Some of these are managed as wildlife reserves, providing a refuge when high tide covers the mudflats.

Mai Po's diverse habitats draw a host of land, water, and shore birds. The spring migration of April and early May attracts the greatest concentration of shorebirds in the world, including rare species like the Asiatic dowitcher and the spoonbill sandpiper. Winter visitors tend toward aquatic species: ducks, egrets, ibises, herons. Arrivals have increased in the last few years as other habitats have vanished. Mai Po provides a unique haven for migratory birds, who are arriving in increasing numbers as wildlife habitat in China is destroyed. It also shelters leopards, civets, mongooses, and otters.

The reserve is administered by the World Wide Fund for Nature (WWF), which runs a visitor center at Mai Po. A government permit is needed to visit the blinds, which lie within the closed border area. Serious naturalists should inquire at the Agriculture and Fisheries Department. The easiest option is to join the three-hour guided tour operated by the WWF, which leads down a floating boardwalk to a viewing hide. Contact the WWF office, 1 Tramway Path, Central, tel. 22526-1011, for details. Kingfisher Tours in Tsuen Wan, tel. 2665-8506, also operates birdwatching tours.

mosaics writhe about the entrance pillars, stone lions and elephants guard the door, and a porcelain menagerie prances across the roof ridges. The temple was transferred from China in 1948, first to Ladder Street on Hong Kong Island, later moving to the Hakka village of Lam Tei.

Inside, painted bas-relief sculptures on the stairway landings depict Buddhist themes. An elaborate dining hall on the second floor serves vegetarian lunches (buy tickets at the desk at the entrance). The main shrine is upstairs, an unusually elegant high-ceilinged room that's an orgy of marble, crystal, and gilt. Walls are inlaid with thousands of gold Buddha plaques, and murals on the ceiling depict Indian-inspired Buddhist scenes. Walk behind the main shrine of the Three Precious Buddhas to view rows of gilt-inscribed ancestor tablets, and a giant Avalokitesvara equipped with 1,000 hands to help the suffering.

Getting There and Around
Easiest transport is the hoverferry from Central's Government Services Pier, which runs every 15-20 minutes 6:30 a.m.-7:40 p.m. and costs HK$12-15 for the 40-minute ride. Otherwise there's Bus 59M (Tsuen Wan MTR to Tuen Mun Pier); 59X (Mongkok KCR to Tuen Mun Pier); or the 60M (Tsuen Wan MTR to Tuen Mun Town Centre). Bus 68X (Jordan Rd. Ferry to Yuen Long) and the 68M (Tsuen Wan to Yuen Long) both run through the center of town, passing by Ching Chung Koon and Miu Fat temples. Finally, the Light Rail Transit system running from Tuen Mun Pier all the way into Yuen Long provides a handy means of transport in the Western New Territories; see the special topic "Riding the Light Rail Transit" for details.

Gold Coast
The Gold Coast Hotel, opened in 1994, has put Tuen Mun on the map, with its own marina, water sports, and conference facilities for 1,200 people. Rooms are HK$1300-1950 s or d; the hotel is at 1 Castle Peak Rd., Tuen Mun, tel. 2452-8888. Most interesting is the 30-minute special ferry to Queen's Pier in Central—a great way to zoom into town. Departures either way are roughly hourly; fare is HK$21.

YUEN LONG 元朗

From Tuen Mun, Castle Peak Road and the LRT run north to Yuen Long, another big, built-up New Town housing a quarter-million people. It's hard to believe this was once a small rural market center ringed by fishponds and marshland. There's little appeal for visitors apart from a typically glossy downtown—perfectly adequate if you haven't yet explored a New Town —but Yuen Long serves as launching pad for some worthwhile side trips: to Kam Tin (described above), Laufaushan, and the Ping Shan Heritage Trail.

Downtown
Yuen Long's old market area lies just northwest of the LRT terminus, off Long Yip Street. Two formerly walled villages—Sai Wai and Nam Pin Wai—constitute the old-fashioned market town of **Kau Hui,** which ranks among the least-touched New Territories settlements. Its dark, isolated streets are seldom visited by outsiders, and there's a protective feel to the old shophouses, many of them closed. Look for the **two old temples** to Tai Wong and Pak Tai on the main lane.

Castle Peak Road is the town's main strip; off it is the central shopping center, **Yuen Long Plaza,** a handy stop for fast-food restaurants and Double Rainbow ice cream. The main **bus terminal** is nearby on On Tat Square. Useful routes from here include the 54 to Kam Tin, the 76K to Sheung Shui, the 68M to the Tsuen Wan MTR, and the 64K to the Tai Po Market KCR. (A smaller bus station at the LRT terminus on the east side of town serves Bus 53 to Tsuen Wan Ferry, the 68 to Jordan Road, the 68X to the Jordan Road Ferry, and Minibus 655 to Laufaushan.) Minibuses leave from the terminal on Tai Fung Street.

Ping Shan Heritage Trail 屏山
In the face of relentlessly encroaching development, government antiquities authorities have managed to preserve more than a half-dozen old structures along a one-km route in Ping Shan, a village a few kilometers northwest of Yuen Long. Opened in late 1993, the Ping Shan Heritage

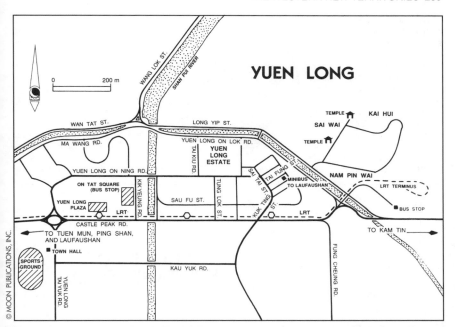

YUEN LONG

Trail includes some exceptionally fine buildings, including ancestral and study halls, some transplanted from other locations. It's a painless way to get a dose of old architecture and culture, as the well-marked trail avoids the need to constantly refer to a map.

Take the LRT to Ping Shan station. Turn right onto Ping Ha Road and follow the leftward curve onto Tong Fong Tsuen Road. Look for the wooden signposts across from the 655 bus stop. (You can also catch Bus 655, 53, or 276 from Yuen Long to here. Leaving, it's easy to take Minibus 655 or 35 on to Laufaushan.)

The trail starts at the **Hung Shing Temple,** built in 1767 in honor of a virtuous government official of the Tang dynasty, posthumously elevated to the status of a deity protecting seafarers. The original open courtyard linking the two halls remains, providing light and ventilation for incense smoke.

Next is **Kun Ting Study Hall,** a beautifully painted high-ceilinged structure which is probably the best-preserved such building in the New Territories. It was built in 1870, before the

area's incorporation into Hong Kong. Boys of the Tang clan studied here for the imperial civil service examination; the hall was also used for ancestor worship. The ornate decor includes carved granite columns, murals, plaster moldings on walls and eaves, and an elaborate altar. Adjoining it is a restored guesthouse for visiting scholars, also superbly decorated.

A little farther up the lane is an open square with two large ancestral halls at the far end. The **Tang Ancestral Hall** on the left is among the finest in Hong Kong, consisting of three impressively large halls linked by two courtyards. Old ancestor tablets rest on the repainted altar at the rear, and there's a photo display outlining clan history. Built around 700 years ago, it was recently restored with funding from the Tang clan. The exquisite detailing includes carved wooden roof beams and Shiwan pottery dragonfish on the roof. Next door is the similar but smaller **Yu Kiu Ancestral Hall,** dating to the early 16th century and commemorating a different branch of the Tang clan.

The trail continues past a small temple dedicated to **Hau Wong,** an impressive black-bearded figure flanked by the Earth God and the patron goddess of expectant mothers, her lap full of pottery children. Passing an old well and a fragment of a walled village, the route winds past vegetable fields to end at **Tsui Shing Lau,** a pagoda built over 600 years ago to ward off evil influences and ensure the success of Tang clan members in civil service exams.

Kun Tin Study Hall, Ping Shan

In accordance with the dictates of *feng shui,* the pagoda was carefully sited at the mouth of a river (long since filled in) and aligned with Castle Peak; one wonders what the housing blocks now looming over it have done to its power.

The hexagonal structure originally had five stories, but the top two were destroyed in a 1954 typhoon. Tsui Shing Lau means "Pagoda of Gathering Stars," and the entrance to each story is inscribed with an auspicious title

PING SHAN HERITAGE TRAIL

TIN FUK RD.

TIN YU RD.

♦ TSUI SHING LAU PAGODA

PING SHAN

FIELDS

SHEUNG CHEUNG WAI

EARTH GOD SHRINE

♦ HAU WONG

HANG TAU TSUEN

FIELDS

OLD WELL

FIELDS

TANG ANCESTRAL HALL

YU KIU ANCESTRAL HALL

KUN TING STUDY HALL

HANG MEI TSUEN

CHING SHU HIN

♦ HUNG SHING

BUS STOP ■

PING HA RD.

TO YUEN LONG

TONG FONG TSUEN

PING SHAN LRT STATION

CASTLE PEAK RD.

0   150 m

© MOON PUBLICATIONS, INC.

like "Over the Milky Way" or "Gathering Star Chamber."

Laufaushan 流浮山
This tiny coastal fishing village seven km northwest of Yuen Long offers excellent seafood, a busy little fish market, and the chance to get out into the countryside, more or less (the area is being overtaken by the giant housing estates of Tin Shui Wai). Laufaushan itself is barely a village: a single alley lined with restaurants and shops purveying the local specialties of dried and live shellfish and bottles of brown oyster sauce. At the far end is the fish market, active only in the morning, and beyond it several centuries of discarded oyster shells, covering a full 500 meters between the village and the seashore.

The shallow, muddy waters of misnamed **Deep Bay** once provided the perfect environment for oyster cultivation, supporting some 3000 hectares of oyster beds, guarded by proprietors against raids by oyster pirates. Sadly, water pollution is poisoning this old tradition.

Across the bay loom the skyscrapers of China's sprawling Shenzhen Special Economic Zone. Deep Bay used to be a popular crossing point for illegal swimmers from China. The bay is fringed by a series of ponds and marshes, culminating in the Mai Po marshes (see the special topic "Mai Po Marshes Nature Reserve"), prime habitat for migrating water birds.

Laufaushan is a good place to eat, being low-key, authentic, and not too touristy or overpriced. Oyster dishes are the specialty, of course, but you'll want your shellfish well-cooked due to pollution. Try **Sun Tau Yuen Restaurant** or the larger and more expensive **Yue Wo Tong.**

To get here, take Minibus 655 from the Yuen Long LRT terminus, or Minibus 34 or 35 from Tai Fung Street. It's a 20-minute ride to the end of Ping Ha Road. Get off at the roundabout and go down the steps behind—there's really only one narrow street. The trip to Laufaushan is easily combined with a stop at the Ping Shan Heritage Trail.

THE EASTERN NEW TERRITORIES

Much of the Eastern New Territories is wild and rugged, a landscape of rocky outcroppings, contorted coastline, and sweeping views. Traditionally undeveloped, this area remains sparsely populated, though this is changing. An increasing number of apartment blocks and Mediterranean-style villas are sprouting up, but for now it remains among the best places to head for scenic views and good walks.

The small coastal settlements along Tolo Harbour and the Sai Kung peninsula have grown rich on the smuggling of VCRs and TVs into nearby Chinese villages, a trade that peaked in the early '90s. Police now control such illegalities with a checkpoint set up at the neck of Tolo Harbour, but villagers have profited from it, accounting for the proliferation of handsome villas with Mercedes parked in front.

CLEARWATER BAY PENINSULA
清水灣

The southeast corner of the New Territories is bordered by Junk Bay on the west and Clearwater Bay on the east. A huge reclamation and housing project slated for Junk Bay will soon house some 400,000 people, and there's talk of extending the MTR out to here. But the gently curving sweep of Clearwater Bay on the peninsula's eastern side remains a good daytrip destination, with a few excellent beaches and an extremely old and important Tin Hau temple. Bring a picnic and enjoy the peace, quiet, and space—except on summer Sundays.

Take the MTR to Choi Hung and catch Bus 91 just outside. The bus stops at the new, ultramodern Hong Kong University of Science and Technology (funded by the Jockey Club with gambling revenues) and passes several film studios and the attractive **Silverstrand Beach**—not so attractive when one considers the recent shark attacks here—before heading onto the increasingly empty peninsula. At Tai Au Mun the road turns south: hikers can get off the bus here and head off onto the trails crossing the peninsula's nearly deserted eastern headland. There are good beaches at **Tai Wan Tau** to the south and **Lung Ha Wan** on the northern tip.

SAI KUNG PENINSULA
AND
CLEARWATER BAY

0   2 km

The 91 terminus is the parking lot above **Clearwater Bay Beach #2;** from here you can walk back up to smaller **Clearwater Bay Beach #1.** Both have clean water and sand and full facilities, but count on crowds on summer weekends.

To Joss House Bay 大廟灣
From Clearwater Bay Beach #2 it's a half-hour walk down the road to the other side of the peninsula and Joss House Bay (Tai Mui Wan). The road winds above the pretty little village of Po Toi O, a favorite destination for pleasure craft. Just beyond is the luxurious **Clearwater Bay Golf and Country Club,** its golf course extending down the manicured headland.

Follow the red-and-white signs to the right of the entrance, pointing down a series of steps to the classic old **Tin Hau Temple** on the southern tip of the peninsula. Set at the outer mouth of the harbor, it was the last stop for outbound crews who anchored here to pray; they called in again on return to give thanks for their safe journey.

The site dates to 1266, making it the oldest of all Tin Hau temples along the Guangdong coast. (A famous carved rock inscription above the temple commemorates the 1274 visit of a Song dynasty government administrator.) It was built by descendents of a pair of brothers who were saved from drowning near here, a miracle they attributed to the statue of the young Fujian girl Lam Tai Kwu, who would later become deified as "Queen of Heaven" (Tin Hau).

The main altar holds triple images of Tin Hau: to the right is the goddess' "bedroom," where each image has its own mosquito-netted bed, washstand, basin, and mirror. Look for the 18th-century model junk inside the main hall, its deck full of carved sailors, and another finely carved gilt junk suspended over the entrance.

The present building dates to 1878, though it was heavily restored after a devastating 1962 typhoon and was renovated again in 1989. The broad waterfront terrace and pier were added by the government to accommodate the crowds of worshippers who arrive by boat on Tin Hau's main festival (usually May). It's quite a sight to see the bay filled with brightly decorated boats, their banners fluttering.

Otherwise it's seldom visited, except for families marching down on weekends to light giant incense sticks. You could do worse than to picnic here, on the pier or out on the rocks edging the bay. Just across the way is **Tung Lung Island** with its old Chinese fortress (see "Tung Lung Chau" under "Other Islands" in the Outlying Islands chapter), with Shek O on Hong Kong Island visible in the distance on a clear day.

Returning, hiking trails lead back to the beaches or bus stop, crossing high bare hills offering splendid coastal views: consult the Country Parks map board near the country club entrance. A trail starting here heads up **Tin Ha Shan,** with side trails descending at several points to the road. Or you could continue all the way across **High Junk Peak** back to Clearwater Bay Road, about six km altogether.

SAI KUNG PENINSULA 西貢

It's hard to believe this wild easternmost outcropping of land with its long rugged coastline exists less than 20 km from urban Hong Kong. For now, at least, it's unspoiled and sparsely populated. Sai Kung serves as Hong Kong's garden—nurseries coax expensive blooms for the Chinese New Year—and its weekend retreat, with luxury marinas holding yachts used for cruising amid the scattered islands. An increasing number of pseudo-Mediterranean villas with red or blue tiles are rising up on the hillsides. Development is moving into this last, biggest, and most accessible chunk of unspoiled land, but the country parks system will hopefully preserve large swatches of Sai Kung's current splendor.

Sai Kung Town, an old fishing port and market village, provides a base for exploring 7,500-hectare **Sai Kung Country Park,** which is divided into East and West sections. (Adjoining **Ma On Shan Country Park** covers the interior of the peninsula all the way up to Shatin.) Sai Kung boasts some 80 km of trails, including the MacLehose Trail, which begins at Pak Tam Chung and immediately heads off into some of its finest scenery.

Sai Kung also has some of Hong Kong's best, most isolated beaches, and makes a great choice for a pleasant day out of town. Have lunch or dinner at Sai Kung's seafood restaurants, and spend the rest of the day exploring one of the options detailed below.

To get to Sai Kung Town, take the MTR to Choi Hung and exit onto Clearwater Bay Road (North). Catch Bus 92 across the street, or the slightly faster air-conditioned Minibus 1 from right in front of the MTR exit. Bus 299 plies between Shatin and Sai Kung.

Sai Kung Town 西貢墟

Despite recent development, this former small fishing village retains its busy harbor packed with boats and sampans, its seafood market and restaurants, and a fragment of the closely packed old town. The main bus terminus and taxi stand is just off the waterfront promenade (Hoi Pong Street). Veer off onto Sai Kung Public Pier for nice views of Sai Kung Hoi (Inner

Port Shelter), full of sampans and boats. The quay may be lined with people fishing with reels of dental floss and bits of worm—it must be the joy of the hunt, rather than the miniscule catch.

Stroll down past a long row of restaurants, which start out fancy and become increasingly simpler. Prices vary, but the food is excellent everywhere. The fish stalls here are virtual aquariums selling every imaginable kind of sea creature: tropical lobsters, clams squirting jets of water, huge iridescent blue-green Napoleon wrasse, mussels, elephant-nose clams, bamboo-bound crabs—even snakes in the winter. You can pick out your meal here and carry it to the restaurant for cooking, still writhing in a plastic bag.

The **wholesale fish market** at the end of the quay is active in the early morning but shuts down by noon. Beyond it, veer slightly right to ex-

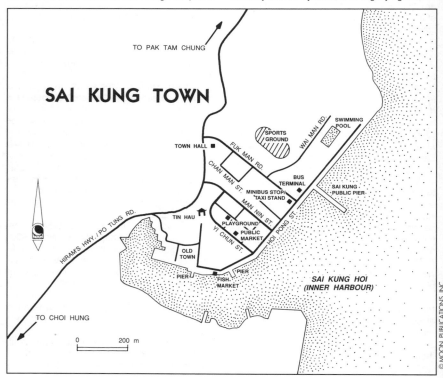

plore the narrow lanes of the **old market town,** where proprietors drowse in open shophouses behind displays of herbal medicine, incense, and fresh-baked sweet buns. Mahjong players secreted on upper floors provide the only noise. Wander up to the **Tin Hau Temple** up Yi Chun Street, founded some seven centuries ago, with a separate hall for fierce, red-faced Kwan Ti, god of all things martial. If you haven't yet visited a public market, check out the one on Yi Chun Street, with a variety of produce and meat.

Food

Sai Kung has a disproportionate number of good restaurants. A fresh seafood meal from one of the many waterfront restaurants is an excellent pretext for a visit to Sai Kung. Just make sure to ask the prices of the live seafood you select! **Tung Kee Restaurant,** 96 Man Nin St., is a popular choice, but really, all these places produce excellent food. **The Shanghai,** across from the Watson's, has good Shanghai food.

If you're not in the mood for seriously fresh seafood, try the pizza and pasta at **Pepperoni's** at 1588 Po Tung Rd. (just off Hiram's Highway), or **Firenze** at 60 Po Tung Road. **Susanna's,** 74 Po Tung Rd., serves good Mexican, Asian, and Western food.

Tiny Sha Tsui Path, which leads from the playground to the market, is looking vaguely European of late, with a string of funky little café/restaurants with open-air tables. There's **Black Sheep,** a small innovative café serving African and veggie food; the **Ali Oli Delicatessen** next door (good coffee) and **Jaspa's,** the best choice, with a delicious international menu. All are inexpensive to moderate.

Inner Port Islands

The islands dotting Sai Kung's Inner Port offer some fine swimming beaches. *Kaido*s run from the promenade: either hop on the regular service to more popular sites, or hire your own—but bargain, and arrange a pickup time.

The most popular destination is **Kiu Tsui Chau (Sharp Island).** There's a good sandy beach with facilities at Hap Mun Wan, and *kaido*s also call at Kiu Tsui Bay on the island's rockier western shore. The island is getting more visitors with the opening of a new Jockey Club-sponsored golf course. Service to the miniscule

sand-fringed specks of **Pak Sha Chau** and **Cham Tau Chau** is less frequent, and consequently they are less crowded, though there are facilities like barbeque pits and toilets. These three islands, plus the Trio beach peninsula, form **Kiu Tsui Country Park.**

*Kaido*s also run over to the tiny island of **Yim Tin Tsai,** where century-old St. Joseph's Chapel serves the island's miniscule but entirely Catholic population. A narrow spit, submerged at high tide, connects it to the bigger island of **Kau Sai Chau,** also served by *kaido*s. Off the east side of Kau Sai Chau is **Rocky Harbour,** dotted with idyllic small islands worth exploring if you've got a private boat. Sai Kung *kaido*s run as far as the High Island beaches of **Tai She Wan** and **Pak Lap;** see below for more on High Island.

Trio Beach, a few kilometers south of Sai Kung Town on a tiny peninsula, is also worth a visit. Get off Bus 92 before town at the luxury development of **Hebe Haven (Pak Sha Wan),** and catch a *kaido* over to Trio. Or walk down Hiram's Highway and take the trail down to the tip of the peninsula, about three km altogether.

Pak Tam Chung 北潭涌

Bus 94 runs from Sai Kung Town north across the peninsula to Wong Shek Pier on Tolo Channel. The road skirts between Sai Kung's two country parks, providing access to many good walks.

The road commences by passing a multitude of roadside barbecue pits. The second parking area on the bus route is Pak Tam Chung, where a big **Sai Kung Country Park Visitor Centre** dispenses information on hiking trails and the natural history of the peninsula (open daily except Tuesday 9:30 a.m.-4:30 p.m.).

The easiest walk is the signposted **Pak Tam Chung Nature Trail,** less than one km in length and designed for schoolchildren. It leads to **Sheung Yiu Folk Museum,** a tiny, compact hamlet of eight houses built some 150 years ago by a Hakka family. Residents earned their living from lime kilns, a local tradition until the market collapsed with the introduction of cement. The last villagers left in 1965, and the houses have been carefully restored by the Regional Council into a mini-museum, outfitted with traditional furnishings to illustrate traditional Hakka life. Displays reveal the great reliance on local plants: the longan trees in front, for instance, provided timber, fruit, and "tea" leaves of a sort, while the nuts were compounded into medicine. The museum is open daily except Tuesday 9 a.m.-4 p.m. Returning, you can loop back via the signposted 1.8-km Family Walk, which starts about 100 meters past the museum.

More ambitious hikers can take in a portion of the 100-km MacLehose Trail, which starts just across the road from the visitor center. Stage One is a three-hour stroll from Pak Tam Chung around High Island Reservoir to a campsite on the white sands of **Long Ke** (the loop around the reservoir makes a fine longer day-hike). Things get even better during Stage Two (five hours), as the trail winds past spectacular coastal scenery and the fine beaches of Sai Wan and Ham Tin to the Bradbury Youth Hostel at Chek Keng (see below).

Past Pak Tam Chung, Bus 94 turns left, cutting across the peninsula to Wong Shek Pier. The countryside is relatively wild, and largely undeveloped apart from a few old farmhouses. This is jungle territory for Hong Kong, with wildlife—cows!—lurking in the underbrush.

Chek Keng and Tai Long Wan 赤徑 , 大浪灣
Get off at the small village of Pak Tam Au to make the hour's hike east to the small coastal settlement of Chek Keng. The **Bradbury Hall Youth Hostel,** tel. 2328-2458, is near here, close to the pier where the Tolo Harbour-Ma Liu Shui ferry calls at 10:20 a.m. and 4:45 p.m.

Ninety minutes' walk farther east down the MacLehose Trail is Tai Long Wan, a long curving expanse of white sand that's the best beach in all Hong Kong, remote enough to remain uncrowded. Small restaurants at nearby **Tai Long** and **Ham Tin** serve food, at least on weekends. Remember to return to Chek Keng in time for the ferry (double-check the departure time on your way in), or you'll have to walk all the way back to Pak Tam Au.

Pak Sha O and Hoi Ha Wan 白沙澳 , 海下灣
Past the little village of Ko Tong the road forks again, with Hoi Ha Road turning off to the left. Minibus 7 runs up it from Pak Tam Chung on Sunday and holidays, but it's easy to walk or hire a taxi. First point of note is the remote hamlet of Pak Sha O, one of the more pastoral New Territories villages. Most of its inhabitants have moved to the city, leaving the buildings to a few elderly caretakers and weekend vacationers. Look for the nicely decorated ancestral hall of the Ho family, walled and crowned by a tower, and the tiny Roman Catholic church built in the 1930s, now renovated as a recreation center. Nearby is the **Pak Sha O Youth Hostel**, tel. 2328-2327, about 30 minutes' walk from the main road.

Hoi Ha Road continues a little farther to Hoi Ha village, set on a small inlet overlooking Jones' Cove. The few old houses here are outnumbered by modern ones. Residents used to farm and produce lime, and two kilns on the east side of the village have been restored for sightseers. The coral-fringed small bay of Jones' Cove (Hoi Ha Wan) is good for swimming and a favorite site for scuba diving. A Marine Park was recently established here, and the World Wide Fund for Nature is now proposing a HK$22 million marine education center, featuring glass-bottomed boats and tide tanks.

Wong Shek and the Long Harbour Ferry
The main reason for staying on Bus 94 all the way to the terminus at Wong Shek Pier is to take the *kaido* up the lovely fjord-like inlet of Long Harbour to the isolated island of Tap Mun Chau (see "Tap Mun Chau" under "Other Islands" in the Outlying Islands chapter). The boat runs roughly every two hours (hourly on Sunday); it's a 30-minute crossing. Returning from Tap Mun, you can take the 5:20 p.m. Tolo Harbour ferry to Ma Liu Shui and walk to the KCR University Station—a superb daytrip if you make all the connections.

BOB RACE

THE OUTLYING ISLANDS

Hong Kong has 235 islands in addition to Hong Kong Island, many of them uninhabited stony specks surrounded by the sea. Other, larger islands hold communities of fisherfolk and farmers. More isolated than the New Territories and sheltered from the impact of motor vehicles, they preserve a bit of old China.

Prehistoric rock carvings and excavated artifacts indicate the islands' history dates back at least to the Stone Age, when sandy beaches were a favorite camping ground for a semi-nomadic population. Well into this century the islands remained havens for fishing fleets and smugglers, but today city life is tempting younger residents to leave the difficult, isolated island life to a few elderly people. A few of the larger and more centrally placed islands have become bedroom communities for Hongkongers who make the daily ferry commute into town in exchange for open space, peace and quiet, and lower rents.

Most popular with visitors are the "big three" islands arrayed southeast of urban Hong Kong: **Lamma,** tiny **Cheung Chau,** and sprawling **Lantau,** which is twice the size of Hong Kong Is-

land. While it's possible to overnight on all these, most visitors are satisfied with a daytrip via ferry from Central. Public ferries go to a total of seven islands, and *kaido* or local ferries to more. A charter boat is expensive, but offers infinite flexibility: it's the only way you're likely to find the desert island of your dreams.

The islands are where Hong Kong goes to play. Locals troop over en masse in the evenings to enjoy the seafood restaurants of Lamma and Cheung Chau, and weekend ferries are packed with cheerful groups of hikers, barbecuers, and young couples headed for an island "holiday flat" and a bit of privacy. You're likely to use the islands in the same way as day-tripping urbanites: for beaches and hikes, fresh air and silence, and excellent cheap seafood. Try to avoid weekends, when ferries, beaches, and hotels are packed and transport and room rates go up. Summer Sundays are especially crowded.

Serious hikers should pick up the *Countryside Series No. 3: Lantau & Islands,* available at the Government Publications Office in Admiralty. The Country Parks Authority puts out a map/brochure of the Lantau Trail, and HKTA

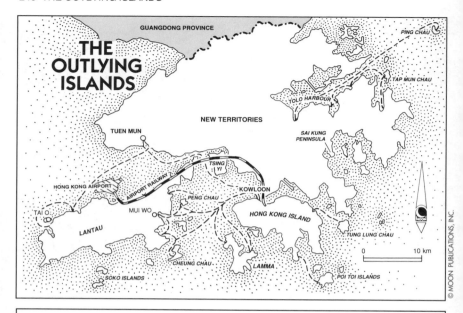

© MOON PUBLICATIONS, INC.

OUTLYING ISLANDS FERRIES

Big double- and triple-decker **ferries** to Lantau, Lamma, Cheung Chau, and Peng Chau depart from the Outlying Districts Services Pier in Central, a ten-minute walk from the Star Ferry terminal. The Kowloon Star Ferry Terminal operates weekend ferries for Lantau and Cheung Chau; see text for details.

Fares are very reasonable, around HK$9 on weekdays for an "ordinary class" ticket on the middle deck. HK$16 buys a deluxe class seat on the top deck, worth it for the better views. Deluxe class is air-conditioned in summer and heated in winter and is outfitted with big picture windows, seats and tables (to play cards on), and an open-air sundeck in back.

The trip out is a pleasure in itself. Drinks and snacks are sold on board, and on sunny days you can sit on the open back deck and watch boats of all descriptions bobbing about in the harbor, as unexpected vistas of Hong Kong Island slide past. People eat, sleep, cuddle, or read the newspaper; kids play; teenagers joke—it's all very relaxed, at least on weekdays, when the huge boats are practically empty. On sunny Sundays city folk descend upon the islands, a good reason to stay away. Fares al-

most double starting Saturday afternoon, and lines can be long, though you can usually get a ticket for the next boat. Buying a roundtrip ticket (available for deluxe class only) will save time waiting in line on return. For more information and up-to-date departure times, call the Hongkong and Yaumatei Ferry Co. at 2310-4091.

Faster and slightly more expensive **hoverferries** to Lantau, Peng Chau, and Cheung Chau depart from the same location. Services are less frequent and may run only on weekdays. The hoverferry to Lantau's Discovery Bay leaves round-the-clock from the Edinburgh Place Ferry Pier near City Hall.

Kaidos—wooden-seated, un-air-conditioned local ferries—ply remoter routes to more untouched places. Details are given in the text. **Inter-island-hopping** is a slightly more complicated matter, though a few *kaidos* run between islands. The ferry service shuttling between Peng Chau, Lantau and Cheung Chau means you can combine several islands into a single day—though given Lantau's sprawling size and the essentially laid-back nature of the islands, it's probably best to enjoy just one at a leisurely pace.

publishes two booklets of detailed commentary accompanied by maps: *Cheung Chau Walking Tour* and *Lantau Island Explorer's Guide*. Another useful guide to Lamma Island is published by Friends of the Earth as part of its Coastal Guide series—it's available at the Government Publications Office.

LANTAU 大嶼山

The island's name means "Broken Head," a reference to two-headed Lantau Peak. More commonly it's called Tai Yue Shan, "Big Island Mountain." In pre-British days Lantau was the most important of all the islands; indeed, the British at one time considered appropriating it rather than Hong Kong Island.

Lantau's history stems back to Neolithic times, when its inhabitants lived along the shoreline. Bronze Age rock carvings have been discovered at Shek Pik, and Sung dynasty relics at Fan Lau on the island's southwest tip. Its mainstays for centuries were fishing, salt panning, and the burning of coral and seashells to make lime. The old port of Tai O served as the center for the latter two industries.

Today Lantau is taking center stage again, with the new airport on its northern coast. Developers are busy buying up coastal land and farms in the hopes that the new train and road links to Kowloon and Central will make the island another bedroom community. While Lantau's northern shore is likely to be transformed beyond recognition, the island's interior is likely to remain as it has always been: mountainous and peaceful, crossed by only a handful of roads, its upper reaches often wreathed in mists. The island is dotted with holy sites, the best-known the flashy Buddhist monastery of Po Lin, but there's also a Trappist monastery and dozens of smaller Buddhist hermitages, many sheltering only two or three retreatants.

It's easy to sense what drew them here. Lantau boasts some of the finest mountain scenery in Hong Kong. Wooded on the lower slopes and bare on the upper, the hills rise straight up from the sea. The island's backbone is formed by the second and third-highest peaks in the SAR: Lantau Peak (933 meters) and Sunset Peak (869 meters). Lantau's 70 km of trails draw both serious and semi-serious hikers. The island is big enough to feel alone on, and the bare mountainsides yield sweeping vistas of sea and sky.

The present population is only around 30,000, but given that Lantau is twice the size of Hong Kong Island, its population density is ridiculously low when compared to the SAR as a whole. People live in scattered small villages set along Lantau's three main roads. The interior of the island—over 50% of its total area—is preserved in two country parks (Lantau South and Lantau North), which are crisscrossed by marked trails. Premier is the circular **Lantau Trail,** which from Mui Wo heads up over the mountains, passing near Po Lin and Tai O and looping back along the south coast. The entire trail takes a total of 23.5 hours walking, and you can overnight at campsites and the few youth hostels along the way.

It's perhaps easier to do selected stretches as day-hikes. The best scenery is found in the middle section over Lantau and Sunset peaks. Pick up the Lantau sheet from the Government Publications Office, or request a leaflet from the Country Parks Authority booth near the Mui Wo ferry pier. Other good hikes include Tai O to Tung Chung, Mui Wo to the Trappist monastery at Tai Shui Hang, and the loop around the isolated southwest corner and Fan Lau.

Other attractions are the big Buddhist monastery of Po Lin and the fishing village at Tai O, which still manages to preserve its traditional atmosphere. Catch an early ferry to allow time for getting around: Lantau's scale is twice as big as anywhere else in Hong Kong, and bus rides are a minimum of 45 minutes one-way.

Silvermine Bay (Mui Wo) 銀礦灣

The name is the best part about it, but Silvermine Bay's 19th-century mines are sealed, never having produced much ore. The town is Lantau's main point of access. Most everyone arrives here on the ferry from Central, and most everyone treats it as a takeoff point, marching straight out to the bus terminal and taxi stand across from the ferry exit.

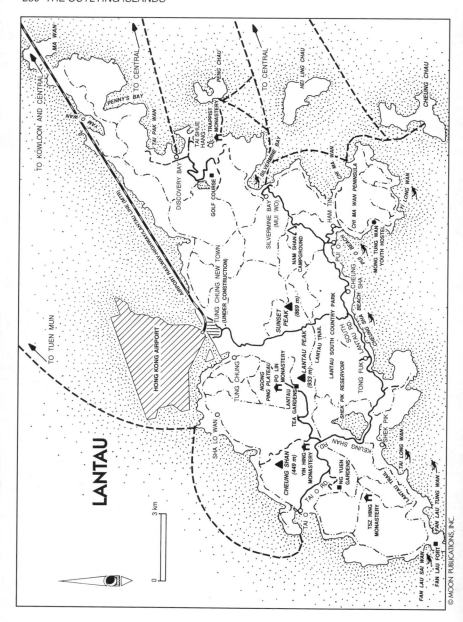

LANTAU

© MOON PUBLICATIONS, INC.

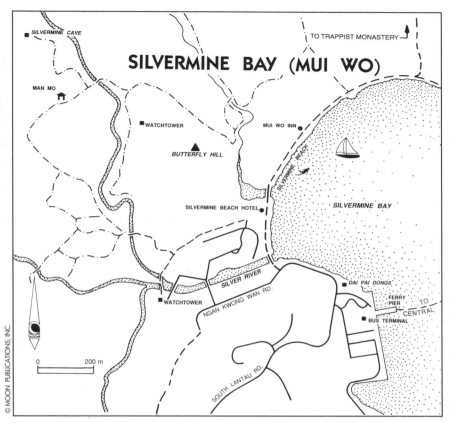

SILVERMINE BAY (MUI WO)

SILVERMINE CAVE

TO TRAPPIST MONASTERY

MAN MO

WATCHTOWER

MUI WO INN

BUTTERFLY HILL

SILVERMINE BEACH

SILVERMINE BEACH HOTEL

SILVERMINE BAY

SILVER RIVER

DAI PAI DONGS

WATCHTOWER

NGAN KWONG WAN RD.

FERRY PIER

TO CENTRAL

BUS TERMINAL

SOUTH LANTAU RD.

0   200 m

© MOON PUBLICATIONS, INC.

Silvermine Bay is actually a collection of small villages strung along the bay, one of which (Mui Wo, or "Five-Petal Flower," a reference to the plum blossom) has lent its name to the ferry terminal. The quaintly scruffy village around the terminal was long ago cleaned up and organized. Across from the ferry exit is a minor "downtown," with a few restaurants and small supermarkets and a post office. Off to the right, a waterfront string of *dai pai dong*s sell cheap, good food until late at night. The path leads down to **Silvermine Bay Beach,** still popular despite the dubious quality of its water. Here are two hotels and some bike rental stands,

though the island is really too steep and big for anything but mountain bikes.

The area around Mui Wo has some minor attractions. Up Mui Wo Rural Committee Road is a 200-year-old Man Mo Temple. Farther down is a little park with a waterfall—a nice place for a picnic, though the water flow is a trickle in the dry winter season—and behind it, abandoned and sealed Silvermine Cave, its brief history described on a plaque. The three old **watchtowers** scattered around town are relics of a modern-day warlord who dominated the island until the 1960s.

THE SOUTH COAST

Sunset Peak 大東山

The island's second-highest mountain (and Hong Kong's third-highest), Sunset Peak is a good choice for a comfortable day-hike. Buses 1, 2, 4, 5, and 7 all run past **Nam Shan Campground,** about 10 minutes out of town. Cross the road to the clearly marked beginning of the Lantau Trail. Steep stone steps, mercifully shaded, eventually give way to open grasslands and vistas of the surrounding island. It's about a two-hour climb to the 869-meter summit. The small stone huts just below are used as summertime retreats by church groups. Returning, you can retrace your steps back to the South Lantau Road, or take a trail dropping down the back side of the slope about an hour to reach Pak Kung Au on the Tung Chung Road. From here, buses run hourly to Tung Chung or Mui Wo.

Cheung Sha Beach 長沙灣

About 15 minutes' ride down the South Lantau Road, the little town of **Pui O (**貝澳 **)** nestles below Sunset Peak. It consists of a long, unlovely string of holiday "villas," apartments, and shops, set across the road from a popular beach. Past the next headland lies what is probably the best major beach in Hong Kong: Cheung Sha, an unusually long (3.2 km), narrow strip of clean white sand facing an open bay. Facilities are excellent here, and the beach isn't crowded on weekdays. Best access is to get off the bus after the 4.5-mile marker, on the outskirts of Tong Fuk village

LANTAU BUS ROUTES

Bus routes out of Mui Wo:

NO.	DESTINATION
1	Tai O
2	Ngong Ping
3	Tung Chung
4	Tong Fuk
5	Shek Pik
7	Pui O
21	Ngong Ping
23	Ngong Ping (Sunday only)

(buses 1, 2, 4, and 5 all run past here). People tend to cluster at the lower end of the beach near Tong Fuk: for privacy, aim for Upper Cheung Sha Beach.

Chi Ma Wan Peninsula 芝蔴灣

Most of this quiet, secluded chunk of land jutting south toward Cheung Chau belongs to Lantau South Country Park. Get off the bus at Pui O and follow the road south toward Ham Tin. Stage 12 of the Lantau Trail from Nam Shan Campground also leads out onto the peninsula, and a *kaido* plying between Peng Chau, Mui Wo, and Cheung Chau calls at a small jetty on the eastern side of the peninsula.

About 45 minutes walk south from Pui O on the western side of the peninsula is **Mong Tung Wan Bay,** with a small IYHA Youth Hostel over-

Tai Long Wan Beach, Lantau

BOB RACE

looking the water. Trails lead south from here, past the cove of Yi Long Wan, where the luxury homes of the exclusive **Sea Ranch** development serve as holiday retreats for Hong Kong executives who commute by private ferry or helicopter. The next bay over, **Tai Long Wan,** has a tiny village and the friendly **Frog and Toad Pub,** site of boozy weekend lunches and a gleefully messy "Mud Olympics" held each October. The pub is open daily 12:30-5:30 p.m., later on summer weekends or holidays. Bar staff will call for a *kaido* from here over to nearby Cheung Chau (HK$60), or it's a 90-minute walk back to Pui O.

Shek Pik 石壁

From Tong Fuk the road heads inland, passing gigantic 5.5-billion-gallon Shek Pik Reservoir (the water is piped to Hong Kong Island via an underground/undersea tunnel). Trails encircling the reservoir make for good walking; there are prehistoric rock carvings in the vicinity, and a mysterious stone circle set on a hillside, not to mention Shek Pik Maximum Security Prison down on the right. The back side of Po Lin Monastery's gigantic Buddha is visible through a notch up in the hills behind.

Soon after the reservoir the road turns north, changing its name to Keung Shan Road and ascending the lower slopes of Lantau Peak. The turnoff to Po Lin Monastery is about two km farther; the Keung Shan Road continues into the coastal fishing village of Tai O.

Fan Lau 分流

Get off the bus at Shek Pik to explore the isolated southwestern corner of Lantau. There's a decent beach at **Tai Long Wan** a little south of Shek Pik. Tung Wan beach to the east is the site of archaeological excavations of prehistoric burial sites.

The Lantau Trail wends along a coastal road that eventually dwindles into a trail, passing campsites and barbecue sites and the good, quiet beaches of

Fan Lau Tung Wan and **Fan Lau Sai Wan.** Between these, strategically sited on the southwestern tip of the peninsula, is an 18th-century **stone fort,** part of a chain of coastal defenses built by Guangdong authorities to protect the Pearl River estuary and Lantau Island against pirates. (The estuary is very shallow in this area, and the only navigable channels run along the Lantau coastline.) The fort has been partially restored and makes an interesting destination—plus you're virtually guaranteed privacy. It's about two hours' walk from Shek Pik, or two and a half hours from Tai O.

Near the fort is a mysterious circle of large, partly buried stones set overlooking the bay and only discovered in 1980. Its purpose and age is unknown, but it may date to the Bronze Age, and may be related to a similar circle found on Lamma Island.

PO LIN MONASTERY 寶蓮寺

This ornate Buddhist temple, among the biggest and grandest in Hong Kong, is without a doubt Lantau's most popular attraction, receiving up to 2,000 visitors each weekend. While touristy, it's undeniably impressive, with brilliantly colored shrines and an active community of about 100 monks and nuns and an equal number of elderly lay residents.

Po Lin or "Precious Lotus" Monastery was founded as an isolated retreat in 1905. Set on the 750-meter-high Ngong Ping Plateau in the shadow of Lantau Peak, it was a tranquil refuge, in those days reached only by a steep footpath from Tai O. It remained modest until a building spree in the early 1970s added a number of opulent buildings.

The orange-and-gold **main shrine** holds gilt figures of the historical Buddha, Shakyamuni, flanked by the Healing Buddha on the right and Amitabha on the left. The finely carved statues were created in 1969 by craftsmen using jade tools. Across the way is a lav-

Po Lin's giant Buddha

CHRIS PARMENTER

*nuns of
Po Lin Monastery*

KERRY MORAN

ishly decorated shrine to Wo Tei, guardian of Buddhist temples. The small original temple behind the main building is still used for daily prayers chanted at 5 a.m and again around 3 or 4 p.m.

Po Lin's latest attraction towers above the newly developed parking lot: the world's tallest outdoor **bronze Buddha statue.** The project took six years and HK$68 million (US$8.8 million) to complete. Its design—a steel framework covered with a 10-mm-thick coating of bronze—replicates that of the Statue of Liberty. Over 200 numbered pieces were shipped from the factory in China to be assembled on the site. Hauling up the enormous load required closing the road for three days. Climb up the steps for fantastic views of the area; there's a small exhibition gallery inside the statue's base.

Po Lin's other main draw is a **vegetarian lunch** of tofu, black mushrooms, and greens, typical of the tasty fare served in many temples. Buy a HK$60 ticket at the booth to the right of the main temple, and find your numbered table in the big restaurant on the left. In the summer months you might opt for the HK$120 lunch served in an air-conditioned restaurant.

The monastery also offers overnight accommodation in men's and women's dorms (HK$200 for three meals and a hard bed). An overnight stay is recommended if you want to get the real feel of the place, as things become considerably more peaceful after the tour buses go home. The other reason for an overnight stay is to climb 933-meter-high **Lantau Peak**

for sunrise views. Slogging up 1,400 steep stone steps before dawn may seem daunting, but the views are impressive as long as the frequent fog stays away. It's a three-hour roundtrip.

Lantau Tea Gardens

A few minutes' walk from the monastery are the Lantau Tea Gardens, a scrubby-looking 160-acre plantation revived several decades ago by a British lawyer. High mountaintops are considered excellent for tea-growing, as the fog is said to nurture supremely flavorful leaves. The local *wan mo cha* ("cloud-mist tea") is served in a small cafe here. The Garden's main emphasis is on tourism, with a paddock for horseback riding, a shabby outdoor roller rink, and some motley looking bungalows. **Lantau Stables** here offers horseback riding, charging from HK$70 for a horseback photo opportunity to HK$360 per hour for trail rides (minimum three horses).

Transportation

Bus 2 from Mui Wo runs roughly hourly up to Po Lin; the trip takes about 40 minutes and lines are often long on Sunday. Bus 2R runs only on Sunday between Po Lin and Tai O. Leaving Po Lin, you may be able to snag a taxi, or consider making the pleasant two-hour hike down to **Tung Chung** and the new airport, passing a less elaborate Buddhist monastery en route. **Tai O** is a longer hike, and you'll probably end up walking along the road a good part of the way.

Ng Yuen 吾圍

Another good hike is to the exquisitely landscaped Chinese gardens of Ng Yuen near the little village of Lung Tsai, south of the Tai O Road. They're part of a millionaire's country estate—the house is closed but the gardens are open to the public. Going direct, take Bus 1 (Tai O) from Silvermine Bay and get off at the Lantau South Country Park Entrance (past the Po Lin turnoff). Head up the paved road and follow the signs to Ng Yuen, at the top of a steep stone staircase. A longer, hillier route (about three hours) starting across from the Po Lin turnoff leads along Stage 5 of the Lantau Trail. Returning, you can follow Stage 6 down into Tai O, about 2.5 km downhill and an hour away.

TAI O 大澳

This old fishing and smuggling port on Lantau's west coast is the island's traditional unofficial "capital." Though its population has dropped considerably since its heyday, it remains the largest settlement, with some 3,000 inhabitants, many of them Tanka "boat people" who have resettled on dry land. It's also Lantau's richest village: smuggling is an old and respected means of supplementing local incomes, and Tai O's proximity to the Pearl River estuary gives easy access to Chinese coastal villages.

Tai O retains its aura of a quaint fishing village, with an old-town atmosphere reminiscent of Hong Kong a century ago. Though concrete boxes are proliferating, there are still houses set on piles over the river, and fishermen cruising the waterways.

Bus 2 from Mui Wo stops outside of town, where old ladies lurking about solicit customers for a short sampan ride up the creek—good for views, but be sure to bargain. Check out the HKTA map board of the area at the terminus, then stroll up the narrow shop-lined lane, where Tai O's fishing village orientation soon becomes clear. Locally made shrimp paste is displayed in glass jars, along with various dried aquatic objects wrapped in plastic for day-trippers to cart back to Hong Kong. Through the 1950s, Tai O was a center of the ancient salt-panning industry and is famous still for its salt fish, the pungent

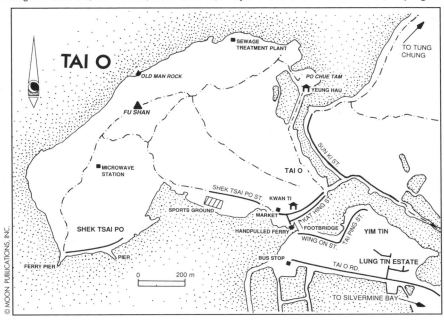

smell of which fills the air. The area is dotted with old salt pans, many of them now converted to fishponds.

The rest of town lies across a creek—actually an ocean inlet, as Tai O lies partly on a small island. The gap is bridged by a rope-drawn ferry, run by local women for a HK50 cent toll. At low tide the barge lies stranded in the riverbed, connected by gangways to each bank. You walk across it—and still pay the toll. There's a new pedestrian footbridge as well.

The other side of town is more compact, with a produce market, several decent restaurants, and a 200-year-old temple dedicated to Kwan Ti, the God of War (a replica of Kwan Ti's horse is here too, and the horse of the Han emperor he served). The primeval-looking Earth God shrines scattered about town are little more than sacred rocks with sticks of incense smoldering in front.

Walk down the lane past the Kwan Ti temple and follow the waterfront to the recently renovated old **Yung Hau Wong Temple,** prettily situated on a little promontory jutting into Pearl Bay. This is the village's most popular temple, dedicated to the minister said to have jumped into the sea holding the last young Sung dynasty emperor in his arms. A big annual festival with Cantonese opera is held here during the sixth moon.

Getting There
Bus 1 runs from Mui Wo to Tai O in about 45 minutes, or it's a two-hour-plus walk from Po Lin. You could also ride the bus down from Po Lin to the junction of Keung Shan and Sham Wat roads and wait for Bus 1 from Mui Wo, or, if you're very lucky, a taxi. Bus 2R runs between Tai O and Po Lin on Sunday and holidays.

Tai O also has a few weekend ferry connections. On Sunday there's a ferry to Tuen Mun and Tsuen Wan at 4:45 p.m., and another to Tuen Mun and Central at 5:30 p.m. On Saturday at 5:45 p.m. there's a ferry to Tuen Mun.

TUNG CHUNG 東涌

Tung Chung, the second of Lantau's two old harbors, is a very old settlement indeed: it was here that the fleeing Sung dynasty boy-emper-

or is said to have set up his court. A handful of local inhabitants still claim descent from those long-ago courtiers.

The fertile coastal plain surrounding the former coastal settlement is changing in a big way, with the construction of the new airport on the former island of Chek Lap Kok. The hugely ambitious scheme, touted as the world's biggest ongoing civil engineering project, includes an eventual two runways, a new terminal, and elaborate transportation links connecting Lantau's north shore with Kowloon and Central. Tung Chung is being developed into a shiny New Town with an eventual population of 150,000.

Sights
About 10 minutes' walk before town along the main road is **Tung Chung Battery (** 東涌炮台 **),** set on a small grassy headland overlooking the bay. Discovered in 1980 beneath dense underbrush, it's little more than a stone wall, part of a series of coastal fortifications developed by the Chinese to fight piracy. About one km farther down the road is **Tung Chung Fort (** 東涌城寨 **),** with muzzle-loading cannons set into its thick granite walls. Its intimidating appearance is belied by an unstrategic location. Records indicate it was built in 1817 as a military administrative center rather than an offensive installation, but the name "fort" has stuck. The building was restored in 1988 and now houses a public school and offices.

A winding footpath leads across the plain to the double-roofed Ming dynasty **Hau Wong Temple,** dedicated to the Sung dynasty minister Yung Hau Wong, the uncle of the ill-fated boy emperor. It boasts a cast-metal bell dated 1765 and fine ceramic roof decorations from the Shiwan kilns.

Getting There
Bus 3 from Mui Wo takes about an hour to Tung Chung. Otherwise, it's a two-hour walk down from Po Lin, passing other monasteries en route, or four to five hours from Tai O via a coastal trail. Ferries run between the Castle Peak Bay jetty in Tuen Mun and Tung Chung three times a day.

It will be a different picture once the airport opens, of course. Apart from flying in on a jet, Tung Chung will be reachable by taxi, bus, or

MTR—the new **Lantau Line** will provide domestic service linking north Lantau to Tsimshatsui and Central.

NORTHEAST LANTAU

Trappist Monastery 熙篤會神樂院

The Trappist Haven of Our Lady of Liesse at Tai Shue Hang provides a Christian counterpoint to Lantau's numerous Buddhist retreats. It was founded in the 1950s by 12 Trappist monks fleeing the communist regime in Beijing. Today the community's main means of support are its dairy cows. Set amid a pine grove halfway up a hill, it's serenely peaceful, as befits the Trappist vow of silence. Mass is said at 10:45 a.m. Sunday in the spare, modern chapel. Overnight accommodation can be arranged by applying in advance to the Grand Master, Trappist Haven, Lantau Island, P.O. Box 5, Peng Chau.

The walk here from Silvermine Bay makes a nice daytrip, either by a three-km ridgetop trail or a longer, lower route skirting the coastline. Heading east from the monastery, it's a 30-minute walk to Nim Shue Wan and the massive housing complexes of Discovery Bay. *Kaidos* run infrequently from the monastery pier to Nim Shue Wan, and six times daily between the monastery and the nearby island of **Peng Chau.**

Discovery Bay 愉景灣

Popularly known as "Disco Bay," this big commercial-residential development set on a secluded cove is popular with Hong Kong expats. It boasts a population of 10,000 and its own marina and golf course, plus a 24-hour hovercraft service to Central. Nearby is the old Hakka village of **Nim Shue Wan,** with a small beach. *Kaidos* run five times daily between here and Silvermine Bay.

PRACTICALITIES

Food

Lantau is too far from Hong Kong Island for the seafood crowd, though there are plenty of decent places to eat, beginning with the *dai pai dong*s along the waterfront at Mui Wo, and Po Lin Monastery's veggie lunch (see above). **Papa**

Doc's pub at 3 Ngan Wan Rd., Mui Wo, serves basic pub food with the pints.

Charlie's in Pui O is a little Australian-run al fresco place serves Chinese and Western food (notable crab Mornay and curries) and stocks a good supply of wine.

Several good cheap Cantonese seafood restaurants are in Tai O, like the friendly and cheerfully noisy **Fook Moon Lam.**

Discovery Bay has the most diverse selection of places to eat; look in Discovery Bay Plaza. Best are **Chili'n Spice,** with delicious Southeast Asian cuisine, and **Jo Jo Indian Restaurant.**

Accommodations

The **Jockey Club Mong Tung Wan Youth Hostel** on the Chi Ma Wan peninsula, tel. 2984-1389, is a 45-minute walk from Pui O. A string of bungalows set on a good swimming beach, it's an exceptionally nice hostel.

S.G. Davis Youth Hostel at Ngong Ping, tel. 2985-5610, is small (48 beds) and often crowded, but nicely situated on a hill behind Po Lin Monastery.

The men's and women's dormitories at **Po Lin Monastery** charge HK$200 for three veggie meals and a bed.

Lantau Tea Gardens, tel. 2985-5161, has shabby a/c rooms for HK$170.

Mui Wo Inn, Silvermine Bay Beach, tel. 2984-8597, is a small, quiet hotel with good rooms for as little as HK$288 Sunday through Friday.

Sea Breeze Hotel, Pui O, tel. 2984-7977, has adequate rooms for HK$300 and up.

Silvermine Beach Hotel, Silvermine Bay Beach, tel. 2984-8295, is probably the nicest hotel on Lantau, though hardly luxurious. There's a pool, terrace, and Western and Cantonese restaurants; rooms are HK$860-1200 s or d, 30% less on weekdays.

Optimistically named **holiday flats** are available at Pui O and Tong Fuk; check at the accommodations booth to the right of the ferry exit or at **Cheung Sha Resort Hotel. Campsites** are found at Pui O, Nam Shan, Chi Ma Wan, and along the south coast; consult the *Countryside Series* map.

Getting There

The MTR's new **Lantau Line,** scheduled to open in 1998 with the new airport, will provide the fastest connection between Central and Lantau, though the ferries will remain the most scenic means of transport.

Ferries and hoverferries run from the Outlying Islands Ferry Pier in Central to Mui Wo, via Peng Chau. Sunday and holidays most ferries go direct to Mui Wo, leaving Central at 7 a.m. and every half-hour 8-11:30 a.m., then hourly. Fare is HK$9, HK$16 on Sunday and holidays.

Weekend ferries run from Tsimshatsui to Mui Wo on Saturday afternoon at 1, 2, 3, 5, and 7 p.m. Departures Sunday and holidays are at 9 and 11 a.m. and hourly 1-6 p.m. **Hoverferries** run every 20 minutes from the Edinburgh Place Ferry Pier to Discovery Bay. From here it's a half-hour walk to the Trappist monastery, and another 90 minutes into Mui Wo.

Transport to more obscure points of access, like Tung Chung and Tai O, are described in the text. An **inter-island service** runs between Cheung Chau, Chi Ma Wan, Silvermine Bay, and Peng Chau: check the schedule at the pier.

Getting Around
Apart from buses, the island also has its own fleet of blue-and-silver taxis, but since there are only three or four dozen of these, don't count on finding them anywhere but around the Mui Wo bus terminal. Call service is 2984-1328. The **Lantau Tour Co.,** tel. 2984-8255, will arrange rental minibuses with drivers.

CHEUNG CHAU 長洲

A visit to Cheung Chau is a great one-day getaway from Hong Kong's urban turmoil. The island is appealingly leisurely (as on Lamma, there are no motor vehicles), and offers the best village of any of the major islands, decent walks, and some okay beaches. It's easily visited, even with a late start from Central: allow an hour to stroll around town, another few hours for a walk if you're in the mood, and finish with dinner in one of the excellent Chinese restaurants.

Cheung Chau lies about 12 km southwest of Hong Kong Island, just across from Lantau's Chi Ma Wan Peninsula. Its 2.4 square km are stretched into a dumbbell shape, with the crowded town set at the island's narrow, curving "waist." Originally Cheung Chau was two small islands, slowly welded together by a tide-formed land bridge. Like Lamma and Lantau, it was once far more important than Hong Kong Island and prospered as a fishing village and smuggling hangout.

Cheung Chau is in the process of becoming developed and uglified, but the cheerful bustle lingers in the warren of old streets, where everybody knows everyone else. The island has become popular with mainlanders seeking peace and quiet: perhaps half of its 35,000 residents commute to work in urban Hong Kong. There are no roads here, only concrete paths, and the only vehicles are lawnmower-like work carts and an ambulance.

Cheung Chau Village
The first sight as you arrive on the ferry is not so charming: hillsides erupting with a new and hideous housing estate, an ugly hint of the future. If the fishing fleet is in, though, the colorful junks make up for this lapse. Cheung Chau's harbor hosts one of the largest remaining communities of fisherfolk, many of whom still live on their boats. They are dwindling in number as small-scale fishing becomes less profitable. Many blame recent dramatic declines in their catch on widespread dredging and dumping in fishing waters.

Disembarking from the ferry, cast a glance at the Cheung Chau map board, which shows popular hiking routes. **Praya Street** runs along the waterfront, lined with shops, restaurants, and little carts advertising holiday flats. The streetside food stalls of the morning and evening street market have been shunted off to the cement-block **Regional Council Cheung Chau Complex.** The big indoor market here is more spacious and less smelly than most. At night, restaurants set up tables outside it, serving reasonably priced seafood dinners with good set menus for larger groups. Behind the market complex at the south end of town is an old Tin Hau Temple, a former pirate outpost.

Wander back down through the interior of town, a few streets lined with shops selling a jumble of goods: brownish-red blocks of shrimp

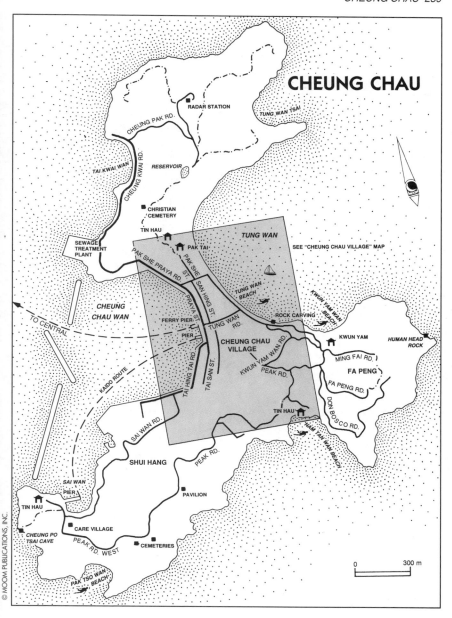

CHEUNG CHAU

RADAR STATION

TUNG WAN TSAI

CHEUNG PAK RD.

TAI KWAI WAN

CHEUNG KWAI RD.

RESERVOIR

CHRISTIAN CEMETERY

TIN HAU

SEWAGE TREATMENT PLANT

PAK SHE PRAYA RD.

PAK TAI

TUNG WAN

SEE "CHEUNG CHAU VILLAGE" MAP

PAK SHE ST.

SAN HING ST.

PRAYA ST.

TUNG WAN BEACH

KWUN YAM WAN BEACH

CHEUNG CHAU WAN

TO CENTRAL

FERRY PIER

PIER

TUNG WAN RD.

ROCK CARVING

KWUN YAM

HUMAN HEAD ROCK

CHEUNG CHAU VILLAGE

MING FAI RD.

KAIDO ROUTE

TAI HING TAI RD.

TAI SAN ST.

KWUN YAM WAN RD.

PEAK RD.

FA PENG

FA PENG RD.

DON BOSCO RD.

SAI WAN RD.

TIN HAU

NAM TAN WAN BEACH

SHUI HANG

PEAK RD.

SAI WAN

PIER

TIN HAU

PAVILION

CHEUNG PO TSAI CAVE

CARE VILLAGE

CEMETERIES

PEAK RD. WEST

PAK TSO WAN BEACH

0   300 m

© MOOM PUBLICATIONS, INC.

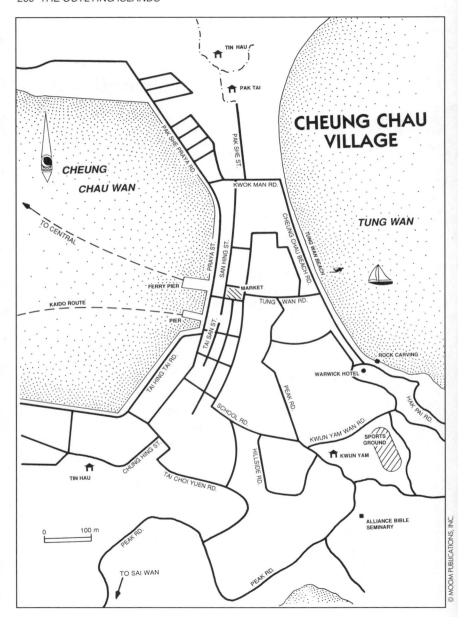

TIN HAU

PAK TAI

CHEUNG CHAU VILLAGE

PAK SHE PRAYA RD.

PAK SHE ST.

KWOK MAN RD.

CHEUNG

CHAU WAN

TUNG WAN

CHEUNG CHAU BEACH RD.

TO CENTRAL

PRAYA ST.

SAN HING ST.

TUNG WAN BEACH

KAIDO ROUTE

FERRY PIER

MARKET

TUNG WAN RD.

PIER

TAI SAN ST.

TAI HING TAI RD.

ROCK CARVING

WARWICK HOTEL

HAK PAI RD.

SCHOOL RD.

PEAK RD.

KWUN YAM WAN RD.

SPORTS GROUND

CHUNG HING ST.

TIN HAU

TAI CHOI YUEN RD.

HILLSIDE RD.

KWUN YAM

0   100 m

ALLIANCE BIBLE SEMINARY

PEAK RD.

TO SAI WAN

PEAK RD.

paste, dried fish, cheap clothes, jade bracelets and gold jewelry, boat equipment, straw hats, and paper funeral offerings (junks figure prominently). There are several small grocery stores, with a heavy emphasis on cold beer for picnickers. The Earth God shrine at the junction of Pak She Street and Kwok Man Road is simply a stone, taking the tradition back to its most primeval roots.

Turn left off the pier, and Praya Street turns into **Pak She Praya Road.** Turn right onto Pak She Fourth Lane (just past the Baccarat Restaurant), and you'll see Cheung Chau's famous **Pak Tai Temple.** It's exceptionally well decorated, with fine gilt wood altarpieces, carved granite pillars, and an elaborate carved and painted wood junk hanging just inside the entrance.

Built in 1783, this Taoist shrine is dedicated to Pak Tai, "Lord of the North," who is said to have saved the village from plague in 1777. Every May the broad platform in front of the temple holds the three tall towers of the Cheung Chau Bun Festival. The god's image stands atop a snake and turtle, symbolizing his rule of the sea. Two side halls feature crude stucco murals of the Green Dragon and White Tiger, important elements in *feng shui*.

The Sung dynasty sword in the glass case to the left of the altar was dredged up in the last century by fishermen and donated to the god. Poke about to find more odd treasures: petrified swordfish beaks, an elaborately carved sedan chair in which the deity's image was once paraded about, and a plaque commemorating the 1966 visit of Princess Margaret.

Back on the waterfront is the industrial end of town: a sewage treatment plant, followed by an ice factory with giant cubes rumbling down a metal chute, and a line of junk repair sheds, where boat hulls are scraped and coated with barnacle-repelling paint. A few craftsmen here still build fishing boats, using a mix of old and new tools and plans straight out of the builder's head.

The North End

The paved path heading out of town hugs the coastline and makes a good cycling route. (Bike rentals are available along Pak She Praya Road, with fat-tired mountain bikes going for around HK$20 an hour.) It's a 15-minute walk to the bay of Tai Kwai Wan. From here you can head up Cheung Pak Road to a small hilltop reservoir offering views of the entire island. Cheung Chau's northern end is virtually deserted and laced with paths—a good place to head for a private picnic.

Tung Wan and Kwun Yam Wan Beaches
東灣海灘, 觀音灣

When you've had enough of town, turn east down Tung Wan Road, passing several good restaurants and an open-air shrine set beneath a sacred banyan tree. The stones raised here represent spirits who are supplicated by neighborhood women for healing and fertility. With its hanging branches taking root, it's not hard to figure out how the banyan gained this association.

Tung Wan Road soon leads to the island's east coast and **Tung Wan Beach,** Cheung Chau's largest and most popular. A lifeguard is on duty here in season and there are full facilities, but the big curving bay tends to retain pollution. You may want to walk down Peak Road to a more remote beach.

The small prehistoric **rock carvings** off Tung Wan Beach can be hard to find unless you raise your gaze—they're four meters above the ground. Take Hak Pai Road, which skirts below the big **Warwick Hotel.** At the end of the retaining wall, a Plexiglas shield protects the stylized geometric forms, which date back to the Bronze Age, about 2,500 years ago.

Just past here is Kwun Yam Wan, a slightly better if smaller beach named after the small, bright-red Kwun Yam Temple up on the hillside behind it. The **Windsurf Centre** on the beach rents windsurfers and ocean kayaks by the hour or day and gives lessons; its cafe is a nice place for a drink.

Fa Peng 花坪

Much of the island's eastern headland has been appropriated by various missionary, church, and youth organizations, which run retreats and summer camps here. From the Kwun Yam temple, follow the signed footpath 15 minutes to "Human Head Rock, Bell Shape Rock, and Vase Shape Rock." These require a great leap of imagination to visualize, but the quiet hillside overlooking the ocean has some good picnic sites. Return in a loop, passing **Kwai Yuen Monastery,** a retreat founded in 1957. Then follow the signs back toward town and the **Kwan Kong Pavilion,** near No. 1 Peak Road. Dedicated to Kwan Ti, it was built in traditional style in 1973, with lacquered wood pillars and gilded carvings.

The South End

Cheung Chau's best walk is the 40-minute stroll up Peak Road. A "Residence Ordinance" once restricted its occupants to Europeans, just like Victoria Peak on Hong Kong Island. The road runs along the island's southern end, passing houses, villas, and fancy vacation homes maintained by hongs for the vacationing pleasure of senior management. Past the Alliance Bible Seminary, steps lead down to small, rocky **Nam Tam Wan** or "Morning Beach."

CHEUNG CHAU BUN FESTIVAL

Cheung Chau's colorful, crowded Bun Festival is one of Hong Kong's finest celebrations, a classic example of a *ta chiu,* a Taoist village festival of peace and renewal. It's held for six days on a date determined by divination each year, generally in early May.

The pièces de résistance are the three 20-meter-high bamboo and paper towers (one each for Heaven, Earth, and Man) raised in front of the island's Pak Tai Temple. They are covered with thousands of round rice-flour buns imprinted with pink symbols, offerings to satisfy unhappy ghosts. In the old days the towers were stacks of solid buns (they're still called "bun mountains" in Chinese). Today austerity reigns, and the bamboo framework is thinly covered with a single layer of buns. After the ghosts have ingested the spiritual essence, the buns are distributed on the last day as lucky talismans. This used to be an exciting event, as swarms of young men charged and scaled the bun towers trying to grab as many as possible. In 1978 a tower collapsed under the assault, injuring people in the process, and since then the buns are distributed to orderly lines of people, a safer if duller event.

Meanwhile, Taoist priests conduct ceremonies inside the temple to appease the restless spirits the buns are intended for. Legend disagrees as to whether these are pirate victims whose bodies were discovered in the 1880s on the island, or the casualties of a typhoon or plague.

Another component of the festival honors the god Pak Tai for his successful intervention in a plague epidemic a century ago. Giant mat sheds raised across from the temple host opera performances, and processions are held through Cheung Chau's streets during the last two days. Sedan chairs carried in front bear the images of the island's main eight deities. These are followed by dancing lions and unicorns, and by a fabulous procession of elaborately costumed and made-up children who seem-

HONG KONG TOURIST ASSOCIATION

"floating" child, Cheung Chau Bun Festival procession

ingly float above the crowd, borne on concealed metal frames anchored by hidden wires. Wander the town's back streets earlier in the day to see the complex preparation process.

The Bun Festival is extremely popular: go early and spend the day on Cheung Chau, but be prepared for jammed ferries and crowds. HKTA sets aside special seating for tourists at the main events. Accommodations are scarce, and only vegetarian food is available for two nights and three days on the island—though given the delicious nature of Chinese vegetarian cooking, this is not exactly a hardship.

Peak Road ascends to yield superb views of the long curve of the island's waist, packed with houses. The small roadside **Chung Lok Garden** features a pavilion dedicated to a local poet. Verses written in tribute to her are carved on surrounding boulders, but unfortunately everything is in Chinese. Next come a series of **cemeteries,** auspiciously oriented facing the ocean, their excellent *feng shui* ensuring the welfare of descendents. The shiny new Cheung Chau Crematorium nearby indicates the graveyards are getting crowded. A little farther, a side trail leads down to small **Pak Tso Wan** ("Italian Beach").

Veer right to Sai Wan, descending through a now-obsolete CARE Village, built by the charitable organization with overseas funding in 1968 to house local fishermen. CARE gradually withdrew from the area as Hong Kong became more prosperous.

Down at Sai Wan's waterfront, pass the pier and follow the signs to **Cheung Po Tsai Cave,** about a ten-minute walk. Set facing the ocean and Lantau's Chi Ma Wan peninsula, this is supposedly the treasure cave of a notorious Ching dynasty pirate, who according to HKTA lore ruled over 40,000 men and several hundred ships. Romantic associations make it a top attraction for day-tripping Hongkongers, but the brutal truth is that the "cave" is only a dark cleft in the rocks, too small to house anything, much less 40,000 men. Exploring it is easier with a flashlight, sometimes rented out by enterprising locals at the entrance—but really there's nothing to see.

Returning, round off your visit with a short detour to the small **Tin Hau Temple,** featuring some exceptionally fine porcelain roof figures. To return to Cheung Chau Village, either wait on the pier for the signed *kaido* back to town, which runs every 20 minutes, or walk back a half-hour along the coastal route. The *kaido,* piloted by an elderly lady in jade bracelets, is recommended: the five-minute ride through the crowded harbor offers close-up views of lines of fishing junks moored in neat rows.

PRACTICALITIES

Food

While not as famous as Lamma's seafood emporiums, Cheung Chau has some excellent restaurants serving food that's fresh, fast, and fairly cheap. Dine outside on mild evenings, to the accompaniment of the roaring wok inside. Try the many restaurants along the Praya or Tung Wan Road, or explore the cheerful, brightly lit *dai pai dongs* that set up at night around the market complex.

East Lake Restaurant on Tung Wan Road has an English menu and a friendly staff. Try the special stuffed tofu. **Betty's Garden Cafe Pub,** a little farther down the road, serves drinks and British pub food at outdoor tables. **Coffee or Tea,** a bit south of the ferry pier, serves Chinese and Western food, while **Kee Yeung** and **Lotus Thai,** on the waterfront just right of the pier, both specialize in Thai food. **Dreyer's Ice Cream** on Tung Wan Road tops off your meal.

A long string of restaurants on Pak She Praya Road all feature English menus and cold beer; try the **Baccarat. The Patio** in the Warwick Hotel on Tung Wan Beach serves Western food on the terrace.

Accommodations

Praya Street is lined with small booths displaying photos of rooms and "holiday flats" for rent, catering to amorous Hong Kong couples (pictures of beds are prominently featured). Most come with bath and kitchen facilities and are clean, verging on spotless, but viewed en masse they're pretty depressing. Rates are around HK$300 on weekdays, up to HK$500 on weekends and holidays.

The **Warwick Hotel** on Tung Wan Beach (tel. 2981-0081, Hong Kong office 2541-7031) is a six-story concrete block with 70 rooms, some with beach views, for HK$620-1120 s or d. A 20% discount is offered on weekdays.

Getting There

Ferries run frequently between the Outlying Islands Ferry Pier and Cheung Chau: the trip takes around an hour. **Hoverferries** make the journey in half the time, leaving Central Mon.-Sat. at 9 and 10:15 a.m. and 12:15, 2:15 and 4:05 p.m. A weekend ferry from Tsimshatsui departs at 4 p.m. Saturday and 8 a.m. and 10 a.m. Sunday. An **inter-island service** runs nine times a day from Cheung Chau over to Chi Ma Wan and Silvermine Bay on Lantau, then on to Peng Chau. Check the schedule at the pier for exact times.

LAMMA 南丫島

The closest of the major islands, a few kilometers across from Aberdeen and only 40 minutes from Central by ferry, Lamma is a good choice for those with limited time. It's the third-largest of Hong Kong's islands, its 13 square km splayed out into a sprawling shape.

Lamma is defined by two settlements. **Yung Shue Wan** on the northwest coast is the principal village, popular with expat residents. On the eastern coast is **Sok Kwu Wan,** its main feature a strip of brightly lit seafood restaurants. Ferries run from Central to both villages, so the obvious thing to do is to arrive at one, hike to the other, enjoy a meal and catch the ferry back. The order you do it in really doesn't matter. Sok Kwu Wan has *kaido*s to Aberdeen supplementing the ferry, while Yung Shue Wan has a wider range of restaurants and more frequent ferries.

Lamma's history is largely invisible but goes back to prehistoric times, when people settled on beaches like Lo So Shing and Sham Wan. With only around 5,000 residents, the island today remains peaceful and largely undeveloped. There are no roads: only concrete paths and trails link the small villages; and the southern half, dominated by the rugged bulk of Mt. Stenhouse, is largely uninhabited. Hiking is a major attraction here, and you'll find a handful of mediocre swimming beaches. Lamma is a pretty, peaceful place, and it would be a lot prettier were it not for its twin eyesores, one on each coast: the giant power plant backing Yung Shue Wan, and the noisy cement quarry, fronted by a fish-farm ghetto, across from Sok Kwu Wan.

Sok Kwu Wan 索罟灣
The main feature of Sok Kwu Wan is the line of open-air restaurants along the waterfront. Over the years these have evolved from simple seafront shanties to fancy dining palaces, with wine lists and enormous round tables set up for up to 24 people. Choose your prey from the bubbling tanks (but check the price first), or order from the extensive menus. Set menus for groups are remarkably reasonable, as little as HK$350 for four to six people. Restaurants do most of their business in the evenings, when cheerful crowds come over from Hong Kong Island.

The daytime view from the tables is disappointing: a noisy cement factory-cum-quarry eating into the hillside, fronted by a bay full of fish-farm rafts, some outfitted with little floating shanties (proprietors paddle out to them on styrofoam floats). Fish farming has been developed since the early 1970s as a safe alternative to open-sea fishing. Imported fingerlings or wild catch are fattened in floating cages and sold to markets and restaurants.

Mo Tat Wan 模達灣
If you'd prefer a more peaceful dining experience, turn left off the Sok Kwu Wan pier and stroll 30 minutes down the concrete path to the next beach, Mo Tat Wan, which is swimmable and altogether more peaceful. The **Coral Seafood Restaurant** here offers the same good food as Sok Kwu Wan's seafood palaces, in a less circus-like atmosphere. The Sok Kwu Wan-Aberdeen *kaido* calls here on its return trip. The tiny old village of Mo Tat lies up on the hillside behind, backed by an ancient *feng shui* wood supposed to protect the village from evil influences.

South End
From Mo Tat, you can continue through the village around to the next cove, **Tung O Wan** (also with a swimming beach), and on to the seldom-used beach at **Sham Wan**. The high sandbar here was the site of an important archaeological site going back 6,000 years. Another path leads steeply up to the 353-meter summit of **Mt. Stenhouse** ("Shan Tei Tong"), about two hours' roundtrip from Sok Kwu Wan.

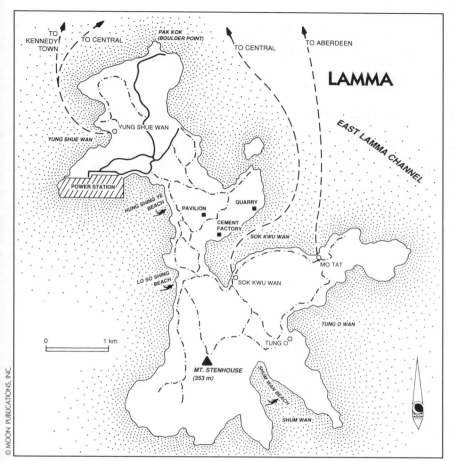

To Yung Shue Wan

The three-km walk between Sok Kwu Wan and Yung Shue Wan is a good way to spend a morning or afternoon. Indulge in frequent stops to pad out the hour or so of actual walking. From Sok Kwu Wan, the paved path follows the coast, then climbs the hill rather steeply, passing the turnoff to **Lo So Shing Beach** about a half-hour from town. This is the biggest and probably the best of the island's main beaches.

The trail continues up to a little tile-roofed Chinese pavilion at the top of the ridge, more or less the halfway mark. It's just barely possible to admire the views from here, if you resolutely turn your back on the power station chimneys looming off the coast. The trail drops down from here, passing small **Hung Shing Ye Beach,** a decent if short stretch of sand with a few hotels. Up in the hills behind here is a mysterious stone circle discovered only in 1956 and possibly dating back to prehistoric times. From Hung Shing Ye it's less than a half-hour into Yung Shue Wan.

Yung Shue Wan 榕樹灣
Lamma's main village, indeed its only real one, "Banyan Tree Bay" is a tidy little cluster of shops, restaurants, and *gweilo*-oriented pubs, with villas and apartment blocks set on the hillside behind. The peaceful ambience is damaged by the ominous-looking twin chimneys of the power plant poking up behind the surrounding hills. The town is slated for big changes if the Hong Kong government presses through with its plans for reclaiming part of the bay, but so far it remains a quiet settlement favored by the more alternative of Hong Kong's expatriates.

A stroll through town takes only a few minutes. Bicycles are available for rent just off Main Street on the way to Hung Shing Ye Beach, but given the limited scope and hilly terrain it's hard to imagine getting much use out of them.

At the far end of Main Street is a **Tin Hau Temple** featuring a veiled image of the goddess in her bridal headdress. To the left is the City God who keeps track of local events, and on the right is the protector Muen Kuen. Up in the hills behind town is a shrine to a local god whose name translates as "Three Mountain Kingdom King."

North End
Yung Shue Wan is the launching point for explorations of Lamma's elongated north end. It's an easy half-hour walk through productive vegetable plots to **Pak Kok** or "Boulder Point" on the northern tip of the island. A *kaido* service runs from here to Kennedy Town on Hong Kong Island. Return via the east coast to get views of the busy East Lamma Channel, crowded with big ships gliding silently past.

LOVE OF NUMBERS

Classical Chinese culture has a fixation on numbers. There are the five elements, for example, as well as the five cardinal points, the five foods, the five colors, and the five 12-year cycles of the 60-year calendar. Many modern political slogans stem back to classical literature's tradition of "four-character slogans," though things like "Store Grain Everywhere" have a less than distinguished ring to them.

The love of numbers, and of skillful punning, spills over into popular culture. Cantonese is rich in homonyms, words that sound alike but have different meanings. The word for "two," for example, sounds the same as "easy." "Three" sounds like "life," and "nine" like "eternity." "Four," on the other hand, sounds like "death," and is to be avoided at all costs. In many buildings (especially hospitals), floor numbers often skip from three to five.

The government plays upon this fetish and annually auctions off license plates bearing lucky numbers (the proceeds benefit charities). A few years ago a bidder paid HK$5 million for the number 8, which is a Cantonese homonym for "prosperity." The plate 8888 earned a bundle too, but the current record is held by the number 9, which sounds like "longevity." The place bearing it brought US$1.7 million in 1994.

The merits of various combinations are pondered as well: 222 means "easy, easy, easy"; 913 means "everlasting life"; 162 "easy all the way"; 168 "prosperity all the way." Shanghai restaurants in particular will often include a series of lucky numbers in their names. The Bank of China opened its new headquarters on the profitable day of 8 August 1988 (8/8/88), which translates as "money, money, money-money." These rules apply to telephone numbers as well, which aren't auctioned off—but could be, if the phone company ever needed to raise a few million dollars.

PRACTICALITIES

Food
You can't go wrong with any of the **seafood restaurants** at Sok Kwu Wan: the **"Lamma Hilton," "Lamma Regent,"** and **Lancombe** are particularly recommended.

Han Lok Yuen at Hung Shing Ye serves Cantonese food on an outdoor patio. It's famous for pigeon—minced, roasted, or special barbecued—which you should order in advance, tel. 2982-0680.

Yung Shue Wan has its own array of waterfront Chinese restaurants, including the excellent **Sampan,** 16 Main Street. There's also a number of decent, not-too-expensive Western restaurants. **The Waterfront** at 58 Main St. has indoor, patio, balcony, and rooftop seating and a diverse menu encompassing Scandanavian

BOB RACE

on Italian, Indian and Mexican. **Toochka's,** 44 Main St., is a casual place with outdoor tables and an international menu; Indian food is best.

Accommodations
In Yung Shue Wan, try **Man Lai Wah Hotel,** tel. 2982-0220, which is just off the pier and has rooms for around HK$400, HK$700 weekends. **Lamma Vacation House,** 29 Main St., tel. 2982-1886, has simple rooms with shared bath for around HK$300 weekdays. There's nowhere to stay in Sok Kwu Wan.

The **Concerto Inn** on Hung Shing Ye Beach, tel. 2836-3388, is an elegant little place aiming for the romantic getaway crowd. Rooms are HK$680-980, with a 30% discount on week-days.

Han Lok Yuen in Hung Shing Ye, tel. 2982-0608, rents rooms for HK$250 and more expensive holiday flats.

Getting There
Ferries run from the Outlying Islands Ferry Pier to Sok Kwu Wan (50 minutes) and more frequently to Yung Shue Wan (40 minutes). There's also a *kaido* service between Aberdeen, Mo Tat Wan, and Sok Kwu Wan, and a less frequent ferry service between Yung Shue Wan and Pak Kok to Kennedy Town and Central on Hong Kong Island.

food, pizza, burgers, and salads. **Banyan Cafe,** 22 Main St., is a small, simple restaurant serving healthy entrees, vegetarian dishes, and desserts —all exceptionally cheap, for Hong Kong. Next door at No. 26 is the **Capital,** another small place specializing in fondue—both the cheese and chocolate varieties. **Deli Lamma,** 36 Main St., has a witty name and an innovative menu that changes nationalities regularly but touches

OTHER ISLANDS

If you're looking to *really* get away from it all, take a ferry or *kaido* out to one of the lesser-known islands detailed below. Most have undergone a recent mass exodus, as residents have emigrated to housing estates, or to run Chinese restaurants in Manchester. They return only rarely, leaving the villages to a few old people, or sometimes to nobody at all.

Peng Chau 坪洲
A miniscule one-square-km speck off Lantau's east coast, Peng Chau hosts a small community of fisherfolk and farmers. Once it was noted for its cottage industries manufacturing rattan and porcelain, but these have been replaced by a less glamorous metal tube factory. In truth

there's little reason to visit: the island is peaceful and car-less, but too small for decent walks, and the **beach** at Tung Wan is only so-so. Points of minor interest include a 1792 **Tin Hau Temple** on Wing On Street, opposite the pier, and a few easy **Family Walks** diagrammed on the map board. Some good, cheap seafood restaurants open up on weekday evenings and all day on weekends. The **Sea Breeze Club** on Wing Hing St. serves good pub food, including steaks, pizzas, and fries.

Most Lantau-bound ferries from Central call at Peng Chau en route, making it easy to stop off here for an hour or so and continue on to Lantau. There's also a *kaido* service between Peng Chau and the Trappist monastery at Tai Shue

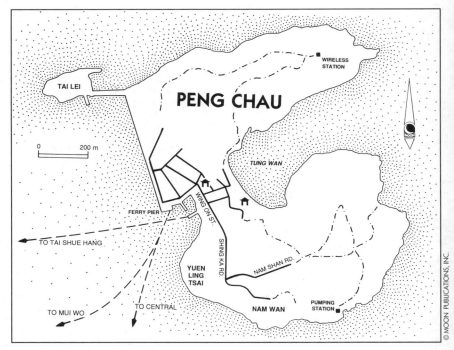

Hang on Lantau, and another *kaido* hookup between Peng Chau, Mui Wo and Chi Ma Chan on Lantau, and Cheung Chau.

Tung Lung Chau 東龍灣

This rugged, picturesque little island across from Clearwater Bay holds the ruins of an old Chinese fortress, plus a very few permanent residents. You can see it from Joss House Bay but, frustratingly, cannot reach it from here. *Kaidos* running from just west of the Sai Wan Ho ferry pier on Hong Kong Island to Joss House Bay call here first, leaving Sai Wan Ho at 8:30 a.m. and 3:30 p.m. on weekends and holidays, and departing Tung Lung Chau at 9:30 a.m. and 5 p.m. Call the Lam Kee Ferry Company at 2560-9929 for the current schedule.

Tung Chau's pier lies midway between its two sights. Climb north to the **old Chinese fort,** built in the early 18th century to protect the passage of Guangzhou-bound junks through Hong Kong's harbor. Two dozen soldiers were once posted here, but it proved difficult to supply and was abandoned in 1810.

A path leads from the pier in the opposite direction to a **prehistoric rock carving** which lies right on the shoreline. It's the earliest recorded carving in the area, mentioned in an 1819 journal, and the largest as well, measuring 2.4 meters wide.

Tap Mun Chau 塔門洲

This remote little island set at the entrance to Long Harbour in the far northeast corner of the SAR offers a rarity in Hong Kong: a high degree of peace. Much of the fun of a visit is the process of getting there, either by *kaido* from Wong Shek Pier or the long but scenic ferry ride up Tolo Channel. Go one way and return the other for the most flexibility.

The Tolo Channel ferry departs at 8:30 a.m. and 3:15 p.m. from Ma Liu Shui Ferry Pier, about ten minutes' walk from the University KCR station. It runs up Tolo Channel between Sai Kung and Plover Cove, passing through some of Hong Kong's most isolated and beautiful scenery before arriving at Tap Mun about 70 minutes later. The return boat is at 5:20 p.m.; there's an additional one on Sunday at 1:45 p.m.

The other option is to head to Sai Kung Town and take Bus 94 to its terminus (Wong Shek Pier), from where a *kaido* runs up Long Harbour to Tap Mun Chau (see "Wong Shek and the Long Harbour Ferry" at the end of the preceding chapter for transport details). *Kaido*s leave Wong Shek Pier every two hours 8:20 a.m.-4:20 p.m., later on Sunday; the trip takes about 20 minutes.

Tap Mun's small harbor is full of fish-farm rafts fashioned from floating plastic jerry cans. Disembarking passengers run the gauntlet past elderly fisherwomen in straw hats and black *samfu,* shrilly hawking dried fish and packets of seaweed. Virtually all of Tap Mun's inhabitants are elderly—the younger ones have gone off to an easier life in the city.

Turn left to explore the small town, its tile-roofed houses beginning to crumble. There are a few shops and a handful of restaurants, the biggest and best being the **New Hon Kee.** Up behind town is a large and important **Tin Hau Temple,** the last stop before the open sea. It's well-maintained if quiet, with superb porcelain roof figures and two more porcelain friezes inside. On the altar is a double image of Tin Hau—big and small versions—fronted by her attending generals, ferocious-looking Thousand-Li Eye and Favorable Wind Ear. On the opposite side of the pier are clusters of slightly newer huddled houses and a Christian chapel off an upper trail.

The grassy hills that form the bulk of the island are crisscrossed with footpaths and dotted with auspiciously sited graves and huts in various stages of construction and disintegration.

It's incredibly, intensely quiet; definitely the slow life, with cows ambling over the green hills that perhaps give Tap Mun its English name, Grass Island.

The small concrete pavilion up on the ridge behind town is a good place to watch the breakers pounding the wild outer coast. Map boards here and near the pier outline walking trails: the island's northern portion is totally uninhabited, while the south half is encircled by a path leading to the strange formation called **Balanced Rock** on the island's eastern tip. Also on the eastern side is **Tap Mun Cave,** believed to be connected by subterranean passage to the Tin Hau Temple.

Wherever you go, be at the pier to meet the Wong Shek *kaido* or the 5:20 p.m. Tolo Harbour ferry, which sometimes pulls out a few minutes early. If you do miss it, you'll have a great adventure in finding someone to put you up for the night.

Ping Chau 平洲

The farthest-flung of Hong Kong's scattered islands, Ping Chau lies in Mirs Bay, very close to the Chinese mainland. This made it a convenient stop for swimmers fleeing China, and a popular smuggling center as well. The illicit trade began during the Korean War, when arms passed through here into China. Later Ping Chau developed into a flourishing center for smuggling duty-free electronic goods into mainland villages.

As late as the 1960s, Ping Chau's population totalled around 3,000; this has since dwindled to near-zero. All that remains are crumbling shrines and a handful of overgrown villages, though a recent renaissance is evident in the smart new bungalows built, it is rumored, with smuggling profits.

Ping Chau comes to life on weekends, with ferry-borne day-trippers and a few locals who return to cater to them. Ferries depart the Ma

fishing junk

BOB RACE

Liu Shui pier at 9 a.m. Saturday and Sunday and 3:30 p.m. Saturday, calling at Ping Chau at 5:30 p.m. for the return trip both days. Double-check the return times and don't miss the Sunday boat, unless you don't mind staying on Ping Chau till the next weekend. The ferry takes nearly two hours to make the scenic trip through Tolo Channel into Mirs Bay. Fare is around HK$70.

Ping Chau's two square km are easy to explore. The ferry docks at Sha Tau, the island's main "village"; it's possible to swim at the nearby beach. Much of the island is now protected in a country park. Trails loop around the coastline to strange **rock formations** at the north and south ends and a **campsite** at Kang Lau Shek on the southeast tip. It's possible to find a bed

and food at Sha Tau and Tai Tong on weekends, when former residents return to set up hostels for visitors.

Po Toi Islands 蒲台島

This group of three islands off the southeast coast of Hong Kong is seldom visited. Not much goes on here, but it's a good choice for peace and quiet, hikes, and excellent seafood.

From Stanley it's a 35-minute *kaido* ride to the main island of Po Toi. (The other two, Beaufort and Sung Kong, are accessible only by private boat.) The Po Toi *kaido* docks at the little bay of Tai Wan, lined by a small collection of fishermen's homes. The handful of seafood restaurants here is a quieter imitation of Lamma's Sok Kwu Wan. On Sunday they're packed

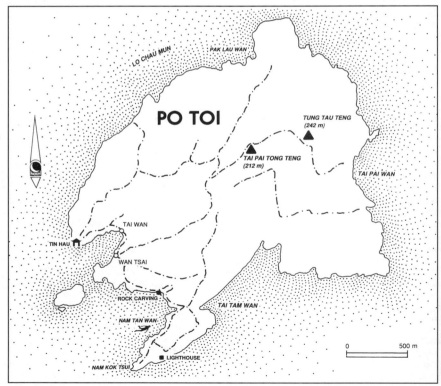

with Hongkongers who come for the excellent cheap food. Turn left from the ferry pier to visit the small **Tin Hau Temple** set on a terrace above the sea, the site of a big annual festival.

Trails are concentrated in Po Toi's southwest corner. Follow the path south through Wan Tsai village and fields of vegetables and bananas, then turn right down a flight of steps to an exceptionally distinct series of prehistoric **rock carvings** in typically geometric patterns. From here it's possible to continue on to horseshoe-shaped **Nam Tan Wan,** where you can swim virtually alone. Another path leads from here around the headland to the isolated point of **Nam Kok Tsui,** passing some interesting rock formations en route. It doesn't take long to return to Tai Wan village.

The Po Toi *kaido* leaves Aberdeen Public Pier at 9 a.m. on Tuesday, Thursday, and Saturday, but it promptly departs Po Toi at 10:30 a.m., mandating an overnight stay (and there's no official accommodation on the island). It's best to visit on Sunday, either on the 8 a.m. *kaido* from Aberdeen or the 10 or 11:30 a.m. *kaido* from St. Stephen's Beach at Stanley (see "Stanley" under "The South Side" in the Hong Kong Island chapter). Sunday afternoon returns are at 3, 4:30, and 6 p.m. (the last goes all the way to Aberdeen). Call 2554-4059 to check the current schedule.

CHINESE ALMANAC

MACAU
INTRODUCTION

Macau will come as a delightful surprise if you're expecting it to be an extension of Hong Kong. A European city with an Asian flavor, it blends Chinese exotica with a leisurely Old World charm. It's more langorous and less sophisticated than Hong Kong, as different as Lisbon is from London. Tucked away in the southwest corner of the Pearl River Delta, it leads its own life, busy yet nowhere near the frantic pace of Hong Kong, and largely ignored by tourists and guidebooks.

Macau's allure springs from its harmonious blending of influences. Portugal's Mediterranean culture is infinitely more graceful and receptive to life on the south China coast than the stiff Anglo-Chinese merger of Hong Kong. In Macau it blends seamlessly into something new—you see it in the Sino-Iberian architecture, in the mellifluous street names, in the Portuguese women bargaining in fluent Cantonese in the markets. The old neighborhoods resemble a Portuguese country town, the cobbled streets

lined with the faded pastel facades of 18th-century houses. Baroque Catholic churches and imposing fortresses, relics of Macau's colonial heritage, dominate the hilltops. The tangible sense of history is rooted in Macau's 1557 founding as a Portuguese trading post, making it the world's oldest remaining imperial relic.

Simply wandering is Macau's finest pleasure. Local architecture is an irresistible mélange of styles: the local "Sino-Iberian" blends with art deco influences and art nouveau touches from the 1920s. Many fine old buildings have been restored and are now occupied by various government offices; others are quietly crumbling away. These colonial treasures are interspersed with magnificent Catholic churches and old Chinese temples with a timelessly authentic feel.

Wandering inevitably works up an appetite, which leads to another Macau attraction: multi-course Portuguese-influenced meals, accompanied by good, cheap wine, excellent bread, and fine coffee. Macanese fare is rich and piquant, combining many different flavors and culinary influences.

The dubious charms of Macau's nightlife and casinos are its main attraction for many visitors. Macau has a reputation as the "Las Vegas of the Far East," but the gambling here is more businesslike than elegant.

Macau's character has so far been preserved from overdevelopment by Hong Kong's economic shadow. Though prosperous, it wields little influence and has until recently remained a sleepy backwater. But a new Macau is emerging, lacking the sparkle and vigor of Hong Kong, but moving into the economic big time nonetheless. With its competitively priced land and labor, Macau is poised to become another gateway into booming south China.

The economic takeoff will inevitably destroy much of its charm, as exemplified by the ongoing Praia Bay reclamation project, and the new airport and container terminals off the islands of Taipa and Coloane. Another threat is Macau's reversion to China, slated for December 1999. While the handover is amicable, Macau's new rulers may not cherish its colonial heritage and palpable sense of history. Go now, rather than later.

THE LAND

Macau is sited across the Pearl River estuary from Hong Kong, 60 km to the southwest and 140 km southeast of Guangzhou. The enclave consists of a tiny chunk of mainland, four km long and less than two km wide, tailed by two islands, Taipa and Coloane. Altogether the territory is 23.5 square km and growing due to land reclamation. It's intensively packed with people. Though Macau never seems as jammed as Hong Kong, it holds the world record for most crowded territory, with 28,343 people per square km. (While the urban Hong Kong neighborhood of Mongkok is 10 times that, its overall population density is less.)

Macau is poised on the cusp of massive physical changes. A recently completed new ferry terminal handles triple the number of visitors. A new container terminal on the back side of Coloane Island has liberated Macau from its shipping dependence on Hong Kong, while the

A weed from Catholic Europe, it took root
Between the yellow mountains and the sea,
And bore the gay stone houses like a fruit,
And grew on China imperceptibly . . .

—W.H. Auden

US$625 million international airport built off the coast of Taipa Island has opened the enclave to international flights. Then there's the US$1.4 billion Nam Van Lakes Project, involving extensive reclamation of the formerly graceful Praia Bay. It's designed to increase the peninsular landmass by about 20%, providing land for housing, offices, hotels, and a six-lane highway. This huge civil engineering and property development project is slated for completion by 1999.

HISTORY

Macau's history predates Hong Kong's by several centuries: its story is part of the seafaring Age of Exploration that brought 15th-century Portugal to glory. Trade was the major motive, specifically the incredible wealth to be gained from the spices and silks of the Orient, which up to that point had been supplied to Europe through Islamic countries. Led by the Portuguese, whose sailing galleons were the most advanced of the age, Europeans sought to expand the boundaries of the known world, to discover new conduits for trade and religious conversion.

By 1498 Vasco da Gama had rounded the tip of Africa and sailed to India's west coast. By 1509 the Portuguese had wrested control of the Asian-European trade from the Muslims and were busy constructing a chain of small fortress-colonies in strategic ports. The west Indian port of Goa was seized in 1510, then spice-rich Malacca.

It was from here that the Portuguese first made contact with the fair-skinned sailors of a land known as "Chin." Captain Jorge Alveres was dispatched to explore the region in 1513. He arrived at the mouth of the Pearl River, near present-day Hong Kong and Macau. It was a re-

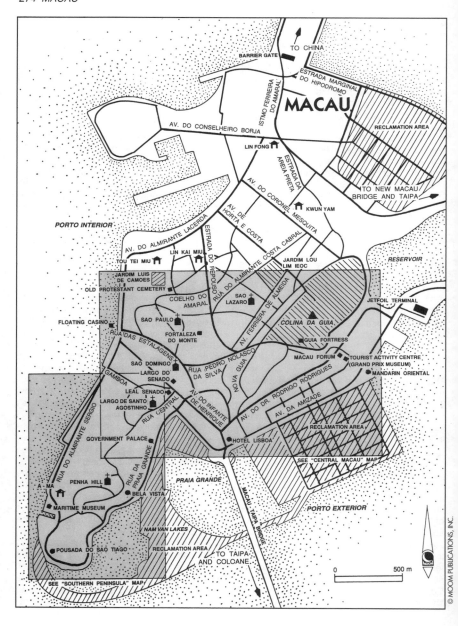

mote outpost of Chinese civilization, but Alveres soon discovered that the potential of inter-Asia trade far exceeded that of Asia-Europe trade.

China's emperor had banned direct trade between Japan and China. The Portuguese stepped into the gap, establishing an extremely lucrative monopoly that was to endure for nearly two centuries. In 1557 Guangzhou authorities gave them permission to establish a base on the little harbor of A-Ma-Go, the "Bay of A-Ma," a local name for the goddess Tin Hau. Here the Portuguese built godowns and homes and developed the inner and outer harbors.

Macau became a pivotal point in the trade of Japanese silver and gold for Chinese silk. Portuguese traders sailed from Malacca with cargoes of European and Eastern goods for sale in Japan and China. Stopping in Macau to load Chinese silks (held in great demand in Japan), they continued on to the Japanese port of Nagasaki, a former fishing village transformed into a major entrepôt. The ships returned loaded with Japanese silver, which traders sold in Guangzhou, using the revenues to purchase Chinese goods for sale in India and Europe. Despite the constant threat of pirates and typhoons, the trade commanded handsome profits: a few voyages and a man could retire for life.

Trade and Religion

Though Macau developed into a rich international port, it was never formally ceded by China. There are no historical records of the agreement reached with the Portuguese, but it probably involved payment of some kind of "rent" to Cantonese authorities. The Chinese also found it expedient to allow the Portuguese to patrol the waters for safe shipping and fight off maurauding Japanese and Chinese pirates.

While prospering as a trade entrepôt, Macau also became a center of Catholic activity in the East. It was proclaimed "the mother of missions" in Asia, with a mandate to cover all of China and Japan. Efforts at mass conversion were only partly successful, sometimes resulting in frightful retaliations like the 16th-century massacre of Japanese Christians by the shogun of Nagasaki. Locally, Catholicism prospered. The first simple churches of bamboo mats evolved into more durable constructions of stone, fronted with pastel-tinted plaster and adorned with rococo altars and elaborate decorations.

The Golden Age

Portugal's trade empire prospered, extending east from Macau to Japan and Manila and west to link India, Africa, and Europe. Predictably, other European countries began to envy the tremendous wealth. The Dutch, who had established themselves in Indonesia, mounted five separate invasion attempts on Macau in the early 17th century, none of them successful.

Responding to the attacks, Macau built a series of forts designed by a French military engi-

Chinese shrine near São Paulo

KERRY MORAN

neer and placed overlooking strategic sea approaches. As throughout the Portuguese empire, the walls were built of a mixture of earth, straw, and crushed oyster shells, packed between wood strips, called *chunambo*. This substance was supposed to be strong enough to withstand a direct cannonball hit, a claim never tested in Macau.

Thick city walls, five meters high, were also built as protection, but these defenses proved superfluous. The Dutch were routed in the decisive Battle of 1622, and no other serious threats occurred. Macau reached its golden age in the early 17th century, ruled by a powerful Senate, its coffers filled by "channels of gold and rivers of silver" from the Japan trade. It was a truly international community, composed of Portuguese colonists; Chinese mandarins and laborers; Japanese Christians; Persian, Dutch, and German traders; and slaves from Portuguese colonies in Africa, India, and Malaya. With few European women in the local community, Portuguese settlers married Christian converts from Japan, Malacca, and China; their offspring became the native Macanese. Chinese laborers were essential to the functioning of the community, but for several decades were forbidden to spend the night in the European district, until a compromise allowed them to settle there—but only in the basements of houses.

The Decline

Feudal politics in Japan ended the lucrative Japan trade in 1639, and this signalled hard times. Macau entered a slow decline, accelerated by internal squabbling and constant quarrels with the Chinese. In the 18th century it developed into a minor pan-European trading post, a base for China merchants, who, forced by edict to leave Guangzhou part of the year, retreated to summer homes in Macau. But with trade liberalization and the opening of the Treaty Ports along the Chinese coast, Macau faded into a quiet backwater.

Modern Times

During WW II Macau, like Portugal, remained neutral. Ignored by the Japanese, it became a haven for refugees from Hong Kong and China. It also served as a hotbed of spies, and developed a reputation for vice and intrigue. In 1966

the turmoil of the Chinese Cultural Revolution spilled over the border into Macau, leading to mass protests and the shootings of demonstrators.

The leftist Portuguese government installed in 1974 was markedly anti-colonial. It divested itself of Mozambique and Angola, and, in a liberal gesture, offered to return Macau to China. China refused the favor, and instead Portugal gave Macau considerable administrative and financial autonomy. A Sino-Portuguese agreement on the territory's long-term future was reached in March 1987. The handover date is set for 20 December 1999. Like Hong Kong, Macau will be a Special Administrative Region (SAR), with its social and economic system guaranteed for 50 years. Unlike Hongkongers, Macanese born in the territory will be entitled to hold a Portuguese passport, giving them right of residence in the EEC (European Economic Community)—and even, the ultimate irony, in Britain.

Government

Since 1976 Macau has enjoyed full internal self-government under Portuguese suzerainty. Officially it's no longer a colony, but a "Chinese territory under Portuguese administration" (call it an enclave or territory for short). The governor is appointed by the Portuguese president and is assisted by a legislative assembly of 23, only one-third of them directly elected. Macau's politics are less tumultuous than Hong Kong's, and China has long played an influential role in things. This, along with the territory's negligible international role, means Macau's impending handover has attracted less attention than Hong Kong's. Since native-born Macanese can get Portuguese (and therefore EEC) passports, there's less trauma involved here, too.

Economy

Macau gradually lost its significance as a trading port as its harbor silted up. Hong Kong's role as the region's premier harbor was strengthened by the advent of bigger ships requiring a deepwater port. The new container terminal off Coloane will allow Macau to reassume its development without having to rely on Hong Kong.

Macau's old role as trade enclave has given way to the gambling and tourism industries. Over seven million tourists arrived in 1995, 80%

of them from Hong Kong. Recent years have seen a growing percentage of mainland Chinese, many of them nouveau riche businessmen and PLA officers drawn by novel attractions like casinos and Russian strippers. The highway and rail links currently being developed between Guangzhou and Macau will only increase China tourism. China has clearly stated that the casinos will continue even after the 1999 takeover, for practical reasons. It's estimated that 20% of Macau's GNP, and one-third to one-half of government revenues, come from the STDM, the private association licensed to run gambling.

Light industry is also important, centering on toys and garments. Hong Kong companies frequently open factories here to take advantage of lower wages and Macau's textile export quotas to the U.S.

PEOPLE AND CULTURE

Macau's population of around 500,000 is 95% Chinese and about three percent Portuguese and Macanese (a complex mixture of Portuguese, Chinese, Malaccan, and Japanese blood). It hosts a fair number of illegal immigrants from China—plenty more Chinese cross the border legally each day to work in Macau's factories—and a considerable population of Thai women employed by the "entertainment" industry.

Language
Cantonese predominates among the Chinese majority, with other dialects spoken by smaller subgroups. The increasing prominence of mainland Chinese tourists means quite a few people speak or at least understand some Mandarin, and a little Mandarin goes a lot farther here than in Cantonese-oriented Hong Kong.

Portuguese was Macau's second official language until 1991, when it was supplanted by English. Related to Spanish, it's the seventh most widely spoken language in the world, and still influences street and shop signs and menus in Macau.

Religion and Festivals
Macau's Chinese temples, or *miu,* are dedicat-

USEFUL PORTUGUESE WORDS

alfaiataria—tailor shop
beco—alley
bilheteira—ticket office
casa de penhores—pawnshop
casa de comidas, casa de pasto—restaurant
casa de cambio—moneychanger
colina—hill
correios—post office
edificio—building
estrada—street
fortaleza—fortress
hospedaria—guesthouse
igreja—church
joalharia—jeweler
largo, praça—square
lavabos—toilet
lavandaria—laundry
mercado—market
museu—museum
ourivesaria—gold shop
pensao—guesthouse
pousada—inn
praia—beach
rua—street
sapataria—shoe shop
travessa—lane
vila—guest house

---

ed to both Taoist and Buddhist deities. As in Hong Kong, religion is strongly practical, with offerings made to obtain worldly benefits. Macau celebrates the same Chinese festivals as Hong Kong, but they tend to be livelier and more authentic. Firecrackers are still allowed, for one thing, so the Lunar New Year is a genuinely noisy Chinese celebration.

In addition, a Roman Catholic population of around 30,000 contributes its celebrations of saints' days and festivals:

Easter Procession of Our Lord of Passos: On the first day of Lent, an image of Christ on the cross is carried from the church of São Augustinho to the Cathedral, returning the following day.

Procession of Our Lady of Fatima: A big procession from São Domingo to Penha churches on 13 May commemorates the 1917 appearance of the Virgin Mary to a Portuguese farm girl. The **Procession of St. John the Baptist** on 10 June honors Macau's patron saint, while the **Feast of St. Anthony of Lisbon** the same month involves a procession from São Antonio church. **All Saints' Day** (1 November) and **All Souls' Day** (2 November) are both public holidays.

PRACTICALITIES

ACCOMMODATIONS

One of Macau's many pleasures is the wide selection of hotels, including the inexpensive and moderate ones that are so hard to find in Hong Kong. Getting a room is easy enough on weekdays, but holidays and weekends (especially in the summer) are crowded. Try to book in advance, especially around Chinese New Year, Easter, and the Macau Grand Prix in late November.

Advance booking may also earn a reduction on room rates in the more expensive hotels at off-peak times. The larger hotels have Hong Kong booking offices, or call them direct from Hong Kong (dial 001-853 to access Macau numbers). The MTIB office in Shun Tak Centre, tel. 2540-8180, can also assist in making reservations. The Macau Hotels Association counter at the airport will make bookings for all three- to five-star hotels, and operates a 24-hour hotline, tel. 703-416.

Room rates fluctuate according to demand, with midweek stays earning a 20-30% discount and winter prices generally lower than summer. Five percent government tax and a 10% service charge are added to bills.

Budget (Under Ptc300)
Cheaper places, often called *vila, pensao,* or *hospedaria,* cater mainly to gamblers and young Hong Kong couples. Proprietors may prefer Chinese guests, mainly because they fear embarrassing communication difficulties (many also have an aversion to "hippie" backpackers). A little Chinese goes a long way in such situations (Mandarin works as well as Cantonese); otherwise just be patient and good-humored.

Given the language barrier it may be difficult to book a room over the phone. You could ask the MTIB office at the Jetfoil Terminal to assist. It's generally easy to show up and find a room on weekdays.

Prices listed below are weekday rates and increase 20-30% on weekends and holidays.

Inner Harbour: This old central neighborhood is full of character and great for simply wandering: it draws many Chinese gamblers and Hong Kong couples, but relatively few foreign tourists. Start at the old red-light district, aptly named the Rua da Felicidade. The old shopfronts here were recently restored and repainted, and the area oozes charm. **Hotel Ko Wah,** 3/F 71 Rua da Felicidade, tel. 375-599, has big, clean, comfortable rooms, though the TV blaring in the lobby can be a problem. Next door at No. 73, **Vila Universal,** tel. 573-247, is also English-speaking and a similarly good value. Around the corner, **Hou Kong Hotel** at 1 Travessa das Virtudes, tel. 937-555, is a pleasant place with balconied rooms. **Vila Veng Va,** at the intersection of Travessa das Virtudes and Travessa Auto Novo, has small rooms, but the owners speak little English and are not very friendly.

Nearby, Praça Ponte e Horta is a formerly dignified little square now given over to shops and a few *vila* which are slowly moving upmarket. Pensao Kuan Heng, 2/F 3 Praça Ponte e Horta, tel. 573-629, is quite small, with basic, clean-enough rooms with VCR and TV for Ptc150 s, Ptc250 d.

There are a few upscale surprises on the way into town. At the small, modern **Hotel Silver Plaza** behind the Kam Pek Casino at 18 Rua Caldeira, tel. 570-456, they speak little English but are friendly enough. Nearby is the **Man Va,** 30 Travessa da Caldeira, tel. 388-656.

THE JESUITS IN ASIA

Trade and religion went hand in hand for the early Portuguese explorers, though most were much more interested in the former. The worldwide spread of Christianity was considered a noble goal, and missionaries accompanied traders and explorers on early voyages.

The Order of the Society of Jesus was at the cutting edge of Europe's Asian explorations. One of the Jesuit order's seven founders was St. Frances Xavier, who was sent by the pope to the Far East. Following three years in Japan (1549-51) he concluded the key to Asian conversion lay in China, which set the lead for all Asia. He died that year of fever on the tiny island of Sanchuang, 80 km upriver from Macau. Xavier's body was transferred to the Portuguese colony of Malacca and later to Goa, where it now reposes. A fragment of his elbow bone is enshrined on a tiny chapel on Coloane.

Xavier's dream of introducing Christianity to China was picked up by his followers, and their story rivals Marco Polo's as one of the most fascinating chapters in the history of West-East relations. Foremost among these adventurers was the priest Matteo Ricci, who arrived in Macau in 1582, and slowly made his way to the Imperial Court in Peking. He studied Chinese, becoming an expert not only on the language but also customs and manners. Dressed as a Confucian scholar, he presented Christianity in Confucian terms and was well accepted, living in the court of Peking for 20 years.

The Jesuits' deep knowledge of astronomy and sciences was a crucial element in their acceptance by China. After Father Adam Schall won a contest to predict the exact time of an eclipse, he was appointed director of the Chinese Almanac. Jesuit control over this institution and the imperial observatory continued until the order's expulsion from China in 1773. The priests hoped to reform the Chinese almanac and eliminate superstition, but while the calendar's precision was improved, the magical influence remained. The Jesuits' knowledge of modern math, astronomy, and geography was respected, but China itself was still quite advanced in the 17th century and was not overly impressed by them.

Along the main road are several older hotels, once moderate or even luxurious, now catering to Chinese gamblers and mainland groups. **Hotel Central,** 26 Avenida de Almeida Ribeiro, tel. 373-888, was once the biggest in town, a haven for gambling and prostitution. Today it's a legitimate hotel with lots of funky character, though rooms may be frankly shabby, and the smallest lack windows.

Pensao Ka Va, 5 Calçada de São João, tel. 574-022, near the cathedral, is nicely located and classier than most places. The **Holiday,** 36 Estrada do Repouso, tel. 361-696, is in a renovated building near São Paulo.

North of the Hotel Lisboa: This is the other main area for budget lodges. It's a well-situated neighborhood, though not as rich in character as the Inner Harbour. **Vila Wai Lei,** 38 Avenida de Dom João IV, tel. 710-199, is a very cheap, friendly place with tiny rooms as low as Ptc130. If it's full, try **Vila Nam Pan,** 8 Avenida de Dom Joãao. Nearby, at 3 Travessa da Praia Grande, is the not-so-friendly **Pensao Nam In,** tel. 710-024.

Vila Kam Loi, 34 Avenida do Infante d'Henrique, tel. 712-561, and **Vila Kimbo,** 57 Avenida do Infante d'Henrique, tel. 710-010, both have small, very cheap rooms under Ptc200.

BOB RACE

São Laurenco Church

Inexpensive (Ptc300-800)

There are plenty of cheap, slightly funky, old places in the Inner Harbor, like **Ruby Pension,** 11 Rua Nova do Comercio, tel. 923-118. **Hotel London,** 4 Praça Ponte e Horta, tel. 937-761, has rooms at the low end of this category. **Hotel Sun Sun,** 16 Praça Ponte e Horta, is a former budget place transformed into a gleaming new high-rise; well-sited for wandering old Macau.

The Grand, 146 Avenida de Almeida Ribeiro, tel. 921-111, is a 1930s-vintage hotel opposite the Kam Pek Casino, catering to mainland Chinese, with rooms at the bottom end of this category. **Hotel Nam Tin,** 4 Travessa da Praia Grande, tel. 711-212, is a pensao with decent bright rooms that have been newly renovated.

Moving up in this category,**Hotel Peninsula,** Rua das Lorchas, 14 Ponte Cais, tel. 318-899, is a classy newish hotel built right on the seawall; some rooms have great views of the Inner Harbour. **Macau Masters Hotel,** 162 Rua das Lorchas (tel. 937-572, Hong Kong tel. 2598-7808), is a modern 75-room hotel aimed at the Chinese market.

Metropole, 63 Rua da Praia Grande (tel. 388-166, Hong Kong tel. 2833-9300), is run by CTS; it has a central location and decent rates.

Hotel Guia Macau, 1-5 Estrada do Engenheiro Trigo (tel. 513-888, Hong Kong tel. 2770-9303), is a small, posh place set on a hillside close to Guia Fortress; the upper rooms offer good views. It's a little out of the way, but a free shuttle bus runs into town.

Hotel Matsuya, 5 Estrada da São Francisco (tel. 575-466, Hong Kong tel. 2368-6181), is similarly perched on a hillside below Guia Fortress; some of its 41 rooms have great views of the Outer Harbour.

Pousada de Coloane, Praia de Cheoc Van, Coloane (tel. 882-143, Hong Kong tel. 2540-8180). Set in a small pine forest overlooking the beach, this popular summertime retreat has only 22 rooms featuring dull decor but splendid balconies. It's somewhat remote and run-down, but undeniably peaceful.

Moderate (Ptc800-1200)

Beverly Plaza, 70 Avenida do Dr. Rodrigo Rodrigues, tel. 782-288, is a new place with 300 rooms, aiming for Chinese customers.

Hotel Lisboa, Avenida da Amizade (tel. 577-666, Hong Kong tel. 2546-6944), is Las Vegas, Chinese style. This is Macau's gambling center, with over 1000 rooms, two casinos, dozens of shops, seven restaurants, and six bars. There's a huge range of room rates, some quite reasonable.

Hotel Fortuna, 63 Rua da Cantao (tel. 786-333, Hong Kong tel. 2517-3728), is a newish mid-market hotel near the Lisboa.

Hotel Grandeur, 199 Rua Pequim (tel. 781-233, Hong Kong tel. 2857-2846), run by China Travel Service, is Macau's tallest hotel, topped by a revolving restaurant-lounge.

Holiday Inn Macau, Rua Pequim (tel. 783-333, Hong Kong tel. 2736-6855), is a big, modern, four-star hotel with rates at the high end of this category.

Kingsway, Rua de Luís Gonzaga Gomes, tel. 702-888, is another big (and ugly) new addition, with restaurants, casino, and a nightclub.

Presidente, 355 Avenida da Amizade (tel. 569-988, Hong Kong tel. 2857-1533). This big full-entertainment hotel has a popular nightclub and disco.

Sintra, Avenida de Dom João IV (tel. 710-111, Hong Kong tel. 2546-6944), is an old standby popular for its good location and service, bay views, and larger-than-usual rooms, some at the low end of this price category.

Royal, 2 Estrada da Vitoria (tel. 552-222, Hong Kong tel. 2543-6426). This nicely located hotel has full facilities and some good restaurants. Rooms are small but decent.

Expensive (Ptc1200+)

Bela Vista, 8 Rua do Comendador Kou Ho Neng (tel. 965-333, Hong Kong tel. 2881-1688). The formerly seedy old colonial hotel has been renovated by the Mandarin Oriental to a stunning level of elegance. There are only eight rooms, all deluxe suites outfitted with antiques.

Ritz Macau, Rua Comendador Kou Ho Neng (tel. 339-955, Hong Kong tel. 2739-6993). Set behind the Bela Vista, this elegant hotel was recently expanded. Rooms on the upper floors have balconies and bay views.

Pousada de São Tiago, Avenida da Republica (tel. 378-111, Hong Kong tel. 2735-3368). This romantic getaway is located inside the 17th-century fortress of São Tiago da Barra at the very tip of the peninsula. The 23 rooms are furnished with reproduction period furniture and offer great views of the channel; other features include a pool, good restaurants, and a 17th-century chapel. A unique experience, though the period decor can be a bit chilly in wintertime.

Mandarin Oriental, Avenida da Amizade (tel. 567-888, Hong Kong tel. 2881-1688). A big, classy hotel with an elegant casino, it's rather impersonal and nowhere near the standards of Hong Kong's Mandarin.

Hyatt Regency Macau, 2 Estrada Almirante, Taipa (tel. 831-234, Hong Kong tel. 2559-0168). Hongkongers visit this five-star resort for its spa, pool, fitness center, casino, and excellent restaurants. Inconveniently located on Taipa, but there's a shuttle bus to the ferry wharf.

New Century, Estrada Almirante Esparteiro, Taipa (tel. 831-111, Hong Kong tel. 2581-9863). A gleaming new 600-room hotel outfitted in Hong Kong-style luxury.

Westin Resort, Hac Sa Beach, Coloane (tel. 871-111, Hong Kong tel. 2803-2015). The big draw is the sports facilities: tennis, health club, and an 18-hole private golf course. Spacious rooms with large terraces overlook the beach.

FOOD

Aside from its architecture, Macau's imaginative cuisine is colonialism's greatest contribution, blending European and African influences with local ingredients. Begin with *caldo verde,* a hearty soup of potatoes, greens, and sometimes sausage. Other appetizers are spicy Portuguese sausages (chouriços), olives, sardines, and crusty fresh bread—a treat in Asia.

Local specialties include African chicken, in which the bird is rubbed with rock salt, marinated in a mixture of coconut milk, garlic, chilies, and peppercorns, and charcoal-grilled. Portuguese chicken is baked with vegetables, olive oil, Indian spices, and saffron. *Arroz gordo* ("fat rice") is a meat stew spiked with prawns, lemon, and chili. From the former Portuguese colony of Goa come spiced prawns, while Brazil contributes *feijoada* (pronounced "feshwada"), a hearty stew of blood sausage, ham, and beans. The former colony of Angola introduced *matapa,*

a saffron-flavored dish of shrimp and spinach. *Bacalhau,* Portugal's beloved salt codfish, appears baked, broiled, stewed, or grilled, while basic cafe dishes like steaks and sardines are served in huge portions. Seafood is superb: giant king prawns, baked or chilied crab, Macanese sole.

Dessert is typically *pudim,* frequently an egg custard. Meals are topped off with small cups of strong brewed coffee. All is washed down with inexpensive wine, served by the glass or bottle: *branco* or white, *tinto* or red (a bit heavy for some), or the quintessentially Macanese *vino verde,* a young, faintly bubbly "green" wine from northern Portugal—Alvarinho is the driest of the lot. Port is served also: white as aperitif, red as digestif. If you prefer beer, look for new local microbrews like Macau Golden Ale and Praia Grande Ale.

Of course, there are plenty of Cantonese restaurants and noodle shops: the fancier Chinese restaurants allow diners to pick their meals out of bubbling tanks, and may display snakes in winter, plus caged raccoons, pangolins, and other sad-looking mammals destined for the cookpot.

Restaurants serve lunch from noon to 2:30 or 3 p.m., and often close for a break before reopening for dinner around 7 p.m. They tend to be small, intimate places, often with a loquacious proprietor. Meals are leisurely, relaxed events, often consumed in friendly groups. Food is much cheaper than in Hong Kong. Even in the finest restaurants it's hard to exceed Ptc200 per person, and that includes wine and the 10% service charge commonly added onto bills.

Food is a highlight of even the shortest trips to Macau, and a good Portuguese meal washed down with wine is a major motive for a quick visit by Hong Kong residents. When looking for a special meal, check the restaurant listings in the Taipa and Coloane sections as well. Taipa in particular has a dense concentration of good restaurants which are well worth the short trip out.

Macanese and Portuguese Food

Most of these serve European and Chinese dishes as well. Telephone numbers are included if reservations are recommended.

A Lorcha, 289 Rua do Almirante Sergio, tel. 313-193, near the A Ma Temple, is reportedly the best Portuguese restaurant in Macau; relatively expensive, but still a great deal.

Afonso III, 11 Rua Central (behind Leal Senado), tel. 586-272, is crowded with locals who come for its unique Portuguese food: try the daily specials.

Bela Vista, 8 Rua do Comendador Kou Ho Neng, tel. 965-333, features terrace dining overlooking the bay—Portuguese and Continental dishes in a lovely setting and at surprisingly reasonable prices, though still expensive for Macau.

Club Militaire, 795 Avenida da Praia Grande, tel. 714-010, has purely Portuguese food in an impressive colonial setting.

Kam Fai Restaurant, 2C Rua de Palha, serves adequate cheap Portuguese food; sit upstairs for fascinating street views.

Henri's Galley, 4 Avenida da Republica, tel. 556-251, is a cozy place famous for its African chicken, curry crab, spicy prawns, and friendly proprietor.

Fat Siu Lau, 84 Rua da Felicidade, tel. 573-585, was the first Western restaurant in Macau when it opened in 1903; it's still in the original building. Specialties are marinated roast pigeon and African chicken.

Litoral, 261 Rua do Almirante Sergio, tel. 967-878, is a cozy Portuguese place with excellent codfish cakes and stuffed crabs.

Solmar, 512 Avenida da Praia Grande, tel. 574-391, is an old favorite, with all the standards on its menu.

A Galera Restaurant, Hotel Lisboa, tel. 577-666, features *azulejo*s on the walls and views of the São Francisco fort. It's relatively expensive.

Chinese Food

Dai pai dongs set up evenings in the Rua da Escola Commercial, north of the Hotel Lisboa, and in a side alley off the Avenida de João IV.

Long Kei, Largo do Leal Senado, is an old Cantonese restaurant with a huge menu (over 350 items) plus dim sum. Other dim sum choices are the **Royal Canton** in the Royal Hotel, **Fu Lai Tau** on Rua Dr. Pedro Jose Lobo, and **Restaurante Palace,** 24 Avenida Almeida Ribeiro. Dim sum is also available at two incredibly quaint old teahouses on the Rua de Cinco Outubro, the **Kun Nam** and the **Tai Long Fong.**

Suen Kong Buddhist Vegetarian, 9 Travessa de Santo Domingos, is a simple, very cheap place with a dozen or so vegetarian dishes on order.

Shanghai 456, in the Hotel Lisboa, has Sichuan and Beijing food as well, and friendly service.

Fook Lam Mun, 63 Avenida da Amizade, tel. 386-388, is highly rated by locals for its extensive menu and expensive Cantonese gourmet food; dim sum is served mornings and afternoons.

Dynasty, in the Mandarin Oriental, is a quiet, elegant place specializing in Beijing food.

Other Asian Food

Thai restaurants catering to women working in the "entertainment" industry are around the Estoril and Royal hotels. Try **Ko Ka,** 21 Rua Ferreira do Amaral, or **Restaurante Thai,** 27E Rua Abreu Nunes, both inexpensive. Slightly more central is the **Kam Kei,** on a side lane off Avenida de João IV. The best Thai restaurant in Macau is the **Baan Thai,** Rua de Henrique de Macedo, with authentically hot food.

Ginza in the Hotel Royal serves not-too-expensive Japanese food, or try **Furosato Nippon** in the Hotel Lisboa or **Sakura** in the Westin Resort.

Restaurante Dilli, 43 Avenida Sidonio Pais, specializes in South Indian food, with a big lunch buffet for Ptc80.

European Food

Os Gatos, Pousada São Tiago, Avenida da Republica, tel. 968-686, has reasonably good Mediterranean food, but what makes it special is the unique setting in a 17th-century fortress. Less formal is the Pousada's **Cafe da Barra,** a coffee shop serving Portuguese and international dishes inside or on the terrace.

Mezzaluna in the Mandarin Oriental, tel. 567-888, is a surprisingly inexpensive way to enjoy superb Italian food.

Pizzeria Toscana, Apaia do Grande Premio de Macau (across from the Jetfoil Terminal) is a superb homey Italian place serving pizzas, pastas, salads, and excellent desserts.

Stow's, 32 Rua Central, has lighter Western fare and a good salad bar along with the usual hearty Macanese menu.

Cafes, Breakfast, and Snacks

Bangkok Restaurant, 11 Travessa de São Domingos, on a quiet street off the Leal Senado square, has excellent coffee and baked goods. On the same street, **Barril Snack Bar** serves simple homestyle dishes like pork ear salad . . . well, try the black-eyed beans with tuna salad.

Establecimento de Comidas Meng Un, Largo do Senado, is a modern little cafe with noodles, cold drinks, and desserts. Next door, **Leitaria I Son** has an enormous array of Chinese-style dairy products, good for snacks and breakfast.

Sun Luen Fat, Rua Sul do Mercado de São Domingos (look for the pink building off the Largo do Senado), is a good place for lunch meat and picnic provisions; it also sells sandwiches, snacks, and ice cream.

Cafe Safari, 14 Patio do Coto Velo (near Leal Senado), is a reliable coffee shop, serving Portuguese and Macanese fare and breakfasts from 8 a.m.

Sopa de Fitas Boa Fortuna, 41 Avenida do Infante d'Henrique, is a cheap, clean, fast diner with an English menu that includes noodle soups, ice cream, and milk shakes.

Pokka, 2/F Yaohan Department Store, Avenida da Amizade, has excellent strong coffee and Japanese cafe food displayed in plastic at the entrance.

Riquexo, inside the Park 'N Shop at 69 Rua Sidonio Pais, is a simple coffee shop with authentic home-cooked food brought in fresh daily by Macanese women—try the daily specials. It opens at noon and is crowded with regulars for lunch.

Hotel coffee shops often stay open 24 hours to serve gamblers. Try **Noite e Dia** in the Hotel Lisboa, or the Holiday Inn coffee shop, which has a good Ptc110 breakfast buffet. In the fast-food line, Macau has four **McDonald's** (the most central at 17 Rua do Campo), and a **Pizza Hut** behind the Hotel Lisboa.

Picnic Fare

Supermercado Days 'n' Days sells all the basics plus Portuguese delicacies like olive oil, olives, sausages, and wine. There's one on Rua da Praia Grande and another on Avenida da Republica. Another supermarket is Mercearia Seng Cheong, behind the Mercado Municipal on Rua Pedro Nolasco da Silva. There's a Park 'N Shop at 11 Praça Ponte e Horta and another at 69 Rua Sidonio Pais. The São Dominogo market sells fresh produce. The Patisserie at the Mandarin Oriental packs picnic lunchboxes, and local bakeries sell Chinese and Western bread (there are lots along Rua Sidonio Pais).

Possible picnic sites include the hilltop grounds of Penha Church, São Francisco Garden, Fortaleza do Monte (with stone tables beneath big banyan trees), Jardim Luís de Camões, and the wooded hill below Guia Fortress. Only a little farther out are Coloane's beaches, especially peaceful Hac Sa with its pine forest, and the park and trails of Alto do Coloane.

RECREATION

Events

Macau's biggest sporting event, the **Macau Grand Prix,** is held in late November, usually the third weekend of the month. It began in 1954, when there were only 300 cars in all of Macau. (Now everyone drives like a Grand Prix racer.) A 6.1-km circuit is set up along the narrow city streets, and crowds flood in to watch the excitement. The event is part of the Formula III World Championship and also involves motorcycle and sports and classic car racing. The city gets incredibly crowded, so book a hotel and a return ticket in advance. Hotel Guia Macau, situated near the dramatic big bend, is a good place for views.

Check with the Tourism Bureau for cultural events, or pick up a copy of its glossy booklet *Welcome to Macau.* The **Macau International Music Festival** (October to November) features concerts at the Macau Forum, Macau University, and the Jardim Lou Lim Ieoc. The **Macau Arts Festival** in February to March features exhibitions and performances by local groups. Chinese dances are performed Sunday and holidays in front of the A-Ma Temple 10:30-11 a.m. and in front of São Paulo 11-11:30 a.m.

The government tourism office sponsors a craft market Saturday afternoons 2-7 p.m. in São Agostinho Square, with demonstrations of skills like kite-making, calligraphy, and Chinese sweet-making. Folk song and dance performances are held Friday and Saturday evenings at 9 p.m.

Shopping

Shopping in Macau is notably cheaper than in Hong Kong (25-30% less), though the selection is not as enormous. Shops are smaller and more casual, people friendlier. Good buys include antiques, porcelain, gold jewelry, knitwear, and clothes.

Antiques: Curio shops sell Portuguese ceramics and pottery, old parchments, carved wooden furniture, Chinese ginger jars, wedding baskets, and silk embroideries. It's a joy to root through the cluttered, dusty shelves, the stock regularly replenished with shipments from China. Beware of fakes from the Ming dynasty, though. Prices are already lower than Hong Kong, so you probably won't be able to bargain sellers down more than 10-15%. Explore the bazaars and flea markets in the narrow streets around São Paulo and the Inner Harbour. Rua São Paulo is especially good for porcelain. Antiques are concentrated along Rua dos Faitioes, Rua da Tercena, Rua Nossa Senhora Do Amparo, and Rua Ervanarios. On the upper end of Rua Almeida Ribeiro are a few stores selling elegant 1930s jewelry and old silver opium pipes.

Clothing: Textiles are a major local industry. The cheapest places to poke about are the stalls along Rua de Cinco Outubro and the Rua San Domingos market. Bins are piled high with sports clothes, mainly for women and children and with a seasonal orientation (lightweight clothes in summer; tights, sweaters, and skiwear in winter). The cobbled Rua Palha is called

---

A GAMBLING GUIDE TO MACAU

Gambling is Macau's major form of nightlife, and day-life too. It's not elegant, however (gambling seldom is)—it's no Monte Carlo or Las Vegas. This is gambling for the serious, gambling "stripped to the bare bones of greed and anxiety," noted one observer.

To dispel any illusions, stroll through a casino and study the faces. Gamblers do not generally look like happy people. Consider why the Hotel Lisboa asks its guests to leave a deposit for laundry and phone calls, and insists they prepay for their rooms. Then note the gold leaf on the ceilings of the more elegant gambling salons, and—the final clue—the abundance of pawnshops in casino neighborhoods, with nervous groups of broke gamblers lurking outside the door, nervously glancing at their watches or cameras.

Legalized gambling has been a lucrative source of income for the Macau government since it was instituted in the 19th century. Government revenues from gambling and betting taxes total half the yearly budget.

Since 1962 the government's gambling franchise has gone to the Sociedade de Turismo e Diversões de Macau (STDM), whose chairman, magnate Stanley Ho, has been called "the unofficial governor of Macau." STDM's current license expires in 1999, but China has repeatedly emphasized that gambling will continue even after Macau's reversion to the mainland. Indeed, many of the gamblers are Mandarin-speaking mainlanders, dazzled by the opportunities their home country doesn't offer—at least so conspicuously.

Games

The basic rule is only bet what you can afford to lose, because you almost certainly will lose it. Games are identical in different casinos, as standard rules are set by the STDM.

Slot machines are the most accessible and popular game, requiring no human contact to play. They're known locally as "hungry tigers"—an apt metaphor, as they relentlessly devour money. No skill is required; just feed in a coin or token and flip the handle. Some illuminating statistics: the odds for three in a row are 1:8,000, four in a row 1:160,000; five in a row 1:3.2 million. Faced with such odds, even laboratory rats would soon give up, but humans keep flipping the lever, hypnotized by the promise of an enormous and rapidly escalating payout displayed in neon figures above.

Blackjack: Also called "21," because players try to collect cards totalling as close to 21 as possible without going over. Winners get their money plus

"Women's Street" because of its many small boutiques.

Gold: The relatively low price of gold is government-controlled. Shops will add a little something for workmanship and profit, so there's some room for bargaining. Twenty-four karat gold is sold by the tael, which equals 1.2 troy ounces. Jewelry is usually 18k gold. The trade is centered along the Avenida Almeida Ribeiro, where gold shops are crowded with mainland Chinese buying gold as a hedge against inflation.

A local peculiarity are the **pawnshops** clustered around the casinos; look for the sign *Casa de Penhores*. Cameras and watches predominate, but of course there are no guarantees. Good deals are possible, but bargain hard and be very careful.

The giant **Yaohan Department Store** on Avenida da Amizade across from the Jetfoil Terminal is a good place for housewares, clothing, and just about anything else you can imagine. **Food** is a favorite purchase of visiting Hongkongers. The Chinese return laden with special sweets and Macau's famous salt fish, the expats with cheap Portuguese wine (Hong Kong customs restricts imports to one liter, but arrivals are seldom checked).

Sports
Bicycling: There's too much traffic in Central Macau to make it enjoyable, but cycles are rented on Taipa Island and can be ridden over to Coloane.

Go-Karting: The new go-kart track built on reclaimed land opposite Coloane Park rents karts to visitors; it's crowded on weekends, when club meetings take place.

50%. **Baccarat** is a more upper-class game, with bets laid on whose hand will total closest to nine points, the bank's or the player's.

Roulette is simple: bettors guess where a ball will come to rest, their choices being 37 holes in a revolving wheel. Payout is 35 times the bet. Winning is more likely, though payout is much smaller, if you simply bet on red or black and odd or even numbers. **Boule** is similar to roulette but uses a larger ball and a different wheel with only 25 numbers.

Fantan is a wildly popular local game involving a heap of porcelain buttons and a silver cup. The buttons are counted off in groups of four, and players bet on how many will be left at the end. Not very sophisticated, but what do you expect from a place where people once bet on the number of pips in an orange? Casinos also sponsor private rounds of *pai kau* or dominoes, taking a set percentage of the win. *Dai siu* means "big-small." Three dice are thrown in a covered container, and players bet on whether the total will show a big number (10-18) or a small one (3-9), or on a particular number. Three of a kind and the bank takes all, unless you've bet directly on it.

Where To Play
Entry to casinos is restricted to those age 18 and above for tourists, 21 and above for locals. A mild dress code forbids shorts, and no cameras or photographs are allowed inside. You'll also note there are no phones, clocks, or windows inside, a deliberate effort to minimize intrusions from the outside world. Most casinos are open 24 hours. Except for the Kam Pek, which takes local currency, betting is in Hong Kong currency, with a minimum bet of HK$50 in most games.

The classiest casinos are at the **Mandarin Oriental** and the **Hyatt**, though the latter is small and not worth going out of the way to visit. The **Kingsway Hotel Casino** is a flashy place with fairly high minimum bets. The **Holiday Inn** has a small upmarket casino featuring blackjack, baccarat, and *dai siu.*

The gaudiest, noisiest, and biggest casino is the **Hotel Lisboa,** which deserves a visit whether or not you actually play. The big smoke-filled rotunda encompasses all sorts of games, while plush semi-private rooms on the sides require minimum bets of HK$1000.

The, er, *ripest* atmosphere is found at the **Kam Pek** on Avenida Almeida Ribeiro and the **Macau Palace Casino,** popularly known as the **Floating Casino** (or in Cantonese Chaak Suen, "Boat of Thieves"). Housed in a converted double-deck ferry in the Inner Harbour, it has a seedy feel entirely appropriate to Macau; highly recommended for a visit.

The **Casino Jai Alai** near the Ferry Terminal draws huge crowds. There's even a small casino (**Casino Victoria**) in the grandstand of the Macau Jockey Club, open weekends and race days.

Golf: For most, the Macau Golf and Country Club behind the Westin Resort will suffice. Serious golfers cross the Chinese border to the superb Zhuhai International Golf Club.

Hiking: Coloane is the best place to hike, either the 8.6-km *Trilho de Coloane* or the 6-km *Trilho Nordeste*.

Horseback Riding: Macau Horse Riding Centre, Hac Sa Beach, Coloane, tel. 828-303.

Ice-Skating and Bowling: Try Future Bright Amusement Park, near Praça de Luís Camões.

Running: You'll see a few persistent runners on the Taipa bridge and the Praia Grande, but the traffic is too heavy to recommend this. The wooded path around Guia Hill is peaceful and shady, and a Fitness Circuit at the top has 20 exercise stations scattered amid pre-WW II gun emplacements.

Swimming and Windsurfing: Hac Sa and Cheoc Van beaches on Coloane are the best, though the water is murky with silt. There are also swimming pools at the beaches. The Hotel Lisboa pool is open to the public.

Tennis and Squash: Courts can be found at the Mandarin Oriental, Hyatt Regency, Westin Resort and New Century hotels, and at Hac Sa Park.

Spectator Sports

Greyhound Racing: Meets are held at the Canidrome near the border every Tuesday, Thursday, and Saturday or Sunday at 8 p.m. Locals take it as seriously as horse racing. The dogs are imported from the U.S., Ireland, and Australia. Admission is Ptc2, and all sorts of odd bets are possible, with the minimum wager Ptc2. For information call 574-413.

Horse Racing: The 18,000-seat Macau Jockey Club racetrack on Taipa hosts races twice a week year-round; for information call 821-188. Tickets are available through hotels or on-site. Admission to the air-conditioned grandstand is Ptc20, and the minimum bet is Ptc10.

Nightlife

Macau's vice has been somewhat cleaned up, though plenty remains, most of it now squarely aimed at the Chinese market. Bar girls, many of them Thai or Filipina, are rented out for a fee, for talking or whatever else.

Hotel nightclubs feature Filipino musicians and foreign dancers (Thai, European, Russian) in varying degrees of nudity. The Presidente Hotel's Skylight Disco and Nightclub is particularly popular, but most famous is the Hotel Lisboa's **Crazy Paris Show,** starring an international troupe of female performers clad in bits of glittering lamé. Shows are nightly at 8 and 9:30 p.m.; Ptc190 tickets are available at various hotels and travel agencies, or call the Lisboa at 377-666, ext. 1193.

Lively local dance clubs provide cleaner fun and are popular with Macanese couples. Hot spots are **Pyratu's** at 106 Rua Pedro Coutinho, where African music reigns; **Talker's Pub** right next door, and **China Pop,** 47 Beco do Sal (near A Lorcha Restaurant), featuring surreal Maoist decor.

GETTING THERE

Traditionally, access to Macau has been via Hong Kong or China. This changed in 1995, with the opening of Macau's new international airport; still, most visitors arrive by sea from Hong Kong.

By Sea

This is by far the most popular means of transport. Seagoing vessels (ferries, catamarans, hoverferries, tricats, and jetfoils), depart Hong Kong for Macau over 100 times a day. Buy your ticket on the 3/F of the Macau Ferry Terminal, Shun Tak Centre, 200 Connaught Rd., Central (near the Sheung Wan MTR and the tram line).

Weekdays you can usually show up and buy a ticket on the next outgoing vessel, but book in advance for weekends and holidays to avoid long lines. Jetfoil and jumbocat tickets can be bought up to 28 days in advance, and jetfoil and high-speed ferry tickets can be picked up at Ticketmate outlets in major MTR stations, Exchange Square in Central, or New World Centre in Kowloon. The jetfoil also allows telephone credit card bookings, tel. 2859-6596. Tickets must be picked up at Shun Tak Centre at least one hour before boarding.

A few words of advice: allow 20-30 minutes for departure and immigration formalities, which take place before boarding and are usually so

BOB RACE

Guia Lighthouse

brief it's easy to forget they're necessary at all. Departure tax (HK$26 or Ptc22) is included in ticket prices and accounts for the slight discount on return fares from Macau. Note that major luggage is not allowed on the jetfoil; if you have a lot of baggage, either arrive early to check it in, or take the high-speed ferry or jumbocat.

Jetfoil is the fastest and most popular means of travel, drawing 75% of all travelers. Boats operated by the Far East Jetfoil Co., tel. 2859-3351, depart every 15 minutes from 7 a.m-5 p.m., then every half-hour until midnight; travel time is 55 minutes. Cost is HK$125 economy class, HK$139 first class on weekdays, HK$129/143 on weekends. There's a 20% additional charge for night service, from 5:30 or 6 p.m. to 3 a.m. Views and legroom from first class on the upper deck are slightly better than second, but are not stunning. The experience resembles an airplane ride, right down to the crowded seating.

Jumbocats are large jet-powered catamarans that also take an hour to travel the 68 km to Macau. Departures are every half-hour 8 a.m.-6 p.m.; economy tickets are HK$125 weekdays, HK$136 weekends; 20 percent extra for night service. Call 2810-8677 for information.

Triple-decker **high-speed ferries** make the trip in 90 minutes. The extra half-hour is not so bad, especially as first class has an outdoor sundeck from which to enjoy the views. The ferries even boast slot machines. They tend to be less crowded than jetcats and are considerably cheaper, with fares HK$59-93 on weekdays, HK$81-116 on weekends. Two ships make five roundtrips daily between 7:30 a.m. and 8 p.m. Contact the Hong Kong Hi-Speed Ferries Co., tel. 2815-3034.

There are also departures from the China Ferry Terminal in China Hong Kong City, Tsimshatsui. Hoverferries are operated by Hong Kong Ferries Co., tel. 2516-9581; departures are every 45 minutes 8:15 a.m.-8:30 p.m., and tickets cost HK$95, HK$110 on weekends; night service is HK$125. Ten **jetcats** depart daily; tickets are HK$112 weekdays, HK$125 weekends. **Jumbocats** depart roughly every half-hour, fare is HK$107-148 weekdays, HK$132-152 weekends.

Helicopter
East Asia Airlines operate 20 flights daily, tel. 2856-3359 in Hong Kong, or 790-7040 in Macau. Travel time is 20 minutes; cost is HK$1202 weekdays, HK$1306 weekends. Helipads are at the Macau Ferry Terminal in Hong Kong and the Jetfoil Terminal in Macau, and bookings can be made there.

MACAU TOUR AGENCIES

Asia Tours: 25B Rua da Praia Grande, tel. 593-844

CTS Macau: Rua de Nagasaki, tel. 705-506

Macau Star Tours: Rm. 511, Tai Fung Bank Bldg., 34 Avenida Almeida Ribeiro, tel. 558-855

Macau Tours: 35 Avenida Dr. Mario Soares, tel. 710-003

Sintra Tours: Rm. 135 Hotel Lisboa, tel. 710-361

By Air

Macau International Airport, on the east side of Taipa Island, is drawing an increasing number of airlines and flights. Currently it's possible to fly in or out to 12 Chinese cities, including Guangzhou, Beijing, Xian, Chongqing, Guilin, and Shanghai. Asian destinations include Bangkok, Kuala Lumpur, Singapore, Ho Chi Minh City, Saigon, and Pyongyang; while European cities include Lisbon and Brussels. All in all, it's cheaper to fly to Hong Kong, however, and catch a boat to Macau.

Departure tax for destinations outside the Chinese mainland is Ptc150. The AP1 bus connects the Barrier Gate, Jetfoil Terminal, Hotel Lisboa, and the airport.

Organized Tours

Organized tours from Hong Kong are of a cookie-cutter sameness, departing around 9 a.m. and returning by 5 p.m. (afternoon tours are 2:30-10 p.m.). These hit all the major sights, but as you might imagine, it's hard to cram Macau's charm into a few over-organized hours. Day tours run HK$760-865, HK$1315-1400 for a 1-day trip. At the very least it's much cheaper to go to Macau on your own and hook up with a local tour company if necessary (see the chart "Macau Tour Agencies").

From China

Two buses a day connect Guangzhou and Macau, a five- or six-hour ride, entering Macau from Gongbei, part of the Zhuhai Special Economic Zone. Bus tickets are available at CITS in Guangzhou.

Arriving In Macau

Boats from Hong Kong dock at the **Jetfoil Ter-** **minal** on Avenida Amizade on the Outer Harbour. Stop in at the visitor information center here for a free map and information. Day-trippers can leave bags in luggage lockers on the ground floor. It's a dull 20-minute walk into town, or catch a taxi or bus in front of the terminal. Buses 3 and 3A run past the Hotel Lisboa and down the main street, Avenida Almeida Ribeiro. (See the chart "Useful Bus Routes for Macau" for a complete rundown of bus routes.)

Buses from Guangzhou usually run into town; if you've crossed the border on foot, Bus 5 runs from the Barrier Gate to Avenida Almeida Ribeiro.

Macau To Hong Kong

Book tickets at the Jetfoil Pier or at the ticket office in the lobby of the Hotel Lisboa. Booking a roundtrip ticket upon departure would save an extra step, but it's easy enough on a weekday to go down and get a seat on the next boat out. Fares from Macau are slightly cheaper than Hong Kong, as the departure tax, included in the ticket price, is only Ptc22.

GETTING AROUND

Macau is small enough to deal with on foot for the most part, and walking, in judicious combination with bus and taxi, is the most enjoyable way of getting around.

Taxi

Taxis, black with beige roofs, are abundant. Fares are metered and charges are clearly outlined on a card in back—Ptc8 for the first 1.5 km, then Ptc1 per quarter-km. There's a surcharge of Ptc5 on trips out to Taipa and Ptc10 to Coloane (none levied on returns, though). Few drivers speak English, so have your hotel staff write down your destination in Chinese, or point it out on a map.

Pedicabs

Green and yellow bicycle rickshaws are a novelty aimed primarily at tourists: be sure to bargain. Rates are Ptc100 or so for an hour around town, Ptc20 for a short ride.

Bus

Public buses run 7 a.m.-midnight and charge a flat fare of Ptc2 on city routes (more out to Taipa and Coloane). Exact change is required; drop it in the fare box on entering. Most buses are air-conditioned 24-seaters, and are not terribly crowded except during rush hour. In-town bus stops are marked; in remoter areas like the islands you can flag them down just about anywhere. MTIB publishes a useful leaflet outlining public bus routes to places of interest.

Car Rentals

There's too much traffic and too little parking to make driving enjoyable, but a rental vehicle can be useful in exploring the islands. Try **Avis Rent-A-Car** in the Mandarin Oriental Macau (tel. 336-789; Hong Kong tel. 2540-2011). A local peculiarity are the small, sporty **mokes,** four-seater soft-top jeeps rented by **Happy Mokes** in the Jetfoil Terminal, tel. 831-212, Hong Kong tel. 2540-8180.

Many hotels offer special rates on rentals. Book in advance and the agency will even deliver the vehicle to your hotel. Weekday rates run around Ptc450 per 24 hours, Ptc500 on weekends. A deposit is necessary, and drivers must be at least 21, with an international driving license or a license recognized in Portugal.

Bicycles

Downtown Macau is too hilly and heavily trafficked to make biking enjoyable; walking is a better alternative. Bikes are available for rent around the Taipa village square for Ptc8 an hour.

By Air

The Macau Aeronautical Association, tel. 307-343, runs flightseeing tours of Macau in ultralight two-seater planes. The landing strip is on reclaimed land across from the Presidente Hotel. Cost is around HK$350 for 10 minutes.

USEFUL BUS ROUTES IN MACAU

BUS NO.	ROUTE
3	Jetfoil Terminal-Hotel Lisboa-Avenida Almeida Ribeiro-Barrier Gate
3A	Jetfoil Terminal-Hotel Lisboa-Avenida Almeida Ribeiro-Rua das Lorchas-Praça Ponte e Horta
5	Barra-Rua das Lorchas-Avenida Almeida Ribeiro-Avenida de Horta e Costa-Lin Fung Miu-Barrier Gate-Jai Alai
9	Rua das Lorchas-Avenida Almeida Ribeiro-Jardim Lou Lim Ieoc-Barrier Gate-Lin Fong Temple/Canidrome-Avenida Sidonio Pais-Flora Garden-Leal Senado-Avenida Almeida Ribeiro-Rua da Praia Grande-Pousada São Tiago-Barra
11	Praça Ponte e Horta-Rua das Lorchas-Avenida Almeida Ribeiro-Hotel Lisboa-Taipa Hyatt Regency-Taipa Village-Macau Jockey Club
26, 26A	Rua das Lorchas-Avenida Almeida Ribeiro-Hotel Lisboa-Taipa Hyatt Regency-Coloane Park-Coloane Village
28A	Jetfoil Terminal-Hotel Lisboa-Hyatt Regency-Taipa-Macau Jockey Club
28B	Jetfoil Terminal-Lisboa-Praia Grande-Barra
AP1	Barrier Gate-Jetfoil Terminal-Hotel Lisboa-Airport

Organized Tours

A number of local agencies put on organized tours: a half-day with lunch at least manages to touch on all the major sights. The price, controlled by the government, is around Ptc100. Agencies do two-hour tours out to the islands as well. Ask MTIB for a list of companies; a few are listed here under the chart "Macau Tour Agencies."

Local companies and CTS also operate day tours across the border to Zhuhai, some visiting the Zhongshan golf course. More elaborate three- and four-day packages around Guangdong are also available.

OTHER PRACTICALITIES

Visas And Customs

Entry to Macau is streamlined. Short-term visitors from many countries don't need a visa, and customs and immigrations formalities are mild. A 20-day stay without visa is granted for visitors from the U.S., Canada, Australia, New Zealand, the U.K, and most European countries, as well as Brazil, India, Japan, Thailand, Taiwan, the Philippines, Malaysia, Singapore, and South Korea. Hong Kong residents who are British Commonwealth subjects get up to 90 days.

Visitors from other countries can purchase visas on arrival in Macau for HK$100. Those from countries without diplomatic relations with Portugal should apply in advance at the Portuguese Consulate in Hong Kong, at Harbour Centre, 25 Harbour Rd., Wanchai, tel. 2802-2587.

Customs procedures are similarly simple: while import and export of weapons, drugs, and other dangerous items is controlled, there are no restrictions on money or goods taken in or out, and no duties on export of locally purchased items. If you're returning to Hong Kong, remember the import limit on wine or alcohol is one liter/quart—but arrivals are rarely checked.

Money
Macau's currency is the *pataca* (written Ptc. or Ptc), made up of 100 *avos*. Coins come in 10, 20, and 50 *avos* and Ptc1 and Ptc5; bills come in denominations of Ptc5, Ptc10, Ptc50, Ptc100, Ptc500, and Ptc1000. The *pataca* is pegged to the Hong Kong dollar and is worth about three percent less (Ptc103.30 = HK$100), but Hong Kong currency is accepted everywhere at an identical rate. For short visits it's easiest to use HK$, unless you're spending a lot, in which case conversion would save you three percent.

You can change money at banks, casinos (24-hour service), and private moneychangers *(casa de cambio);* scams are less common than in Hong Kong, but as usual, check rates carefully beforehand. Don't overload on local currency: even Hong Kong banks don't want *patacas,* and they can be hard to change once you leave Macau.

American Express has offices at 23B Rua de St. Paulo and at the Barrier Gate (Istmo Fereira do Amaral, Jardins do Mar Sui). There's also a 24-hour office in the Hotel Lisboa.

PLANNING A MACAU TRIP

Macau is a world away from Hong Kong, but only an hour away by jetfoil—that's less time than it takes to get to Lantau Island. It's remarkably easy to visit: customs and immigrations formalities are so streamlined as to be unnoticeable, and you can travel there on a weekday virtually at whim. Weekends and holidays are more crowded and may require advance planning. Hotel prices go up 20-30% at these times, so it's better to visit during the week.

A daytrip to Macau is possible, though an overnight stay is recommended, and three or four days allows its pleasures to unfold at leisure. Indeed, leisure is the essence of a Macau visit. No point in rushing about trying to see everything at once: instead, enjoy selected sights, the relaxed ambience of its old streets, and a meal or two at one of the excellent inexpensive restaurants Macau is famous for. If you've only got a day, concentrate on the older neighborhoods around the Largo do Senado, São Paulo, and the Inner Harbour.

Communications
The antique facade of the General Post Office on the Largo do Senado hides a wide range of modern services, including poste restante and a fax counter. Hours are 9 a.m.-6 p.m. Mon.-Fri., Saturday 9 a.m.-1 p.m. There are post offices on Taipa and Coloane as well, and one at the Jetfoil Terminal.

Local telephone calls can be made for free from private phones in shops and restaurants; pay phones are Ptc1 for five minutes, though they're less than abundant. Look around Largo do Senado, near the Jetfoil Terminal, or along the Praia. Pay phones allow International Direct Dialing and Home Direct service to some countries. Most hotels have in-room IDD. Phonecards in denominations of Ptc50, Ptc100, and Ptc200 can be used for local and international calls from yellow Cardphones around Largo do Senado and the Jetfoil Terminal, as well as the 24-hour telephone office inside the GPO. They're available from Companhia de Telecomunicacoes (CTM) offices, located in the GPO and at 25 Rua Pedro Coutinho.

Health

Macau's water is treated with chlorine and is quite safe to drink. Bottled water is widely available, and hotels supply thermoses of boiled water, Chinese-style.

Local pharmacies *(farmácia)* are similar to Hong Kong's. The Government Hospital, tel. 514-499, on Estrada São Francisco (north of the Hotel Lisboa) is probably the best choice for English speakers.

Media

Local papers are in Cantonese and Portuguese, but Hong Kong's *Post* and *Standard* are sold in newsstands along Avenida Almeida Ribeiro. Macau has two Cantonese radio stations and one Portuguese; Hong Kong TV and radio stations come through as well. The local Teledifusao de Macau (TdM) has some English programing, though most is in Portuguese and Cantonese: check Hong Kong papers for daily listings.

Information

Pre-departure, you might want to investigate the Macau government tourist office's Website: http://turismo.macau.gov. Several offices of the **Macau Tourist Information Bureau** dispense leaflets and advice. There's one at the Hong Kong Airport; another on the third floor of Shun

Tak Centre, 200 Connaught Rd., Central, tel. 2857-2297. This office will also assist with reserving mokes and arranging hotel accommodations or tours.

In Macau, there's a **visitor information center** at the Jetfoil Terminal, tel. 726-416; the main tourist office is downtown on the Largo do Senado, tel. 315-566, and there are smaller tourist information counters at Guia Fortress and Fortaleza do Monte. All stock free sightseeing brochures, maps, and information on bus transport and hotels, and provide advice on sightseeing. Other publications to look for are *Macau Travel Talk,* oriented to the tourist trade, the

MACAU TOURIST INFORMATION BUREAU OFFICES

USA: 3133 Lake Hollywood Dr., P.O. Box 1860, Los Angeles, CA 90078, tel. 213-851-3402, 800-331-7150
P.O. Box 350, Kenilworth, IL 60043-0350, tel. 847-251-6421
Suite 316, 70A Greenwich Ave., New York, NY 10011, tel. 212-206-6828

Canada: Suite 157, 10551 Shellbridge Way, Richmond, B.C., V6X 2W9, tel. 604-231-9040
13 Mountalan Ave., Toronto, Ontario, M4J 1H3, tel. 416-446-6552

U.K.: 6 Sherlock Mews, Paddington St., London W1M 3RH, tel. 071-224-3390

Australia: 449 Darling St., Balmain, Sydney, NSW 2041, tel. 02-9555-7548

New Zealand: P.O. Box 42-165, Orakei, Auckland 5, tel. 64-9-575-2700

France: Atlantic Associates SARL, 52 Champs-Elysees, 75008, tel. 331-4256-4551

Germany: Shafergasse 17, D60313 Frankfurt-am-Main, tel. 49-69-234-094

Spain: Gran Via 27, 1/F, 28013, Madrid, tel. 341-522-9354

Japan: 4/F Toho Twin Tower Building, 5-2 Yurakucho 1-chome, Chiyoda-ku, Tokyo 100, tel. 03-3501-5022

DRAGON LORE

Dragons have been strongly associated with the Chinese people for some 4,000 years, serving as a powerful symbol of the renewal of natural energies. The dragon is one of the four supernatural creatures of Chinese folklore, along with the turtle, unicorn, and phoenix. It is found carved atop fiddles and bells, embossed on stone tablets, engraved on sword hilts, or set writhing across the roofs of buildings—folklore has it in order to prevent fire.

The dragon is said to possess the power of invisibility—a good explanation as to why we never see one. However, sightings of giant dead dragons were reported as recently as the 1920s in China.

Dragons reportedly have phosphorescent bodies that emit tiny flames. Their breath is of fire or water, and their voice "like the jingling of copper pots." One account describes them as having "a camel's head, a deer's horns, a rabbit's eyes, cow's ears, a snake's neck, a frog's belly, a carp's scales, a hawk's claws, and a tiger's palm."

Invariably they are depicted sporting with or pursuing a sphere, which is variously described as the Pearl of Wisdom, the sun, the moon, or the embodiment of rolling thunder—all various manifestations of power. Power is the dragon's leitmotif, but his talent at transformation also makes him a symbol of renewal. He can change size at will, from "as small as a silkworm to as large as heaven and earth."

Dragons are said to live in the sky in springtime, when they cavort in storm clouds. A typhoon is considered a battle between two dragons, while an eclipse means a dragon has swallowed the sun. In autumn the creature moves into the water, with which it has a strong association. During a drought he's said to sleep, while a flood signifies his anger.

Three types of dragons are described in ancient texts. The *li* dwell in crystal palaces under the ocean, where they guard wealth, much like the underwater *naga* serpents of Hindu mythology. The smaller *chiao*, found in mountains and marshes, are azure or green in color and are related to *feng shui*. Most powerful is the fire-breathing *lung*, which dwells in the sky and produces wind and rain. Rendered in hues of red and gold, it appears as the imperial symbol.

The dragon has been an emblem of imperial power since the Han dynasty. The emperor's hand was "The Dragon's Claw," his offspring "The Dragon's Seed," his throne "The Dragon Seat." Rather than simply dying, it was said that the emperor had "ascended upon the dragon."

The imperial dragon possesses five claws, as opposed to four claws for ordinary dragons. It appears all over the Imperial Palace in Beijing, carved on furniture, embroidered on robes, painted on porcelain, and adorning palace architecture. There is a particular concentration in the imperial throne room, where the walls, ceiling, screens, and pillars are writhing with dragons. The throne itself is made entirely of dragons, and appears quite uncomfortable to sit upon.

While the imperial dragon fell into disrepute after the Manchu regime was toppled in 1911, the Chinese fascination with the dragon continues. The Year of the Dragon is always a popular one for births, marriages, and new enterprises, as it signals the strongest yang sign in the entire 12-year cycle. Those born during this year are said to have a vital and decisive character. The last dragon year was 1988, the next 2000.

Dragons are also deeply involved in *feng shui;* indeed, the goal of geomancy is to harness the dragon's breath embedded in the earth. Gently undulating hills or ridges are considered the dragon's body, streams and pools his blood. Geomancers seek to discover the dragon's point of union with the female energy (the "white tiger"), as this is where huge quantities of *chi* are produced.

As the dragon's breath signals luck and wealth, it must not be dispersed. Water halts the dispersal of *chi;* the ideal building site thus faces slow-moving water, is flanked by hills on either side, and is protected by hills or trees from the bad influences emanating from the north.

Viewed symbolically, all of the Kowloon Peninsula is considered a dragon: the head is Tsimshatsui, and Hong Kong Island the pearl it sports with. Alternately, the Nine Dragons of Kowloon's hills are said to protect Hong Kong's good fortune and to give it excellent *feng shui*.

booklet *Macau Focus,* and *Welcome to Macau,* a glossy newspaper describing current events, festivals, and activities.

Bookstores are better in Hong Kong, unless you read Portuguese; only a handful stock English-language books. Try Livraria São Paulo, 115 Rua da Praia Grande; Portuguese Bookshop and Cultural Centre, Rua Pedro Nolasco da Silva; or Livraria Portuguesa, 18 Rua de São Domingos. World Book Co. on Rua Mercadores sells very expensive English-language magazines. Newsstands sell Hong Kong papers and international newsmagazines.

Maps
The free *Mapa Turistico* distributed by the MTIB is adequate for most purposes, though it doesn't show bus routes. Universal Publications' *Map of Macau and Zhuhai* is quite good and widely available in Hong Kong. Eric Stone's handdrawn *Streetwise Macau* (subtitled "A Map and Guide for the Seriously Curious") shows restaurants, hotels, and points of interest, with commentary.

Miscellanea
Business hours: Government offices are open 8:40 a.m.-1 p.m. and 3-5 p.m. Mon.-Fri., Saturday 8:40 a.m.-1 p.m. Bank hours are 9 a.m.-4 p.m., Saturday 9 a.m.-noon.

Electricity: 220 volts, AC50 Hz; plugs take three round pins (sometimes square).

Film Processing: Try Photo Princessa on Avenida Infante d'Henrique.

Laundry: Local *lavandarias* charge by weight and are generally quite reasonable. Lavandaria Wah Kong, 39E Rua de Mercadores (off the São Domingo market) does laundry and drycleaning. Your hotel will wash your clothes, too, but you can bet it's expensive.

Time: Same as Hong Kong, eight hours ahead of GMT.

Tourist Complaints: Call the MTIB hotline at 340-390, daily 9 a.m.-6 p.m.

SIGHTS

Orientation
The old part of town lies on the southern tip of the peninsula, a tangle of narrow streets set with old churches, fading mansions, and art-deco buildings and shophouses from the 1930s building boom. The peninsula's eastern side is bounded by the **Porto Exterior** or Outer Harbour, where boats from Hong Kong dock at the Jetfoil Terminal. The old **Porto Interior** or Inner Harbour on the western side is the original settlement, and old-style buildings and atmosphere still predominate. The north end of town is more residential, packed with new housing blocks and local businesses. The outlying islands of Taipa and Coloane are more spacious getaways, but there's not all that much to see on them: a single short day will suffice for both.

CENTRAL MACAU

Around the Jetfoil Terminal
Stepping off the jetfoil, you may wonder momentarily if you're in the right place: the Outer Harbour area around the terminal lacks character and charm, its shiny new hotels and shopping centers spiritless clones of Hong Kong's. The **Cyberfountain** in a reservoir across from the ferry terminal erupts with lasers and fireworks on festival days. A sound and light show plays nightly except Friday, 9-9:30 p.m. View it from stands on the rooftop of the Tourist Activity Centre.

Macau Forum
This new building across from the Jetfoil Terminal includes a giant exhibition hall and a **Tourist Activity Centre.** So far the latter includes a **Grand Prix Museum** detailing the 40-plus years of the race's history, with original and replica cars and an interactive racecar simulator with 3-D animation, sound effects and movement. Unlike a real race, you get to continue on after crashing. It's Ptc20 a go, and so harrowing that kids under 12 are not allowed. The museum is open 10 a.m.-6 p.m., admission is Ptc10.

Across the hall is the **Museu do Vinho** or Wine Museum, a brilliant concept for food- and drink-crazy Macau. Exhibits display Portugal's

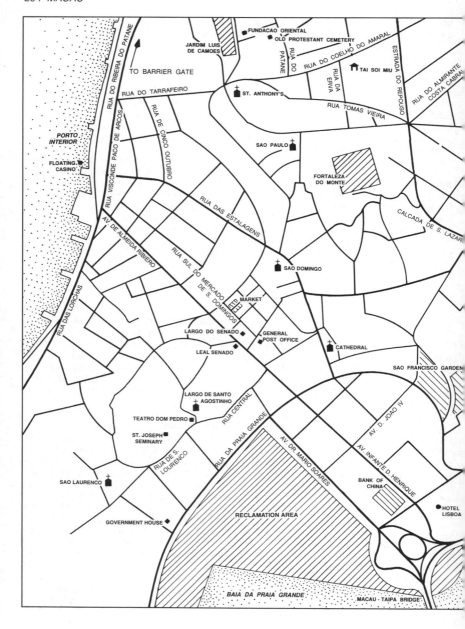

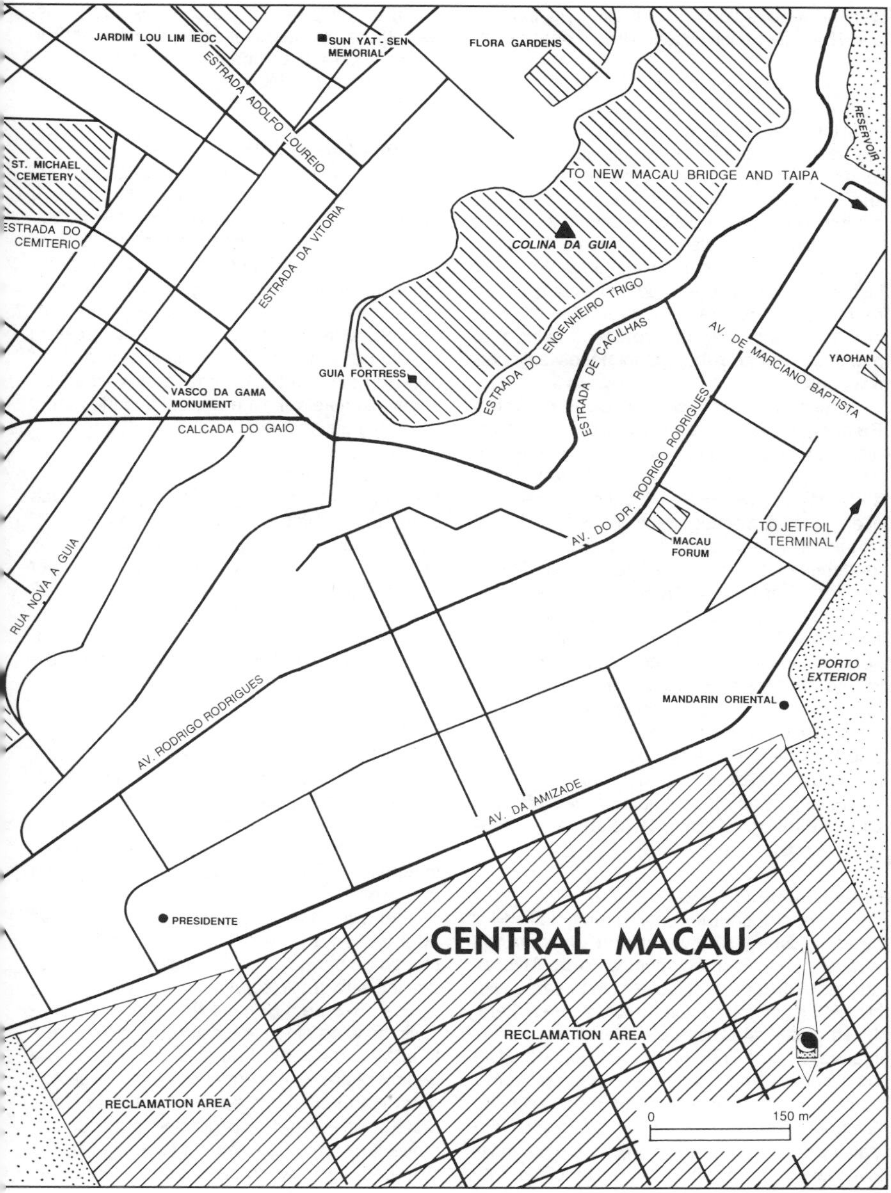

JARDIM LOU LIM IEOC

ESTRADA ADOLFO LOUREIO

SUN YAT - SEN MEMORIAL

FLORA GARDENS

RESERVOIR

ST. MICHAEL CEMETERY

ESTRADA DO CEMITERIO

ESTRADA DA VITORIA

COLINA DA GUIA

TO NEW MACAU BRIDGE AND TAIPA

ESTRADA DO ENGENHEIRO TRIGO

ESTRADA DE CACILHAS

AV. DE MARCIANO BAPTISTA

YAOHAN

GUIA FORTRESS

VASCO DA GAMA MONUMENT

CALCADA DO GAIO

RUA NOVA A GUIA

AV. DO DR. RODRIGO RODRIGUES

MACAU FORUM

TO JETFOIL TERMINAL

PORTO EXTERIOR

AV. RODRIGO RODRIGUES

MANDARIN ORIENTAL

AV. DA AMIZADE

PRESIDENTE

CENTRAL MACAU

RECLAMATION AREA

RECLAMATION AREA

0   150 m

© MOON PUBLICATIONS, INC.

wine growing regions, wine-making equipment, and 750 vintage bottles, each with a description.

Around the Hotel Lisboa 葡京酒店

Built in 1970, this symbol of modern Macau is a local landmark: a barrel-shaped concrete building painted mustard and white, with walls corrugated like a waffle and roofs fashioned to not-so-subliminally resemble roulette wheels. Check out the collection of oddities adorning the lobby: a small dinosaur skeleton, giant junks of carved ivory and jade, a tapestry of the Great Wall. The Lisboa also has a huge shopping arcade, seven restaurants, six bars, a sauna, a popular striptease show, and a crowded casino that merits observation, though not necessarily participation.

Across the street rises the **Bank of China Building,** an excessively modern construction of pink granite and glass that's tall enough to see from across the border. The bank's proximity—and political sensitivity—influenced the removal of an equestrian statue which until recently stood on the traffic roundabout in front. It was a noble rendering of the notoriously aggressive Governor João Ferreira do Amaral, depicted in his mortal battle fighting off Chinese assailants with a whip (he lost, and his assassins hauled his head off to Guangzhou to collect a reward). Following protests by China's Macau Affairs Office, the statue was shipped to Lisbon in 1992.

Across the street from the Hotel Lisboa is the São Francisco Barracks, backed by the **São Francisco Gardens,** a pretty park that's good for a picnic. The elegant salmon-pink **Military Club Building,** raised in 1872, adds an architectural grace note.

Praia Grande 南灣街

The standard itinerary until recently called for heading along the waterfront Avenida da Amizade up to the monument to **Jorge Alvares** (the first Portuguese to set foot in the area with his 1513 landing on a nearby island). From here, the **Rua da Praia Grande** curves along the bay in a breezy, tree-lined promenade set with inviting benches. What used to be a leisurely stroll or pedicab ride, especially pretty in the evening, has been effectively ruined by the ongoing **Nam Van Lakes Reclamation Project.** This massive development effort will turn the bay into two artificial lakes ringed by housing, hotels, and offices. It's slated for completion by 1999; in the meantime the once-peaceful bay is full of earth-moving machines and construction equipment.

Avenida Almeida Ribeiro 新馬路

This is the city's main street, stretching from the Outer to the Inner Harbour. With modern businesses moving out to the newer Porto Exterior, the street has managed to preserve its original character. It begins as the Avenida Infante do Henrique, lined by gold and leather shops, and becomes progressively more intriguing. At its upper end, lined by old arcaded shophouses, old shops sell silver opium pipes and art nouveau bric-a-brac, and wonderfully seedy old hotels like the Central and the Grand cater to mainland gamblers.

Macau Cathedral 天主教堂

Halfway down on the right, the Rua da Sé leads to Macau's old cathedral (or *sé*), a boxy 1938 reconstruction of the original Church of Our Lady raised here in 1576. It was declared the mother church of the Macau diocese, meant to cover all of China and Japan. History is more interesting than the reality of the dull neo-Gothic building, but the stained glass windows inside add a splash of color.

Leal Senado 市政廳

One block farther up is the old Senate House, the traditional seat of government and center of town. Macau's Senate was composed of citizens appointed for life to "assist" the governor. In reality the governor, who doubled as captain-major of Portugal's Japan Voyage, allowed the Senate to administer Macau, until the arrival of a full-time appointee in 1623 touched off a battle for power. The Senate still exists, though it's been reduced to a municipal council dealing with public services.

The 1875 Leal Senado is a simple yet majestic building of white plaster and green shutters. Macau's coat of arms is embossed on a pediment above the entrance, with the slogan "Nao Ha Outra Mais Leal"—"There Is None More Loyal"—which was granted in recognition of Macau's steadfast refusal to recognize the 17th-century Spanish occupation of Portugal.

Step inside to examine the imposing foyer, a stone staircase lined by exquisite blue-and-white tiles *(azulejos)* leading to a small raised garden. Upstairs is the panelled Senate Chamber, hung with portraits of past governors, and a library with rare books and ancient local newspapers. A small art gallery next to the entrance foyer displays works by local and foreign artists; there's another exhibition gallery on the second floor.

Largo Do Senado 議事亭前地

The public square across the street has an almost European feel: residents gather around the central fountain to pass the time and people-watch. The old arcaded buildings lining the square include the white plaster confection of **Santa Casa da Misericordia,** "Holy House of Mercy," the headquarters of a 15th-century order of nuns established to care for widows and orphans. The nuns here still maintain an old people's home, soup kitchen, and clinics, while the reception hall in the building displays oddities like a bishop's skull. The main office of the **Macau Tourism Information Bureau** is in a mustard-yellow building opposite. The enormous old **General Post Office** on the corner contains a small museum on the second floor displaying early postal and telecommunications equipment.

Church of São Domingo 玫瑰堂

Behind the Long Kei Restaurant, Rua Sul do Mercado de São Domingo and the streets around it are crammed with open stalls selling cheap clothing and all sorts of food. At the center is the Municipal Mercado de São Domingo, Macau's biggest, packed with food and flowers. The elegant old market building was recently demolished to make way for something more modern. Wander through it and emerge at the northeast end on Largo São Domingos, with its impressive 17th-century Dominican church. The cream-colored plaster building is set with stucco molding and green shutters; inside, a baroque altar holds a statue of the Virgin and Child, while side altars enshrine statues of saints with hands and faces of carved ivory.

Facade of São Paulo 大三巴牌坊

Take the Rua Palha past São Domingo and turn right into cobblestoned Rua São Paulo, past small shops selling porcelain wares and wooden toys. At the head of the open square and up a majestic flight of stone steps are the remains of the Jesuit church of São Paulo, once described as "the greatest monument to Christianity in all the Eastern lands," and compared by admiring visitors to St. Peter's in Rome.

The original church burned down in 1601, and an ornate replacement, designed by an Italian architect, was inaugurated on Christmas Eve of 1603. It featured three naves and three chapels, completely lined with wood, with wooden pillars and a fantastically carved gilded and painted roof. The elaborate stone facade was added in the 1620s.

Facade of São Paulo

The cathedral's grandeur faded after the Jesuits were expelled from Macau in 1762. In 1831 a kitchen fire from a nearby army barracks burned down the entire complex and much of the neighboring fortress as well. Only the intensely symbolic facade, carved by Japanese and Chinese Christian masons, remains as Macau's most famous landmark.

The intricate stone carvings deserve close examination. The top tier holds a bronze dove symbolizing the Holy Spirit, surrounded by stars and flanked by the sun and moon. Below stands a statue of Christ holding a fleur-de-lys and chrysanthemum, the latter the contribution of Japanese masons. He is flanked by angels bearing symbols of the crucifixion: cross, scourging pillar, crown of thorns, and whip. The third layer is exceptionally elaborate, with the Virgin in the middle, surrounded by angels. To the right is a seven-headed dragon and a supine skeleton, a reminder of death; to the left a Portuguese galleon and a fallen devil. Below, four bronze statues of Jesuit saints are set in niches: from left to right they are Loyola, Xavier, Francis Borgi, and Aloysius Gonzaga. The church's original name, Madre de Deus, is indicated by the "Mater Dei" carved above the central door.

Behind the facade, recent excavations of the church's ruins are now displayed under glass. In the **Museum of Sacred Art,** the tomb of the church's founding father, Jesuit Alessandro Valignano, is enshrined in a rather eerie display, along with the bones of various martyrs. The museum also includes oil paintings by 17th-century exiled Japanese Christian artists and various sacramental objects. The museum is open daily 9 a.m.-5 p.m., admission is free.

Fortaleza Do Monte 大炮台

Beside the church, a path and a series of steep stone steps lead up a grassy hill to the Fortaleza do Monte, built by the Jesuits around the time of São Paulo's construction to fend off anticipated Dutch attacks. Its cannons were fired only once, in 1622, when the defending Jesuits scored a lucky direct hit on the main Dutch powder magazine. Later, Macau's governor evicted the Jesuits and appropriated the structure as his personal headquarters.

The fortress was largely destroyed in the 1835 fire that devastated São Paulo, and today only the massive battlements remain, their cannons now aimed precisely at the Bank of China and a noisy primary school. The steep walk up is compensated by expansive views, which can be admired from stone benches set beneath spreading banyans. A meteorological observatory is housed in a rambling old colonial building, and in the entrance gatehouse is a small tourist information office with a cafe selling drinks. Construction work has started for a new **City Museum** here, which will document Macau's rich history and culture.

São Lazaro 聖母堂

From the Fortaleza you can work your way north through the restored district of São Lazaro (off Rua do Campo), with some fine examples of pastel-tinted Macanese terrace houses. Nearby is the Catholic **St. Michael's Cemetery,** its ornate tombs adorned with sculptures of angels, some Grecian style, others resembling Kwan Yum. Up the busy Avenida do Conselheiro Ferreira de Almeida are several more fine 1920s buildings, now restored and housing the National Archives and National Library.

Jardim Lou Lim leoc 盧廉若花園

This former residence of the wealthy Lou family was restored by the Macau government and opened to the public in 1974. Modelled on the famous gardens of the Chinese city of Suzhou, it's designed to encapsulate a miniature landscape, with concrete mountains, bamboo groves, and a lotus pond with a zig-zag bridge meant to deter the passage of evil spirits. The elegant pavilion in the middle of the pond often hosts art exhibitions. The garden is open 6 a.m.-10 p.m.; admission is Ptc1. It's located off Avenida do Conselheiro Ferreira de Almeida and Estrada Adolfo Loureiro.

A few blocks away at the corner of Avenida de Sidonio Pais and Rua de Silva Mendes, is the **Sun Yat-sen Memorial Home,** the former residence of the founder of the Chinese republic. Sun practiced medicine in Macau for several years before the 1911 revolution toppled the Qing dynasty. The house is an elaborate Moorish-style cement replacement of the more modest original: inside is a collection of historica relating to Sun's life, including newspaper clips and photos. It's not exactly compelling, but will help while away a half-hour or so. Hours are daily except Tuesday 10 a.m.-1 p.m., Sat.-Sun. 10 a.m.-1 p.m. and 2:30-5 p.m.

A little farther up Avenida Sidonio Pais is Macau's largest park, the **Flora Gardens,** occupying the grounds of an old Portuguese mansion (it was destroyed in a 1931 fire generated by the explosion of a neighboring firecracker factory). The landscaped gardens hold a minor zoo, an aviary with some miserably kept birds, and a small outdoor cafe. From the back side of the park a flight of steep steps leads up to the road encircling Guia Hill.

Guia Fort and Hill 松山燈塔
Colina da Guia is Macau's high point, and the 17th-century Fortress of Guia atop it provides wonderful views of the entire peninsula. It's a steep but pleasant climb up the forested hill to the top, following the paved "Path of 33 Curves" past joggers, picnickers, and tai-chi practitioners.

The fortress was built in 1638 as part of a system of defenses to protect against the Dutch. The original barracks and a few old brickwork turrets remain, along with a single cannon (the rest were sold for scrap by an impoverished government in the last century). In pre-radio days, typhoon signals were raised here, and the curious black metal forms still dangle inside the fort's gatehouse.

The interior of the fort is dominated by the smooth tapered barrel of **Guia Lighthouse,** the oldest on the China coast (circa 1865). The original was lit with a paraffin lamp; today its electrified beams reach far onto the Pearl River estuary. The other sight, though it's usually closed, is the tranquil 17th-century **Chapel of Our Lady of Guia,** its whitewashed walls enclosing an altar with an image of the Virgin holding a star and the infant Jesus. A tourist information office and drink stand here sells wine and espresso, and a coin-operated telescope looks out over crowded St. Michael's Cemetery.

THE INNER HARBOUR 澳門內港

For lovers of atmosphere, this is the best part of Macau. The Inner Harbour, or Porto Interior, was the settlement's original anchorage, used for centuries before the recent development of the Porto Exterior. The neighborhood's funky China coast mystique is almost dense enough to package and sell: the opening scenes of *Indiana Jones and the Temple of Doom* were filmed here.

The waterfront road, **Rua das Lorchas** (火船頭街), has a seedy 1930s feel that's only partially dissipated by the roaring traffic. The waterside is still lined with godowns. On the opposite side are cheap flophouses and old-style shophouses, their upper floors holding balconied living quarters, the bottom-floor shops purveying ship-oriented merchandise and Macau's famous dried fish. A few blocks north of Avenida Almeida Ribeiro is the **Floating Casino** (澳門皇宮), more properly titled the Casino Macau Palace, a smoke-filled thieves' den operating 24 hours a day.

Stroll south down Rua das Lorchas to the A-Ma Temple and explore the tangle of quaint inner streets. **Rua Felicidade** used to be the red-light district, described by Ian Fleming as "one great and continuous street of pleasure." Today its pleasures are mild, principally small guesthouses and stalls selling the famous Macanese treats that visiting Hongkongers are expected to bring back for friends and relatives: egg rolls, salt fish, luridly colored squares of dried beef and pork, and sesame and almond cakes. The Macau Cultural Institute recently restored many of this street's old shophouses, with their red-painted carved wooden shutters.

The atmosphere spills across Avenida Almeida Ribeiro. Don't miss the **Rua de Cinco Outubro,** with its roomy old tea shops and a traditional apothecary at No. 146. It leads into the Bazaar de Pagode, an open-air market for clothes, housewares, and produce. Beside the square is the busy and popular **Hong Kong Miu** (no relation to Hong Kong), built in 1860 and dedicated to a Han dynasty general evolved into a Taoist deity. Wander off onto Rua das Estalagens, then left onto Rua Nossa Senhora do Amparo, an increasingly narrow street cluttered with flea-market stalls.

Jardim Luís De Camões 賈梅十花園
This rocky wooded garden, full of old men and birds in the early morning, provides a delightful refuge from the crowded streets and heat. Fortune-tellers sit in the square outside the en-

trance on Praça Luís de Camões; opposite is the gray bulk of St. Anthony's Church, a dull recent reconstruction of the ancient church, founded in 1558.

The garden is everything a Sino-Iberian bower should be, a luxuriant collection of ferns, palms, bamboo, and banyans. It's dedicated to the great 16th-century Portuguese author of the epic *Os Lusiados,* a romantic paean to the great age of Portuguese exploration. Camões was a troublemaker more or less exiled to outskirts of the farflung Portuguese empire. Legend insists he visited Macau and strolled among the garden's rocks, though there's no historical evidence of this.

A bust of Camões, with two stanzas of *Os Lusiados* carved on the pedestal, stands in a little grotto. Opposite, carved on stone slabs set amid twisted banyan roots, is a collection of florid poems praising the poet and Macau ("Gem of the Orient earth and open sea/Macau! That in thy lap and on thy breast . . ."). Atop a wooded hill, in a little pavilion set with stone benches overlooking the Inner Harbour, old men play checkers and argue cheerfully among themselves.

Fundaçao Oriental

The Jardim de Camões originally belonged to the 18th-century colonial villa which now stands in a separate compound alongside it. The building was once rented by the British East India Company to house visiting dignitaries. Recently renovated, its parquet floors and white arches provide a serene backdrop for a collection of Portuguese-influenced porcelain and paintings. In front is a lovely garden with a pond of enormous goldfish. The art gallery is open daily 9:30 a.m.-6 p.m.; admission is free but visitors must sign in at the gate.

Old Protestant Cemetery

Next door, hidden behind a high wall, is the peaceful small cemetery established in 1821 by the East India Company to resolve the problem of Protestant burials—problematic because staunchly Catholic Macau refused to accept Protestant graves in its official cemeteries, and the local Chinese objected to burials taking place anywhere else. Notable residents include China coast painter George Chinnery (1774-1852) and Robert Morrison (1782-1834), the

first Protestant missionary to China, who translated the Bible into Chinese. The small, simple chapel here is dedicated to him. Mostly, though, the graveyard is full of American and European sailors, many of whom met an unexpectedly early demise ("Murdered by the Chinese" and "Fell from mast" are common inscriptions). With its weathered granite slabs and twisted banyan trees, it's a quiet sanctuary full of atmosphere. Ring the bell if the gate isn't open.

Around the corner in an incongruous juxtaposition is the shiny new "Future Bright Amusement Complex," with an ice rink, games, rides, and a McDonald's, all deserted on weekdays.

Lin Kai Miu 蓮溪廟

A few worthwhile old Chinese temples are within walking distance of the Camões grotto. The 17th-century Lin Kai Miu, "Stream of Mourning Temple," is on Travessa da Corda, off Estrada do Repouso. Exceptionally fine carvings decorate the entrance; inside are a half-dozen halls full of the gambling friends of the temple keepers and dusty images of deities. Look for black-faced Wah Kwong, the protector against fire and patron of opera troupes, Kwun Yam and Kwan Ti, and a row of folk statues of 15 goddesses associated with childbirth and child-rearing, whose laps are swarming with children.

Tai Soi Miu 大帥廟

This ranks high on the list of best temples in Macau and Hong Kong, though it's nearly impossible to find, tucked away on a side street between Rua Coelho do Amaral and Rua Tomas Vieira (a tip: turn down Rua dos Cavaleiroes, and look for Rua da Figueira). The remote location protects it from tourist crowds and gives the site an ageless feeling. Dusty altars are piled high with auspicious gold and red offerings—oranges, apples, cooking oil, incense. There are shrines to Pao Kung, the Taoist god of justice, and Kwun Yam, flanked by a retinue of folk goddesses presiding over pregnancy and childbirth. The sixty Tai Sui reign in another hall, while in the main hall, up a steep flight of steps, is the image of the reclining Buddha which gives the temple its name, "Temple of the Sleeping Buddha" (actually the reclining image is associated with the Buddha's death). Tai Soi Miu is exceedingly old, timeless, and peaceful, recommended for aficionados of the authentic.

SOUTH PENINSULA: BARRA 關閘

The wooded hill around Barra is the oldest settled area in Macau, home to a community of Fukien fishermen as early as 1557. The inhabitants prospered as shipbuilders for the Portuguese, and some of their descendents remain here today, speaking a Fukienese dialect along with Cantonese. The older neighborhood extending to the southern tip of the peninsula is definitely worth exploring. Allot half a day for a leisurely stroll past the sights, plus a meal at one of the good restaurants around here.

Largo De Santo Agostinho

Rua Central, opposite the Largo do Senado, leads past an old cobbled square set with a number of old buildings. The yellow and white church of São Agostinho was founded in 1586 by Augustinian friars; its spacious interior holds lit candles on the altar and statues of suffering saints in side alcoves. The central image of Christ bearing the cross is paraded about town in the annual Passos procession.

Look for a strange epitaph carved on a granite plaque and set on a wall to the right of the altar: "In this urn are the bones of the bodies of Maria de Mura de Vascondellos and her daughter Dona Ignes and of the right arm of her husband Antonio D'Albuquerque . . ." D'Albuquerque was a dashing captain (and later governor of Macau) who wooed Maria away from other suitors. A jealous rival wounded him in the arm, which had to be amputated. The couple was married despite the fuss and lived happily for several years until Maria died following the birth of the baby.

Across from the church is the mint-green confection of the **Dom Pedro V Theater,** the first European playhouse on the China coast, once visited by touring troupes. It was recently renovated to perfection and now hosts performances by visiting artists and popular amateur revues. Beside it, **St. Joseph's Seminary** is a rambling Jesuit sanctuary filled with musty old books, manuscripts, and abandoned classrooms. Founded in 1728 to train Chinese priests, it continued until disrupted by the Cultural Revolution in 1966. The seminary's chapel, with three baroque altars in Iberian style, dates back to 1758 and is next to a cloistered garden.

Continue down past the fashionable twin-towered church of São Laurenco, where Macau society gathers for Sunday mass. Behind here is a cluster of cheap local restaurants, stores, and *dai pai dong*s set up in the evenings. The road eventually leads out onto Rua do Almirante Sergio near the Barra bus terminal.

A-Ma Temple 媽閣廟

Situated according to the dictates of *feng shui* on a thickly wooded hill overlooking the Inner Harbour, this is the oldest temple site in Macau, dating back at least six centuries. Legend says a fishing junk that had taken aboard a poor girl seeking a boat ride was the only vessel to survive a violent storm. The boat eventually landed here, and the girl manifested as A Ma or Tin Hau, the Queen of Heaven. (The name Macau is derived from A-Ma Gau, the "Bay of A Ma.") An image of the boat that carried the girl is carved onto a boulder in the entrance courtyard, surrounded by more rocks carved with inscriptions. A sample: "Because of her virtue, ships can sail safely on the oceans like seabirds in fine weather."

The complex has developed over the centuries into a network of small shrines linked by winding paths. The first is to A Ma, flanked by her attendants, Golden Boy and Jade Girl, then Tei Chong Wong ("King of Hell") and Wai To ("Protector of the Law"), with the topmost dedicated to Kwun Yam. Incense is stuck everywhere, along with paper offerings representing supplications from women hoping for children. Big coils of firecrackers sold in the main temple are set off in a deafening racket meant to scare away evil spirits. The Macau Tourist Bureau sponsors lion dance performances in front of the temple at 10 a.m. on Sunday and holidays.

Maritime Museum 海事博物館

On the waterfront opposite the temple, the excellent Maritime Museum is housed in a building designed to evoke a ship, with sail-shaped walls and windows like portholes. Inside are well-presented displays of all things associated with the sea: oyster beds, deep-sea fishing and navigation, junk building, and the great exploratory journeys of Vasco da Gama and the 15th-century Chinese admiral Cheng Ho. Behind the museum are exhibits of actual boats moored at the pier, and a quayside cafe where you can sip a

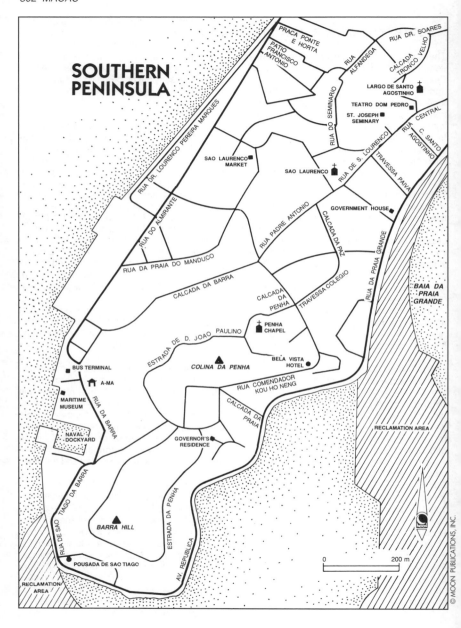

SOUTHERN PENINSULA

PRAÇA PONTE E HORTA

PATIO FRANCISCO ANTONIO

RUA DR. SOARES

RUA ALFANDEGA

CALCADA TRONCO VELHO

LARGO DE SANTO AGOSTINHO

TEATRO DOM PEDRO

ST. JOSEPH SEMINARY

RUA CENTRAL

RUA DO SEMINARIO

C. SANTO AGOSTINHO

RUA DE S. LOURENCO

TRAVESSA PAIVA

SAO LAURENCO MARKET

SAO LAURENCO

RUA DE S. LOURENCO

GOVERNMENT HOUSE

RUA DR. LOURENCO PEREIRA MARQUES

RUA DO ALMIRANTE

RUA PADRE ANTONIO

CALCADA DA PAZ

RUA DA PRAIA DO MANDUCO

CALCADA DA BARRA

CALCADA DA PENHA

TRAVESSA COLEGIO

RUA DA PRAIA GRANDE

BAIA DA PRAIA GRANDE

ESTRADA DE D. JOAO PAULINO

PENHA CHAPEL

COLINA DA PENHA

BELA VISTA HOTEL

RUA COMENDADOR KOU HO NENG

BUS TERMINAL

A-MA

MARITIME MUSEUM

RUA DA BARRA

CALCADA DA PRAIA

RECLAMATION AREA

NAVAL DOCKYARD

GOVERNOR'S RESIDENCE

RUA DE SAO TIAGO DA BARRA

BARRA HILL

ESTRADA DA PENHA

POUSADA DE SAO TIAGO

AV. REPUBLICA

RECLAMATION AREA

0   200 m

© MOON PUBLICATIONS, INC.

beer or espresso and watch boat traffic in the Inner Harbour. Half-hour harbor tours on a converted fishing junk run from nearby Wharf Number One (tours are currently Sat.-Mon. at 10:30 and 11:30 a.m. and 3:30 and 4:30 p.m.; call 595-481 for information and reservations). The museum is open daily except Tuesday 10 a.m.-5:30 p.m.; admission is Ptc5, Ptc15 including the boat ride.

Pousada De São Tiago 聖地牙哥酒店

From the Maritime Museum, the Rua de São Tiago da Barra curves around the peninsula. Set on a hillside at the very tip is the old Fortaleza da Barra, built in 1629 to guard the Inner Harbour, which was then much narrower.

The old fortress had long been abandoned when the government came up with the idea of installing a private inn. The result is the impressive Pousada de São Tiago, sensitively designed to combine old character and modern luxuries. The interior is decorated like an 18th-century colonial home, with fittings and furnishings imported from Portugal and China. Step inside to admire the dramatically-lit stone entrance tunnel vaulting up from the cellar, and the 17th-century chapel of St. James, now a

popular venue for society weddings. The reasonably priced Cafe da Barra here serves coffee shop fare, tea and cakes.

Along the Praia

Round the corner onto Praia Grande and you'll join the old waterfront promenade, its charm now largely destroyed by the Nam Van Lakes reclamation project. The best thing about it to date is the **Gate of Understanding,** two interlocking black granite arches raised in 1993 to symbolize China's relationship with Macau. The road passes the old **Governor's Residence,** a two-storied mansion facing the sea, built by a wealthy Macanese family in 1846 and now painted the goverment-regulation salmon pink.

A little farther down, atop a hill overlooking the bay, is the **Hotel Bela Vista,** the grande dame of Macau lodgings. Built in the 1880s, it's gone through many incarnations, from hotel to boarding school for government cadets to refugee haven to a hotel again, by that time rundown but gloriously cheap. Finally purchased by the government of Macau, it was turned over to the Mandarin Oriental, which has remodelled it into a gem holding only eight deluxe suites. Stop by for a drink or meal on the terrace; as in all Macau's restaurants, prices are startlingly reasonable.

Penha Hill 西望洋山

Behind the Bela Vista is Penha Church, dramatically set atop a steep hill overlooking the bay. The present gray stone chapel dates only to 1935, but a church has stood here since 1622. The chapel is open daily 10 a.m.-4 p.m., and while there's not much to see inside, the fantastic views of central Macau and the Inner Harbour justify the climb up. Next to the chapel is the imposing bishop's residence, appropriately termed a "palace." Souvenir and drink stalls and a tourist information office stand in front of the church.

Back on the Rua da Praia Grande, what used to be a romantic evening stroll or pedicab ride has been effectively ruined by the

BOB RACE

Penha Church

ongoing reclamation project, which is eating into the gracious curve of the bay. The road passes beneath the stately pink **Palacio Do Governo,** or Government House: no entry allowed, but you can peer through the gates.

NORTH PENINSULA

The northern half of the peninsula is more modern and residential, the streets less quaint. Sights are more widely scattered but still walkable—or take buses to avoid the boring stretches. Bus 5 is particularly useful, running from Avenida Almeida Ribeiro down Rua do Campo and Avenida de Horta e Costa to the Barrier Gate.

Kwun Yam Temple 望夏觀音堂
Take Bus 5 to Avenida Horta e Costa, then walk northeast two blocks to Avenida do Coronel Mesquita. This large, wealthy temple complex ranks among the most historically important in Macau. Founded in the 13th century, it has evolved into a maze of passages and shrines. A vast ancestral hall on the left holds rows of dusty wooden tablets, while huge incense coils smoulder in the three central shrines. The first is dedicated to Sakyamuni, Amitabha, and the Medicine Buddha; the second to the Buddha of Longevity; and the third to Kwun Yam in a beaded veil and embroidered silk bridal robes. She is flanked by figures of the 18 wise men of China; the first image on the far left, the one with popping eyes and a mustache, is supposed to be Marco Polo.

The temple is backed by a terraced garden of bamboo and banyans. At a round stone table here, the Viceroy of Guangzhou and an American envoy signed the first U.S.-China treaty in 1844, forcing China to give Americans access to their ports. Guides are fond of pointing out that the table, like the treaty, is lopsided.

Lin Fong Miu 蓮峰廟
Walk north down Avenida do Coronel Mesquite, passing another ancient but active Kwun Yam temple a few blocks later, adorned with elaborate woodcarvings. Turn right on Avenida do Almirante Lacerda, the **Canidrome,** where greyhound races are held at night. Across the street is Lin Fong Miu, the only Taoist shrine in Macau. This very old complex dates back to 1592, and features an exquisite facade of bas-relief clay tableaux made in Shiwan in the 19th century. The spacious, high-ceilinged halls are dedicated to Tin Hau, Kwan Ti, and Kwun Yam; outside, crowds of blue-jacketed old men huddle about newspapers and checker games. The stone statue here commemorates the visit of Chinese mandarin Lin Zexu: the temple was once a favorite stopping point for Chinese officials from neighboring Zhongshan county.

Barrier Gate 關閘
Continuing north from here, the busy Istmo Ferreira do Amaral leads to the Macau-China border, marked by the elaborate 19th-century plaster Barrier Gate. Its old name, Portas do Cerco, "Gate of Siege," was no misnomer: Chinese officials would periodically shut it for several weeks at a time in sporadic attempts to starve the Portuguese colonists, who purchased all their food from China.

Up until a few years ago the border was a popular tourist sight, but its mystique has vanished with the advent of easy access into China. A big new terminal has been built before the gate, crowded with trucks and people going in both directions. It's easy enough to get a one-day Chinese visa on the spot, though the raw new buildings of the Zhuhai suburb of **Gongbei** across the border are less than inspiring. A brief look around may serve to make you appreciate Macau's rich history and culture all the more.

THE ISLANDS

Taipa and Coloane, the two small islands tailing off the southern end of the peninsula, provide Macau with some much-needed breathing space. Though their open countryside is rapidly being taken over by new high-rises and resort hotels, the islands' little main villages have a sleepy feel, with barely any traffic. In truth there's not much going on, but it's easy to visit both islands in a short day. Plan to have a meal out here, perhaps at Taipa, which has a number of superior restaurants.

Island Transport

Buses 11, 28A and 33 run to Taipa, Bus 26 to Taipa and Coloane, and Bus 26A through both and on to Coloane's beaches. Perhaps the easiest place to catch them is in front of Hotel Lisboa. Private shuttle buses also connect the Hyatt Regency on Taipa with the Jetfoil Terminal.

Taxis from central Macau charge an extra Ptc5 for trips to Taipa and Ptc10 for Coloane, but no fee is levied on return fares. Bicycles are available for rent on Taipa, but for obvious reasons are not allowed on the Macau-Taipa Bridge: even riding the Taipa-Coloane Causeway can be an unsettling experience.

TAIPA 冰仔

Tiny Taipa was once two separate hilly islands, the harbor in between them providing a protected anchorage for small ships engaging in the China country trade. The original channel has long since silted up, providing equally valuable land. Until the construction of the 2.5-km Macau-Taipa bridge in 1969, Taipa was reached by small ferries and sampans. Its residents were mainly Chinese fishermen and junk builders, workers in a local firecracker factory, and a few Eurasian Macanese families employed in the government.

New developments have almost erased the sleepy old fishing village, and the dwindling remnants are likely to change further with the new **Macau International Airport** constructed on reclaimed land off Taipa's east coast. A four-lane bridge provides a second point of access between here and the peninsula: eventually it will connect with a Macau-Guangzhou highway.

The North End

A bas-relief monument depicting Macau's history stands atop a knoll at the Taipa end of the bridge, its high location providing a nice panorama of the city. Buses stop near the **Hyatt Regency Macau,** which features landscaped grounds, a swanky casino, and several good restaurants. Behind it and to the west is the **Po Tai Un Temple (** 菩提園廟 **),** a wealthy century-old Buddhist establishment that is one of Macau's finest temples. The main hall features early images of the Three Precious Buddhas; pavilions and statues are scattered about the manicured grounds; and excellent vegetarian lunches are served in the dining hall.

Taipa Village 冰仔市區

Buses continue into Taipa Village, stopping near the main square with its open-air cafes and some quaint advertising devices—giant Fanta and Coke "bottles" fashioned out of painted plaster. Check out the ornate central hall of the Tin Hau Temple off the square, which dates back to the 1820s. Behind is Largo do Camões, with a big Pak Tai Temple. The narrow, quiet streets around here merit a half-hour or so of exploration, past peeling elderly buildings and a shoreline lined with shanties.

The yellow-and-white **Our Lady of Carmel Church** dominates a cobbled square atop the hill between the village and the old praya (take the road across from the Panda Restaurant). The church is generally closed except for Sunday mass, but a zigzag walkway from here leads down through a formal European garden to the old **Avenida da Praia,** a treelined promenade overlooking the old bay, now a shrub-filled mudflat.

The five old mint-green and white mansions here once housed wealthy Portuguese families. One has been restored as **Taipa House Museum (** 屋宇博物館 **)** (Casa Museu), representing a typical China coast mansion of the 1920s. The

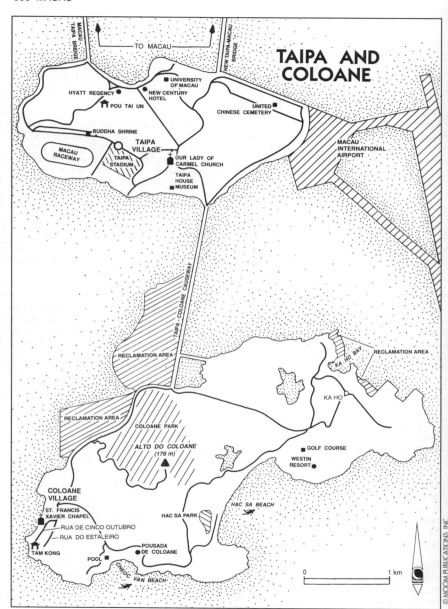

TAIPA AND COLOANE

TAIPA RESTAURANTS

Eating is a big reason to visit Taipa, and informal, inexpensive restaurants are all over the place. The service is personal, the atmosphere intimate, the food excellent and even cheaper than in central Macau. Rua da Cunha has gained a reputation as "Food Street" for its line of eateries, while the town square features several open-air cheap cafes.

The **Po Tai Un Temple** near the Hyatt puts out wonderful vegetarian lunches, fresh from the temple's garden, in a pretty restaurant.

O Santos, 20 Rua da Cunha, is a locally popular cafe serving massive portions of Portuguese food, very cheap.

Leong Un, 46 Rua da Cunha, is rated Macau's best Italian restaurant, with great pizza and pasta and Macanese food too.

Galo, 45 Rua da Cunha, tel. 827-423, set in a delightful old house, is a reasonably priced and informal place to try Portuguese food. Sample the giant "Island Mixed Grill" or the Macau crabs.

Cozinha Pinocchio, 4 Rua do Sol, tel. 327-128, is a large and roaringly popular place packed with locals at lunchtime. House specialties include chilied crab, pepper-salt prawns, and roast quail.

Panda, 4 Rua Carlos Eugenio, tel. 827-338, serves Macanese and Portuguese-Chinese food in a sprawling old pink building.

Moçambique, 28 Rua dos Clerigos, features an interesting menu of Macanese dishes and colonial specialties from Angola and Goa—the African chicken and *matapa* are recommended.

A Petisqueira, 15 Rua San João, emphasizes personal service and fresh food, right down to the homemade cheese and Portuguese tapas.

decor combines European and Chinese elements (blackwood furniture and small Christian altars), while the architecture is tailored to the steamy climate, with deep verandahs and cool high-ceilinged rooms. Eventually the other mansions will be restored and opened as well. Taipa House is open daily except Monday 9:30 a.m.-1 p.m. and 3-5:30 p.m.

Taipa East and West

The eastern half of the island is easily reached via bicycle (rented on Taipa's main square), but with the new airport construction there's little of scenic value apart from the **United Chinese Cemetery** (華人墳場), with its 10-meter-high statue of the Earth God and a garden full of moongates and deities. The road follows along reclaimed coastline past the Taipa-Coloane Causeway and back into town.

Returning buses loop about to the west around the **Macau Raceway** (澳門賽車場), a huge track developed in 1989 to give Hong Kong some gambling competition. At the edge of the vast parking lot, stalls sell flowers and incense which bettors offer to a Thai-inspired Four-Faced Buddha shrine, reputed to bring luck.

COLOANE 澳門賽車場

This island was once the abode of pirates who preyed on the lucrative China trade. The last pirate raid was in 1910, its repulse commemorated by a village monument. Coloane is even less developed than Taipa, larger (7.2 square km) but with a population of only around 6,000. Much of it is protected parkland, crisscrossed with trails that make for good rambling. Things are changing here too, especially on the northeast side, where a giant container terminal has been built off the little village of Ka Ho.

Coloane Park 路環市區

This 20-hectare enclave in the center of the island features gardens, a fitness circuit, a playground, and a walk-in aviary. A reforestation program was begun here 30 years ago after the island's dominant pines were devastated by disease, and today the area features over 1,000 species of plants and trees. Nature trails and a road lead up to the heights of **Alto do Coloane,** a good choice for picnics and views. A map at the roadhead details trails: the main route is the **Trilho de Coloane,** an 8.6-km circuit that takes about three hours to complete but can be done in sections. The slightly shorter **Trilho Nordeste de Coloane** loops about the mountain, ending near Ka Ho.

Coloane Village 路環村

Buses stop near Coloane village square, where open-air restaurants enliven the scene at night. At the far end of the square the waterfront Rua de Cinco Outubro overlooks a channel full of sand barges. China is visible in the background, the new buildings of Zhuhai looking dismally raw and unfinished. Turn right and walk up to the pier to view boats unloading and get a feel for Coloane's fishing-village past. Shops display dried fish, a local specialty.

Turn left down the waterfront to visit the tiny **Chapel of St. Francis Xavier** (聖方濟各聖堂), dedicated to the founder of the Jesuits, who died in 1522 on an island near Macau. A silver reliquary enshrines a precious fragment of his arm-bone, and the bones of European and Japanese Christians crucified by the shogun of Nagasaki in 1597 are displayed in glass cases in a Sacrarium. In the square in front, a monument with embedded cannonballs commemorates villagers' July 1910 victory over a final pirate attack.

It's a pleasant stroll down the banyan-lined waterfront to the **Tam Kong Temple** (譚公廟) at the end of the road. The 120-year-old building was recently restored. Inside is a six-foot whalebone carved in the form of a dragon boat with crew, and another carved and gilded boat bearing the Eight Taoist Immortals. Behind the temple, the tree-lined Rua do Estaleiro leads past tumbledown houses and two smaller temples Kwun Yam and Tin Hau. The rest of town is very minor—the unpaved streets barely deserve their grand names—but there are some excellent restaurants.

Beaches

Just over the the hill from town is **Cheoc Van Beach** (竹灣), with swimming either in the murky ocean or a saltwater swimming pool (open 9 a.m.-10 p.m.). On Coloane's east coast is **Hac Sa Beach** (黑沙灣) ("Black Sand Beach"), the biggest and best in Macau. Though again the water is murky with silt from the Pearl River Delta, the black sand mixes interestingly with the golden, making it a fine place for a walk. There are picnic tables in the pine forest backing the beach.

The **sports and recreation complex** here has an Olympic-sized pool, roller-skating rink, a

---

COLOANE RESTAURANTS

Lord Stow's Bakery, 1 Rua da Tassara (just off the town square), sells tasty bread, sandwiches, pastries, and box lunches. Pick up some of their famous egg tarts.

Restaurante Pirao, off Estrada do Campo, is locally popular for its farmhouse-style Portuguese food.

Cacarola, 8 Rua das Gaivotas (off the main square), offers excellent Portuguese food in a charming setting.

Nga Tim Café, an open-air place well-sited alongside St. Xavier's Church, has great ambience and a diverse Chinese-Portuguese menu.

Balichao, beside the aviary in Coloane Park, serves well-prepared European and Portuguese dishes in a quiet country setting that's especially lovely for lunch.

Pousada de Coloane, Praia de Cheoc Van, tel. 882-143, has terrace dining: enjoy ocean views along with the famous stuffed squid and *feijoada*. Open for dinner only, or try the wonderful Ptc100 Sunday lunch buffet.

La Torre, a few minutes walk along the beach from the Pousada, serves pizza, pasta, and delicious Italian ice creams and espresso.

Fernando's, Hac Sa Beach (near the bus stop), is a famous, casual place serving great Portuguese food: spicy fried clams and crab casserole the house specialties. Friendly Fernando himself will help you order.

---

playground, tennis courts, and miniature golf (open 9 a.m.-9 p.m., 10 p.m. on weekends). You can rent windsurfers here as well, and there's a string of restaurants near the bus stop, **Fernando's** being the most famous. The **Macau Horse Riding Centre,** tel. 828-303, rents out retired nags from the Taipa Jockey Club for riding on hillside trails or the beach. Rates are Ptc250 per hour, with a minimum of two hours and two people.

To get to the beaches, catch Bus 26 or 26A, bike (there are rental stalls around the village square), or walk: Cheoc Van is only 1.5 km from the Tam Kong Temple.

BOB RACE

GUANGZHOU

The Pearl River Delta is the traditional gateway to China, an open and outward-looking region since the first foreign traders arrived in its ports over 1,500 years ago. Its main city is Guangzhou, better known to the West as Canton, after a British mispronunciation. Guangzhou is China's sixth-largest city and the capital of wealthy Guangdong Province. It lies 120 km northwest of Hong Kong, a few hours by train or jetcat or a leisurely journey by night ferry. A stay of several days is preferable, but even a daytrip reveals the economic vitality that characterizes the emerging new China.

Guangzhou has been visited by traders from Southeast Asia, India, and Arabia since at least the seventh century. The flow has been two-way: Guangzhou's natives were among the first Chinese to emigrate, and today form the backbone of overseas Chinese communities across the world.

With its lively streets and shops, Guangzhou is as busy as Hong Kong, and its people share many of the same characteristics: talkativeness, a spirited sense of entrepreneurship, a love of good food. But it's distinctly a different country.

Like Hong Kong, Guangzhou exudes a tremendous sense of vitality, but without the glossy modern facade. Much of the city is reminiscent of the 1940s, in fact, though more new office towers push upwards each year. Hong Kong's proximity exerts surprisingly little influence upon daily life in Guangzhou, which remains simple.

With a quarter of the world's population, China's basic reality deserves to be confronted by virtue of its size if nothing else. Guangzhou is fascinating enough for what it represents: more than that, it's a society that's obviously going somewhere. All of one's fantasies about pagodas and mandarins crumble when assaulted with the tough truth of a big, teeming, vigorous Chinese metropolis.

The Cantonese have taken to heart Deng's dictum: "To get rich is glorious." Guangdong Province is in the midst of an economic explosion, with an industrial growth rate averaging 25% annually. South China's economic boom is one of the biggest stories of the '90s, heralding China's emergence as an economic superpower. Hong Kong and Guangzhou both have vital roles to play in this process: Hong Kong as the marketing and management center, Guangdong as the manufacturing base. In 1997 the artificial delineation of the border was re-moved, reaffirming the truth of the traditional saying: "Hong Kong and Guangzhou are as close as lips to teeth."

SIGHTS

Guangzhou will easily fill two or three days of sightseeing. There are museums, historical monuments (the city has more than its share of Communist memorials), temples, a big zoo, some of China's best restaurants, and plenty of spacious green parks. As usual, though, simply wandering the streets is the best choice, letting you absorb the atmosphere of the busiest and most outward-looking of China's great cities.

Spend some time in the downtown districts, where arcaded old shophouses lend a 1920s feel to the cityscape. Guangzhou's economic vitality is apparent in its small shops—an increasing number of them glossy Hong Kong spinoffs—and in street vendors selling clothing and Mao memorabilia, giving haircuts, and polishing shoes. When the crowds get too claustrophobic, duck down a quiet residential backstreet to observe how people live. Here the atmosphere is casual and low-key: people are out playing with their children, hanging laundry out to dry, lounging in front of their homes in pajamas chatting with a neighbor. There's the smell of cooking, the sizzle of woks, the sound of music from a tape deck—it could be Canto-pop or Chinese opera that's playing.

Orientation
Guangzhou is a big, busy, sprawling city, but its orderly street system and strategic landmarks make it easy to navigate. Main streets are identified by direction: Huanshi Donglu is East Huanshi Street (*dong* being east, *lu* street). "Zhong" in a street name indicates the central portion of that street, "Xi" the western end, and "Bei" and "Nan" indicate north and south. Oc-casionally streets are numbered by blocks: Zhongshan 4-Lu is the fourth block of Zhong-shan Lu.

Downtown Guangzhou is divided into quadrants by north-south Jiefang Lu and east-west Zhongshan Lu. The railway station and a number of major hotels are in the north section of town, which is being intensively developed with new shopping centers. Concentrate on exploring the busy shopping streets south of Jiefang Lu, an area dense with interest and amenable to walking. Near the north bank of the Pearl River, neighborhoods feature arcaded shop-houses reminiscent of the 1920s. The old foreign enclave of **Shamian Island** is pleasant for strolling as there are few cars, and it keeps its focus on foreigners with a number of hotels and restaurants. The wide, muddy Pearl River is spanned by several bridges and a system of small ferries. The southern shore, once lined with gambling and opium dens, now holds busy suburbs.

NORTH OF ZHONGSHAN ROAD

Chen Family Temple 陳家祠
This sprawling complex lies between Lihua and Zhongshan roads, off Chen Jia Si Lane. Built in the early 1890s, it is one of the few ancestral halls to have been spared the ravages of the Cultural Revolution. The ornate buildings are topped with glazed pottery decorations and feature wood and stone carvings and iron castings.

The complex was built in the early 1890s with the donations for members of the extensive Chen clan. It traditionally served as a center for ancestor worship and education. After the revolution, it was declared a folk arts museum, displaying collections of ceramics, embroidery, papercuts, carvings in various mediums (including plum pits), lacquer, and porcelain. The enormous main hall still holds a shrine, which ordinarily would be surrounded by ancestral tablets, but such things aren't done in modern China, at least publicly.

Guangxiao Temple 光孝寺
The origins of this temple date back to the late fourth century. As an old maxim has it, "Before there was Goat City (Guangzhou), there was Guangxiao." The site is rich in history, having seen the initiation of Hui Neng, the seventh-century master who became the Sixth Patriarch of Zen Buddhism.

Today it's among the nicest temples in Guangzhou. Its spacious grounds, located near the Liu Rong Temple on Jinghui Lu off Zhongshan 6-Lu, are set with spreading shade trees and stone benches. The broad-roofed buildings have been carefully restored. The airy main hall used to hold a paleontology exhibit; now giant images of the Three Buddhas have been reinstated in an impressive and actively worshipped display.

A small iron pagoda near the eastern wall dates from A.D. 967. Nearby is the stone "Pagoda of the Sixth Patriarch's Hair," said to have sprouted from the spot where Hui Neng buried his hair after the ritual monastic head-shaving.

Liu Rong Temple 六榕寺
This "Temple of the Six Banyan Trees," located on Liu Rong Lu, just off Jiefang Beilu behind the Number One Guesthouse, dates back to perhaps the fifth century. It was rebuilt in the tenth century following a disastrous fire, and shortly after was visited by the famous Northern Song dynasty poet Su Dongpo, who so admired the courtyard's spreading banyan trees that he wrote out the phrase "Six Banyans" (liu rong) in large characters. A stone tablet with a reproduction of his calligraphy can still be seen today. Adding to the temple's fame, it's said the famous monk Bodhidharma spent the night here. Today Liu Rong Si is an active Zen temple, home to a community of gray-robed, shaven-headed monks.

The central feature is the "Flowery Pagoda" (Huata), a 60-meter-high octagonal tower of nine external and 17 internal stories. Behind it is the main shrine, rebuilt in 1984 and holding three giant seated Buddhas. Young people stand in front to pray and offer incense, a bit sheepishly,

it seems. Off to the side is a smaller shrine holding an A.D. 989 image of the Sixth Patriarch, Hui Neng, seated in meditation, and another statue of the goddess Kwun Yam.

Huaisheng Mosque 六榕寺
This Muslim complex was built around A.D. 627 by Arab traders on what was then the waterfront, and testifies to Guangzhou's ancient history as an international trading center. It's said to commemorate an uncle of the prophet Mohammed, who came here as a missionary in the seventh century. The plain, undecorated minaret is colloquially referred to as Guangta, "Bare Tooth." There is also a "Tower for Watching the Moon," Kan Yue Lou, used as an observation point for calculating the lunar calendar.

The mosque is still active today with local Chinese Muslims. It's on Guangta Lu, east of Renmin Zhonglu. The ferocious gatekeeper may not admit foreigners. Just down the road is the Mishi Lu food market, featuring skinned bunnies dangling from meat hooks and other culinary atrocities.

Five Genies Temple 五仙觀
This Taoist temple is tucked into a courtyard off Huifu Xilu, near the mosque. It's said to have been built on the very site where Guangzhou's legendary five rams appeared. The temple dates to the Ming dynasty, though the present buildings are much newer. Four stone statues of rams stand in the courtyard, much enjoyed by local children who clamber all over them.

AROUND THE CHINA HOTEL

North-central Guangzhou features many of the city's hotels, clustered around the Guangzhou Trade Fair complex. The fair originated in the late 16th century as a means of channeling trade revenues through the government. The economic reforms of the late '70s increased opportunities, and the fair became a major meeting ground for foreign and Chinese companies. The increasing liberalization of the economy has reduced its importance, but it still attracts thousands of foreign businessmen each spring and fall.

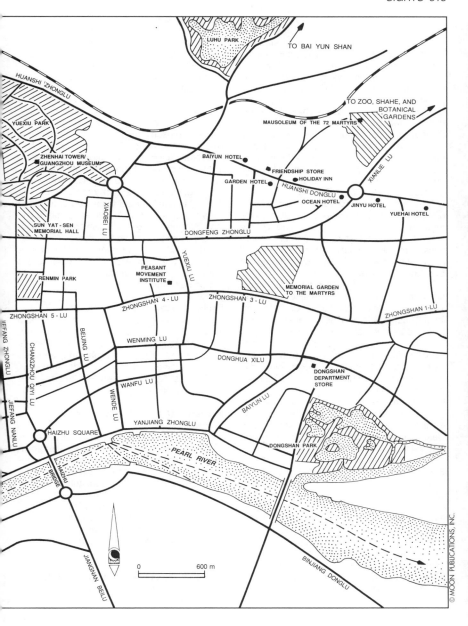

LUHU PARK

TO BAI YUN SHAN

HUANSHI ZHONGLU

TO ZOO, SHAHE, AND
BOTANICAL
GARDENS

MAUSOLEUM OF THE 72 MARTYRS

YUEXIU PARK

XIANLIE LU

ZHENHAI TOWER/
GUANGZHOU MUSEUM

BAIYUN HOTEL

FRIENDSHIP STORE
HOLIDAY INN

GARDEN HOTEL

HUANSHI DONGLU

OCEAN HOTEL

JINYU HOTEL

YUEHAI HOTEL

XIAOBEI LU

SUN YAT - SEN
MEMORIAL HALL

DONGFENG ZHONGLU

YUEXIU LU

PEASANT
MOVEMENT
INSTITUTE

RENMIN PARK

MEMORIAL GARDEN
TO THE MARTYRS

ZHONGSHAN 4 - LU

ZHONGSHAN 3 - LU

ZHONGSHAN 1-LU

ZHONGSHAN 5 - LU

JIEFANG ZHONGLU

BEIJING LU

CHANGZHOU QIYI LU

WENMING LU

DONGHUA XILU

DONGSHAN
DEPARTMENT
STORE

WANFU LU

WENDE LU

BAIYUN LU

YANJIANG ZHONGLU

HAIZHU SQUARE

DONGSHAN PARK

JIEFANG NANLU

PEARL RIVER

HAIZHU
BRIDGE

0   600 m

JIANGNAN BEILU

BINJIANG DONGLU

© MOON PUBLICATIONS, INC.

Yuexiu Park 越秀公園

The biggest of all Guangzhou's parks, Yuexiu encompasses a 30,000-seat sports stadium, an Olympic pool, a roller coaster, and artificial lakes with rowboats for hire. It's easy to spend a morning or afternoon wandering about its 93 hectares. Sunday is the busiest and most interesting day for people-watching.

Among the park's supposed highlights is the ugly concrete **Sculpture of the Five Rams,** a Guangzhou icon. Legend holds that centuries ago, at the founding of the city, five celestial beings astride rams appeared and presented stalks of rice as a symbol of the area's freedom from famine—and indeed Guangdong Province is exceptionally fertile.

Near the statue is **Zhenhai Tower** 鎮海樓 (Zhenhailou), a last remnant of the old city wall, rebuilt as a watchtower in 1686. In front of the broad five-story structure is a line of old cannons, some of them dating from the British and French occupation of Guangzhou during the Second Opium War.

The tower houses the **Guangzhou Municipal Museum,** a moderately interesting account of local history with different floors devoted to various dynasties and political movements. Climb up to the top floor for views from the balcony.

South of here, atop a small hill that used to hold a Kwun Yam temple, is the **Sun Yat-sen Monument,** a tall stone obelisk commemorating the Cantonese revolutionary who led the overthrow of the Qing dynasty. The topmost floor of the structure offers more views. Sun's last testament is engraved in stone at the base: ". . . The revolution has not yet been successfully completed. Let all our comrades follow the principles set forth in my writings. . . ."

Sun Yat-sen Memorial Hall 孫中山紀念堂

South of Yuexiu Park is this massive building, constructed in 1930 with donations from local and overseas Chinese on the site of the Qing dynasty governor's residence. The building is rendered in ornate traditional style and roofed with blue Shiwan tiles. The best part is the gaudy external architecture. Inside is a dilapidated auditorium used for performances and conferences, and a cryptic display of historical photos captioned only in Chinese.

Nanyue Museum 南越王漢墓

This new museum ranks among the best in China. It's built around the mausoleum of Chao Mei, the ruler of the Kingdom of Nanyue (137-122 B.C.), a local empire which arose following the first brief unification of China in 214 B.C. Construction workers digging here in 1983 discovered the king's intact tomb, filled with 1,500 objects and the skeletons of sacrificial victims—concubines, cooks, musicians, courtiers, guards—who had been buried along with him to serve him in the afterworld.

Exhibits begin with a videotape documenting the discovery of the tomb. There's an excellent collection of 200 ceramic pillows, and well-organized displays of tomb artifacts (including a burial shroud fashioned of tiny jade squares) captioned in Chinese and English. The tomb itself, set in the hillside behind the museum building, can be entered for another Y5.

Admission to the museum is Y10 for foreigners; hours are 9 a.m.-6 p.m. It's located across from the middle of Yuexiu Park, just south of the China Hotel.

Orchid Garden 蘭圃

This quiet little grove opposite the entrance to Yuexiu Park off Jiefang Beilu is a pleasant, shady refuge that's seldom crowded. There's a carp pond, a small tea pavilion, bamboo groves, and plenty of potted orchids. Admission is Y2. The park is closed Wednesday and around lunchtime.

Mohammadan Tomb and Cemetery 穆罕默德墓

If you need peace and quiet, seek out this overgrown little cemetery with its wildly overgrown groves of banana trees, poinsettia, and bamboo. There is never anyone here. Beneath the long grass are the square stone tombs of Muslim imams, including that of the seventh-century missionary who founded the Huaisheng Mosque. Head down the lane past the entrance to the Orchid Garden, and look for the stone gate with red lettering on the right.

Liuhua Park 流花公園

Set behind the Dongfeng Hotel on Renmin Beilu, this is one of Guangzhou's nicer parks, with a giant artificial lake and the Guangzhou Children's Palace.

ALONG THE PEARL RIVER

The north bank of the Pearl River is among the oldest and most interesting areas. At night portions of it are almost a praya, crowded with young lovers and families out for a stroll. In the daytime it's fun to observe the wide variety of working boats that constantly ply the muddy, wide river.

Take a ferry ride for more of the same. Tourist boat rides are occasionally operated by the White Swan Hotel, or it's easy to catch a cheap, local ferry. Try the 15-minute ferry ride to **Zhongshan University** (中山大學), in the southern suburbs. Ferries depart from the foot of Beijing Lu and dock at a pier at the north end of the campus. Return immediately on the same boat or spend an hour strolling around the green university grounds, where you may meet students bent on practicing their English.

Roman Catholic Cathedral 石室教堂
The imposing twin Gothic spires of the Sacred

PEARL RIVER DELTA

© MOON PUBLICATIONS, INC.

0   25 km

Heart Cathedral come as a surprise, rising above blocks of shophouses on Yide Xilu, a few blocks back from the river. The largest Roman Catholic church in China, it was designed by a French architect, built on land leased to the French, and consecrated in 1888. In Chinese it's called Shi Shi, "House of Stone." During the Cultural Revolution the building was used as a warehouse. It's been reopened since but is usually closed except for Sunday mass.

Cultural Park 文化公園

This amusement park holds an odd range of performances, displays, and exhibitions. There's a big "Han Dynasty City" of historical tableaux (admission an extra Y5), chess and pool halls, a reading room, a roller rink, kiddie rides, opera performances, public storytellers, and flower displays. It's best visited at night (it's open till 10 p.m.), when there's a sense of vitality; in the daytime it's mainly full of old men playing chess. Ad-

mission is Y2, more for some displays. The park is on Liuersan Lu, across from Shamian Island.

Shamian Island 沙面

With its crumbling old colonial buildings, many of them now serving as offices, Shamian Island retains the quaint air of the old foreign quarter it once was. The Chinese leased this bad *feng shui* site, originally little more than a fever-haunted mudbank, to English and French traders in 1859. The colonists built up the embankments, planted banyan trees, and transformed it into a private, shady enclave for some 300 European and American traders. It remains quiet and peaceful, a good place to stroll. A narrow, filthy canal separates it from the city; you can see vegetables being "washed" here for sale in the nearby Qingping Market, though the water is so thick with filth you can almost walk on it.

The back side of the small island holds the White Swan Hotel, built on a chunk of reclaimed

---

SHENZHEN'S SPECIAL ECONOMIC ZONE

The brash face of a new China is embodied by Shenzhen, a booming frontier community just across the border from Hong Kong. The contrast is the reverse of what you'd expect—the peaceful green fields and fishponds of Hong Kong set beside the boomtown metropolis.

Shenzhen looks a little like a down-at-the-heels New Town, with its starkly new skyscrapers, high-rise hotels, lots of shops (an inordinate number of gold stores), and fancy cars. Buildings are under construction everywhere you turn; giant billboards advertise motorcycles, makeup, and appliances, and the streets are full of fashionably dressed young people. Shenzhen is on the cutting edge of Chinese economic change: by some accounts, it's the future China.

Shenzhen is one of the original four Special Economic Zones established in 1980 (the other three being Zhuhai, Shantou, and Xiamen). In these isolated little havens China was able to experiment with capitalism on a small scale. The Special Economic Zones were supposed to adopt the positive material benefits of Western capitalism while filtering out the negative aspects of Western culture.

The biggest and best of the SEZs is Shenzhen. Twenty years ago it was a local market town of

some 20,000, surrounded by green countryside. Ten years ago the town was a dusty if burgeoning little dump of a place. Today Shenzhen City is home to over 700,000 workers from all over China, drawn by the promise of incomes 5 or 10 times higher than they could earn anywhere else. Gold-diggers of other nationalities can be found here also, including Russian bar hostesses and Pakistani laborers. Shenzhen's insatiable urge to get ahead has given rise to a modern aphorism: "There's nothing a Beijingese won't say, a Shanghaiese won't wear, a Cantonese won't eat—and a Shenzhen resident won't do for money."

The Shenzhen SEZ has been expanded the length of the Hong Kong border to cover some 2,000 square km and 3 million people. Shenzhen has its own port and international airport, its own rotating restaurant, a number of glossy hotels rivaling Hong Kong's in style, and a get-ahead spirit that's extraordinary even for industrious south China. The government is forced to restrict internal access to it, but has had little luck in controlling immigration: two thirds of Shenzhen residents lack official permission to live there.

Ninety percent of the Shenzhen SEZ's foreign investment is from Hong Kong. Much of the rest is from land along the riverbank. One of the more elegant hotels in China, it's worth a stop to admire the indoor waterfall in the lobby.

Qingping Market 清平市場

This fantastic market is among Guangzhou's main attractions, though certain streets may upset the tender-hearted. Qingping Lu itself is devoted to dried medicinal herbs and ingredients—crushed pearls, sea horses, pungent star anise and licorice root, stacks of shredded tobacco. Side streets radiating out from here purvey ordinary goods—fish, vegetables, fruit, and meat (flayed dogs dangling from meat hooks are a common sight in winter months). Deep in the recesses are more unusual animals destined for the pot: monkeys, frogs, owls, tortoises, cats, rabbits, unfortunate live deer trembling in wire cages. You can buy tiger paws for around HK$300 a pound (an average paw weighs over four pounds) or a whole bear for around HK$7000. It's stinky,

lively, disturbing, and undeniably authentic. Qingping Lu is across from Shamian's second bridge.

EAST GUANGZHOU

Peasant Movement Institute 農民運動講習所

This Communist party institute was established in 1924 to train young party members from all over China. Mao served as its director, and Zhou Enlai was a lecturer during its brief operation (it was shut down in 1927 by the Kuomintang). Today it's been transformed into a "Revolutionary Museum," with a facsimile of Mao's quarters and some pretty dull displays of early party documents and photos. The building is at 42 Zhongshan 4-Lu.

Memorial Garden To the Martyrs 烈士陵園

One block east down Zhongshan Lu is this big park, laid out on the site of the execution

---

overseas China, mainly Taiwanese. Hong Kong companies have set up some 10,000 factories in Guangdong Province, employing more workers than in all of Hong Kong. The Hong Kong-Shenzhen highway is lined with new factories and full of trucks bringing in cloth, leather, plastic and electronic parts, and hauling out finished garments, shoes, toys, and electronic gadgets. The boom has spread beyond the boundaries of the SEZ to penetrate deeper into the countryside, where labor costs are even cheaper.

Sights

In all truth it must be said Shenzhen is not much of an attraction. If you want to see China—as opposed to a Chinese version of Hong Kong—you're better off going to Guangzhou, even if only for a day.

That said, you may end up passing through Shenzhen with a few hours to spare. It's reached in under an hour from Hong Kong's Hung Hom KCR station. Take the KCR to Lo Wu (you need a Chinese visa to get even this far), pass through immigration and customs, and walk over to Shenzhen's towering new railway station. Trains depart for Guangzhou every half hour.

Stalls around the railway station sell Chinese goods—thermoses, quilts, roast ducks, porcelain—to Hongkongers looking for bargains. Many uppercrust hotels are visible from here, most notably the

glizty **Shangri-La Hotel** on Jianshe Lu, where rooms start at US$100. The McDonald's on Jiefang Lu was the first in China.

Shenzhen lacks cultural or aesthetic value: it's almost entirely a manmade monument to the power of economic forces. A very few old shophouses remain amid the new skyscrapers. The town's grid layout is deadly dull and obviously recently planned. Downtown Shenzhen, with its glossy restaurants and fancy hotels, lies along the east side of the railway tracks, around Renmin Nanlu. Jianshe Lu, and Shennan Lu. There are a few parks in the north part of town.

Shenzhen's biggest tourist attraction (very popular with Hong Kongers) is **Splendid China,** a miniature theme park in the western corner of the SEZ near Shenzhen Bay (minibuses leave regularly from the Shenzhen railway station). Here, 5,000 years of history are compressed into miniature renditions of Chinese sights: the Great Wall, Suzhou's gardens, Guilin's rock formations. Next door is the **China Ethnic Culture Demonstration Villages,** where the costumes and villages of Chinese ethnic minorities are displayed. The 8:30 p.m. parade of nationalities is impressive, according to at least one reader, who also cited performances of dancing, martial arts, and exotic skills like barefoot climbing of a pole equipped with knife-sharp steps.

vendors at the Qingping market

KERRY MORAN

grounds used by the Kuomintang during the bloody suppression of Guangzhou's 1927 Communist uprising, in which some 5,000 people died. The pretty gardens hold a boating lake and a stone book inscribed with calligraphy by Zhou Enlai. There is also a "Pavilion of Blood-Cemented Friendship of the Sino-Soviet Peoples" and another dedicated to Koreans, commemorating the Soviet consular officials and Koreans who died in the uprising.

Mausoleum of the 72 Martyrs
黃花岡七十二烈十墓
Out the backside of the park and up Xianlie Lu is the "Memorial of Yellow Flowers," a 36-acre park commemorating the failed uprising of 1911, one of many attempts to topple the Qing dynasty. The monument encompasses a mishmash of styles and eras, including copies of an Egyptian obelisk, the Liberty Bell, the Trianon of Versailles, and the Statue of Liberty, with some Chinese themes thrown in for good measure.

Guangzhou Zoo 廣州動物園
Farther up Xianlie Lu is a large zoo housing some 2,000 creatures—not exactly an attraction, given the terrible conditions for the animals.

AROUND GUANGZHOU

The surrounding countryside offers some moderately interesting excursions if you've more than a few days to spend in Guangzhou. Hire a taxi on your own, take a public bus, or ask CITS to arrange transport. Or just rent a bicycle and ride out past city limits into the green countryside, though nowadays you have to go farther and farther to escape the urban sprawl.

Bai Yun Shan 白雲山
These "White Cloud Hills," 15 km northeast of the center of town, are the only slopes of any note in the flat Guangdong region—which isn't saying much. The highest, optimistically dubbed Mo Xing Ling or "Star-Touching Hill," is around 400 meters in elevation. The shady hills are a favorite weekend getaway. A cable car line takes about 10 minutes to ascend the hill; it's near the terminus for Buses 36 and 24.

> *When one is in China one is compelled to think about her with compassion always, with despair sometimes and with discrimination and understanding very rarely. For one either loves or hates China. . . . If one comes to China, one feels engulfed, and soon stops thinking. One merely feels that she is there, a tremendous existence somewhere too big for the human mind to encompass, a seemingly inconsequential chaos obeying its own laws of existence.*
>
> *—Lin Yutang, My Country and My People*

The road up Bai Yun Shan passes **Lu Lake,** where paddleboats are rented on weekends, then ascends past **Cheng Precipice,** a favorite lookout point over the city. A footpath from here leads up to Mo Xing Ling in around 15 minutes, or you can continue by road, passing various scenic rocks and viewpoints.

Nanhu Amusement Park 南湖樂園
Just west of Bai Yun Shan, this small park is designed to entertain mainly children with its rides, but its restaurant and park-like setting is a good place to relax on less-crowded weekdays. Minibuses run directly from the railway station to here, or you can incorporate it into a trip to Bai Yun Shan.

Shahe 沙河
This northeast suburb is famous for the **Shahe Noodle Restaurant** (沙河粉店) at 79 Shahe Dajie. Here, rice noodles are prepared according to a 600-year-old recipe and served in 40 different varieties. It's about a 20-minute taxi ride from downtown if traffic isn't heavy.

South China Botanical Garden 南華植物公園
The largest botanical garden in China, this features 3,000 varieties of tropical and subtropical plants, including palms, bamboo, and conifers. There's a small teahouse on the grounds, quite peaceful on weekdays but crowded on weekends. Take Bus 28 from Shahe.

Foshan 佛山
The ancient town of Foshan lies 25 km southwest of Guangzhou, an hour's bus ride or a 40-minute train ride away. For well over a thousand years it served as an important Buddhist center (the name means "Buddha Hill"), as well as a major market town and a center for crafts like silk-weaving, paper-cutting, and metalwork. The famous pottery industry in nearby Shiwan (now a suburb of Foshan) dates from the Han dynasty. Shiwan wares, especially lifelike figurines, were exported all over China and earned fame abroad as well.

Today Foshan serves as a major ceramics center, making and selling statues and tableaux as well as bathroom fixtures and glazed tiles. The city is situated on an apparently inexhaustible deposit of reddish-brown clay that stretches for miles out into the countryside.

The town's main sight is the **Ancestor Temple** (祖廟) or Zu Miao on Zumiao Lu, a complex of prayer halls, pavilions, gardens, and courtyards. The main hall is constructed of interlocking wooden beams fitted together without a single nail. The structure dates to the 11th century but has obviously been rebuilt and renovated since. Inside is a massive 2,500-kilogram bronze image of the "Northern Emperor," Bei Di.

Nearby, the former Renshou Temple has been converted into the **Foshan Folk Art Institute** (佛山文俗工藝學院), where craftsmen produce and sell papercuts, paintings, paper lanterns, and carvings. You might also visit the **Lianhua Market,** which is smaller than Guangzhou's Qingping but displays a similar variety of animals.

There's no compelling reason to overnight in Foshan, but there are plenty of hotels, including the **Pearl River Hotel** on Chenren Lu, across from the post office, tel. 8287-512, and the flashier **Rotating Palace Hotel** across the street, tel. 8285-622.

Buses to Foshan regularly depart Guangzhou from the railway station bus terminal, and take around an hour. They stop at the Foshan railway station, which lies north across the river from town, less than two km from the Ancestor Temple. The Guangzhou-Foshan train is more comfortable and takes only 30 minutes. Foshan lies on the Zhaoqing line. There are now two direct express Foshan-Hong Kong trains daily.

Conghua Hot Springs 中華溫泉
This spa on the banks of the Liuxi River is another popular weekend getaway. The mineral-laden hot springs are said to be good for all sorts of disorders. The water is pumped direct into the bathrooms of villas and hotels for private basking. Hotels here include **Guangdong Hot Springs,** tel. 8683-338, **Gualu,** tel. 8252-354, **Pine Garden,** and **Hubin Guesthouse.**

Conghua lies around 80 km northeast of Guangzhou, about a 2.5-hour bus ride. Catch a bus from the long-distance bus station on Huanshi Xilu, near the railway station. Make sure the bus is going to the hot springs (Conghua Wenquan) and not the town of Conghua; otherwise you'll have to catch another bus to bridge the 16-km gap between the two.

PRACTICALITIES

ACCOMMODATIONS

If Hong Kong is bad for budget travelers, Guangzhou provides little relief. No guesthouse is as cheap as any in Tsimshatsui, and there is only one budget youth hostel. The cheapest hotels are usually reserved for Chinese travelers.

The good news is that there's a wide selection of mid-range tourist hotels, which are decently equipped if old-fashioned. At the top end, Guangzhou has some of China's finest hotels—not quite up to Hong Kong-standard of luxury, but comfortable all the same, and far more reasonably priced.

Hotels are often booked solid for the first week of the Guangzhou Trade Fair held each April and November. Hoteliers draw most of their profit from those months, when normal room rates may double. In winter months, expect discounts up to 50% on published rates. Corporate discounts of around 25% are easily netted with a professional demeanor and a business card.

Price categories are for double rooms.

Budget (Under Y250)
Guangzhou Youth Hostel, 2 Shamian 4-Jie, tel. 8188-4298. This modest place across from the White Swan Hotel is extremely popular with backpackers, with smallish dorm rooms, a few singles, and decent doubles. Go early in the morning and put your name down on the list for a room.

The other good budget neighborhood is near the railway station. Zhanqian Lu has a whole string of cheapish new hotels, rather institutional in decor, but well-priced. Try the **Zhanqian Hotel,** 81 Zhanqian Lu, tel. 8667-0348; **Leizhou Hotel,** 88 Zhanqian Lu, tel. 8669-1668; or the Jinhuan Hotel at 101 Zhanqian Lu, tel. 8668-9510. The **Friendship Hotel** at 698 Renmin Beilu, tel. 8667-9898, is another option.

Mid-Range (Y250-500)
Many of these are older but perfectly adequate hotels, catering mainly to groups of overseas Chinese.

Starting on Shamian Island, there's the **Pearl Inn,** 50 Shamian Nanjie, tel. 8188-9238, a fancy place with a restaurant and disco. Next door is the simpler and perhaps quieter **Shamian Hotel,** tel. 8188-8124. **Victory Hotel,** Shamian Beijie, tel. 8186-2662, is housed in an ornate building typical of the island's old colonial architecture.

Aiqun Hotel, 113 Yanjiang Xilu, tel. 8186-6668, is an excellent choice if you want atmosphere. The big, old-fashioned stone building dates to 1937 but the interior has been renovated to Chinese modern standards. It's nicely situated on the river. More expensive rooms have river views. At the high end of this price category.

Other classy old places in the heart of downtown include the **Bai Gong Hotel,** 13 Renmin Nanlu, tel. 8188-2313, and, across the street at 4 Renmin Nanlu, the 1920s-vintage **Xinhua Hotel,** tel. 8188-4722. The **New Asia Hotel,** 10 Renmin Nanlu, tel. 8188-4722, is new and fancy, catering to groups from Hong Kong.

Around the railway station, Zhanqian Lu is a good place to look, with mid-range places like the **New Mainland Hotel,** 78 Zhanqian Lu, and the **Sinochem Hotel,** 58 Zhanqian Lu, tel. 8667-2288. The big old **Liuhua Hotel,** tel. 8666-8800, across from the railway station at 194 Huanshi Xilu is a busy, echoing place full of Chinese travelers.

The elite northeast quadrant of town is full of expensive hotels, but there's a few more reasonable ones scattered in amid these high-rise towers. **Hua Shan Hotel,** 420 Huanshi Donglu, tel. 8776-3868, is a good choice, with a few single rooms available as well. **Guangdong Jinye Hotel,** 422 Huanshi Donglu, tel. 8777-2888, is another option. The older **Bai Yun Hotel,** 367 Huangshi Donglu, tel. 8333-6498, is located right beside the Friendship Store.

Expensive (Above Y500)

Top hotels like the Garden, the White Swan, and the China rank among the country's best, with slick management and Hong Kong panache. Most of the others in this category are older and less impressive.

Northeast Guangzhou is packed with luxury hotels. **Garden Hotel,** 368 Huanshi Donglu, tel. 8333-8989. This monster joint venture boasts an ornate lobby, over 1100 rooms, a conference hall for 1400, a dozen bars and restaurants, sports facilities (including two swimming pools), and lots of shops. It's glittery bordering on luxurious—top-of-the-line for Guangzhou.

Equally impressive, with the title of tallest building in China, the **Gitic Plaza Hotel** at 347 Huanshi Donglu, tel. 8331-1888, towers above its neighbors at 63 stories. Equally interesting for locals, it houses the city's first McDonald's.

Ocean Hotel, 412 Huanshi Donglu, tel. 8776-5988, is a moderately luxurious hotel with rooms at the lower end of this category. **Holiday Inn,** 28 Guangming Lu, tel. 8776-6999, is located just west of the Ocean Hotel, and is popular with business travelers.

White Swan Hotel, 1 Shamian Nanjie, tel. 8188-6968, was China's first joint-venture hotel, and it remains impressive, although other hotels have overtaken it in terms of elegance. Facilities include two outdoor pools, tennis courts, some good restaurants, and a waterfall in the lobby that still draws crowds. Also near the river is the **Furama Hotel** at 316 Changdi Lu, tel. 8186-3288.

Near the railway station is the **China Hotel** on Liuhua Lu, tel. 8666-6888, an ultramodern establishment with more than 1,000 rooms, 18 restaurants and bars, sports facilities, and very efficient service. **Hotel Equitorial,** 931 Renmin Beilu, tel. 8667-2888, is less slick and expensive

but still quite nice. **Dong Feng Hotel,** 120 Liuhua Lu, tel. 8666-9900, adjoins the China Hotel and looks positively clunky in comparison, though it was once the most prestigious place in town.

FOOD

While it's not up to Hong Kong standards in terms of diversity or class, Guangzhou still has some of the best food in China. See the Hong Kong section for a description of its indigenous Cantonese cuisine, considered China's best. Sunday mornings at crowded, noisy dim sum restaurants are a local institution, and Hong Kong-influenced fast food has been eagerly embraced.

A local quirk is the pronounced taste for exotica, or "wild flavor" cuisine, relatively uncontrolled compared to Hong Kong. Enough money will purchase a meal of bald eagle or tiger meat or bear paws or pangolin (a mammal covered in horny scales, resembling an armadillo). In addition to the large local market, even more is exported into Taiwan. A more homey specialty is rat: rodent kebab, or rat fried with raccoon or boiled in rat broth, is the house specialty of at least one Guangzhou restaurant.

Fast Food and Restaurants

Small local bakeries dispense sweet buns and dim sum treats. There are good bakeries at the White Swan and China Hotels; the latter also has a deli counter.

For a cheap, light meal look for small places displaying trays of fresh noodles or meat dumplings *(jiaoze)*. Small restaurants also sell boxes of rice-and-dish for takeout, a la Hong Kong. Muslim restaurants, like the **Huimin Fandian** at 325 Zhongshan 6-Lu, are informal and inexpensive places to eat; they specialize in mutton.

Street vendors and small restaurants set up around the Aiqun Hotel and near the railway station on Liuhua Lu. Given the lack of English menus, point-and-eat. More refined and perhaps easier to deal with is **Food Street** in the China Hotel, an air-conditioned food mall with a variety of Chinese food stalls, open 7:30 a.m.-1 a.m.

For fast food, there's Hong Kong's Fairwood chain, a McDonald's on Huanshi Donglu near the Bai Yun Hotel, and a Kentucky Fried Chicken, complete with plastic Colonel, on Changdi Damalu near the Aiqun Hotel.

Restaurants on Shamian Island have outdoor seating at night; there are several on Shamian 4-Jie down from the Guangzhou Youth Hostel, including the excellent **Li Qin,** and a cheap canteen with an English menu in front of the White Swan Hotel. The restaurant in the Victory Hotel serves good morning dim sum. **Lucy's** in front of the Shamian park has a Western-style bar and menu.

Yijingyuan on Haizhu Square is a moderately priced informal restaurant serving Chinese food. **Taipinguan,** at 344 Beijing Lu, is another reliable standby, serving Chinese and Western dishes.

Hotel restaurants provide an air-conditioned safe haven. The **White Swan** has a breakfast buffet for Y60, while the morning buffet at the China Hotel's **Verandah Coffeeshop** is Y95.

More offbeat places include the **Wild Animals Restaurant,** 247 Beijing Lu, which serves bear paws, dog, and snake. The venerable **Snake Restaurant** (She Canguan), 43 Jianglan Lu, serves 30 different serpent recipes, including "Dragon-Tiger-Phoenix Soup," composed of simmered snake, cat, and chicken. If these prospects sound less than delightful you may want to try a vegetarian restaurant, like **Caigen Xiang,** 167 Zhongshan 6-Lu, where tofu is transformed into dishes that look and taste exactly like meat.

Top Restaurants

Guangzhou's culinary heritage is embodied in its *jiujia* or "wine houses," some of which date back to the last century. They may be expensive (determine the price of everything beforehand and check the bill carefully) but they're worth it. Go with a Chinese friend if possible, but don't be afraid to try them on your own—they're used to catering to foreign tour groups.

Datong, 63 Yanjiang Xilu (just off Renmin Lu). This multi-storied, gaudy restaurant is famous for its roast suckling pig and dim sum.

Guangzhou Jiujia, 2 Wenchang Nanlu. Once renowned as the top restaurant in town, and still extremely popular, it's located in a big modern building right in the middle of the city.

Bei Yuan, 202 Xiaobei Lu. Another "famous house," conveniently located behind Yuexiu Park. Across the river at 142 Qianjin Lu is its cousin, the **Nan Yuan** or "South Garden," with a Chinese garden and traditional dining halls.

Panxi, 151 Longjin Xilu. This huge place is built around a little lake and garden and is renowned for its wide array of elegant dim sum, served throughout the day.

Taotaoju, 288 Xiuli 2-Lu. Another highly reputed old establishment, with superb dim sum and tea made with water imported from the Bai Yun Hills to the north.

ENTERTAINMENT

Shopping

Generally speaking it's best to shop in Hong Kong, where the China products emporiums stock a far wider range of goods. Guangzhou is good for kitschy propaganda posters (try the Xinhua Bookshop at 376 Beijing Lu) and Mao artifacts peddled by street vendors.

The government-owned Friendship Store next to the Bai Yun Hotel provides foreign goods to local people with money. There's a big supermarket on the first floor and tourist-oriented wares up on the third floor. The city's first shopping mall, the Nam Fong International Plaza, is just east of here. Another busy Friendship Store is in the China Hotel.

Major shopping areas are the downtown stretches of Beijing Lu, Zhongshan Lu, and Jiefang Lu. Department stores include the Nanfang Dasha on Yanjiang Xilu off Haizhu Square and the Guangzhou Department Store at the corner of Beijing and Xihu Lu. Hong Kong chains like Wing On and Giordano's are also expanding into Guangzhou.

Nightlife

While it's nowhere near as flashy as Hong Kong's, Guangzhou's nightlife is a world ahead of Northern China's. Discos were introduced here over a decade ago and have become increasingly more sophisticated, adopting Hong Kong music and mores. There are lively discos at the Chinese-run Ocean, Dong Fang, and Guangzhou hotels, and more Western-oriented ones in the Garden and China hotels. Karaoke lounges are also locally popular.

Western-style bars are found in the hotels, like the China Hotel's Corner Bar, the British pub in the Garden, and the Holiday Inn's TGIF, popular with local expats. The Riverside Lounge at the White Swan is more low-key. Red Ants, on Guangzhou Dadao across from the Ramada Pearl Hotel, wins the prize for best name; it's extremely popular with foreigners.

The usual thing to do at night is eat, then stroll the busy streets. In the steamy summer months, nighttime is the only tolerable time to be outside and people stay up till late chatting and socializing. Visit the night market on Er Ma Lu: the street is blocked off to traffic so that pedestrians can stroll past theaters and restaurants. Another good place is the Cultural Park on Liuersan Lu, which livens up at night with performances and exhibitions.

Festivals and Events

China's traditional cultural events were devastated by the Cultural Revolution. Even today celebrations and festivals are more authentic in Hong Kong. Lunar New Year remains the biggest holiday, three days stretching into a week where nothing much happens for outsiders. It's not a good time to visit as there's not much to see, crowds make it difficult to travel, and restaurants and shops are closed. Most of the other holidays are less than exciting government-sanctioned events like International Labor Day (1 May) and National Day (1 October), which is marked by parades and displays of military might.

GETTING THERE

Visa and customs requirements have been streamlined and transport options broadened to make Hong Kong-Guangzhou travel easy. Train or boat (either the night ferry or the faster jetcat) are the best choices. Transport is crowded on weekends, and on holidays like the lunar New Year and the Mid-Autumn Festival, vast hordes trample both ways across the border—avoid traveling then at all costs. If trains or boats are full, try booking through CTS (HK), or Hong Kong agents specializing in corporate travel, like Swire, Farrington, American Express, P&O, or American International Travel.

Travel by bus is less pleasant, but the new six-lane Shenzhen-Guangzhou highway has cut travel time three hours. The new route is helping weld Hong Kong, Shenzhen, and Guangzhou into a single sprawling metropolis—everywhere you look out the window, new factories are sprouting up on what used to be farmland. Eventually you'll be able to drive your own car from Hong Kong to Guangzhou.

By Train

The Kowloon-Guangzhou express train takes 2 hours 40 minutes and is preferable to the slower local train, which requires changing in Shenzhen. There are four express departures daily from Hung Hom, currently at 7:50 and 9:50 a.m. and 12:23 and 2:22 p.m. (The 9:50 a.m. train is "semi-high speed" and takes only two hours). Returning, trains depart Guangzhou at 8:15 and 10:10 a.m. and 4:50 and 6:15 p.m.; check again as times can change. Tickets are HK$200 one-way, HK$220-250 for the high speed train. In Hong Kong, book tickets at CTS or the Hung Hom KCR station; in Guangzhou from CITS or the railway station.

Guangzhou's railway station is a sprawling monstrosity built in the early '60s and typical of Communist architecture. In recent years it's become a mecca for rural migrants in search of a better life. Surrounded by bundles of clothing and bedding, they camp on the station's vast forecourt as they search for jobs and living quarters. They may stay here for months or even years, eating, sleeping, and living out on the pavement. Some have even found a niche peddling goods and services to other squatters.

Express trains depart from a siding on the east side of the station compound (near the CAAC office). Look for the green "Guangzhou-Kowloon Through Train" sign by the pedestrian underpass. Tickets for both express and local trains are available from the second floor of the adjoining building. Different windows accommodate purchases in RMB or HK$.

If you opt for the cheaper local train, take the KCR from Hung Hom up to Lo Wu (HK$29), cross the border into Shenzhen, and catch a Guangzhou-bound train from Shenzhen's giant new station. A soft-seat Shenzhen-Guangzhou ticket costs HK$110. Avoid local trains during holidays, when they're packed with Hongkongers bearing consumer goods for Guangzhou relatives. Express trains are a better choice at those times.

By Bus

CTS buses travel daily from Hong Kong to Guangzhou in three hours; fare is HK$200 one-way, slightly cheaper if you buy a return ticket. Book tickets at CTS offices or travel agencies. Citybus also operates a Hong Kong-Guangzhou bus service; inquire at the company's office in China Hong Kong City, 33 Canton Rd., Tsimshatsui, tel. 2736-3888.

In Guangzhou, the bus station is on Huanshi Xilu, across from the railway station. Regular government buses are on the terminal's east side; private minibuses (generally faster and more comfortable) on the west side. Buses and minibuses run to Shenzhen (two hours) and Zhuhai (four hours), and to various destinations in southeast China, including Guilin and many coastal cities.

rush hour on Renmin Bridge

Travelers from Macau can buy bus tickets to Guangzhou from the Kee Kwan Motor Road Co. office on Rua des Lorchas, near the shuttlebus station, or the CTS office on Rua de Nagasaki. Fares are around Ptc60. Or simply cross the border on your own, and catch one of the many minibus running from Zhuhai to Guangzhou.

By Boat

To/From Hong Kong: Jetcat and overnight ferries depart daily from the China Ferry Terminal in China Hong Kong City, Tsimshatsui. In Guangzhou they dock at Zhoutouzui Wharf, which is near the south end of the Renmin Bridge, about 15 minutes' walk from Shamian Island.

The jetcat takes 3 hours and departs Hong Kong daily at 8:15 a.m.; fare is HK$270. The Guangzhou-Hong Kong jetcat leaves Zhoutouzui at 1 p.m.

Overnight ferries take eight hours, departing both places at 9 p.m. and arriving at 6 a.m. the following morning. Aside from the romance of a leisurely cruise up the Pearl River, it saves the cost of a night's hotel. Tickets cost HK$200 for a third-class seat (not recommended), HK$250 for the second-class dormitory (clean and decent), and HK$300 for a semi-private cabin.

Try to buy tickets at least a day in advance. In Hong Kong, tickets are available at the ferry terminal (departures are on the 1/F) or through CTS or travel agencies. In Guangzhou, buy tickets at Zhoutouzui Wharf or through CITS.

By Air

Both Cathay Pacific and CAAC's regional airline, China Southern Airlines, make several daily flights between Hong Kong and Guangzhou. The flight is only 30 minutes, but add some time for customs and immigration. Fares are around HK$600 one-way. Flights land at Guangzhou's new international airport at Huadu, 28 km from the city center. CAAC runs very cheap buses between the airport and its office at 181 Huanshi Lu, near the railway station. Taxis are available, but drivers often try to extort ridiculous fares from arriving foreigners.

Guangzhou is connected by air with several dozen domestic flight destinations, including Beijing, Changsha, Changzhou, Chengdu,

Chongqing, Dalian, Guilin, Haikou, Hangzhou, Harbin, Hohhot, Kunming, Liuzhou, Nanjing, Ningbo, Shanghai, Tianjin, Urumqi, Wuhan, Xiamen, and Xian. Buy tickets through CITS, or at the CAAC office, which is at 181 Huanshi Zhonglu, just east of the railway station, tel. 8666-2969 domestic, 8666-1803 international.

Organized Tours

While exploring Guangzhou on your own is probably easier than you think, an organized tour eliminates all hassles and may be worth considering if your time (or patience) is very limited. In Hong Kong, check with CTS or private tour companies like Gray Line. CTS trips can be booked through independent travel agents, or you can sign up for a privately operated independent tour. Prices vary somewhat between companies but will usually include China visa, transport, lunch, and fees. Book at least one or two days in advance to allow for visa arrangements.

Daytrips out of Hong Kong are necessarily limited in scope. Shenzhen is the likeliest destination, though it's not very appealing. A typical tour includes a visit to an art gallery, the Shenzhen reservoir, a local market or kindergarten, and prefab tourist attractions like Splendid China and China Folk Culture Village. Average cost is HK$650-790.

CTS also runs one-day excursions to Guangzhou (some *very* fast sightseeing for around HK$1200), and two to four-day trips to Shenzhen, Macau, Guangzhou, and "scenic" destinations like Zhaoqing's Seven Star Crags and Lotus Mountain. More expensive individual tours can also be arranged.

GETTING AROUND

On foot is recommended for the interesting areas, but it must be combined with some means of public transport to get about the sprawling metropolitan area.

Bus

Public buses, often electric trolleys, are crowded and slow, though very cheap and usefully routed. Ticket prices depend on the distance you travel. Tell the conductor where you want to go and she or he will charge you accordingly—and hopefully notify you when to get off. City maps sold in hotel bookshops and in front of the railway station detail common bus routes. Useful ones include Bus 31, which runs from the railway station down Renmin Lu; and Bus 5, which again starts at the railway station and runs down Renmin Lu, then turns west on Liu'ersan Lu, providing access to Shamian Island. Minibuses ply set routes, with destinations written in front in Chinese; they're useful for hops to major places like the train station.

Taxi

Metered taxis are all over the place. If you can't find one on the street, look at a major hotel. Flagfall is Y7-9; fares may vary slightly according to the make of the car. A small supplement may be charged after midnight; no tipping is necessary. Make sure the driver uses the meter, and don't believe him when he insists on Hong Kong dollars. It's wise to have your hotel staff write out your destination in Chinese, as English is rare. You can also hire a taxi for a half or full day at a prearranged rate.

Bicycle

This is arguably the best way to get around town, though heavy traffic can make it terrifying at times. The established bike lanes are so crowded that cycling in them is akin to drifting downriver in a fast current. One tip: always keep moving. There's a bike rental place on Shamian Island right across from the Guangzhou Youth Hostel. It charges Y1 an hour and requires a deposit or passport as ransom. The hostel also rents bikes to its guests.

Parking around town, beware of theft and always use the provided lock. Park only at designated lots, where an attendant will give you a ticket and will guard the bike for a few *mao*. Otherwise you may find the police have hauled off your bike for obstructing pedestrians, and it's hell to get it back.

Ferry

These dumpy old-fashioned boats are a great way to cross the Pearl River and get a glimpse of life on the outskirts of town. Bicycles can be transported on the lower deck. Tickets cost only a few *mao* and are sold from windows at the pier.

VISAS

You'll need a Chinese visa to visit Guangzhou, obtainable from CTS or through Hong Kong travel agencies (see "Travel Agents" under "Getting Around" in the Hong Kong Basics chapter). Cheapest is Type A, HK$130 for a single-entry Chinese visa provided in two working days. It costs HK$190 to get the same visa in one day, HK$280 for same-day service, HK$360 for a few hours. Dual-entry visas cost an additional HK$150. You'll need one photo, available on the spot if you don't happen to have one.

It's slightly cheaper to avoid CTS altogether and get the visa yourself from the Visa Office of the Chinese Ministry of Foreign Affairs, located on the 5/F, East Wing, China Resources Bldg., Gloucester Road, Wanchai, tel. 2827-1881. It's open 9 a.m.-12:30 p.m. and 2-5 p.m. Mon.-Fri., Saturday 9 a.m.-12:30 p.m.

In Macau, the main CTS office on Rua de Nagasaki, tel. 700-8888, issues visas and arranges tickets.

Visas are generally valid for one month, and are good for one month from date of issue. To extend while in China, apply at any Public Security Bureau; one-month extensions are easy to get.

Chinese customs are generally straightforward. You may be asked to declare valuable items like computers, tape recorders, or cameras on a form, and to show these items upon leaving the country. People may ask you to carry in cigarettes, alcohol, or mysterious packages, but it's best to avoid doing strangers such a favor.

CHINA TRAVEL SERVICE

Travel in China is aided, and sometimes impeded, by two monster tourist organizations. CITS, or China International Travel Service (Luxingshe in Chinese), is a state-run company established to deal with foreign tourists. Its counterpart is CTS or China Travel Service, which handles "Overseas Chinese," including Hongkongers and Taiwanese. In places where CITS is not established, as in Hong Kong, CTS will also handle foreign tourists.

CITS differs from CTS in that it's supposed to have English-speaking staff, who will buy train and plane tickets, arrange hotel rooms, tours, and vehicles, and provide general information. The CITS office in Guangzhou is at 179 Huanshi Lu, beside the railway station, tel. 667-7151. Office hours are 8:30-11:30 a.m. and 2-5 p.m. Staff here are reportedly less than helpful, and touts may come up to help arrange matters at special prices. Avoid them, and buttonhole the staff instead.

There is no CITS office in Hong Kong, so CTS handles foreigners' requests for visas, transport tickets, and tours. The CTS head office is at 4/F, CTS House, 78 Connaught Rd., Central, tel. 2853-3533. Branch offices are at 2/F, 77 Queen's Rd., Central, tel. 2525-2284, and 1/F, 27 Nathan Rd., Tsimshatsui, tel. 2721-1331, and 1/F, China Hong Kong City, 33 Canton Rd., Tsimshatsui, tel. 2736-1863.

MONEY

The basic unit of currency is the yuan (informally called *kuai*), which is divided into *jiao* (informally called *mao*) and *fen*. Ten *fen* make one *mao*, ten *mao* one *kuai*. The exchange rate in mid-1997 was Y8.32 to US$1.

In January 1994 China announced it was scrapping its much-loathed system of dual currencies, which assigned one type of money (*renminbi* or RMB) to "the people" and another (Foreign Exchange Certificates or FEC) to tourists. While the yuan is not yet fully convertible and probably won't be for several more years, this is a major step on the road to a market-style economy.

Hong Kong currency is also common in south China, especially Shenzhen, where taxi drivers may insist on it. Hong Kong dollars are legally allowed in the Special Economic Zones of Shenzhen and Zhuhai—in fact, an estimated 20 to 30% of Hong Kong's currency supply is circulating in China.

Travelers can change money at the Bank of China, which has branches in large hotels. Rates are the same everywhere, and no commission is charged. The bigger hotels also change money for guests, charging only a small commission. Hong Kong banks and money-changers also sell and buy yuan.

OTHER PRACTICALITIES

Communications

The Chinese postal system is reliable and efficient. Write the destination country in capitals and underline it (or learn the Chinese characters). The rest of the address can be written in English. Airmail takes 5-7 days from Guangzhou. The main GPO is alongside the railway station (poste restante is located here), and there are post offices in major hotels.

Local telephone calls are often free from hotels. There are few pay phones around town, so ask at a shop or restaurant. Make long-distance calls from hotels, or from the telecommunications office on Huanshi Zhonglu across from the railway station.

Health

No vaccinations are required to enter China unless you're arriving from an area infected with cholera or yellow fever. You might, however, consider vaccines for common diseases like hepatitis (A and B) and tuberculosis.

Tap water is treated in Chinese cities, and should theoretically be safe, but most people still avoid drinking it in China. Thermoses of boiled water *(kai shui)* are provided in hotels and restaurants. Chinese prefer it to drinking cold water, which is said to slow the digestion, and also use it to rinse chopsticks, bowls, and teacups in more dubious restaurants.

Respiratory illnesses due to cold, dust, and pollution are another biggie among China travelers, but Guangzhou, with its moist warm climate, is better than most cities.

Western medical treatment and medicines are readily available: standards are not bad and cost is minimal. Guangzhou No. 1 People's Hospital on Renmin Beilu, tel. 8333-3090, has been designated for use by foreigners. Or you could try traditional Chinese herbal medicine or acupuncture.

Maps and Information

Before leaving Hong Kong, pick up a copy of Universal Publications' *Guangzhou Touring Map,* which has major roads and sights marked in English as well as in Chinese. In Guangzhou,

hotels and local bookstores sell city maps, as do vendors at the railway station, but make sure they're not entirely in Chinese. CTS puts out a multi-colored tourist map of Guangzhou, good mainly for its entertaining mistranslations.

Little English reading material is available in Guangzhou, so stock up beforehand. Kiosks in major hotels sell foreign newspapers, magazines, and some books at inflated prices, as well as *China Daily,* the government-issued English language newspaper. The Foreign Language Bookstore at 326 Beijing Lu has cheap translations of Chinese works and Western classics.

Safety

The major problem is theft, usually by the pickpockets who lurk on public buses and in other crowded places. They may use crowding or a distraction to rip you off; others simply snatch bags. Guangzhou's black-market moneychangers were known for ripping off foreigners but with the demise of FEC the black market has vanished.

Female travelers should find Guangzhou quite easy to deal with—harassment of women is rare, apart from an occasional grope. The main complaints from travelers of both sexes are the ubiquitous Chinese habits of spitting (at a decibel level loud enough to wake the dead), staring fixedly at foreigners, and pushing in crowds.

Details

Business Hours: Shops and offices open around 8 or 9 a.m., then close for two hours after lunch for *xiuxi,* the institutionalized Chinese siesta. They reopen around 2-3 p.m. and close again at 5 or 6 p.m. China works a six-day week: Sunday is the weekly holiday, though CITS offices and bank branches may be open Sunday morning.

Consulates: There's a U.S. Consulate in the Garden Hotel on Huanshi Donglu.

Electricity: 220 volts, 50 Hz. Outlets are designed for three flat prongs rather than three round ones as in Hong Kong.

Film Processing: Film is available in major hotels, although the selection is limited. Film and developing costs are cheaper in Hong Kong.

Weights and Measures: China is basically

metric, but old measurements are used in markets to weigh produce and meat, and even dumplings in restaurants. The most common are the *liang* (37.5 grams) and the *jin* (roughly one pound or a half-kilo).

Time: All of China, from Shanghai on the east coast to far Western Tibet, is on Beijing time, which is 8 hours ahead of GMT and 13 hours ahead of New York EST.

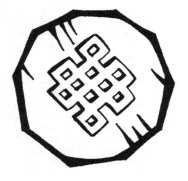

GLOSSARY

amah—an all-purpose maid and nanny, formerly a Chinese woman, now probably a Filipina

cheongsam—slinky tight-fitting women's dress, high-collared and slit up the leg

chim—set of numbered bamboo sticks used to tell fortunes

chi—vital energy

chop—engraved seal used as personal or official stamp

congee—Anglo-Indian term for a bland porridge of soaked rice, a favorite breakfast dish

cumsha—"tip" given in advance to expedite a desired result

dai pai dong—open-air food stall

dim sum—South China specialty; small savory and sweet tidbits served for breakfast or lunch (see the special topic "Dim Sum")

expat—expatriate, a foreigner working in Hong Kong

feng shui—the art and science of Chinese geomancy

godown—warehouse

gweilo—literally "foreign devil," a general term for Westerners (see the special topic "On *Gweilo*")

hong—one of the major trading houses, originally British-owned

junk—traditional flat-bottomed Chinese ship with a high poop and battened sails

kaido—wooden ferryboat, usually motorized

mahjong—Chinese game similar to bridge but using tiles instead of cards (see the special topic "Mahjong")

pai kau—Chinese dominoes

praya (also praia)—Portuguese term for waterfront promenade

samfu—a loose-fitting collarless top *(sam)* worn with loose, straight trousers *(fu)*, an outfit still favored by elderly women

sampan—small flat-bottomed wooden boat (the term literally means "three planks"), nowadays often fitted with an outboard motor

shroff—originally a moneychanger or banker, nowadays a parking lot cashier

ta chiu—a Taoist village festival of peace and renewal

tai chi—martial arts exercise involving a graceful, slow series of movements, practiced to cultivate balance and energy (see the special topic "Tai Chi")

taipan—boss of a *hong* or major company

tai-tai—wife of a taipan

tofu—soybean curd

wet market—public market supplying fresh meat, fish, and produce

yin/yang—the female and male energies; together these constitute the vital life force

CANTONESE PHRASES

With so many people speaking English in Hong Kong, it's unnecessary to learn *any* Cantonese —but any effort you make will be warmly welcomed. At minimum, try to absorb a few polite phrases and greetings. Numbers are useful for understanding prices and bargaining in street markets; fortunately Chinese numbers are more straightforward than English.

The words and phrases provided below are only an approximation of the correct pronunciation, which depends heavily on the nine tones of Cantonese. Ask a native speaker to pronounce these for you, then listen carefully and mimic the intonation. For more on Cantonese, including advice on studying, see the section on "Language" in the Introduction.

Politesse

The all-purpose "thank you" for minor favors and transactions is *mm'goy*. The major "thank you" to express gratitude for a gift, dinner, or a big favor is *do jeh*.

good morning	*jo san*
good night	*jo tau*
hello, how are you	*Nei ho ma*
very good	*ho ho*
not good	*mm ho*
pretty good	*gei ho*
goodbye	*joi geen*
What's your name?	*Nei gwai sing ah?*
Have you eaten yet? (a common greeting)	*Nei sik fan mei ah?*
please	*cheng*
would you please . . .	*mm'goi nei/cheng nei . . .*
excuse me (prefacing a question)	*cheung mun*
excuse me (getting someone's attention)	*mm'goi*
excuse me (I'm sorry)	*dui mm'jyu*

yes	*hai* or *hai-ah*
no	*mm'gai* or *mm'hai-ah*
OK?	*dat um dat?*
Hong Kong	*heung gong*
China	*chung kwok*
England	*ying kwok*
America	*mei kwok*
Canada	*ga la dai*
France	*fat kwok*
Germany	*dat kwok*
I am American	*Ngo seung mei kwok yan*
Where is the . . .?	*. . . hoi bin doh ah?*
bank	*ngan hong*
hospital	*yi yun*
hotel	*lui dim, jau dim*
policeman	*chai yan*
police station	*chai gok*
telephone	*din wah*
toilet	*chi sor*

Transportation

airplane	*fei gay*
airport	*fei gay cheung*
bicycle	*dan che*
bus	*ba si*
car	*hei che*
ferry	*go hoi syu*
MTR	*dai har tit*
taxi	*dik si*
train	*fou che*
train station	*fou che zham*
tram	*din che*

Peak Tram	*lam tse*	this one	*lee goh*
a little farther	*yun di*	that one	*goh goh*
turn right	*jyun yau, mm'goi*	How much is it?	*Gai do chin?*
turn left	*jyun cho, mm'goi*	HK$	*mun*
straight on	*chek hoi*	one dollar	*yat mun*
hurry up	*fai di*	ten dollars	*sup mun*
slow down	*man di*	too expensive	*ho gwai*
be careful	*sui sum*	so cheap	*ho peng*
stop the car	*ting che*		

Numbers and Shopping

Chinese use classifiers with numbers when referring to nouns. These vary according to types of objects; the most generic is *goh* and can be applied to everything. Thus, one thing is *yat goh;* two things, *leung goh,* ten of something, *sap goh.*

1	yat
2	yi (for counting), leung (item)
3	sam
4	sey
5	mm
6	lok
7	chat
8	bat
9	gau
10	sap
11	sap yat
12	sap yi . . .
20	yi sap
30	sam sap . . .
100	yat bak
1,000	yat chin
10,000	yat man
100,000	sup man

Dates

week	*lie by*
month	*yuet*
year	*nien*
Monday	*lie by yat*
Tuesday	*lie by yi*
Wednesday	*lie by sam*
Thursday	*lie by sai*
Friday	*lie by ng*
Saturday	*lie by lok*
Sunday	*lie by tin*

Food and Restaurants

restaurant	*fan dim*
menu	*choy dan/chan pai*
table for two	*leung wai*
. . . for three	*sam wai*
. . . for four	*sei wai*
Bill, please.	*Mai dan, mm'goi.*
breakfast	*jou chan*
lunch	*mm chan*
dinner	*man chan*
Chinese food	*tong choy*
Western food	*sai tsan choy*
steamed white rice	*bak fan*
fried rice	*chau fan*

noodles	*mein*
fried noodles	*chau mein*
soup noodles	*tong mein*
beef	*ngau yuk*
chicken	*gai*
pork	*jyue yuk*
seafood	*hoi sin*
jasmine tea	*heung peen*
black tea	*bo lei cha*
milk tea	*nai cha*
lemon tea	*ling mong cha*
coffee	*gai fay*
milk	*niou nai*
water	*seui*
beer	*bai jau*
liquor	*jau*

BOOKLIST

CULTURE

Baker, Dr. Hugh. *Ancestral Images.* Hong Kong: *South China Morning Post,* 1979. Also look for *More Ancestral Images* and *Ancestral Images Again.* These hard-to-find books contain Baker's brief, informative newspaper columns on Chinese culture. They're the perfect way to pick up entertaining tidbits on subjects as diverse as ducks, incense, and suicide.

Bard, Dr. Solomon. *In Search of the Past: A Guide to the Antiquities of Hong Kong.* Hong Kong: Hong Kong Urban Council, 1988. No temples, unfortunately, but a goldmine of information on old villages, forts, ancestral halls, and inscriptions. Accompanied by detailed maps and appendixes on Chinese architecture and *feng shui.*

Blofeld, John. *The Chinese Art of Tea.* Boston: Shambhala Publications, 1985. Poems, stories, and musings on tea, in far more detail than you'd ever imagine. Nicely illustrated and designed.

Chang, K.C. (editor). *Food in Chinese Culture.* New Haven: Yale University Press, 1977. Chapters on the historical and anthropological meanings of food, each focused on a different perspective: exotic food, rice, the imperial diet, daily menus. Scholarly and fascinating.

Hartman-Goldsmith, Joan. *Chinese Jade.* Hong Kong: Oxford University Press, 1986. One of the *Images in Asia* series on aspects of Chinese culture, this is a detailed, interesting, and well-illustrated discussion.

Lim, Liliane Kim. *The Chinese Dragon.* Hong Kong: Pencoed Ltd., 1987. An illustrated exposition of dragon mythology, exploring the meaning underlying the symbolism.

Pan, Lynn. *Truetoform.* Hong Kong: FormAsia, 1995. Exquisitely detailed look at Chinese crafts in clay, wood, bamboo, stone, celebrating their exquisite beauty and taste.

Reid, Daniel P. *Chinese Herbal Medicine.* Boston: Shambhala Publications, 1993. Beautifully illustrated, comprehensive introduction to the world's largest and oldest pharmacopea, with an illustrated list of more than 200 herbs and explanations of the basic premises of diagnosis and application.

Savidge, Joyce. *This Is Hong Kong: Temples.* Hong Kong: Hong Kong Government Press, 1977. Interesting trivia and stories about popular local temples.

Thompson, Patricia, and Betty Maloney. *The Game of Mah Jong.* Kenthurst, NSW: Kangaroo Press, 1990. An illustrated introduction to this Hong Kong passion.

Ward, Barbara E., and Joan Law. *Chinese Festivals in Hong Kong.* Hong Kong: The Guidebook Company, 1993. The complete festival-watchers' handbook, with explanations of origins and descriptions of what to see, where, and when. Beautifully photographed.

Williams, C.A.S. *Outlines of Chinese Symbolism and Art Motives.* New York: Dover Publications, 1976. An illustrated dictionary-style assemblage of Chinese motifs, mythology, and history, first published in Shanghai in 1941.

HISTORY

Cameron, Nigel. *Hong Kong: The Cultured Pearl.* London: Oxford University Press, 1978. One of the best historical accounts, eminently readable and with period illustrations.

Coates, Austin. *Myself a Mandarin.* Hong Kong: Oxford University Press. Amusing account of the author's stint as a New Territories magistrate in the 1950s, enhanced by his command of Cantonese and enlivened by his insights into local culture.

Crisswell, Colin. *The Taipans.* London: Oxford University Press, 1981. A look at the early country traders and their evolution into "merchant princes," tracing the development of the still-powerful hongs to the present day.

Inglis, Brian. *The Opium War.* London: Hodder and Stoughton, 1976. A clear and detailed examination of the antecedents to the infamous Opium Wars.

Turner, J.A. *Kwang Tung, or Five Years in South China.* Hong Kong: Oxford University Press, 1982. Originally printed in 1894, this volume contains firsthand observations of life in turn-of-the-century south China by an English Wesleyan missionary.

Waley, Arthur. *The Opium War Through Chinese Eyes.* London: Allen & Unwin, 1958. This translation of the diary of Commissioner Lin provides an alternative to the standard British version of the Opium Wars.

Warner, John (compiler). *Hong Kong Illustrated Views and News 1840-1890.* Hong Kong: John Warner Publications, 1981. Miscellaneous collection of Hong Kong-related engravings and articles from the British press; amusing and wonderfully illustrated.

Welsh, Frank. *A History of Hong Kong.* London: Harpercollins, 1993. A comprehensive (600-plus pages) historical overview, from "barren island" to the uncertain future.

CONTEMPORARY ISSUES

Hong Kong Government. *Hong Kong.* Hong Kong: Hong Kong Government Press, 1997. Official annual yearbook stuffed with essays, statistics, and information.

Hughes, Richard. *Hong Kong: Borrowed Time-Borrowed Place.* London: Andre Deutsch, 1968. The title itself is borrowed from Han Suyin. A dated but still interesting overview written in a breezy style.

Morris, Jan. *Hong Kong: Epilogue to an Empire.* New York: Viking, 1988. If you get only one book on Hong Kong, make it this elegant blend of travelogue and analysis. Highly recommended.

Patrikeff, Felix. *Mouldering Pearl: Hong Kong at the Crossroads.* London: George Philip, 1989. An entertaining look at the territory's history and economy and what makes it tick, and a survey of its future prospects—bleak, as the title implies. Heavy on the betrayal aspect and the semi-tragic parallels with Shanghai.

Rafferty, Kevin. *City on the Rocks.* New York: Viking, 1991. Beefy overview emphasizing economics, politics, and 1997; a good primer on many basic issues.

Rand, Christopher. *Hong Kong: The Island Between.* New York: Alfred A. Knopf, 1952. An entertaining, anecdote-packed account of the early Communist days, when rumors flourished.

Wilson, Dick. *Hong Kong! Hong Kong!* London: Unwin Hyman, 1990. Another solid overview, this one emphasizing the business aspect and 1997.

Various editors. *The Other Hong Kong Report.* Hong Kong: Chinese University Press, 1997. This annual volume is meant to counterbalance the yearly government report and provide a broader perspective. Chapters review the year's events in government, culture, education, economy, industry, and the environment.

PEOPLE

De Mente, Boye. *Chinese Etiquette and Ethics in Business.* Chicago: NTC Business Books, 1989. Witty, comprehensive look at various aspects of modern Chinese culture, written with the business traveler in mind.

Pan, Lynn. *Sons of the Yellow Emperor.* London: Martin Secker and Warburg, 1990. The Shanghai-born author blends history, travel, and reflections in this examination of the overseas Chinese and the essence of Chineseness. There's a particularly good chapter on Hong Kong and the mentality that's supported its success.

Seligman, Scott D. *Dealing with the Chinese.* New York: Warner Books, 1989. Another good guide for the business traveler, everything from meetings and banquet etiquette to dealing with graft. Practical and down-to-earth, it does much to demystify the culture.

LANGUAGE

Bruce, R. *Teach Yourself Cantonese.* London: Hodder and Stoughton, 1992. Probably the best language book around, with a clear transliteration and tonal system and useful situational dialogues.

Newnham, Richard. *About Chinese.* New York: Pelican Books, 1971. Superb little volume explicating the mysteries of the Chinese language. Interesting for the nonlearner and invaluable for the student.

GUIDEBOOKS

Girling, Barry. *Time Out: Sightseeing Ideas for Hongkongers and Visitors.* Hong Kong: Kowloon-Canton Railway Corp. and *South China Morning Post,* 1993. Reprints of over two dozen of Girling's popular newspaper columns on offbeat places to visit in Hong Kong—ancestral halls, hikes, temples—complete with mini-maps and transport information.

Heywood, G.S.P., and Richard Gee. *Rambles in Hong Kong.* Hong Kong: Oxford University Press, 1992. Heywood's 1938 classic reissued with a modern commentary by Gee. It outlines good walks, most in the New Territories, and is full of description, background, and practical details, plus lots of interesting sidebars. For the dedicated walker rather than the casual tourist.

Isaacson, Shelley, and Matt Hackett. *The Book: The Kids' Guide to Hong Kong.* Hong Kong: The Guidebook Company, 1992. HK from a kid's point of view: sights, sports, fun places to go, and lots of comments from kids themselves.

Moores, Alan (editor). *Another Hong Kong: An Explorer's Guide.* Hong Kong: Emphasis Hong Kong, 1989. Highly recommended, if you can find this out-of-print volume. Loving descriptions of Hong Kong's nooks and crannies by local writers.

Schepel, Kaarlo. *Magic Walks* (Vol. 1, 2, and 3). Hong Kong: Phileon Entertainment, 1990. Lots of ideas for local hikes.

RESTAURANT GUIDES

Hong Kong Tatler's Best Restaurants 1998. Hong Kong: Illustrated Magazine Publishing Co., 1997. Annual rundown of the top 150 restaurants in Hong Kong, nominated by readers and reviewed by food critics. Great for up-to-the-minute reviews for serious diners.

The Post Guide to Hong Kong Restaurants. Hong Kong: *South China Morning Post,* 1997. Another useful annual restaurant guide.

SHOPPING GUIDES

Gershman, Suzy. *Born To Shop: Hong Kong.* New York: Bantam Books, 1991. A cheerfully bouncy guide, savvy and fun to read, oriented towards the pricier end of the market.

Goetz, Dana. *The Complete Guide to Hong Kong Factory Bargains.* Hong Kong: Delta Dragon Publications, 1995. Regularly updated, handy little guide to bargains you'd never find on your own.

FICTION

Clavell, James. *Tai Pan.* London: Coronet, 1966. This dull but popular novel dealing with the founding of a fictional hong fails to capture any of the atmosphere of Hong Kong. *Noble House* is the contemporary followup, with more dull subplots involving espionage, drugs, arms, kidnapping, and corporate takeovers.

Elegant, Robert. *Dynasty.* London: Fontana, 1978. A history lesson in novel form, a sweeping family saga involving a prominent Eurasian family linked to a hong and the changes they undergo from 1900-1970.

Le Carre, John. *The Honourable Schoolboy.* London: Pan, 1977. Typically engrossing plot and characterizations set in an authentic Hong Kong atmosphere.

Mason, Richard. *The World of Suzie Wong.* Glasgow: Fontana, 1957. Entertaining if dated tale of a British artist who falls in love with a Cantonese hooker-with-a-heart-of-gold. Lots of period atmosphere involving the lives of Wanchai bar girls.

Mo, Timothy. *An Insular Possession.* London: Chatto & Windus, 1986. Thick novel that's a witty and well-done portrayal of the lives of foreign traders in 19th-century China. Also look for Mo's *The Monkey King,* the engaging story of an upper-class Chinese family in 1950s Hong Kong.

Suyin, Han. *A Many-Splendoured Thing.* London: Jonathan Cape, 1952. Romantic novel of a Eurasian doctor and her lover, a British journalist, set in postwar Hong Kong.

COFFEE-TABLE BOOKS

Hong Kong: Return to the Heart of the Dragon. Hong Kong: O&A Editions, 1993. Big, beautiful, glossy collection of essays and photos—so big it's hard to read, but still beautiful.

Brown, Rick, and James Marshall (editors). *Hong Kong: Here Be Dragons.* New York: Stewart, Tabori and Chang, 1992. Its intention is to "capture the spirit of Hong Kong," a phrase repeated like a mantra throughout the book—and it does, quite successfully. The photos and a perceptive essay by Simon Winchester provide a realistic look at the territory, affectionate but not sentimental. One of the best overall photo books on Hong Kong.

Girard, Greg, and Ian Lambot (photographers). *City of Darkness: Life in Kowloon Walled City.* London: Watermark, 1993. Photos accompanied by a collection of essays drawing on four years of interviews, all done prior to the 1992 clearance of the infamous Walled City. Though the Walled City is now demolished, this sensitive, realistic examination of urban life still applies to many in Hong Kong.

Hahn, Werner, and Dean Barrett. *Aberdeen: Catching the Last Rays.* Hong Kong: Perennial Press, 1974. A dated but timely look at Aberdeen's community of boat people—25,000 strong when written, and now much reduced.

Robson, Michael. *The Potent Poppy.* Hong Kong: FormAsia, 1992. Gorgeously illustrated story of the seductive drug that brought Hong Kong into being.

Wiltshire, Trea. *Echoes of Old China: Traditional Shops in Contemporary Hong Kong.* Hong Kong: FormAsia. Hong Kong's traditional culture through its vanishing old shops—jade, calligraphy, tea, weddings, rice—a good idea, beautifully photographed and sensitively interpreted.

Wiltshire, Trea. *Old Hong Kong* (two volumes). Hong Kong: FormAsia. Sepia photographs from the 1860s reveal a colonial past of palanquins, coolies, and elegant colonial buildings—all long gone.

Wolfendale, Stuart. *Hong Kong: The Way We Are.* Hong Kong: FormAsia. 250 photos from various photographers, beautifully laid out, captures Hong Kong on the cusp of change.

MACAU

Coates, Austin. *A Macau Narrative.* Hong Kong: Heinemann, 1978. The colony's history from the time of the Portuguese explorers and Jesuit missionaries, a fascinating if somewhat rambling account.

CHINA

Bonavia, David. *The Chinese.* New York: Viking, 1981. Good basic introduction to all aspects of this enormous and baffling country.

Butterfield, Fox. *China: Alive in the Bitter Sea.* London: Coronet, 1983. A journalist posted in China reveals the country's not-so-nice side, in terms of political repression and human suffering.

Kristoff, Nicholas, and Sheryl WuDunn. *China Wakes.* Random House, 1995. Up-to-date (for now) observations on modern China by a husband-and-wife team of reporters. Probably the best for current events.

Schell, Orville. *To Get Rich is Glorious.* New York: Pantheon, 1984. A non-technical overview of China's revised economic policies, a bit dated but readable.

Thubron, Colin. *Behind the Wall: A Journey through China.* London: Heinemann, 1987. A beautifully written account of the author's perceptive encounters with various Chinese cities and people, already dated in some ways, but illuminating and sensitive.

Zhang, Xinxin, and Sang Ye. *Chinese Lives: An Oral History of Contemporary China.* London: Macmillan, 1987. Frank and fascinating interviews with 60 ordinary Chinese of all ages and professions. Skillful translation and editing allows the individual voices to be heard.

INDEX

Page number in *italics* indicate information found in maps, charts, sidebars, or captions.

ABOUT THE AUTHOR

Kerry Moran received a Bachelor of Journalism degree from the University of Missouri-Columbia in 1981. Following a year in Paris and a stint as a newspaper editor in Northern California, she moved to Guangzhou in 1984 to teach English at Zhongshan University. The following year she moved to Kathmandu, Nepal, where she has lived ever since.

She works as a freelance writer and editor. Her articles have appeared in *The Asian Wall Street Journal* and a number of inflight and travel magazines. Her *Nepal Handbook* (Moon Travel Handbooks, 1991) won the 1991 Lowell Thomas Travel Journalism Award for Best Guidebook from the Society of American Travel Writers. Her other books are *Kailas: On Pilgrimage to the Sacred Mountain of Tibet* (Thames and Hudson, 1989) and *Introduction to Nepal* (Odyssey Publications, 1994).

NOTES

LOSE YOURSELF IN THE EXPERIENCE, NOT THE CROWD

For 25 years, Moon Travel Handbooks have been the guidebooks of choice for adventurous travelers. Our award-winning Handbook series provides focused, comprehensive coverage of distinct destinations all over the world. Each Handbook is like an entire bookcase of cultural insight and introductory information in one portable volume. Our goal at Moon is to give travelers all the background and practical information they'll need for an extraordinary travel experience.

The following pages include a complete list of Handbooks, covering North America and Hawaii, Mexico, Central America and the Caribbean, and Asia and the Pacific.To purchase Moon Travel Handbooks, check your local bookstore or order by phone: (800) 345-5473 M-F 8 am.-5 p.m. PST or outside the U.S. phone: (530) 345-5473.

"An in-depth dunk into the land, the people and their history, arts, and politics."
—*Student Travels*

"Amazingly detailed in a style easy to understand, the Handbooks offer a lot for a good price."
—*International Travel News*

"Moon Travel Handbooks' line of travel guides adds wisdom to one's wanderings."
—*Excursions*

"Outdoor enthusiasts gravitate to the well-written Moon Travel Handbooks. In addition to politically correct historic and cultural features, the series focuses on flora, fauna and outdoor recreation. Maps and meticulous directions also are a trademark of Moon guides."
—*Houston Chronicle*

"Moon [Travel Handbooks] . . . bring a healthy respect to the places they investigate. Best of all, they provide a host of odd nuggets that give a place texture and prod the wary traveler from the beaten path. The finest are written with such care and insight they deserve listing as literature."
—*American Geographical Society*

"Moon Travel Handbooks offer in-depth historical essays and useful maps, enhanced by a sense of humor and a neat, compact format."
—*Swing*

"Perfect for the more adventurous, these are long on history, sightseeing and nitty-gritty information and very price-specific."
—*Columbus Dispatch*

"Moon guides manage to be comprehensive and countercultural at the same time . . . Handbooks are packed with maps, photographs, drawings, and sidebars that constitute a college-level introduction to each country's history, culture, people, and crafts."
—*National Geographic Traveler*

"Few travel guides do a better job helping travelers create their own itineraries than the Moon Travel Handbook series. The authors have a knack for homing in on the essentials."
—**Colorado Springs *Gazette Telegraph***

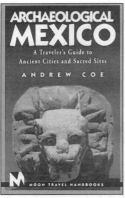

MEXICO

"These books will delight the armchair traveler, aid the undecided person in selecting a destination, and guide the seasoned road warrior looking for lesser-known hideaways."

—*Mexican Meanderings* Newsletter

"From tourist traps to off-the-beaten track hideaways, these guides offer consistent, accurate details without pretension."

—*Foreign Service Journal*

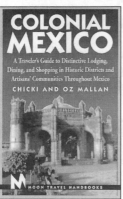

Archaeological Mexico	**$19.95**
Andrew Coe	450 pages, 25 maps
Baja Handbook	**$15.95**
Joe Cummings	380 pages, 44 maps
Cabo Handbook	**$14.95**
Joe Cummings	265 pages, 18 maps
Cancun Handbooks	**$13.95**
Chicki Mallan	270 pages, 25 maps
Colonial Mexico	**$16.95**
Chicki Mallan	300 pages, 38 maps
Mexico Handbook	**$21.95**
Joe Cummings and Chicki Mallan	1,200 pages, 232 maps
Northern Mexico Handbook	**$16.95**
Joe Cummings	590 pages, 68 maps
Pacific Mexico Handbook	**$17.95**
Bruce Whipperman	580 pages, 69 maps
Puerto Vallarta Handbook	**$14.95**
Bruce Whipperman	330 pages, 36 maps
Yucatan Handbook	**$15.95**
Chicki Mallan	470 pages, 62 maps

LATIN AMERICA AND THE CARIBBEAN

"Solidly packed with practical information and full of significant cultural asides that will enlighten you on the whys and wherefores of things you might easily see but not easily grasp."

—*Boston Globe*

Belize Handbook	**$15.95**
Chicki Mallan	390 pages, 45 maps
Caribbean Handbook	**$16.95**
Karl Luntta	400 pages, 56 maps
Ecuador Handbook	**$16.95**
Julian Smith	450 pages, 43 maps
Costa Rica Handbook	**$19.95**
Christopher P. Baker	780 pages, 74 maps
Cuba Handbook	**$19.95**
Christopher P. Baker	740 pages, 70 maps
Dominican Republic Handbook	**$15.95**
Gaylord Dold	420 pages, 24 maps
Honduras Handbook	**$15.95**
Chris Humphrey	330 pages, 40 maps
Jamaica Handbook	**$15.95**
Karl Luntta	330 pages, 17 maps
Virgin Islands Handbook	**$13.95**
Karl Luntta	220 pages, 19 maps

NORTH AMERICA AND HAWAII

"These domestic guides convey the same sense of exoticism that their foreign counterparts do, making home-country travel seem like far-flung adventure."

—*Sierra Magazine*

Alaska-Yukon Handbook	**$17.95**
Deke Castleman and Don Pitcher	530 pages, 92 maps
Alberta and the Northwest Territories Handbook	**$17.95**
Andrew Hempstead and Nadina Purdon	530 pages, 72 maps,
Arizona Traveler's Handbook	**$17.95**
Bill Weir and Robert Blake	512 pages,54 maps
Atlantic Canada Handbook	**$17.95**
Nan Drosdick and Mark Morris	460 pages, 61 maps
Big Island of Hawaii Handbook	**$13.95**
J.D. Bisignani	370 pages, 23 maps
British Columbia Handbook	**$16.95**
Jane King and Andrew Hempstead	400 pages, 65 maps

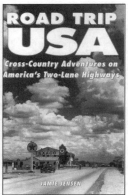

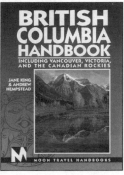

Colorado Handbook	**$18.95**
Stephen Metzger	480 pages, 59 maps
Georgia Handbook	**$17.95**
Kap Stann	370 pages, 50 maps
Hawaii Handbook	**$19.95**
J.D. Bisignani	1,030 pages, 90 maps
Honolulu-Waikiki Handbook	**$14.95**
J.D. Bisignani	380 pages, 20 maps
Idaho Handbook	**$18.95**
Don Root	610 pages, 42 maps
Kauai Handbook	**$15.95**
J.D. Bisignani	320 pages, 23 maps
Maui Handbook	**$14.95**
J.D. Bisignani	410 pages, 35 maps
Montana Handbook	**$17.95**
Judy Jewell and W.C. McRae	480 pages, 52 maps
Nevada Handbook	**$16.95**
Deke Castleman	500 pages, 40 maps
New Mexico Handbook	**$15.95**
Stephen Metzger	360 pages, 47 maps
New York City Handbook	**$13.95**
Christiane Bird	300 pages, 20 maps
New York Handbook	**$19.95**
Christiane Bird	780 pages, 95 maps
Northern California Handbook	**$19.95**
Kim Weir	800 pages, 50 maps
Oregon Handbook	**$16.95**
Stuart Warren and Ted Long Ishikawa	540 pages, 33 maps
Road Trip USA	**$22.50**
Jamie Jensen	800 pages, 165 maps
Southern California Handbook	**$19.95**
Kim Weir	750 pages, 30 maps
Tennessee Handbook	**$17.95**
Jeff Bradley	530 pages, 44 maps
Texas Handbook	**$17.95**
Joe Cummings	620 pages, 70 maps
Utah Handbook	**$17.95**
Bill Weir and W.C. McRae	490 pages, 40 maps
Washington Handbook	**$19.95**
Don Pitcher	870 pages, 113 maps
Wisconsin Handbook	**$18.95**
Thomas Huhti	590 pages, 69 maps
Wyoming Handbook	**$17.95**
Don Pitcher	610 pages, 80 maps

ASIA AND THE PACIFIC

"Scores of maps, detailed practical info down to business hours of small-town libraries. You can't beat the Asian titles for sheer heft. (The) series is sort of an American Lonely Planet, with better writing but fewer titles. (The) individual voice of researchers comes through."

—*Travel & Leisure*

Australia Handbook	**$21.95**
Marael Johnson, Andrew Hempstead, and Nadina Purdon	940 pages, 141 maps
Bali Handbook	**$19.95**
Bill Dalton	750 pages, 54 maps
Bangkok Handbook	**$13.95**
Michael Buckley	244 pages, 30 maps
Fiji Islands Handbook	**$13.95**
David Stanley	280 pages, 38 maps
Hong Kong Handbook	**$16.95**
Kerry Moran	370 pages, 39 maps
Indonesia Handbook	**$25.00**
Bill Dalton	1,380 pages, 249 maps
Japan Handbook	**$22.50**
J.D. Bisignani	970 pages, 213 maps
Micronesia Handbook	**$14.95**
Neil M. Levy	340 pages, 70 maps
Nepal Handbook	**$18.95**
Kerry Moran	490 pages, 51 maps
New Zealand Handbook	**$19.95**
Jane King	620 pages, 81 maps
Outback Australia Handbook	**$18.95**
Marael Johnson	450 pages, 57 maps
Pakistan Hanbdook	**$19.95**
Isobel Shaw	660 pages, 85 maps
Philippines Handbook	**$17.95**
Peter Harper and Laurie Fullerton	670 pages, 116 maps
Singapore Handbook	**$15.95**
Carl Parkes	350 pages, 29 maps
Southeast Asia Handbook	**$21.95**
Carl Parkes	1,000 pages, 196 maps
South Korea Handbook	**$19.95**
Robert Nilsen	820 pages, 141 maps
South Pacific Handbook	**$22.95**
David Stanley	920 pages, 147 maps

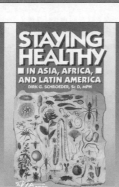

Tahiti-Polynesia Handbook	$13.95
David Stanley	270 pages, 35 maps
Thailand Handbook	**$19.95**
Carl Parkes	860 pages, 142 maps
Tibet Handbook	**$30.00**
Victor Chan	1,104 pages, 216 maps
Vietnam, Cambodia & Laos Handbook	**$18.95**
Michael Buckley	720 pages, 112 maps

OTHER GREAT TITLES FROM MOON

"For hardy wanderers, few guides come more highly recommended than the Handbooks. They include good maps, steer clear of fluff and flackery, and offer plenty of money-saving tips. They also give you the kind of information that visitors to strange lands—on any budget—need to survive."

—US News & World Report

Moon Handbook	$10.00
Carl Koppeschaar	141 pages, 8 maps
Moscow-St. Petersburg Handbook	**$13.95**
Masha Nordbye	259 pages, 16 maps
The Practical Nomad: How to Travel Around the World	**$17.95**
Edward Hasbrouck	575 pages
Staying Healthy in Asia, Africa, and Latin America	**$11.95**
Dirk Schroeder	197 pages, 4 maps

THE PRACTICAL NOMAD

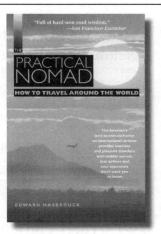

✈ TAKE THE PLUNGE

"The greatest barriers to long-term travel by Americans are the disempowered feelings that leave them afraid to ask for the time off. Just do it."

✈ TAKE NOTHING FOR GRANTED

"Even 'What time is it?' is a highly politicized question in some areas, and the answer may depend on your informant's ethnicity and political allegiance as well as the proximity of the secret police."

✈ TAKE THIS BOOK

With experience helping thousands of his globetrotting clients plan their trips around the world, travel industry insider Edward Hasbrouck provides the secrets that can save readers money and valuable travel time.
An indispensable complement to destination-specific travel guides, *The Practical Nomad* includes:

airfare strategies

ticket discounts

long-term travel considerations

travel documents

border crossings

entry requirements

government offices

travel publications

Internet information resources

WHERE TO BUY MOON TRAVEL HANDBOOKS

BOOKSTORES AND LIBRARIES: Moon Travel Handbooks are distributed worldwide. Please contact our sales manager for a list of wholesalers and distributors in your area.

TRAVELERS: We would like to have Moon Travel Handbooks available throughout the world. Please ask your bookstore to write or call us for ordering information. If your bookstore will not order our guides for you, please contact us for a free catalog.

Moon Travel Handbooks
P.O. Box 3040
Chico, CA 95927-3040 U.S.A.
tel.: (800) 345-5473, outside the U.S. (530) 345-5473
fax: (530) 345-6751
e-mail: travel@moon.com

IMPORTANT ORDERING INFORMATION

PRICES: All prices are subject to change. We always ship the most current edition. We will let you know if there is a price increase on the book you order.

SHIPPING AND HANDLING OPTIONS: Domestic UPS or USPS first class (allow 10 working days for delivery): $4.50 for the first item, $1.00 for each additional item.

Moonbelt shipping is $1.50 for one, 50 cents for each additional belt.

UPS 2nd Day Air or Printed Airmail requires a special quote.

International Surface Bookrate 8-12 weeks delivery: $3.00 for the first item, $1.00 for each additional item. Note: We cannot guarantee international surface bookrate shipping. We recommends sending international orders via air mail, which requires a special quote.

FOREIGN ORDERS: Orders that originate outside the U.S.A. must be paid for with an international money order, a check in U.S. currency drawn on a major U.S. bank based in the U.S.A., or Visa, MasterCard, or Discover.

TELEPHONE ORDERS: We accept Visa, MasterCard, or Discover payments. Call in your order: (800) 345-5473, 8 a.m.-5 p.m. Pacific standard time. Outside the U.S. the number is (530) 345-5473.

INTERNET ORDERS: Visit our site at: www.moon.com